Reuben van Rensburg, Zoltan Erdey
Thomas Schirrmacher (Editors)

**"Be Focused ...
Use Common Sense ...
Overcome Excuses and Stupidity ..."**

World of Theology Series

Published by the Theological Commission of the World Evangelical Alliance

Volume 22

Vol 1   Thomas K. Johnson: The First Step in Missions Training: How our Neighbors are Wrestling with God's General Revelation
Vol 2   Thomas K. Johnson: Christian Ethics in Secular Cultures
Vol 3   David Parker: Discerning the Obedience of Faith: A Short History of the World Evangelical Alliance Theological Commission
Vol 4   Thomas Schirrmacher (Ed.): William Carey: Theologian – Linguist – Social Reformer
Vol 5   Thomas Schirrmacher: Advocate of Love – Martin Bucer as Theologian and Pastor
Vol 6   Thomas Schirrmacher: Culture of Shame / Culture of Guilt
Vol 7   Thomas Schirrmacher: The Koran and the Bible
Vol 8   Thomas Schirrmacher (Ed.): The Humanisation of Slavery in the Old Testament
Vol 9   Jim Harries: New Foundations for Appreciating Africa: Beyond Religious and Secular Deceptions
Vol 10 Thomas Schirrmacher: Missio Dei – God's Missional Nature
Vol 11 Thomas Schirrmacher: Biblical Foundations for 21st Century World Mission
Vol 12 William Wagner, Mark Wagner: Can Evangelicals Truly Change the World? How Seven Philosophical and Religious Movements Are Growing
Vol 13 Thomas Schirrmacher: Modern Fathers
Vol 14 Jim Harries: Jarida juu ya Maisha ya MwAfrika katika huduma ya Ukristo
Vol 15 Peter Lawrence: Fellow Travellers – A Comparative Study on the Identity Formation of Jesus Followers from Jewish, Christian and Muslim Backgrounds in The Holy Land
Vol 16 William Wagner: From Classroom Dummy to University President – Serving God in the Land of Sound of Music
Vol 17 Thomas K. Johnson, David Parker, Thomas Schirrmacher (ed.): In the Name of the Father, Son, and Holy Spirit – Teaching the Trinity from the Creeds to Modern Discussion
Vol 18 Mark Wagner and William Wagner (Ed.): Halfway Up the Mountain
Vol 19 Thomas K. Johnson: The Protester, the Dissident, and the Christian – Essays on Human Rights and Religion
Vol 20 Thomas K. Johnson: Humanitarian Islam, Evangelical Christianity, and the Clash of Civilizations
Vol 21 Thomas K. Johnson: Christian Ethics in Secular Cultures, Vol 2
Vol 22 Reuben van Rensburg, Zoltan Erdey, Thomas Schirrmacher (Ed.): "Be Focused ... Use Common Sense ... Overcome Excuses and Stupidity ..." Festschrift in Honor of Dr. Manfred Waldemar Kohl
Vol 23 John W. Ewing. Goodly Fellowship – A Centenary Tribute to the Life and Work of the World's Evangelical Alliance 1846–1946

Reuben van Rensburg, Zoltan Erdey
Thomas Schirrmacher (Editors)

"Be Focused ...
Use Common Sense ...
Overcome Excuses and Stupidity ..."

Festschrift in Honor of
Dr. Manfred Waldemar Kohl

On the occasion of his 80th birthday

Essays on Holistic Biblical Ministries

WIPF & STOCK · Eugene, Oregon

Wipf and Stock Publishers
199 W 8th Ave, Suite 3
Eugene, OR 97401

"Be Focused... Use Common Sense... Overcome Excuses and Stupidity..."
Festschrift in Honor of Dr. Manfred Waldemar Kohl:
Essays on Holistic Biblical Ministries
By van Rensburg, Reuben and Erdey, Zoltan
Copyright © 2022 Verlag für Kultur und Wissenschaft Culture and Science Publ.
All rights reserved.
Softcover ISBN-13: 978-1-6667-4515-3
Hardcover ISBN-13: 978-1-6667-4516-0
Publication date 6/13/2022
Previously published by Verlag für Kultur und Wissenschaft Culture and Science Publ., 2022

Contents

Preface: Overcome Excuses and Stupidity
by Thomas Schirrmacher 9

Vorwort: Ausreden und Dummheit überwinden
by Thomas Schirrmacher 11

PART 1: THE NEGLECTED IMPORTANTS 15

The Holistic Child Development Movement: Lasting Fruit, Uncertain Future
by Dan Brewster 17

Child-Focus in Theological Education: A Neglected Core
by Jessy Jaison 35

Theological Education and the Church
by Roger Kemp 47

Settler Colonialism, Conflict and Reconciliation
by Salim J. Munayer 61

Thinking Constructively
by Perry Shaw 77

A Framework for Christian Child Advocacy
by Johannes Malherbe 97

Education and Learning in Christian Perspective
by Thomas Schirrmacher 117

PART 2: THEOLOGICAL TRAINING 135

A Galilean Movement: For Such a Time as This
by Joe Handley 137

Theological Education as Mission
by Christopher J. H. Wright 151

Mission and Theological Education for the Extension of the Kingdom of God
by Antonio Carlos Barro 163

Theological Education: Which Way?
  by Ashish Chrispal 177

Reconciliation in the Context of Corruption
  by Johannes Reimer 185

Innovation in Seminary Theological Education: An Overview of
Contributing Forces
  by Scott Cunningham 195

Training of Pastors: A High Priority for Global Ministry Strategy
  by Ramesh Richard 211

A Salute to Manfred Kohl: In Pursuit of Excellence in Theological
Education
  by Wilson W. Chow 223

Affirming Quality in Theological Education
  by Steve Hardy 235

Theological Education as Worship
  by Taras N. Dyatlik 249

PART 3: THE WORD OF GOD, INTEGRITY AND HUMILITY 259

Itching Ears and Willing Learners: Balancing the Clarity and
Complexity of Scripture
  by Bruce Barron 261

Confronting Lying Biblically in Honor- and Shame-Oriented
Cultures
  by Ajith Fernando 267

Faithful Ministry: An Exposition of 2 Timothy
  by Kevin G. Smith 279

God's Word for God's World: Toward a Gospel-Centered Faith
  by Samuel Richmond Saxena 293

Plumbing the Sacred: Narrative Approaches to Understanding
Non-Western Christian Ethical, Political, and Theological
Discourse
  by Thomas Alan Harvey 305

Integrity and World Evangelization: What is the Connection?
  by David W. Bennett 323

Living in Global Integrity: Moral Wholeness for a More Whole World
by Kelly O'Donnell and Michèle Lewis O'Donnell 335

The Book of Romans as a Charter for World Missions—Why Mission and Theology Have to Go Together: Thoughts on the Relationship of Theology, Missiology and Mission
by Thomas Schirrmacher 353

PART 4: BIBLICAL MINISTRY AND SERVANT LEADERSHIP 379

Dissent: Global Transformation on Shaky Ground
by Janet Wootton 381

Jesus Inaugurates the Kingdom: Proclaim the Gospel in Word and Deed
by Richard Howell 397

Lifelong Learners in the School of Grace: The Pedagogy of Grace
by Paul Sanders 411

Re-Forma: Solving a Desperate Need
by Reuben van Rensburg 425

Transregional Mission from Bad Liebenzell: Piety, Pioneering and Priority of Maria Von Rausch in Hong Kong Mission
by Wai-Yip Ho 435

The Bible as the Foundation of Life: Sacramental Realism
by Sergii Sannikov 449

Humble Integrity: The Work of God in the Life of Job
by Brad Smith 461

The Power of Servant Leadership
by Dan Aleshire 473

The Churches Need Healthy, Well-Formed Leaders—How Shall We Now Train?
by Paul Allan Clark 485

Servant-Leadership of Ezra and Nehemiah
by Joseph Shao 509

PART 5: THE CHURCH 521

The Covid-19 Pandemic as a Test Case for the Unity of the Worldwide Church and for Solidarity in Ecumenical Diakonia of All Christian Churches—15 Theses
by Dietrich Werner 523

Lessons Drawn from the Precarious Existence of the Church under Pressure
by Peter Kuzmič 543

A Tribute to Manfred Kohl: A Developer of Leaders
by Theresa R. Lua 553

A Prayer for Manfred Kohl
by Bill Houston 559

APPENDIX: BIOGRAPHY AND BIBLIOGRAPHY 561

Preface:
Overcome Excuses and Stupidity

In 2005, Manfred Kohl helped to start an MBA program in *Biblical Stewardship and Christian Management*, based in the Philippines and Brazil. The name of this program—along with a third term, *institutional development*—sums up the impact of Manfred's life and why he has meant so much to the many people he has taught, mentored, instructed or influenced.

These topics were inspired from two sides, as his professional experience and academic training included both theology/Christian ministries and business/management. Manfred is a master of both. His long list of professional publications is a mix of very pious thoughts, including most areas of theology as well as management and institutional development.

Manfred has taught theology and institutional development in all kinds of structures and systems, from Harvard University to seminaries in the bushes of Africa. He has visited more than 490 theological institutions in 125 countries. He has also been a lifelong learner—M.Div., M.Th., Th.D., D.Min.

Manfred has received honorary doctoral degrees and theological awards from leading institutions in Ecuador, Brazil, the Central African Republic, Kenya, South Africa, India and Croatia. Each year he seemed to be studying something new. The last entry in his long list of official trainings completed is from 2021, when he was 79 years old.

Manfred lived in and learned from multiple cultures, including Germany, the USA, Africa and Canada. He absorbed the best of each of them into his leadership. He lectured in many countries and trained many leaders around the globe, most often on a one-to-one basis. But his was never just a private counseling enterprise. He was always guiding leaders to focus on how to evaluate and restructure their organizations to ensure sustainability and the fulfillment of long-term strategies.

I say this as someone heading up a global organization, the World Evangelical Alliance, where I mainly use a structure that Manfred initially proposed as a consultant to an internal reform process. This departmental structure was installed in 2016 by my predecessor as WEA Secretary General, Bishop Efraim Tendero, in reaction to the large expansion of WEA ministries. As Secretary General, I have gladly retained this structure.

Manfred also serves WEA as chair of Re-Forma, a global training initiative for Christian leaders, and (together with Bishop Tendero, Global Ambassador of WEA) he co-chairs the Integrity Network of WEA and the Lausanne Movement. Manfred is passionate about integrity because for him, corruption is an utter evil and the opposite of everything he teaches churches and institutions about stewardship, responsibility and accountability.

Manfred has been known as a scholar, mentor, advisor and friend who never minced words. He is known to rely on the simple but essential phrases "Be focused" and "Use common sense" when dealing with colleagues on every level. Many times he has told his listeners, "Stop being a *Dummkopf*" or "Overcome excuses and stupidity." He is known for speaking candidly and not "through the flowers," as he calls it. However, as numerous colleagues have testified, Manfred has always displayed a deep love and concern for each individual or Christian ministry with whom he interacts. In his unique way, he has made many, many friends.

In 1969, Manfred married Barbara Marie Kohl, B.A., M.Div., D.Min., a passionate and gifted guidance counselor and a native of Nova Scotia, Canada, where the two have lived for the past quarter-century. Everyone acquainted with Manfred and Barbara knows that their relationship spans all I report here and has been the most important vital dormant pole and force in his very active life.

After serving as field director for World Vision in West Africa, with 100 projects in 10 countries, a $2 million annual budget and 80 staff, Manfred accepted the challenge of founding and building up the German branch of World Vision from 1979 to 1993. When he left World Vision, he handed over 25,000 monthly child sponsors and an additional 150,000 donors. During this time, he also started branches of World Vision in Austria (1981), Switzerland (1983) and the Netherlands (1986). In the end he was responsible for six national offices with 100 full-time staff and an annual budget of $20 million. Today, World Vision Germany is one of the largest donor organizations in that country, with a budget of $160 million in 2019. From 1986 to 1993, he was also one of the vice presidents of World Vision International, today one of the largest development NGOs in the world with a yearly budget of $2.9 billion.

Others would have stayed in that role until retirement. But Manfred felt called repeatedly to something new. As people were just getting acquainted with his brainchild Re-forma as part of WEA, he was already moving on to the next global initiative, the Galilean Movement. You will surely hear more about it soon.

After leaving World Vision, he was Vice President of International Development for the Overseas Council from 1994 to 2008; after retiring from there, he stayed on as the OC's ambassador. In that position, he helped numerous large and small theological institutions around the globe to restructure their management, financing, educational and outreach pro-

Preface / Vorwort

grams. Hundreds of institutions might not have survived without his fundraising skills and his willingness to teach these highly strategic skills to others. In 1996 he helped to start the German branch of the OC, of which he remains the chair.

Few people know that while Manfred was pastor of a Congregational church in the USA long ago, he left his mark in writing in the leading journals of the global congregational movement.

Manfred Kohl has left an indelible mark on global Christianity, fusing biblical insights together with practical models for today.

Thomas Schirrmacher, Secretary General, World Evangelical Alliance

Vorwort:
Ausreden und Dummheit überwinden

Im Jahr 2005 half Manfred Kohl, ein MBA-Programm für *Biblische Haushalterschaft und christliches Management* auf den Philippinen und in Brasilien ins Leben zu rufen. Der Name dieses Programms – zusammen mit einem dritten Begriff, der *institutionellen Entwicklung* – fasst zusammen, was Manfreds Leben geprägt hat und warum er für die vielen Menschen, die er gelehrt, betreut, unterrichtet oder beeinflusst hat, so viel bedeutet hat.

Diese Themen wurden von zwei Seiten inspiriert, da seine berufliche Erfahrung und akademische Ausbildung sowohl Theologie/Christliche Dienste als auch Wirtschaft/Management umfasste. Manfred ist ein Meister in beidem. Seine lange Liste von Fachveröffentlichungen ist eine Mischung aus sehr frommen Überlegungen, den meisten Bereichen der Theologie, sowie Management und institutioneller Entwicklung.

Manfred hat Theologie und institutionelle Entwicklung in allen möglichen Strukturen und Bereichen gelehrt, von der Harvard University bis hin zu Seminaren in den Wäldern von Afrika. Er hat mehr als 490 theologische Einrichtungen in 125 Ländern besucht. Außerdem hat er sein ganzes Leben lang gelernt: M.Div., M.Th., Th.D., D.Min.

Manfred hat Ehrendoktorwürden und theologische Auszeichnungen von führenden Institutionen in Ecuador, Brasilien, der Zentralafrikanischen Republik, Kenia, Südafrika, Indien und Kroatien erhalten. Jedes Jahr schien er etwas Neues zu studieren. Der letzte Eintrag in seiner langen Liste der abgeschlossenen offiziellen Ausbildungen stammt aus dem Jahr 2021, als er 79 Jahre alt war.

Manfred lebte und lernte in verschiedenen Kulturen, darunter in Deutschland, den USA, in Afrika und Kanada. Er hat das Beste aus jeder dieser Kulturen in seine Führungsprinzipien einfließen lassen. Er hielt Vorträge in vielen Ländern und bildete viele Führungskräfte rund um den Globus aus, meist in Einzelgesprächen. Aber seine Arbeit bestand nie nur in privater Beratung. Er leitete die Führungskräfte stets an, sich darauf zu konzentrieren, wie sie ihre Organisationen bewerten und umstrukturieren können, um Nachhaltigkeit und die Umsetzung langfristiger Strategien zu gewährleisten.

Ich sage dies als jemand, der eine globale Organisation, die *Weltweite Evangelische Allianz*, leitet, in der ich hauptsächlich eine Struktur verwende, die von Manfred vorgeschlagen wurde, als er einen Reformprozess beriet, in dem der damalige Generalsekretär der WEA, Bischof Efraim Tendero, im Jahr 2016 die gegenwärtige Struktur der Abteilungen einrichtete und damit auf die große Expansion der Dienste der WEA reagierte, eine Struktur, mit der ich als Generalsekretär der WEA immer noch gerne arbeite.

Manfred dient der WEA auch als Vorsitzender von Re-Forma, einer globalen Ausbildungsinitiative für christliche Führungskräfte, und ist (zusammen mit Bischof Tendero, dem globalen Botschafter der WEA) Co-Vorsitzender des *Integritätsnetzwerks* der WEA und der Lausanner Bewegung. Manfred setzt sich leidenschaftlich für Integrität ein, denn für ihn ist Korruption ein absolutes Übel und das Gegenteil von allem, was er Kirchen und Institutionen über Haushalterschaft, Verantwortung und Rechenschaftspflicht lehrt.

Manfred ist als Gelehrter, Mentor, Berater und Freund bekannt, der nie ein Blatt vor den Mund nimmt. Er ist bekannt dafür, dass er sich im Umgang mit Kollegen auf allen Ebenen auf die einfachen, aber wichtigen Sätze „Sei konzentriert" und „Benutze den gesunden Menschenverstand" verlässt. Viele Male hat er seinen Zuhörern gesagt: „Hör auf, ein Dummkopf zu sein" oder „Überwinde Ausreden und Dummheit". Er ist dafür bekannt, offen zu sprechen und nicht „durch die Blume", wie er es nennt. Wie jedoch zahlreiche Kollegen bezeugt haben, hat Manfred immer eine tiefe Liebe und Sorge für jeden Einzelnen oder jede christliche Gemeinde gezeigt, mit der er zu tun hatte. Auf seine einzigartige Weise hat er viele Freunde gewonnen.

1969 heiratete Manfred Barbara Marie Kohl, B.A., M.Div., D.Min., eine diplomierte und begabte Beraterin, die aus Nova Scotia, Kanada, stammt, wo die beiden auch wieder seit einem Vierteljahrhundert leben. Jeder, der Manfred und Barbara kennt, weiß, dass sich ihre Beziehung über all das erstreckt, was ich hier berichte, und dass sie der wichtigste ruhende Pol und die wichtigste Kraft in seinem sehr aktiven Leben war und ist.

Preface / Vorwort

Nachdem er als Feldleiter für World Vision in Westafrika tätig war, mit 100 Projekten in 10 Ländern, einem Jahresbudget von 2 Millionen Dollar und 80 Mitarbeitern, nahm Manfred die Herausforderung an, den deutschen Zweig von World Vision von 1979 bis 1993 zu gründen und aufzubauen. Als er World Vision verließ, übergab er 25.000 monatliche Kinderpatenschaften und weitere 150.000 Spender. In dieser Zeit gründete er auch Niederlassungen von World Vision in Österreich (1981), der Schweiz (1983) und den Niederlanden (1986). Am Ende war er für sechs nationale Büros mit 100 Vollzeitmitarbeitern und einem Jahresbudget von 20 Millionen Dollar verantwortlich. Heute ist World Vision Deutschland mit einem Budget von 160 Millionen Dollar im Jahr 2019 eine der größten Geberorganisationen in diesem Land. Von 1986 bis 1993 war er auch einer der Vizepräsidenten von World Vision International, heute eine der größten Entwicklungs-NGOs der Welt mit einem Jahresbudget von 2,9 Mrd. $.

Andere wären bis zu ihrer Pensionierung in dieser Funktion geblieben. Aber Manfred fühlte sich immer wieder zu etwas Neuem berufen. Als die Menschen jüngst sein Kind Re-forma als Teil der WEA kennenlernten, fügte er bereits die nächste globale Initiative hinzu, die *Galileische Bewegung*. Sie werden sicher bald mehr darüber hören.

Nachdem er World Vision verlassen hatte, war er von 1994 bis 2008 Vizepräsident für internationale Entwicklung beim Overseas Council; nach seiner Pensionierung blieb er dem OC als Botschafter erhalten. In dieser Position half er zahlreichen großen und kleinen theologischen Einrichtungen rund um den Globus bei der Umstrukturierung ihres Managements, ihrer Finanzierung und ihrer Bildungs- und Outreach-Programme. Hunderte von Einrichtungen hätten ohne seine Fundraising-Fähigkeiten und seine Bereitschaft, diese hochstrategischen Fähigkeiten an andere weiterzugeben, vielleicht nicht überlebt. 1996 half er mit, den deutschen Zweig des OC zu gründen, dessen Vorsitzender er noch immer ist.

Nur wenige wissen, dass Manfred Kohl als Pastor einer kongregationalistischen Kirche in den USA längst seine schriftstellerischen Spuren in den führenden Zeitschriften der weltweiten kongregationalistischen Kirchen hinterlassen hat.

Manfred Kohl hat das weltweite Christentum geprägt, indem er biblische Einsichten mit praktischen Modellen für heute verbindet.

Thomas Schirrmacher, Generalsekretär, Weltweite Evangelische Allianz

PART I:
THE NEGLECTED IMPORTANTS

The Holistic Child Development Movement: Lasting Fruit, Uncertain Future

Dan Brewster

1. Introduction

It is a pleasure for me to write some short reflections in honor of my friend Manfred Kohl. Our friendship has extended for some four decades. We both served in World Vision in Africa in the late 1970s and early 1980s. Manfred's exploits in West Africa were, from time to time, the subject of conversations regarding his "get-it-done" style. Like our boss at the time, Dr. Stan Mooneyham, Manfred didn't move slowly when it came to implementing program solutions and innovations to help the needy.

More recently, Manfred was one of the most influential champions of the movement for Holistic Child Development (HCD), some of the history of which I document in this paper. Manfred recognized that training in HCD and related subjects was very much lacking in the typical seminary curricula. He worked tirelessly as a strong advocate and voice for HCD, the "4/14 Window," and other approaches which drew the attention of seminary leadership to the needs, nurture and significance of the child in the ministries of the future leaders who were being equipped in their theological institutions.

2. Holistic Child Development—Antecedents and Inspirations

What came to be known as the HCD movement began in Compassion International in 2001. Although Compassion had (and has) immense resources and commitment to child development, in reality at the time they employed few people with specific tertiary academic training in its core ministry of *Christian, holistic* child development.

Compassion is the largest Christian organization specifically caring for needy children. Three major distinctives characterize their approach: Christ-centered, Church-based, Child-focused. The second of these—being Church-based—highlights the fact that nearly all of the now two million or so children sponsored by Compassion are cared for in a program administered by a local church. That being the case, Compassion has always invested heavily in training and equipping of local pastors and church leaders to give them the necessary tools and motivation to care holistically for children in their churches and communities. Most of this training was done in ad hoc ways by the local leadership of the many offices Compassion has in countries around the world.

But there was a need for something more and different from most of the equipping done for pastors and church personnel. There were many training programs for Sunday School workers. There were also many training programs and approaches for child and family development workers at the church and local level. Moreover, there were lots of seminary and Christian undergraduate programs focusing on child evangelism, child spirituality, and Christian nurture, and even studies in "child theologies" and other theological reflections on the child. But something different was needed, not only for Compassion church partners but for others seeking to combine theological insights and developmental theory with holistic, developmental practice. And there was much in Compassion's ethos and commitments which set the stage for global innovation and leadership in what became the HCD movement.

The true beginning of the HCD movement came out of a conversation I had with Dr. Bambang Budijanto, then the Asia Director for Compassion, in 2001. Reflecting on the energy we invested in our training programs for pastors and church leaders in our projects, we observed what a good thing it would be to go "back upstream" in the equipping of future church leaders, giving them a mindset about the importance of ministry to children and youths *before* they became leaders—that is, while they were still studying.

Bambang asked me to engage with the Malaysia Baptist Theological Seminary (MBTS), not far from us up the winding coastal road in Penang, Malaysia, about the possibility of pioneering such courses. In dialogues, chapel presentations, and other forums, we made our case with the President, Dr. John Ong, the Academic Dean, Dr. Sunny Tan, and Dr. Rosalind Tan. We agreed to develop a master's-level HCD program for which Compassion would provide some resources and some aspiring students and MBTS would provide the academic and administrative framework and expertise.

There was some surprise on the part of the MBTS leadership, ("What? Children as part of seminary training? You don't get it, do you? We are a SEMINARY and seminaries deal with Bible, theology ... we train pastors") but there was also a readiness. MBTS already had a program called Early Childhood Care and Education (ECCE), begun by Dr. Rosalind Tan. They already had a mindset that ministry with children is an essential core of seminary training.

2.1. First course, Penang, 2001

An interesting, serendipitous event gave the opportunity for a lasting and characteristic feature of HCD programming. The first courses were planned for November 2001, and professors were lined up to teach. Two were to come from the USA. However, after the 9/11 attacks in New York City in September, both of those professors bowed out. Neither was willing to travel to a Muslim country to teach at that time. It was a big blow, and I was inclined to postpone the course. However, Bambang encouraged me to proceed.

Casting about for others who might help, I decided to call Dr, Keith White. Keith had presented a landmark paper titled "A Little Child Shall Lead Them"[1] at the 2001 Cutting Edge conference in De Bron, Holland. I asked if he would come to teach a course on Biblical Foundations.

The call came as a surprise to Keith, but he later wrote that my call "seemed to bear some resemblance to the vision that the apostle Paul had when he was at Troas. There was the same sense of urgency; this was not about long-term planning and strategy, but a plea to drop everything and to go."[2]

Thus the call proved to be a very pivotal decision for both of us. Teaching with us that year and in many subsequent years gave Keith a forum and opportunity to expand and deepen the biblical reflections on the child, leading eventually to the formation of the Child Theology Movement. And the inclusion of Child Theology became a crucial distinctive of HCD programming in many seminaries around the world, immeasurably enriching the HCD movement over the years.

Dr. Rosalind Tan was the Director of that first HCD program at MBTS. In 2002 she set up an office at the seminary to support the HCD ministry. This office was later named the *Holistic Child Development Institute* (HCDI); to this day it still facilitates the HCD initiatives. More than 200 students from some twenty countries have taken degrees, and at least that many studied in the on-campus or extension programs.

With promising feedback from the MBTS program, Bambang and I decided it would be good to do this in seminaries all over the world. He deployed me to pursue it, marking the beginning of the efforts to which I devoted the last fifteen years of my work in Compassion, and some years beyond—developing seminary programs in HCD.

---

[1] http://prevetteresearch.net/wp-content/uploads/image/churches-children/A%20Little%20Child%20Shall%20Lead%20Them.pdf.
[2] Keith White, "Reflections on Child Theology and Holistic Child Development in Repairers of Broken Walls." (Bangalore. CFCD-India.2014), p. 178.

2.2. The Global Alliance for HCD

There was, though, a problem with Compassion doing advocacy and providing leadership for an *academic* movement. Obviously, as an international NGO, Compassion had no "standing" to promote academic programming in seminaries. A new, separate entity was needed. At the first global HCD "summit" held in Chiang Mai, Thailand in May of 2007, the HCD Global Alliance (GA) was formed so that that HCD promotion in the seminaries was done from a "neutral" platform.

In Chiang Mai I was asked to be the global General Secretary of the GA. Mr. Enrique Pinedo, Rosalind Tan, Dr. Jesudason Jeyaraj and Mr. Shiferaw Michael were appointed as the Regional GA coordinators for Latin America, Southeast Asia, South Asia and Africa, respectively. Regional Alliances for HCD comprised theological institutions that supported the mission of the HCD Global Alliance by advancing and promoting holistic child development in their regions. We defined the GA as "a voluntary partnership of Seminaries, Bible Colleges, and other Christian academic institutions working together with researchers, trainers, practitioners and other Christian leaders to create a global movement for the development of academic programs in Holistic Child Development."

The Global Alliance Partners (the participating institutions) were encouraged to contribute to the development of HCD resources, including curricula, syllabi, books, articles, websites and other items, to raise standards, improve content, ensure accreditation, and develop administrative/governance guidelines which would enable and enhance HCD programs.

In a paper prepared for Chiang Mai, Keith White captured for us the intent for the institutions at that gathering—Jesus seeks to place a child right in the midst of your seminary. And he does this not to provide a comforting object of admiration and comfort, but to challenge what you stand for—your priorities—and to shed light on all that you are doing in his name. In time every part of what you do will be reformed. That includes the way you do things (the process) and the content, including your historical, biblical, systematic, and practical theology. And Jesus is longing for you to do this. And the church and children are waiting.[3]

The Chiang Mai consultation was followed by two other global GA consultations, in Pasadena (hosted by Fuller Seminary and spearheaded by Drs. Doug McConnell and Dave Scott) and at SAIACS in Bangalore, India

---

[3] Keith White, "The Contribution of Child Theology to the HCD Course and Beyond." Unpublished paper presented to HCD Summit, Chiang Mai, Thailand, May 13, 2007.

where Dr. J. B. Jeyaraj provided leadership. Numerous regional consultations followed over the next few years.

There was remarkable enthusiasm and resourcefulness on the part of the participants over the years, and many seminaries went on to offer courses or develop full HCD programs in their respective institutions. The quarterly GA "*Communique,*" which I compiled and published for several years, highlighted the programs being offered and the HCD resources being developed by various people and institutions around the world. The January 2014 *Communique*[4] indicated 121 institutions engaging in more than 132 HCD Initiatives worldwide, including 12 each in Southeast and East Asia, 25 in Latin America, 3 in North America, 23 in Africa, 3 in Europe, 48 in South Asia, and 2 in the Middle East. Meanwhile, the Global Alliance website had over 200,000 resource downloads in the space of about three years.

An early consensus was that this was something new and necessary for the seminary context. It began to be recognized that children feature prominently in Scripture (and are therefore a legitimate topic for emphasis and exploration), always with a consistent message to protect and nurture them to become what God intends. But with the input from Child Theology reflections, it came to be recognized that children are also significant "pointers" to understanding the Kingdom of God. Manfred Kohl's voice was an influential and passionate one in a chorus in support of such emphases in seminaries.

Beyond the scriptural mandate, it was becoming clear that relevance in the "real world" demands that seminaries equip students to carefully reflect on the strategic importance of children.

3. HCD. What was it and what was it not?

As seminary leaders began to see the value of incorporating HCD programming into their curricula, it also quickly became apparent that "HCD" programming needed definition and clarity. GA members wanted HCD to learn from, but to be different from other training activities and events which sought to equip practitioners and caregivers on behalf of needy children. But how, if at all, were HCD programs to differ from other child-focused training, workshops, and curricula? ("If everything is HCD, then nothing is HCD.") How should we clarify whether course offerings were "true HCD" courses or not?

---

[4] Produced quarterly from 2010 to 2014.

As things progressed, we generally settled on some working definitional distinctives which, taken as a whole, differentiated an HCD program from most other training and equipping programs.

For example, we agreed that HCD programs would be:

- *Academic*, normally taking place in an academic institution and normally part of the course mix of the hosting institution—and thus more than, and different from, typical workshops or in-service trainings. An HCD program would typically be designed to lead the student toward some kind of academic credentialing or other recognition.
- Known for an emphasis on *research* and *scholarship*. As an academic course (as opposed to practicum training), students would be expected to engage in reflection on, for example, the theoretical frameworks of holistic child development. They would also do quality research on matters such as the needs of children in light of Scripture, culture and theology; the systems and structures of poverty in communities, and the way in which these affect children; and the relationship of Christian child development programs and strategies to the wider context of the mission of the Church.
- *Cognizant of the Church as God's instrument for transformation,* and emphasizing the role of the Church in carrying out ministry to children in need. An HCD program would recognize that the Church is uniquely able to do true Holistic Child development, because only the Church can adequately address both the physical and the spiritual needs of children. Thus, while the students might be from Christian NGOs or other non-church entities, an HCD program would seek to equip future church leadership to be strong advocates and spokespersons who supported and emphasized the unique and crucial role of the church in ministry on behalf of needy children.
- *Distinctive in scope*—inclusive of children both *inside* and *outside* the church. It would be intentional about equipping the students to care for children not yet in the church, such as those from other faiths, or those needy children in the communities around the church but who are not part of church-going families.
- *Understanding of the strategic mission component of ministry to children.* An HCD program would view ministry to a child as very strategic, recognizing the importance of such ministries to the mission of the church, to church growth and to furthering the kingdom. An HCD

program would recognize the opportunity that ministry to children represents in terms of reaching the whole family—not in a manipulative or scheming way—but rather as an informed view of the "big picture" of how such "great commandment" ministries fit into the Great Commission as well.

4. Child Theology and the Child Theology movement

Even more fundamental to the distinctiveness of HCD programming was the theological importance of the child. Rosalind Tan, whose essential contributions in leading the pioneering program at MBTS in Malaysia were invaluable in developing the HCD program throughout the Southeast Asia region, said that the distinguishing "signature" of HCD training programs was their objective to form theological minds so that those who minister to children can faithfully work out the God-children connection, and also research on contextual issues as a means of prophetic challenge for Christian ministry to children. Whereas other training programs often include biblical foundations or other biblical references to children and our responsibility to care for them, an HCD program would provide the opportunity for deeper biblical and theological reflection.

The process meant that all courses taught are not only based on theoretical data but seriously reflect from what God is communicating to us when he calls us to be responsible for the children in our midst.[5]

It was Keith White who most persuasively argued for and articulated the theological component of the early HCD programming. He often noted that although in most "Christian" child development training, components of biblical reflection were included, they were always more or less only one piece of a puzzle or mosaic. He argued that the theological/biblical reflection in an HCD program should not be just as an add-on or stand-alone "puzzle" piece, but more like threads in a fabric running through and informing the whole. The early inclusion of "Child Theology" (CT) (as defined and developed by Keith and Professor Haddon Wilmer of Leeds University) in the HCD movement gave CT a fertile field in which to test, ripen and grow. The first two global CT consultations were in Penang. Other early regional consultations included those in Addis Ababa, San Jose, Bangalore, India, and Houston, Texas. Many other such consultations have

---

[5] Rosalind Tan, 'An Introduction to the Working Group Discussion on the Contextual Needs of HCD Programs in South East Asia.' Unpublished paper presented to SEA HCD Program Implementation Consultation, Session 2, June 6, 2009.

taken place in recent years. The proceedings of each were captured in compendia which were published and distributed.[6]

Child Theology as developed by White and Willmer began with "the child that Jesus placed in the midst" (Matt 18:1-3). It was quite different from "children's theologies," or theological reflections on the child, or child spirituality, or any other such previous manifestations. Indeed, CT didn't even focus on the child or on children. Rather, it was an exercise in "looking at God through the lens of the child." In other words, "CT stresses that the child Jesus placed in the midst of his disciples is not intended as the object of analysis or adoration but as a sign or clue to a great understanding of God and his kingdom."[7]

Keith provided this working definition:

> Child Theology is an investigation that considers and evaluates central themes of theology—historical, biblical and systematic—in the light of the child standing beside Jesus in the midst of the disciples. This child is like a lens through which some aspects of God and his revelation can be seen more clearly. Or, if you like, the child is like a light that throws existing theology into new relief.[8]

As White and Willmer's approach to CT ripened, others around the world began to engage in their own reflections. For example, Dr. Jeyaraj used the incarnation of Jesus as the basis and starting point to explore more of its dimensions. He explored the topic from the standpoint of Christological, sociological, political, ecclesiastical and missional dimensions.

Except during the Christmas season, we always see Jesus an adult. That is why we often miss seeing through him as a child. To me, placing Jesus in the midst of us as Immanuel—that is, incarnation—gives the Christological, sociological, political, ecclesiastical and missional bases. Jesus is a lens to reflect on theologies, doctrines and practices, and he asked later to see through the lens of a child by placing the child in the midst of his disciples.[9]

---

[6] See https://childtheologymovement.org/ for access to these and other CTM resources.

[7] Haddon Willmer, *Experimenting Together: One Way of Doing Child Theology*, (London: Child Theology Movement, 2007), p. 10. See also Keith White and Haddon Willmer, *Entry Point* (London: WTL Publications, 2013).

[8] Willmer. 2007. p. 4.

[9] J. B. Jeyaraj, "Child in the Midst: Incarnation and Child Theology," in Jesudason Jeyaraj et al. (eds.) *Children at Risk: Issues and Challenges.* (Bangalore: ISPCK, 2009), pp. 49-72. See also J. B. Jeyaraj, "Churches and Kingdom of God: Relationship and Development of Children," HCD Study Document Series (GA-HCD South Asia Unit, 2013).

Other very insightful contributions were made and developed by scholars in Latin America, Africa and elsewhere.

5. HCD implementation

The years 2007 to 2014 saw significant growth in the HCD movement. With the support of Dr. Scott Cunningham and Manfred Kohl of the Overseas Council (see below), and other initiatives, more than 100 seminary presidents and academic deans heard about HCD, Child Theology, and related topics. It was not an obviously good idea or good fit for all. Some leaders resisted personally "engaging" in child development. They felt neither called nor gifted for such ministries (as was the case even for me). At the same time, many relished the engagement with new, fresh, robust theological reflection. Of course, the goal was not to turn seminary leaders into children's workers, but that they would become fervent and well-versed advocates for children, able to speak out and lead with passion and solid biblical, practical and strategic conviction about the needs, nurture and potential of children.

For those for whom it did seem to be a good fit, there were immense challenges in implementation. Any thriving seminary will already have full dockets, courses and programs, and their teachers will have full loads with little margin for adding anything new. The Global Alliance (GA) members in every region grappled with these and other obvious and understandable challenges.

Moreover, the HCD movement itself was learning and evolving. More fundamental questions were posed: How were we to hold institutions to the above distinctive approaches? Were the distinctives we talked about useful and appropriate? How should we ensure high-level, academic content, inclusive of theological and missiological reflection? How could or should meaningful tracking of HCD programming be done? How do we upgrade the value and consequence of GA membership, such that it carried more weight and meant something important to participating seminaries? Attention was given to defining and refining membership mechanisms, member maintenance, and renewals. Also, work was done to make HCD more accessible to the many church leaders who do not go to seminary or a "normal" theological institution for their training. Various approaches were explored to find ways to make HCD training more accessible at the grassroots level.

GA participants wrestled with these and many other matters. But the movement grew. The GA-HCD conducted frequent regional meetings in South Asia, Europe, Southeast Asia, Africa and Latin America calling the leaders of the seminaries to learn about the HCD curriculum and introduce this training in their seminaries.

Among the most active and productive were the efforts of Dr. Jeyaraj and his colleagues in South Asia. Jeyaraj and others formed an indigenous committee called the Christian Forum for Child Development (CFCD) to develop the curriculum and promote concern for holistic child development. Under the auspices of this CFCD, they tirelessly promoted HCD programming and consulted on curriculum planning and resource development. They were prolific in producing curricula, books and other resources for use throughout the Indian sub-continent.

Dr. Jeyaraj particularly zeroed in on resources addressing advocacy and HCD education, faculty orientation, networking and involvement in other activities connected to children. Several outstanding course books and HCD resources were developed, including a noteworthy reader with a South Asian flavor called *Children at Risk,* and an even more remarkable book called, *Holistic Child Development Education,* providing extensive information and bibliographies on various possible courses for HCD at the different levels (Certificate, Diploma, MA, M.Th., Ph.D.)[10]

The list of South Asia seminaries engaged in HCD development is long and impressive. Of particular interest was the commitment of the Serampore Senate that all Serampore affiliated seminaries were to include some HCD programming.

Elsewhere, through the efforts of Enrique Pinedo and others, twenty-five Latin American Seminaries offered courses including the outstanding programs at SEMISUD in Quito, the CGST in Jamaica and elsewhere. More than forty institutions came together in July 2014 in San Jose, Costa Rica for the purpose of furthering HCD throughout the Latin American and Caribbean regions. The Southeast Asia HCD Institute (HCDI) was and is the "arms and legs" of the GA (Torchbearers) movement in Southeast Asia and China.

HCD was ably promoted in East and West Africa through the efforts of Shiferaw Michael, Jonas Sawadogo and others. SATS and PETRA offered extensive programs in Southern Africa and elsewhere. The 2008 and 2012 consultations in Ouagadougou, Burkina Faso and Lome, Togo brought leaders from eighteen seminaries and organizations from Burkina Faso, Benin, Togo, Mali, Niger and Senegal, where they agreed to develop common foundational and distinctive West African syllabi and courses for their seminaries.

---

[10] See J. B. Jeyaraj, "Child in the Midst: Incarnation and Child Theology," in Jesudason Jeyaraj et al. (eds.), *Children at Risk: Issues and Challenges* (Bangalore: ISPCK, 2009). Also see J. B. Jeyaraj, *Holistic Child Development Education* (Bangalore: ISPCK, 2009).

Advocacy and HCD guest lecturing were done in Odessa (Ukraine), Moscow, Beirut, and elsewhere. HCD was a catalyst for other kinds of reflections, such as "Reimagining the Seminary" spearheaded by the late Dr. Corneliu Constantineanu.

It was becoming clear that including programs in HCD could ensure a high level of real-world relevance to seminary programming.

6. Key Partnerships and Spin-offs

Several key partnerships provided additional energy to the HCD movement. The Child Theology movement mentioned above is the most obvious and significant. But there were others.

6.1. The 4/14 Window movement

The term "4/14 Window"[11] piggybacked, of course, on Dr. Luis Bush's "10/40 Window." In fact it was a Korean pastor in New York, Dr. Nam Soo Kim, who along with Bush organized the first "4/14 Window Summit" at Kim's Promise Church in New York in September 2009. He recruited several people to lead various tracks.

I had the privilege of leading the Academic and Theological Transformation (ATT) track along with Jesudason Jeyaraj. The goals and approaches for the ATT track neatly paralleled those we sought to accomplish through the GA, most importantly to seek to ensure that the value and strategic importance of children were recognized in seminaries and theological institutions. Manfred Kohl's support, contributions and affirmations were a consistent source of encouragement in support of the initiatives which arose.

The ATT track was active in six global 4/14 Window "summits" and many National and Regional 4/14 Window Consultations, including Beirut, Jordan, Mongolia and Kenya. In two key consultations, the proceedings were captured in conference compendia.[12]

---

[11] See Dan Brewster, "The 4/14 Window: Child Ministries and Mission Strategies," in Phyllis Kilbourne, *Children in Crisis: A New Commitment*. (Pasadena: MARC, 1996).

[12] See Siga Arles et al. (eds.), *Now and Next Conference and Compendium* (Penang: Compassion 2011), and also the 4/14 Window Missiology Conference Compendium from Seoul, in Dan Brewster and John Baxter-Brown, (eds.), *Children and Youths as Partners in Mission* (Penang: Compassion International, 2013).

6.2. Overseas Council International (OCI)

A second very important partnership for the HCD movement was with Overseas Council International (OCI). OCI is an organization specifically dedicated to developing the vision and leadership skills of seminary leaders. Part of their approach is to conduct multiple "Institutes for Excellence" in regions around the world. They require that participants be the academic deans or principals/directors of the institutions they represent, so that the participants are the true leaders.

Here again, Manfred had a key role. He introduced me to Dr. Scott Cunningham, who then had the responsibility for designing and implementing the Institutes for Excellence. I met with Scott in Indianapolis and he invited me to do presentations on HCD in all ten of their upcoming Institutes in 2008. We did so, and virtually everywhere the reception was open and thoughtful. (In informal surveys, we found that the vast majority of the leaders had themselves come to Christ in the "4/14 Window," thus validating the strategic importance of that "window.")

Scott reflected on Manfred's role in promoting HCD programming:

> Manfred's thought was that the area of HCD had been almost totally neglected in the typical seminary curriculum and needed increased attention. OC could service this need, along with HCD resources, to seminary leaders for their consideration during the Institute sessions. This eventually led to our invitation to Dr. Dan Brewster to participate in each of our regional Institute for Excellence workshops held worldwide in 2008.
>
> For Overseas Council, this was an important step. One of our emerging values for theological education was that it must be missional. It must be missional in the sense that the seminary needed to exist, not for its own sake, but for the sake of the Church. And so the theological education provided by the seminary needed to be responsive to the realities of the Church. The fact was that, though the Scriptures provide theological perspectives on children, the Church by and large had neglected this mission field for outreach and discipleship.[13]

Following up the many contacts made in those consultations and responding to invitations to teach or consult was what kept me occupied for many years and a major driver of HCD growth around the world.

---

[13] Scott Cunningham, personal correspondence, March 30, 2021.

6.3. Asia Theological Association (ATA) consultations

As HCD programming in Asia matured, it became useful to also seek to influence the leadership of the Asia Theological Association (ATA). The roles of the ATA (and other regional theological associations) in seeking to ensure theological soundness and encouraging and facilitating academic innovation suggested the importance of raising awareness about the possibilities and importance of HCD programming. Dr. Theresa Lua invited me to make presentations at several ATA gatherings. I worked to ensure a "place at the table" for Compassion and for advocating for HCD among the member seminaries. The ATA published chapters I wrote on aspects of the HCD movement in some of their publications.[14]

6.4. The International Council for Evangelical Theological Education (ICETE)

While seminaries and theological institutions are under the umbrella of their regional theological associations, those associations are themselves under a global umbrella called the International Council for Evangelical Theological Education (ICETE). Having networked with the regional associations, I was invited to their triennial global gatherings, leading workshops or panel discussions in Chiang Mai, Thailand (2006); Sopron, Hungary, (2009); Nairobi, Kenya (2012); and Antalya, Turkey (2015). Here again, Manfred Kohl was a helpful advocate and door opener.

6.5. Denominational implementation

Advocacy for and promotion of HCD programming also took place among denominational leadership. The impact on two particular denominations is useful to note.

6.5.1. Church of God (Cleveland, Tennessee)

Dr. David Ramirez, former bishop of the Church of God in Latin America and now Assistant General Overseer, was a particularly enjoyable and enthusiastic HCD "convert." He was an energetic advocate for HCD in the

---

[14] See for example "Leadership *from* the Next Generation," published in Bruce Nicholls et al. (eds.), *Leadership in an Age of Turmoil* (Manila: Asia Theological Association, 2012), pp. 161–176.

seminaries of his own denomination as well as others. He wrote about his invitation to visit the Baptist Seminary in Malaysia:

> Without a doubt, the Holy Spirit dealt with me and the leadership of SEMI-SUD to engage in the process of offering the HCD degree. Immediately, we started designing and developing the HCD master's degree at SEMISUD. The program gave us a tool for advocacy and acceleration for 4/14 geographical, generational, and missional reach.

As a result, Lee University, the premier academic institution for the Church of God, expressed interest in the SEMISUD HCD program. The curriculum received accreditation from the Southern Association of Colleges and Schools (SACS) and is now offered at the university.[15]

6.5.2. The Church of the Nazarene

Apart from the outstanding and ongoing HCD programming in the Malaysia Baptist Seminary, perhaps the most significant and enduring work has been done in the commitments and in the seminaries of the Church of the Nazarene.

Dr. Floyd Cunningham (no relation to Scott Cunningham above) served as President of the Asia Pacific Nazarene Seminary (APNTS). Floyd participated in the Chiang Mai conference, but in fact was not aware of the longstanding commitment of his own denomination to children. He wrote of his dawning realization while at the "Cutting Edge" Conference at Wheaton College in July 2008:

> The Church of the Nazarene made up the largest single group at that conference. One person said that she had never been in the Church of the Nazarene, and knew nothing of our teachings. The only thing that she knew about the Church of the Nazarene was that we were the church that cared for children in crisis. Amazing! When I informed them of APNTS's plan for a holistic child development graduate degree the response was, "yes, of course, you are Nazarene."[16]

Floyd went back to Manila and began work with others at APNTS to develop an HCD program. Key to the program's success was the appointment of a full-time professor in holistic child development: Dr. Nativity Petallar,

---

[15] Personal correspondence, March 30, 2021.
[16] Floyd Cunningham, "Opportunities and Challenges for Holistic Child Development," unpublished paper regarding observations from Nazarene Compassionate Ministries Conference, Olivet Nazarene University, July 14, 2016.

one of their own graduates. "Natz" was working as a project director for Compassion International in Davao City. The perfect choice, it has turned out to be. Together they worked with the Philippine government to set up a Holistic Child Development major within our existing Master of Arts in Religious Education. Floyd remarked on the significance of this program:

> This is more than simply Sunday School ministry, as important as that is. Master of Divinity students, who tend to be men, who have taken subjects such as Child, Church and Mission, Intervention Strategies for Children in Crisis, Learners with Special Needs, and Holistic Nurture of Children have expressed the incredible benefit of these classes for both their outlook on life and their entire ministry. These subjects force us to lift our eyes beyond the local church to families, community, and society.[17]

Then, more ambitiously, in 2009, in cooperation with the Asia Graduate School of Theology, APNTS launched a 60-credit-hour Ph.D. degree in Holistic Child Development, one of the few programs like it around the world. Because they viewed the program as a hybrid of education and missions, they chose to call the degree a Ph.D. In January 2012 they received Philippine government permission or "recognition" to officially grant Ph.D. degrees in holistic child development.[18]

In this ongoing program, to date, seven students have received Ph.D.'s in HCD from APNTS, including two from Africa and two from India. Currently, there are twenty-three active Ph.D. students from ten different countries.[19]

7. Conclusion: Lasting Fruit and Uncertain Future

Seminaries are (or should be) a prophetic voice to the churches. They should help set the agenda for the churches. Seminaries today are concerned about survival and relevance. HCD programs can help their feet touch the ground. It was hoped that HCD could provide new "wind in the sails" for seminaries which are striving for survival and relevance.

Compassion International pioneered the HCD movement and had a unique niche. No other large NGO was as well-known as Compassion for exploring and developing the biblical foundations for ministry to children, or for promoting the whole new discipline of "Child Theology." However, in 2014 Compassion withdrew its support for many of its advocacy

---

[17] Cunningham, "Opportunities and Challenges."
[18] Floyd Cunningham, "What Has This to Do with Me? Holistic Child Development at Asia-Pacific Nazarene Theological Seminary." *Barnabas*, 2010. [No pages]
[19] Nativity Petallar. personal correspondence, April 9, 2021.

initiatives including the HCD programming. Sadly, this left a big gap in the support and promotion for the HCD movement and related initiatives and understandably interrupted its momentum around the world.

Did HCD provide such new wind in the sails for seminaries? Was HCD really integrated into the fabric of seminary offerings? Was a child placed right in the midst of seminaries, challenging what they stood for and shedding light on all they were doing? Perhaps here and there, but certainly not as widely as was envisioned and hoped for. Undoubtedly, the HCD movement bore lasting fruit, some of which this review has highlighted. Indeed, much is still happening. But for now, the HCD movement lacks a global champion. While I would say that its future is uncertain, a seed has been planted, and we will not despise the day of small things.

Floyd Cunningham draws attention to a critical ongoing challenge:

> In educational institutions, the danger is for holistic child development to become institutionalized, for it to simply become one part of the curriculum added on to all the others, rather than at the center of our ministry and mission. How can children become and remain a central part of our attention whether we are teaching biblical studies, theology, church history, preaching, pastoral counseling, or other subjects? School presidents must be sold on the idea of the centrality of children in the school curriculum, and deans must keep it before the faculty.[20]

Experience showed that providing programs in HCD can have a revolutionary effect on students and on the institutions themselves. The real strength of HCD was in changing mindsets in those institutions.

Dr. Sunny Tan, the Academic Dean of MBTS, said, "Not only has this program transformed the lives of many students, but the seminary itself has changed. The key leaders in the seminary have a new vision for the strategic significance of children in their own equipping and mission strategies."[21]

Similarly, Scott Cunningham of OCI noted three major outcomes for OCI through its engagement with HCD programming: (a) Seminaries were introduced to HCD as a field of study and training, with many of them introducing courses and even entire degree programs focused on this area of study, at various academic levels. (b) Several seminaries became involved in the Global Alliance for HCD, adding capacity and global diversity to the movement, and to its theological reflections. (c) Through our own consideration of HCD, OC, as an organization, became more finely tuned to

---

[20] Cunningham, "Opportunities and Challenges."
[21] Global Alliance brochure.

the values of missional and contextual theological education. In some ways, HCD was an impetus for OC's recognition that seminary curriculum needed to be more attentive to the context of churches and communities.[22]

Floyd Cunningham of APNTS summed up the lasting effect of the movement at APNTS, which captures my own feelings about the overall global impact of the movement. He writes:

> The Holistic Child Development program has made a deep and lasting imprint on the life of APNTS both inwardly and outwardly. The program has helped us to look at the context of ministry where we are located and to devise means of reaching out to our community. This outreach is both a laboratory for students and a model that they can take back with them to their local churches and ministries. At the same time, no matter what their academic program, every graduate of APNTS in the last few years has gone on to ministries, whether as pastors, teachers or missionaries, with hearts for children.[23]

I am grateful to all who have been a part of the HCD movement and the contributions all have made to that remarkable endeavor. Thanks especially to you, Manfred. Your passionate support and commitment were a constant motivation and your insights always provided trustworthy guidance.

---

[22] Scott Cunningham, personal correspondence, March 30, 2021.
[23] Floyd Cunningham, excerpted from "Opportunities and Challenges," April 7, 2021.

About the Author

Throughout his life, Dan's passion was speaking for and about the needs of children. Dan worked for World Vision and Compassion International managing child-focused relief and development programs.

In 1995, Dan coined the term "4/14 Window" which focuses ministry on the 4 to 14 age group. It highlights the reality that most people who will ever decide to follow Christ will do so before their 15th birthday. The "4/14 Window" is now a significant global movement in missions.

In 2007, Dan helped found the Global Alliance for promoting Holistic Child Development and Child Theology in seminaries and theological institutions, and he served as the General Secretary for the Alliance for eight years.

Dan had a doctorate in Missiology from Fuller Seminary. He taught "Child, Church and Mission" in more than twenty seminaries, and he chaired or convened numerous consultations relating to the child, child theology, family and mission in a variety of contexts around the world. He worked as an advisor/consultant, promoting Christian HCD and other ministries to, for and with children and youth.

Dan traveled to 120 countries and was involved in planning and monitoring child and family development or relief projects in more than 50 countries. He and his wife Alice lived in Penang, Malaysia for 22 years until his passing in 2021.

Child-Focus in Theological Education: A Neglected Core

Jessy Jaison

1. Introduction

I have known Rev. Dr. Manfred Waldemar Kohl as the Ambassador for Overseas Council and a catalyst for integrity and anti-corruption with Lausanne. Having been a member of the board of Re-Forma has made me appreciate his transformative vision for theological education more closely. Indeed, it is a privilege to have been invited to contribute to this Festschrift in honor of Kohl's life, work and ministry.

This paper addresses a "neglected important" in theological education, i.e., children. "Child-focus," though supposed to decorate the central place in all forms of training in this rapidly shifting global culture, has been a neglected core in theological academia. We contend that, without this essential in place, the mission and sustenance of the church are at stake. Placing this matter for more deliberation, however, we do not envision this paper as a theological or historical treatise. As I write these lines today, every form of Christian ministry is facing unprecedented setbacks due to the persisting disruptions of the Covid-19 pandemic. Academia is already heeding the inevitable need for educational revolution, certainly beyond all of its routine curricular modification. Perhaps this is a clarion call for theological educators to capture the worthy motif of *child-focus*, irrespective of the contexts we represent. Let us examine here how intentional the place of children in our thinking and training is and should be. The following sections discuss the elitist curriculum that divorces itself from the actual needs of the church, present a case of responsiveness from India, and invite the church and theology schools to envision the future with the "child in the midst."

2. Is Academic Inflexibility and Elitism Jeopardizing Child-Focus?

The evangelical theological guild over the decades has acclaimed firmly the slogan "As goes the seminary, so goes the church." Yet we continue to search in the dark, wondering what exactly is going on between the two institutions. Even after decades-long debates and consultations, many theological institutions are still conveniently revolving around the rigid observances of the "clerical paradigm." We hesitate to embrace "the community of faith paradigm" that values the meaning, mission and context of the constituencies in the church, which leaders like Tan defined as "the expansion of the whole people of God."[1] Insider assessments in theological education are no novelty. Let us survey a few comments that reflect the damaging, elitist shifts in theological education.

The World Missionary Conferences in Tambaram, held in 1938, called theological education the "Cinderella of mission."[2] At the dawn of the twenty-first century, we heard the voice of Athyal, an Indian theological educator who lamented, "Seminaries exist to serve the church, but they have become prodigals doing their own thing."[3] Heywood quoted Newbigin about the "Babylonian Captivity"[4] of theological education, indicating, "Theologians are often out of touch with the needs of the church in society at large." Thomas addresses this multi-dimensional issue and mentions the unhealthy influence of the university model on theological institutions[5] that makes them produce scholars who are independent of the church, insensitive to their communities and immersed in their own inquiry interests. Lloyd-Jones stated, "Theological teachers and tutors have often been academics who know nothing about church life, who now nothing about handling people, and often, who cannot preach."[6] All this points to either the obscurity and neglect of theological education, or the damaging elitist direction it could take in the institutionalized, professional, scholastic training patterns.

In the fixed and loaded traditional curricula and in the priorities of courses, contents relating to children and youth are often labelled as "irrelevant," "unnecessary" or "less important." Modules on Child Theology

---

[1] Derek Tan, "Theological Education in Asia: Present Issues, Challenges and Future Opportunities," 35–51 in *Biblical Theology and Missiological Education in Asia*, edited by Siga Arles, Ashish Chrispal and Paul Mohan Raj (Bangalore: TBT, 2005), 46.

[2] Lesslie Newbigin, "Theological Education in a World Perspective," *Churchman*, Vol. 94, p. 105. The article forms the substance of a paper given to the conference of the staffs of the Church of England Theological Colleges on January 3, 1978.

[3] Saphir Athyal, "Missiological Core of Theological Education," *UBS Journal*, Vol. 1, No. 2, September 2003, 55.

[4] David Heywood quotes Lesslie Newbigin in "A New Paradigm for Theological Education?" *Anvil*, Vol. 17, No. 1 (2000), 19.

[5] Jaison Thomas, "Church Ministry Formation in Theological Education," unpublished Ph.D. thesis, Queens University of Belfast, UK, 2008.

[6] Martyn Lloyd-Jones, *Training Men for the Ministry Today* (London: London Theological Seminary, 1983), 8.

or Holistic Child Development barely find a slot in the mainstream theological curricula, and hence an academic program specializing in children would only remain an unrealistic prospect. Keith White identified the development of child theology as a challenge to seminaries. He hopes to see that the child placed by Jesus is received today as a theologically important sign. The quality of church leadership is hugely impacted by the training they undergo in the seminaries. For White, "many pastors seemed ill-equipped and ill-prepared to relate to children and families appropriately. Such preparation was not simply about the content of teaching, but the ethos of the institutions themselves."[7] There are several roadblocks to finding space for child-focus in the seminary educational system. Unless guided by a visionary direction, traditional churches tend to remain adult-oriented in much of their work. Affinity to children/youth ministry domains or developmental topics are viewed as secondary skills and not as a leadership potential.

Marcia Bunge recorded in 2008 that the scholars in diverse areas of biblical studies, religious studies and theology were beginning to focus attention directly on children and childhood in the United States and Europe.[8] The 4/14 Window and Holistic Child Development vision became globally influential concepts around the same time. However, studies showed that the Asian and particularly Indian theological curriculum was revisited and revised a few times based on this, yet for many this "re-envisioning of the educational core" still remains a distant reality. The *core* refers to the locus of the actual needs of the church. Adaptation of a set of curricula is not likely to ensure formation or transformation. By monopolizing the mechanisms of an inflexible academic curriculum, "the theological education in Asia and particularly India has failed to produce effective ministers to face the global challenges in the local contexts,"[9] Nayak observed. Educators need to read the culture, the missional needs of the church, and the changing socio-political scenario of human daily engagement and equip ministers and leaders who are committed to grappling with those realities both in theory and praxis. Beyond the contextual, linguistic or regional differences, "child-focus" stands out as a distinct priority. In fact, every program, course and ministry practicum needs to integrate this crucial

---

[7] Keith J. White, "An Introduction to Now and Next," in *Now and Next*, edited by Siga Arles et al. (Singapore: Compassion International, 2011), 11.

[8] Marcia J. Bunge, "Introduction," in *The Child in the Bible*, Marcia J. Bunge, general editor (Grand Rapids, Michigan: Eerdmans, 2008), xvi.

[9] Biren Kumar Nayak, "Curriculum: The Heart and Tool for Indian Theological Education," in *Towards Indigenous Mission and Theological Education*, edited by Siga Arles and Gnanaraj D. (Bangalore: CFCC, 2012), p. 252.

component. Children set for us the measure by which we assess the impact (the long-term effect) of training, because they paint the future and lead beyond the *now*. Kohl reminds us:

> The lives of church members and the ministries in which they are involved will reflect what is taught in seminaries. The direction in which a seminary is moving, any failure to communicate basic and essential elements of the faith or of ministry, any undue emphasis on particular formations or functions of ministry will be replicated in the ministries of students.[10]

In other words, what is neglected in the content, resources and direction in learning will be neglected in the ministry of the church.

3. From Neglected Corners to Adorn the Core

"Children are a nuisance! I don't like to be around children because they are so demanding and annoying." The book *Precious in His Sight*[11] starts this way, portraying the annoyance little children might cause. Amandeep Kaur, my Indian student in a Master of Theology class, said that not even a single church in her locality had a Sunday School or any form of service to children. No one to speak for children; literally, no one cared. Many churches have traditionally kept children in the margin of the margins with little or no facilitation, engagement, focus or funds. Stories of seminaries too are not very different. Nakah and Malherbe studied the obstacles faced by African seminaries in moving "child theology" from the margins to the mainstream of theological education. For them, both the church and the seminary need to tackle the challenge of numbers, needs, history, diversity, culture and marginalization of African children as they engage in theology and praxis.[12] Maybe we should keep asking ourselves, "What are seminaries supposed to do if their central purpose is serving the church and her mission?"

Children as a neglected important in theological education would be perceptible to anyone who scanned through the learning contents,

---

[10] Manfred Waldemar Kohl, "Theological Education: What Needs To Be Changed," in *Educating for Tomorrow: Theological Leadership for the Asian Context*, edited by Manfred Kohl and A. N. Lal Senanayake (Bangalore: SAIACS Press, 2007), 29.

[11] Roy B. Zuck, *Precious in His Sight: Childhood and Children in the Bible* (Grand Rapids, Michigan: Baker, 1996).

[12] Victor Nakah and Johannes Malherbe, "Child Theology: A Challenge to Seminaries," in *Now and Next*, edited by Siga Arles et al. (Singapore: Compassion International, 2011), 135–149.

ministry internship programs, library collections, and program specializations. Many questions are there to reflect on. Is not "building up the next generation of the church" an urgent mandate with Gen X, Y, Z and the Alphas? What if we keep failing to recognize children as a worthy motif in theological education? Can the integration of child-focus be a game changer in the post-Covid church and theological education? Lamenting our own detrimental flaws of the church in forgetting the significance of youngsters and youth, and being left with a few faithful elderlies in church pews, does not appear to be capable of resolving anything. Child neglect is a global reality; it is only the attitudinal and practical intensity that varies. Rensburg reports on the neglect of children and child realities in the South African context as follows:

> It is time for the South African seminaries to carefully re-examine their course content, to measure it against what children and youth are experiencing and then to deploy experts in these fields to write courses that will address what have now degenerated into critically important issues. If they do not, we will simply perpetuate the cycle of seminaries producing pastors and Christian leaders who are ill-equipped (or not equipped at all) to deal with these maladies, thereby making the church less and less relevant.[13]

Part of the problem may be the elitist content and outlook of theological education our schools have succumbed to over the decades. Theology, intending to be a life-giving source rather than a rigid set of concepts, should fall to the ground, die and sprout afresh. Seminaries continuing to be the "ivory towers" that inherit an unexamined passion to *train scholars to produce more scholars* with the top-rail education in isolation from the ground reality are the challenge. White said:

> It cannot be denied that the way much theology is done in seminaries communicates to ordinary Christians that it is a discipline for a few, and that it tends to be more concerned with words and formulations than with action. We cannot allow it to be falsely defined in this way. It reflects western philosophical traditions and it is understandably a problem to ordinary Christians seeking faithfully to live out their faith in the real world.[14]

---

[13] Reuben van Rensburg, "The Realities of Children and the South African Seminaries," in *Repairer of the Broken Walls,* edited by J. B. Jeyaraj, Rosalind Tan, Sheferaw Michael and Enrique Pinedo (Delhi: ISPCK, 2014), 265-277.
[14] Keith White, *Introduction to Child Theology* (Malaysia: Compassion International, 2010), 10.

Theological education should change gears to address the realities of the world and equip the whole church for action and change. More than at any other time in history, this Covid pandemic is bidding us revisit all of our life, and particularly the ways in which we educate people in the new era named "post-Covid" or "Covid-accompanied." The context and culture of all kinds of education are changing, and theology cannot be an exception. A generation with distinct digital curiosities and faith crises is opening up new vistas for "digital ecclesiology." The church is exploring ways to affirm, integrate, inspire and equip this generation for the future, with a deep-felt realization of her limited access to the current generation. If formal training in seminaries fails to address this need, non-formal training practices will emerge to keep the momentum of discipleship and mission formation in church.

4. Seminaries Capturing the Generational Vision: A Case from India

At this point, my own experience of responding to the need to integrate child-focus in a traditional theological setting in India seems to be worth sharing. This case might serve as a pointer or motivator to some. Mapping an unknown path with a team, then mobilizing ourselves to walk on it despite the hurdles was simultaneously exciting and challenging. A theological curriculum with child-focus was obviously something that the team did not imagine, at least in the worst of scenarios.

In 2010 at the New India Bible Seminary in Kerala, India, we, the faculty and leadership, raised difficult questions among ourselves regarding the status of church-seminary relationships. Does the church seek the seminary's service in anything?[15] To what extent is the seminary responsive to the pertinent needs or challenges of the church? "If not for the church, why should a seminary exist?"[16] Realizing that the seminary curriculum needed radical restructuring and not mere cosmetic improvement, we started exploring the top mission needs in the country to which the church must be equipped to respond authentically. From this informal unconventional inquiry was birthed a residential M.Th. program in Practical Theo-

---

[15] Jessy Jaison, "Evaluation and Innovation: Possibilities in Theological Education," paper presented with Jaison Thomas at the OC Institute of Excellence, Colombo, August 8, 2014.

[16] Kohl, "Theological Education: What Needs to be Changed," establishes the centrality and necessary procedures in strengthening the church-seminary relationship through theological education.

logy, specializing in Holistic Child Development. The initial deterrence from the theological academia, the student constituency and the sending churches gave clear indications of an imminent downward momentum of the seminary. Several voices forewarned that child-focused programs are seldom found in the hierarchy of theological disciplines, and therefore making it a core discipline would be like inviting the hasty ruin of the elevated structure. In spite of the ongoing issues of lack of textual resources, lack of full-time specialized faculty, fears of applicants about future ministry placements, and the issues in obtaining accreditation, a full-fledged master's program was launched in 2011, the first of its kind in India.[17] Things started turning positively after four years, with churches seeking to send their choicest candidates to this program, and every single graduate being appointed to key roles in the churches as assistant pastors, youth directors, Sunday School superintendents, family ministers, Bible Study directors and community service managers. This confirmed the enormous need for training in the church to which seminaries are bound to respond. This innovation achieved a four-sided impact:

Establishing a training model that affirms and realizes the dignity of children/youth	Educating the church to appreciate and accept children as signs of the Kingdom
Empowering families to lead children into responsible Christian living for themselves	Ensuring children's presence and enhance their participation in God's mission

Often, the resistance to curricular innovation hinders the responsiveness and growth of theology schools. Right at the student recruitment phase in the program, we realized the immense needs for such a focus in the local contexts of students. Slowly they developed an ardent desire to understand God's plan for the emerging generation and explore intervention strategies for those who are losing their childhood and purpose in families, churches and communities. One of my students, named Nehemiah, completed his project in Andhra Pradesh on the societal restoring of children who were rescued from sex trafficking in his neighborhood. Another student, William, explored the context of village churches in Northeast India that lost all their children at early adolescence. Sam developed a church

---

[17] This program was evaluated and accredited by the Asia Theological Association. The academic assistance of Dr. Dan Brewster and Dr. J. B. Jeyaraj in this initiative was commendable.

help center for parents of acutely autistic children who were in an endless struggle with daily life management and ultimate theological questions regarding their suffering. Sharmily went further to reside with the children of HIV victims in Tamil Nadu, to study what life and faith meant to them. Year after year, the vision of "child-focus" is transforming the culture of theologizing in context, multiplying the impact on churches and communities with more topics such as digital addictions, suicidal tendencies, father-absent homes, and so on. These are leaders, made on the ground where they can touch for themselves and become one with the human realities.

This experience reformed and revitalized the faculty's perception about the way we learn and teach theology. Learning continues on to engagement and to transformation of the church and society. Defining *theological education* beyond the function of the seminary and *ministry* beyond the walls of the church seemed crucial. Transcending the irrelevance of theology in the ecclesial and public arena becomes useful when a pertinent theme such as "child-focus" is addressed in training. Tangibly, this new track released the traditional theological content from its intellectual (erudite) and ecclesial confinements. Even apart from the traditional nomenclatures, the program integrated every aspect of theology in meaningful ways and addressed several of the real-time concerns of the church. It also taught us how graduates' ministry placement turns into a natural and dynamic momentum when the program is highly responsive to the needs of the church and the society at large.

5. Envisaging Future with the Child in the Midst: The Post-Pandemic Mandate

At the heart of the church are children. We have multi-dimensional expositions on Matthew 18:2-5, concerning "the child in their midst"[18] articulating it. A question posed to the participants in a theology consultation was "Where is the heart of the church?" The litany of responses identified "children" as the heart, but "the neglected heart." Subsequent analysis brought to light attitudinal problems in the church including adult orientation at the expense of children, labeling children as spiritually inferior,

---

[18] "Child in the midst" is based on Matt 18:2-5. For more discussion of this, see Keith White, "He Placed a Little Child in the Midst: Jesus, the Kingdom and Children," in *The Child in the Bible,* Marcia J. Bunge, general editor (Grand Rapids, Michigan: Eerdmans, 2008), 353-374.

and counting children as a means to certain structural ends.[19] Education and training have an important role to play in making the church grow as a child-friendly community that upholds the standards of the Kingdom of God. Hobson termed such a task as the "re-engineering" of curricula and church relationships, emphasizing a thoughtful move from the "Classical Model" to the "Missional Model," equipping theological education in Asia to address issues faced by the church and the society.[20]

Being more concerned about its own grandiose identity, theology's tendency to become less and less responsive to the world around should concern us. Clark's recent reflection on the great reversals in the Kingdom, symbolized by "the cup of cold water," appears to be a fitting insight here. For him, "Theological education in the majority world needs to consider giving a 'cup of cold water' to reverse this world's tendency to higher and more exclusive forms of theological and ministry formation."[21] Educational settings enslaved by an ever-growing schema of upward professionalism often fail to realize when and how they make theology unreachable and incomprehensible to the community of believers. According to Prevette, "Theology is not just finding the best words to describe God, Christ, sin and Redemption, it requires a conscious and serious engagement with the text, context and living human persons including children."[22] The shape of theological education in the majority world needs to adopt a certain amount of flexibility due to the diversity of children's realities that vary from context to context. The churches in each region are to tackle the lived reality of their children and youth, which could be of poverty, addictions, natural disasters, child labor, child prostitution, child abuse and many more. These are the realities in which the church lives and serves—although, slowly, *child* is capturing our theological imagination lately, calling the church and seminaries not to relegate children to the receiving end of our sympathy but as the dynamic signs of God's Kingdom, and as partners in the mission of God. When the church is not able to see her children as her invaluable resource in hand, there is an obligation for

---

[19] Referring to the Penang Child Theology Consultation in 2006. See Dan Brewster, "Characteristics of a Child-Friendly Church," In *Marriage, Family and Church*, HCD Vol-2 (Delhi: ISPCK, 2014), 213.

[20] Steve Hobson, "Creative Leadership Development: Breaking out of the Traditional Seminary Model," in *Educating for Tomorrow*, edited by Manfred Kohl and A. N. Lal Senanayake (Bangalore: SAIACS Press, 2007), 5–21.

[21] Paul Allan Clark, A "Cup of Cold Water," unpublished paper; Overseas Council, June 2021.

[22] Bill Prevette, "Child Theology and the Reflective Practitioner," in *Repairer of Broken Walls* (Bangalore: CFCD, 2014), 156.

the theological community to initiate theological thinking and praxis in that direction.

Child-focus in theological education will change the paradigm of training. It is a ground-shaking initiative that calls for a reshaping and re-envisioning of the curriculum. As the saying goes, "It is easier to change the location of a cemetery than to change the school's curriculum." We acknowledge that the central objective of theological education includes educational service to the church, equipping leaders for the church, and training for the advancement of Christian mission in the world. These are the loudest pleas before the church and seminary today.[23] With child-focus, we will address three critical needs in theological education:

- Dynamic relationship between church and seminary
- Strategic leadership development for the future
- Impact-oriented advancement in Christian mission

A comprehensive curriculum that meets these objectives is a mirage for most of the traditional seminaries.

Renewal in theological education does not occur by repeated affirmations of successes in the past; it happens when leaders start discerning the needs of the time, changes in the society and the new steps in responding to God's plan for the world today. For educators, Pattison's reminder is "Mourn the 'great' past of theology and then leave it behind to grasp new possibilities and challenges. The past, with the methods and assumptions it has bequeathed to theology, often hangs like a millstone round its neck."[24] Authentic leadership recognizes the capability of inherited patterns of ministry and training in preventing us from seeing the essentials of the moment or the futuristic predicaments. Unperceptive safeguarding of the status quo is not of much help; to most institutions. it is the sign of slow internal death. In a world that is witnessing technological transitions, religious and socio-cultural paradigm shifts, do we find ourselves with a dearth of abilities to observe, listen and respond? This long-heard plea for change in the way seminary education is done is not just to teach people to do programs for children and youth. It is about instilling the vision of God for children and endowing the God-given dignity that is due to them, and enabling them to be partners in God's mission. There are rays of hope,

---

[23] Jessy Jaison, *Towards Vital Wholeness in Theological Education* (Cumbria: ICETE-Langham, 2017).
[24] Stephen Pattison, *The Challenge of Practical Theology* (London: Jessica Kingsley Publishers, 2007), 223.

as in the words of Cannell: "Today many churches frustrated with the graduates of theological schools are challenging the existing systems and joining their efforts to find new models."[25] Seminaries as learning communities and serving institutions must hear and see the particular areas where the church is in dire needs for trained ministers.

6. Summary and Conclusion

Theological leadership should take courage to move out of the world's enthralling standards that blindly maintain the status quo of the higher academic trajectory and seldom reach down to the ground of the community of faith. Jesus' radical ministry for and with the latter, which involved children, women, and the most vulnerable, must inform our theology and theological education. Matthew 18 resonates within us that learning with "the child in the midst" will augment and not diminish our growth. Theological scholarship that disregards the significance of children in God's plan would do so for its own irreversible loss. We are in the business of building leaders who will, in turn, build a responsive church in a suffering and confused world. For this, theological training should embody an intentional and explicit focus on its neglected cores, in which *child-focus* has always been at the top of the list. Child-focus in training is intensely theological, missional, prophetic and transformative. It acknowledges *child* as the symbol, the message, the sign, and the standard of the Kingdom of God, and hence capable of impacting the adult disciples. Humility, wisdom, courage and vision come together here in a perfect blend, as we are called not only to be mindful of the little ones, but to welcome them and, further, to learn from them. This could be a challenging reversal for many, but will be worth it for the sake of the Kingdom of God.

Any authentic self-assessment of the challenges of the church in leadership, socio-political engagement, digital cultural/ecclesial crises, sustenance of generations in faith, or whatever challenge the context may present, will often point us to the need to focus on *child*. Ignoring this would be hazardous, as it would constitute ignoring God's mission mandate to the church in the present moment. Child-focus is deeply a divine agenda, with which we can have a privileged partnership. Those who wait for a favorable season to embrace this vision may run the risk of waiting forever. Church-seminary collaborative learning, listening to local contexts, cross-sectional synergizing, strategic planning and publishing are key in this

---

[25] Linda Cannell, *Theological Education Matters: Leadership Education for the Church* (Newburgh: EDCOT Press, CanDoSpirit Publishing, 2006), 18.

process of re-envisioning. Resource development from a wide range of specializations seems crucial in the formation of ministry leaders, practitioners, teachers and child advocates for the multifaceted needs in the church and society. Theological education has to break out of the shells of conventional models to serve the church in radically deeper purposes and patterns by envisioning her most neglected cores, where one would certainly identify *children*.

About the Author

Jessy serves as the Professor of Practical Theology and Director of Advancement at New India Bible Seminary, Kerala, India. She gained her M.Th. (Oxford) and Ph.D. (Queens, Belfast) and completed post-doctoral projects at Asbury and Fuller Seminaries in the USA. She also serves alongside the Lausanne Theology Working Group, ICETE Senior Consulting Initiative and Re-Forma, envisioning the transformative integration of the formal and non-formal modes of theological education and the vital missional engagement between church and seminary. Jessy and her husband Dr. Jaison Thomas (Regional Director, Overseas Council, South Asia) are blessed with two sons, Abraham and Aquil.

Theological Education and the Church

Roger Kemp

1. Introduction

I believe it is the right of every group of believers in Jesus to be taught regularly from the Bible by someone who has had some training in Scripture. Unfortunately, for many, it is not the case—especially for those believers who are part of the growing insider movement.[1] The focus of most literature on the subject is on the traditional understanding of theological education and the church. There is little written directly on the insider movement. There are good reasons for this. The insider movement is, by its nature, unconventional, and so demands a different approach to leadership training. I hope to make a small contribution to the ongoing conversation on the issue. First, I define the terms "theological education" and "church" and then trace the strong relationship between the two. The heart of what I have to say is to explore possible ways to train leaders of believers in the insider movement. It involves using cultural beliefs and practices and linking them with Scripture so that the lessons learned are not only true to the Bible but are also meaningful to the believers in that culture. I submit several examples as evidence that this approach has value.

2. Definitions and history

The term "theological education" has many meanings. There is no universally accepted definition. In this chapter I am defining it as the training of church leaders that enables them to be effective in ministry. Likewise, the term "church" has a history of different meanings. I use it here to mean a community of believers in Jesus who exist for the purpose of worship and fulfilling Jesus' Great Commission,[2] in ways that are appropriate to their culture. This definition particularly reflects the insider movement, which

---

[1] The insider movement in missiological terms refers to mission using contextual methods and expression. It is most common in countries with major religious blocs such as Muslim, Hindu or Buddhist. The emphasis is on empowering followers of Jesus to express their faith in their own cultural ways.
[2] As found in Matthew 28:18–20.

is the focus of my discussion. It is my intention to explore the link between theological education and church as I have defined those terms.

In the New Testament, there are references to church leaders but not a great deal of data on how they were equipped to do their job. If, as I believe, Jesus' disciples were chosen to lead the fledging church, then we can see how Jesus trained them for their task. He used a variety of teaching methods including parables, illustrations, questions, discussion, lectures, object lessons and debates. He used whatever method was appropriate for the occasion. He was flexible in his methods—some would say contextual.

So it is unsurprising that the early church at first did not use formal training—perhaps because initially the use of spiritual gifts was preeminent. Writings such as the Didache and Shepherd of Hermas give "evidence of the charismatic nature of the ministry of 'apostles, prophets and teachers,' a ministry which hardly called for formal training."[3]

However, with the more formal subdivision of clerical orders beginning in the second century, and the need to debate heresies such as Gnosticism, the need arose for more formal ministerial training. Once the canon of Scripture had been recognized, there was a need for training in authoritative interpretation—something that is true to this day.

Down through the centuries, the training of leaders has been linked to the Church in one way or another, whether to edify believers, defend the faith or promote the gospel.

This chapter examines that relationship, albeit as expressed in ways that are not as obvious as in traditional contexts.

Over twenty years ago, the International Council for Theological Education published a "manifesto."[4] The second of twelve sections relates to the Church:

> Our programs of theological education must orient themselves pervasively in terms of the Christian community being served. We are at fault when our programs operate merely in terms of some traditional or personal notion of theological education. At every level of design and operation, our programs must be visibly determined by a close attentiveness to the needs and expectations of the Christian community we serve. To this end, we must establish multiple modes of ongoing interaction between program and church, both at official and at grassroots levels, and regularly adjust and develop the program in the light of these contacts. Our theological programs must become manifestly of the church, through the church and for the church. This we must accomplish, by God's grace.

---

[3] H. Rowdon, "Theological Education in Historical Perspective," *Vox Evangelica* 7 (1971): 75.
[4] For the full text of the manifesto, see www.icete.info.

The message is clear: theological education and the church are inextricably linked. The question that has dominated throughout the relationship is how theological education can best serve the church. So we need to deal with some of the issues that endeavor to answer the question. The large number of groups of believers in Jesus that are emerging in many countries as part of the insider movement are challenging the traditional meaning of "church." Such groups don't identify with any formal expressions of church because those are a long way from a relevant cultural expression of what it means to be a follower of Jesus. Such churches normally reflect the form of the church that the "outsider" missionaries introduced. In that sense, they are foreign to the local culture.

The question then is how theological education relates to this emerging expression of "church."

3. Major Issues

3.1. The nature of Church

"The nature of the church has been tightly intertwined in the fabric of the insider debate from the very beginning."[5] There are different opinions as to the meaning of the term *ekklesia* as found in the New Testament. The term itself only occurs three times in the Gospels but 114 times in the New Testament. It was common in first-century society, where it referred to a gathering of like-minded people. So, like other secular terms such as *logos*, the term was invested with a deeper meaning by the early believers. Perhaps the most significant use of the term in the Gospels is in Matthew 16:18, where Jesus states that he is going to build his *ekklesia*—church. It is Jesus' church, his assembly, bearing his authority and presence.

Of the other references in the New Testament, most are found in Paul's letters. There is no doubt that in Paul's mind, an *ekklesia* is a community of believers who regularly gather (1 Cor 11:18). But they are no ordinary communities. They have divine significance—referred to as the "church of God" (1 Cor 1:2). As such, they have a purpose, and that purpose is to be on mission for God. "In the emerging ecclesiology, *the church is seen as essentially missionary.*"[6]

The understanding of the true nature of the church is helped by the way it is expressed in the New Testament. Paul, for example, refers to the

---

[5] S. T. Antonio, *Insider Church: Ekklesia and the Insider Paradigm* (Littleton: William Carey, 2020), xxi.
[6] David Bosch. *Transforming Mission* (Maryknoll: Orbis, 1991), 381.

church as a building (Gal 2:18), a temple (1 Cor 3:16-17), a field (1 Cor 3:9), a family (Gal 4:4-7), and the body of Christ (Rom 12:12-17). Peter adds to the picture by referring to the church as the people of God—elect (1 Pet 1:1), called (1 Pet 1:15), and God's sheep (1 Pet 2:25). Perhaps the most significant description of the church is found in 1 Peter 2:9 where the people of God are referred to as "a chosen race, a royal priesthood, a holy nation, a people for his own possession."

Such an understanding of the church is crucial for the ever-increasing insider movement, because, as we will discuss, it affects the way leaders are trained.

There are several matters to discuss first.

3.2. The kingdom of God

The church and kingdom of God are closely linked. The best way to think of the kingdom of God is to see how God relates to believers in Jesus. For such believers, God is king. Jesus was aware that the term "kingdom of God" could be used to mean different things. He made it clear in his preaching and teaching that the kingdom of God involved the sovereignty of God; that it was a "present reality wherever individuals acknowledged it by obedient submission to his will."[7] The "concept of the kingdom of God implies a community ... a group of people who own him as king and the establishment of a realm of people within which his gracious power is manifested."[8] So the connection between the kingdom of God and the church is a close one. The kingdom emphasizes the concept of the rule of God while the church emphasizes the fellowship of believing men and women.

Such a relationship is important for believers in the insider movement. For many, the expression of community is determined by their local contexts, and as such, it may be difficult in the extreme, or even impossible, to meet physically. However, they can assure themselves that they are in the kingdom, along with all the other believers in the world who claim God as king. For them there is a sense of worldwide fellowship even if they are unable to express that physically in the local context.

One aspect of the kingdom of God that is especially reassuring for the communities of believers where physical fellowship is not always possible

---

[7] O. Evans. "Kingdom of God," in G. Buttrick (ed.), *The Interpreter's Dictionary of the Bible* (New York: Abingdon Press, 1962), 20.

[8] H. Marshall. "Church," in J. Green and S. McKnight (eds.), *Dictionary of Jesus and the Gospels* (Downers Grove, IL: InterVarsity, 1992), 122-125.

is the eschatological one. This aspect was predominant in Jesus' teaching of the kingdom. His words spoken in the upper room[9] when he inaugurated the Last Supper are an encouragement to such groups. The present difficulties of meeting physically are overshadowed by the fact that when Jesus comes again, all believers will enjoy true fellowship, both with each other and with Jesus.

3.3. Identity

For all believers, realizing who they are in Jesus is an important aspect for their well-being. Being able to identify with a group of fellow believers is very encouraging—especially during times of difficulty and stress. There is no substitute for the encouragement of one another. In the Bible, believers are exhorted to bear one another's burdens (Gal 6:2), to encourage one another (1 Thess 5:11) and to pray for one another (Jas 5:16). This is best expressed within a local community of believers—the local church. And it is an important aspect of being community—in times of need—to help each other, but also in times of celebration such as when someone comes to faith or a sick person is healed.

However, for many such fellowships in the insider movement, this is difficult, because they cannot meet regularly, and communication is difficult at best.

Many such fellowships are therefore isolated—spiritually as well as physically. Identity is therefore important to them. For most of them, someone from a culture other than their own introduced them to Jesus. Such cultural outsiders (intercultural workers), being sensitive to current missiological thinking, would most likely have used contextualized methods when sharing the gospel, so that the believers now follow Jesus in their own way, rather than reflecting the culture of the outsider. The believers "own" Jesus for themselves—the news of Jesus is not seen as a foreign gospel. Naturally, they express their faith in their own cultural ways. So each insider fellowship is different from the next one. The intercultural workers do not impose the structure or methodology of their church on the new fellowship. If they did, it would be seen as foreign and therefore largely irrelevant.

It is only natural, then, that such fellowships would like to know where they stand in relation to others. They ask important questions: do other such fellowships exist? If so, are they like them or are they different? Are

---

[9] Mark 14:25: "Truly I tell you, I will never again drink of the fruit of the vine until that day when I drink it new in the kingdom of God."

there others with whom they can relate? In other words, they search for their identity as believers in Christ.

Those who look on this situation from a distance could well argue that the intercultural workers should give a lead and inform the fellowships that whatever their situation, it is a *fact* that they are part of the body of Christ. And therefore, they have family members throughout the world. While it is true that the fellowships are part of the body of Christ, to be simply *told* it is so without experiencing it for themselves is simply imposing ideas on them from outside.

The dilemma, then, is to enable the believers in these fellowships to answer the questions for themselves, and this involves "theological education," or leadership training. It is a challenge as large as any other that has faced the Christian faith since its inception. There are attempts to meet the challenge, and this is what the rest of the chapter addresses.

3.4. Leadership training (theological education)

As defined earlier in this chapter, I am using the term "theological education" to refer to training that will enable persons to become more effective in ministry in the church. Most such training is found in formal institutions such as theological colleges and seminaries. How related that training is to the needs of the church is a matter of great debate. In recent years, there has been a move away from the more formal aspects of training to other, informal, and non-formal approaches—even within institutions. So an emphasis on small group study, seminars with open discussion, field trips, and experience-based learning are all methods being used by institutions around the world.

Yet a direct relationship between such learning and the church's needs is not always to be found. There is little, if any, discussion with the church as to its leadership needs and how they may be met. As a result, some local churches have begun their own training programs to bridge that gap. "Training capable leaders inside the church provides a stability that cannot be replaced."[10] A brief survey of the internet with the subject "leadership training in local churches" results in thousands of possible websites and/or articles with all kinds of attractive titles including "Be a better leader in 8 weeks," "The importance of leadership training in the local church," and "Effective leadership training—the new way to train lea-

---

[10] R. F. Ginnan, *Developing a Leadership Training Program for the Local Church in the Twenty-first Century*, unpublished D.Min. thesis, Liberty Baptist Theological Seminary, 2003.

ders." There are many reasons why local churches are training their own leaders, one of which is that institutional training programs have by and large been irrelevant to the needs of churches.

> My reading pointed to the fragmentation and contextual irrelevance of most ministerial training programs ... student after student entering college passionate for ministry and leaving passionate for academia, with little idea how to empower the church and often with no genuine desire to do so.[11]

It comes down to the main reason for the existence of any training program, whether it is institutional or not. Using my definition of theological education, it seems that there are major challenges for institutional programs. I believe those challenges can be overcome and institutions can be effective in preparing students for ministry in local churches. Perry Shaw outlines ways by which the Arab Theological Seminary in Beirut has been successful in doing so although it took a major overhaul of the curriculum.

When Steve Hardy worked with training institutions in his role with Overseas Council International, one of the questions he asked was "Did they have a plan for strengthening a curriculum that equipped quality students for effective ministry?"[12] Indeed, the manifesto of ICETE, referred to earlier, under section 11 (Equipping for Growth) talks of the importance of preparing students for effective life-long ministry. "We need to design academic requirements so that we are equipping the student not only to complete the course but also for a lifetime of ongoing learning and development and growth."

As we consider the faith fellowships of the insider movement, we quicky recognize that while such outcomes for leadership training are necessary, the methods used to reach those outcomes cannot be guaranteed to be able to do so. Indeed, it is improbable, if not impossible, that theological institutions can achieve what is required. Factors such as language, worldview and learning styles come into play, not to mention cost. The challenge is so great that a more appropriate term is being used for such training in faith fellowships, namely intercultural discipling.

> Intercultural discipling is the long-term, intentional process in which Christians from one cultural background walk alongside people from another

---

[11] Perry Shaw, *Transforming Theological Education: A Practical Handbook for Integrative Learning* (Carlisle: Langham Partnership, 2014), preface.

[12] Steve Hardy, *Excellence in Theological Education: Effective Training for Church Leaders* (Green Point, UK: Modern Printers, 2006), p. 13.

culture, sharing life with them in order to help them in their journey of getting to know Christ and growing in their relationship with Him.[13]

This type of theological education fits naturally in majority world cultures where the norm for learning is oral, not written.[14] Faith fellowships of the insider movement are by and large found in the majority world. Using print learning will not benefit faith fellowships to any large degree. Using art forms such as proverbs, stories, dance and music will be most effective. The problem is that theological educators in these cultures come mainly from the West—where learning is done using written materials rather than those mentioned above from oral cultures. Two questions arise from this. How can a Westerner be part of intercultural discipling, and is it possible for those from the insider culture to be the theological educators? It is my belief that the answer to both those questions can be expressed in the affirmative.

3.5. Intercultural discipling

The Bible is a written record of a story—God's story. "If our lives are to be shaped and formed by Scripture, we need to know the biblical story well, to feel it in our bones."[15] In order to "feel it in our bones," the story must be told in ways that make sense to us culturally. In order for someone from the West to disciple persons within an oral culture, it must be the oral culture that determines what and how it is done. For example, it won't be done in a term or semester. It is an ongoing, open-ended *way of life*. In other words, it must be based on a relationship, not on an accumulation of knowledge. "Good discipling happens in the context of a relationship that integrates practical matters with knowledge and character with ministry skills so that the whole of the disciple's life is affected."[16]

Once a relationship has been formed between the person doing the discipling and those being discipled, the issue remains as to how best to disciple—how to integrate knowledge of Scripture with character-building traits: theological education. As mentioned above, the best way is to use the art forms of the host culture.[17]

---

[13] Evelyn and Richard Hibbert, *Walking Together on the Jesus Road: Intercultural Discipling* (Littleton: William Carey, 2018), 5.
[14] W. Jay Moon, *Intercultural Discipleship* (Grand Rapids: Baker Academic, 2017), 5.
[15] Craig Bartholomew and Michael Goheen, *The Drama of Scripture* (Grand Rapids: Baker Academic, 2004), 197.
[16] Hibbert and Hibbert, *Walking Together on the Jesus Road*, 11.
[17] The term "host" refers to the culture in which the people who are being discipled reside.

It ought to be understood that such discipling is best done using the host language, but unfortunately it isn't always the case. Misunderstandings and false conclusions will be common unless the host language is used. A movement cannot be recognized as "insider" if a foreign language is used. Some of the most common art forms of an oral culture are symbols, rituals, stories, proverbs, music, dance and drama. It is beyond the scope of this chapter to deal in detail with each of those, but a brief discussion of several will be helpful.

Symbols are used by people of all cultures to create meaning out of the world around them. They "can bring the theoretical and remote to the center of things."[18] Symbols are things that are seen to point to something that is unseen. For those wanting to disciple within the insider movement the use of symbols is a necessity. "It seems clear. That effective cross-cultural discipling requires working with symbols."[19] Symbols are varied in their description. They can be ceremonies (rituals), songs, drama, or dance. It behooves the intercultural worker to dig deep into the meaning and significance of symbols in the host culture, because the same symbols can mean different things in two different cultures.[20] In discipling, symbols point to matters of faith as expressed in Scripture. A good discipler will use the symbols of the host culture to communicate an important point from Scripture. For example, in Thailand, the Buddhists have a ceremony (symbol) in which a person ties a piece (or more) of string around the wrist of another person. It can be done between two people, or a group of people. The ceremony is used for a variety of significant occasions, such as to welcome someone into a new group, or when someone is about to leave the group or community. The string represents the bond between each other—a bond that will remain through all circumstances. The string is usually left on the wrist for several days. The ceremony has been used by disciplers to illustrate the bond that occurs between a person and God when the person accepts Jesus as their savior. The ceremony would not mean anything to anyone else but the Thai people. By using the ceremony to communicate a biblical principle, a powerful message is proclaimed.[21] Guiding a believer

---

[18] Mathias Zahniser, *Symbol and Ceremony: Making Disciples across Cultures* (Monrovia: MARC, 1997), 76.

[19] Zahniser, *Symbol and Ceremony*, 75.

[20] For example, a village woman sweeping the dirt around her hut is not "cleaning" it—as would be expected in Western culture. She is clearing away any spirit that could impact her life that day.

[21] I have had the privilege of being involved in a number of these ceremonies in Thailand—especially with the faith community in the insider movement in northern Thailand.

to scriptures such as John 15 indicates the principle involved and helps the believer grow in his or her faith.

Jay Moon[22] refers to symbols as only one way to disciple believers. He talks about rituals, stories, proverbs, music, dance and drama as other cultural practices that can be used in discipling new believers. The challenge for intercultural workers working within insider movements is to know their host culture well enough that they can use appropriate practices in a way that illustrates biblical principles and points believers to scripture. This is the appropriate way to disciple and bring believers to maturity.

The process of making disciples within insider movements can begin with either cultural practices (as in the string-tying ceremony mentioned above) and proceeding to Scripture, or it can begin with Scripture and connect with cultural practices. An example of the latter comes from northern Thailand.

Groups of believers from a Buddhist background have emerged from a ministry begun over twenty years ago by a team of Australian Baptists using insider movement principles. The believers come from quite a few villages in a wide area. Due to the large distances between the villages, the believers can only come together several times each year in a central location for fellowship and training (discipling). This is their "church"[23] although that is not the term they use for their gatherings (though they fit my definition of church). They simply call their gatherings "workshops." The training in the workshops was initially done by the intercultural team leader or another member of the intercultural team, but more recently the believers themselves have led sessions.

The team leader has made a practice of linking cultural practices with Scripture in the discipling process. On one occasion several years ago, I attended one of their workshops led by the resident intercultural worker. The workshop was conducted in Thai (and translated for me). Several steps were taken in the learning session. The first was to choose a passage, and Mark 4:1–9 was chosen. Then the passage was read in Thai several times by different members of the group. To enhance the experience, the leader divided the group into pairs and had each person tell the story to their partner. The leader then explained the context of the story: the people involved, the location of the story and what happened before and after the story.

---

[22] Moon, "Intercultural Discipleship."
[23] There are several denominational churches in the region. However, they are institutional, reflecting the culture of their founders, so they have little connection to village culture.

Knowing that the villagers were farmers, the leader then asked the members of the group if there was any cultural event from their traditional life—a ritual, poem, story—that came to mind as the story was told. The responses from the group were enlightening. One person said that special prayers would be offered to Buddha at certain stages of planting and reaping. Another person described a ritual that would be enacted to enable the farmer to know the best day to sow the seed.

The group members were then asked to draw a picture of the story as they understood it. Once that was done, the members were given the opportunity to voluntarily explain their drawing to the rest of the group. Several did so, one saying that now that he was a believer, he prayed to God rather than Buddha throughout the process.

The final step was to ask the group members to meditate on the story and ask themselves several questions: what is God saying to me in this story? What was the main character in the story feeling? What do you think is the main point of the story? They were encouraged to share their answers with other group members outside the group session.

The group members regularly hold meetings in their homes where non-believers from their village are invited to come and hear stories about Jesus. They use the method just described as the basis for the way they lead their home groups—with the aim of bringing more into a relationship with Jesus.

Another example of this kind of theological education comes from central Australia and the work being done by a team of Baptist intercultural workers to train aboriginal pastors of churches in communities.[24] The format is based on Hiebert's critical contextualization model.[25] The learning is done in what they call training camps.

The church leaders come from communities that are separated by long distances—over 1000 kilometers between several of them. Frequent training is therefore virtually impossible, so the leaders are brought together

---

[24] Culture demands that the pastors be male. Training courses for women leaders are run along similar lines at different times.

[25] Paul Hiebert, *Anthropological Reflections on Missiological Issues* (Grand Rapids: Baker, 1994), 75–92. The process of critical contextualization within a culture involves four stages once a topic is chosen. Stage one is to exegete the culture regarding the topic; stage two is to exegete the Bible regarding the topic; stage three is to bring the results of stages one and two together and allow people of the culture to critically analyze the issues, resulting in a response; stage four is an optional stage whereby a new contextualized practice may result. The process must involve people of the particular culture and may also involve someone from outside the culture to facilitate activities.

at a central location several times each year—a week at a time—the location being rotated so that no one group is constantly disadvantaged. Local cultural practices dictate the training. For example, for each session a campsite in a remote area is chosen.[26] Camping is basic: sleeping bags, straw mattresses, and a campfire for cooking are sufficient. There are no books and no planned schedule. Clock time is ignored. Meetings take place when the church leaders are ready and conclude when all are satisfied that it is a good time to take a break. The language medium is English because the leaders come from different tribes, but all have used English in their general education.

To begin the week, a local person is invited to come and share something to the group about the significance of the area where the camp is situated: for example, a description of the tribal group who traditionally lives or lived in the area—telling of significant events that may have taken place at the location.

Before the week begins, the church leaders choose a topic that is of significance to them at the time, and about which they need to learn something. Sometime during the first day, the group members get together and tell stories from their background that relate to the chosen topic. If there is an intercultural worker present, he will include stories from his culture. The stories are told without any interpretation or lesson. Questions can be asked for clarification, but no value judgments are made. This carries on throughout the day with breaks for meals. Usually at night there is a campfire when the participants simply talk to each other—usually personal stories.

Once the stories from their experiences are exhausted, stories from the Bible that relate to the topic are told by the intercultural worker and the pastors if they desire to do so. As with the cultural stories, they are told without any value judgment being made. The stories speak for themselves. When those stories have been exhausted, the pastors are left to discuss the topic using the stories from culture and the Bible as the basis. If there is an intercultural worker at the camp, he would leave before this stage took place, to allow the pastors time and freedom to talk openly among themselves.

Usually by the end of the week the discussions have taken their course and the pastors and intercultural worker come together for a final session—which can take a day or more—to find out what each pastor has learned during the week. They may also come up with a practical suggestion as to

---

[26] Meeting under trees in a rural setting is the cultural way of learning. It is also how cultural interaction takes place.

what they could do as pastors to help their church members. On the one occasion I was present at such a training camp, the topic was anger. The final day was an eye-opener for me. From my cultural standpoint, I was doubtful that anything could be learned, but as I listened to each pastor share his thoughts and ideas from the week's discussion, I realized that this was what theological education is all about: helping church leaders learn things from Scripture and life generally—things that they can share with their people and lead them onward in their spiritual journey. On this occasion, they also decided that action needed to be taken to rebuke the anger that was present in a particular community. They decided they would all assemble in the community and lead a procession to bring the two parties together for reconciliation. This was church leadership in action.

4. Conclusion

It is obvious that to enable every group of believers to fulfill the right to have regular teaching from Scripture, there is still much to be done. Statistics indicate that there is a huge lack of properly trained church leaders. "The biggest crisis facing the evangelical, global church today is the fact that most pastors, missionaries, and Christian leaders are under-educated or not educated at all."[27] But there is more to it than increasing the numbers being trained. The method of training is also important. If the training is not appropriately contextual, then the teaching will be worth little. This applies particularly to the insider movement, but also to theological education generally.

There needs to be further research and writing on developing the learning potential of linking cultural practices and scriptural truths. If this chapter motivates others to get involved in such activity, then it has done its job.

---

[27] Part of the front page of Re-Forma website: www.re-forma.global.

About the Author

Roger Kemp holds a Th.D. from UNISA. He was the founding principal of the Evangelical University in Ndola, Zambia. Roger has lectured in missiology at several seminaries in Australia and Europe. He has served Australian Baptists (Global Interaction) in intercultural ministry for the past 26 years, mentoring team leaders and church leaders around the world. He is currently intercultural mission advisor with Global Interaction. He holds the view that every church community has the right to hear regular teaching and preaching from within their own context.

He is married to Barbara, a schoolteacher, and has two grown children and six grandsons.

Settler Colonialism, Conflict and Reconciliation

Salim J. Munayer

1. Introduction

Many peace initiatives have failed to achieve their goals and transform the reality within the Palestinian–Israeli conflict. For many, within and outside Palestine/Israel, this reality fosters a hopeless attitude regarding the attainment of peace, reconciliation, and justice.

However, this failure stems from a wrong diagnosis of the Palestinian–Israeli conflict which yields inappropriate treatment. Thus, only a reform of analysis concerning the Palestinian–Israeli conflict can lead to apposite and authentic reconciliation. This paper argues that the proper assessment of the conflict is that of a conflict between settlers and natives, otherwise known as settler colonial conflict. Moreover, reconciliation is the remedy for the Palestinian–Israeli conflict.

First, I will present the Palestinian–Israeli conflict as a settler colonial conflict, then demonstrate the transformative effects of reconciliation on settler colonial conflicts by using the observations of social scientists.

2. What Is Settler Colonialism and How Is It Different From Colonialism?

Settler colonialism and colonialism both refer to the domination of a native or indigenous people by another group that comes from somewhere else, and there is no clear cutoff between the two terms.[1] In fact, settler colonial projects usually developed out of colonial campaigns. However, the focus of settler colonialism is on land, whereas colonialism focuses on resource extraction. In other words, settlers come to stay.[2] They are concerned with setting up a new homeland rather than simply enriching

---

[1] T. A. LeFevre, "Settler Colonialism," in J. Jackson (ed.), *Oxford Bibliographies in Anthropology*, (Oxford University Press, 2015).

[2] P. Wolfe, "Structure and Event: Settler Colonialism, Time and the Question of Genocide," in A. D. Moses (ed.), *Empire, Colony and Genocide: Conquest, Occupation and Subaltern Resistance in World History* (Berghahn Books, 2008).

themselves. Therefore, whereas colonial projects are focused on exploiting the native population, often through slave labor, settler societies are more concerned with getting rid of the native people altogether.

Another way of explaining this difference is by saying that in colonial projects, the native population is indispensable. They are required for cheap or forced labor to produce wealth and extract resources from the land that the colonial power can then bring home. For settler colonial projects, on the other hand, the native population is dispensable because the settlers are concerned with setting up a new and permanent home.[3] This means taking control of the land for themselves, which often requires taking that land away from the native people, rather than exploiting the natives themselves. Their goal is to replace the current inhabitants with a settler society.[4] The replacement process is often carried out using violent means or other more subtle forms.

3. What Relation Does Settler Colonialism Have to Conflict?

Conflict between settlers and indigenous peoples is inevitable. As the settler society expands, it will make more and more claims on the land that is currently owned by the native people. Historically, native peoples have ascribed great importance to the land. The land provides them with sustenance and a home. In many cultures, land is ascribed a spiritual importance and is tightly entwined with a sense of identity. This relationship to the land has often been denied by settlers, frequently on the grounds that the natives do not have the same conception of private property and therefore were not seen to "own" the land in the European sense of the word.

The causes of settler colonial conflict are insecurity, inequality, private incentives, and perceptions of history and identity. They all stem from the settlers' desire to control the land and exclude the native.[5]

---

[3] P. Wolfe, "Settler Colonialism and the Elimination of the Native," *Journal of Genocide Research*, 8:4 (2006), 387–409.
[4] L. Veracini, *Settler Colonialism: A Theoretical Overview* (London: Palgrave Macmillian Press, 2010).
[5] E. Lutz, "Indigenous Peoples and Violent Conflict," *Cultural Survival Quarterly* (2005), https://www.culturalsurvival.org/publications/cultural-survival-quarterly/29-1-indigenous-peoples-and-violent-conflict.

3.1. Insecurity

Settlers rarely show any desire to include native people in political or judicial decision making. They are excluded and often dehumanized in ways that make it easier for settlers to resort to violence as a means of expropriation. The native people are forced to react with violence that makes dialogue very difficult. Human rights violations are justified through the "othering" of the native, justified by explicit or implicit appeals to racial superiority or the labeling of natives as terrorists. Violence produces feelings of insecurity which justify more violence, creating a vicious cycle.

3.2. Inequality

In the early period of settlements, the natives are likely to outnumber the settlers; however, the settlers have more material power. Their material and military dominance allows them to act in an unrestricted way towards the native. When combined with narratives that dehumanize the native and stress the racial superiority of the settler, and with a desire for land, violence is inevitable. Even after a settler state is established, economic inequality between settler and native usually remains. These real or perceived differences in the wealth distribution often lead to unrest. Any economic dissatisfaction can be manipulated by leaders to intensify group identity and persuade them to use violence to further their goals.

3.3. Private Incentives

The personal interest of politicians and private companies often leads to a continued desire for land expropriation. They desire natural resources or land that can be used for agriculture. This drives more expropriation and therefore more exclusion of the natives from their own land, feeding the vicious cycle of violence and insecurity, and also increasing inequality between settler and native. Poor young men and boys are drawn to the conflict due to a lack of opportunities elsewhere, as a life of soldiering can be relatively lucrative. Together, these factors produce a large incentive for conflict.

3.4. Clashes in Perceptions of History and Identity

As we will see in the next section, colonists arrive with a perception of both themselves and the native population which provides a justification for the use of violence against that population. Once they arrive and the expropriation of land begins, their perceptions clash with those of the native people. The history and identity of indigenous peoples has always been closely tied to the land, so the physical clash represented by the expropriation of their land can simultaneously be considered an attack on their identity. This existential threat has driven many indigenous peoples to violence as a means of preserving their identity, history, and land.

Once the cycle of violence begins, both sides assume an "us versus them" mentality. The conflict becomes zero-sum in nature, which erodes trust and hinders attempts at resolution. As time passes, the conflict becomes increasingly integrated into the history and identity of each side. As this happens, the historical legacy of violence becomes a reason to be fearful of the "other" in the future, justifying violent preventative measures. This is especially true when the settler colonial group has the means to enforce such measures. Therefore, historical perceptions feed the sense of insecurity that we saw earlier as a root cause of settler colonial conflict.

4. Settler Colonial Perceptions and Justifications for Violence

Understanding settler colonial perceptions of themselves and the native is crucial in understanding the narratives that have justified violence and produced conflict in the past. This will help us to identify these perceptions and address them as a way of dealing with conflict today. The most prominent justifications of settler colonial societies have been the religious and racial superiority of the settlers, over against the natives, and the notion of "returning" to a promised land, all of which delegitimizes the natives' claim to their own land.

4.1. Religious Superiority

Settlers have always claimed that it was divinely ordained that they should occupy the new land.[6] For example, European settlers in North America referred to themselves as the "new Israelites" while the indigenous people were the "new Canaanites." The conquests of South Africa, the East Indies and North Africa all relied on similar narratives. Although many settlers went for economic reasons, an appeal to religious superiority provided a justification for mistreatment of the natives already living there. In South Africa, the indigenous African residents were labeled as the descendants

---

[6] R. Reuveny, "The Last Colonialist: Israel in the Occupied Territories since 1967," *Independent Review*, 12:3 (2008), 325–374.

of Ham by the Afrikaners. Consequently, they were condemned to be "hewers of wood and drawers of wood in perpetuity."[7] On the other hand, religion provided an ideological tool that imbued the settler project with meaning and encouraged social cohesion.

4.2. Racial Superiority

The racial superiority of the settler is another narrative that is present in all settler colonial projects and usually goes hand in hand with religious superiority. For example, for the Afrikaner settlers of South Africa, the term "Christian" was synonymous with "White" and "European." There are three common components.[8] The first is the belief that the settler's culture is superior to that of the native. Second is the use of this belief as a justification for the exploitation or elimination of the native for the settler's benefit, involving a "civilization mission." Adopting the settler religion was considered a prerequisite for becoming civilized. Third, these differences are presented as a matter of fact or objective truth. Historically, this belief in the racial superiority of the settlers has played an important role in the dehumanization of the natives, portraying them as primitive and in need of "civilizing."

4.3. Returning

Settler societies have often appealed to the notion of "returning" home to land that was once theirs in the past.[9] Therefore, they are within their rights to take it back from the native. This view simultaneously delegitimizes the native, reversing the roles as they come to be seen as the occupiers. This was true of the French conquest of Algeria and the Italian conquest of Libya, and even settlers in Minnesota appealed to the idea that Vikings from Europe had once occupied the land there but had been killed by the current inhabitants.

4.4. Disconnecting the Native from the Land

Settlers also produced narratives that delegitimized the native population, denying them their connection to the land and therefore their identity.

---

[7] J. Schechla, "Ideological Roots of Population Transfer," *Third World Quarterly*, 14:2 (June 1993), 239–275.
[8] D. Loyd, "Settler Colonialism and the State of Exception: The Example of Palestine/Israel," *Settler Colonial Studies*, 2:1 (2012), 59–80.
[9] L. Veracini, "Israel-Palestine Through a Settler-Colonial Studies Lens," *Interventions*, 21:4 (2019), 568–581.

The doctrine of *terra nullius* (empty land) was a common way of achieving this.[10] The idea is very simple; according to the settlers, the land they found was empty. There was nothing wrong with their settling there because there was nobody to dispossess. If they admitted that a native population existed, they often claimed that the natives were originally from somewhere else or that they did not represent one contiguous community. Therefore, they could not be considered indigenous to the land.[11] Furthermore, European conceptions of property ownership meant that nomadic or hunter-gatherer communities were considered to be detached from the land they inhabited. If they were not permanent residents of the land, then the Europeans did not believe that they could "own" it, making it easier to justify the occupation of that land.

5. How Have Indigenous Peoples Been Treated?

The justifications of domination that have been outlined facilitated policies that aimed to exclude and deprive the natives of their identity, either physically through violent means or using more subtle legal and bureaucratic methods. This is what Patrick Wolfe has labeled the "logic of elimination."[12] It has been manifested in a number of ways throughout history, ranging from rapid extermination or genocide to the appropriation of native land, to the subjugation of the native population as a source of cheap labor and finally to assimilation of the indigenous identity into the settler society.

During the colonization of North America, the settlers often made treaties with the native tribes and even allowed "occupancy" rights to the land, but not full ownership.[13] These treaties were rarely respected by the settlers, however, leading to conflict between settlers and natives. Once conflict had broken out, this provided a pretext for the settlers to expropriate the native land using violent means. This pattern was very common throughout the European expansion in both North America and Australia and continued until Europeans had taken effective control of the whole of both continents.

Once there was no longer a "frontier," or new land where the settlers could expand their enterprise, the means and methods used to exclude the native usually changed. In the United States, this occurred around 1870.

---

[10] Lutz (2005).
[11] Veracini (2019).
[12] Wolfe (2006).
[13] Ibid.

The settler government began enacting draconian legislation that enclosed native peoples on reservations and forced their children to leave the reservations and be educated in boarding schools. This should be interpreted as an attempt to assimilate the native children into the settler society rather than allowing native people self-determination and the ability to preserve their own history and identity. This approach to assimilation can also be seen in the government's differing approaches to African American and Native American identity. African Americans were considered black as long as they had a single ancestor who was black, regardless of how they looked or identified. In contrast, Native Americans were considered half-breeds, or not real Native Americans, as long as their heritage was not 100% native. Both these approaches represent a form of oppression; however, the denial of Native American identity was an attempt to eliminate that form of identity altogether. This legacy is an approach to the logic of elimination.

6. Settler Colonialism and the Israel-Palestine Conflict: A Case Study

The study of settler colonialism may be useful in how we approach the Israel-Palestine conflict. Scholars generally agree that this framework can help us understand the Israeli approach in the West Bank, and indeed to the whole of historical Palestine. Some Zionists have appealed to their religious beliefs as justification for the occupation of Palestinian land. Likewise, many Zionists appeal to the idea of "returning home" to the previous kingdom of David promised to the Jewish people by God.[14] This fits with the religious justifications used by other settler colonial societies.

Lorenzo Veracini argues that Israel should be analyzed within a settler colonial framework rather than a colonial one because the main period of conquest is in the past. By this he refers to the wars of 1948 and 1967, where Palestinian land was taken by the Israeli military. Since then, the settler project has been concerned with the appropriation of new land in the territories through legal and bureaucratic methods, and also the Judaization of the land that they currently control.[15] Furthermore, there is a gaping economic disparity between Israelis and Palestinians, who have often been forced to work in low-level, menial jobs. The Palestinian economy is completely reliant on Israel, leading to

---

[14] Veracini (2019).
[15] Loyd (2012).

disproportionately high levels of poverty.[16] Once again, these are common features of settler colonial states.

7. The Logic of Elimination in Israel

The logic of elimination can be seen most clearly during the wars of 1948 and 1967. In 1948, 750,000 Palestinians were expelled from their homes or forced to flee and then denied the ability to return to their homes. The use of violence to appropriate Palestinian land ended in 1979 when Palestinians were forcefully removed from the town of Elon Moreh. They appealed to the Supreme Court in Israel, and it judged that this action was unlawful.

Since then, the appropriation of land has taken different forms, including declaring land to be absentee property and requiring that Palestinians provide proof of ownership to prevent the government from acquiring the property in the West Bank. Land has also been turned into nature reserves, declared "public property," or declared needed for military use in order to appropriate it. Moreover, the Israeli government has often turned a blind eye to "unauthorized" settlements built on Palestinian land illegally by settlers.[17] Meanwhile, ever since 1967, Palestinians have been unable to expand their own towns and settlements or develop them in any way despite their growing population.

The logic of elimination is also present within Israeli territory through the Judaization of that territory. For example, measures have been taken to fragment Palestinian communities within Israel. Those who did not leave their homes during the 1948 war have been kept under strict military surveillance and have had their freedom of movement restricted. Communities of Palestinian Christians, Druze and Muslims were cut off from each other and allowed to leave their towns only with a military permit that was very hard to obtain.[18] There are even instances of the Israeli Defense Forces (IDF) allowing—and sometimes encouraging—violence between these communities. The physical separation and fragmentation of communities within Israel has contributed to the breakdown of their Palestinian identity as well.

---

[16] Reuveny (2008).
[17] Ibid.
[18] M. Shihade, "Settler Colonialism and Conflict: The Israeli State and Its Palestinian Subjects," *Settler Colonial Studies*, 2:1 (2012), 108–123.

8. How Is the Israeli Case Different from Other Settler Colonial Societies?

Scholars also highlight the features of the Israel/Palestine case that differentiate it from other instances of settler colonialism. In the case of Israel, there is no central metropole as Britain was for its conquests in North America, Australia and around the world.[19] The Zionist movement did not originate from some pre-existing territory, although it was a predominantly European movement. Historically, Israel has considered itself a European nation.

Secondly, Zionist acquisition of land began primarily through purchase rather than conquest, which distinguishes it from most other colonial projects. As Wolfe argues, that did not necessarily mean that land acquisition was conducted fairly with respect to Palestinians.[20] Furthermore, land acquisition did eventually take the form of conquest during the war of 1948.

Lastly, unlike other current settler colonial societies such as the United States and Australia, Israel has not concerned itself with the assimilation of the native population into the settler state. Instead, it has aimed to keep its land Jewish and focused on excluding the native population. In conclusion, Israel should be considered a settler colonial society, but this analysis does not prevent us from understanding the unique and individual features of the conflict.

9. Perspective from Political Science

Often, when Palestinians approach the concept of reconciliation as a form of resolving the conflict, they point to South Africa and the end of apartheid as a model to implement in the Israeli–Palestinian conflict. This is especially true for those who support the movement calling on the world to boycott, divest from and sanction (BDS) Israel, and who claim that reconciliation efforts are normalizing the conflict and oppression of Palestinians. According to this logic, any encounter, collaboration, or partnership between Palestinians and Israelis maintains the injustices.

In his book *Neither Settler nor Native*, Mahmood Mamdani examines the link between nation states and colonialism. Palestine/Israel and South Africa are studied and analyzed as case studies. Among his many conclusions,

---

[19] P. Wolfe, "Purchase by Other Means: The Palestine Nakba and Zionism's Conquest of Economics," *Settler Colonial Studies*, 2:1 (2012), 133–171.
[20] Ibid.

Mamdani argues that apartheid in South Africa was ended by many factors, not just the boycott efforts, such as

> the anti-apartheid boycott was one dimension of the anti-apartheid movement, and not the main one at that. The South African moment was most of all a political engagement, one that went beyond earlier efforts to form cross-racial coalitions and instead mobilized a nonracial one. This movement did not simply make moral arguments about the wrongness of South Africa apartheid, as earlier activists had. It demonstrated what the alternative to that moral wrong looked like: diverse people working toward a united political future.[21]

To create change in the conflict, Palestinians need to engage in politics that go beyond advocacy and move to the realm of creating alternative visions for society, corporations, and institutions. Therefore, some of the principles and processes of reconciliation ought to be implemented for the transformation of the political reality in the Palestinian–Israeli conflict. If a movement is to be politically effective and transformative, there needs to be some form of engagement between Palestinians and Jews that envisions an alternative future. Advocacy and non-violent resistance through boycotts alone are not sufficient for the political change needed in Palestine–Israel.

For this reason, Palestinians also need to work in reconciliation efforts and not only through advocacy and BDS. There is a need to develop personal relationships and address fear and obstacles, bridging the historical narratives and building a vision for the future for all inhabitants. Thus, engaging with Israelis is crucial to bring justice to Palestinians.

10. Perspective from Social Science

Dr Nadim Rouhana, Professor of International Negotiation and Conflict Studies at the Fletcher School of Law and Diplomacy at Tufts University, argues for a paradigmatic shift in conflict analysis in regard to the role of reconciliation in the Israeli–Palestinian conflict. He argues that the current understanding of the players in the field, namely a conflict between Zionism and the Palestinian National Movement, misrepresents the dynamic on the ground, which makes any strides towards reconciliation merely impossible. Rouhana asserts that the conflict should be understood in a settler-colonial framework. According to this new lens,

---

[21] M. Mamdani, *Neither Settler nor Native: The Making and Unmaking of Permanent Minorities* (London: Harvard University Press, 2020), 350.

reconciliation in this conflict is conceived as decolonization within a transitional justice framework.

The term "reconciliation" is vaguely applied across many disciplines but is rarely used in the context of transitional justice. Reconciliation when applied within the politics of transitional justice is "the transformation of authoritarian regimes and regimes involved in mass human rights violations into democracies that face their histories and seek to overcome past atrocities by introducing social reconciliation and restorative justice."[22]

The focus of Rouhana's piece is on reconciliation as opposed to conflict settlement or conflict resolution, which are two qualitatively different processes, varying in end goal, degree of public involvement, nature of the desired societal and political relationships, importance of mutual acceptance among the parties, examination of past injustice and collective responsibility, and the prerequisites for changes in political institutions and constitutional arrangements. Rouhana argues that the latter two approaches "avoid tackling core issues such as historical responsibility, justice, truth, and other transitional justice-related issues."[23]

In contrast, Rouhana describes reconciliation as "a process that seeks a genuine, just, and enduring end to the conflict and a profound transformation of the dynamics of relationships between the societies through a course of action involving intertwined political and social changes."[24] According to this definition, reconciliation addresses political structural issues, such as distribution of power, as well as intangible concerns regarding "historical truth and historical responsibility."[25] At its core, reconciliation is founded on mutual legitimacy, achieved through a "new moral and political framework."[26] The process of reconciliation is in essence social and political, in that "it demands reaching agreements not only based on restructuring the power distribution, democratic arrangements, and constitutional guarantees for equality and human rights within a frame of restorative justice, but also on reaching intersubjective agreements on historical truths and reckoning with the historical responsibilities for the mass violations of human rights that have occurred."[27]

---

[22] N. Rouhana, "Decolonization as Reconciliation: Rethinking the National Conflict Paradigm in the Israeli-Palestinian Conflict," *Ethnic and Racial Studies* 41: 4 (2018), 643–662.
[23] Rouhana (2018), 645.
[24] Ibid.
[25] Ibid.
[26] Ibid.
[27] Rouhana (2018).

Rouhana identifies four key issues that must be addressed for a reconciliation process to achieve its goals: "justice, truth, historical responsibility, and restructuring the social and political relationship between the parties within a framework that guarantees constitutional rights, democracy, and equality of groups and individuals."[28]

11. Reconciliation as Decolonization

Rouhana, guided by the settler-colonial paradigm, proposes that reconciliation should be pursued as decolonization within a framework of transitional justice. Understanding the conflict through this lens can shed light on why the pursuit of a political settlement based primarily on partition has failed thus far. Rouhana's proposed conceptualization of reconciliation between Israelis and Palestinians is grounded in the understanding that the Zionist project is in essence a settler-colonial project with features of a national movement. Understanding this as the paradigm for the conflict, reconciliation between the parties in a settler-colonial conflict should be approached with the intention of decolonialization. This paradigm rejects the symmetrical analysis that is most often applied to both sides of this conflict, namely as two equals fighting over land. Instead, Rouhana argues that reconciliation as decolonization addresses "power structures and asymmetry between colonized and colonizer as the point of departure, with the explicit goal of transforming them into structures of equality and reciprocity in a new democratic political order."[29]

This new framework would be a dramatic departure from the current understanding of the conflict, which is why a shift towards this new intellectual paradigm will take time. This shift would provide the mechanisms for "examining the history of settler colonization, the moral and political framework that propelled it, the injustice it caused to the native population, how responsibility for this project should be assigned, and what mechanisms will be available for restorative justice."[30] This approach should also define the privileges colonizers enjoy by virtue of their ethnic affiliation as well as the framework for a new political order in which both national groups will obtain mutual acceptance, equal status and security.

Rouhana outlines four interrelated processes that should be included in the framework:

---

[28] Ibid.
[29] Rouhana (2018), 657.
[30] Rouhana (2018), 658.

The moral imperative: This will be based on decolonization within a transitional justice context, seeking to transform the power structures that characterize colonizers and the colonized and address the asymmetrical injustice and massive human rights violations. The new moral foundation is defined by social justice, truth, historical accountability, and the establishment of institutions that reflect this framework. Such a framework makes use of tools of transitional justice appropriate to this particular conflict, including truth commissions, measures for restorative justice and reparations, historic reckoning and the use of apology or acknowledgment. These tools cannot be applied mechanically, without negotiations within the new moral framework. The challenges of transitional justice usually take center stage. How do we advance transitional justice without threatening a new democratic arrangement established on these foundations?

The political: Reconciliation as decolonization is a process in which new democratic institutions are created and constitutional transformations are introduced in order to guarantee a future based on equality and democracy and protect against violations of human rights. The constitutional form that guarantees such a future—whether it is integration, federation, binationalism, autonomy, or something else—will be founded on restorative and distributive justice, fair distribution of resources, and power sharing.

The social-psychological: The reconciliation process entails cognitive, emotional, and behavioral changes that support the transformation. These changes become possible within the broader process. These are mainly consequences of the reconciliation framework, although once instigated, they promote its continuation. Similarly, psychological healing can be facilitated and easier to achieve within such moral and political frameworks.

The involvement of publics and elites: These processes are public and involve new political behavior on the part of the publics and elites of both societies. Within such frameworks, state institutions can be legitimately employed to generate public and open support that translates into mutual legitimacy for these frameworks and the transformation they guided.

Finally, this type of reconciliation will enable the legitimacy of the Jewish-Israeli presence in Palestine. This will require an explicit, open, and public acceptance of the Israeli-Jewish national group on fully equal terms and a completely legitimate basis within the new order. The mutual recognition that some scholars so tirelessly but hopelessly argued for will become more likely after decolonization in a joint and mutually accepted political framework. Admittedly, though, there are currently no significant political forces on the ground pushing in this direction.[31]

---

[31] Rouhana (2018), 16–17.

12. Conclusion

The Palestinian–Israeli conflict is one of the most notoriously intractable conflicts in the world. For many the conflict seems unresolvable and the idea of reconciliation as naïve and superfluous; this is true for the population living within the conflict and without. This approach is partially due to the failed peace efforts of many politicians, organizations, and initiatives. These endeavors are unsuccessful since their approach is incorrect regarding the conflict.

This paper has sought to illustrate that the correct approach to the conflict is one of settler colonial conflict. Through this analysis, there can be appropriate facilitation of reconciliation between Palestinians and Jews which will lead to political transformation. By drawing on social scientists' observations, reconciliation is a necessary tool for envisioning a more peaceful and just future. For instance, reconciliation can dissolve oppressive systems such as apartheid and aid in decolonization. Thus, by viewing the conflict in the suitable manner, reconciliation can be a transformative political and social activity.

My hope is twofold. First, it envisions developing new conversations among organizations, initiatives, and individuals who are involved in peace and reconciliation work. More dialogue and understanding cultivates better approaches to peace and reconciliation efforts, which can build on the strengths and avoid the weaknesses of past endeavors. This is particularly vital in settler colonial conflicts akin to the Palestinian–Israeli one since wrong attitudes or perceptions can lead to harmful dynamics. My second hope is to expand the notion of being peacemakers among the Christian church. One of the essential acts of discipleship and core principles of the kingdom of God is pursuing reconciliation and being peacemakers. This paper illuminates that reconciliation is to be pursued also on a political and communal dimension, a point that is often overlooked in many of our churches. Bearing witness to the Prince of Peace does not mean reconciling only on an individual level, but also concerning all aspects of the communities we are a part of. Moreover, theologians reflecting on the topic of reconciliation must recognize and address the political and social aspects of conflicts.

About the Author

Salim J. Munayer, Ph.D. is executive director and founder of Musalaha Ministry of Reconciliation, which has been bringing Israelis and Palestinians together since 1990 and creating a forum for reconciliation. He served as academic dean of the Bethlehem Bible College from 1989 to 2008 and is a professor at the college. Salim is also an adjunct professor at Pepperdine University and the Hebrew University of Jerusalem. In 2021, Salim was appointed coordinator of the Peace and Reconciliation Network for the Middle East and North Africa region under the umbrella of the World Evangelical Alliance.

Thinking Constructively

Perry Shaw

1. Introduction

The words we use matter. The terms we choose can shape the ethos and mood that pervade the learning space. The thrust of this article is to suggest that, particularly for those involved in Christian higher education in the Majority World, the language of "constructive thinking"[1] provides a healthier trajectory than the language of "critical thinking" that has been inherited from the wider Minority World[2] academy.

It is important from the outset to provide a narrative context. I come to this topic not as a Christian philosopher, but as a missionary educator, shaped by thirty years of cross-cultural immersion with a particular focus on Christian training in the Middle East. As a result of the extraordinarily innovative approaches we developed at the Arab Baptist Theological Seminary,[3] and thanks to the spaces opened for me by Manfred, my cross-cultural experiences have become increasingly global in consultancy and training.

Over my years of international work in theological education, I have been deeply concerned to observe the ubiquitous nature of the following:

- The legion of complaints I have heard from leaders of Majority World schools as to the "arrogant dismissal" by visiting Minority World lecturers of the quality of education and product of local students. Too many visiting teachers come with the assumption that if local students do not follow Minority World patterns of academic work, then their work is somehow substandard.

---

[1] From the outset, I must make it clear that my use of the term "constructive thinking" is not alluding to constructivist understandings of learning. Rather, I am advocating an approach to thinking and action that seeks to build up the community through positive and productive outcomes.

[2] Throughout this essay, I will use the term "Minority World" rather than the more common "West" or "Global North" to emphasizes that the perspectives that so often are taken as normative actually represent minority, culturally driven assumptions as to the appropriate underpinnings of educational priorities.

[3] Documented in P. Shaw, *Transforming Theological Education: A Practical Handbook for Integrative Learning* (Carlisle, UK: Langham, 2014), 1–13.

- The expectation of visiting lecturers that students elsewhere in the world should follow Minority World patterns of knowledge construction, often without any awareness of the long and rich legacy of local knowledges.[4] In particular there is often a dismissal of the circuitous and indirect approaches of narrative reasoning, so foundational to thinking in much of the Majority World.[5] Likewise, the strong heritage of spiritual engagement that undergirds much of African and Asian society is viewed by many Minority World teachers as a substandard framework for interpreting text and life in the theological academy, rather than a pathway toward growth in discipleship.
- An assumption that Minority World approaches to critical thinking are the best pathway to healthy church life and the accomplishment of the mission of God. It is particularly ironic when instructors who come from contexts where the church is struggling to survive despise more vernacular approaches to teaching and learning used by students coming from situations where the church is growing rapidly.

A collection focused on Christian training cross-culturally[6] includes thirty position pieces from across the globe and finds as its central theme "humble listening" as the imperative for Minority World instructors who teach in the Majority World. This is hardly surprising. What is more striking is the advice given in several of the local pieces to teachers coming from elsewhere: "Don't come!" The strong feelings based on negative experiences of perceived arrogance from outsiders are palpable.

My own experience of teaching in the Middle East has further contributed to a disquiet about the global exportation of Minority World perspectives on knowledge and learning. Many of our students in Lebanon come from highly collectivist societies in which respect for elders is paramount, and critique of existing leaders generally results in mistrust of the young graduate or even ostracism. Given our commitment to strengthening the local churches for missional impact, the indiscriminate importation of Minority World understandings of critical thinking can have profound negative consequences.

---

[4] C. Lopes, "Nurturing Emancipatory Local Knowledges," in P. Shaw and H. Dharamraj, eds., *Challenging Tradition: Innovation in Advanced Theological Education* (Carlisle, UK: Langham, 2018), 145–165.

[5] S. Black, "Scholarship in Our Own Words: Intercultural rhetoric in Academic Writing and Reporting," in Shaw and Dharamraj, eds., *Challenging Tradition,* 127–143.

[6] P. Shaw, C. Lopes, J. Feliciano-Soberano, and B. Heaton, eds., *Teaching across Cultures: A Global Perspective* (Carlisle, UK: Langham, 2021).

These manifold experiences have catalyzed numerous questions in my mind about the largely unquestioned value placed on autonomous critical thinking that I myself experienced in my studies, and whether a more holistic outcome for Christian higher education might be found. My primary audience for this chapter is the leadership of theological colleges in the Majority World, and my desire is to affirm local patterns of knowledge construction. I also come to the topic as an educationalist concerned that the patterns of teaching and learning that take place are relevant and impactful for local realities. I believe that Minority World educational leaders can benefit enormously from listening in on a conversation built from Majority World realities. However, given the almost sacred nature of autonomous critical thinking in the Minority World academy, I suspect that many will have difficulty understanding the issues at stake for Majority World educators, particularly for those who have been deeply steeped in the European philosophical heritage.

From the outset, I must acknowledge the great benefit I have gained from my own higher education experiences, and I consequently see much of benefit in the critical training I have received. I also believe that elements of critical thinking are invaluable for every culture and context, and in fact I will be using a form of critical thinking to critique critical thinking. My point is not that critical thinking is wrong *per se*, but rather that in our Christian educational endeavors we need to take what is good in critical thinking, temper our conclusions with humility in community, and seek wisdom through richer and more constructive approaches to learning.

2. Defining "Critical Thinking" Is Problematic

Due to the ongoing hegemony of the Minority World academy, the revered learning outcome of critical thinking has been exported across the globe. Critical thinking is frequently prominent among our desired educational goals, even in theological education. The term is ubiquitous in Western education, even though many students seem to have only a vague understanding of what "critical thinking" means.

The term "critical thinking" is extremely "murky." Brett Murphy describes it as "paradoxical," asserting that you generally cannot understand "critical thinking" until you know how to do it.[7] In some of the better-known tests of critical thinking, the term centers on the ability to resolve

---

[7] B. Hunt, "Unpacking the Critical Thinking Conundrum," *The Teaching Professor* 32 (7), 2018, 1, 7.

logical syllogisms.[8] In most popular usage, however, critical thinking is generally seen to involve some or all of the following:

- The ability to engage in a balanced evaluation of sources.
- The ability to differentiate between factual statements, normative statements, interpretive statements, and causal statements in the development of arguments.[9]
- The ability to discern logical and illogical thought patterns in what is seen or heard.
- The ability to place an issue in the broader context of ideas and practices.
- The ability (to borrow Bloom's taxonomy) to move from mere knowledge and understanding to more complex analytic, synthetic, evaluative, and creative thinking.
- The ability to develop an argument that considers multiple perspectives and goes beyond surface-level quoting and dichotomist statements.

In whatever way we define "critical thinking," it is generally understood as a skill each individual needs to develop as an individual, and it is generally seen predominantly if not exclusively as a cognitive exercise.

Many students confuse critical thinking with being critical, as if critical thinking simply means finding fault in the other. This is exacerbated when literal translations are made of the term into other languages, particularly where the local term used for "critical" has universally negative connotations. In some cases, the end result is a somewhat conflictual environment in the classroom. Some Minority World teachers welcome argument and controversy in the classroom as "robust" discussion; but for those with greater relational sensitivity, notably those from more collectivist societies, such "robust" discussions are often perceived as aggressive, antagonistic, and disunifying, and hence unhelpful. I will return to this issue later.

---

[8] Widely used examples are the Cornell Critical Thinking Test (CCTT) or the Sample Reasoning Mindset Test (SRMT).
[9] J. Fitzgerald and V. Baird, "Taking a Step Back: Teaching Critical Thinking by Distinguishing Appropriate Type of Evidence," *PS: Political Science and Politics*, 44 (3), 2011, 619–624.

3. Historical Background

The contemporary Minority World emphasis on the development of critical thinking skills exists with good reason. Although advocacy for critical thinking has deep roots that go back to ancient times, events of the twentieth century have brought critical thinking to the fore in Minority World education systems. In little more than 100 years, we have witnessed two catastrophic world wars, the subsequent Cold War, and numerous subsequent conflicts, and these have all contributed to a profound suspicion of authority figures. Our promotion of critical assessment is related to a healthy desire to avoid at all costs the sort of tragic loss of life that resulted from these conflicts, catastrophes that often emerged from mindless obedience to authority and conformity to questionable cultural norms. More recently, the "echo chambers" of social media and the rise of populist leaders have made even more crucial the ability to assess critically the material we hear and see.

In the world of education, probably the most significant influence on contemporary understandings of critical thinking has been the work of John Dewey, who consistently pressed the importance of "reflection," which he defined as the "active, persistent and careful consideration of any belief or supposed form of knowledge in the light of the grounds that support it and the further conclusion to which it tends."[10] Perhaps even more significant in recent years has been the influence of Paulo Freire, who embraced the importance of developing a "critical pedagogy" as a pathway for empowering the oppressed and disenfranchised.[11] Abusive relationships exist where personal individuality is denied, and critical response can be a crucial factor in the pathway to liberation and justice.

There are good reasons for critical thinking to be promoted as a significant educational goal!

4. Thinking Critically about Critical Thinking

But we must also ask ourselves what forms of teaching and learning best serve God's mission in the world. I will not present a rigorous philosophical

---

[10] J. Dewey, *How We Think: A Restatement of the Relation of Reflective Thinking to the Educative Process* (Boston: Heath and Co., 1933), 9.
[11] P. Freire, *Pedagogy of the Oppressed* (New York: Continuum, 1970); P. Freire, *Pedagogy of Freedom: Ethics, Democracy and Civic Courage* (Lanham, MD: Rowman & Littlefield, 1998).

argument, but rather some suggestive observations generated during my years of living in the Majority World and thinking back on my Minority World education. I invite those who are better qualified to add rigor to what I can offer.

The issue of "autonomy" is a crucial starting pointing for reflecting in a Christian fashion upon critical thinking. In numerous sources on educational philosophy, the end goal of critical thinking is the development of the autonomous individual. Whether the desire for autonomy is a human universal need observed across cultures or an issue of cultural particularity to more individualistic societies is a matter of considerable controversy.[12] What is rarely discussed, even among Christian philosophers, is a theological assessment of whether autonomy can be seen as a human "good." Sadly, despite our strong theological bases for doing so, a concern about the emphasis on autonomy in critical thinking has not been particularly notable among Christian scholars. Rather, the main critique has come from a number of secular feminist writers who have pressed for a greater relational emphasis in our educational paradigms, one group coining the seemingly oxymoronic term of "relational autonomy."[13]

Although we recognize that our unique individuality is a reflection of God's awesome creativity, the desire for autonomy is a quite different matter. Is it not a desire for autonomy that catalyzed the Fall? Autonomy by definition alludes to being a law unto oneself without master. I doubt that many of us want to train our students to be autonomous in the sense of creating their own individual determination of rights and appropriate practice. Rather, our trinitarian God has created us in the divine image as communal beings, and the divine imperative of love presses us to go beyond the autonomy of critical thinking to the engagement in quality reflection that functions in humility as a part of community.

---

[12] See for example V. Chirkov, "Culture, Personal Autonomy and Individualism: Their Relationships and Implications for Personal Growth and Well-being," in G. Zheng, K. Leung, and J. G. Adair (eds.), *Perspectives and Progress in Contemporary Cross-Cultural Psychology: Proceedings from the 17th International Congress of the International Association for Cross-Cultural Psychology*, 2008, https://scholarworks.gvsu.edu/cgi/viewcontent.cgi?article=1005&context=iaccp_proceedings; D. Rudy, K. Sheldon, T. Awong, and H. Tan, "Autonomy, Culture, and Well-being: The Benefits of Inclusive Autonomy," *Journal of Research in Personality* 41 (5), 2007, 983–1007.

[13] See for example C. Mackenzie and N. Stoljar, eds., *Relational Autonomy: Feminist Perspectives on Autonomy, Agency and the Social Self* (New York: Oxford University Press, 2000); A. C. Westlund, "Rethinking Relational Autonomy," *Hypatia* 24 (4), 2009, 26–49; H. Baumann, "Reconsidering Relational Autonomy: Personal Autonomy for Socially Embedded and Temporally Extended Selves," *Analyse & Kritik* 30, 2008, 445–468.

A focus on autonomous critical thinking necessitates an emphasis on the broad "tolerance" of every other view, since everyone is entitled to their own personal opinion. Where there are no shared societal values, it is not possible to address foundational disagreements through common philosophical frameworks. All views are legitimate, and the imposition of one view over another is perceived as "an action of violence."[14] In that all views are seen as equally valid, the expectation is "tolerance" of all other views unless deemed "harmful to society." Tolerance is seen as the only pathway by which an acutely individualized society can deal with the diversity of ideas that are generated through an approach to critical thinking that denies the place for collective authority. Generally, the only alternative to "tolerance" offered is "intolerance," and frankly I don't know very many people who would enjoy being seen as intolerant. And so, either consciously or unconsciously, many Christians have come to see tolerance as a supposedly Christian value.[15]

The problem arises where there is difference of opinion as to what is considered harmful to society. Muslims think gay advocacy should not be tolerated, while gays think traditional views of sexuality are bigoted; some see voluntary euthanasia for those with terminal sickness as humanizing, while others see it as a dangerous precedent on the pathway to murdering those who are born with physical or intellectual challenges. The examples are legion. With no way to negotiate these differences, so-called tolerance often morphs into efforts to silence competing voices. We should not be surprised to see that the increased emphasis on tolerance in Minority World societies has led to a commensurate rise in censorship of divergent opinion—if not at the formal legal level, certainly through shaming on social media. Without a mooring in a transcendent reality, tolerance quickly devolves into a shouting war of all against all in the realm of discourse, in which the loudest voice seeks to silence dissenting voices.

Not so long ago, a graduate student orator in his commencement address at a major American university lamented, "They tell us that it is heresy to suggest the superiority of some value, fantasy to believe in moral

---

[14] The concept of metanarrative as violence is common in "postmodern" thought, perhaps most clearly seen in Jacques Derrida's *Of Grammatology*. *De la grammatologie*, trans. by G. Spivak, Baltimore: (Johns Hopkins University, 1967/2016), and Jean-François Lyotard's *The Postmodern Condition*, trans. by G. Bennington and B. Massumi (Manchester: Manchester University Press, 1984).

[15] It is noteworthy that the only times when any of the cognates of "tolerance" appear in the Scriptures is where Jesus says that "it will be more tolerable for ... on the day of judgment than for ..." (Matt 10:25; 11:22; 11:24). In each of these contexts the word of "tolerance" is actually a word of judgment.

arguments, slavery to submit to a judgment sounder than your own. The freedom of our day is the freedom to devote ourselves to any values we please on the mere condition that we do not believe them to be true."[16] Najla Kassab (now President of the World Communion of Reformed Churches) once commented, "Critical thinking can lead to silence."[17] Tolerant autonomous thinking may help us avoid being driven by populist demagogues, but rational, critical, autonomous thinking without humility and love can divide and isolate individuals and destroy communities. Although I know that correlation does not necessarily mean causation, it is noteworthy that with the increasing emphasis on autonomous thinking, we have also seen a growing fragmentation of society and escalating rates of divorce and suicide.

Although Jesus always modeled respect toward the other, the primary value he presented was not tolerance but love. Love is more powerful than tolerance as it embraces a place for truth-telling and healthy growth, as we see in the response of Jesus to the woman caught in adultery, "Neither do I condemn you. Go your way, and from now on do not sin again" (John 8:11). Most people don't actually want to be "tolerated" but loved and respected. Tolerance assumes that the other person is a pain in the neck who needs to be endured, rather than a fragile, damaged image of the living God who needs to be cherished. A simple but significant example: my wife loves me intensely, and, yes, a part of her love is the tolerance of certain negative idiosyncratic patterns. But inasmuch as she tolerates these patterns, I cannot grow. I can grow only when she gently and graciously points out the negativity of these patterns, and their potential cumulative destructiveness to me and to others, and then helps me develop an action plan and prays with me in implementation. But I would never accept the critique if I did not first know of her unconditional love for me. Love needs to precede critique.

I wonder how this sort of love might be a stronger Christian paradigm than tolerance in our broader societal relationships. Certainly, the starting point must be the building of personal loving relationships with those with whom we differ. Where this is not possible, an empathetic reading of the other's story in context can help us come to alternative perspectives with wisdom and grace. I am struck by a leading Christian woman at the time of the 2019 Australian referendum on same-sex marriage, who began by

---

[16] Quoted by Arthur Zakonc in P. Palmer and A. Zajonc, *The Heart of Higher Education: A Call to Renewal; Transforming the Academy Through Collegial Conversations* (San Francisco: Jossey Bass, 2010), 63.

[17] Najla Kassab, personal communication, 2007.

reaching out in love to a number of gay people she knew. When she was excoriated by the press for her opposition to same-sex marriage, she was publicly defended by one of these gay friends: "We disagree with her perspective, but you leave her alone. She loves us as real people, which is more than can be said for most of you journalists!"

Critical thinking is also presented as rational and logical. Since no one wants to be seen as irrational and illogical, we can too easily embrace a purely rational and empiricist cognitive emphasis as the primary end goal of our teaching. In contrast, biblical epistemology is always both holistic and relational,[18] seeing cognition as balanced with heart relationship and obedient action, a learning that goes beyond "faith seeking understanding" to "faith seeking intelligent action."[19] Jesus' great commandment (Mark 12:30) does not begin, "Love the Lord your God with all your mind," but "with all your heart," a perspective echoed in Paul's claim that justifying belief occurs through the heart, not the mind (Rom 10:10). The broad biblical use of the term "heart" to embrace thinking, feeling and acting points to a holistic and transformational understanding of learning and growth. To know God is to be changed by God. And it is a knowledge that emerges in community: to "know" in the Scriptures is to have relationship—the relationship between God and a person, between God and the community, between person and person—a knowing relationship that finds its source in God's self-revelation to us: it is not a matter of *us* discovering truth, but of us coming to know *only as we are already known* (1 Cor 13:12).[20]

This holistic understanding of learning and knowing presses us to make biblical wisdom a prominent value. Paul emphasizes that Christian wisdom is not some form of abstract philosophizing, but a posture of humility and weakness before God, empowered by the Spirit (1 Cor 1:20-25; 2:6-14). Christian wisdom assumes the presence of a community within which we take both rational and autonomous thinking seriously but also critique it. Within a community of wisdom, we can step back and see how some ideas are problematic in practice. Christian wisdom goes beyond right thinking to right attitude and right action, and in this communal dance of thought, affect, and practice broader nuances are realized that

---

[18] T. Schirrmacher, "Education and Learning in Christian Perspective," *Evangelical Review of Theology* 39 (2), 2015, 100-12.
[19] S. Bevans, *Models of Contextual Theology* (Maryknoll: Orbis, 2002), 73.
[20] Relational knowledge forms the epistemological foundation for Parker Palmer's seminal educational text, *To Know as We Are Known: A Spirituality of Education* (San Francisco: Harper & Row, 1983).

rationality alone fails to comprehend. Proverbs 3:5–6 advises us that the "fear of the Lord is the beginning of wisdom." Being renewed through wisdom can provide a much-needed lens for assessing rational critical thinking and for promoting the common good. Only wisdom can provide guidance to the fruitful life, a life enriched by relationships and meaning.

Paul was profoundly concerned that Christians not be conformed to the patterns of the surrounding society, but the alternative to conformity he presented was not "I need to think for myself," but rather a call to "be transformed by the renewing of the mind, so that you may test what is the will of God—what is good and acceptable and perfect" (Rom 12:2). Some Christian scholars have seen in Paul's "renewing of your mind" some sort of biblical justification for autonomous, rational critical thinking. However, a careful exegesis of the text finds that Paul's priority is not the establishment of a personal intellectual perspective but an active obedient response to the will of God. The term he uses here, *dokimazein*, points not to intellectual analysis but to the ability to "test" or "prove" experientially what is God's will. Paul continues in Romans 12 to speak of humility, the gifts in the body of Christ, and wisdom for Christian living; in short, the "renewing of the mind" is demonstrated in changed attitudes and obedient action. Gerhard Maier captured something of this when he wrote, "A critical method [in interpreting Scripture] must fail, because it presents an inner impossibility. For the correlative or counterpart to revelation is not critique but obedience; it is not correction ... but it is a let-me-be-corrected."[21]

5. From Individual Critical Thinking to Collective Constructive Thinking

The unspoken assumption that autonomous critical thinking is the measure of quality work has been exported around the globe. This is particularly the case where the educational agendas have been shaped by Minority World accreditation systems or (worse) when Majority World colleges are led by white Minority World males. However, I sometimes wonder whether the normative expectation of autonomous critical thinking has overtones of neo-colonial cultural imperialism.[22] It is a decidedly Minority

---

[21] G. Maier, *The End of the Historical-Critical Method*, trans. E. Leverenz and R. Norden (St. Louis: Concordia, 1977), 23.

[22] L. Semali, L. M. Semali, and J. Kincheloe, *What is Indigenous Knowledge? Voices from the Academy* (Milton Park, UK: Taylor & Francis, 1999), 31; S. Merriam, "An Introduction to Non-Western Perspectives on Learning and Knowing," in S. Merriam

World notion with a heritage deeply rooted in Greek philosophy and atomistic individualism, a heritage that is not shared globally,[23] and which has generated highly problematic outcomes in many parts of the world.[24]

In his seminal work on intercultural rhetoric, Robert Kaplan[25] offers a set of foundational questions that influence patterns of discussion and argument in different cultural contexts:

- *What may be discussed?* What sorts of limitations are there on acceptable and unacceptable topics of discussion and research? In some settings, the limitations may be related to social concerns, while in others they may be in terms of how narrow or broad a discussion topic should be.
- *Who has the authority to speak/write?* In what ways do social, political, and religious authority structures influence the shape and content of what is talked about or studied?
- *What form(s) may the writing take?* To what extent are the rhetorical patterns of surrounding cultures allowed to influence the forms in which students write?
- *What is evidence?* Minority World patterns of linear empiricist logical argumentation are found to be offensive and distasteful in societies that place greater value on life experience, wisdom, and story.
- *What arrangement of evidence is likely to appeal (be convincing) to readers?* To what extent is argumentation expected to be explicit in your students' presentation of their work, or are implicit approaches preferred?

The answers to these questions are profoundly shaped by culture, and what constitutes good reasoning varies across contexts.[26] There is a wide

---

and Associates, *Non-Western Perspectives on Learning and Knowing* (Malabar: Krueger, 2007), 1–20; S. Egege and S. Kutieleh, "Critical Thinking: Teaching Foreign Notions to Foreign Students," *International Education Journal* 4 (4), 2004, 75–85.

[23] See for example J-Q. Chen, "China's Assimilation of MI Theory in Education," in J-Q. Chen, S. Moran, and H. Gardner (eds.), *Multiple Intelligences Around the World* (San Francisco: Jossey-Bass, 2009), 29–42.

[24] See for example the various articles included in Shaw and Dharamraj, *Challenging Tradition*.

[25] R. Kaplan, "Foreword," in C. Panetta, ed., *Contrastive Rhetoric Revisited and Redefined* (New York: Routledge, 2008), ix.

[26] J. Ichikawa and M. Steup, "The Analysis of Knowledge," in E. Zalta, ed., *The Stanford Encyclopedia of Philosophy* (Summer 2018 Edition), https://plato.stanford.edu/archives/sum2018/entries/knowledge-analysis/; S. Stich and R. Nisbett, "Justifi-

variety of interpretative frameworks that can make sense of the world, each based on a different set of assumptions.[27] In particular, I have been struck by the fundamentally different understandings of the first two questions between collectivist and individualistic societies. In more individualistic societies, such as Australia and United States, the normative assumption is that it is right and healthy to promote the development of a strong autonomous voice in students. We encourage students to speak with confidence, question assumptions, and challenge those in authority, without reference to their relationship to the broader community. In most parts of the world such individualistic assumptions would be seen as disrespectful, divisive, and destabilizing.[28]

Collectivist societies begin with an understanding that the young need to see older people as a great source of deep wisdom. This stands in stark contrast to the dominant narrative often delivered to young people in the Minority World, where aging means increasing irrelevance. A pervasive assumption in the Middle East, Africa, Asia, and elsewhere is that young adults do not have the maturity to speak with authority. They should first spend time learning from the elders, and perhaps at a later time their experience and quality of life will earn them the right to speak independently and with authority.

Given these assumptions, a focus on rote learning makes sense. Students begin by learning and embracing the perspective of those who have acquired the wisdom that comes from long years of living.[29] The opinions

---

cation and the Psychology of Human Reasoning," in *Collected Papers*, vol. 2: *Knowledge, Rationality, and Morality, 1978-2010* (Oxford: Oxford University Press, 2012), 36–48; J. Weinberg, S. Nichols, and S. Stich, "Normativity and Epistemic Intuitions," *Philosophical Topics*, 29, 2001, 429–460.

[27] W. Merrifield, "Culture and Critical Thinking: Exploring Culturally Informed Reasoning Processes in a Lebanese University," Ph.D. dissertation, George Fox University, 12.

[28] S. Black, "Scholarship in Our Own Words: Intercultural Rhetoric in Academic Writing and Reporting," in Shaw and Dharamraj, eds., *Challenging Tradition*, 127–143.

[29] In much of the world the dominant culture of learning is the master-disciple approach, as against the independent learning approach, promoted in European-influenced education systems. See for example L. Senanayake, "The Imperative of Cultural Integration in Advanced Theological Studies: Perspectives from the Majority World," in Shaw and Dharamraj, eds., *Challenging Tradition*, 109–126. Margaret Kumar has observed that moving from a more collectivist master-disciple model to an independent learning approach is one of the major challenges facing international students coming to study in Australia. See M. Kumar, "International Candidates' Transition to a 'Doctorate Downunder'," In C. Denholm and T. Evans,

and perspectives of the young are rarely taken seriously, even when they are better educated than their elders. Comparable patterns are observed through much of the Majority World. For example, in a study of self-directed learning in the Korean context, a context greatly influenced by Confucianism, most Minority World educational values were seen as inappropriate. Rather, "a person becoming independent of his or her parents, teachers or other people, tends to be considered threatening [to] the stability of a community he or she belongs to ... Becoming independent without being interdependent passes for immaturity or self-centeredness."[30]

I discovered this when teaching in Beirut. A notable feature of education in the Middle East (as in much of the world) is an emphasis on rote learning. I received the bulk of my formal education in Australia and the United States, with a strong focus on the development of autonomy through critical thinking. With some ethnocentric arrogance, I initially viewed the local education systems in the Middle East, Africa, and large swaths of Asia as backward and destructive. I saw the education systems resulting from and contributing to the sort of authoritarian dictatorships that prevail in so many parts of the world. Over time, however, I have gained a more nuanced appreciation of local learning approaches and I believe there are elements that Minority World educators may do well to reconsider.

The implications for higher education are profound. Kaplan observes, "In the United States composition tradition, anyone—even a lowly student—has the authority to write and to hold and express an opinion, but in more traditional cultures, the young have no such authority." Kaplan suggests this may be a major reason why such students quote published sources extensively rather than offering more independent insights. These students are often "accused of failing to exercise critical thinking, but they may not see themselves as authorized to undertake such an act."[31]

In observing highly collectivist societies at first-hand I have realized that healthy multigenerational communities cannot function without a strong sense of authority, respect for elders, and a focus on wisdom. The idea that all opinions have the right to be spoken compromises the overall quality of conversations within the community.

Doctorates Downunder: Keys to Successful Doctoral Study in Australia and Aotearoa New Zealand, (Camberwell: ACER, 2012), 155.

[30] Y. Nah, "Can a Self-Directed Learner Be Independent, Autonomous and Interdependent? Implications for Practice," *Adult Learning*, 11(1), 1999, 18–25. Compare with S. Fabiano, "Reflective Judgment and Critical Thinking in a Collectivist Cultural Context," Ph.D. preliminary paper, Trinity International University, 2011.

[31] Kaplan, "Foreword."

We can learn much from the African concept of *ubuntu*, which is foundational to traditional African educational philosophy and practice. *Ubuntu* expresses concern for human welfare in the context of community in which one affirms one's own humanity by recognizing the humanity of others— "I am because you are." The purpose of education then becomes focused less on developing an autonomous individual voice, and more on the development of virtues such as kindness, generosity, compassion, benevolence, courtesy, respect, and concern for others.[32]

Although the students I taught in Beirut came from these sorts of collectivist, deferential societies, they were also being educated to assume significant Christian leadership roles. Consequently, they needed to move from rote learning to developing a meaningful and well-informed voice so that they could work productively and be listened to in their communities, while still honoring and respecting the current leadership of their communities. My colleagues and I at the Arab Baptist Theological Seminary (ABTS) also sensed a need to develop in our students the ethical commitment to challenge leadership that is corrupt, dishonest, and abusive. But such a voice needs to be constantly tempered by respect and an element of submission: if our students were to return to their homes and be perceived to be openly criticizing the existing leaders, they would run the risk of being silenced or even ostracized. For their voices to be heard, they needed to speak constructively within a respectful relationship with the leaders and the wider community.

Finding the balance between a voice that acknowledges its own limited maturity and life experience while speaking up and providing leadership is a challenging teaching assignment. But after seeing our graduates in action and speaking with those in their communities, we believe that ABTS has made progress in addressing this challenge. In a faculty meeting in February 2018 we identified the following as some of the many processes that we have used at ABTS to help our students develop a clear and respectful voice in their community.[33]

The teacher's perspective is crucial. Students in collectivist societies defer to authority, but authority is easily abused. When students show respect for authority, it is easy for a teacher to take advantage of that respect and not return it in full measure to the students. Concerned about the arrogance and power differential that often comes from a position of

---

[32] P. Higgs, "Towards an Indigenous African Educational Discourse: A Philosophical Reflection," *International Review of Education* 54, 2008, 445–458.

[33] The ideas given here emerged from a faculty discussion held at the Arab Baptist Theological Seminary on 20 February 2018.

authority, we placed an emphasis on teachers speaking with both humility and confidence. Modeling good listening was key. Also significant were actions that evidenced an attitude of service to the students, even as simple as picking up a book that a student had dropped—acts that would not normally take place in their home contexts, but which demonstrated pathways to servanthood in leadership.

We also encouraged students to challenge one another graciously and sought to demonstrate how that can be done with respect and humility. We wanted our students to become equipped to respectfully challenge abusive power dynamics wherever they exist. We looked for opportunities to train students in constructive and meaningful critique. Being a theological college, we had daily chapel gatherings, which we intentionally made the responsibility of the students. Several times a week the student leaders and chapel speakers were critiqued publicly by the other students and privately by individual professors. Placing students in the position of teaching their professors was counter-cultural and intimidating for our students, but it helped them build confidence and develop their voices.

Shifting from lecture to small-group discussion became a model for an alternate form of leadership and decision-making for our students. However, rather than individual students sharing their own individualized perspective, feedback from small-group discussion came through a group spokesperson. Being the spokesperson gave students the opportunity to practice finding a voice that speaks respectfully for the community represented by their group.

Likewise we promoted the use of group projects rather than individual assessment, recognizing that a significant part of our desired hidden curriculum was to develop the ability to work together towards a common goal, rather than working in competition with one another.[34] Working collaboratively both respected the collective nature of the society our students came from and encouraged the development of a respectful voice.

We structured our policies and official communications formationally rather than legislatively. For example, the academic integrity policy at ABTS begins with a narrative acknowledging the difficulty of moving from a rote-learning culture to one that expects students to develop a personal voice while also showing respect for existing experts. When students break the policy, processes are step-by-step and pastoral, recognizing the pathway to integrity is a journey.

---

[34] Shaw, *Transforming Theological Education*, 79–92.

6. Practical Implications

There is a widespread perception that "the West knows best and tells the rest," but the time has come for a level of reciprocity as together we learn from one another through the richness that the global church has to offer. Surely the development in our students of a constructive voice in respectful community should be central not just to theological education in more collectivist societies, but even in more individualist cultural contexts such as Australia, North America, or Europe—all the more as the proportion of non-Anglo membership grows in many Minority World churches.

At ABTS we began with students trained not to speak, and we needed to help them to develop a respectful but thoughtful voice. Minority World educators face the opposite challenge of students arriving at college who have been socialized by the broader educational and social environment to say what they think, not always with reason or respect.

Here are a few suggestions, many of which I have already seen practiced in many Minority World schools, but which need to be affirmed and more fully developed.

Students should be encouraged to speak more tentatively, understanding how much they have yet to learn and that wisdom comes with life experience. A loss of intergenerational respect can be a major deficiency in many students' learning. One useful exercise may be to ask students to share a research paper or even classroom notes with an older person in the community. The elder would be invited to respond to the student's ideas in light of their more extensive life experience, and then evaluate the students in terms of both the clarity and respect with which they have functioned.

Approach class participation with more caution. We assume that when students make comments and express their opinions and ideas, this is a sign of engagement. Indeed it may be. However, these opinions are often expressed without concern about whether they make sense, if the opinion has evidence to support it, or the impact such an idea would have on the wider community. Having students first discuss their ideas in small groups or even in pairs can improve the caliber of their comments and the tone in which they are presented.

Move away from a debate mentality with its need to "win the argument" towards working in diverse teams which seek win-win solutions that serve the whole community. One of the regular themes in the educational literature is that the information revolution, and in particular social media, has not led to the original utopian hope of greater mutual understanding, but rather greater polarization, antagonism, and the development of echo chambers.[35] A debate mentality can easily feed into the toxic nature of much that appears on Facebook, Twitter, and the like, with many people (including many Christian leaders) seeing these platforms as an opportunity for unexpurgated criticism of those with whom they disagree. I do wonder whether our emphasis on critical rather than constructive thinking feeds into such postures. The contemporary technological environment makes it even more imperative that teachers encourage students to develop solutions that consider the impact their personal words and actions have on the wider community.

The use of case studies and problem-based learning as a basis for stimulating and developing reflective judgment can stimulate high-quality multidimensional reflection.[36] When these approaches are structured as a group exercise, the end goal becomes not so much individual critical thinking but collective resolution of problems. Having students discuss essays or research tasks in groups before tackling them individually, or having students work jointly on written tasks, promotes teamwork and collaboration, and a potentially gentler voice.

"Speak the truth with love" (Eph 4:15). Although the principle of developing genuine care and respectful speech has applicability in any classroom, those involved in theological education in particular should embrace these words. This requires restraint and wisdom along with courage. Our own practices as teachers can model truth in love, as can the behaviors we require from our students.

Some of the key ideas on moving from critical to constructive thinking are summarized in Table 1:

---

[35] See for example E. Stetzer and A. MacDonald, "How Can and Should We Reach and Train Our Future Pastors and Christian Leaders?" *Christian Education Journal*, 17 (1), 2020, 160–176; G. Lukianoff and J. Haidt, *The Coddling of the American Mind: How Good Intentions and Bad Ideas Are Setting up a Generation for Failure*, (New York: Penguin, 2018), 131.

[36] P. King and K. Kitchener, *Developing Reflective Judgment: Understanding and Promoting Intellectual Growth and Critical Thinking in Adolescents and Adults* (San Francisco: Jossey Bass, 1994), 147; John Jusu, "Problem-Based Learning in Advanced Theological Studies," in Shaw and Dharamraj, eds., *Challenging Tradition*, 209–231.

From Critical Thinking	To Constructive Thinking
Individual and autonomous	Collaborative and collective
Primarily cognitive dimension of learning	Engages cognitive, affective, and behavioral dimensions of learning
Emphasis on rationality	Emphasis on wisdom, obedience, and the good of the community
Accountability is to self and the academy based on individual assessment	Accountability is to the community based on broad intergenerational assessment
Deconstructive without a requirement for reconstruction	Includes deconstruction, but critique is unacceptable without constructive alternative
From above	From below
Danger of pride and self-righteousness	Danger of blind acceptance of evil

Table 1: *From Critical Thinking to Constructive Thinking*

7. Conclusion

The words we use matter. If you gain nothing else from the ideas presented here, I hope that the next time you encounter the term "critical thinking" you will think twice, and perhaps consider the richer alternative of "constructive thinking." Manfred's passion has always been the strengthening of the global church. Likewise, I would urge educational leaders in the Majority World to be very cautious in adopting Minority World educational perspectives. Rather, as we seek local models that nurture holistic and contextually significant teaching and learning, there is rich potential for our training paradigms to more effectively serve God's mission in this world.

About the Author

Dr. Perry Shaw is Researcher in Residence at Morling College, Sydney, and author of *Transforming Theological Education*. Prior to moving to Australia, Perry and his family served in the Middle East from 1990 to 2019, the final decade as Professor of Education at the Arab Baptist Theological Seminary (Lebanon). While at ABTS, Perry was closely involved in the development of their highly innovative curriculum, while also becoming increasingly involved in international consultancy for theological education. Perry has published extensively in the fields of theological education, intercultural studies, and Christian leadership.

An earlier version of this article was published as "Moving from Critical to Constructive Thinking," *Evangelical Review of Theology* 45, no. 2 (May 2021): 128–40.

A Framework for Christian Child Advocacy

Johannes Malherbe

1. Introduction

In a perfect world, there would be no need for advocates—all would be treated with dignity, respect and fairness. But our world is far from perfect, and especially not "fit for children" (cf. Yates 2012, 61-3). We therefore need child advocates to draw attention to the value and needs of children.

Manfred Kohl is an advocate for children. This was already evident from his focus on children at risk when he served in various leadership positions with World Vision (cf. *Gründer von World Vision*, 2020). It also found expression in his research and publishing over the years (cf. Kohl 1985, 1990, 2015), as well as in his connections with several strategic child-focused organizations and movements. At Overseas Council, Manfred ensured a greater focus on children and children's ministry in the curricula of theological training institutions around the world. In his special address to graduates of the South African Theological Seminary in 2018, Manfred highlighted the special treatment of children as a key characteristic of "The Seminary of Jesus Christ" (South African Theological Seminary 2018). He also actively supported the teaching ministry of his wife, Dr Barbara Kohl, in the area of teenage sexuality.

To honor these and many other efforts of Manfred Kohl on behalf of children, this chapter presents a framework for Christian child advocacy (CCA). It starts with an overview of relevant terms and approaches, followed by an overview of the biblical foundations of CCA and a brief exploration of CCA in history. The next part provides some detail about the position of children on the African continent. The final section explores five core activities of CCA, which are anchored in the ministry and teaching of Jesus and as such part of the discipleship journey intended for all his followers. Throughout, special attention is given to the African context where there is a great need for effective CCA.

2. Key terms

Children and childhood

Although we frequently refer to children and childhood, it is very difficult to define these terms. In Africa, a seventeen-year-old could be someone without any formal education or someone who has matriculated. She could be a minor in a traditional family with no voice or agency, or she could be a mother of two or three. He could be a soldier or a prisoner, a slave or an informal business entrepreneur, a famous artist or a self-taught software expert. These may be extremes, but they illustrate the limited value of biological age and the classifications built on it. Fixing the point of division between childhood and adulthood at eighteen years (CRC, Art. 1) is important for legal purposes, but says nothing about the character, social position, agency or spiritual status of younger people. These are shaped by personal and social factors, varying from one person to the next. In the present context, we use the terms child, children and childhood as general references to the early phase of human life when most of our growth occurs, when our limited experience, power and agency may make us more vulnerable, and when we can make unique contributions, because we are not yet fully conditioned to the conventions of adult life.

The discovery of childhood

Several scholars refer to the discovery of childhood, though there is considerable diversity in how this is defined, located and dated. The idea originated with Philippe Ariès who argued that this discovery was an extended process that started in medieval Europe in the thirteenth century and continued to the seventeenth (1962, 47, 33, 125). Most would agree that in recent centuries children emerged from being hardly noticed minors in their respective extended families to human beings in their own right, social agents with their own characteristics, needs and dreams (cf. Cunningham 1998, 1197; Bunge 2001c, 2; Westerhoff 2008, 355).

The factors that contributed to radical changes in the general position of children in Africa include the slave trade, the industrial revolution, colonialism, Christian missions, and the rise of secularism. Severed from the protection of their families and communities, children became easy prey—slaves for the export market, workers for farms, mines and factories, soldiers, concubines for warlords, orphans, migrants, refugees, people living on the streets, prostitutes and, more recently, consumers and subscribers.

Child advocacy

It has been claimed that there are no orphans in traditional African communities—assuming that the extended family and broader community cherish their children and attend to their needs (cf. Foster 2002, 2007; Mafumbate 2019, 9). The reality is that the suffering of children is more prevalent and severe in Africa than on any other continent (see below). There is, therefore, a desperate need for child advocacy—people who can raise the alarm, speaking out on behalf of children at risk and ensuring that appropriate action is taken.

The term advocacy has its origins in ancient Latin where it referred to the action of speaking (mostly in court) on behalf of another. Over the last century or so, the application of the term has broadened to refer more generally to "public support for an idea, plan, or way of doing something" (Cambridge Dictionary 2008). It is often linked to basic human rights and social justice, and presented as a citizen-centered action that challenges those who hold power to change policies and practices in the interests of the disadvantaged (cf. UNICEF Wiki).

Many of these elements are reflected in the definition of child advocacy proposed by Wright and Jaffe (2014, Chapter 1):

> Acting as the voice of children, advocacy often involves calling things as they are and identifying problems. It also involves calling on those who hold positions of authority in society to engage and involve them in solving problems for children.

Christian child advocacy

The addition of the qualifier "Christian" could specify a context for child advocacy, without necessarily changing its essence. This could refer to the agents of the task (i.e., Christians who do child advocacy), its target audience (i.e., Christians who should be mobilized for more effective engagement with children), or both—which is often the case. The present study argues that there is more to the adjective than merely denoting social context—it claims that CCA has distinctive characteristics, derived from the Bible, and aspired to by Christians. This is explained in some detail below.

3. Basic approaches in childhood studies

The discovery of children and childhood also spread to the academic world with increasing focus and intensity since the second half of the twentieth century. Theological studies joined this process quite late, but there are signs of growing interest in issues of childhood over the last two decades (Bunge 2001c, 3-4). This section briefly outlines four different scholarly approaches in childhood studies. The focus is on the last of the four, of which CCA is a sub-category.

The *philosophical approach* focuses on childhood as an abstract concept (cf. Gheaus et al. 2019). The emphasis might be on the development of this concept in history (e.g. Ariès 1965; Cunningham 1995; Kennedy 2006), the definition and meaning of key terms related to childhood (e.g., James and James 2012), the key characteristics of childhood (e.g., innocence, dependence, malleability, vulnerability, spontaneity, creativity), and its significance for ethics (e.g., Walls 2010) or for theology (e.g., White and Willmer 2013).

The *developmental approach* deals with childhood as a path along which children go through a series of stages or past specific milestones. This approach is dominant in education, psychology, health and welfare. While there has been considerable variation in the naming and demarcation of the stages and milestones over time and across schools of thought, the basic assumptions remain that children progress along a standard pathway en route to adulthood and that they could and should be assisted to ensure optimal growth.

The *contextual approach* focuses on ways in which children are affected by their physical, social and cultural environments. This could range from empirical research on the position and experiences of children in specific contexts to trends affecting children on a national, continental or global scale. The latter can be seen, for example, in generational studies, highlighting the impact on children of factors unique to a particular period (cf. Rudolph et al. 2020; Punch 2020; Valentine 2019).

The *relational approach* focuses on different types of engagement between children and others. These engagements can be informal, formal or professional, between children and their family members, or between children and others, between children and other children, or children and adults. Child advocacy is understood as a relational approach referring to the engagements between adult professionals and children.

4. Professional engagement with children

We can identify five types of professional engagement, arranged according to an increasing level of child agency (see diagram below). They are all denoted by prepositions, each emphasizing a specific aspect of the engagement with children. Three of these—*to*, *for* and *with* children—are taken from an article by John Westerhoff III (2008), but they are adapted, expanded, and applied to fit the present context.

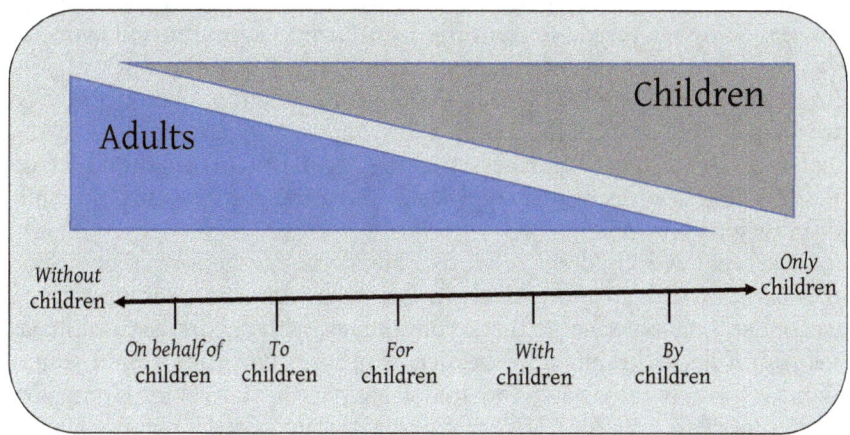

The type "on behalf of children" refers to engagements in which children are passive and absent, which means the lowest level of child agency. It presupposes some level of engagement with children and issues of childhood, but the action mainly targets adults, hoping to inspire them to greater involvement with children. Examples include raising funds for child-focused projects, researching, writing and publishing on issues of childhood, and child advocacy, the focus of the present study. Child advocacy can be further subdivided according to the social context of its application into legislative, legal, media, and organizational (Wright and Jaffe, Chapter 1). It can also be subdivided according to the scope of its application. *Micro* advocacy deals with a specific child or project, *mezzo* advocacy focuses on communities' engagements with their children, and *macro* advocacy deals with children issues on state/provincial, national or international levels (ibid, Chapter 2). The latter requires collaboration between people and organizations with compatible goals and values (cf. Jenkins-Smith et al. 2018).

The type "to children" refers to engagements in which children are passive and present, which means a low level of child agency. Westerhoff proposes an assembly line as the underlying metaphor with children being the raw material worked into a final product. Influential champions of this approach include John Locke, who argued that children enter the world as an empty slate, and B. F. Skinner, generally regarded as the father of behaviorism. Typical examples of this type of engagement would be earlier approaches to basic education as well as medical care to severely ill children.

The type "for children" refers to child engagements that acknowledge the potential of and natural growth in children. Westerhoff proposes the greenhouse as the underlying metaphor, with children being the plants or flowers being nurtured. He identifies Jean-Jacques Rousseau and Jean Piaget as early champions of this approach. We may add the work of Urie Bronfenbrenner (1979) who inspired the development of the concept of "a world fit for children" (cf. Gruskin 2001; Todres 2002; Cascardi et al. 2015). Examples of this type of professional engagement with children include more recent approaches to child welfare, basic education and the children's rights movement.

The type "with children" refers to professional engagements that include collaboration with children, who help shape the interaction. For Westerhoff, the underlying metaphor is that of pilgrimage, with children and adults as fellow travelers. This might be the ideal of progressive forms of basic education, such as those associated with Rudolf Steiner/Waldorf, Maria Montessori and Reggio Emilia. In the Christian context, this approach is espoused in the intergenerational faith formation movement (cf. Yu 2018, 143–72; Weber and De Beer 2016; Roberto 2015; Roehlkepartain 2015; Merhaut 2013).

The type "by children" allows the maximum agency to children while adults are present, though mostly passive. Examples of professional adult roles of this type include sports coaches, conductors of children choirs and orchestras or directors of plays, all of whom may help prepare children for performances in which the adults would be in the pavilion, in the audience or watching on television.

While child advocacy belongs to the type of "on behalf of children," it can include aspects with greater levels of child agency, as long as the children's participation is constructive, voluntary, respecting their privacy and preferences, and in no way exploiting their vulnerability to achieve quick results (e.g., coercing hearers to contribute).

5. Biblical foundations

The Bible portrays God as the one who entrusts children as blessings to families. God also acts when children are at risk—as in the case of the young Ishmael, exposed to the blazing heat of the desert (Gen 21:17) or the Egyptian ruler's strategy of killing Hebrew infants (Exod 1:15–17). In Deuteronomy, God instructs the ancient Israelites to care for the orphans who are mentioned six times, always with widows and foreigners (10:18; 24:17, 19, 20, 21; 27:19). The sacrifice of children opens the list of nine abominations prohibited in Deuteronomy 18:9–14. The prophets identified child sacrifice as one of the reasons why God punished his people and sent them into exile (e.g., Jer 7:31; 19:5; 32:35; Ezek 16:20-21, 36; 20:26, 31; 23:37, 39). The book of Jeremiah shows a keen awareness of how the calamities the prophet announced would affect children.[1]

In the poetic books of the Old Testament, leaders are commanded to "defend the cause of the poor and fatherless" (Ps 82:3 NET Bible; cf. Prov 31:8-9 and Job's claim in 31:17, 21). This standard is repeated in James 1:27 where the care for orphans and widows is described as "pure and undefiled religion before God the Father" (NET Bible).

According to the four Gospels, children assumed an important position in his teachings and ministry (cf. Abera 2021; Gundry 2008; Carroll 2008; Thompson 2008). The most comprehensive passage on the topic is Matthew 18:1-14, which relates how Jesus called a child and had it stand among his disciples as a model for entering the "kingdom of heaven" (verse 3). He added that whoever treats children as he did[2] would effectively welcome him (verse 4). He then warned his disciples not to cause "one of these little ones who believe in me to sin." While the term "little ones" may refer more generally to marginalized disciples (cf. Orton 2003), it at least includes children (cf. Miller 1992, 39). Marcia Bunge (2001c, 26) observes that Jesus' teaching is "striking because at that time children occupied the lowest rung on the social ladder." Though there is nothing in the biblical text suggesting that the child at the center of this account was needy in any way, Jesus may have chosen a child because of the generally low social position of children at the time (cf. Laes 2011; Sigismund-Nielsen 2013; Fitzgerald 2016). This would assign to Jesus the function of child advocacy. CCA derives its ethos and values from the example of Jesus, as well as the command and mandate given to his followers—then and now.

6. Christian child advocates in history

The groundbreaking study *The Child in Christian Thought* explores the views on childhood expressed by prominent figures in the history of Christianity. Editor Marcia Bunge points out that some of these figures "strongly connect care of and advocacy for children to their vision of Christian life and faith" (2001c, 25), which is the essence of Christian child advocacy. However, there is little evidence of macro advocacy in the period before

---

[1] Cf. Jer 2:9; 5:17; 6:11, 21; 7:6, 31; 9:21; 10:20; 11:22; 13:14; 14:16; 15:7-9; 16:1-4; 18:21; 19:3-9; 22:28; 23:34; 29:32; 31:15, 29; 32:18; 36:31; 38:23; 39:6; 44:7; 47:3; 48:4, 46; 49:2; 50:30, 45; 51:3, 22.
[2] The Greek 'in my name' could refer to Jesus' mandate or example.

the Reformation. Martin Luther set a new standard by placing the highest priority on the needs of and ministry to children (cf. Strohl 2001).

In terms of CCA, Luther's achievements were surpassed by John Amos Comenius (1592-1670), a Czech philosopher, theologian and educator, considered by many as the father of modern education. Comenius chose to focus *primarily*, even *exclusively*, on issues affecting children, as the following statement shows:[3]

> I may here mention my endeavors to promote the education of youth. Many considered them unworthy a theologian's time; but I thank Christ, my everlasting love, for inspiring me with such affection towards his lambs and for regulating my exertions in the form set forth in my educational works. I trust that when the winter has passed they will bring forth some fruit to his church.

August Francke (1663-1727), an accomplished biblical scholar and theologian, is also remembered mainly for establishing orphanages and schools for needy children, later known as *Franckesche Stiftungen* (cf. Bunge 2001a). George Müller (1805-98) was born in Germany but spent most of his adult life in England where he served as a pastor, distributed Christian literature and supported missionary work. He established orphanages and schools to care for thousands of needy children during the second industrial revolution. Booker T. Washington (1856-1915), in his later life in the dominant African-American community, devoted most of his life to the Tuskegee Institute that provided educational opportunities to African-American students ranging from teenage years to midlife. He was a pragmatic Christian who promoted Christian values and lifestyle through formal education. Maria Montessori (1870-1952) was an Italian physician who inspired an influential education movement that focuses on helping children to learn naturally.

Starting around 1930 in the United States, the term child advocacy was introduced as a more general reference to work with children in need. It eventually became directly associated with the work of a network of "child advocacy centers" that provide multi-professional support for traumatized children in the United States and many other countries of the world (cf. NCAC website).

The concept of child advocacy also features prominently in Compassion International (CI). Since about 2010, CI has presented itself as a "Christian child advocacy organization" (Compassion International website). Shiferaw Michael, CI's former director for Ethiopia, had played a key role in CI's embracing of this term. Before joining CI, he was a practicing

---

[3] Comenius 1896, 12, footnote by Will S. Monroe.

lawyer, served a term as the minister of justice in the Ethiopian government, and was a respected leader in his national denomination as well as the Ethiopian Evangelical Fellowship (Richter and Bull 2020, 88-92). Shiferaw relates how, after accepting the CI appointment, God impressed it on his heart to start the ministry with children "in the heart of church leaders and workers." To him, this meant that he should not focus on funds, skills, facilities or organizations, but rather on the beliefs, attitudes and values of Christian leaders. Once they discovered the value of children, not only for what they may become one day but for what they already are, their engagements with children would be transformed. For Shiferaw this was the birth of the concept and strategy of CCA (Michael 2021).

Over the years that followed, he shared the vision with key CI leaders. This led to the establishment of a Child Advocacy department at the CI headquarters, the appointment of regional advocacy directors in 2003, and ultimately the organization embracing the term as describing its core business. In an internal policy document, dated May 2014, advocacy is described as "a powerful complementary strategy that works alongside our core strategy [of helping children in poverty] to achieve our mission" (Debenport et al. 2014, 3). This "complementary" strategy focused on local churches, as the proposed purpose statement shows: "Advocacy raises awareness of God's heart for the poor and God's heart for children and mobilizes local churches to prioritize holistic discipleship of children in poverty" (ibid, 4). The document emphasizes the important role of prayer and spiritual discernment for all aspects of CCA. The ambitious vision for expanding CI's impact through advocacy to 400 million children in extreme poverty was not carried through—in 2016 CI closed its advocacy unit, leaving its Latin American region as the only area where this function continues (Wong 2021). While the strategy has changed, CI continues to market itself as a Christian child advocacy organization.

This overview briefly explored traces of child advocacy in the history of Christianity. It showed that the core function was known and promoted at various points in history. More recently it has emerged as an important function within child-focused organizations, especially NGOs, NPOs and FBOs that depend on community support for their functioning and survival.

7. Children of Africa

Africa is home to about 615 million children, which is 26 percent of the children of the world or more than the children of the Americas, Europe and Central Asia combined. Children make up 47 percent of the African population, compared to 24 percent in North America, Europe and Central

Asia (UNICEF 2021, Table 1). It is predicted that Africa's child population will reach 1 billion in 2055 (UNICEF 2019).

As observed elsewhere, "Life is hard for the children of Africa. They face HIV/AIDS and malaria, floods and famine, child labor and violence, crime and corruption" (Malherbe 2016, 44). The statistics in *The State of the World's Children* (UNICEF 2021) paint a dismal picture of Sub-Saharan Africa. On average, 26 percent of girls have a child before their eighteenth birthday (Table 5, global average: 15); a total of 1.5 million children under 15 years are living with HIV (Table 6, constituting 88 percent of the world total); the average illiteracy rate among youth is 21 percent (Table 11, global average 7); 17 percent of girls are subjected to female genital manipulation, 11 percent of girls are being married before they turn fifteen, 26 percent of children are involved in child labor, and 84 percent are subjected to violent discipline (Table 12).

The precarious position of children in Africa is reflected in the infant mortality rate, widely regarded as a reliable indicator of child wellness in any community. According to recent statistics (UNICEF 2021, Table 2), out of every thousand live births in Sub-Saharan Africa, 52 will die before their first birthday. This is 17 times more than the rate for Western Europe, 10 times higher than for North America and 86 per cent higher than the global average of 28. The picture is even worse with the under-five mortality rate—the 20 countries with the highest percentage of children dying before their fifth birthday are all from Sub-Saharan Africa!

The problem is not that these challenges are unknown—tens of thousands of organizations are involved in various initiatives aimed at helping African children. They handle a considerable portion of an estimated US$65 billion of annual foreign aid to the continent.[4] The question is to what extent children have benefited from the massive amounts of foreign aid and how much it has contributed to building African families and communities' capacity to care for their children (cf. Malherbe 2016, 29–63).

There is no shortage of Christians and churches on the continent. The growth of Christianity in Africa is one of the most astonishing religious changes of the twentieth century (cf. Jenkins 2011). The result is that Africa is the continent with the highest number and percentage of Christians (cf. Johnson et al. 2018). The uneven spread of Christians on the continent may play a role—the prevalence of children at risk in Africa is significantly higher in areas with a predominantly Muslim population, such as Somalia, Sierra Leone, Guinea, Mali, Chad, Central African Republic, and South

---

[4] The top ten Official Donor Assistance (ODA) donors gave US$52 billion to Africa in 2017 (OECD 2019, 2).

Sudan. However, large numbers of children facing extreme hardship are found within proximity of vibrant, often wealthy Christian communities all over Africa.

One cannot escape the conclusion that generally, Christians on the African continent fail to see the connection between the faith they confess and the expression of that faith in caring for children at risk in their communities. A recent doctoral study explored the treatment of children in and by one of the largest Protestant denominations in Ethiopia. It found that, generally, children are neglected in the practical ministry of the selected local churches in Addis Ababa (Abera 2021, 120–2). A decade ago, another doctoral thesis explored the views of senior practical theologians in South Africa. It found that children are a neglected and peripheral theme in theological training and research (Yates 2012, 279–315; 376–7).

This presents us with a huge paradox—the continent with the highest number and percentage of Christians is simultaneously the one with the highest prevalence of children at risk. One of the most promising solutions, as Compassion International had proposed, is that of CCA, primarily targeting African Christians and their leaders to mobilize and equip them for constructive involvement with the millions of African children at risk.

8. Christian child advocacy in practice

In structuring practical CCA, we follow and adapt the Prosci method of individual change management as developed by Jeff Hiatt (2006). It is also known as the ADKAR model, an acronym of its five key outcomes (awareness, desire, knowledge, ability and reinforcement). The six-step model for advocacy proposed by Wright and Jaffe (2014) includes helpful additional information, especially for preparatory steps to the actual CCA process.

8.1. Awareness

As a change management strategy, the Prosci model starts with the important reality that adults need to know why change is needed. In the context of CCA, this means that people need to *see* children—their value and their needs. Jesus included children in his ministry and thereby ensured that his disciples had authentic encounters with them. Because the model was counter-cultural and uncomfortable, they did not immediately grasp it, but the seeds were planted and the fruit is evident in the accounts of the four Evangelists.

A very effective way to raise awareness of children is to facilitate authentic encounters with children—through physical encounters or indirectly, through narration, multimedia productions or virtual connections. These should be handled with the greatest care, avoiding the reduction of children to mere objects of pity or violating their rights to dignity and privacy. Another effective approach, especially when addressing Christian leaders, is to facilitate the study of biblical passages and themes related to children. When addressing (potential) practitioners, it is recommended to expose them to models of child engagement.

The process of raising awareness will only work when those targeted through CCA would sense in the child advocate an authentic love and compassion for children and a genuine commitment to serve them, or what Hiatt calls "the credibility of the sender" (2006, 21).

8.2. Desire

Awareness is bound to dim and die unless it is joined by a desire to bring about real change. It is this desire that will drive someone to take the first crucial step to a new way of thinking and doing. The crucial point in CCA is that this desire is not seated in human emotion, nor just "intrinsic motivation" (Hiatt 2006, 27). It is ignited by God himself when he shines his truth into our hearts, challenging our limited understandings and practices. Jesus told his disciples, "Truly I tell you, unless you change and become like little children, you will never enter the kingdom of heaven" (Matt 18:3 NIV). The Greek word used here for change is the same used in the Septuagint for the change that happened to Saul when God's Spirit came over him (1 Sam 10:6) and the change of heart mentioned by Jeremiah (34:15). Unless God changes us to not only become like children but to see children as he sees them, our CCA might turn out to be fruitless. This emphasizes the need for CCA to be carried by prayer and conducted under the guidance of the Holy Spirit.

8.3. Knowledge

I once discussed with a prominent senior academic with decades of experience in designing and facilitating learning in the field of counselling the possibilities of incorporating into his work a stronger focus on children in need. His response stunned me: "I am afraid I am not qualified for that." This was not a lame excuse or false humility. Neither was it simply the wisdom of staying within one's field of expertise. He knew how sensitive, complex and demanding child counselling is, not to mention the training of child counsellors. This applies to most types of child engagement—few of us are properly equipped for tasks that often affect children very directly.

The need for knowledge flows naturally from the preparatory steps of awareness and desire in the CCA process. This follows basic principles of adult learning, which include that adults want to understand why they need to learn something, need to collaborate in the learning process and require the learning content to be relevant to their lives and circumstances (cf. Freire 1968; Lippitt et al. 1984; Brookfield 1991; Vella 2002; Ferreira and MacLean 2018). Since the learning is mostly of a practical or applied nature, it would be most effective when done in real contexts and led by facilitators with appropriate expertise and experience (cf. Kolb 2014).

The typical Christian child advocate is usually not the ideal facilitator of learning. This is because of the complexity and diversity of professional child engagement, because the facilitation of adult learning may not be their area of expertise, and because the settings in which CCA usually takes place, may not be ideal or conducive to learning. The Christian child advocate can help identify the specific type of learning each person or situation may require and then help link them with the right training provider. The training may range from short to long term, from informal to formal, from basic skills training to high-end academic training—all depending on the needs of the trainee and their specific type of child engagement.

8.4. Ability

Jeff Hiatt (2006, 32, 36) provides a case study of a company that changed its marketing strategy, requiring its salespeople to move from selling hardware to selling customer solutions. During training, about one-third of them expressed reluctance about the new approach, another third were "optimistic, but uncertain" while the final third "left confident and ready." Only about 20% of the salespeople successfully implemented the new strategy. This somewhat resembles Jesus' parable of the sower, with only one portion of the seed yielding a crop, making up for what was lost elsewhere (Matt 13:1-9 and parallels).

The key is *ability*, which Hiatt describes as "the act of doing, such that the desired objectives of the change are realized ... visible in action or measurable in terms of effect" (2006, 36). Other terms used in this regard include capacity building, leadership development, application, internship, mentoring and coaching. The purpose is to see awareness, desire and knowledge constructively and consistently applied to the point that it becomes part of new ways of thinking, believing and acting. It involves the overcoming of psychological, physical, intellectual and resource obstacles and limitations (ibid 36-9). The process is demonstrated in the way Jesus equipped his followers to become leaders in the early church. He lived, travelled and ministered with them over two or three years, modelling a new type of leadership and establishing a new ethos and mandate, including a new way of seeing and treating children.

In CCA the process of enhancing ability involves the establishment of strong personal relationships with key individuals and, ideally, joint practical engagements with children or at least child-focused organizations, movements or events. It also involves the exchange or sharing of relevant resources. In terms of practical strategy, we can learn much from the approach of Paul as he shared the gospel and planted churches along the northern coast of the Mediterranean Sea for about ten years (cf. Allen 2006). Guided by the Holy Spirit, he focused on key individuals based in key trade centers. He stayed at each point for periods ranging from a couple of days to a few years, in most cases following up with personal visits and maintaining contact through epistles and specially mandated messengers. This was so effective that he could remark that "from Jerusalem all the way around to Illyricum, I have fully proclaimed the gospel of Christ ... there is no more place for me to work in these regions" (Rom 15:19, 23, NIV).

8.5. Reinforcement

All four Gospel writers relate the story of how Peter denied Jesus (Matt 26:47-56; Mark 14:43-50; Luke 22:47-53; John 18:3-11). Had the account ended there, the time Jesus spent in equipping his most enthusiastic disciple would have been in vain. John provides a moving description of how Jesus turned this failure into an opportunity for reinforcement. Just as Peter had denied Jesus three times, Jesus provided him with three opportunities for a new confession of his loyalty and commitment (John 21:15-19).

Along the CCA journey, we might also experience challenges and disappointments which could likewise be turned into opportunities for reinforcement and renewed commitment. There will also be opportunities to celebrate special achievements and breakthroughs. The rewards are seldom in material terms—the rewards are in witnessing the impact of our work in the lives of children.

Experience has shown that professional child engagement is enhanced when the good work done at the local level is noticed and presented to others as examples and models. It also helps if those who have had practical success are allowed to share their experience with those who are eager to learn. This inspired the concept of learning by teaching. Finally, professional child engagement is enhanced by joining, establishing and expanding networks, forums or communities of practice.

9. Conclusion

The nurture and the protection of children are the responsibility and privilege of the families into which they are born or incorporated. This fundamental truth is often misunderstood, ignored and even intentionally violated, with tragic consequences for millions of children. This demands action, including advocacy—stepping up and speaking out on behalf of children in need and at risk.

The Bible shows that child advocacy is anchored in the heart and character of God and was demonstrated in the ministry and teaching of Jesus. It is expected of everyone claiming to be part of God's people and acknowledging his Son as Savior and Teacher. Like several other aspects of the Christian ethos and lifestyle, advocacy seldom appears naturally; it has to be cultivated. It should therefore form an essential part of Christian discipleship and theological teaching.

References

Abera, Abera Abay. 2021. "A Theological Evaluation of Views on Children and Childhood in the Ethiopian Full Gospel Believers' Church, with Special Reference to the Gospel According to Luke." Ph.D. dissertation, South African Theological Seminary.
Allen, Roland. 2006. *Missionary Methods: St Paul's or Ours?* 5th ed. Lutterworth Press.
Ariès, Philippe. 1965. *Centuries of Childhood: A Social History of Family Life*. Vintage.
Bronfenbrenner, Urie. 1979. *The Ecology of Human Development: Experiments by Nature and Design*. Harvard University Press.
Brookfield, Stephen D. 1991. *Understanding and Facilitating Adult Learning: A Comprehensive Analysis of Principles and Effective Practices*. Reprint edition. Jossey-Bass.
Bunge, Marcia J. 2001a. "Education and the Child in Eighteenth-Century German Pietism: Perspectives from the Work of A. H. Francke." Pages 247–78 in *The Child in Christian Thought*. Eerdmans.
Bunge, Marcia J. 2001b. *The Child in Christian Thought*. Religion, Marriage, and Family Series. Eerdmans.
Bunge, Marcia J. 2001c. "The Child in Christian Thought: Introduction." Pages 1–28 in *The Child in Christian Thought*. Eerdmans.
Bunge, Marcia J., Terence E. Fretheim, and Beverly Roberts Gaventa, eds. 2008. *The Child in the Bible*. Eerdmans.

Cambridge University Press. 2008. *Cambridge Advanced Learner's Dictionary*. 3rd ed. Cambridge University Press.

Carroll, John T. 2008. "'What Then Will This Child Become?' Perspectives on Children in the Gospel of Luke." Pages 177–94 in *The Child in Christian Thought*. Eerdmans.

Cascardi, Michele, Cathy Brown, Svetlana Shpiegel, and Ariel Alvarez. 2015. "Where Have We Been and Where Are We Going? A Conceptual Framework for Child Advocacy." *SAGE Open* 5:215824401557676.

Comenius, Johann Amos. 1896. *School of Infancy: Education of Youth during the First Six Years*. Heath. https://archive.org/details/comeniusschoolof00come.

Compassion International. n.d. "Compassion International: About Us." https://www.compassion.com/about/about-us.htm.

Cunningham, Hugh. 1995. *Children and Childhood in Western Society since 1500*. Longman.

Debenport, Russ, Todd Scott, and Menchit Wong. May 2014. "Global Advocacy Strategy." Compassion International.

Ferreira, Dan, and George R. MacLean. 2018. "Andragogy in the 21st Century: Applying the Assumptions of Adult Learning Online." *Language Research Bulletin* 32:11–19.

Fitzgerald, J. T. 2016. "Orphans in Mediterranean Antiquity and Early Christianity." *Acta Theologica* 23:29.

Foster, G. 2000. "The Capacity of the Extended Family Safety Net for Orphans in Africa." *Psychology, Health & Medicine* 5:55–62.

Foster, G. 2007. "Under the Radar: Community Safety Nets for AIDS-Affected Households in Sub-Saharan Africa." *AIDS Care* 19:54–63.

Freire, Paulo. 1968. *Pedagogy of the Oppressed*. Translated by Myra Bergman Ramos. Seabury Press. http://www.amazon.com/Pedagogy-Oppressed-30th-Anniversary-Edition/dp/0826412769.

Gheaus, Anca, Gideon Calder, and Jurgen De Wispelaere, eds. 2019. *The Routledge Handbook of the Philosophy of Childhood and Children*. Routledge Handbooks in Philosophy. Routledge, Taylor & Francis Group.

Gruskin, Sofia. 2001. "A World Fit for Children: Are the World's Leaders Being Passed on the Fast Lane?" *Health and Human Rights* 5:1.

Gründer von World Vision; Portrait Über Manfred Kohl; Bibel TV Lauf Des Lebens. 2020. https://www.youtube.com/watch?v=u8RQJx91myw.

Gundry, Judith M. 2008. "Children in the Gospel of Mark, with Special Attention to Jesus' Blessing of the Children (Mark 10:13-16)." Pages 143–76 in *The Child in the Bible*. Eerdmans.

Hiatt, Jeffrey M. 2006. *ADKAR: A Model for Change in Business, Government and Our Community*. 1st edition. Prosci Research.
James, Allison, and Adrian L. James. 2012. *Key Concepts in Childhood Studies*. Sage.
Jenkins, Philip. 2011. *The Next Christendom: The Coming of Global Christianity*. 3rd ed. Oxford University Press.
Jenkins-Smith, Hank C., Daniel Nohrstedt, Christopher M. Weible, and Karin Ingold. 2018. "The Advocacy Coalition Framework: An Overview of the Research Program." Pages 135–72 in *Theories of the Policy Process*. Westview Press.
Johnson, Todd M., Gina A. Zurlo, Albert W. Hickman, and Peter F. Crossing. 2018. "Christianity 2018: More African Christians and Counting Martyrs." *International Bulletin of Mission Research* 42:20–28.
Kennedy, David. 2006. *Changing Conceptions of the Child from the Renaissance to Post-Modernity: A Philosophy of Childhood*. 1st edition. Edwin Mellen Press.
Kohl, Manfred Waldemar. 1985. *Menschenskinder: Hilfe Direkt*. Neuhausen-Stuttgart: Hänssler-Verlag.
Kohl, Manfred Waldemar. 1990. *Kinder der Welt sagen danke*. Neuhausen-Stuttgart: Hänssler-Verlag.
Kohl, Manfred Waldemar. 2015. "A Boy Called Jesus." *International Congregational Journal* 14:115–24.
Kolb, David A. 2014. *Experiential Learning: Experience as the Source of Learning and Development*. FT Press.
Laes, Christian. 2011. *Children in the Roman Empire: Outsiders Within*. Cambridge University Press.
Lippitt, Gordon L. and Malcolm S. Knowles. 1984. *Andragogy in Action: Applying Modern Principles of Adult Learning*. Wiley.
Mafumbate, Racheal. 2019. "The Undiluted African Community: Values, The Family, Orphanage and Wellness in Traditional Africa." *IKM* 9:7–13.
Malherbe, Johannes S. 2016. *Saved by the Lion? Stories of African Children Encountering Outsiders*. 2nd ed. Aboutchildren.net.
Merhaut, Jim. 2013. "Emerging Models for Intergenerational Ministries." *Lifelong Faith*, 49–64.
Michael, Shiferaw. Personal correspondence, February 2021.
Miller, Gordon Goldsbury. 1992. "A Baptist Theology of the Child." D.Th. thesis, UNISA. http://uir.unisa.ac.za/bitstream/handle/10500/17460/thesis_miller_gg.pdf;jsessionid=3A41FCD8B76766716DA99AA45016309B?sequence=1.
NCAC. n.d. "NCAC: History—National Children's Advocacy Center." https://www.nationalcac.org/history/.

OECD. 2019. "Development Aid at a Glance: Statistics by Region: Africa 2019." https://www.oecd.org/dac/financing-sustainable-development/development-finance-data/Africa-Development-Aid-at-a-Glance-2019.pdf.

Orton, David E. 2003. "We Felt Like Grasshoppers: The Little Ones in Biblical Interpretation." *Biblical Interpretation* 11:488–502.

Punch, Samantha. 2020. "Why Have Generational Orderings Been Marginalised in the Social Sciences Including Childhood Studies?" *Children's Geographies* 18:128–40.

Richter, Fanie, and Laetitia Bull. 2020. *Destined to Be Change-Agents: "Ordinary" People Serving Significantly*. Digital on Demand.

Roberto, John. 2015. *Reimagining Faith Formation for the 21st Century: Engaging All Ages and Generations*. Lifelong Faith Associates. https://www.lifelongfaith.com/uploads/5/1/6/4/5164069/reimagining_faith_formation_book.pdf.

Roehlkepartain, Jolene. 2015. "Building Intergenerational Relationships between Children and Adults." *Lifelong Faith*, 8–13.

Rudolph, Cort W., Rachel S. Rauvola, David P. Costanza, and Hannes Zacher. 2020. "Generations and Generational Differences: Debunking Myths in Organizational Science and Practice and Paving New Paths Forward." *Journal of Business Psychology*. https://doi.org/10.1007/s10869-020-09715-2.

Sigismund-Nielsen, Hanne. 2013. *Slave and Lower-Class Roman Children*. Oxford University Press. http://oxfordhandbooks.com/view/10.1093/oxfordhb/9780199781546.001.0001/oxfordhb-9780199781546-e-014.

South African Theological Seminary. 2018. *Dr Manfred Kohl: The Seminary of Jesus Christ*. https://www.youtube.com/watch?v=LXRI-sTPkOY.

Strohl, Jane E. 2001. "The Child in Luther's Theology: 'For What Purpose Do We Older Folks Exist Other than to Care for … the Young?'" Pages 134–59 in *The Child in Christian Thought*. Eerdmans.

Thompson, Marianne Meye. 2008. "Children in the Gospel of John." Pages 195–214 in *The Child in the Bible*. Eerdmans.

Todres, Jonathan. 2002. "The Challenge of Creating 'A World Fit for Children.'" 10, no. 1: 18-21.

UN General Assembly. 1989. "Convention on the Rights of the Child." United Nations General Assembly. https://www.ohchr.org/EN/ProfessionalInterest/Pages/CRC.aspx.

UNICEF. January 2019. "Children in Africa: Key Statistics on Child Survival and Population." UNICEF and African Union.

UNICEF. 2021. *The State of the World's Children 2021: On My Mind: Promoting, Protecting and Caring for Children's Mental Health.* https://data.unicef.org/resources/sowc-2021/.

UNICEF Wiki. n.d. "What Is Advocacy?" *UNICEF Wiki.* http://www.advocate-for-children.org/advocacy/laying_a_conceptual_foundation/what_is_advocacy.

Valentine, Gill. 2019. "Geographies of Youth: A Generational Perspective." *Children's Geographies* 17:28–31.

Vella, Jane. 2002. *Learning to Listen, Learning to Teach: The Power of Dialogue in Educating Adults.* Revised edition. Jossey-Bass.

Wall, John. 2010. *Ethics in Light of Childhood.* Georgetown University Press.

Weber, Shantelle, and Stephan De Beer. 2016. "Doing Theology with Children in a South African Context: Children as Collaborators in Intergenerational Ministry." *HTS Teologiese Studies/Theological Studies* 72. http://www.hts.org.za/index.php/HTS/article/view/3572.

Westerhoff, John H. (III). 2008. "The Church's Contemporary Challenge: Assisting Adults to Mature Spiritually with Their Children." Pages 355–65 in *Nurturing Children's Spirituality: Christian Perspectives and Best Practices.* Cascade Books. https://childrenyouthnkc.files.wordpress.com/2012/01/westerhoff-churchs-contemporary-challenge.pdf.

White, Keith J., and Haddon Willmer. 2013. *Entry Point: Towards Child Theology with Matthew 18.* WTL Publications Limited.

Wong, Menchit. Personal correspondence, October 2021.

Wright, Amy, and Kenneth Jaffe. 2014. *Six Steps to Successful Child Advocacy: Changing the World for Children.* Sage. https://sk.sagepub.com/books/six-steps-to-successful-child-advocacy.

Yates, Hannelie. 2012. "Die Promovering van Kinderregte: 'n Prakties-Teologiese Ondersoek." D.Th. thesis, Stellenbosch University. http://scholar.sun.ac.za/handle/10019.1/71759.

Yu, Hui Er. 2018. *Translating Nephesh in the Psalms into Chinese: An Exercise in Intergenerational and Literary Bible Translation.* Langham Monographs.

About the Author

Johannes Malherbe is a senior academic at the South African Theological Seminary. His areas of expertise include Old Testament Studies, Leadership Development, and Children's Ministry. The seeds for the latter were planted during his term as leader of Petra Institute. Over the years he has engaged with Christian leaders from all over the African continent to advocate more effective ministry with children. This inducted him into the task of Christian child advocacy, the topic of the chapter he contributed to the present volume. He is married to Annelie, a music teacher, and they have four adult children and one grandchild.

Education and Learning in Christian Perspective

Thomas Schirrmacher[1]

I. The Bible and Holistic Education[2]

The question of education is inseparably bound up with the central meaning of the written Word of God for Jesus' church. The particular New Testament text which most clearly teaches the divine inspiration of the Holy Scriptures unmistakably describes the educational mandate of the Bible: "All Scripture is God-breathed and is useful for teaching, rebuking, correcting [or teaching] and training in righteousness, so that the man of God may be thoroughly equipped for every good work" (2 Tim 3:16-17). The verses prior to the ones just quoted (2 Tim 3:14-15) address the practical task of educating the next generation. The Old Testament law, in its own name for itself, had already significantly addressed the need for education. This is seen in the fact that the Hebrew word for "law," which is *torah*, actually means instruction. God instructs people through his Word and his law. This Old Testament theme is developed in the New Testament, where we are told that the law was designed to be a tutor (Greek: *paidagogos*) to lead us to Christ (Gal 3:24).

Is education as described in the Bible only a matter of conveying biblical knowledge? Does it only have to do with educating character and spiritual qualities? Is it only a matter of education in the intellectual sense? No, it has to do with all these things simultaneously. That is to say, it has to do with comprehensive, holistic formation and education, including all the spheres of life, and with making an individual "thoroughly equipped for *every* good work" (emphasis added). This holistic orientation to education is seen in both the Old Testament *torah* and in the New Testament description of God's purposes for giving us the Scriptures. This holistic orientation should influence even how we define what theology is. John

---

[1] Translated by Richard McClary; revised by Thomas K. Johnson.
[2] This essay was originally in the German language in which the terminology for education (usually school-oriented) and child rearing (usually family-oriented) are more closely linked with each other than is usually the case in English terminology. In this light, the author perceives close links between the theological and ethical principles of parenting and the principles of schooling. Ed.

Frame appropriately defines theology as "the application of the Word of God by persons to *all* areas of life" (emphasis added).[3]

Many Christians have a divided faith. While the Bible is responsible for internal, religious questions, varying standards are followed in questions relating to commerce, education, politics, or church policy. As fathers in the home, some may live according to other values than they do as representatives in parliament; as businessmen, some may live according to other values than they do as church elders. Christians all too often have separated their knowledge of character, their knowledge of ethics, and their doctrine from each other. What is so often asked for today—at least in the area of education—is a comprehensive, holistic view of life and the world, precisely what is often missing. Christian *parents*—at least in many cases when it comes to practice—educate the character of the child, while the *church* teaches them biblical knowledge and the *school* conveys learning. Too seldom do we ask if these three entities educate according to different standards and to what extent this is helpful for the child.

In the Bible the comprehensive responsibility for education lies with the parents. They are responsible for teaching the children biblical knowledge, while the church's educational programs can only be a supplement. Parents are to provide education to their children and to deal responsibly with this, in such a manner that teachers are always only an extended arm, mediating knowledge on behalf of the parents.

2. What is to be learned (examples)

- Deuteronomy 31:12: "so they can listen and learn to fear the Lord your God and follow carefully all the words of this law."
- Proverbs 1:2: "for attaining [or learning] wisdom and discipline"
- Proverbs 15:33: "teaches a man wisdom, and humility comes before honor."
- Isaiah 26:9: "learn righteousness."
- Isaiah 32:4: "know and understand."
- Titus 3:14: "learn to devote themselves to doing what is good"

In the Bible the words know, learn, understand, and teach are all terms which include one's intellectual side as well as the ability to correctly

---

[3] John M. Frame, *The Doctrine of the Knowledge of God*, Phillipsburg NJ, 1987, p. 81.

practice what has been learned.[4] This becomes particularly clear with the fact that the word "know" also can be used to designate the consummation of marriage (Gen 4:1, 17, 25; 19:8; 24:16; 1 Kgs 1:4; Matt 1:25).[5] At this point, knowing equally comprises intellectual, emotional, spiritual, and physical aspects. John M. Frame has shown that knowing in the Bible always expresses a covenantal relationship; for that reason, knowing God not only includes knowing something about God but also having a personal relationship with him and following him.[6] In the Bible, knowledge is always both holistic and relational.

Can an individual, however, truly educate a child with only a Bible in his hand? Of course, the answer is "no," for the Bible does not say anything about children's health problems, about the necessary amount of sleep, about polite manners, about the age at which to begin schooling, or about pocket money, not to mention mathematics, chemistry, or how to play the flute. The Bible gives us the divine sense of and the foundational orientation of educating a child, but nowhere does it go into detail about the specifics of a child's education. In the same way, the Bible otherwise prescribes an ethical framework but does not prescribe exactly how to live life. Parents should bring up children "in the training and instruction of the Lord" (Eph 6:4). They should make God and his Word dear to them (2 Tim 3:14–17) and prepare them to live a life on their own under God's authority within the order of creation. However, underneath this basic orientation there are only isolated commandments and pointers relating to the education of children. Christian parents are also called upon to implement this basic orientation toward education in daily life. In order to do this, they revert to the experience of past generations (tradition) as well as to advice and studies in the present, and they utilize their God-given talents in order to find the best possible path for their children.

For example, it is God's desire and command that every individual utilize his God-given abilities and gifts (Exod 31:1–6; 35:30–35; 1 Pet 4:11). However, how should parents put this into practice other than by utilizing their reason and by observing and learning from others how to find out which talents and preferences their children have and then encouraging, challenging, and accompanying their children in them?

---

[4] Comp. Lawrence O. Richards, *A Theology of Christian Education*, Grand Rapids MI, 1975, pp. 32–34.
[5] Also according to Friso Melzer, *Das Wort in den Wörtern*, Gießen 1990,² pp. 112–113.
[6] Frame, *Doctrine*, pp. 40–49.

I consider child rearing to be an example of a certain authorization of the so-called "natural law"—admittedly only valid in a relative and mitigated sense. With that said, child rearing provides an authorized location for a natural ethic as well as for a manner of situational or experiential ethic.[7] If the basic biblical mandate for child rearing is accepted, parents will simply learn much from the "nature" of things. The growth and physical and spiritual development of a child provide many decisions to consider, leading parents to compare their children with others' children—even if this cannot be done completely. And many dimensions of child development can be accurately described by people who are not Christians, so that it is proper for Christian parents to take counsel from such people, even while we acknowledge that their descriptions of child development may be influenced by worldviews we do not accept.

The Old Testament book of Proverbs is an example of a large educational book in the Bible (e.g., Prov 4:1–9), and it is not by chance that it draws from the wisdom of many cultures, not only from the earlier parts of the Bible or other Hebrew sources. Comprehensive education found there includes the ability to survive in everyday life independently. This is comprised of work, forethought, working for peace, and bringing about justice. Everything, however, leads back to this point of departure: "The fear of the Lord is the beginning of knowledge" (Prov 1:7).

3. Christian Education and Ethics between the Millstones of the Spirit of the Age and Evangelical Pharisees

Are Christian child rearing and ethics conservative or progressive? Christianity is very conservative when it comes to the preservation of God's creation ordinances, but it is very progressive and revolutionary when it comes to surmounting false traditions and unjust regulations which stand against God's Word, wrongly lay claim to be God's commands, and enslave people. A pure conservatism to appease the older generation is as foreign to the Bible as is change in order to satisfy the younger generation.

Christians should neither be automatically conservative nor automatically progressive but should attempt to pursue education and child rearing from a biblical perspective. This means they should not try to overcome

---

[7] For a more detailed explanation, see Thomas Schirrmacher, *Leadership and Ethical Responsibility: The Three Aspects of Every Decision*, The WEA Global Issues Series, vol. 13, Bonn (Germany) 2013. Online: http://www.bucer.org/resources/details/leadership-and-ethical-responsibility.html.

the spirit of our age with the spirit of a previous age and should not try to overcome the spirit of a previous age with the spirit of this age. Following Romans 12:2, they know that only the person who is ready and willing for constant growth through the renewal of the mind by means of continuing examination of the will of God is set free from the scheme of any age: "Do not conform to the pattern of this world, but be transformed by the renewing of your mind. Then you will be able to test and approve what God's will is—his good, pleasing and perfect will."

Justice in the godly sense in society has to be maintained at every price; injustice has to be combated and eliminated, regardless of whether this is perceived to be conservative and outmoded or progressive and subversive. The biblical picture of lifelong monogamy is perceived in Germany today to be backward-looking and conservative, and in Saudi Arabia it can be charged that it would destroy an established thousand-year culture in a revolutionary way. Whoever wants to practice Christian ethics based on the Bible today cannot let it be defined according to a pattern that is conservative or progressive, as one directed toward restoration or revolution, as one oriented toward the past or the future. Christian ethics cannot allow itself to be grist for the mill between today's millstones of the spirit of the age and the millstone of Evangelical Pharisees. To emphasize the point: Christians cannot conquer today's spirit of the age with yesterday's spirit of the age, nor *vice versa!*

We can take as an example the effects on education of the so-called "1968" student revolt in Germany, along with similar events at that time in other Western countries. Not everything prior to that time was good, but not everything before that time was bad. Conservative Christians tend to romanticize earlier times, and progressive Christians tend to demonize those same earlier times. However, whoever thinks in terms of the Bible cannot allow himself to be pressed into such a template. At those points where the 1968 student revolt toppled immoral authorities or brought about the collapse of bourgeois facades, Christians should be grateful. At those points where biblical values were destroyed, Christians should have regrets. To be more specific, take the concrete example of anti-authoritarian education. Anti-authoritarian education was taken *ad absurdum* by some who were influenced by the ideas of "1968," but today it is rarely practiced in a comprehensive manner. There are still many who give lip service to the ideology of the student revolt, but in the realities of family life, kindergartens, schools, and professional life, the values now promoted are the abilities to co-exist, to integrate, and to exercise self-discipline, lest one receive a bad evaluation. Because Christians believe in creation, in which God, the highest authority, established the state and parents as secondary authorities, they have never been able to straightforwardly endorse anti-authoritarian child rearing and education. And Christians should not be surprised that social realities have led many to step back from fully implementing the ideas of "1968."

However, does that automatically mean that what was previously practiced as authoritarian child rearing was entirely correct with nothing to improve? Was the penchant for draconian punishment and the use of force sometimes unbridled? Was parental authority sometimes viewed as unlimited, without judging whether it served the goal of the well-being and the growing self-responsibility of the child? And were children all too often treated according to fixed formulas without taking their individual differences into account? Besides the negative side effects, has it not also been a benefit of modern pedagogy that every child is seen as an individual and that education is to be adjusted to every child? Is it not also a benefit that we today treat children in a manner corresponding more to their age, specifically calibrating educational material according to their age, and not just offering doctored-up, adult-oriented material?

Apart from that, one has to note that on the side of Evangelicals, the word authority is used often. However, there are seldom elaborations about what authority actually means when taken in the context of the Bible. In spite of a lack of good sources, Hans-Georg Wünch has analyzed the concept of "authority in the Christian school"[8] commonly brought into the recent Christian school movements. Wünch has shown that Evangelical schools—as they often call themselves—are shaped by modern anti-authoritarian pedagogy to a much larger degree than they are often aware. They have also only achieved very little in the way of justifying a biblical-theological sense of their understanding of Christian pedagogy and biblical authority. Wünch surely differentiates among schools at this point, but that changes little as it relates to the overall result. Wünch shows how much can be said with the Bible as the *norma normans* as far as authority is concerned[9] and how little of this has been developed and assimilated by Evangelical schools. Looking at this question more than fifteen years later, there is nothing which has essentially changed with respect to this situation.

Paul makes it clear in two passages that child rearing does not give parents *carte blanche*. Rather, authority is for the child's best and will be measured against a future goal. Here are the two passages: "Fathers, do not

---

[8] Hans-Georg Wünch, *Autorität in der christlichen Schule*, Bonn 1995; the English translation of the title is *Authority in the Christian School.*
[9] Ibid, 186–255.

exasperate your children; instead, bring them up in the training and instruction of the Lord" (Eph 6:4). "Fathers, do not embitter your children, or they will become discouraged" (Col 3:21). How is it that so often in Christian circles there is talk of necessary obedience on the part of children but so seldom mention of the warning against hard-hearted education which provokes children to rebellion (Eph 6:4) or takes away their courage to live (Col 3:21)?

Love for the well-being of the one to be educated is recognized in the Bible as the central motivation for education (Prov 3:12; 1 Thess 2:7-12).[10] Child rearing and education are not primarily about punishment. Rather, light punishments (in contrast to the punishments the state can impose) are only permissible and appropriate if they are embedded in what is essentially a loving relationship and are avoidable for the children by the parents' having set up sensible and understandable rules beforehand.

The necessity of correction and punishment is justified in many biblical texts by saying that the child has evil possibilities or malicious plans or is otherwise in some manner a threat to himself because of negative developments (e.g., Prov 20:30; 22:15; 23:13-14; 29:15). The teaching of original sin is of great significance for Christian pedagogy. If children are evil from the time they are small (see Gen 8:21 and Ps 51:5), and sin, as in Sodom and Israel, can be committed by "young and old" and by "the least to the greatest" (Gen 19:11; Jer 8:10), it is also appropriate to address the problem of evil inside a child.

However, it is too one-sided when Christian child rearing only emphasizes this aspect, as correct as it might be. Authority never exists for its own sake. Rather, it is always given by God and is to be measured against the good for which God has given it. And is it not God the Creator who has made children so diverse and who has endowed them with the most various gifts and abilities?

Judeo-Christian anthropology (the understanding of human nature) exists in a certain tension. On the one hand, humankind is created as the image of God and endowed by God with unbelievable abilities and diversity. On the other hand, as sinful, humankind has turned from God and is capable of unbelievably evil thoughts and actions.[11] Corresponding to this two-sided understanding of human nature, there are two complementary

---

[10] For details, see Thomas Schirrmacher, *Moderne Väter*, Holzgerlingen 2009, pp. 64-72.

[11] This sinful or evil direction within human nature must be addressed both by limitation/restraint and by forgiveness/grace, both by law and by the gospel.

sets of educational goals which, in our view, belong together, even though some have separated these goals. On the one hand, education and child rearing should develop the self-sufficiency and God-given potential of the individual; on the other hand, education should develop the integration and obedience of the individual into society, restraining sin. Christian instructional method should implement a thoroughgoing complementarity of principles.

Children, in both family and school, are viewed as images of God needing direction and encouragement so that the abilities they have been given by God can unfold and be fully utilized. These are abilities which are artistic and literary as well as interpersonal. And even a self-reliant personality under the Creator as the goal of child rearing and education is not an end in itself. Rather, the limited goal of unfolding the talents of the individual has a further goal, not only responsibility for oneself but also for other people as well for the development of the created potential of society.[12]

Children, in both family and school, are likewise seen as people who, owing to sin, no longer live according to their original God-given purpose and design. For that reason, they need to be trained away from evil. This includes limits and punishments as much as it does counseling, assistance, and gracious pastoral care. Christianity is very self-critical, as well as very critical and mistrustful of sinful human nature. It assumes that every individual—parents and teachers as well as those entrusted to our care—not only allows himself the occasional blunder now and then; rather, in normal everyday life, every individual is characterized by egoism which injures the self and others.[13]

All too often, authoritarian child rearing has lost sight of the fact that each child is a distinct and unique personality created by God and that the goal of every form of child rearing is the healthy unfolding of abilities into independence as a member of a community. Authoritarian child rearing has sometimes placed the holder of the office in an absolute position without measuring him against the purpose for which he received his authority—no wonder that without God man is ostensibly the final authority. Authoritarian child rearing assumes that if one has driven away or restrained

---

[12] This part of our philosophy of education corresponds with the part of our political philosophy in which we emphasize human rights and human dignity.

[13] This part of our educational philosophy corresponds with the part of our political philosophy where we talk about provisions for accountability for those who rule via a separation of powers so that even government officials can be indicted by another branch of government.

evil, something good has been achieved. Authoritarian child rearing too often became an end in itself, where the father has a right to be served after a strenuous day and obedience has value in itself. This is the only way to explain that the army has been praised as the "school of the nation," even with its often brutalizing tendencies.

The 1968 generation built upon an opposite and extreme educational theory arising from belief in the good in humanity, thinking this goodness would develop on its own. All that had to be done was not to stand in its way and to get all authorities out of the way. Suddenly authority itself was perceived as evil, and setting limits no longer served to protect against what was wrong or to learn the good and the useful. Authority was described as something sinister. The old insight of experience had been lost, that whoever is raised in a loving, good, and intensive manner often becomes a more self-confident person with backbone, whereas little supervision in childhood can lead to unsure and easily manipulated adults.

Christian child rearing and education should consciously build upon a set of significant complementarities: law and grace, encouragement and boundaries, self-sufficiency and leadership belong together. Whoever only sees the positive side as the scheme education should follow will be brutally overrun by evil in child rearing (and likewise in school). Whoever only sees the negative side declares child rearing and punishment to be ends in themselves and loses sight of the goal.

Christian educators in the family, school, and elsewhere have the opportunity to practice the balance and complementarity of encouragement and demands, of freedom and limits, of self-sufficiency and integration/submission, and of consolation and admonishment.

I am convinced that biblical complementarity is appealing for all people, whether Christians or not. We all know how unpleasant it is either to have authorities who are bitterly hard or who never take a stand. We know we did not want parents who always said "no" or parents who always said "yes." We know that our children expect real authority from us, as well as real personal love and support. We can love neither the harsh sergeant nor the dish rag. And, as a Christian, I am of the opinion that God created us in this way.

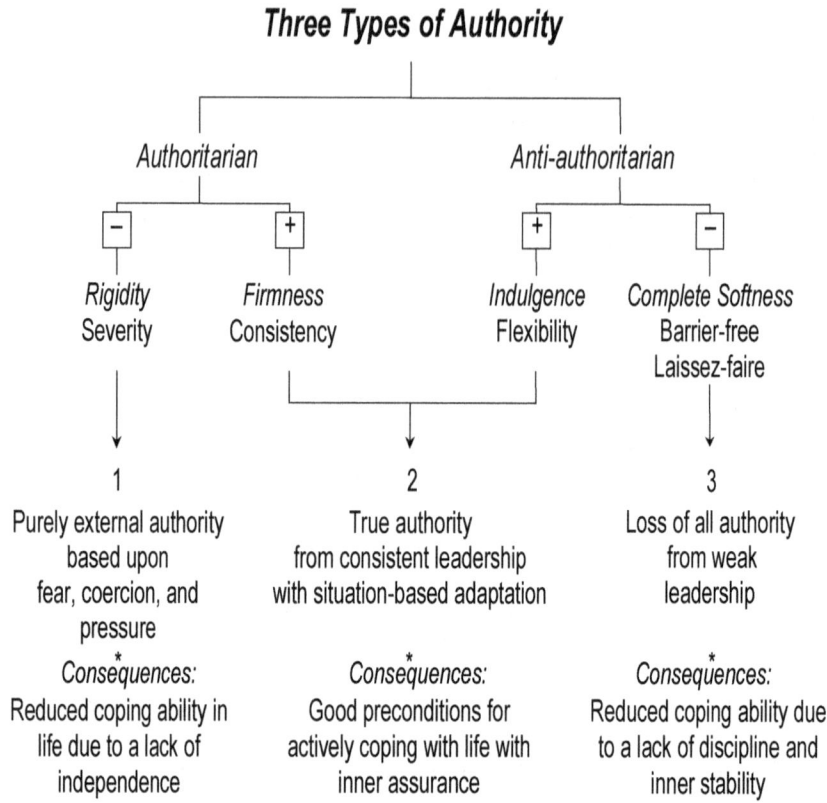

4. Use of Reason

Our starting point has been the Bible, therefore faith, but we must also take up the role of reason. However, our discussion of faith and reason is not that of the secular world in which reason, often under the influence of a secular ideology, is seen as evaluating faith-based or Bible-based truth claims. Rather, our discussion of reason starts within the Bible. And in the New Testament a Christian is taught to be consciously and willingly a thinking individual.[14] It is impossible to list all the terms and texts found in the New Testament in which thinking is described as indispensable for living out the life of faith. Christians know, discern,

---

[14] For details, see Thomas Schirrmacher, "Wie erkenne ich den Willen Gottes," Nürnberg 2001, pp. 115–134; Schirrmacher, "Leadership and Ethical Responsibility," pp. 21–29; John R. W. Stott, *Your Mind Matters: The Place of the Mind in the Christian Life*, 2nd edition, Wheaton, 2007.

learn, teach, question, answer, ask for wisdom and prudence, understand, grasp, test, and declare.[15]

In the Old Testament, the God-fearing individual is a person who reflects on life, who does not thoughtlessly live for the moment. There is an emphasis on the use of reason before God. This is repeatedly emphasized in the book of Proverbs—for example, when the topic of speaking is addressed: "The heart of the righteous weighs its answers, but the mouth of the wicked gushes evil" (Prov 15:28). Self-control, which both the Old and New Testaments extol, has to do with not following one's impulses but first thinking and then acting. "A simple man believes anything, but a prudent man gives thought to his steps" (Prov 14:15). For that reason, Paul calls upon Christians, "Brothers, stop thinking like children. In regard to evil be infants, but in your thinking be adults" (1 Cor 14:20). Indeed, in the Bible it is a matter of submitting all thought to God in obedience (2 Cor 10:3–6). However, that does not mean that one thinks less. Rather, the fact is that one reflects more.

5. Schools, the School System, and Home Schooling

European Pietistic Christians in centuries past, along with Evangelical Christians worldwide, have always been involved in a wide variety of school systems. And they have given a significant impetus to the whole range of school systems. Committed Christians have always been active as teachers at state schools, while they have also repeatedly started new private schools using completely different approaches. And they have also been active around the world in the home schooling movement for several different reasons. Even if these ways can be viewed as parallel paths for Evangelicals around the world, indeed leading to intense discussion among themselves, there are still some common denominators of Evangelical involvement:

1. The great significance of well-thought-out and comprehensive child rearing, i.e., of immense commitment to the next generation.
2. The great significance which is attributed to self-sufficiency and religious freedom for the next generation operates on the assumption that a real Christian is an individual who can decide for himself at a

---

[15] Comp. the good overview by Otto Michel, "Vom Denkakt des Paulus," pp. 211–213 in Otto Michel, *Dienst am Wort: Gesammelte Aufsätze*, Neukirchen 1986.

mature age.[16] For that reason, there is no movement which emphasizes religious freedom as strongly as does Evangelicalism because it begins with one's own children.
3. The considerable importance which is attributed to parental responsibility and which, in relation to the state, comprises an extended and controlling arm rather than any entity which stands over it.
4. A holistic view of child rearing and education not divided into knowledge, character, and becoming self-reliant. Rather, Evangelical education includes all aspects of life.

6. Values and the limits which are associated with them are again in demand in Germany

In the meantime, the "1968" student uprising in Germany, which substantially contributed to the development of the first Evangelical schools in Germany, is over and has been proved to have been on the wrong track, even though no one should say that very loudly, because many of the old '68 generation still hold the reins of power. Now many, even some not usually regarded as either Christian or conservative, are talking about the need for boundaries, values, rules, or discipline within education. Some of the examples are striking.

Focus (a major German weekly magazine) had the following on its cover page (8/2005): "*Verzogen oder erzogen? Kinder brauchen Grenzen,*" translated, "Spoiled or Educated? Children Need Boundaries." However, no one is supposed to name the inappropriate values being rejected in order to re-establish boundaries. Nor should one name the culprits who undermined value-based boundaries and continue to call them in question.

Der Spiegel (also a major German news magazine), which as one of the great promoters of the 1968 movement is certainly not above suspicion, has written about the current day school situation in a detailed article entitled "*Pfusch am Kind,*" translated "Botching It with Children."[17] In the section called "*Auch Disziplin ist eine Schlüsselqualifikation*" (Discipline Is Also a Key Qualification), it included the following on the consequences of the

---

[16] This is true as this is expressed in the teaching of adult baptism or in emphasizing the idea of confirmation introduced by Martin Bucer as the personal confirmation of a child's baptism.

[17] Jochen Bölsche, "*Pfusch am Kind,*" *Der Spiegel* 20/2002, pp. 96–116, here p. 104; also comp. "*Ende der Kuschelpädagogik,*" *Der Spiegel* Nr. 22/2002, pp. 58–64.

1968 movement as far as schools are concerned—whereby it was certainly high-mindedly silent with respect to its own complicity:

> Many politicians involved in education have underestimated ... the force of the change in values which changed the school system in the wake of the student uprisings. Many an individual has not mustered the courage to self-critically learn from mistakes in the past and to make the overdue policy adjustments ... This attitude still characterizes many old leftists in the education system today, although school has radically changed in the meantime. Even the mildest punishment at school can only be enforced with difficulty, and similar to giving someone detention, these so-called social behavior grades (for the form of behavior during instruction) only have a scarcity value. Even stubborn truants—estimated to be 250,000 throughout Germany—remain largely undisturbed. For this reason, the much "cherished concept of an enemy" of long ago, the "crammer school," with its "teaching approach based on direct instruction," is something which the left has to "urgently say good-bye to." Hans-Peter Bartels, an SPD (Social Democratic Party) member of the German Bundestag, has called upon his colleagues to do the following: "Thirty years of continual anti-authoritarian inspired reform have instead brought about the farthest reaching erosion of limits, de-formalization, and de-canonization within the practice of instruction in the school system. Therein, and not in the manner of the alleged authoritarian teacher, lies the problem nowadays." There is now a heavy price to be paid for progressive pedagogues, for whom writing counted as something elitist, and from time to time only had little writing done and declared a written form of expression secondary in so-called minor subjects.

World War II ended in 1945. The new constitutions of the German states and then finally the constitution of the Federal Republic of Germany all contain the right to Christian private schools. And yet, for twenty-five years there was a type of paralysis in the school question across large sections of Evangelical Christianity. It was not until the almost legendary 1968 uprising that a turn came. Scientists began to "out themselves" (as it is now called) as adherents of creation. For the first time, private trans-denominational theological universities (e.g., the STH Basel, the FTH Gießen) and study centers (the Albrecht Bengel Haus, the Friedrich Hauß Study Center, among others) emerged initially as an alternative or complement to state theological schools, and the weighty tradition of Christian educational theory returned to the scene.

That what began with the first schools on a biblical basis would become a movement with over 100 schools, for which *Focus* and *Die Welt* predict rosy times, was not suspected by anyone then. While at that time there was a struggle for each individual family and discussions in Christian churches became very emotional, nowadays the Evangelical school movement, as well as the entire private school movement, is decidedly not limited by one thing: a lack of parental interest.

Finally, in Germany the first Evangelicals in the sphere of educational theory left their self-imposed ghetto at the end of the 1970s and the beginning of the 1980s, and their belief was put to the test in the middle of society and everyday life with their own schools. From the beginning, the schools were intensively used by non-Evangelicals and non-Christian families, even though, strangely enough, the most frequent charge to be heard was that these schools were ghettos. Nowadays many of these schools are so integrated into their cities and communities that the charge has become self-defeating. This is because only a tiny number of the schools are insider schools that only serve children from Christian families. The Evangelical school movement has contributed significantly to getting Christians out of the ghetto of their church circles. Belief is no longer an affair only within a believing church community when the devout are among themselves. Rather, it has to stand the test in everyday life, taking positions on all the questions with which our society has to deal, continually answering before a critical public.

Christian schools have a long and largely beneficial history to exhibit around the world. Whether it is schools from the early days of Christianity, the schools of the Reformation, or missionary schools around the world, it has always been a matter of course for Christians everywhere to grant their children a good education and to offer this as well as to those who believe differently.

7. The Notion of Humanity in Educational Theory

A reason that Christians cannot simply leave the education and rearing of their children to the state, even if the children go to a state school, is that every educational theory is determined by its notion of man and a related form of ethics. There is no pedagogical approach without an approach to ethics and without a worldview by which the respective educational theory orients itself. Eckhard Meinberg has for that reason written in his book entitled *Das Menschenbild der modernen Erziehungswissenschaft* (translation of the title: *The Conception of Humanity in Modern Educational Science*) "about the indispensability of notions of man for mankind."[18] That behind every educational theory there is a form of ethics, a notion of humanity, indeed

---

[18] Section 1.1 in: Eckhard Meinberg, *Das Menschenbild der modernen Erziehungswissenschaft*, Darmstadt 1988, pp. 1–3.

a religion and a worldview to be found, does not only apply to such obvious examples as the "educational theory of the Greens." Rather, this is rather generally made clear, for example, in the study by Karl Dienst entitled "Streams of Educational Theory: Worldview Positions and Notions of Man."[19] Siegfried Uhl has aptly noted:

> Each of these views of humanity is simultaneously the "hidden center" of a "system of educational theory." For this reason, the respective 'concept of humanity' is the appropriate key for getting through to the details of the tenets of educational theories and to grasp them ... with respect to their inner required coherence.[20]

In other words: There is no value-free, neutral form of child rearing. Every form of child rearing is oriented toward a certain ethical ideal and rests upon a certain notion of what humanity is, so that rearing the child thus occurs in the direction of this notion of humanity. Christian child rearing will always include the idea that Christian standards and the biblical notion of humanity form the foundation of the education of children.

Children are not only shaped by the actual curriculum, which prescribes the material to be conveyed. In addition to the official educational theory, the mere necessity of co-existence and cooperation in school has a shaping function educationally, in a positive or a negative sense. This is mostly overlooked, for which reason some speak about a "second" or a "secret" curriculum.[21]

> The second curriculum could be designated as the unofficial or even as the secret curriculum since it largely escapes the attention of school educators. This secret curriculum also reflects a happy medium: a basic course in social rules, regulations, and routines. Pupils as well as teachers have to appropriate this basic course if they want to make their way through the institution, which is the school, without incurring great loss.[22]

---

[19] Karl Dienst, "Pädagogische Strömungen der Gegenwart: Weltanschauungspositionen und Menschenbilder," Information Nr. 70 (X/77), *EZW*, Stuttgart, 1977.
[20] Siegfried Uhl, *Die Pädagogik der Grünen*, München/Basel 1990, p. 46 using a quote by Otto Friedrich Bollnow.
[21] Comp. in particular Jürgen Zinnecker (ed.), *Der heimliche Lehrplan: Untersuchungen zum Schulunterricht*, Weinheim/Basel, 1975.
[22] Philip W. Jackson, "Einübung in die bürokratische Gesellschaft: Zur Funktion der sozialen Verkehrsformen im Klassenzimmer," pp. 19-34 in Zinnecker, *Lehrplan*, p. 29; also comp. John Taylor Gatto, *Dumbing Us Down: The Hidden Curriculum of Compulsory Schooling*, Philadelphia, 1992.

How does one solve problems? How does one respond when one is an outsider? How does one speak with people who represent other views? What is it that counts in order to be acknowledged by fellow classmates? What is truly important in life? How are boys and girls to get along with each other? These and many other questions are not covered in class. Rather, they are answered in the schoolyard. At many schools, the question of how pupils are to get along with each other and how teachers and pupils are to get along with each other has long since no longer been answered by educational principles and high ideals. Rather, it is answered by the law of the jungle. With the increasing decay of Christian values in our society and the exceedingly limited room for maneuver on the part of teachers and pupils at state schools, it is often no longer possible to come to a positive relationship between teachers and pupils. Indeed, sometimes there cannot even be an orderly flow of instruction in the classroom. Teachers at state schools hardly have the opportunity to instruct their pupils when it comes to character and to exercise any influence on how pupils get along with each other beyond the hours of instruction.

8. Being a Role Model

According to the Bible, being a role model is of great significance for whatever upbringing is involved. Parents are supposed to set an example for what they expect from their children. The elders of a church should live according to biblical requirements so that they have the authority to lead God's community (1 Pet 5:1–4). Dietrich Bonhoeffer once wrote the following about the church of the future:

> One must not be allowed to underestimate the meaning of the human "role model" (which has its origin in the humanity of Jesus and was so important in the case of Paul!); their words receive their emphasis and power not through concepts but rather through "role modeling." ... This thought has almost completely escaped us![23]

From this it becomes clear just what a Christian school is. It is not simply a school which only Christians attend, or which is only under the ownership of Christians, or in which only "born-again" teachers give instruction. In an impressive book, Jay Adams makes it clear that a Christian school is

---

[23] Dietrich Bonhoeffer, *Widerstand und Ergebung*, München 1958[8], p. 262.

above all a school in which Christian content is conveyed, lived out by example, and practiced.[24]

Suggestions for further thought and study:

1. To what degree does the Christian worldview lead to its own form of educational theory?
2. Discuss the quotation by Dietrich Bonhoeffer regarding the term "role model" in the penultimate paragraph above.
3. Is there a biblical-theological justification for the table found in the text above?

---

[24] Jay E. Adams, *Back to the Blackboard: Design for a Biblical Christian School*, Phillipsburg NJ, 1982. This is more clearly defended for a Christian college by Arthur F. Holmes, *The Idea of a Christian College*, Grand Rapids MI, 1987.²

About the Author

Archbishop Prof. Dr. theol. Dr. phil. Thomas Schirrmacher, PhD, DD (born 1960) is Secretary General of the World Evangelical Alliance, which represents Protestant churches belonging to 143 National Evangelical Alliances with altogether 600 million members. Before that he served WEA in different leadership roles the last two decades, the latest being the Associate Secretary General for Theological Concerns and Intrafaith and Interfaith Relations. He has been ordained and consecrated in Anglican tradition and is archbishop of the Communio Messianica.

Schirrmacher earned four doctorates in ecumenical theology, in cultural anthropology, in ethics, and in the sociology of religion and has received honorary doctorates from the USA and India. He has authored and edited 102 books, which have been translated into 18 languages.

He is President of the International Council of the International Society for Human Rights (Frankfurt) and Co-President of Religions for Peace (New York) and extraordinary professor of the sociology of religion at the state University of the West in Timisoara (Romania) and at the University of Oxford (Regent's Park College).

Part 2:
Theological Training

A Galilean Movement: For Such a Time as This

Joe Handley

1. Introduction

As I reflect on the life and ministry of Dr. Manfred Kohl, I am consumed by a challenge he laid out for several of us at the beginning of 2021. Dr. Kohl believes that we need to equip many more biblically formed, character-based leaders for the Church worldwide. This Festschrift is a fitting place to ponder that challenge, explain why it is imperative today, and provide potential solutions for the problems it presents. This article, in appreciation of Dr. Kohl, attempts to cast the vision and frame the rationale for such a movement.

2. A Call for More Christlike Leaders

"Today we need a global leadership summit for the purpose of finding, training, mentoring, and commissioning a million women and men for the needed ministry every year." Dr. Manfred Kohl suggested this following a series of gatherings with some of the top leadership development catalysts in our world today.[1]

Estimates from the Global Alliance for Church Multiplication (GACX) suggest that millions of new churches are springing up rapidly and are in desperate need of leaders. GACX believes that five million more churches are still needed.[2]

The Cape Town 2010 Lausanne Congress also highlighted the need for quality Christian leadership. According to the Lausanne Leadership Development Working Team, the current lack of mature leading pastors could prove tragic:

> Having Christlike leaders is a necessity. Providing opportunities for leaders to grow is critical to a healthy, vibrant, transformational and multiplying

---

[1] Kohl, M. "A Global Challenge for Evangelical Christianity." Unpublished Document (2021, July 7).

[2] GACX News. (2015, November 3) *Toward a Global Alliance* https://gacx.io/news/towards-a-global-alliance.

Church. Unless we find, make available, promote and multiply the very best in leadership development opportunities throughout the globe, the results will be tragic. The staggering weight of poor leadership will hold back the advance of the gospel.[3]

As South African theologian Stephanes Sigemindus Loots observes, "Church planting is moving at the speed of a bullet train with leadership development following on a bicycle."[4]

Exacerbating the issue is the need for change, especially given the impact of the coronavirus pandemic. Mark Dyer notes, "About every 500 years the empowered structures of institutionalised Christianity, whatever they may be at the time, become an intolerable carapace that must be shattered in order that renewal and new growth may occur."[5] Jerry Pillay further highlights the importance of change for church leadership:

> Historical church structures were designed for a cultural context in which change was more predictable and occurred at a slower pace. When things happen suddenly and unexpectedly, as in the case of COVID-19, the church needs organisational structures that are flexible and flat—that is, capable of adjusting to changing needs and circumstances to allow for timely and appropriate responses. This phenomenon has an impact on any institution, sacred or secular. Hierarchical structures are thus increasingly problematic, because decision making has to go through a chain of command and levels of control. People find themselves boxed into structure. Vertical relationships are emphasised at the expense of horizontal engagement. Hierarchies at times paralyse initiative and are ponderous in responding to unanticipated challenges.[6]

If we are going to best equip the body of Christ for future ministry, we need to equip leaders to engage every sector of society. Os Hillman captures this for the marketplace sector:

> We've spent too much time equipping our workplace people to do our ministries rather than equipping them to do the ministry God has called them to in the first place. ... The workplace is the greatest mission field of our day,

---

[3] Overstreet, Jane. "We Have a Problem!—But There Is Hope!" *Cape Town 2010 Advance Paper*, Leadership Development Working Group, (June 10, 2010), p. 7.

[4] In January 2021 Dr. Manfred Kohl invited fifteen key theologians and church leaders to explore how to begin such a new global initiative. It was during this meeting that Dr. Loots made his statement.

[5] Pillay, Jerry. "COVID-19 Shows the Need to Make Church More Flexible," *Transformation* 37(4): October 6, 2020, p. 266.

[6] Ibid, p. 273.

and yet we do not train our workplace leaders on how to effectively integrate faith into their workplace.[7]

We do not only need more equipped pastors. We need Christian leaders who are equipped for the vast growing Church worldwide, serving in every sphere of society and every sector of the world. If we only equip for traditional church space, we will miss areas of society that are crucial for the Gospel's advance. The church of the future must take forms that traditional equipping structures are not addressing.[8]

3. Christlike Leadership: Integrity, Character and Spiritual Formation

In the Lausanne Working Team Leadership Development survey, leaders list "the most pressing issues facing Christian leaders as personal pride, lack of integrity, spiritual warfare, corruption and lack of infrastructure."[9] The global survey also indicates that the most frequent causes of failure in Christian leaders to "finish well" as a Christ-centered leader include: a) burnout; b) abuse of power; c) inappropriate use of finances; d) inordinate pride; e) lack of growth in their spiritual life, and f) sexual sin.[10]

Dr. Kohl is championing an effort to address these issues of integrity and anti-corruption. He advocates for a deeper reflection through examining ourselves:

> We, as followers of Christ, must not simply accept the reality of corruption in the world. We need to be concerned. We are called to be the light of the world (Matt 5:14), and there are many ways in which we can fight corruption. However, there is another side of this issue: the need to examine ourselves. Corruption is simply the reflection of a lack of integrity.[11]

It is encouraging to see how the Lausanne Movement is strengthening this initiative. David Bennett highlights a modern-day Daniel from Malaysia as a prime example of Christian leadership from within the secular

---

[7] Hillman, Os. "What Every Pastor and Church Leader Should Know," *Faith Work*, (Aslan Press, 2004), Kindle Loc. 990–993.
[8] Moynaugh, Michael. "An Introduction to Theology and Practice," *Church for Every Context* (SCM Press, 2012).
[9] Overstreet, Jane. "We Have a Problem!—But There Is Hope!" p. 2.
[10] Ibid, p. 4.
[11] Kohl, Manfred. "Do We Care about Corruption?" *Lausanne Global Analysis*, 8/3 (2019), p. 4.

government sphere of society. In doing so, Dr. Bennett champions the vital importance of living with integrity and character for leaders of the Church today.[12]

The Lausanne Working Team paper on Leadership Development digs deeper into the best practices of developing leaders:

> When growing in areas of character development, discipleship, worldview and modifying core values, however, experiential learning has a great deal to offer. Factors that make this type of learning most effective include a motivated learner:
>
> – Who wants and needs to change;
> Who gets to try out something new, or apply it in her life;
> Who gets feedback on how she did when she tried;
> Who then has the opportunity to make sense of it through seeing results.
>
> The leader/learner who has the opportunity to participate in this type of experiential learning has, by far, the greatest chance of actually changing her beliefs and behavior. Excellent leadership development must include, but go beyond just acquiring information and include this type of experiential learning.[13]

From the vantage point of the mission I serve, Asian Access, the needs in the Church include the following:

- More Christlike pastors to lead the church with vision, character, and competence.
- Pastors who are better equipped to lead their congregations in countries where Christians are persecuted.
- Pastors who are less likely to end ministry due to burnout or moral failure.
- More pastors with the vision for multiplying churches that will enfold new believers across the most populous continent in the world.

Key to this type of change is nurturing a deep, abiding love relationship with God. This paradigm shift revolutionizes our personal life, family life, and ministry. It is the foundation for becoming a more Christlike leader. Transformation in society, in the city, in the state, in the neighborhood, in the church, always begins with transformation in the lives of individuals—and this usually ignites from the transformation of the leader.

---

[12] Bennett, David. "Integrity, the Lausanne Movement, and a Malaysian Daniel," *Lausanne Global Analysis 4/1* (2015).
[13] Overstreet 2010, pp. 4–5.

Leadership development needs to be infused with robust spirituality, a spirituality that builds great character and formed on the bedrock of living in a love relationship with Christ. That is why leaders like Matthews A. Ojo are calling for a deeper spirituality:

> There is a disconnection between Christian spirituality and the quest to provide leadership for the continent. Leadership in Africa with the exception of a few has not been exemplary or sacrificial. It has not been the Nehemiah model nor the Jesus model nor the Pauline model, but that which resembles the traditional African tribal chieftaincy structure with all its privileges and power but less of trust and accountability. ... Unless the above disconnections are addressed, it is doubtful if Christianity could impact positively and substantially on the nation and the society in the twenty-first century.[14]

David Singh argues for a stronger spirituality following the models of Sadhu Sunder Singh and Narayana Vamana Tilak from India who focused more on the transforming encounter and relationship with Christ than the importance of church expansion: "By moving from an institutional and polemical model of Christianity and Christian mission to one that is based on discipleship and enlightenment while engaging people personally, devotionally and sacrificially, a mission more reflective and formed by the Indian context could be realised." He concludes, "Regardless of what we call it, we have seen that authentic discipleship is crucial to sustain effective mission. Mission spirituality cannot exist without authentic discipleship."[15]

The development of Christlike character in a leader is foundational, as Dr. Kohl points out: "To address corruption and integrity, one must begin with the condition of one's own life. Do I strive to practice integrity, to be open to re-formation by God, to become more holy? It is not enough to condemn big bribery scandals or power-seeking individuals. We also have to examine ourselves."[16] This self-examination practice is crucial to our lives as Christlike leaders. Our integrity is what is on display for the world to see (2 Cor 3:2-3). Our Lord has called us to be salt and light; to be that salt and light, we must have a life filled by his Spirit displaying the fruit of integrity.

---

[14] Ojo, Matthews A. "African Spirituality Socio-Political Experience and Mission." In Ma, Wonsuk and Kenneth R. Ross (eds.). *Mission Spirituality and Authentic Discipleship* (Oxford: Regnum, 2013), pp. 47–61.

[15] Chan, Kim-kwong. "The Back to Jerusalem Movement: Mission Movement of the Christian Community in Mainland China." In Ma, Wonsuk and Kenneth R. Ross (eds.). *Mission Spirituality and Authentic Discipleship* (Oxford: Regnum, 2013), p. 237.

[16] Kohl, Manfred. "Do We Care about Corruption? How Integrity Can Tame the Beast of Bribes and Extortion," *Lausanne Global Analysis*, 8:3 (2019), p. 7.

4. The Struggle for Authentic Change

At a 2015 workshop, Dr. Kohl shared how weak theological education was producing ethically challenged leaders. He highlighted many of the glaring gaps in theological education and called for renewed emphasis on the importance of integrity and character.[17]

I was encouraged that week, despite the difficult assessment. Formal and non-formal theological educators had come together, continuing a dialog about how to better synergize and draw from one another's strengths. Formal educators could bring valid research and in-depth study while non-formal groups focused more on character transformation, spiritual formation and leadership dynamics.

That said, change is hard. Studies at Harvard over the past decade have found that very few leadership development efforts prove successful. Robert Kegan and Lisa Lahey point out that even those who desire to make changes—even at crisis stages of life—often do not make the best or right choices.[18] They state, "It requires more than learning new skills; it requires the ability to grow and reach new levels of mental complexity: the development from a 'socialized mind' via a 'self-authoring mind' to a 'self-transforming mind.'"[19] This reminds me of Romans 12:2, "Do not conform to the pattern of this world, but be transformed by the renewing of your mind. Then you will be able to test and approve what God's will is—his good, pleasing and perfect will."

The global Church has entered a new era of mission within a world context that has never seen such rapid change. We need radically different paradigms of church and mission leadership. The complexities of the current *sitz im leben* require a dexterity that wasn't needed even a decade ago.

This is one of the most dynamic and complex eras in which to lead. As the *Global Trends 2030—Citizens in an Interconnected and Polycentric World* report states, "The world is undergoing a massive transition, particularly in terms of power, demographics, climate, urbanization and technology. In this context, the opportunities are huge; but so are the uncertainties and challenges to the well-being of citizens."[20] The US National Intelligence

---

[17] Kohl, Manfred. "The Relevance of Theological Education: Reflections on 50 Years" (Workshop Presentation at ICETE 2015, Antalya, Turkey).

[18] Kegan, Robert and Lisa Lahey. *Immunity to Change: How to Overcome it and Unlock the Potential in Yourself and Your Organization* (Cambridge, MA: Harvard Business School Press, 2019).

[19] Ibid, pp. 16–21.

[20] *Global Trends 2030—Citizens in an Interconnected and Polycentric World: Report of the European Strategy and Policy Analysis System* (European Union, October 2011), p. 1.

Council concludes that we are living through a transformative period that is "equal to if not greater than the aftermath of the political and economic revolutions of the late eighteenth century."[21] We need a dynamic compass with which to orient ourselves in this sea of turbulent change.

There is a crying need for leaders who can discern the times and serve as trail guides on the contours of global change. According to *The Global Trends Survey by the Intelligence Council*:

> Leaders and their ideas matter: No history of the past hundred years can be told without delving into the roles and thinking of such leaders as Vladimir Lenin, Josef Stalin, Adolf Hitler or Mao Zedong. The actions of dominating leaders are the hardest element to anticipate. At several junctures in the 20th century, Western experts thought liberal and market ideas had triumphed. As demonstrated by the impacts of Churchill, Roosevelt, and Truman, leadership is key even in societies where institutions are strong and the maneuvering room for wielding personal power is more constrained. ...
>
> Leadership Will Be Key: As we indicated at the beginning of the study, human actions are likely to be the crucial determinant of the outcomes. Historically, as we have pointed out, leaders and their ideas—positive and negative—were among the 99 biggest game-changers during the last century. Individually and collectively over the next 15-20 years, leaders are likely to be crucial to how developments turn out, particularly in terms of ensuring a more positive outcome. As we have emphasized, today's trends appear to be heading toward a potentially more fragmented and conflicted world over the next 15-20 years, but bad outcomes are not inevitable. International leadership and cooperation will be necessary to solve the global challenges and to understand the complexities surrounding them.[22]

Peter Northouse reminds us:

> Globalization has created a need for leaders with greater understanding of cultural differences and increased competencies in cross-cultural communication and practice.[23]
>
> Although all of us have an ethical responsibility to treat other people as unique human beings, leaders have a special responsibility, because the nature of their leadership puts them in a special position in which they have a greater opportunity to influence others in significant ways.[24]

---

[21] *Global Trends 2030*, p. 2.
[22] *Global Trends 2025—"A Transformed World"* (US Government, Nov. 2008), pp. 5, 98–99.
[23] Northouse, Peter. "Leadership: Theory and Practice" (February 2012), Kindle loc. 8149.
[24] Ibid, Kindle loc. 8320.

The role of leaders in shaping the next phase of ministry, mission and life is vital. It is critical that we move beyond the current norms for leadership and yet retain the values inherent for leadership that endures.

5. Listening to Unheard Voices

Dr. Kohl has called for a Galilean Movement to raise up millions of new leaders with integrity and character who are willing to listen to the margins in our world today. It's imperative that we hear from those serving on the edges of society. For those of us engaged in leadership development, we would be wise to learn from Robert Kegan and Lisa Lahey as they articulate how to overcome the inherent immunity to change.

To help us reframe our mindsets and reset our agendas, the voices where the church is growing the greatest have much to inform us. As Dr. Kohl aptly assessed, our institutions are inadequate when it comes to fully meeting the needs and addressing the core issues the Bible addresses. Critical for learning is a process of inclusion that values those within a variety of networks, listening to them and letting their voices be part of the process. Oxford Leadership emphasizes being conversational in leadership, where collaboration moves beyond the hierarchy and away from directional forms of communication. Leaders become co-creators with their teams, learning together as sojourners. Dialogue becomes how everyone is engaged, and the full diversity of a movement can be heard. This allows all levels of expertise to share empowering every corner of the organization to play their part in the direction they are heading.[25]

Kelly Malone's research from Japan illustrates this principle. He found that many approaches to leadership training for church planters were unidirectional in nature, highlighting an arrogance about what was proper to pass along and to be learned. Instead, he encouraged trainers to listen to local leaders in their process of developing vision, strategy, and training. As trainers implemented a listening framework, their objectives proved more successful over time. These collaborative approaches to training employed deeper levels of listening to indigenous leaders thus serving as a more inclusive polycentric process overall.[26]

---

[25] Hurley, Tom. "Collaborative Leadership" (Oxford Leadership, 2016), https://www.oxfordleadership.com/wp-content/uploads/2017/07/OL-White-Paper-Collaborative-Leadership.pdf.

[26] Malone, Kelly. "Releasing Indigenous Leaders: Empowerment vs. Enlistment," EMQ 48(4), 2012, https://missionexus.org/releasing-indigenous-leaders-empowerment-vs-enlistment/.

This listening paradigm could prove transformative in changing the way we do leadership training. It is an emergent model for overall leadership, based on a new theoretical model that I proposed called *Polycentric Mission Leadership*.[27] I believe that polycentrism provides a stronger leadership model for leading mission movements in an interdependent, globally networked world. In reviewing recent developments in mission history[28] and studies in polycentric governance,[29] I discovered six important themes that form an emerging theoretical leadership model. Given the complexities we face today, I am convinced that a collaborative, communal approach to leadership that empowers multiple centers of influence and a diverse array of leaders is better suited to addressing the challenges during this era of globalization.

Ronald Heifetz and Marty Linsky provide outstanding insights into leading during times of rapid change and chaotic circumstances. We would be wise to listen to their wisdom when it comes to adaptive leadership to better equip those who are serving Christ's Church today.[30] Heifetz and Linsky state, "Hierarchical structures with clearly defined roles are giving way to more horizontal organizations with greater flexibility, room for initiative and corresponding uncertainty. Democratization is spreading throughout organizations as well as countries."[31] Given the chaotic, rapid-change pace of the world in which we find ourselves today, the need for these flexible models of leadership is essential.

6. A Galilean Movement

Recently, a group of Evangelical leaders gathered to discuss their concern about the lack of theologically trained pastors. At that gathering, Dr. Kohl stated, "The biggest crisis facing the evangelical, global church today is the fact that most pastors, missionaries, and Christian leaders are under-

---

[27] Handley, Joseph W. "Polycentric Mission Leadership," PhD Diss., Fuller Theological Seminary, School of Intercultural Studies (ProQuest; 27745033, 2020).
[28] Koschorke, Klaus and Adrian Hermann. "Polycentric Structures in the History of World Christianity / Polyzentrische Strukturen in der Geschichte des Weltchristentums" (Harrassowitz, 2014).
[29] Ostrom, Elinor. "Beyond Markets and States: Polycentric Governance of Complex Economic Systems," *American Economic Review*, 100 (3), June 2010, pp. 641–72.
[30] Heifetz, Ronald and Marty Linsky. "Leadership on the Line: Staying Alive through the Dangers of Leading" (Harvard Business, 2002).
[31] Ibid, p. 4.

educated or not educated at all."³² This concern is compounded by the need for further theological reflection on the leadership theories that many Christian leaders espouse. Banks and Ledbetter voiced this concern in reviewing many of the approaches and cast a vision for strengthening leadership development: "Little attention is also given to a theological evaluation of current views of leadership."³³

How then are we to proceed? It is encouraging to see groups like ICETE pursuing conversations and, hopefully, collaboration between formal and non-formal theological education. We need more, and it needs to expand beyond the traditional fields of pastoral training. It is also encouraging that Dr. Kohl has championed standards across the spectrum through the launching of Re-Forma. Dr. Reuben van Rensburg shared, "There are many programs which attempt to train pastoral leaders, but up until now there has not been a global standard. Re-Forma was established to do that."³⁴

More is necessary. As Dr Thomas Schirrmacher said, "Globally there are 50,000 new baptized believers each day, and if one takes an average of fifty believers to start a new church, that means we need 1,000 new pastors every day!"³⁵ The excellent work on standards and new approaches to leadership development are significant, but to keep up with the fast-growing church in our world today, the development of significant numbers of new leaders will be paramount.

To better mobilize and equip leaders for this fast-growing movement, a gathering to galvanize the interest and propel the leadership development networks and organizations should prove helpful, *if those from the margins take center stage and their voices are heard*. Thus, Dr. Kohl's call for a new global congress has merit. Movement theory, a framework for launching and sustaining social movements, affirms this potential. Zald and Asher suggest, "The coalition pools resources and coordinates plans, while

---

[32] Schirrmacher, T. "Ten Elder Statesmen of Evangelical Theological Education Establish Re-Forma to Encourage Untrained Pastors," thomasschirrmacher.net https://www.thomasschirrmacher.net/blog/ten-elder-statesmen-of-evangelical-theological-education-establish-re-forma-to-encourage-untrained-pastors/ (July 4, 2019).

[33] Banks, Robert and Bernice Ledbetter. *Reviewing Leadership: A Christian Evaluation of Current Approaches* (Grand Rapids: Baker, 2004), p. 11.

[34] Van Rensburg, Reuben. Personal correspondence, August 20, 2021.

[35] In his plenary at the Lausanne Consultation on Theological Education, June 2014, Thomas Schirrmacher presented the view of WEA and its Theological Commission that about 50,000 people (that do not come from a Christian background and do not have any basic Bible knowledge) are baptized each day in evangelical churches worldwide. See https://www.thomasschirrmacher.net/category/theology/.

keeping distinct organizational identities."[36] Blumer magnifies the importance of something that can galvanize a movement:

> Social movements can be viewed as collective enterprises seeking to establish a new order of life. They have their inception in a condition of unrest, and derive their motive power on one hand from dissatisfaction with the current form of life, and on the other hand, from wishes and hopes of a new system of living. The career of a social movement depicts the emergence of a new order of life.[37]

If we are going to attempt to meet the demand of the fast-growing Christian movements worldwide, this type of collective endeavor will prove helpful. Jehu Hanciles noted that "[Movements] do not have a commander and chief. There is no one person who can claim to speak for the movement as a whole, any more than there is one group that represents the movement. Movements are actually 'polycentric' or 'polycephalous' with multiple leaders."[38] The idea that leadership in flourishing movements is shared or collaborative will prove pivotal to pulling these forces together.

Listening will prove essential. According to Jopling and Crandall,

> Perhaps the most critical thing for leaders to do is listen well to their followers, for it is they who will carry the burden of bringing the network to life and realizing its intent. Structuring meaningful dialogue and framing questions that elicit felt concerns and make explicit the perspectives of the followers are essential to successful network leadership.[39]

Kärin Primuth highlights how a gathering like the one Dr. Kohl suggests can prove beneficial. "Networks offer a context to build trust across cultures and to genuinely listen and learn from our partners in the Majority World. They provide a platform for dialogue with our brothers and sisters in the Global South to mutually define what the North American Church can contribute to today's mission movement."[40]

---

[36] Zald, M. N., and R. Ash. "Social Movement Organizations: Growth, Decay and Change," *Social Forces* 44 (3), 1966, pp. 327–341.

[37] Blumer, H. *Symbolic Interactionism: Perspective and Method* (Upper Saddle River, NJ: Prentice Hall, 1969), p. 99.

[38] Hanciles, Jehu J. *Beyond Christendom: Globalization, African Migration, and the Transformation of the West* (Maryknoll, NY: Orbis, 2009), pp. 40–47.

[39] Jopling, Michael and David Crandall. "Leadership in Networks: Patterns and Practices" (NCSL 2006), p. 5.

[40] Primuth, Kärin. "Mission Networks: Connecting the Global Church," EMQ 51 (2), 2015, p. 215.

A global platform, like the Galilean Movement Dr. Kohl is advocating, has great potential. In an unpublished working draft, he proposed the following seven questions as part of a needs assessment to discern how we can move forward:

- What is presently being done in training pastors/leaders in formal and in informal theological training ... country by country?
- What is a church ... a house church ... a fellowship group ... a believer's gathering ... an internet fellowship ... a student worshiping team ... and so on?
- What are the approximate numbers of additional pastors and kingdom leaders that are actually needed?
- What is the best term/description/title for women and men leading the flock? We must not be influenced by our Western terminology and traditional thinking. How do we address emerging kingdom movements outside of the traditional church?
- What are the best ways forward of bringing together the countless organizations presently working in the field of leadership development without anyone claiming to be the right or the only one?
- What is the best way of starting new initiatives according to the established needs? How best can we multiply our present leadership development efforts?
- How can we mobilize the entire "evangelical family" to be engaged in a new wave of leadership development as envisioned in the Galilean Movement?[41]

Pulling together an event to galvanize a new movement of leadership development for the global Church is worthy of our attention and engagement. If we can listen well to those seeing the need most readily before them, there is great potential.

7. Conclusion

Similar to how Mordecai encouraged Esther ("who knows but that you have come to your royal position for such a time as this?"), this might be one of those moments in history in which the global Church can rise to the occasion and help foster a movement to equip leaders for the vast growing church worldwide. Our rallying call for the Galilean Movement comes from Jesus' concern to send forth workers into the harvest:

---

[41] Kohl, Manfred. Correspondence on July 8, 2021.

> Jesus went through all the towns and villages, teaching in their synagogues, proclaiming the good news of the kingdom and healing every disease and sickness. When he saw the crowds, he had compassion on them, because they were harassed and helpless, like sheep without a shepherd. Then he said to his disciples, "The harvest is plentiful but the workers are few. Ask the Lord of the harvest, therefore, to send out workers into his harvest field." (Matt 9:35-38)

The call from Dr. Kohl for a global congress to raise up more Christlike leaders is fitting. The harvest is abundant today and the need for workers immense. I pray that we can seek the Lord's face in this venture and follow his lead to mobilize and empower many new leaders for the fields that are ripe! As Phill Butler reminds us:

> Spiritual breakthroughs are not a game of guns and money. No human effort, expenditure of resources, or brilliant strategy will alone produce lasting spiritual change. Our partnerships must be informed and empowered by God's Holy Spirit in order to be effective. The challenges of relationships, cultural and theological differences, technical and strategic issues, and sustainability can only be dealt with in a process rooted in prayer.[42]

A movement like the Galilean Movement to prayerfully seek a breakthrough in developing Christlike leaders for the fast-growing global Church is critical to serve the vast harvests that lie before our world today. Dr. Kohl's challenge to research the needs, marshal the forces who currently serve, and catalyze endeavors to multiply our efforts to equip leaders for the future is important. The time is ripe and the potential is strong for us to give collective attention to this urgent need.

If we pay heed to the challenges ahead and we have the wisdom to listen to those who remain on the margins, together we can marshal the collective energies of the Christian leader development world and galvanize our forces to raise up a new generation of Christlike leaders who are well-trained, are biblically formed, and exhibit the fruit of the Spirit for the growing Church around the world.

A global congress like the one Dr. Kohl envisions has potential to be the lightning rod rallying us toward this end. The Galilean Movement could result in a world better served by solid, capable, biblical women and men. I am grateful for Manfred and his dream: a million new Christlike leaders per year for the global Church. May this dream come to fruition!

---

[42] Butler, Phill. *Well Connected: Releasing Power, Restoring Hope through Kingdom Partnerships* (Waynesboro: Authentic, 2006), p. 101.

About the Author

Rev. Joseph W. Handley, Jr., Ph.D. is the president of Asian Access. Previously, he was the founding director of Azusa Pacific University's Office of World Mission and lead mission pastor at Rolling Hills Covenant Church. He co-led one of the first multi-national high-school mission congresses in Mexico City in 1996 and served as a contributing blogger for the Billy Graham Center's Gospel-Life Blog. Joe serves as catalyst for the Lausanne Movement in Leader Development and on the advisory teams for the Nozomi Project and DualReach as well as the boards for BiblicalTraining.org and ReIgnite Hope. Joe strives to accelerate leaders for mission movements.

Theological Education as Mission[1]

Christopher J. H. Wright

Introduction

Who are we and what are we here on earth for?

These two questions are the simplest way I have found to help Christians understand the identity and mission of the church. To answer them from the Bible means to understand how God called his people into existence in order that we should participate with God in his great agenda for the world—the blessing of all nations and the ultimate redemption of all creation. At its simplest, a biblical ecclesiology must be missional. We are God's people created and called by God for God's purpose and God's glory, both in history and in the new creation.

The Cape Town Commitment puts it like this:

> God calls his people to share his mission. The Church from all nations stands in continuity through the Messiah Jesus with God's people in the Old Testament. With them we have been called through Abraham and commissioned to be a blessing and a light to the nations. With them, we are to be shaped and taught through the law and the prophets to be a community of holiness, compassion and justice in a world of sin and suffering. We have been redeemed through the cross and resurrection of Jesus Christ, and empowered by the Holy Spirit to bear witness to what God has done in Christ. The Church exists to worship and glorify God for all eternity and to participate in the transforming mission of God within history. Our mission is wholly derived from God's mission, addresses the whole of God's creation, and is grounded at its centre in the redeeming victory of the cross. This is the people to whom we belong, whose faith we confess and whose mission we share.[2]

If the people of God, then, are collectively a missional community by God's intention, how are they to be shaped and equipped to live in, or live up to, that calling? The Bible insists that one primary means of doing that is

---

[1] This is a shortened and adapted version of an earlier paper included in Dirk R. Buursma, Katya Covrett and Verlyn D. Vergrugge (eds.), *Evangelical Scholarship, Retrospects and Prospects. Essays in Honor of Stanley N. Gundry* (Grand Rapids. Zondervan, 2017), pp. 225-254.

[2] Cape Town Commitment, I.10a. This is the statement from the Third Lausanne Congress on World Evangelization, Cape Town, 2010.

through the teaching done by men and women whom God gives to his people for that purpose. In both Testaments, God's people need godly teaching and godly teachers and are very vulnerable when both are lacking.

The biblical importance of teaching among God's people

The Bible provides robust support for this conviction.

The Old Testament. "The Old Testament is the oldest and longest programme of theological education." This remarkable affirmation was made by Professor Andrew Walls in an unpublished presentation given at the Mission Leaders Forum at the Overseas Ministry Study Centre, New Haven, Connecticut. Throughout the whole Old Testament, for a millennium or more, God was shaping his people, insisting that they should remember *and teach to every generation* the things God had done ("what your eyes have seen") and the things God had said ("what your ears have heard"). He gave his people priests as teachers of the Torah, and prophets to call them back to the ways of God, and Psalmists and wise men and women to teach them how to worship God and walk in godly ways in ordinary life. When reformations happened in Old Testament times (e.g., under Jehoshaphat, Hezekiah, Josiah, and Nehemiah-Ezra), there was always a return to the teaching of God's word. God's people were supposed to be a community of teachers and learners, shaped by the word of God, as we see so emphatically in the longings of the author of Psalm 119.

Jesus. It is no surprise, then, that Jesus spent years doing exactly the same—constantly teaching his disciples as the nucleus of the new community of the Kingdom of God. Even as a twelve-year-old boy, he showed that he was rooted in the Scriptures and was able to engage with the rabbis in the temple. And in the Great Commission, he mandates his apostles to teach new disciples to observe all that he had taught them. Teaching was at the heart of Jesus' mission and ministry.

Paul. The importance of biblical teaching in the missionary work of Paul can hardly be missed. There is his personal example of spending nearly three years with the churches in Ephesus, teaching them "all that was needful" for them, as well as "the whole counsel of God," and combining that with systematic teaching in the public lecture hall (Acts 19:8-10; 20:20, 27). There was his personal mentoring of Timothy and Titus to be teachers of the Word. There was his mission team, including Apollos whose primary training, gifting and ministry was in church teaching. Apollos's missional curriculum in Corinth included Old Testament hermeneutics, Christology

Theological Education as Mission

and apologetics (Acts 18:24-28). And Paul insisted that his own work as a church-planter and Apollos's work as a church-teacher (watering the seed) "have one purpose" (1 Cor 3:8). Evangelism and theological education are integral to each other within the mission of the church.

The Bible as a whole, then, highlights the importance of teaching and teachers within the community of God's people—teaching that is rooted in, and shaped by, the Scriptures and which in turn brings health and maturity to God's people and shapes them for their missional life in the world. Teaching within the church in all its forms, including what we would now call theological education, is an intrinsic part of mission. It is not an extra. It is not merely ancillary to "real mission." The ministry of teaching has to be included within our obedience to the Great Commission. The Bible itself commands it.

Once again, the Cape Town Commitment carefully expresses this vital link.

> The New Testament shows the close partnership between the work of evangelism and church planting (e.g., the Apostle Paul), and the work of nurturing churches (e.g., Timothy and Apollos). Both tasks are integrated in the Great Commission, where Jesus describes disciple-making in terms of evangelism (before "baptizing them") and "teaching them to obey all that I have commanded you." Theological education is part of mission beyond evangelism. (Col 1:28-29; Acts 19:8-10; 20.20, 27;1 Cor 3:5-9)
>
> The mission of the Church on earth is to serve the mission of God, and the mission of theological education is to strengthen and accompany the mission of the Church. Theological education serves *first* to train those who lead the Church as pastor-teachers, equipping them to teach the truth of God's Word with faithfulness, relevance and clarity; and *second*, to equip all God's people for the missional task of understanding and relevantly communicating God's truth in every cultural context. Theological education engages in spiritual warfare, as "we demolish arguments and every pretension that sets itself up against the knowledge of God, and we take captive every thought to make it obedient to Christ" (2 Cor 10:4-5).
>
> a) Those of us who lead churches and mission agencies need to acknowledge that theological education is *intrinsically* missional. Those of us who provide theological education need to ensure that it is *intentionally* missional, since its place within the academy is not an end in itself, but to serve the mission of the Church in the world.
>
> b) Theological education stands in partnership with all forms of missional engagement. We will encourage and support all who provide biblically faithful theological education, formal and non-formal, at local, national, regional and international levels.
>
> c) We urge that institutions and programmes of theological education conduct a "missional audit" of their curricula, structures and ethos,

to ensure that they truly serve the needs and opportunities facing the Church in their cultures.

d) We long that all church planters and theological educators should place the Bible at the centre of their partnership, not just in doctrinal statements but in practice. Evangelists must use the Bible as the supreme source of the content and authority of their message. Theological educators must re-centre the study of the Bible as the core discipline in Christian theology, integrating and permeating all other fields of study and application. Above all theological education must serve to equip pastor-teachers for their prime responsibility of preaching and teaching the Bible. (2 Timothy 2.2; 4.1-2;1 Timothy 3.2b; 4.11-14; Titus 1.9; 2.1)[3]

The missional goals of theological education

Since theological education is an integral part of the wider ministry of teaching within the church, what should be the outcomes of theological education if it is going to truly reflect the goals of teaching that the Bible itself envisages?[4]

I suggest three focal points. Each of the following sections is connected with a Bible character who was either commissioned to teach, or commissioned others to do so—Abraham, Moses, and Paul.

Abraham: teaching for mission, in a world of many nations

> Abraham will surely become a great and powerful nation, and all nations on earth will be blessed through him. For I have chosen him, so that he will direct his children and his household after him to keep the way of the Lord y doing what is right and just, so that the Lord will bring about for Abraham what he has promised him. (Gen 18:18-19)

In a world going the way of Sodom and Gomorrah (Gen 18:20-21; 19; Isa.1:9-23; Ezek 16:49-50), God wanted to create a community that would be different—not just religiously different, but *morally and socially distinctive* (committed to righteousness and justice). That is the reason God chose and

---

[3] Cape Town Commitment, IIF.4 (biblical references are part of the original).
[4] These questions were very much brought to the fore at the Triennial Conference of the International Council for Evangelical Theological Education (ICETE), in Antalya, Turkey, 2015. See http.//www.icete-edu.org/antalya/index.htm. The materials from the conference are available at http.//theologicaleducation.net/articles/index.htm?category_id=77.

Theological Education as Mission

called Abraham and commissioned him to instruct and teach his own household and descendants (see Gen 18:19).

But *why* did God want such a community to exist in the world? Why did God create a nation chosen in Abraham and taught by him? It was to fulfill God's promise to Abraham, that through him and his descendants *all nations on earth would find blessing* (v. 18, echoing, of course, Gen 12:3). That is God's ultimate purpose. Abraham is the launchpad of the mission of God.

There is, then, a *universal and missional context* here to the teaching mandate given to Abraham. Notice that Abraham was to instruct his people not only *about* God, but also about the ethical character of God and how God wants people to *live*. In other words, this is *missionally focused ethical teaching* to shape a people through whom God can fulfill his mission among the nations. This long-term eschatological vision is clearly expressed in the syntax and logic of verse 19. There are three statements in verse 19 joined together by two "so that's." "I have chosen him, *so that* he will direct ... *so that* the Lord will bring about what he has promised." God's election flows through human teaching within God's people towards God's ultimate mission of blessing all nations.

So the *ethical purpose* of teaching in Old Testament Israel is governed by *the missional purpose* behind Israel's existence in the first place. In the midst of many nations, *this* nation is to be *taught* how to live as the redeemed people of God, ultimately for the sake of the nations, and as part of the mission of God for the nations. That fundamentally missional purpose of teaching surely still applies to the goal of theological education within the church.

Moses: teaching for monotheism, in a world of many gods

There is a strong emphasis on teaching in Deuteronomy. Moses himself is repeatedly presented in the book as the one who teaches Israel the requirements of their covenant God (to be followed by the Levitical priests, Deut 33:10). And the primary content of Moses' teaching was that YHWH God of Israel was *the one and only, unique and universal God, beside whom there is no other* (Deut 4:35, 39). For that reason, the first and greatest commandment, as Jesus said, is to love that one whole single God with your one whole single self—with heart and soul and strength. And then that primary love command is immediately followed by *the necessity of teaching*—teaching that is to apply to the personal realm (hands and foreheads), the family realm (the doorposts of the home), and the public arena (the "gate") (Deut 6:4-9).

Such teaching was necessary because of the polytheistic culture that surrounded the Israelites. Monotheism, in its proper biblical sense (i.e., not just the arithmetical conviction that only one God exists, but the specific affirmation of the identity and universality of YHWH, God of Israel), is *not* an easy faith to inculcate or sustain (as the rest of the Old Testament shows). But since this crucial affirmation is both the primary *truth about God* and the primary *obligation and blessing for God's people* (the privilege of knowing, loving and worshipping the one true creator and redeemer God), then whatever threatens that biblical monotheistic faith must be vigorously resisted at any cost. Idolatry is the greatest threat to biblical mission, for God's people cannot bear witness to the true and living God if they are obsessed with the worship of the gods of the cultures around them (whether in OT Israel or in today's church).

Therefore, the whole of Deuteronomy 4 is a sustained challenge to *avoid idolatry*, and the emphasis on *teaching* within the chapter is strong and repeated. It is worth reading that chapter carefully noting how the two themes (idolatry and teaching) are interwoven, since each is integral to the other. The way to avoid idolatry is to pay attention to the teaching; and the purpose of the teaching is to keep future generations from idolatry. The missional goal and outcome of the teaching that God wanted to happen in Israel was to keep people from idolatry and preserve their monotheistic faith and covenant obedience for the sake of the nations who had yet to come to know this truth about the living God.

Paul: teaching for maturity, in a world of many falsehoods

When we talk about church growth, we usually mean numerical growth through successful evangelism and church planting. But if you had asked the apostle Paul, "Are your churches growing?" I think he would not have understood the question in that way. For Paul, evangelistic growth was simply "gospel growth" (Col 1:6).

The kind of church growth Paul prayed for was *growth in maturity*. Here's how Paul describes the kind of qualitative church growth that he prayed for in his churches. In Colossians 1:9-11, Paul prays for three kinds of maturity:

- Paul wants the believers in Colossae *to know God's story* (v. 9; the will and purpose of God). That involves "head knowledge" of the whole great narrative of God's plan revealed in the scriptures.
- Paul wants them *to live by God's standards* (v. 10). That involves their practical lives and moral choices and behavior.
- Paul wants them *to prove God's strength* (v. 11). That involves their spiritual commitment to Christ and perseverance in spite of suffering.

So for Paul, growth in maturity could be measured: (1) by increasing knowledge and understanding of the faith; (2) by a quality of living that was ethically consistent with the gospel and pleasing to God; and (3) by perseverance under suffering and persecution. And all of those would be necessary if the believers in Colossae were to participate in God's mission in the surrounding pagan culture of their region.

But how will such Christian maturity be attained? Through sound teaching by those whom Christ has gifted to the church. Paul instructs Timothy and Titus to be teachers themselves, and trainers of teachers, with a view to *opposing false teachings and practices* of all kinds. Then as today, Christian believers were surrounded by competing worldviews and seductive alternatives to the true confession of faith. All kinds of false teaching were around. Then as today, the apostolic remedy and protection against false teaching was sound teaching rooted in the Scriptures.

Paul is very clear about this in Ephesians. There he affirms that the teaching ministry within the church (within which we could now include the work of theological education), is *a Christ-ordained gifting*. Theological education is not an end in itself (that is the temptation of academia, which can easily become an idolatrous seduction), but rather *a means to an end*, namely the goal of equipping God's own people for *spiritual maturity* and effective mission in the world. This combination is the main thrust of Ephesians 4:11-16.

The unique ministry gifting of pastor-teachers, according to Paul, is precisely to equip the rest of the people of God for *their* ministries—their many ways of serving God in the church and in the world. So, in theological education, we do not train people for a *clerical* ministry that is an end in itself, but for a *servant* ministry that has learned how to train disciples to *be* disciples in every context in which they live and move.

Are we teaching future pastors to think like that? Do we give them the missional task of *training others for ministry and mission*? Do we encourage and equip them to shape their preaching and teaching and pastoral ministry for that goal—to be equippers of the saints for *their* ministry? Do we inculcate in them the understanding that their own calling is not to do all the mission or ministry themselves, but to train and equip the rest of God's people for mission and ministry in the world?

To summarize, then, God has ordained that there should be teachers and teaching within the people of God:

- so that God's people as a whole should be a community fit for participation in God's own mission to bring blessing to the nations (the Abrahamic goal);

- so that God's people as a whole should remain committed to the one true God revealed in the Bible (as YHWH in Old Testament Israel, and incarnate in Jesus of Nazareth in the New Testament), and resist all the surrounding idolatries of their cultures (the Mosaic goal); and
- so that God's people as a whole should *grow to maturity* in the understanding, obedience and endurance of faith, and in effective mission in the world (the Pauline goal).

The questions we have to ask of our theological educators at this point, then, are as follows. What kind of graduates would we need to be producing from our programs, if we wished to show that our theological education is being effective and fulfilling its these biblical objectives? What should be our goal in our theological training, if we want to be faithful to the purposes for which God has ordained and provided for the teaching ministry among his people? What outcomes should we want to see emerging from our theological education investments?

Surely, we ought to be seeing men and women graduate and go out into their own pastoral and teaching ministry in the churches who are:

- *committed to mission* (in all its multiple biblical dimensions), eager to participate with God in his mission and to lead the communities they serve in the mission entrusted to the church.
- *faithful to biblical monotheism*, totally committed to the God of the Bible alone, and able to discern and resist the false gods that surround us. This includes not only the ability to understand and defend the uniqueness of Christ in contexts of religious plurality (and where necessary to bear costly witness to that faith), but also the spiritual insight to discern many idolatries that are more subtle in all cultures (e.g., consumerism, ethnocentrism, nationalism, etc.).
- *marked by maturity*, in understanding, ethics and perseverance, able to do the things Paul urges Timothy and Titus to do; men and women who are taking care of their life and their doctrine, and building up others in maturity, by godly example and steady biblical teaching.

So I ask: is that actually the kind of *goal* we have in mind as we shape our curricula and construct our syllabi, and develop our lecture courses and hold our seminars and workshops—across the whole range of our theological disciplines and departments? Is that what we are trying to achieve? Are we aiming to produce people who are biblically mission-minded, biblically monotheistic, and biblically mature?

The contemporary need of the church

The *Cape Town Commitment* identifies several ways in which we, as Christians, have failed to live up to our calling:

> When there is no distinction in conduct between Christians and non-Christians—for example in the practice of corruption and greed, or sexual promiscuity, or rate of divorce, or relapse to pre-Christian religious practice, or attitudes towards people of other races, or consumerist lifestyles, or social prejudice—then the world is right to wonder if our Christianity makes any difference at all. Our message carries no authenticity to a watching world.[5]

What has contributed to this failure? Surely the moral confusion and laxity of the global church are a product of a "famine of hearing the words of the Lord" (Amos 8:11), that is, a lack of biblical knowledge, teaching and thinking, from the leadership downwards. As in Hosea's day, there are many of God's people who are left with "no knowledge of God"—at least, no adequate and life-transforming knowledge. And this is so for the same reason as Hosea identified, namely the failure of those appointed to teach God's word (the priests in his day) to do so (Hos 4:1-9).

Without good biblical teaching rooted in a missional hermeneutic (that is, biblical teaching that is conscious of its own purpose, namely to shape God's people for their mission in the world), people forget the story they are in, or may never know it in the first place. They may know that their sins are forgiven and that they are "on the way to heaven." But as for how they should be living now, engaging with God in God's mission in today's world—of that story and its demands and implications, they know nothing. Lack of missionally focused Bible teaching inevitably results in absence of missional interest or engagement.

Decades ago, John Stott believed that this lack of biblical teaching, more than anything else, was to blame for the ethical and missional weakness of the contemporary church. And he believed that the key remedy, "the more potent medicine" as he called it, was to raise the standards of biblical preaching and teaching, from the seminaries to the grassroots of the churches. Here is an extract from a document I found among his papers, dated 1996, expressing his personal vision for the work of Langham Partnership (which he founded):

> If God reforms his people by his Word, precisely *how* does his Word reach and transform them? In a variety of ways, no doubt, including their daily

---

[5] Cape Town Commitment, IIE.1.

personal meditation in the Scripture. But the principal way God has chosen is to bring his Word to his people through his appointed pastors and teachers. For he has not only given us his Word; he has also given us pastors to teach the people out of his Word (e.g., John 21:15-17; Acts 20:28; Eph 4:11-12; 1 Tim. 4:13). We can hardly exaggerate the importance of pastor-preachers for the health and maturity of the church.

My vision, as I look out over the world, is to see every pulpit in every church occupied by a conscientious, Bible-believing, Bible-studying, Bible-expounding pastor. I see with my mind's eye multitudes of people in every country world-wide converging on their church every Sunday, hungry for more of God's Word. I also see every pastor mounting his pulpit with the Word of God in his mind (for he has studied it), in his heart (for he has prayed over it), and on his lips (for he is intent on communicating it).

What a vision! The people assemble with hunger, and the pastor satisfies their hunger with God's Word! And as he ministers to them week after week, I see people changing under the influence of God's Word, and so becoming more like the kind of people God wants them to be, in understanding and obedience, in faith and love, in worship, holiness, unity, service and mission.

That was John Stott's vision. But it is very close to how the apostle Paul also saw the primary task of those who were appointed as elders and pastors within the churches. After all, what should a pastor be able to do? What should a pastor-in-training in a seminary be trained and equipped to do? We can start to answer that question by consulting the list of qualifications that Paul gives for elders/overseers in the churches he had founded which were now being supervised by Timothy and Titus. We find extensive lists of qualities and criteria in 1 Timothy 3:1-10 and Titus 1:6-9.

What is striking is that almost all the items Paul mentions are matters of character and behavior—how they should live and conduct themselves and their families. Pastors should be examples of godliness and faithful discipleship. Only one thing could be described as a competence, or ability, or skill: "able to teach." The pastor above all should be a teacher of God's Word, able to understand, interpret and apply it effectively (as Paul further describes in 1 Tim 4:11-13; 5:17; 2 Tim 2:2, 15; 3:15-4.2; Tit 2:1-15). The pastor's personal godliness and exemplary life give power and authenticity to this single fundamental task. The pastor must *live* what he or she *preaches* from the Scriptures. But preaching and teaching the Scriptures is the fundamental task and competence for those who are called into pastoral leadership in the church. That is very clear.

So then, if seminaries are to prioritize in their training what Paul prioritizes for pastors, they ought to give very careful attention to two primary things: (1) *personal godliness* and (2) *ability to teach the Bible*. To be very frank at this point, whenever theological education neglects or marginalizes the teaching of the Bible, or squeezes it to the edges of a curriculum that has become crammed with other things, then that form of theological education has itself become unbiblical and disobedient to the clear mandate that we find taught and modeled in both testaments. Theological education that does not produce men and women who know their Bibles thoroughly, who know how to teach and preach the Scriptures, who are able to think biblically through any and every issue they confront, and who are able to feed and strengthen God's people with God's Word for God's mission in God's world—whatever else such theological education may do, or claim, or be accredited for, it is failing the church by failing to equip the church and its leaders to fulfill their calling and mission in the world. That kind of theological education is failing to fulfill the very biblical mandate for which it exists.

Now of course there are many other things that pastors have to do in the demanding tasks of church leadership. They will need basic competence in pastoral counseling, in leading God's people in worship and prayer, in management and administration of funds and people, in articulating vision and direction, in relating to their particular cultural context, etc. And good, comprehensive training for pastors should undoubtedly pay attention to all these in some measure. But above all else, Paul emphasizes what they must *be* (godly and upright in their personal life) and what they must commit themselves to *do* (effectively preach and teach God's Word).

If that is our aim, then one necessary component of achieving it will be to bring the Bible back to its central place both in the regular teaching and preaching ministry of local churches, and in the world of theological education in seminaries.

The Cape Town Commitment calls for this, quite emphatically, twice:

> We long that all church planters and theological educators should place the Bible at the centre of their partnership, not just in doctrinal statements but in practice.[6]
>
> We long to see a fresh conviction, gripping all God's Church, of the central necessity of Bible teaching for the Church's growth in ministry, unity and maturity. We rejoice in the gifting of all those whom Christ has given to the Church as pastor-teachers. We will make every effort to identify, encourage, train and support them in the preaching and teaching of God's Word. In doing so, however, we must reject the kind of clericalism that restricts the ministry of God's Word to a few paid professionals, or to formal preaching in church pulpits. Many men and women, who are clearly gifted

---

[6] Cape Town Commitment, IIF.4.d.

in pastoring and teaching God's people, exercise their gifting informally or without official denominational structures, but with the manifest blessing of God's Spirit. They too need to be recognized, encouraged, and equipped to rightly handle the Word of God.[7]

Knowing that Manfred Kohl shares these convictions and is actively involved through his Re-Forma initiative in practical response to those last two sentences, I am pleased to offer this essay in his honor with gratitude and respect.

About the Author

Christopher J. H. Wright M.A., Ph.D., is the Global Ambassador for Langham Partnership. He taught in India for five years, and at All Nations Christian College, England, for thirteen. As well as commentaries on several Old Testament books, his books include *Old Testament Ethics for the People of God; The Mission of God;* and *The God I Don't Understand*. Chris was the chief architect of *The Cape Town Commitment*—from the Third Lausanne Congress in October 2010. Chris and his wife Liz have four adult children and eleven grandchildren and live in London, as members of All Souls Church, Langham Place.

---

[7] Cape Town Commitment, IID.1.d.1.

Mission and Theological Education for the Extension of the Kingdom of God

Antonio Carlos Barro

1. Introduction

The first time I met Manfred was long ago; I do not remember where or what the purpose of that meeting was. I believe it was something important judging by the number of people from all parts of the world attending it.

One thing I do remember very vividly. When I got home and we had a faculty meeting at the South American Theological Seminary, Brazil, I informed the group about Manfred. I spoke to them about the German theologian who was in charge of the Institutes provided by Overseas Council.

I told them something like this: "This man is very hard to deal with, because he has a very strong personality and he likes precision and order. Let us hope that he does not come to visit us. I am sure you are not going to like to have him around our school."

This article deals with Manfred beyond the surface. A man of God, with whom I have had the privilege of traveling to many places of the world, hosted in my home, translated his lectures, and together we have edited seven books on God's mission and leadership.

Manfred is a "one of a kind" type of Christian leader. He exhibits a concern for holistic commitment to the Gospel. He is conversant with all aspects of what makes life meaningful in God's Kingdom and especially in theological education, where he thrives the most due to his unbelievable experience of knowing schools in more than 150 countries around the globe.

In this article, I will explore his contribution to the understanding of the *missio Dei* and his involvement with theological education, and I will engage in a conversation with him on these topics.

2. The Mission of God in Contemporary Society

The mission of God is the *leitmotif* for the existence of the church. It means that the church does not have a mission of its own but one that originates from God's throne of grace.

The change of this *locus theologicus* from *missio Ecclesiae* to *missio Dei* that occurred in the last decades brought a new perspective to the reason to exist for the community of faith. Mission often carried the stigma of being at the service of imperialistic nations, and it meant to conquer peoples all over the earth. In this sense, this change brought freshness and new enthusiasm for mission. Jürgen Moltmann says, "It is not the church that has a mission of salvation to fulfill in the world; it is the mission of the Son and the Spirit through the Father that includes the church."[1]

Manfred Kohl in a succinct way, much in his style, declares, "Mission lies at the center of God's purpose for the church."[2] If the mission is from God and the church has its origin similarly in God, it is only natural that the task of the church is to obey God's command fulfilling the Great Commission. The mission needs to be true to the person of Jesus Christ. Following Karl Barth, Kohl states, "Christ is the true missionary and, in union with Christ, the church participates in the reconciliation."[3]

Following this theological understanding of God's mission, Kohl goes on to consider what he presupposes to be principles that give direction to mission on Earth. These are important principles in every culture and in every ecclesiastical tradition. They are also principles that have accompanied the church since the early Christian days, and they are important to remember and to reflect on.

First, the mission is integral or holistic.[4] Looking at the person of Jesus as model and inspiration for today, the mission of the church needs to address all human beings as a whole person. The message is concerned with all that pertains to life.

Kohl points to the core of Jesus' ministry, that is, his compassion. He says: "Christ's compassion for the poor and the oppressed should be an integral part of the gospel proclamation in his name."[5] This is an important issue that the evangelical church has been struggling for decades or even longer. The debate about priority in God's mission has divided scholars and practitioners. In Latin America today this question is present and the majority of the Christian churches do not accept that the Gospel of Christ

---

[1] J. Moltmann, *The Church in the Power of the Spirit: A Contribution to Messianic Ecclesiology* (London: SCM Press, 1977), p. 64.
[2] M. W. Kohl, "Radical Transformation in Preparation for the Ministry," *Haddington House Journal*, 2 (2007), p. 161.
[3] M. W. Kohl, "Missão: O Coração da Igreja para o Novo Milênio," in M. W. Kohl and A. C. Barro (eds.), *Missão Integral Transformadora*, p. 50 (Londrina, Brazil: Editora Descoberta, 2nd edn, 2006).
[4] In Latin America we prefer the term integral.
[5] Kohl 2006, p. 51.

addresses all facets of humanity. To write that the church has a social obligation puts one under suspicion of being in favor of communism.

Manfred Kohl clarifies the issue:

> There is no separation between the spiritual and the social. The integration between evangelism and merciful works and development must be effective, since the strategic goal is the construction of God's Kingdom."[6] Here there is an agreement with John Stott as he formulated the same issue: "His [Jesus'] words and deeds belonged to each other, the words interpreting the deeds and the deeds embodying the words. He did not only announce the good news of the kingdom; he performed visible signs of the kingdom."[7]

Unfortunately, the church in Latin America and elsewhere has a long road to travel on this important understanding of the gospel.[8]

The second principle to give direction to mission is ecclesiology.[9] Having in mind that Kohl stated above that mission has its origin in God (*missio Dei*), he nevertheless focuses on mission as the heart of the church. Here the central point is that the church is not only a local group of believers, but also one group that belongs to a global church and as such, we share the same responsibility.

Here he makes an important observation that has been overlooked by Christian leaders, especially those from the Global North, that is, all the resources of the global church are common resources, and consequently they have to be used for a common mission—a mission that belongs to the people of God elsewhere. One can see only that this understanding seldom becomes a reality. The poor churches of the Global South continue to struggle to survive and to make ends meet, while the rich churches are using God's resources as they see fit. The discourse from the Global North needs to lead into an effective solidarity with brothers and sisters from the rest of the world to become credible.[10]

---

[6] Kohl 2006, p. 51.

[7] John R. W. Stott, *Christian Mission in the Modern World* (Downers Grove: InterVarsity Press, 2008) p. 29. See also J. B. Nikolajsen, "Beyond Sectarianism: The Missional Church in a Post-Christendom Society," *Missiology* 41(4), 2013, pp. 462–475.

[8] To be acquainted with the Latin America context, these authors are essential: C. R. Padilla, *Mission between the Times: Essays on the Kingdom* (Langham, 2010); O. E. Costas, *Christ Outside the Gate: Mission beyond Christendom* (Wipf and Stock, 2005); Samuel Escobar, "Mission in Latin America: An Evangelical Perspective," *Missiology* 20, no. 2 (1992), pp. 241–253.

[9] Kohl 2006, p. 51.

[10] As early as 1973, Orlando Costas called attention to this aspect, in "Mission Out of Affluence," *Missiology*. 1, no. 4 (1973), pp. 405–423. Another important book on this

Thirdly, Manfred Kohl outlines the principle of engaging in partnership and pleading for the unity of the church. Drawing from the Lausanne Covenant, he recognizes the need to practice partnership and to search for Christian unity as part of the biblical mandate to build up the Kingdom of God.

This has to go hand in hand with one of the principles above. There is a need, an urgent one, to be intentional in our efforts to work together. As members of the Global South, we often feel the indifference in the treatment to which we are subjected when we participate in world congresses and conferences. Our perception is that our participation is just symbolic.[11] That is exactly what Manfred Kohl wants all of us to grasp.

In sequence, Kohl calls our attention to another important aspect of God's mission, that is, focus on leadership. Here he has in mind a strategic plan to train biblically and professionally national leaders who are willing to be accountable for the resources bestowed on them.

It is imperative for the future of the church and the mission that local leaders, both pastors and lay people, be trained for ministry. Kohl argues that this type of training is more effective than sending and sustaining foreign workers.

The next important principle has raised many questions regarding the context of mission, which is focus on the poor and on the rich. Mission theology when done in the Global South has a tendency to point to the poor as the object of God's love and therefore the church's obligation toward them. Kohl concurs: "Today the poor, the persecuted, the so-called voiceless and faceless are often marginalized, ignored or forgotten."[12]

This is a sad picture of those people, and the church, in general, does very little to remedy this situation. However, moving in another direction, Kohl calls attention to those who are rich in our society. They also need God's love: "For Jesus, the desperately poor and the many rich—and all between the two extremes—needed to be confronted with the good news of salvation so that each one could make a personal decision."[13]

Kohl is right to point in this direction. There are many rich people in our society in Latin America despite rampant poverty, and they need to hear the gospel as well. This idea, however, is also applicable for the rich

---

issue is J. Bonk, *Missions and Money: Affluence as a Missionary Problem—Revisited* (Maryknoll, NY: Orbis, 2006).

[11] See C. R. Padilla, "Global Partnership and Integral Mission," In *Mission in Context: Explorations Inspired by J. Andrew Kirk*, ed. John Corrie and Cathy Ross (New York: Routledge, 2016), pp. 47–60; Samuel Escobar, *A Time for Mission: The Challenge for Global Christianity* (Langham, 2013).

[12] Kohl 2006, p. 53.

[13] Ibid, p. 54.

Christian people in our churches, because many of them are reluctant to apply the concept of the Kingdom of God when the issue is about finances.

Another important principle for Manfred Kohl is that mission must have a human face. Here he addresses an important issue that really matters for the members of the church: "Many Christians are not satisfied with simply praying and giving for missions; they want to be personally involved."[14] Church leadership needs to pay more attention to this aspect, as God's people want to be involved, and without this involvement the enthusiasm and interest for missions tends to decrease drastically. The reverse is also true:the more personal involvement, the more enthusiasm and commitment will be seen in our churches. Eddie Arthur states, "When we invite people to be involved in God's mission, we must not minimize the fact that it will inevitably involve some sort of sacrifice. Those who pray, give or go will almost certainly find themselves facing some sort of hardship if they are truly involved and truly effective."[15]

Mission, as Kohl always likes to emphasize in his lectures and meetings with local leaders, needs to make responsible use of the resources allocated for this purpose. Seminars and mission organizations must consider carefully for what purpose they are using the financial resources placed in their hands.

Many unnecessary expenses have brought seminaries and mission agencies to a situation where their ministries are no longer effective. Kohl states, "Research shows that mission supporters are often frustrated if they discover how their donations have been used and that many would want to invest far more if mission organizations were more transparent and efficient with respect to resources."[16]

Finally, Kohl explains the last principle that should guide the mission of God performed by the church in its pilgrimage on earth: the mission must emphasize meaningful communication and factual publicity. The indication here is that

> Communication can mean sharing difficulties, problems and pains, also multiplying joys, successes and achievements. It should include details of problems as well as solutions. Anyone who is part of the Great Commission, investing prayer, experience and finances in a mission, wants to be informed of the great obstacles and failures as well as the solutions and after-effects.[17]

---

[14] Kohl 2006, p. 54.
[15] Eddie Arthur, "Missio Dei: The Mission of God," (2009), https://www.academia.edu/2282856/MISSIO_DEI_THE_MISSION_OF_GOD, p. 6.
[16] Kohl 2006, p. 56.
[17] Kohl 2006, pp. 56–57.

These eight principles became fundamental to the ministerial praxis of Manfred Kohl. He applied them profusely in his meetings, lectures and writings during his journey through so many places and diverse contexts. In the following, it is my intention to show how these principles applied especially in the life and administration of theological seminaries that he visited in more than 150 countries around the world.

3. Theological Education: An Important Tool for the Mission of God

We can confidently say that there is no other Christian leader in the world who has visited more schools of theology than Manfred Kohl. Some schools, like the South American Theological Seminary, he visited more than fifteen times.

If one puts this in perspective, knowing that he has visited schools in over 150 countries and some more than once, then we can say that he is the person who best knows the reality of theological education around the world. Remembering that these schools range from small biblical institutes to universities, independent non-denominational and denominational, new and old, poor and rich, small and large schools.

The slogan that guided Kohl's perspective was very simple but profound at the same time: "Theological education is at the center of Christianity—as the seminary goes, so goes the church."[18] He saw theological education right at the center of the *missio Dei*. This firm foundation finds its reason in the Great Commission given by Jesus Christ to all his followers: "Make disciples ... teaching them to keep all my commandments" (Matt 28:18–20). The task of the school of theology is simply this: to prepare men and women to disciple people of all nations. Kohl then gives this important warning:

> The direction in which a theological school is moving, any failure to communicate basic and essential elements of the faith or of ministry, any undue emphasis on particular formations or functions of ministry will all be replicated in the ministries of the students. It is therefore essential to take a closer, in-depth look at the emphases in current theological education in order to determine whether future Christian leaders are receiving the best possible training for ministry.[19]

---

[18] Manfred Kohl, "Theological Education: What Needs to Be Changed," Torch Trinity Journal 12, no. 1 (2009), p. 149.
[19] Kohl 2009, p. 149.

We turn our attention to reflecting on how Manfred Kohl, based on his understanding of God's mission as seen above and together with his large knowledge of the field, envisioned a solid and prosperous theological training.

A theme that stands out in Manfred Kohl's speech is the distance found between the church and theological schools. Churches complain that the theological education offered by schools does not make sense for the development of their ministries and has only slight relevance for the proclamation of the gospel in contemporary society. On the other hand, Christian educators are frustrated and disappointed by the churches' lack of interest in pastoral formation. The church is reluctant to collaborate with this important task of ministerial training. Ashish Chrispal makes this acute observation about the situation in India:

> The divide between the church and theological education has widened. In the last 30 years in India there has been an explosion of church growth, much of it, especially in North India, through Christian workers who have no connection with the traditional denominations and seminaries. As a result, these leaders are not being equipped by the seminaries, nor are the leaders of the seminaries well acquainted with the needs and challenges of the emerging churches.[20]

To remedy the polarized situation, Kohl makes a few suggestions on how we can have a better theological education that will produce the solid and firm leadership that is much needed in the church and will bring satisfaction for those involved in the training. He recommends the following items for further reflection.

3.1. Changes in subjects to be taught

Here, Kohl addresses what is fundamental in any school of theology, namely the curriculum. The curriculum will determine the excellence of leaders being trained for the ministry of the church. This is his observation:

> Most seminaries measure success by pure academic standards, minimizing the requirements for developing spiritual maturity and ministry experience. Character formation, servant leadership, and spiritual modeling are

---

[20] Chrispal A. "Restoring Missional Vision in Theological Education: The Need for Transformative Pastoral Training in the Majority World" (Lausanne Global Analysis 8, no. 5, Sept. 2019, https://lausanne.org/content/lga/2019-09/restoring-missional-vision-theological-education.

not automatic outcomes of academic excellence. Academic achievement should, at most, take second place to the development of these personal characteristics.[21]

In this respect, I believe it is necessary to explore a partnership between the theological institution and the church regarding the spiritual formation of theology students. The church cannot leave the development that leads the student to reach Christian maturity solely under the responsibility of the school.[22] The school has an academic role and it must take care to provide the best education possible. It is true that the school also needs spaces in its curriculum to encourage elements of spirituality in its students. In the third principle for mission outlined above, Kohl talks about engaging in partnership. I believe this principle applies here. A partnership between the church and the seminary in the formation of new ecclesiastical leaders is then necessary. Pastors and leaders should interrogate their students on how they are progressing with their theological studies.

Based on the Murdock Study, ten subjects were named as fundamental for a sound theological education. They are ministry and spirituality, English Bible (or national language), historical overview of Christianity, Christianity and culture, evangelism and mission, spiritual leadership, hermeneutics, theology of ministry, personal growth, and communication.[23]

Regardless of whether these disciplines are still the most essential today or not, because we need to take into account the different contexts of the world, what is important is the concept being discussed here, namely that the theological curriculum cannot be stymied by any circumstance. Princeton University President Woodrow Wilson once said, "It is easier to change the location of a cemetery than to change the school curriculum."[24] Moreover, this has been the problem with most schools of theology everywhere, in the Global North as well as the Global South. Theological seminaries are reluctant to modify their curriculum and this for several

---

[21] Kohl 2009, p. 152.
[22] The issue of spirituality in theological formation has generated a wide range of literature. R. J. A. Doornenbal, for instance, puts the question as follows: "To what extent and in what way may spiritual formation be said to be mandatory, and how can this be assessed?" Doornenbal, *Crossroads: An Exploration of the Emerging-Missional Conversation with a Special Focus on Missional Leadership and Its Challenges for Theological Education*. (The Netherlands: Eburon Academic Publisher, 2012), 234.
[23] Kohl 2009, p. 153.
[24] Perry Shaw, *Transforming Theological Education: A Practical Handbook for Integrative Learning* (Langham Global Library, 2014), 18.

reasons, such as the lack of qualified professors, lack of energy to face the new, being unaware of what is happening in the church and especially in society, and loyalty to the denomination or to the missionaries who founded the school. The truth is that the topics taught these days do little to help pastors to be effective in a church that has changed (and the seminary has not) and has to minister to a rapidly changing society. According to Perry Shaw, many "academics are fearful of approaches that require them to move outside their specialist areas or that challenge them to emphasize the practice of ministry as well as academic excellence."[25]

3.2. Changes in missiological emphasis

There is an ongoing debate about the place of missiology in theological education courses—in my view, a fruitless and unnecessary debate. Without mission, there would be no need for the existence of theology. Without mission, there is no reason to devote time to studying theology, since the church is not carrying out its missionary task. It is the growing church in the world that provides subsidies for doing theology, not just any kind of theology, especially the one developed only within a small circle of theologians who communicate with each other without regard to the context of the church, but a theology derived from evangelical praxis. In other words, a missional theology.[26]

Manfred Kohl joins Robert Banks, Orlando Costas and David J. Bosch in calling for a dialogue between theology and missiology, as both are equally important in developing pastoral leadership. The problem as I see it, from a Latin American perspective, is that there is a theological education that is ideal—the one from the epochs of the missionaries who came, especially from the United States, and established seminaries in Latin America implementing the same curriculum they studied in the United States. These curricula, over the years, became sacred and many denominations are reluctant to contextualize them to our realities. Therefore, they have no missiological emphasis but perpetuate the great importance of systematic theology, church history, and the original languages of the Bible. The student graduates as a theologian and not as a pastor for a local church. For this reason, many of them will fail as leaders of the people of God.

---

[25] Ibid., 18. For more discussion about the curriculum see Doornenbal, *Crossroads*, 259–261; H. Jurgens Hendriks, "Contextualising Theological Education in Africa by Doing Theology in a Missional Hermeneutic," *Koers* 77, no. 2 (2012), pp. 1–8; Kruger P. Du Preez, Hans J. Hendriks, and Arend E. Carl, "Missional Theological Curricula and Institutions." *Verbum et Ecclesia* 35, no. 1 (2014): 1–8.

[26] For this, see Doornenbal, *Crossroads*.

3.3. Changes in the area of fieldwork

Borrowing from the field of medicine where students are required to complete training periods in hospitals and under the supervision of experienced professionals, Kohl suggests that the same model be applied to theology students. He goes on to describe areas where this training will take effect:

> The student (pastor-to-be or missionary-to-be) learns his future work step by step. He learns from his mentor how to prepare a sermon, how to begin the practice of prayer and fasting, how to engage in a devotional or "quiet" time, how to handle staff, finances, and board meetings, how to deal with both supportive and critical deacons. He sits in on counseling sessions, participates in weddings and funerals, and his functions continue wherever the pastor leads him.[27]

Again, as we engage in a conversation with Manfred Kohl we need to take the context into consideration. Most of the historical denominations require this type of internship. The Presbyterian Church of Brazil requires one to three years of work in a local church under the supervision of an experienced pastor. The Lutherans and the Methodists have a similar requirement.

The current problem is that the ecclesiastical context has changed significantly in recent years. Each church has its own style and way of dealing with its students. What we think is an ideal education it is not what churches think and do.

Another thing is that it is not up to theological seminaries to demand internships. The function of the seminar is to provide formal training and it is up to each church to determine the requirements for pastoral and missionary ordination. Every denomination has its own rules to apply for ordination. In relation to the practical work, another illustration comes from Brazil. The Brazilian government requires theology students to have 300 hours of practical work either in church or in Christian organizations. This certainly helps a lot in ministerial formation, even if it is not ideal.

One more issue here in which Kohl is correct is that every school should require its teachers to be more involved with local churches. It is not possible to produce a theological formation distant from the church and its mission.

---

[27] Kohl 2009, p. 154.

3.4. Changes in organizational structures

With his vast experience, Kohl suggests that schools think boldly about their organizational structures. The days when seminarians went to a theological seminary, lived on its premises, and finally returned to their hometown and church are now in the past. With rapid changes at all levels of society and also in churches, the theological institution can no longer passively wait for students to come to it. This happened, and to some degree still happens, with seminaries that belong to a denomination. Nevertheless, the vast majority of schools now need to develop student recruitment programs.

There needs to be a change in the mentality of the schools towards things that we had no idea could exist today. What is the future of large libraries taking up massive physical space? What is the need for buildings and classrooms if today students prefer to stay at home and have the same quality of education? The most varied contexts move us to think boldly and move towards the future. If we think about a theological education for today, we are already late.

I again bring an illustration from Brazil. In our country, schools were required to hire full-time professors to receive accreditation by the Minister of Education. Today, there is a change in our laws and the schools can hire professors by the hour. What are the implications of this change? One, for sure, is the reduced cost that the schools incur in terms of salaries and fees to the government. The other one is the quality of the teaching. Professors will no longer be available to guide and mentor students; they will not devote time to research and writing and will come to school only to teach their classes.

Manfred Kohl goes on to make suggestions on how to organize the school around important areas, explaining the role of the institution's principal and the board of directors. He concludes this important area by saying, "Any theological institution that has not developed a clear institutional development concept, with a strategic plan as its outcome, will struggle to be effective; it may not even survive."[28] To this warning, everyone involved in theological education should pay careful attention.

3.5. Changes in dealing with financial resources

If there is a particular area where Kohl thrives, it is financial resources. His vast experience in Europe working for World Vision gave him perspectives and insights hard to find in anyone else.

---

[28] Kohl 2009, p, 158.

The first comment he makes here is certainly true. Theological institutions in the West, or most of them, have financial resources from tuition, large donations and especially money generated by endowments. This is not the case with schools in the majority world. We do not have the luxury of having those sources available to us.

For this reason, theological institutions "must begin to develop their own financial resources."[29] One of the first steps to remedy this situation is to include in the curriculum of the seminary classes on stewardship and giving to the ministry. There is still a need, especially in countries outside the Global North, to inculcate in students' minds a sense of gratitude for their *alma mater*. Few graduates contribute financially to their educational institutions. It is also necessary to create the alumni association to keep graduates close to the school.

Another important theme mentioned by Manfred Kohl is the issue of fund-raising. It is true that all theological schools depend on student enrollment, tuition and donations from individuals, churches and foundations for the qualified maintenance of the pedagogical project. However, even knowing what needs to be done, it is not always possible even with good intentions in this direction. In the countries of the Global South, our schools deal with a very limited budget for setting up a fund-raising department. Another difficulty is the lack of people with training in this area, which is very specific.

On the other hand, Kohl is right to raise the issue of lack of interest on the part of many schools in giving due attention to the challenge of maintaining the ministry of teaching. School leadership very often is not determined enough in leading the institution to seek financial independence from sources outside their own country. Schools that still rely on foreign resources for more than 50% of their budget will have problems in the future when these resources are no longer available.

Those of us who minister in the Global South must bear this in mind: "Christian leadership formation is a topic which can be presented in an exciting and appealing way."[30]

4. Conclusion

For Manfred Kohl it is very important that theological education be at the service of mission and as such, the school needs to be in constant dialogue with its constituencies. The school needs to hear the graduates in the field,

---

[29] Kohl 2009, p. 158.
[30] Kohl 2009, p. 160.

pastors, laypeople, missionaries and even people who are not part of the church.[31]

This will help the seminaries to fulfill the *missio Dei* in complete obedience to the Great Commission. Mission is the fuel of theological education, and theological education is the guardian of the gospel doctrines.

Yes! Eventually Manfred Kohl came to our school and we became good friends.

He challenged us, rebuked when necessary, taught new skills, encouraged us to keep moving despite all the adversities, promoted our ministry worldwide and always prayed for us.

Manfred Waldemar Kohl, an ambassador for Christ!

About the Author

Antonio Carlos Barro was born and raised in Brazil and ordained as a Presbyterian pastor in 1981. He worked as a missionary in the Amazon jungle for two years and pastored churches for 25 years.

He is the founder of South American Theological Seminary in Londrina, Brazil in 1994, where he continues to serve as professor and president. He serves as mentor for South African Theological Seminary in Johannesburg, South Africa.

He has written and edited several books on the mission of the church, leadership and pastoral ministry. His areas of research are missiology, leadership, pastoral ministry and theology.

---

[31] "In the light of the missional-ecclesial vision for theological education, it is important that the voices of local churches be heard." Shaw 2014, p. 57.

Theological Education: Which Way?

Ashish Chrispal

1. Introduction

At the outset I want to submit that I believe in scholarship, but with a purpose. I am reminded of my spiritual mentor, Dr. John R. W. Stott, who had a vision of "scholar saints." Secondly, I believe in the "and/also" rather than the "either/or" way of looking at realities.

This analysis of theological education is based on my forty-four years of involvement in ministry and theological training. My thinking has been sharpened by my involvement with more than twenty seminaries in various nations of Asia as I served with the Overseas Council during the past twelve years. It has been accentuated by the challenges posed by the first-generation new believers who are now forming the emerging churches in India and many other nations in Asia and the majority world. I also edited this against the backdrop of the massacre of God's people worshipping on Resurrection day in Sri Lanka. Also, a comedian who professes to be an atheist, was elected as the President of Ukraine (and a large number of Evangelicals voted for him). How does the Church respond to pain and death at its most inhuman extent, on the day when we celebrate the defeat of death and principalities and powers? How do we explain the response of believers in Ukraine?

2. Challenges for Traditional Theological Education

Let me begin with some historical background. Theological education as it exists today in our theological colleges and seminaries is the product of the nineteenth-century Enlightenment era. In many ways it is the paradigm set by Schleiermacher of Germany. He wanted the Church's ministry education to be recognized by the university—the academia, which led to compartmentalized silos of the Old Testament, New Testament, Theology, History of Christianity, and Practical Theology with some dimension of the study of religions. It was molded by its heritage of Aristotelian logic and higher literary criticism of the Bible.

The Indian case study shows the beginning of theological education by 1818, with the establishing of the Serampore College, founded by William

Carey, Joshua Marshman and William Ward. The college became a full-fledged university by the Charter of the Danish King in 1827. This was followed by prominent denominational theological colleges and divinity schools in various parts of India (Bishop's College, Kolkata, Leonard Theological College, Jabalpur, United Theological College, Bangalore, Orthodox Theological Seminary, Kottayam, and so on). However, because of their antecedents, these colleges were preferred avenues for the ministry training of the historical/traditional churches. As higher literary criticism became stronger and as many nationals received their higher academic credentials from Germany and the West with liberal persuasions, the colleges became training grounds for the "priests of the cult" ... Christianity, slowly taken over by pluralism as its vanguard.

With this backdrop, one saw the beginning of evangelical theological education. Most of the Evangelical missions had smaller Bible schools for their training of national evangelists and pastors. It was at Yavatmal, Maharashtra, during the spiritual revival of 1953, that the Evangelical Mission bodies came together to form the Union Biblical Seminary (now in Pune, Maharashtra since 1983). The vision was formation for mission and ministry with academic excellence. The foundations were Christocentric, Bible-centric, missional and ministry training. In the years to come, other Pentecostal and Evangelical seminaries with similar vision took root in the nation. One can recognize similar patterns in other Asian nations. However, these Evangelical colleges and Bible schools had missionaries as their faculty.

The new beginning of higher academic credentials for nationals within the Evangelical seminaries happened from the 1970s. Rev. Dr. John R. W. Stott, as the Founder-Secretary of the Evangelical Fellowship within the Anglican Communion (EFAC), invited prospective scholars to come and study in the United Kingdom under Evangelical scholars or sympathizers of the Evangelical cause. By the end of 1980, EFAC became the Langham Scholarship which today is the Langham International. The efforts of one servant of God, followed by many others committed to the cause of the evangelical scholarship, has resulted today in there being a great number of Evangelical scholars in the majority world.

The Evangelical Institutions took seriously their heritage of training or theological education as formation for ministry and mission with academic excellence. This phenomenon saw the rise of respected Evangelical leadership in India and many other nations during the 1980s and 1990s. However, one begins to see the shift after the mid-nineties and in the new millennium.

The divide between the church and theological education (TE) has widened. The student's vision in many cases has changed. It is a normal pattern to hear at graduation exercises that nearly 60% of graduates are aspiring to "further studies," rather than ministry. One can also see another pattern: students completing their first and secondary degrees in theology, serving in one of the Bible schools or seminaries for a year or two and then doing their master's degree with a view to being absorbed by one of the mushrooming seminaries.

The real danger we face in Evangelical theological education today is the overtaking by academia, without the vision for mission and ministry. In many countries like Indonesia, South Korea, Philippines, Thailand, for example, the governments have forced theological education to move into higher education or university modes. This has further forced it to academia with overemphasis on cerebral learning rather than professional training similar to studies in medicine, law, engineering, and so on. The faculty are pressed either by the governments or by the demand of scholastic pursuit to the dictum: "Publish or Perish." There is a weakening of the understanding of theological education as a formation for mission and ministry. Spiritual and character formation have become appendages. Since the demand of faculty by academia is overwhelming, so the mentoring of students is suffering.

As a result of the above shift, the mission agencies and mega-churches have started their own theological training programs, to keep their DNA alive and kicking. Some even say, "Seminaries are cemeteries." One mission leader told me that our woe is that we send good church planters for training but after the study they want to settle down in a church with no zeal for church planting.

3. Grassroots Workers' Training in Mission and Ministry

At the present time it can be seen that most of the emerging churches are made up of first-generation believers. Therefore, they come with totally different sets of worldviews. Their faith most often is based on healing from illness, or release from demon possession, or an answered prayer in a crisis situation. So, they know Jesus as the Healer or Miracle Worker! What is lacking is to lead them into deeper discipleship and the Lordship of Jesus Christ in their lives. This means transformation of their worldviews. The teaching of God's Word, therefore, is of paramount importance. However, because they come from the downtrodden communities, their school education is minimal and discipling them is our priority. There is a significant leadership deficit in many regions where the Church is rapidly growing.

This leadership deficit has been quantified by research conducted by the Center for the Study of Global Christianity, at the Gordon-Conwell Theological Seminary:

- 2.2 million Protestant pastors in the Majority World lack formal biblical training.
- 90% of churches worldwide are led by brothers and sisters in Christ who have no formal training.
- 50,000 people accept Christ every day in the Majority World, creating a need for 1,000 new pastors daily.

First, while formal theological education makes a critical contribution to the long-term health of the Church, non-formal approaches address the large and growing numbers of those needing basic pastoral training but for whom formal training is neither accessible nor appropriate.

Non-formal training organizations and programs can benefit from the right kind of partners offering the right kind of assistance.

Secondly, most of the grassroots pastors or mission workers who can speak people's heart language are also educationally deprived, but they are on the fire for the Lord. They need training, but with the recognition that it has to be in the vernacular, much of it will have to be orally transmitted and the learning methods are different.

Thirdly, the materials from the West are good, but based on the pattern of traditional theological education. This means it is based on Aristotelian logic, teacher-centered, and dependent upon the writing ability of the student. It also fails to address the worldview questions, and hence we see very little transformation among students.

Fourthly, we need adaptable materials with a profound biblical base, yet which are easily transferable according to the needs of people.

Fifthly, there is evidence of how the Asian and African students learn; namely, they are neither analytical nor field-independent. This means the synthetic dimension and learning dependence on their context become necessary in how we develop training.

Sixthly, Bloom's taxonomy which has given rise to cognitive concerns as supreme in TE has not helped the churches. We need training based on biblical wisdom that undergirds the character and spiritual formation as well as giving equal importance to competency building.

Finally, the ownership needs to be shifted to the learners; not a ready-made TE which in form is non-formal but apes the formal. We need to begin by challenging the grassroots pastors as to what is their perceived need in discipling themselves and their congregations and how can they be equipped to do better in fulfilling the task the Lord has given us.

4. Conclusion

The time has come for us to recognize the following, if evangelical theological education is to be impactful and not become a fossil.

First, theology is for the whole Church: Paul and other New Testament writers wrote for the grounding and rooting of the Church in God's word (Col 2:6, 7). It is not for the pursuit of few to be elitist leaders within the Church.

Secondly, theology as theos-logos (the study of God) needs transformation as theos-eulogeo, (the praise of God). Today theological education has become a cerebral pursuit. Some even call theology a Christian philosophy rather than a way of life.

Thirdly, it is important to note that when Paul wrote to Timothy and Titus, his emphasis was on their character formation, undergirded by biblical theology.

Fourthly, the present pattern of student fees, donations (fund raising in the West) and expense is no longer viable for two reasons. First, students who can make a difference in the society tend to be bi-vocational as they are disillusioned by the church leadership and want to stay away from courses of three to four years of residential theological education. Secondly, the new millennial donors are more interested in outcome- and impact-based learning rather than traditional status-quo theological degrees.

Fifthly, we need to re-envision theological education as discipling the disciplers. There is an urgent need to focus intentionally upon transformative theological education, with focus on an outcome that is rooted in missional and ministerial formation.

Sixthly, theological education needs to also look at the emerging churches where many new believers come from a marginalized and oppressive background. The pastors who minister to them have minimal formal school education. But they speak the heart language of people and are able to present the gospel effectively to plant churches. What about their training? The need for theological education in the vernacular, with oral communication as the key and their learning patterns to be taken seriously, is the need of the growing mass of people at the grassroots.

Lastly, struggle like the early Church with a question: Do gentiles first become Jews to learn and follow Jesus Christ? Do the pastors and evangelists, those interested in learning God's Word, have to first be English-speaking and have Aristotelian logic with an analytical mind as their prerequisite? The early Church lived as a minority among the people of other faiths; they suffered trials and persecution and yet communicated the wisdom of God in both written and oral forms. Majority believers were from a marginalized and despised background, but they responded to the Good News. Is this not the reality of the present-day world and especially the majority world? Can we free people from the Western captivity of theological education and allow it to flourish and take shape in the earthen vessels of different soils, that the living waters of the Lord may quench the thirst of many who are dying without Christ?

My pain is like the book of Acts, chapter 15. Why should gentiles first have to become Jews to be full-fledged disciples of Jesus Christ? So why should new believers and grassroots pastors have to first be trained in Aristotelian logic, Western philosophical categories, writing skills on essays and exams, and primarily know English before they can undergird emerging churches to be rooted and built up in the Word and be engaged in the world to disciple others? I cry for alternative synthetic thinking in place of analytical thinking but having the Word as the critical tool for hermeneutics. Can there be an alternate way of assessing their competency? Can their reflective practices be given value?

For me the TE needs to re-orient itself away from the Enlightenment era of Schleiermacher when academic recognition became the goal. I am not anti-scholarship. But scholarship for what? What is the focus of TE today? I am going to be stark in my expression, so please forgive me. Before Constantine the Church, a persecuted and suffering community, took the people of other faiths seriously. Look at Origen and Tertullian, for example; they wrote to communicate the gospel. But since Constantine and until today we teach and speak from the Christendom mentality and mindset. The very theological education that has brought the Church in the West, especially Europe (France and Germany), Canada, and the USA to its bankruptcy and decay—why should that methodology and process continue to dominate theological education for the new believers?

I'm once again forced to think that we as theological educators have failed. While we concentrated on higher education with cerebral-academic excellence, we forgot and neglected the "grassroots" in every sense of the word. Lord, forgive us for forgetting that knowing you (in the Hebrew sense) means to obey you, and help your Church to know you. We have become elitist and emphasized our education for intelligentsia, searching for approval by the accrediting and affiliating agencies of higher-level education. We have failed to relate knowing God with obeying his command, in the sense that we lacked public and political theology and failed to help people to interpret God's Word in everyday life. We need to regain the grassroots by making theology for all, that undergirds our faith and its outworking in life.

When we fail to speak and act against corruption and bribery and only try to protect our ghetto understanding, we fail people! We need to complement our theological learning with applied theology that takes ethics as an equal partner with the Lord in our life.

We are facing the upsurge of craving for credentials rather than writing, speaking and training our young ones in the Church, to live our faith combining heart, head and mind. Look at the sequence Paul has in Romans chapter 12—body, mind and attitude/practice. We have also forgotten the people who live near us who are of no faith or other faiths. We need to regain the Church that lived as a minority and shared the Good News at the expense of their life. We are too complacent and speak and teach the language of majoritarian Christianity, which is far from reality today.

It was the persecuted, suffering Church, which manifested God's power in her own powerlessness, that sang about Jesus "who, though he was in the form of God, did not count equality with God a thing to be grasped, but emptied himself, by taking the form of a servant, being born in the likeness of men. And being found in human form, he humbled himself by becoming obedient to the point of death, even death on a cross. Therefore God has highly exalted him and bestowed on him the name that is above every name, so that at the name of Jesus every knee should bow, in heaven and on earth and under the earth, and every tongue confess that Jesus Christ is Lord, to the glory of God the Father" (Phil 2:6–11).

May we lift up our Crucified and Risen Lord as our Healer, Counsellor and Master who answers our prayers and asks us to follow him, learning and teaching all he has commanded us to disciple all the nations.

Theological education, which way? We need a two-pronged approach and must not be just elitist and traditionalist educators who do not recognize the need for transformation, but ones who will lead the Church of our Lord Jesus Christ to be rooted and grounded in his word.

About the Author

Ashish Chrispal has served as a pastor and Theological educator. He has served at the Union Biblical Seminary (Pune) and SAIACS (Bangalore) as a teacher of contextual and Pastoral Theology. He is a Langham Scholar receiving his PhD from the University of Aberdeen. He has served with the Overseas Council for the last fifteen years, as the Regional Director for Asia and now as the Senior Advisor. He lives in Bangalore. He is presently involved in preparing the curriculum and courses for the church-based Grassroots Training for Mission and Ministry.

Reconciliation in the Context of Corruption

Johannes Reimer

1. Introduction: A Man with a Prophetic Vision

It is a great honor for me to contribute an article to this Festschrift. I have known Manfred Kohl since the 1990s. Together with a number of other young Evangelicals I founded Logos International, a mission agency set to plant educational structures for the Church in the Soviet Union and the Commonwealth of Independent States (CIS). Manfred represented the Christian College Coalition, and it did not take much to find out how well informed this man was and how deep his interest in issues beyond the ones commonly known. In fact, I have seldom met a Westerner with such an impressive prophetic mind. Manfred was driven by the passion to not just copy existing institutions of the West, but rather to develop effective solutions for each individual context. And as soon as he saw the advantages of a proposed structure, he invested all his energy in their realization. Over the years I have observed a similar behavior in all of Manfred's undertakings. One of them is the creation of the Integrity Network, a timely Evangelical venture set to fight corruption in the church and the world. Thank you, Manfred, for having invited me to participate.

In my contribution I will define corruption theologically and examine the effects corruption has on a given culture and on the development of unjust and abusive systems dividing whole nations and creating zones of conflict and war. And I will describe the special mission of the church in reconciliation and peacebuilding for such zones.

2. Living in a war zone

The world around us is a "world of war" as John H. Yoder properly puts it.[1] This world is marked by egoism and a constant strife for personal gain, even if this means quarrel, fight, not to mention killing. The apostle James writes:

> What causes fights and quarrels among you? Don't they come from your desires that battle within you? You desire but do not have, so you kill. You

---

[1] John Howard Yoder, *He Came Preaching Peace* (Eugene, OR: Wipf & Stock, 1998), 17.

covet but you cannot get what you want, so you quarrel and fight. You do not have because you do not ask God. When you ask, you do not receive, because you ask with wrong motives, that you may spend what you get on your pleasures. (Jas 4:1–3 NIV)

Putting personal gain first in order to satisfy our own pleasures is what motivates conflict and creates the zones of war, claims the apostle. He describes the process as a common human-worldly process encompassing the social and religious dimensions. Even those who pray may do this out of very egoistic motives. Sure enough, personal gain-centered prayers will stay unanswered and people using them are called adulterous and deemed to become enemies of God, living under the rule of satanic powers (Jas 4:4–7).

The world as a zone of conflict is determined by the egoistic nature of men misled by demonic powers. Today, we rather speak of corruption broadly defined "as the abuse of entrusted power for private gain" which "erodes trust, weakens democracy, hampers economic development and further exacerbates inequality, poverty, social division and the environmental crisis."[2] Corruption is a central factor shaping the zones of conflict in the world.

And the world is the place we Christians live in and are sent to. Jesus himself determines the context in which his followers exist and are sent to by saying, "As you sent me into the world, I have sent them into the world" (John 17:18 NIV). And this is an evil world in which "you used to live when you followed the ways of this world and of the ruler of the kingdom of the air, the spirit who is now at work in those who are disobedient," writes the apostle Paul in Ephesians 2:2–3 (NIV). "All of us also lived among them at one time, gratifying the cravings of our flesh and following its desires and thoughts. Like the rest, we were by nature deserving of wrath." The demonically corrupted world is desire-centered, gratifying the cravings of our flesh and, therefore, promoting anger and distorted relationships.

The church sent into such zones will have to name and fight corruption. In fact, any meaningful transformation of a society to what the Great Commission calls "making disciples of nations" (Matt 28:19) will require an elaborate missional response of the church to corruption. Understanding the source and nature of corruption will inform the development of both (a) a strong resistance among Christians toward corruption and (b) a meaningful tool to fight corruption.

---

[2] https://www.transparency.org/en/what-is-corruption (accessed March 23, 2021).

3. Corruption, Conflict and Reconciliation

Corruption evolves, biblically speaking, from a sinful human nature depraved "from its primary purity."[3] Corrupted by the deceiver, Adam and Eve laid a foundation for moral deterioration or decay. Disobedience to God's rule with the goal of self-satisfaction drove Eve to follow the voice of the deceiver (Gen 2–3). This resulted in the loss of paradise. And soon sin and moral decay determined the course of our human history. Their son Cain even killed his brother in an attempt to concentrate God's blessing on himself (Gen 4:1–16). Sin and corruption entered the world created so perfectly by God. And God himself states after the fall of the first humans, "Every inclination of the human heart is evil from childhood" (Gen 8:21b).

Corruption is a result of sin, godlessness, disobedience and self-determination. Today it is often identified with fraud, bribery, money laundering and the like, with an expressed interest to gain power over those in authority or receive their favors.[4] But corruption is not limited to illegal financial transactions. There are many ways to abuse power and promote favoritism. Corruption has many faces and is widely spread all over the world in both democratic and non-democratic societies, in secular as well as religious settings. In some countries it develops to a system permeating all strata of society.

I grew up in the Soviet Union. While on the one hand corruption was banned and vetoed from the lowest to the highest authority levels by law, it permeated all, literally all, strata of society. Nearly every act of promotion, be it intellectual, social, political or economic, required bribery. Corruption became a system by which society existed. Only when one paid an extra amount of money did things become possible.[5] Bribery became a norm of behavior.

The situation in Russia and the non-Baltic former Soviet republics is not much better today.[6] Ukraine, for instance, is seen as the most corrupt

---

[3] See the discussion in A. Heidenheimer, *Political Corruption: Readings in Comparative Analyses* (New Brunswick: Transaction Books 1970), 3–64.
[4] S. Cavill and M. Sohail, *Accountability Arrangements to Combat Corruption* (Leicestershire, UK: WEDC Publications, 2007), 1.
[5] See for instance the report of Constantin Simis, a leading Soviet expert on criminal law, in Rudy Maxa, "USSR Corruption: An Insider's View," *Washington Post*, October 24, 1982, https://www.washingtonpost.com/archive/lifestyle/magazine/1982/10/24/ussr-corruption-an-insiders-view/a9aa8a7a-2442-4e88-8004-4cd1567c8362/.
[6] Günther G. Schulze and Nikita Zakharov, "Corruption in Russia—Historic Legacy and Systemic Nature," CES Info Working Paper 6864, January 2018 (Munich: Society for the Promotion of Economic Research, 2018).

country of Eastern Europe, right after Russia. Recently a Ukrainian friend of mine living in Germany received a call from his mother at home; she was brought to a hospital but did not receive any treatment. Well, he took the next plane to Kiev, went to that hospital and was bluntly informed that if the family did not come up with a certain amount of money, no one would be able to help his mother any longer. "People die here in the hospital because of false treatments," the doctor explained. "You'd better pay." My friend paid. What else would you do? And things like that happen by the hour everywhere throughout the country. Ukraine is completely overtaken by systemic corruption.

Obviously, many cannot pay this extra money. Some are too poor. Others are refugees who lost all their possessions in the Russian-Ukrainian war. There is nothing they have to satisfy the corrupt system. They are often left with their naked bodies only, and feel forced to sell themselves to bribe corrupt authorities in order to assure even a basic existence for their children. The injustice around them creates hatred, anger and crime. As a result, conflicts, violence, even killings are on the rise. And Ukraine is by no means the most corrupted system. By far the majority of the countries in the world face corruption.[7]

In the midst of all of this, the Church of Christ is seeking to proclaim the gospel of the kingdom, to live a holy life and avoid compromise and corrupt ways of living and business. Yet how does one do this in a country overtaken by systemic corruption? What are practical ways to confront the system and yet manage to stay alive? And how effective can a church fighting corruption be?

4. The Mission of the Church in Zones of Conflict

The Church of Christ is sent to the world as God's agent of transformation, entrusted with the word of reconciliation and peace. To the church in Corinth, a troubled church with many inward and outward challenges, the apostle Paul wrote:

> So from now on we regard no one from a worldly point of view. Though we once regarded Christ in this way, we do so no longer. Therefore, if anyone is in Christ, the new creation has come: The old has gone, the new is here! All this is from God, who reconciled us to himself through Christ and gave us the ministry of reconciliation: that God was reconciling the world to

---

[7] See the Corruption Index of Transparency International: https://www.transparency.de/cpi/?L=0 (accessed March 24, 2021).

himself in Christ, not counting people's sins against them. And he has committed to us the message of reconciliation. We are therefore Christ's ambassadors, as though God were making his appeal through us. We implore you on Christ's behalf: Be reconciled to God. God made him who had no sin to be sin for us, so that in him we might become the righteousness of God. (2 Cor 5:16-21).

The apostle defines the state of the Church in the world by (a) clarifying who we Christians are and what informs our behavior, (b) pointing to the basic ground for our identity, (c) naming the missionary task of the Church, and (d) describing the culture by which the Church exists in the world.

Identity

Followers of Jesus are a new social reality in the world. Paul states clearly that being in Christ suggests that a new creation is set in motion and this new identity is no longer informed by the world, but rather by Christ.[8] The world shapes a culture of self-centered pleasure, of egoistic thoughts, thus ignoring zones of conflict (Eph 2:1-3; Jas 4:1-4). Christ, on the contrary, has the mind of a servant giving his whole life for the benefit of his neighbor (Phil 2:5-11). Those who are in Christ will have the same mind of Christ (Phil 2:5). Egoistic motives are gone—loving your neighbor as yourself is now the suggested program (Lev 19:18; Mark 12:29-31).

Foundation

The new identity is only possible because of God's salvific act of reconciling the world with himself through Christ Jesus, who bore the sins of the world to the place of utmost punishment—the cross. He died for us so that we may live!

It is Jesus who sets humans free from worldly dominance and a culture of self-satisfaction and corruption. Jesus does not leave any doubt about who sets people free when he claims, "So if the Son sets you free, you will be free indeed" (John 8:36). The end of slavery is marked by Jesus. Reconciliation with God precedes reconciliation with one another. The chains of a system of sin and corruption can only be broken by God in Jesus Christ.

---

[8] See more in John C. Majors: *True Identity: Finding Significance and Freedom Through Who You Are in Christ* (Grand Rapids: Bethany House, 2017).

Mission

The new identity in Christ is more than a state—it is a commission. The Church is called out of the world in order to accept the responsibility for the world (Matt 16:18). She is God's ecclesia, God's parliamentarian community set aside to deal with all the issues of a given community.[9] She does not exist for herself, but rather as *salt for the Earth* and as *light for the world* (Matt 5:13–15). Reconciled with God, Christians become ambassadors for reconciliation and are sent to the world to make all nations of the world disciples of Christ (Matt 28:19). And their mission follows the mission of their master. "As the Father has sent me, I am sending you," says Jesus to his disciples (John 20:21). And this includes:

(a) *martyria* = witness as living a culture of peace in the midst of conflict. Jesus, God in person, became human and then people saw his life and glory (John 1:1–14);

(b) *diaconia* = service and comfort to the troubled and restless. Jesus claims that he did not come to be served, but to serve those in need (Mark 10:45);

(c) *dialog* as engagement in conversation for peace. Jesus commanded his disciples always to first look for a person of peace who makes their house a base of mission in the community (Matt 10:5–15);

(d) *prophecy* as naming of critical issues. Jesus came to dispose of and destroy the forces of darkness (Mark 1:24);

(e) *evangelism* as healing of the wounded. Jesus came to preach the gospel of the kingdom (Matt 4:23).[10]

Culture

And last but not least, the Church in the world is God's mirror of what righteousness and a good and godly life is all about. She is, in the words of Lesslie Newbigin, "a sign, instrument and a foretaste of the reign of God."[11] She testifies to God's current presence in the world, displays her changed life in front of the world, points to the eschaton and works to win the world for God's reign. Newbigin states:

---

[9] Johannes Reimer, *Missio Politica: The Mission of the Church and Politics*. (Carlisle: Langham 2017), 42–63.

[10] See details in Johannes Reimer, "The Mission of the Church in a World of War," *Anabaptist Witness* 6, no. 1 (April 2019), 56–62.

[11] Lesslie Newbigin, *The Open Secret: An Introduction to the Theology of Mission* (Grand Rapids: Eerdmans, 1995), 110, 150.

The community that confesses that Jesus is Lord has been, from the beginning, a movement launched into the public life of mankind. The Greco-Roman world in which the New Testament was written was full of societies offering to those who wished to join a way of personal salvation through religious teaching and practice. There were several commonly used Greek words for such societies. At no time did the church use any of these names for itself. It was not, and could not be, a society offering personal salvation for those who cared to avail themselves of its teaching and practice. It was from the beginning a movement claiming the allegiance of all peoples, and it used for itself with almost total consistency the name "ecclesia"—the assembly of all citizens called to deal with the public affairs of the city. The distinctive thing about this assembly was that it was called by a more august authority than the town clerk: it was the "ecclesia theou," the assembly called by God, and therefore requiring the attendance of all. The church could have escaped persecution by the Roman Empire if it had been content to be treated as a *cultus privatus*—one of the many forms of personal religion. But it was not. Its affirmation that "Jesus is Lord" implied a public, universal claim that was bound eventually to clash with the *cultus publicus* of the empire. The Christian mission is thus to act out in the whole life of the whole world the confession that Jesus is Lord of all.[12]

The Church of Christ is God's alternative to the sinful and corrupt nature of the world. And she is given the task of living out the alternative in the midst of the worldly zones of conflict, publicly resisting "to conform to the pattern of the world" (Rom 12:2).

5. Conclusion: Mission as Reconciliation Confronts Corruption

Christians live in a world of conflict and corruption. It is their divine task to bring reconciliation with God and the world to the attention of all and announce the end of corruption. Her mission is a political mission as well.[13] And it must, therefore, address the issue of corruption since corruption, as seen above, is the source for unrest and injustice in the world.

How can this be done practically? Following the markers set above, we may establish a praxis theory which proposes the following steps:

(1) The Church must live by her divine identity and consequently withdraw from any corrupted pattern of the world in order to be a trustworthy witness of God's just and divine reign.

---

[12] Ibid, 16–17.
[13] See more in Reimer, *Missio Politica*.

Kingdoms are recognized by their cultures, "their way of life,"[14] their "design for living"[15] across the material (what people have), social (what people do), intellectual (what people think) and religious (what people believe) levels of life. As a rule, the system of belief informs the way people think, and a worldview informs behavior and results in material status.[16] All of those levels can be affected by sin and corruption. Corrupted beliefs shape corrupted thinking and result in corruptive behavior, leaving behind victims of corruption. A systemic corruption unfolds.

The Church of Christ refuses to follow the cultural pattern of corruption. Moreover, not being involved in corruption the church and her members—even in countries ruled by systemic corruption—sends the most powerful signal to a society in conflict zones. I vividly remember young Kazakh believers and businessmen who decided to withdraw from any corruptive behavior as soon as they became followers of Jesus. Some of them suffered the loss of their business. At the same time thousands of Muslims in Kazakhstan admired them and became interested in Jesus. Soon an unprecedented movement began.

(2) Church members will serve those who are victims of corruption by sharing their lives and their possessions with them.

It is the diaconic nature of God's people which opens people's hearts and eyes for God's alternative lifestyle. Helping people in need is not an option—it is the Great Commandment of Jesus (Matt 20:28). And nobody set a better example than our Lord himself (Mark 10:45). While the church refuses to participate in corruption, her members will engage in assisting the poor and needy, sharing with them materially and socially out of unconditional love and far beyond the classic societal conditions shaped by the corruptive spirit of the world. And as soon as people see the good deeds of God's people, they may start to praise our Father in heaven (Matt 5:16).

(3) The Church will enroll in a creative dialog for transformation and change, especially in countries with systemic corruption.

Very often people cannot see any change around them, simply because every step of life requires bribery. In the church the cycle is interrupted, a community of caring people is established, and a model for a society

---

[14] Wendy Chriswold, *Cultures and Societies in a Changing World* (Thousand Oaks: Pine Forge, 2012), 8.

[15] Luis J. Lutzbetak, *The Church and Cultures: New Perspectives in Missiological Anthropology* (Maryknoll, NY: Orbis, 1989), 59–60.

[16] See the four-level model of culture in Gary Ferraro and Susan Andreatta, *Cultural Anthropology: An Applied Perspective* (Belmont: Wadsworth, 2009), 18.

beyond corruption is set. Entering the dialog and discussing practical options for the community will encourage interest and trigger change. Christian mission properly understood will always opt for inclusive approaches. It is less interested in working *for* the people, but rather *with* the people.[17] And working hand in hand for transformation of a given society and observing the koinonitic[18] spirit among Christians will soon trigger curiosity in the good life as offered by God.

(4) The Church will raise her prophetic voice and confront society with its bad ways of life and corruptive systems.

The Church is God's prophetic voice in the world.[19] She is called to lay open the evil structures of a corrupt world. This might mean that systems turn against the Church and persecution follows. But didn't exactly this happen to Jesus, our master? And he said, "A servant is not greater than his master. If they persecuted me, they will persecute you also. If they obeyed my teaching, they will obey yours also" (John 15:20). Persecution can never stop the Church from being prophetic. Wherever the Church silences her prophetic voice, society goes astray.[20]

(5) The Church will offer society a way to confess sin and to experience the healing of the land, as God promised it to his own people (2 Chron 7:14).

And finally, knowing the fact that no lasting transformation of community is possible without a principal reconciliation between God and humans, the Church will proclaim the gospel, inviting people to enter a relationship with God. Evangelism follows peaceful witness, meaningful service of love, joint acts of community change and bold uncovering of evil structures. It is a natural ending of a missional process of change and naturally the last act towards ending corruption. Evangelism brings reconciliation and peace and opens doors for good living in which no sin and corruption develops.

---

[17] See my discussion on inclusive mission in, Johannes Reimer: "Inklusive Mission—Widerspruch oder Notwendigkeit," *Theologisches Gespräch* 3 (2016), 11–125.
[18] From koinonia, the New Testament term for a mutual caring fellowship. See the definition in Strong's *Old and New Testament Greek Lexical Dictionary*, #2842, κοινωνία.
[19] See for details Reimer, *Missio Politica*, 57–59.
[20] See, for instance, insight from South Africa in M. S. Kgatle, "The Prophetic Voice of the South African Council of Churches: A Weak Voice in Post-1994 South Africa," *HTS Teologiese Studies/Theological Studies* 74, no. 1 (2018), https://doi.org/10.4102/hts.v74i1.5153.

About the Author

Dr. Johannes Reimer is Professor of Missions Studies and Intercultural Theology at the Ewersbach University of Applied Arts in Germany and the University of South Africa. Reimer studied theology in Germany, Belgium, the USA and South Africa. He founded and co-founded numerous churches and agencies, including Logos International in Germany, plus Bible colleges and universities such as the St. Petersburg Christian University in Russia (SPCU) and the Lithuanian Christian University (LCU) in Lithuania.

Reimer is married to Cornelia, is father of three children and has two grandchildren. The couple lives near Bonn, Germany.

Since September 2016, Johannes Reimer has led the Peace and Reconciliation Network of the World Evangelical Alliance. He is personally involved in several conflict resolution programmes, and has written extensively on integral mission and peace. His books have been published in 15 languages.

Innovation in Seminary Theological Education: An Overview of Contributing Forces

Scott Cunningham

1. Introduction

Let me begin this exploration into this subject with a personal observation.

I find all too common in the West a perception of the typical seminary in the Majority World[1] as it commonly existed decades ago. It is a perception of a traditional school of higher education characterized by "four walls and four years." That is, it is imagined that the typical seminary offers a predictable curriculum over an inflexible four-year period (or two or three years). This curriculum is taught to residential students who live on a physical campus on which exist typical "four-wall" classrooms where the teaching takes place. This is the "traditional residential" model. This idea of the seminary, based on this straw-man characterization, is dismissed from being an important contributor to the health of the global Church and attacked as being disconnected from the Church, irrelevant, and out of touch.

There are instances where this model does persist. And in many of these cases, the criticism of being irrelevant to the leadership needs of the churches they are meant to serve is justified. Such schools focus on maintaining the status quo. Worse, they think of growth and development in terms of imitation rather than innovation. Leaders of such schools may look to important Western seminaries as models to which to aspire (often not realizing that there is more to the Western seminary than "four walls and four years"). Or they compare themselves to the well-known flagship seminaries within their own region and imagine that their goal should be to duplicate what already exists. Sometimes, school leaders are bound to a traditional approach to theological education, perhaps because this is the

---

[1] The focus of this paper is on institutions of higher learning (with the main academic programs at the post-secondary level) located in the Majority World, which includes, for the purposes of this paper, Latin America, Africa, the Middle East, Eastern Europe, and Asia.

only experience or model they know, teaching the same curriculum they were taught. "After all, the Bible doesn't change."

Thankfully, however, such schools constitute a minority of seminaries. More than a decade ago, Overseas Council (OC) noticed a number of schools that appeared to be engaging in theological education in unusual, innovative, and at times provocative ways. To understand these innovative approaches more deeply, OC commissioned research that took place in 2011–2013.[2] Although the research did not focus on the prevalence of innovation in theological education, it provided a foundation for understanding the phenomenon of "unconventional" theological education through an appreciative inquiry into nine seminaries.

OC has continued to observe the growing prevalence of innovation, particularly in aspects of curriculum, and it undertook further research in 2019, this time with survey responses from over 100 seminaries in the Majority World.[3] Survey results confirmed that over 75% of seminaries were providing some sort of non-formal ministry training. Indeed, over 40% of total students being trained by these seminaries were enrolled in non-formal programs. The picture of the prevalence and wide variety of ministry training being offered in these key seminaries undermines the traditional, "four walls, four years" image still held by some. Thankfully, innovation is happening and appears to be expanding.

While the research just mentioned explores the prevalence and diversity of the innovation, the purpose of this essay is to seek a deeper understanding of the forces that appear to motivate these new approaches to theological education.

---

[2] The results of this research are contained in Meri MacLeod, "Unconventional Educational Practices in Majority World Theological Education" (Overseas Council, unpublished paper, 2013). The report may be accessed by contacting the author of this essay at scott@overseas.org.

[3] A summary of the results of this research can be found elsewhere in this volume, in the essay by Paul Allan Clark, "The Churches Need Healthy, Well-formed Leaders—How Shall We Now Train?" Focusing on "non-formal" does not mean to imply that all innovation within the curriculum takes place in non-formal programs, or that all non-formal programs are necessarily innovative. However, because of the inherent nature of formal programs, with characteristics of equivalences, transferability, and academic laddering, the breadth of innovation would seem to be somewhat more constrained.

2. What is "Innovation" in Theological Education?

In exploring the topic of the forces that motivate innovation, we do not choose to overly limit the educational or institutional practices we consider to be "innovative." That is, we are not seeking examples of an approach which is unique or has never existed, either in a different time or different place. Rather, since our focus is on the motivation and not the phenomenon itself, we are considering innovation from a more expansive and inclusive perspective. For the purposes of this essay, we will share the definition employed by OC's initial research on unconventional methods, as "an idea, practice, or object that is perceived as new by an individual or another unit of adoption," such as close peers or one's family, community or organization.[4] In using this definition, we may reference educational and institutional practices which are not unique, perhaps not even uncommon, but which are, nonetheless, new endeavors for the particular school employing them. To repeat, our primary interest is not so much what the practice is, as much as the motivational forces that lie behind it.

Innovation can take place in different aspects of the seminary. However, one of the most fruitful areas of innovation (that is, in terms of the variety of innovation and the perceived missional impact) is in the area of curriculum. By this, we mean curriculum writ large, including all aspects of the formational programs of the seminary which are intentionally employed by the seminary to accomplish its mission.

Curricula can be notoriously difficult to change, for all sorts of reasons, from faculty turf battles to donor perception to alumni and board conservatism. Calvin Coolidge, former U.S. president, supposedly once quipped, "Changing a college curriculum is like moving a graveyard—you never know how many friends the dead have until you try to move them!" In spite of the challenges, there are numerous possibilities for curricular innovation.

Traditionally, curriculum was held together by a coherent center, epitomized by the physical campus. It was in this location that students, faculty, and resources (such as the library) converged, and thus where the teaching and learning took place over a prescribed period of time. Hence, the traditional "four years, four walls." However, due to various factors, technology being primary, higher education is experiencing a remarkable "deconstruction" of this model,[5] with far-ranging impact on the shape of

---

[4] Everett M. Rogers, *Diffusion of Innovations*, 4th edn. (New York: Free Press, 1995), p. xvii, cited by Macleod, "Unconventional," p. 12.
[5] Other terms for this phenomenon can be used including "decentralization," "disaggregation," "unbundling," and "distributed."

the curriculum. Because of the possibility of remote teaching and learning, students and faculty no longer need to be at the same place at the same time. Books no longer need to be in one location. Indeed, they do not even need any physical presence at all, if they are available digitally. And the delivery of the typical prescribed courses over a prescribed time period is a model that is also breaking down. Once the whole is broken down into its constituent parts that no longer need to hang together, the process of reconstruction of the curriculum can result in a wide variety of expressions, as it moves away from a one-size-fits-all model dependent on a coherent center to a collection of distributed bits which can be reconstituted depending on the available resources, needs and local contexts.

Nearly forty years ago, Evangelical theological educators took notice of the possibilities for curriculum innovation and embraced this as a value in the "ICETE Manifesto on the Renewal of Evangelical Theological Education."[6] The third heading of the "Manifesto," on "Strategic Flexibility," addresses three areas of the curriculum: the need to serve the formation of more than only one type of leader (pastors); the need to take into account different academic levels; and the need to embrace a variety of educational modes, not only a traditional approach.

Another way of exploring possibilities for innovation in the curriculum is through the familiar who, what, when, where, why, and how questions:[7]

- Who are our students? Who could be our students? Who should be our students? Who needs training but is not now able to access it? Who does the teaching and mentoring of our students? Who could they be?
- What are the subjects in our curriculum? What are the affective, behavioral and cognitive objectives of our courses and programs? What is the profile of our graduate? What will the context of ministry look like for our projected graduates in five or ten years?
- Where does the teaching and practice learning take place? Is there a physical location, or a virtual meeting space? What does this place look like, and how does that facilitate the teaching and learning? Where is the expected ministry location, and what does it look like?

---

[6] International Council for Evangelical Theological Education, "ICETE Manifesto on the Renewal of Evangelical Theological Education" (1983, rev. 2002), https://icete.info/resources/manifesto/.

[7] This approach is followed by Brian E. Woolnough, "Rethinking Seminary Education: Bridging the Field and Academia," Lausanne Global Analysis 8.5 (2019), https://www.lausanne.org/content/lga/2019-09/rethinking-seminary-education.

- When does the teaching and learning take place? Is it synchronous or asynchronous? Does it take place only during prescribed classes or at other times also? What is the cadence of the teaching and learning? Do teaching and learning take place after the prescribed period of the formation program?
- Why do we exist as an institution? To what end are we providing these teaching and learning opportunities and programs? In what ways do we intend for our graduates to serve the churches who send them?
- How do our students learn and become formed as ministers and how, then, do our teachers teach with this in mind? What are we doing intentionally to form our students? What are we doing unintentionally? What are we intentionally not doing?

Though not commonly included in this list of questions, there is another which can be fruitfully asked in considering innovation: with whom? Who are our partners in our formational endeavors? How do we partner with churches? How are we partnering with other seminaries or academic institutions? Are there other organizations that we can fruitfully partner with? With whom are we intentionally connecting students to be part of their life-long formation process?[8]

Responding to these questions from a fresh perspective can open a multitude of avenues for curriculum innovation. As we have seen, many schools are already asking and answering these questions in fresh ways. But what is their motivation? What prompts them to ask these questions in the first place and answer them in unconventional ways? We turn to three important forces leading to innovation.

3. The Challenge of Accessibility

Research in the global Church has concluded that approximately nine out of ten churches are led by individuals who do not have formal theological

---

[8] This is the question asked by Julia Freeland Fisher: "This new wave has less to do with just transforming how students learn, and instead has the potential to revolutionize how they connect—to experts, mentors, and peers." See "The Next Decade of Disruption in Education? Unlocking Networks" (Christensen Institute, 2020), https://www.christenseninstitute.org/blog/the-next-decade-of-disruption-in-education-unlocking-networks/.

education.⁹ While research has not investigated the proportion of church leaders globally who have no form of ministry training whatsoever, we may use the confirmed data point of the "nine out of ten" as an indicator of a significant missiological challenge—the deficiency of trained church leaders in the Majority World. We refer to this challenge, which is probably the greatest missiology task for today's Church, as the Church's Global Leadership Challenge.

Behind the deficit is actually a positive observation—the remarkable growth of the Church in the Global South, which is one of the underlying disruptive forces for innovation in theological education. The high-level statistics are well known. In Africa, for instance, Christianity grew from 9% of the population to nearly 50% in the last century.¹⁰ In just the last fifteen years, Christianity in Africa has increased by 50%, with an average of 33,000 individuals becoming Christians or being born into Christian homes each day.¹¹ The building of equipped leaders is simply not keeping pace with this growth of the Church. Typically, leaders do emerge in these newly planted churches. To be clear, the result is not so much a deficiency of leaders as a gap in the training of leaders. The long-term outcome, if unaddressed, is unhealthy, doctrinally vulnerable, stagnant, and sometimes fading congregations.

Our observations suggest that most often emerging leaders do not lack a desire for equipping for ministry; rather, they lack the opportunities for accessing ministry training programs in their current form. This is due to numerous barriers which stand in the way:

- Educational. Formal programs, by definition, require a certain educational achievement in order to progress to the next level on the academic ladder. One benefit of non-formal programs is increased flexibility in educational prerequisites for participation.
- Geographic. Schools that use a physical campus where the teaching and learning take place limit access to students who can be physically present. One of the advantages of online learning is the elimination of this barrier. Use of extension programs also helps to

---

[9] Todd Johnson, "Majority World Pastors" (email to Eddy Thomas), June 15, 2018. Dr. Johnson refers to research conducted by the Center for the Study of Global Christianity, of which he is the director.

[10] Gina A. Zurlo, "African Christianity," Gordon-Conwell Theological Seminary, https://www.gordonconwell.edu/blog/african-christianity-101/.

[11] Krish Kandiah, "The Church Is Growing, and Here Are the Figures That Prove It," *Christianity Today* (2015), https://www.christiantoday.com/article/a-growing-church-why-we-should-focus-on-the-bigger-picture/49362.htm.

mitigate against this barrier. One seminary in Sri Lanka maintains seven extension centers throughout the island, which serve 43% of their total students.
- Financial. Students often lack sufficient resources to enroll. This is primarily due to the relatively high costs of providing higher education, particularly in traditional approaches. Schools attempt to lower the cost for students through lowering the cost of the educational program itself or raising funds from other sources besides student tuition. Since financial sustainability is such a significant challenge, we will look at this issue more closely later.
- Linguistic. Formal programs tend to use the "national language of higher education." This can be a barrier to students whose educational experience has taken place in other local languages. This obstacle can be overcome by designing alternative programs aimed at a group of students who are fluent in a localized language.
- Family and ministry involvement. Often students cannot relocate themselves or their families due to commitments in their current location. Among others, these commitments might be the student's ministry commitment, their own employment or that of a spouse, or the education of their children. Educational models that do not require physical presence on a campus overcome this barrier. It is sometimes mitigated by programs offering courses which are intensive or modular in nature, requiring only short amounts of time away from home.
- Technological. Although the offer of online programs can overcome some barriers, it can also introduce other technology-related obstacles, such as the potential student's lack of Internet connectivity, the cost of technological devices or connectivity, or the lack of technological fluency.
- Gender-related. Biases against training women for ministry can lead to subtle obstacles related to their family, church, and community. Schools can offer targeted support and assistance to women to assist them in their desire for ministry training.[12]

---

[12] Since 2013, OC has distributed nearly $500,000 for scholarship assistance to seminaries specifically for the training of women in theological education. OC's research has determined that schools which offer targeted scholarship assistance to women, on average, have a higher proportion of female students than those schools which do not offer scholarships only for women.

If seminaries are to assist students to overcome these barriers, they must see those who need training but who face such obstacles as their potential students. This relates to a question we posed earlier: Who could and should be our student? Often this requires a change in way the seminary views its own mission. When seminary leaders see their mission as not "to offer a master's degree in theology" but "to serve the church by providing appropriate ministry training for those who need it," this missional shift serves as motivation for seeking innovative ways to overcome such barriers. The challenge of providing access to students who need training but are currently outside the reach of current programs has previously been identified in OC's research as a critical motivating force for innovation in the seminary's educational programs:

> Stakeholders across all schools expressed a passionate vision for serving the church by providing accessible theological education for the working adult student. Board members, administrators, and faculty alike expressed concern for unmet educational needs essential for a healthy church. It seemed central to their sense of call to provide accessible and relevant theological education. This burden for the church, coupled with an awareness of the changing context, seemed an important catalyst that pushed them toward new and unproven approaches.[13]

This more expansive sense of mission, combined with the identification of potential students who need ministry training for the health of the Church and the obstacles they face in accessing that training with current models, is a primary motivating factor in innovation in theological education.

4. The Challenge of Contextualization and Relevance

Ultimately, the mission of the seminary is to serve the mission of the Church.[14] The seminary doesn't exist for itself; it exists for and must be intentionally shaped to serve the Church. Hence, the forms and outcomes of theological education must be aligned with the context of the churches which the seminary serves.

To the extent that this does not happen, the seminary is rightly judged as disconnected, irrelevant, or out of touch with the realities of the church

---

[13] Macleod, "Unconventional," p. 10.
[14] The Lausanne Movement's *Cape Town Commitment* (2011) puts it this way: "The mission of the Church on earth is to serve the mission of God, and the mission of theological education is to strengthen and accompany the mission of the Church" (section IIF.4).

which it exists to serve. At times, seminaries appear to have been designed to serve a church of a different place or a different time. This is somewhat understandable. Missionaries who established centers for ministry training tended to replicate or at least base new institutions on patterns which were most familiar to them in their home countries. "National" faculty trained in countries other than the ones they serve in might find the replication of the way they were taught to be the most straightforward approach in their own teaching.

Similarly, curricula designed decades ago may have been shaped with the context of that time in mind. However, given the pace and breadth of cultural change, if the curriculum has changed little since then, it has probably lost much of its relevance to current cultural and church realities. Given the inertia of the curriculum, it is understandable if programs and curricula fail to keep pace with the changes in the context of the churches which they intend to serve.

However, the very nature of the gospel and the Church demands that our ministry training must be responsive to the realities of our contexts.[15] We can say that the disruptive force underlying the challenge of contextualization is the very nature of the gospel and Church. If the seminary exists to serve the mission of the Church, then it must frequently check to see that its formational programs are appropriate to the contextual realities of the Church and its mission of speaking and living the gospel in the world.

As an example of the Church's innovation compelled by its understanding of the gospel, it's appropriate here to reference an enormously significant innovation and gift to humanity on the part of the early Church—the hospital.[16] Though early civilizations may have had the material resources, knowledge of medicine, and doctors, they never established hospitals. It was the very nature of the gospel and the mission of the Church which was the foundation for this invention by the Christians. The Christian's understanding of human dignity, the Second Great Commandment, the pattern

---

[15] See Evan Hunter, "On the Shoulders of Giants: Traditioned Innovation and Leading Change," *InSights Journal for Global Theological Education*, 3.1 (2017). Hunter builds on the work of Greg Jones on "traditioned innovation." Hunter notes, "However, as contexts, theological questions, societal needs, and student objectives have changed, schools must continue to adapt and change their curricula as well" (p. 12).

[16] I'm grateful to Dr. Gregory Jones for pointing me to this instructive parallel in the history of the Church. For a brief history, see Mike Aquilina, "How the Church Invented Health Care," *Angelus* (July 15, 2019), https://angelusnews.com/voices/how-the-church-invented-health-care/.

of Jesus as healer, and the command to show hospitality all formed the theological foundation. Because of this, the Church felt compelled to respond to the context of its world, particularly widespread illness. And so, in the fourth century, Christians established the first hospitals, the most well-known being that of Basil of Caesarea. Because Christians were proximate to the need of the hurting world and due to their understanding of the gospel and the mission of the Church, Christians "had to" invent the hospital to meet this need. In a parallel manner, seminaries, seeing the needs for leadership development in their context and recognizing the inadequacy of current models, respond to those needs innovatively.

Deeply embedded in this challenge of contextualization and relevance is the need for the seminary to be willing and able to listen carefully to the Church in its context. If the seminary is to serve the Church well, it must learn to listen well. Evan Hunter, in his article summarizing the work of Govindarajan and Trimble on "reverse innovation," relates the story of how Mahindra became the dominant tractor manufacturer in India (over the competing John Deere products from the US). Mahindra did so by carefully identifying the needs of their clients and then building a product that met those particular needs.

In the same way that Mahindra relied on teams to explore the needs of their market, theological educators need to listen closely to the differing and changing needs of the Church in diverse contexts and to remain open to fresh approaches. Discoveries may lead to new designs that depart from previous iterations but also prove more effective in equipping leaders for ministry in new contexts.[17]

5. The Challenge of Sustainability

A third force for innovation in the seminary stems from the challenge of financial sustainability. We do not mean by this that the goal of every seminary should be "self-sustainability," as though a seminary should operate only on revenue from student-derived tuition. Nor do we suggest that financial donations should be limited to the particular churches that directly benefit from the services of the seminary. Rather, for our purposes, financial sustainability is a state of equilibrium between the mission of the school, its educational program, and its financial resources. The goal is to achieve reliable sources of revenue which will allow fulfillment of the school's mission through its educational programs.

---

[17] Evan Hunter, "Reverse Innovation: In Search of Better Solutions Than Best Practices," *InSights Journal for Global Theological Education*, 1.2 (2016), p. 12.

Because the traditional seminary is patterned on the university,[18] they share similar financial models and, thus, many of the same financial challenges. This financial model includes high costs for buildings and other infrastructure, high fixed costs for faculty and other staff, and revenue from student tuition, donations, and other income. Most schools, even in the best of circumstances, will find that achieving financial sustainability is a challenge. For this reason, we would suggest that the underlying disruptive force behind this source of innovation is the inherently unsustainable financial model of the university. Recognizing these challenges, seminaries have sought innovative ways to reduce expenses, increase revenue, and modify educational programs (or even the school's mission) to achieve financial sustainability.[19]

Numerous factors have contributed to a situation where financial sustainability is becoming even more difficult:

- At a time when missionaries were a higher proportion of the staff, the school was not responsible for significant staff compensation. Gradually, missionaries were replaced with staff indigenous to the region, along with responsibilities for compensation and other expenses (such as government-mandated payments).
- Missionaries were not only "free labor" (that is, free to the seminary), but they also brought donor interest and other financial assistance from the churches that supported the missionary. The departure of the missionary thus had a double effect—higher salaries to be paid and a decrease in donations from the missionary's network.
- Accreditation has become important for many seminaries. To achieve this goal, expenditures increased for additional (and more credentialed and thus more expensive) faculty and staff, library holdings, and other facilities.

---

[18] We hesitate to call the university a "Western" model. Though the centuries-old history of the university began in Europe, universities are now found in every country.

[19] There is now a wealth of material on the topic of financial sustainability for the seminary. Much of this is a result of the early partnership of Overseas Council and ScholarLeaders International (SLI) in the Vital Sustainability Initiative. This project has continued to grow under the leadership of SLI. Numerous articles on the topic can be found in the *InSights Journal for Global Theological Education* here: https://insightsjournal.org/topic/finances/. The single most helpful book on the topic is Emmanuel O. Bellon, *Leading Financial Sustainability in Theological Institutions: The African Perspective* (Eugene, OR: Pickwick, 2017).

- In some places, government regulations have had a major impact. This includes not only mandated government taxes and payments, and compliance with other government regulations and labor laws, but also staff and facilities requirements for government recognition or accreditation.
- Competition has increased for some seminaries. In some cases, this includes competition for students, as well as for donors. With the increased use of online education, the seminary's competition is not just the school in the same town, but schools on the other side of the world. Free theological education courses are being offered online, and even by a few residential programs of well-supported, missionary-run seminaries. This limits the ability of other seminaries to charge tuition.
- Adding higher-level academic programs also adds to costs (for additional library holdings and for faculty with higher credentials). The trend of increased numbers of seminaries in the Majority World offering programs at the doctoral level has been documented.[20]

These factors have stimulated creative paths toward financial sustainability. Generally, this means seeking either to lower costs or to raise revenue.

One approach is to reduce the number of core faculty and instead use part-time (less expensive) adjunct faculty. A consortium of Francophone schools exchanges some faculty members. A seminary in Ukraine relies heavily on visiting professors from the West who come for intensive summer programs—and bring additional donations with them. With the growth of online education, visiting professors can be sourced from nearly anywhere.

Some schools are exploring joining together in consortia. Such agreements could facilitate the sharing of courses and faculty. A consortium is being formed in Northeast India around a shared online platform allowing for the sharing of IT costs, but potentially also the sharing of faculty, students, and courses.

Some schools have sought to reduce the burden of electricity costs through the installation of solar panels—a large up-front capital expense which might be funded by donations.

---

[20] Evan Hunter, "A Tectonic Shift: The Rapid Rise of Ph.D. Programs at Evangelical Theological Schools in the Majority World," *InSights Journal for Global Theological Education*, 1.2 (2016), pp. 41–60.

In terms of increasing revenue, examples of creative fund-raising efforts abound, and schools have gradually increased in their sophistication in this area, many now with multi-staffed departments for fundraising.[21]

Several decades ago, schools began exploring "third-stream" revenue,[22] in which existing (or purchased) facilities and resources are used in a for-profit manner to benefit the school. A number of schools operate guest houses (sometimes repurposing dormitories) and conference halls. A seminary in Zambia once used their land for a banana farm. A seminary in Ethiopia uses their valuable location on an urban boulevard to rent space in its campus building to businesses.[23] Computer schools, Internet cafés, and English language schools leverage for profit capacity that the school already possesses. At times schools find that third-stream projects attract donors who see the potential of providing endowment-like funding to an institution, rather than indefinite operating funds. However, many schools have learned that they do not have the expertise to operate a business profitably and resort to using the profit to hire such expertise. Others have learned that their business also suffers from unpredictable economic downturns and business competition, which reduce their profit margins.

Some schools have sensed that there may be an opportunity to grow student numbers through online courses. It is thought that, once the upfront costs for online programs are paid, larger numbers of students will more than cover the initial outlay. However, schools are finding it difficult to charge for online courses, especially when so many are available at no cost whatsoever.

Just as with the challenges of accessibility and contextualization, the challenge of financial sustainability is ongoing and widespread. Because sustainability involves so many different factors—educational program, mission, and costs and revenues—and because it is such a powerful motivator, we expect that it will be a continued area of innovation, as schools seek to utilize the resources of the school effectively and efficiently, toward continuing their mission.

---

[21] It would be appropriate here to mention that the honoree of this *Festschrift*, Dr Manfred Kohl, consistently and persuasively argued for the establishment of fundraising departments in seminaries in the Majority World. Much of the success of such programs finds its roots in this aspect of Dr. Kohl's work.

[22] That is, a third source of revenue after student tuition and donations.

[23] Desta Heliso, "Third Stream Income: The Case of the Ethiopian Graduate School of Theology," *InSights Journal for Global Theological Education*, 1.1 (2015), pp. 38–43.

6. Innovation and the Pandemic

With the global spread of the Covid-19 pandemic, forces converged and were accentuated, which brought about widespread disruption to Majority World seminaries during 2020 and into the present. These disruptive forces were both educational and financial.[24]

With government restrictions on in-person gatherings and on travel, along with the government closure of schools, most OC-related seminaries, at least for a time, closed fully to in-person classes. For those schools that were primarily teaching in-person, this completely disrupted the usual mode of educational delivery. Schools scrambled to find new ways to provide accessibility for students, at first rapidly shifting to some form of emergency remote teaching and then gradually employing more robust forms of online theological education.

As the pandemic persists and most schools are now on the path toward making successful adjustments to their educational programs, the financial disruption is perhaps even more challenging, with all the factors of sustainability going from bad to worse. Entire economies were disrupted with the loss of jobs in the host countries, leading to the inability of students, families, churches, and donors to provide tuition or donations. In addition, there were unexpected costs: paying for protective equipment, assisting families who were infected or lacked money for living, as well as costs related to implementing remote teaching.

Thus, the impact of the pandemic has been a major disruption of the entire educational and financial models of the seminary. So, if the seminary were to survive and if it were to continue to fulfill its educational mission, it would need to adapt, change, and innovate in significant ways. In this respect, the pandemic "forced" innovation. Many schools, having in pre-pandemic days dipped their toes into the world of online theological education and even having expressed intentions to pursue this at a later date, were now thrown without warning into the proverbial deep end, to either sink or swim. Schools were forced to ask questions, challenge assumptions, and overcome constraints in these new, unfamiliar waters.

Many have described the pandemic as a pivotal or liminal moment. This suggests that many of the changes being "forced" upon schools because of the pandemic will persist. Some will persist because the effects of

---

[24] The impact of Covid-19 on seminaries, along with a hopeful response, is well described by Evan Hunter, "Responding to the COVID-19 Crisis: Moving from Desperation to Hope in Theological Education," *InSights Journal for Global Theological Education*, 6.1 (2020), pp. 21–30.

the pandemic may be longer-lasting than originally expected. Other innovations will persist because schools have observed positive outcomes which will also benefit them in "normal" times. For example, four schools in Nepal, India, and Bangladesh have formed a consortium to provide online learning to their students, allowing them to share costs, faculty training, and IT support. In the future, they could also share students, courses, and faculty. A seminary in Lebanon, primarily residential for its pre-pandemic programs, has shifted permanently to a hybrid approach, using intensive on-site residential modules combined with online learning. Fully one-third of OC-related seminaries have experienced a growth in the number of students after a year of the pandemic, mostly by providing access to theological education through online modes to students who could not access traditional programs. One seminary in Sri Lanka notes that their new offering of online courses has helped them fulfill a long-time objective of reaching students in other countries, with expatriate ethnic Sri Lankans now taking classes online. There are compelling reasons to think that many such changes will be long-lasting. Some innovations forced by emergency conditions have demonstrated that many of the changes previously considered off limits or imagined only in long-range planning are, in fact, quite implementable and potentially beneficial for the long term.

7. Conclusion

Some, upon surveying seminary theological education in the Majority World, express pessimism or are even dismissive of its positive contribution to the health of the global Church. The seminary, in their minds, is largely inaccessible to those who need ministry training, disconnected from the life of the Church, and built on an unsustainable financial model. This essay offers a different perspective. Although seminaries are not without legitimate criticism, we have argued, beginning with evidence of widespread innovation (particularly in the area of non-formal ministry training offered by the seminary), that in three respects, we see strong forces that are leading to further innovation. Behind these forces stand important realities for the Church:

- Behind the challenge of accessibility is the reality of remarkable Church growth and the need to equip additional leaders.
- Behind the challenge of contextualization and relevance is the very nature of the gospel and the Church, which compels us to respond

to the changing realities of a broken world so as to fulfill the Church's mission.
- Behind the challenge of sustainability is the inherent difficulty of the university's financial model, leading schools to explore creative ways to find equilibrium between the school's mission, finances, and educational programs.

These are enduring challenges and realities (which were only accentuated by the current Covid-19 pandemic). But by God's grace, motivated by these challenges, seminaries in the Majority World are discovering innovative ways to better serve the mission of the Church.

About the Author

Scott has served in global theological education for over 40 years. He first trained church leaders in New Testament in a Nigerian seminary. Following his Ph.D. work at Dallas Seminary, he accepted an invitation to serve seminaries throughout Africa with ACTEA, now called the Association for Christian Education in Africa. This role deepened his interest in understanding how seminaries might better serve the Church. For the past dozen years, his ministry in this direction has been through Overseas Council, now a ministry of United World Mission.

Scott now serves as OC's Executive Director.

Training of Pastors: A High Priority for Global Ministry Strategy[1]

Ramesh Richard

I. Preamble

After each meeting with our celebrant Dr. Manfred Kohl, I have often come away with the conviction that God raised a keen *strategist* for Christ's Great Commission for the latter part of the twentieth and early part of the twenty-first century. Search for "strategists" and in the positive sense, they are independent, organized, and decisive. Manfred Kohl fits that description. There are many strategic *thinkers*, but he is also a strategic *doer*. Rarely have I experienced a man more aware of needs, who identifies opportunities in them, generates ideas for potential solutions, mobilizes key individuals, and facilitates conversation and collaboration in action toward implementation.

Case in point? Re-Forma, an organization founded by Manfred Kohl to develop global ministry outcomes so non-formal training efforts can be credibly validated. His worldwide exposure to formal theological education, with relevant research on its (in)effectiveness, and the rise of many leadership initiatives drove the founding of this organization, still fledgling at this writing. Based on the needs voiced and opportunities presented at the 2016 Global Proclamation Congress for Trainers of Pastors in Bangkok, Thailand, Manfred asked to meet with the board of RREACH (the pastoral ministry training organization I lead) to affirm the uniqueness of what he was sensing in that momentous event dedicated to the pastor-training "industry." He then explored the possibility of a way to address the need for validation of those trained by the hundreds, perhaps thousands, of training initiatives with Trainers of Pastors International Coalition (TOPIC). TOPIC would have been an ideal platform to carry out his idea, though their focus was limited to *pastoral* leaders. Could a new and

---

[1] This article significantly updates and expands a version in the *Lausanne Global Analysis* in late 2015 (https://lausanne.org/content/lga/2015-09/training-of-pastors) which, at that time, anticipated the 2016 GProCongress for Trainers of Pastors. We now write from the perspective gained from the event with four years of documenting activity undertaken by a world of pastor-trainers.

neutral entity, committed to the validation of any and all leadership training, be established?

2. Introduction

Re-Forma's website (www.re-forma.global) opens with the realities which generated the need for convening trainers of pastors from every sector:

> Studies show that over 90% of all pastors do not have a formal theological education. According to statistics, that equates to well over 2 million Protestant pastors worldwide. In addition, every year thousands of new Protestant churches are established, very often without a trained pastor or preacher. The biggest crisis facing the evangelical, global church today is the fact that most pastors, missionaries, and Christian leaders are under-educated or not educated at all. Re-Forma has set as its goal to fundamentally remedy this situation.

While pastors, then, are still first and in the core of Re-Forma's ministry, all Christian workers are in their view. I am grateful for a personal friendship with Dr. Kohl. By cultural reticence, I still wonder if I should call him by his first name, or by the familial title of "Brother," or with the full-fledged title of Dr. Manfred Kohl. I am even more thankful for the strategic overlap of a ministry calling, yes, a burden to call the world of evangelicalism to establish the training of a large number of pastoral leaders as a high priority in global ministry strategy.

Our priority is built on a biblical conviction. The ascended Messiah sovereignly distributed pastors and teachers "for the equipping of the saints for works of service, to the building up the body of Christ" (Eph 4:11–12).

Theologically, then, pastors and teachers (along with the extensional roles of evangelists and the foundational roles of apostles and prophets; Eph 2:20) are critical for the health of Christ's Church. The health of a church is directly affected by the health of whoever functions in pastoral leadership.

Can the priority of training pastoral leaders also be strategically critical for global missions and ministries today? We know that congregations without healthy pastoral leaders are detrimental to God's purposes. If pastoral leaders are more healthy, their congregations become healthier too, with church health affecting societal health, as believers impact their spheres of influence for the ascended Messiah, the Lord Jesus Christ.

In this article, I consider the strategic priority of the training of pastors for intentional and collaborative global missions and ministry obedience.

I also propose practical considerations for both strategists and practitioners in pastoral training—whether individuals or churches, but especially for formal and institutional programs as well as non-formal organizational initiatives.

3. Local Examples

The National Fellowship of Born Again Pentecostals informally contacted the Kampala (Uganda) Evangelical School of Theology to help with basic training for their pastors—30,000 of them. Can an opportunity like this be effectively seized by a fledgling institution such as the local seminary, or indeed by more mature residential models in Africa and beyond? With the onset of the global pandemic (2020 and beyond), campus-based theological education came to a halt anyway, with the need to urgently fine-tune delivery strategy.

Or take São Gonçalo, a suburb of Rio de Janeiro, which once averaged a new church plant every weekday. Who would shepherd these congregations in Latin America beyond the initial investment of effort? After church planting, what follows?

I remember meeting about 200 Nepali pastors and wives for one day of refreshment and restoration after earthquakes devastated Nepal (April–May 2015). They had hardly slept or eaten well. However, they had labored well. Having comforted their congregations during the horrific loss of lives and property, they continued to rally believers to serve communities *outside* the faith, all while being publicly suspected of the ultimate, bad motive of "Christian conversion." Instead and regardless, they were concerned for the well-being, rebuilding, and eventual flourishing of their communities.

Like-minded readers could supply several such anecdotes where the health of the pastor is critical to the health of the church (and vice versa too), with the health of the church, positively or negatively, in turn affecting the health of the community.

4. Global Realities

Four, plus one,[2] global realities continue to shape thoughtful decisions and decisive action concerning this global ministry strategy:

---

[2] Post-GProCongress research adds one more reality to the previous version of this article for consideration in global ministry strategy.

4.1. The world

My population app shows that the world contains 7.8 billion individuals at this time of writing, in mid-2021. A comparison to highlight the immensity of this number: just over one billion minutes have passed since the time of the Lord Jesus, and not too much over two billion minutes from Moses until now. Large numbers of people mean large-scale opportunities with proportionate losses in tragedies and, worst of all, massive eternal lostness.

We need a "scalability" strategy of global scope and local impact to promote the Lord Jesus to large numbers of individuals worldwide.

4.2. The faith

Some 2.5 billion self-identified Christians currently comprise the faith. "Census" Christians, i.e., choosing "Christianity" as their religion over and against other options, do not all belong to the Lamb's Book of Life. The World Evangelical Association's Theological Commission estimates 50,000 new baptized believers daily.[3] How may we influence nominal Christians toward personal salvation and Christian discipleship? How could we nurture the embryonic faith of so many, especially in re-evangelizing a formerly Christianized region? Who might facilitate a "spreadability" strategy to reach nominal Christian family and friends anywhere?

4.3. The Church

The Global Alliance of Church Multiplication continues to raise a most serious concern about newly planted congregations as the primary challenge facing the church planting movement. First expressed in October 2013, when they envisioned the planting of 5 million churches by 2020, they surmise an astounding fail rate of up to 70% within the first year. How could we go about preserving the fruit of incredible church planting efforts? How can church health keep pace with church growth? How do we address "sustainability" issues to justify the enormous human and financial costs of these amazing labors and responses?

---

[3] "In his plenary at the Lausanne Consultation on Theological Education, June 2014, Thomas Schirrmacher (Secretary General of the World Evangelical Alliance since March 2021) presented the view of the WEA and its Theological Commission that about 50,000 people (that do not come from a Christian background and do not have any basic Bible knowledge) are baptized each day in evangelical churches worldwide." http://www.thomasschirrmacher.net/tag/theological-education/.

4.4. Pastoral leaders

Though primarily referring to those popularly labeled "pastor," I've learned to use "pastoral leader" for depth and breadth of understanding along with honor due to them. "Pastor" is restricted in many contexts. However, the word "leader" is simply too wide. In many if not most contexts, shepherding roles are performed by more than those ordained or titled as pastors. I recommend calling them "pastoral leaders."

More than 2.2 million pastoral leaders (and as many as 3.4 million by some estimates) presently minister whereas "only 5% are trained for pastoral ministry"[4] according to the Center for Study for Global Christianity.[5]

Thus at least 2 million pastoral leaders need immediate strengthening for their pastoral ministries. Furthermore, if a pastoral leader can initially provide pastoral care for a group of 50 believers, 1,000 *new* pastors are needed daily to serve the 50,000 new believers baptized every day. We are rather behind. We will never catch up at this pace and need a "speedability" strategy. How may we quicken the pace of pastoral training (a challenge to formal pastoral training models) while increasing the quality (a challenge to ad hoc, non-formal pastoral training initiatives) everywhere?

---

[4] "The CSGC [Center for Study of Global Christianity] estimates a total of 5 million pastors/priests in all Christian traditions worldwide (Catholics, Orthodox, Protestants, and Independents, including bi-vocational). Of these, we estimate that 5% (250,000) are likely to have a formal theological training (undergraduate Bible degrees or master's degrees]. This is based on incomplete responses in survey results from colleges and seminaries in our Global Survey on Theological Education. Roughly 70% of these pastors are in Independent congregations. Independent pastors, in particular, have a little theological training, even in the West" (https://www.gordonconwell.edu/center-for-globalchristianity/research/quickfacts/).

[5] From the author's personal correspondence and confirmation with researcher Todd Johnson, Director, Center of Study for Global Christianity, July 8, 2015; and again reinforced on April 16, 2021 by Todd Johnson in communication with Michael Ortiz, International Director of the International Council for Evangelical Theological Education (ICETE), about the 5 million figure: "We estimated that approximately 2.2 million of these would be Evangelical, Independent, Protestant, or Pentecostal (these categories overlap). We don't have a separate estimate for each of these. We also believe that only about 5% of these have had formal ministerial training (Bible college and/or seminary)."

5. Intentional and Collaborative Training

May I suggest that intentional and collaborative pastoral training of large numbers of pastoral leaders can effectively and efficiently address the opportunities and dangers embedded in the above four realities?

Precisely such a burden was informally brought up at Cape Town in 2010. All involved in pastoral training, whether through formal institutional or non-formal organizational channels, were invited by word of mouth to a lunch-hour meeting. Hundreds of leaders showed up to share the vision for pastoral training and support the calling. The doors had to be closed and a second lunch meeting scheduled. Again, dozens showed up for introductions and conversations.

A one-page *Cape Town Pastoral Trainers Declaration* was framed with special reference to the commitment of formal and non-formal pastoral trainers to intentionally work together in the spirit of the Lausanne Movement. Although not part of the *official* history of Lausanne II, its finale was graciously featured in the *Lausanne Global Analysis* of September 2015. Below is the full statement for the reader to process well since it sets the stage for the next strategic moment in the global training of pastors.

Pastoral Trainers Declaration
October 2010
Cape Town, South Africa

In the spirit of the Lausanne Movement, we pastoral trainers at Cape Town 2010, declare our renewed commitment to the training, forming and strengthening pastors for Christ's Church.

Strategic Assumptions in Pastoral Training

- The local church is God's primary instrument on the earth for implementing the Great Commission of our Lord Jesus Christ.
- The ascended Messiah has given pastors and teachers to shepherd His Church to growth and health.
- While set in the broad context of leadership development, pastoral training is uniquely related to local church ministry.
- The rapid growth of the Christian faith especially in Asia, Africa, and Latin America requires pastors who faithfully fulfill the demanding responsibilities of local church ministry.

- Massive numbers of pastoral leaders have been called, gifted and placed by the Holy Spirit in their congregations but lack skills, tools, and relationships for ministry.

Ministry Affirmations in Pastoral Training

- Local pastors provide a formidable labor force for obeying Christ's commission worldwide.
- The spiritual health of the local church depends on the health of the pastoral leader.
- Formal and non-formal training play strategic roles in specific ways to address pastoral and church health needs, especially where the Church is growing.
- The non-formal training of pastors needs the depth and quality of formally trained pastoral trainers.
- The formal training of pastors cannot keep up with the breadth and quantity of large numbers of untrained pastors.
- The long-term usefulness of pastors calls for both formal and non-formal delivery mechanisms to enrich their ministry effectiveness.

Declaration

Since the formal and non-formal sectors of pastoral training have knowingly and unknowingly allowed ourselves to be divided in heart and efforts, we declare together that we shall endeavor to build trust, involve each other, and leverage the strengths of each sector to prepare maturing shepherds for the proclamation of God's Word and the building up of Christ's Church in all the nations of the world.

6. Pastor-Trainers

The *Global Proclamation Congress for Pastoral Trainers*, held in June 2016 in Bangkok, Thailand, further extended the momentum for the training of large numbers of pastoral leaders.

This specific and task-focused event brought more than 2,500 trainers of pastors from more than 100 countries representing both the formal and non-formal pastor-training sectors. The objectives of the GProCongress were to: build community, explore opportunity, discover resources, and exchange encouragement in the ministry of training pastors.

As part of a decade-long goal by RREACH to reduce the deficit of trained pastoral leaders by 5%, the GProCongress was prepared by and predicated on strategic international and national cohorts of younger trainers of pastors. The goal questions were as follows: Could there be 100,000 more pastors better trained over four years? Could 1,000 pastor training resources be found in the six major UN languages?

Driven by the conviction that "pastoral health affects church health; and church health affects societal health," the GProCongress created global awareness and national interest in the urgent need to prioritize the training of pastoral leaders. Every level of missions and ministries agrees that *local* pastoral leaders inform and influence decisions on fruitful Christian work anywhere and everywhere in the world.

At the final session of the eight-day event, delegates were challenged and committed to reduce the deficit by training *an average* of twenty-five pastoral leaders a year for the following four years. An event without follow-up would be more a memory to applaud than a cause to accomplish. Without solid documentation of post-event activity, there would be no confidence of objectives met.

An extensive and intensive follow-up program of encouraging and documenting activity by fellow pastor-trainers yielded major findings. To cover errors in duplication, replication, or exaggeration, RREACH's four-year process set out to count 500,000 pastoral leaders better trained for pastoral ministry, and then to an extremely conservative 80 percent error rate to meet the goal of 100,000 better-trained pastoral leaders. By July 1, 2020, definitive training reports, even after applying the error rate, recorded over 280,000 better trained pastoral leaders between 2016 and 2020. Also, 14,000 pastor-training resources in twenty-nine languages were posted on relevant websites for access, downloads, and learning.

With reports of pastor-training activity from every nation-state and territory (248) in the world, but prioritizing 147 nations from which reports flowed, the goal was surpassed, under budget and ahead of time, to the glory of God and the health of his shepherds and of Christ's Bride.

The amazing fruit of the labors of trainers of pastors all over the world was presented at a virtual global gathering for trainers of pastors in mid-2021. A substantial Global Integrated Report gave the current status of pastor training, especially where Christ's Church is growing. Immense numbers of pastors are being trained by various pastor-training organizations and institutions, churches, and individuals. This 2020 report also highlights the great need and opportunity in the training of pastoral leaders. Over 1,000 trainers of pastors celebrated their accomplishments, but more so to envision the next decade till 2030. Trainers of pastors can discern direction for ministry and geographical ordering of respective initiatives into their next season of fruitful work.

If intentional and collaborative, "stackability" as a strategy may be added to pastoral training efforts. Non-formal pastoral training facilitates speed for quantity. It can find, filter, and feed all those who should receive better quality formal preparation so that they in turn become future trainers of pastors, all while serving as pastoral leaders. Training "delivery systems" may be intentionally stacked to prevent random admission of any person who accidentally discovers an ".edu" website and applies for formal training. An overall strategy with policy for the selection, training, and placement is necessary.

The global pandemic provided for, even required, the formal sector to justify and value non-formal training as part of their program offerings, without forcing the non-formal sector to act like their formal siblings. Fortunately, almost all effective non-formal pastoral training of which this author is aware seems to be led by those who themselves have been formally trained for ministry. Pastor-trainers and pastoral leaders may thus work intentionally and collaboratively, innovatively and cooperatively to "stack" the advantages and mitigate the disadvantages of courses and programs for the sake of pastoral health and church health in a location.

7. A Global Strategic Priority for Missions and Ministries

Would the reader consider a sixth "s," a principle more than a strategy, to fulfill scalability, spreadability, sustainability, speedability, and stackability criteria for the faster delivery to more pastoral leaders of better training at lower costs?

I borrow the principle of "subsidiarity" from the relationship of central and local authorities in politics[6] to build a practical actionable strategy for this call to prioritize pastor training as an integral part of all ministry portfolios.

Simply speaking, a "subsidiarity" strategy emphasizes contiguity of contact and continuity of impact. Our actionable assumption is that those closest to a situation are most aware of local needs and, *if properly selected, trained, and resourced*, are willing and able to deliver good solutions for best

---

[6] "The general aim of the principle of subsidiarity is to guarantee a degree of independence for a lower authority in relation to a higher body or for a local authority in relation to central government." https://www.europarl.europa.eu/factsheets/en/sheet/7/the-principle-of-subsidiarity.

effect upon local need. In the pastor-training industry, such "local and lower" pastoral leaders would have the greatest impact on their people, and those people on their neighbors.

What if we could select, train and resource both local pastoral leaders and local pastor-trainers for this multiplicative process? Much good will be delivered on-site, with most relevance, over a longer term and in a much less expensive way.

On average, over any following ten years:

- if one pastor-trainer trains a minimum of one pastoral leader a year, and
- one pastoral leader develops a minimum of one church leader a year, and
- one church leader equips a minimum of one believer to spiritual health a year, and
- one growing believer shares the gospel with a minimum of one unbeliever a year,
- it leads to 10,000 exposed to Jesus' salvation over ten years. Such exponential multiplication is possible because of proximity, contiguity, and subsidiarity, since it is the local pastor-trainer who begins this sequence of consequence.

An absolute minimum expectation defines each role and covers all attrition beyond which the process cannot be reduced. If a pastor-trainer does not train even *one* pastoral leader a year, a pastoral leader doesn't develop even *one* church leader per year, and if a church leader doesn't equip even *one* believer a year, should they be considered trainers or leaders in any ministry sense at all?

Sadly, the weak link in the chain is the believer who does not verbally share the gospel with even one unbeliever each year. He is still a believer, albeit immature and unfruitful, since God's gracious, eternal salvation is never conditioned on erratic, human performance.

It is a safe assumption that each *healthy* believer, leader, pastor, trainer will minimally reach one a year at the next level of life and ministry influence. Fortunately, losses and lacks at any layer in this sequence, where less than one does not give credibility to each role, are covered and compensated by the surplus of others' good works across the whole range.

Increase the number of pastor-trainers and more unbelievers are reached. What if we could train and resource 100,000 trainers of pastors over ten years?

8. Conclusion

I conclude this festschrift to a missionary strategist with our mutual concern for this third decade of the third millennium: the strengthening of pastoral leaders—forming, training, and uniting them—needs to be of higher priority in missions endeavors and a higher proportion of ministry attention among the many methodologies, strategies, and proposals in making disciples of all nations today. Indeed, social ministries, evangelistic presence, and church planting need to be undergirded with pastoral training initiatives regarded as their apex. Why is this?

Initially, entrance into cultures and peoples may come through compassion initiatives—whether in medicine, education, relief and development, justice, or human trafficking issues.

Then, building on these long and short, big and small goodwill platforms, evangelization does take place (or else we resemble secular nongovernmental organizations).

After that, beyond evangelism, comes church planting. However, after church planting, what follows?

Strengthening pastors should stand at the pinnacle of missions and ministry strategy because strategists and practitioners often go through local pastoral leaders for endorsement and counsel about where to dig wells, show movies about Jesus, and plant new churches.

In summary, I commend pastoral training as a necessary complement to and the highest priority for implementing all ministry proposals and plans globally and locally:

- It justifies the cost and preserves the fruit of the other sacrificial and successful ministry efforts.
- It protects churches from the spiritual health disaster that otherwise awaits them.
- It depopulates hell from the highest numbers of people in an earthly situation and facing an eternal destiny without Christ.
- It helps correct creedal and cultural misperceptions of Christianity when local believers permeate their social spheres.
- It prevents church growth from being a mere sociological phenomenon.
- It multiplies and sustains the future leadership of the faith.

Often, underserved and isolated pastors are on-site for the long term; they are the least expensive and most relevant to their contexts. They are thus our key co-laborers who urgently need skills, training, and relationships. Therefore, prioritizing a global strategy for faster delivery of better training to more pastors at lower cost as the focus and framework of ministry and missions efforts significantly accomplishes the final mandates of our Lord Jesus. Enhancing pastoral health everywhere accelerates church health anywhere and delivers spiritual health to large numbers of individuals worldwide.

About the Author

A global spokesman for the Lord Jesus Christ, Ramesh Richard serves as founder and president of RREACH and professor of Global Theological Engagement and Pastoral Ministries at Dallas Seminary. RREACH envisions changing the way *one billion individuals* think and hear about the Lord Jesus Christ by personal, media and local proclamation. He founded TOPIC to champion non-formal pastoral training and convened the first Global Proclamation Congress for Pastoral Trainers to accelerate church health where Christ's Church is growing.

Ramesh holds a Th.D. in Systematic Theology from Dallas Seminary and a Ph.D. in Philosophy from the University of Delhi. He and his wife, Bonnie, have three children and three grandchildren.

A Salute to Manfred Kohl: In Pursuit of Excellence in Theological Education

Wilson W. Chow

1. Introduction

On the occasion of the eightieth birthday of Dr. Manfred Kohl, I join his many colleagues and friends in extending to him our most sincere congratulations. I wish him and his dear wife Barbara many more years of good health, happiness and active ministry for the Lord. It gives me great joy to contribute this paper to the Festschrift in honor of Dr. Kohl for his contributions to global evangelical theological education. This paper serves as an expression of my deepest personal appreciation and salutation to him.

The writer counts it a blessing and privilege to have served with him together for almost two decades in theological education. I am grateful that he brought me into the ministry team at Overseas Council International and involved me in the work of the Institute for Excellence.

In this article I will tell my story of working with Manfred and will express my appreciation of him for who he is: a friend, a promotor of theological education in pursuit of excellence, a pioneer in exploring new horizons, and a partner in serving theological schools in the Chinese-speaking world and, in particular, mainland China.

2. Manfred the Man

I would like to begin with a word of appreciation to Manfred the man. Manfred is human in every sense of the word. He is a straightforward person, says what he means and means what he says. Those who know Manfred can testify that he is always kind and gentle, but he can be blunt and rough at times. He cannot stand nonsense, for like Nathanael, he is a true Israelite in whom there is nothing false, nor any deceit (John 1:47). Manfred is not an impatient man, but he always emphasizes punctuality and expects works to be done on schedule. He does not accept mediocrity. He expects people to respond to his emails in a reasonable time and is impatient with people who delay unduly in answering his requests and questions. More than once he has expressed to me that he cannot understand why people take so long replying to him.

Next, my words of appreciation to Manfred as a friend. He is a trustworthy and caring person. The Chinese have an idiom, "One doesn't visit a temple without a cause," which means figuratively that one doesn't come to you unless he wants to ask you for a favor, or with an ulterior motive, or with a hidden agenda. A true friend does not call on you simply for his personal gain or in his personal interest. I hear from Manfred from time to time. He writes to send me greetings from him and his wife Barbara, and to touch base with me and my wife. Indeed, we are friends and we are co-workers, but our friendship is not functional; it is not built on working relationship. A true friend speaks the truth out of love.

One time during our conversation, we talked about our family and I mentioned "my son." The words just slipped out of my mouth. Manfred corrected me immediately. He asked, "Why did you say 'my son' and not 'our son'?" It never occurred to me that it was a slip of the tongue. He reminded me that when I talk about our son, his mother should not be dismissed. One may think that this is a trivial matter and that Manfred is a bit picky. But I don't think so. I learned a lesson and I take his advice seriously.

This is the Manfred Kohl I have come to know as a person and value as a friend.

When Manfred retired from Overseas Council International as Vice President of Development at the end of 2007, I wrote him a personal note to express my profound sense of gratitude and appreciation. I would like to quote my letter below. Yet it is only a summary of what I want to say.

> You are an agent, or better still, an angel, of encouragement. Both in your public lectures and in private conversations, you have always encouraged me in my ministry of theological education. I have learned so much from you. Your insights and experiences have inspired me to embark on new ventures. Since I attended the Institute for Excellence in Hong Kong in February 2004, I have been following one of your advices in writing a monthly report to the chairman of the Board of Directors of China Graduate School of Theology to share with him the highlights of my activities every month. I am sure that my chairman now knows very well what a seminary president does. My travel with you in China in March 2007 is an unforgettable experience. We visited Shanghai, Nanjing and Beijing. I could see your interest in and concern for theological training in China mainland, and your willingness and readiness to offer your service. I pray that your vision for China will bear much fruit in the near future.
>
> Manfred, thank you for your past fifteen years of service to OCI and to its many partner institutions. Many theological educators benefit from your ministry and are blessed by the Institute. We want to say "thank you" to you from the depth of our hearts.

Finally, I wish you happy retirement. The Chinese phrase for "retirement" is made up of two words (two characters). They stand for "stepping down" and "getting rest." I think "stepping down" is for you, also slowing down and doing less, but please continue to make yourself available to needy people and needy situations.

Manfred continued to serve as Ambassador for OCI. What I share in the following pages is a continuation of what I had said in the above-quoted personal letter. But this time it is made public, and my story concerns events which mostly happened after 2007.

3. Manfred the Theological Educator

Manfred believes in the strategic importance of quality holistic theological education. He has a passion for the training of future servant-leaders of the Church. He achieves this purpose through the Institute for Excellence, in which he plays a significant role. My association with him throughout these years has helped me to come to understand him as a person as well as his aspirations for theological education.

Manfred promotes evangelical theological education globally. His insights and experience as a theological educator himself give him the credentials to instruct, advise and guide seminary leaders to pursue excellence in theological education. When we think of a seminary, we see training as its core and key program, which requires a campus, a library, a qualified faculty and a relevant curriculum. These are all necessary but may not be sufficient. Manfred sees a theological school as more than an academic institution. He has interesting analogies, and he compares theological training to a manufacturing enterprise. The industrial model consists of at least three departments: the process of production, management and marketing. When applied to theological education, the production line covers all the training programs, the teaching and learning aspects on the academic, spiritual and practical dimensions. Yet we cannot stop there. A theological school as an organization needs to be well managed in terms of personnel and finance, and operate smoothly. Then no matter how good the products are, it will amount to nothing unless there is a market for them. Marketing is important. When this concept is translated to theological education, it means that besides and in addition to quality theological training, there are the issues of governance, administration, financial sustainability, development and student placement that a seminary must take into consideration in the ministry of theological education.

As a consultant, Manfred travels globally to hold seminars on issues of concern to theological educators. Many welcome his advice. Yet some of his ideas are not easy to grasp, and some people may find them difficult to implement. For instance, Manfred has clear definitions of the functions of a seminary Board of Directors and the role of a seminary President. He draws the boundary between the two. The Board is usually the legal body of the seminary, makes policy decisions, sets the annual budget and bears ultimate responsibility. However, the Board of Directors is not a management board and does not intervene with the everyday operation of the school. Manfred would maintain that of all the faculty and staff of the school, in the eyes of the Board of Directors, they only "hire" one person, that is, the President of the seminary. The President acts for and on behalf of the Board and executes the decisions of the Board. The chain of organizational command is clear. The Board does not bypass the President in reaching out to the faculty and staff in the affairs of the school, and vice versa. Of course, this does not mean there is no channel of communication or appeal other than going through the President. What it means is that the faculty and staff are accountable to the President, while the President is held accountable to the Board. In this respect, the President works closely with the Chairman of the Board of Directors.

Manfred has a particular view of the role of the President. He compares a seminary president to an orchestra conductor. Whereas the conductor directs and coordinates the members of the orchestra in performing a piece of music, the seminary president likewise directs and coordinates the faculty and staff of the school in theological training. The conductor may be a seasoned musician and performer, a pianist or violinist, yet as conductor his main role is not to give a musical instrument performance, but to conduct the whole orchestra. Only on certain occasions and for a period of time does the conductor sit down and play the piano or violin. The seminary president may be a renowned scholar and professor, but as president his main role is not to teach but to lead and direct the school for its well-being. Of course, he may still continue his academic career as time permits. Yet his priority is clear and defined.

Whenever Manfred speaks of the role of a seminary president as described above, there is always a strong reaction and mixed feelings among the audience. People understand the analogy, but they find it difficult to put into practice. In most situations in Asia, the seminary president is a well-respected scholar with academic achievements. There is the traditional Confucian model: those who do well in an academic career are fit to become government officials. It is unthinkable that the seminary president should put aside his teaching and focus on administration, development and fund raising. Many seminary presidents express that they have the heart to take Manfred's suggestion, but in reality the president cannot afford not to teach because of the shortage of faculty. At any rate, Manfred's idea arouses much discussion and reflection, and it is satisfying to see that many take his advice seriously and work toward that goal.

Manfred always stresses the importance of finding the right person doing the right thing the right way. One of his favorite illustrations is taken from his family furniture business, a centuries-old tradition of which he is very proud. His early years as a carpentry apprentice tell him that when making an item of furniture, if a piece of wood is found too short to fit well, the only thing to do is to throw away the wood and get another piece that will fit. Manfred said from experience that no matter what one does to that piece of wood, it just does not fit, and there can be no remedy. To continue working with that unfit piece will only be a waste of time. His point was that for any position or task, one must get the right person who is suitable, promising and with great potential for the job. In this respect, Manfred has a special gift in reading people. He does not judge or criticize people, but he is so perceptive that he is able to see beyond the surface and the obvious. He knows how to evaluate people and is able to find the right people to work with him. No wonder that under his leadership OCI had a team of good people serving as Regional Directors for Europe, Africa, Middle East, South America and Asia. As a theological educator, Manfred believes in teamwork and gathers these co-workers around him in planning, organizing and operating the Institute for Excellence.

My acquaintance with OCI can be traced back to the early time of Dr. Charlie Spicer. When OCI President Dr. John Bennett kindly invited the China Graduate School of Theology to be one of its partner schools, my close association with OCI began, which led to my appointment as OCI Senior Consultant for Chinese Asia in 2008. The year before that was crucial in my working with OCI, and in particular with Manfred. In March 2007, I took Manfred for the first time to visit China. The trip included the four cities of Guangzhou, Shanghai, Nanjing and Beijing. It opened the door and prepared the way for more visits and serving China in subsequent years. Then in September I was invited to attend an OCI Institute held in Frankfurt, Germany. What happened after the Institute was a memorable experience. Manfred organized a retreat for all the OCI Area Directors, myself included, at a mountain resort in the village of Gries in Austria. The purpose of the gathering was team building. We all enjoyed the beautiful scenery, the food, the rest and the fellowship. One day we went hiking in the hills. We made a few stops here and there along the way, and we paused for short moments of prayer. It was a retreat both for the physical and the spiritual.

We deeply appreciated the way Manfred connected with us and provided the opportunities to connect with each other as co-workers.

4. Manfred and Chinese Theological Education

Manfred did a great service to the Chinese Church in Southeast Asia by introducing the Institute for Excellence to the Chinese-speaking seminaries in that region. The Institute was sponsored by the Overseas Council International (OCI), and it was the first of its kind ever held. Manfred was able to gather theological education leaders, presidents and deans to come together for a four-day institute for learning, sharing and peer tutoring. The Institute was hosted by a local seminary as the venue for the meetings, and lodging was provided in a nearby hotel. All the expenses for the Institute were underwritten by OCI, including registration, rooms, and meals. Participants needed to pay only for their own travel. Manfred wanted to make sure that decent accommodation was arranged for the participants so that they were comfortable and could rest well during those few days.

As for the content of the Institute, important topics included Seminary Governance, the Role of the Board of Directors and the President, Curriculum Design, Strategic Planning, Fund Raising and Alumni Relations. All the sessions were conducted in the Chinese language, except for Manfred and Dr Ashish Chrispal, Asia Director for OCI, who were the main speakers, and other specialists Manfred brought in to speak on particular issues. We were privileged to have had distinguished guest speakers such as Dr. Perry Shaw of the Arab Baptist Theological Seminary, Chip Zimmer of Peacemaker Ministries and Dr. Dan Brewster of Compassion International.

The first Institute was held in Hong Kong in February 2004, hosted by the China Graduate School of Theology, which was planning to launch a Ph.D. program and sought the help of OCI in sponsoring a two-day conference on how to prepare for doctoral programs. The next Institute was held in Macau in 2005, and after that it was held every year from 2008 to 2013 for a consecutive period of six years, altogether twelve Institutes. The locations included Hong Kong, Taiwan, Singapore and Malaysia, attended by the presidents or deans of nearly thirty seminaries. The mere fact of bringing together these key theological education leaders for a conference is itself quite an accomplishment, not to mention the far-reaching impact it generated. For these, we are indebted to Manfred and his team and OCI.

The following is a summary of the Institute of Excellence listed in chronological order, with the dates, locations and themes.

- February 2004
  Hong Kong, hosted by China Graduate School of Theology. Theme: Doctoral Programs
- October 17–21, 2005
  Macau, hosted by Macau Bible Institute. Theme: Meeting the Needs of Our Community and Church
- October 13–17, 2008
  Taipei, hosted by China Evangelical Seminary. Theme: Leadership Development
- May 11–12, 2009
  Hong Kong, hosted by China Graduate School of Theology. Theme: The Board and the President
- May 14–15, 2009
  Taipei, hosted by China Evangelical Seminary. Theme: The Board and the President
- October 23–24, 2009
  Singapore, hosted by Singapore Bible College. Theme: Role of the Seminary and the President
- April 6–9, 2010
  Taipei, hosted by China Evangelical Seminary. Theme: Curriculum Design and Development
- November 30–December 1, 2010
  Kuala Lumpur, hosted by Malaysia Theological Seminary. Theme: Seminary Governance
- April 11–14, 2011
  Hong Kong, hosted by Evangel Seminary. Theme: Seminary Development
- April 16–19, 2012
  Hong Kong, hosted by China Graduate School of Theology. Theme: Financial Sustainability and Institutional Changes
- May 21–22, 2012
  Hong Kong, hosted by Evangel Seminary. Theme: Moving Beyond 80 Years
- April 22–24, 2013
  Taipei, hosted by China Evangelical Seminary. Theme: Spirituality

5. Manfred and Theological Education in Mainland China

Manfred's contributions to the Chinese-speaking world are unique. He not only introduced the Institute for Excellence to the Chinese seminaries in Southeast Asia, but he also brought it to mainland China, thanks to his patience, persistence and skill in establishing a relationship of trust with the leaders of the Three Self Patriotic Movement Committee (TSPM) and the China Christian Council (CCC).

After the Cultural Revolution and since the implementation of the "reform and opening up" policy in China in the late 1970s, the Church in mainland China has been growing rapidly. Bible schools were reopened and there was a great need for training pastors and workers for the Church. Many well-intentioned people outside look at China as a vast "mission field," because of her 1.4 billion population. There are people who try to go into China, by various means and methods, to evangelize or to conduct training. Yet China made it clear that the Church in the nation is self-governing, self-supporting (financial independence from foreigners) and self-propagating (indigenous missionary work). These are the well-known three-self principles. Like the people in China, the Church has also stood up.

My ministry in China began in the early 1990s. It was a calling to serve the Church in China. Yet as someone outside the mainland, I understood that it was not my business to go to the mainland to do whatever I want in the name of "vision" from God. It was my conviction that first, it is purely serving the Church there out of love, with no other motives or hidden agenda; secondly, whatever I do must be open, public and legal; thirdly, I only do what I am asked to do by the Church leaders on the mainland, who know best what the real needs are, instead of doing what I think best for them. Manfred agreed with me completely, and on the basis of these convictions we worked together for and in mainland China.

Manfred and I first visited the leadership of the national TSPM and CCC in Shanghai in 2007 to establish a cordial working relationship. We also traveled in the country and paid visits to seven Bible schools and seminaries. After laying down the groundwork, we proposed to work with the Training Department of the national CCC to bring together the presidents and deans of the twenty Bible schools and seminaries in China for a five-day conference in theological education. The national TSPM and CCC were cautious, but open to working with an outside body when they were assured of the latter's sincerity and willingness to serve. It would be the first of its kind. Such a gathering itself was of great significance and provided the occasion for these seminary leaders to meet, learn and share together. Key issues were introduced in the conference. Among them were seminary Board structure and membership, governance, curriculum, faculty development, standards of excellence, and library development. All the participants shared these same concerns and expressed keen interest in exploring approaches and solutions to these issues. Although Bible schools and seminaries in China have their own infrastructures and prescribed policies, it was a good exercise for the participants to engage in discussion openly on these issues. They were aware of their situations and limitations, but they also saw the need for changes and reforms.

Altogether, three institutes were held in Shanghai in partnership with the national CCC for three consecutive years in 2009, 2010 and 2011, listed below chronologically:

- October 26–29, 2009
  Shanghai, hosted by the Training Department of the national CCC.
  Theme: Governance in Theological Education
- November 1–5, 2010
  Shanghai, hosted by the Training Department of the national CCC.
  Theme: Effective Theological Training
- December 5–9, 2011
  Shanghai, hosted by the Training Department of the national CCC.
  Theme: The Idea of Higher Education in Theological Education in China

6. Conclusion

As we look back to these conferences, we ask ourselves: what did we achieve? I think Manfred's fine efforts were well rewarded. One of his goals was to cultivate among the national TSPM, CCC and seminary leaders an increasing sense of openness to principles, models, values and practice of theological education outside China, especially to the evangelical heritage. Little did people know that Manfred was also instrumental in opening the door that led to a subsequently developed friendly relationship between the national TSPM and CCC and the World Evangelical Alliance (WEA). It was gratifying to know that, for example, the Nanjing Union Theological Seminary considered requesting WEA to help recruit evangelical scholars from the West to teach at the seminary.

Our experience in serving China deepens our understanding of Revelation 3:7–8: "These are the words of him who is holy and true, who holds the key of David. What he opens no one can shut, and what he shuts no one can open. See, I have placed before you an open door that no one can shut. I know that you have little strength, yet you have kept my word and have not denied my name."

Indeed, Christ holds the key. We cannot decide, much less control, what is possible and not possible. It is God who opens the door and it is also God who shuts the door. When the door opens, we must respond and act promptly, seize the day, and get hold of the opportunity. When the door is closed, we need not force our way in or think of ways to knock it down. We wait. Yet we do not wait idly. We prepare and always get ready. What was not possible before is now taking place. What cannot be done today may be possible tomorrow. We need to be patient, remain hopeful, always look up to God and be encouraged.

There is another contribution that Manfred has made to theological education in mainland China. It is the China Book Project, which he initiated after discussing it with Rev. Kan Boping, Executive Secretary of CCC, and Rev. Bao Jia-yuen, Director of Theological Education, at a meeting in November 2010. Although I was not personally involved in this project and cannot provide the details, yet my story is incomplete without mentioning the Book Project. A list of updated theological books was first prepared, primarily in Chinese. With funding available in 2012, the pilot project was launched with four seminaries as recipients of 350 to 500 books based on their selection of books from the list. In the following years, more schools were added to receive books. This project has substantially increased book acquisition by the libraries of several major seminaries in China,

In conclusion, I would like to quote the words of the late TSPM Chairman Elder Ji Jian-hung when he last met Manfred. After some years of acquaintance, Elder Ji told Manfred that when he first got to know him, he regarded Manfred as a friend. As time went by and friendship developed, they worked together and Elder Ji called Manfred a co-worker. Finally in terms of their working relationship, Elder Ji treated Manfred as a partner. A friend, a co-worker, a partner. There is no better way to describe Manfred's standing with regard to theological education in China.

About the Author

Wilson was born in China, grew up in Hong Kong and studied in the USA. He and his wife Stella and their son's family now live in Hong Kong.

Wilson holds a Ph.D. from Brandeis University. He is currently President Emeritus of China Graduate School of Theology and serves as Advisory Pastor of the Kowloon Tong Chinese Alliance Church.

He devoted his life to theological education, participating in the Asia Theological Association and the Theological Commission of the World Evangelical Fellowship. He was Senior China Consultant for Overseas Council International. His publications include commentaries on Ruth, Judges and Micah.

Affirming Quality in Theological Education

Steve Hardy

1. Introduction

Evangelical peer-level accreditation affirms how well an institution is doing in effectively equipping people for ministry within specific contexts. The process of self-evaluation is helpful for renewal. Evaluation should begin with revisiting one's values and purposes. It should be comprehensive, using standards and guidelines developed by other institutions doing similar things at similar levels. ICETE's "Standards and Guidelines of Global Evangelical Theological Education" (discussed later in this essay) is an excellent tool for evangelical training programs. Our affirmation of quality is not adequate. We may need the affirmation of educational or government-level authorities. We definitely need the affirmation of the community being served. Affirmation of quality from peer institutions leads to international credibility. When an evangelical institution does well in preparing people for the ministries to which they have been called, the best affirmation is from God himself.

I know of no one who has visited more theological schools globally than Dr. Manfred Kohl. For a number of years, Manfred and I worked together with the Overseas Council's Institute for Excellence in Global Theological Education.[1] The Institute began in the mid-1990s with a conversation between Manfred and John Bennett regarding the care of overworked and undertrained leaders of OCI-related partner programs. The Institute for Excellence in Global Theological Education was designed to equip school leaders in issues of curriculum, faculty development, strategic planning, governance, fundraising and other practical areas, as well as to strengthen global networks of theological training institutions.

One of those global networks of theological institutions is the International Council for Evangelical Theological Education (ICETE). ICETE is a network of networks, linking regional evangelical accreditation associations around the world. Verifying and certifying quality in evangelical theological institutions is one of the purposes of ICETE. As the former director

---

[1] Overseas Council now functions as a part of United World Mission. Its Institute for Excellence is currently run by Dr. Paul Clark. Further information on Overseas Council can be found at https://uwm.org/overseas/.

of OCI's Institute for Excellence and as a current senior advisor to ICETE, in this chapter I would like to look at ways to use evaluation to foster quality (and not just academic excellence) in the training done by evangelical theological institutions.

God encourages excellence in all that we do. Interestingly, most training programs tend to consider themselves excellent. But as I wrote in *Excellence in Theological Education,* we are not excellent simply because we think that we are, because we are the best (or only) program that we know, or even because we once were.[2] A theological training program is excellent to the extent to which it achieves what it intends to do.

The most visible proof of success in a training program is in its graduates. Students receive diplomas, certificates and academic awards for their educational efforts. But as master educator Jane Vella asked of students, "How do they know that they know?"[3] And how do we know whether they have really learned anything of significance from our educational efforts? How can we measure whether graduates and the churches and organizations they serve are making an impact for God and for good in their communities?

About ten years ago, Overseas Council Australia developed a project to research the impact of theological training. Various institutions shared their conclusions at the ICETE Consultation in Antalya, Turkey in 2015. The reality is that it is difficult to determine one's role in what God is doing. Even when things don't go well, it isn't always so obvious why something did or did not occur. We trust and pray that God will use us, but to what extent can we determine or measure whether our efforts or structures were a significant factor in what God has done? Have our students grown in faith, character and ministry skills because of the educational activities we planned? Or has growth occurred simply because God was at work in them? Or is the answer some combination of the two?

2. The importance of evaluation

Careful and thorough evaluation will help us discover answers to these questions. Through evaluation we should be able to affirm whether or not there is quality in our theological education, as we observe and measure the results of the right people doing the right things in right ways—under the grace of God.

---

[2] Hardy, Steven A. *Excellence in Theological Education* (Langham, 2016), pp. 3–4.
[3] Vella, Berardinelli and Burrow. *How Do They Know They Know?* (Jossey-Bass, 1998).

Evaluation is an essential part of the fabric of any academic community. When there is an institutional culture of learning, evaluation is done regularly in every area. Institutions evaluate prospective students to see if they are qualified to enter the institution. Evaluation, through observation, personal relationships, exams or assignments, allows students and teachers to affirm that learning is happening. Evaluation helps teachers to teach better. It can also identify those who cannot teach at all. Evaluation helps programs to modify their curriculum, eliminating those courses that are no longer needed and adding those that are. Evaluation helps us to see the impact of both the visible and the invisible curriculum. When an institution has done a careful self-study, it will have a critical self-awareness that allows it to affirm its quality.

Nevertheless, if ours is the only voice saying that we are doing well, our credibility is still at stake. We need the affirmation of others. On our part, this involves sharing data and telling stories of our history as well as stories of the achievements and lives of our grads, professors and staff. Those whom we are trying to serve need to see that our graduates are competent for ministry. They need to see not only that the ministries of our graduates are thriving, but that our graduates and their families are thriving. When the community served is satisfied with our students as they graduate, our programs are validated by the community. This affirmation is essential as without the validation by one's constituency or stakeholders, an institution really shouldn't exist at all.

Re-Forma has offered a way for a theological institution to demonstrate that its graduates have competencies that churches and Christian organizations want in areas of character, skills and knowledge. This is a validation that carries the endorsement of the World Evangelical Alliance.

The affirmation or validation of government-level educational entities can be good (and sometimes necessary). Official commendation or accreditation involves a legal dimension. Being granted a charter or a license to function allows an institution to receive students and fees and gives it authority to grant degrees. Accreditation by government or regional educational agencies assumes a certain level of demonstrable quality; the institution has established that it has the resources, teachers, finances and structures for its programs to work as intended. This official recognition allows students to transfer into other programs operating at equivalent levels and lets graduates move seamlessly into upper-level programs elsewhere.

However, while having a charter may be a legal requirement, there can be a hesitancy to submit to government-level accreditation because of fears of interference in curriculum or concerns that secular authorities might force theological schools to admit students or to hire faculty with non-evangelical lifestyles or beliefs. But even if there were minimal or no interference, affirmation of educational quality by non-evangelical organizations or by departments of education will not indicate whether our graduates have matured in Christian character or are appropriately and theological equipped to serve the church. Furthermore, in some parts of the world, charters can be purchased or acquired through "knowing" someone, rather than earned by demonstrated quality. So while a license to exist is a good and often necessary thing, there still may be unanswered questions about quality and credibility for a church-focused evangelical institution of learning.

3. But is accreditation even worth it?

Not everyone is excited about accreditation. In the early 1990s I heard it said at a global missions conference in South Africa that accreditation was actually the enemy of good training. Sadly, this accusation can be true if a school determines its quality only by looking at numbers and process: Are there enough books and periodicals to support the program? Do the class sessions meet for the correct number of minutes? Are there enough properly sequenced credits to justify the program? Is the paperwork in order to show that all instructors, staff and students are appropriately qualified? Are all of the accounts in order?

Moreover, isn't it enough to have community validation—the affirmation of satisfaction by those we are serving? Doing a thorough internal evaluation takes time and effort, as documenting one's quality requires more than great stories. It involves a comprehensive assessment of vision and purpose, process, and results. These are important questions. Yet I would argue that there are benefits to a thorough institutional assessment. Paul Bowers, one of the founders of both ACTEA and ICETE, has defined accreditation as "a collaborative effort among programs of theological education to achieve and demonstrate a quality that is credible."[4] The value of the accrediting process is in its help to "achieve" quality. As Dr. Bowers noted, the process of working towards accreditation is a catalyst for renewal. Taking the time and effort to ask the right questions in order to examine and document one's quality is worthwhile as it encourages renewal.

---

[4] "Accreditation as a Catalyst for Renewal in Theological Education," in Part 2 of *Evangelical Theological Education: An International Agenda* (ICAA, 1994), pp. 26–41.

4. Credibility through the affirmation of others

As we noted earlier, credibility doesn't come if a theological program is the only voice declaring its own quality. The ICETE standards defining quality are not something invented or imposed by one isolated institution or individual. Institutions with similar values and purposes, functioning at similar academic levels and with significant input from their stakeholders, have been the ones to collectively define what quality should look like. While demonstrating that one is functioning in accordance with those standards is an internal effort, credibility comes as this process is done in cooperation with other theological schools. To the extent to which the standards for theological training are equivalent at a global level, having one's quality recognized by one's peers gives international credibility.

Nevertheless, quality is not documented by showing how well you are doing in going backwards. If the institution's primary concern is with perfecting what was inherited from the past, it probably will have ceased to serve today's church. If teachers simply look for better ways to teach the same things that they were taught in ways similar to those in which they were taught, learning will not be focused on the realities and the context of the students. Bible schools and seminaries will only be perfecting academic content that has come from other times and different cultures. Programs can get lost within their own traditions.

That is not to say that it is not a good thing to improve what we are trying to do. But while an internal evaluation may show that the school is doing brilliantly what it intends to do, a better starting point is to be aware of the extent to which what it is trying to do is worth doing. Given that the realities of today are significantly different from those the program was originally created to respond to, we need to know that we are doing the right things now. It is simply not helpful to discover better and better ways to provide answers to questions that no one is asking any longer. There will be no community validation if few outside the institution perceive value in the training that we are doing. Accordingly, an evaluation of a program must be done within the context of equipping students to respond effectively to the community and church needs of today and tomorrow.

5. Accreditation by ICETE

Accreditation is done by ICETE's regional members in Africa, Latin America, the Caribbean, North America, Western Europe, Euro-Asia, Asia and the Middle East and North Africa. A strength of the accreditation process within the ICETE family is its use of the long-established practice of peer-level accreditation. Rather than letting an external examiner determine one's quality, peer-level accreditation requires institutions to affirm their own quality through a thorough self-evaluation, documenting the quality of their programs against standards and processes developed or adapted by training institutions in the region that function at the same levels and with similar purposes. A visitation by an ICETE-related accreditation team is not an independent external examination as much as an external affirmation that the self-evaluations have been well done.

One huge advantage of working with an accreditation agency that shares our ethos and our evangelical theology is that someone with sympathetic understanding will read through a self-evaluation report carefully. It is only when both the school and the accrediting agency feel that the institution is ready for an accreditation visit that a team comes to verify that what the school feels about itself is true. A visit also comes with suggestions and advice for improvement and renewal. This external evaluation is an affirmation of one's own internal evaluation.

The ICETE family has given global value to these accreditation processes by its affirmation that regional standards and processes by its member agencies are functionally equivalent. To make this more transparent, ICETE convened a global consultation in Rome in September 2017 to review the ICETE recognition process standards and develop a common global framework for the accreditation of evangelical theological education, including global indicators of quality assurance and comparability of regional degree specifications. The document that grew out of this consultation, "Standards and Guidelines for Global Evangelical Theological Education,"[5] was approved by ICETE's board in February 2019. This document was updated and approved at the board meeting in June 2021 to include doctoral-level training and distance education.

Principles and values are at the beginning of a self-evaluation. For ICETE, these principles are expressed in a document first developed in 1983 and then published in 1984 as the *ICETE Manifesto on the Renewal of Evangelical Theological Education*.[6] The manifesto focuses on the impact of all aspects of an educational program, not only what happens in a classroom. Quality in theological education goes beyond academic issues. *The*

---

[5] The "Standards and Guidelines of Global Evangelical Theological Education" were approved at the ICETE board meeting in June 2021. It is accessible on the ICETE website: https://icete.info/resources/sggete/.

[6] Also available on the ICETE website.

Manifesto is designed to help institutions evaluate the excellence of their programs in the context of their vision by examining the following:

1. *Contextualization.* Context matters, so within the context of an institution, how should one teach students who come from a variety of contexts and who will minister in specific contexts?
2. *Orientation to the church.* If the theological institution exists to serve the church, how does leadership listen to and work in cooperation with the church they are trying to serve?
3. *Strategic flexibility.* Rather than continuing to do what has always been done, how does the institution creatively prepare people for various roles and responsibilities that exist now and that will come to exist in the future?
4. *Solid theological foundations.* Is the institution laying a solid biblical and theological foundation for the lives and ministries of its students? To what extent does the institution's theology provide a foundation for not only the courses being taught, but also its structures, relationships and methodologies?
5. *Continuous evaluation.* To what extent is the theological institution structured to learn continuously from what it does?
6. *Life and learning in community.* Too much learning has been focused only on the individual. So, to what extent is the educational program designed to function in community, with learning done as a community?
7. *Integrated curriculum.* How do classes and all planned activities relate to each other so that learning is holistic, coming from the total package of educational experiences?
8. *Development of servants.* How is character formation included and modeled in the curriculum and in the life of the institution so that transformational learning occurs?
9. *A variety of learning methodologies.* To what extent do teachers use a variety of creative ways to encourage learning?
10. *A mind that thinks Christianly.* To what extent are students being taught to think as Christians, and not simply to memorize and repeat things that others have learned?
11. *Life-long learning.* To what extent is the program designed to help its students to keep on learning for the rest of their lives?
12. *Cooperation.* To what extent is the institution learning from and cooperating with other training programs and organizations?[7]

---

[7] This document can be found on the ICETE website at https://icete.info/resources/manifesto/.

From the perspective of the ICETE family, these are values that should shape the vision and structures of a theological program. Quality should be visible in the impact of the integrated package, not just in the content of what is being taught. As the context changes, one's purposes and vision need to change. As the world changes, it is important to note that even this manifesto is being updated. ICETE is currently revising it with plans to discuss it within its global family and then to hopefully approve a new version of the ICETE Manifesto at the ICETE international gathering scheduled for November 2022.

6. Documenting quality

It is important to document the qualifications of the teachers, to describe the nature of the academic program and to list how many students have graduated. But even more important is to show how one's process illustrates good vision and a relationship to the church and the context being served. How well are we doing in getting where we want to go? Have we recruited the right students, with the right set of gifts, so that the end result of the training effort is of benefit to the church?

Affirming quality involves looking at the complex package that includes student maturity, character formation and skill development in the context of the learning community. The evaluation process needs to look at the integration of an entire curricular process as it effectively equips real people for ministry within the contexts to which they have been called. We look at the impact of the whole process while telling the stories of community validation.

As ICETE's Standards and Guidelines indicate, this involves a "common global framework" with "global indicators of quality assurance and comparability of regional degree specifications."[8] More than mere academics is visible through bearing in mind the importance of character education, holistic learning and being a prophetic voice. As the Standards and Guidelines state, this includes "integrating principles, quality measures and assessment of character education into our global indicators, within our vision of holistic theological education."[9]

A good way to systematically do an institutional evaluation is the self-study review that is part of ICETE's accreditation or re-accreditation process. This provides a series of comprehensive questions based on standards of practice that are internationally acknowledged as indicators of quality in the training of leaders for ministry and the church. Teams of people

---

[8] From the ICETE website: https://icete.info/resources/sggete, p. 5.
[9] Ibid.

working through the questions and documenting the extent to which these standards are being met is a good way to collectively perceive strengths and weaknesses.

ICETE's Standards and Guidelines document lists core standards that represent agreed common denominators in quality assurance work of global theological education. It embraces all levels of theological education, including undergraduate and postgraduate theology degrees as well as research degrees and doctoral level degrees. The Standards and Guidelines encompass the work done in the ICETE Beirut Benchmarks (2010) and the Bangalore Affirmations (2011), conferences that dealt with research and professional doctoral-level programs.

Standards deal with both numbers and process. Evidence documenting conformity to standards comes largely from examples. If there is quality in the institution, there should be an abundance of examples to look at. For example, in looking for ways to see if context has been taken seriously, the Standards and Guidelines suggest the following as some of the places where evidence can be found:

- community character covenants
- disciplinary regulations and procedures
- social gatherings, small groups, care groups
- pastoral care provision
- board of governors' representation
- student, faculty and staff involvement in local churches, including placement opportunities for students
- integration with local communities in ministry placements
- consultation events and attendance at civil and stakeholder community events
- promotional materials
- written policies on contextualization
- social and community involvement
- contact and dialogue with other educational institutions
- application forms with references from churches
- student handbooks, faculty handbooks, internal and external policy repositories, course information, fee schedules, board minutes, budgets, employment opportunities, general publicity
- communication policies[10]

---

[10] From the ICETE website: https://icete.info/resources/sggete. 13–14.

Beyond numbers and processes, quality should be visible in one's institutional identity. Evangelical training should be known for its embrace of the gospel. Accordingly, the ICETE standards want the identity of an institution to be clear, so the standard for Section A1.1, "Identity," states:

> Institutions understand themselves as providers of tertiary level evangelical theological education, subscribing to an evangelical statement of faith and integrating core Christian values into their operations and programmes. Biblical grounding is evident in all programmes.[11]

The results of one's educational efforts come from the interaction of many different factors. Much of what students learn does come from things that were never said in class or memorized for exams. The ICETE standards recognize that learning comes from who we are as God's people as well as from how we do what we do. Being Christian should be visible in a school's leadership, in its administrative staff and in its teaching team.

Concerning leadership and management, section A2.2 of the Standards and Guidelines states:

> Effective leadership is contextually sensitive in adopting various leadership styles, optimizing the human resources of the institution, reflecting adaptability to contextual factors, administering finances and facilities, inspiring Christian character in the learning community and operating within the context of board-approved policies. Institutions consciously seek to model Christian patterns of leadership and community in the ways that leaders at all levels relate to each other, their subordinates and to all members of the educational community.[12]

In other words, how an educational institution views and handles finances will probably be the way that our students will view and handle finances in their churches when they graduate. The size of the president's office will potentially shape how large a graduate's office will be when he becomes a pastor. The way leaders treat students and staff will be reflected in the leadership behaviors of graduates as they become pastors.

Concerning teachers and staff, the ICETE standards reflect that we have an adequate team of qualified people who have the knowledge, experience and methodological competence to teach and serve well. They also should model the Gospel. As section A3.3 says, "Educational staff understand and

---

[11] Ibid. 8.
[12] From the ICETE website: https://icete.info/resources/sggete, p. 9.

accept the institution's educational philosophy and are adequately qualified, spiritually mature and demonstrate Christian character."[13]

We need pastor-teachers and mentors. The teachers and staff become the curriculum for our students as our students will look like their teachers. Future pastors and missionaries will learn about relationships in ministry from the way an educational institution treats issues like status or ethnicity, the way men treat women, or how senior administrators treat their staff. They will learn to teach and counsel by observing how their teachers teach and give advice. They will learn about confession and forgiveness by living in community with those who teach and serve them. If we are going to document quality, one needs to show this in relationships within the educational community, as those relationships have much to do with the credibility and outcome of one's programs.

Quality Christian institutions hire good people and invest in them. A3.3 continues:

> Institutions assure themselves of the competence of their educational staff. Teachers should understand student-centered learning, facilitate high-quality student experience and be able to actively promote the acquisition of knowledge, the development of generic and specific competences and contribute to nourishing spiritual and character formation.[14]

Quality evangelical organizations function as learning communities. As Standard 4.1 states:

> Institutions foster a healthy sense of community life among their members. This includes strategies to develop healthy relationships, provide student support systems, facilitate graduate employment and alumni care and nourish a community where character is modelled and can be emulated. These strategies relate to all modes of educational delivery and all program levels. Institutions consider community life as a core component of theological education and all students, members of staff, faculty and the governing board are actively engaged.[15]

Who the community is becomes a "core component" of education. This isn't just a requirement for some students. Staff, faculty, students and even the governing board are actively engaged in the learning community of a quality institution. None of this denies academic quality. Like any good university or school, the Standards and Guidelines assume documentation

---

[13] From the ICETE website: https://icete.info/resources/sggete. p. 11.
[14] Ibid.
[15] From the ICETE website: https://icete.info/resources/sggete, p. 11.

that students have "subject knowledge and understanding" and that they "develop intellectual virtues and abilities such as critical thinking, ability to find information and ability to apply knowledge."[16] Students should be "motivated and equipped to be lifelong learners with the skills and competencies to do well professionally."[17]

But the most important factors for graduates to have impactful ministries will come from their character, attitudes and healthy relationships. These are not competencies for which schools can give exams. They are competencies that build on classroom instruction and grow out of the environment in which learning is done. This is education that is holistic and integrative. It can be observed and documented. Thus, one of the important ICETE standards affirms that "Institutions form their students within a holistic approach to theological education, carefully integrating spiritual formation, character education, academic achievement and practical training."[18]

7. Conclusions

Evangelical peer-level accreditation affirms whether an institution has documented how well it is doing in effectively equipping people for ministry within specific contexts. The process of self-evaluation is helpful for renewal as an institution sees where it can and should improve. This kind of evaluation starts with revisiting one's values and purposes. It should be comprehensive and works best when done using standards and guidelines that have been developed by other institutions doing similar things at similar levels. ICETE's Standards and Guidelines are an excellent tool for evangelical training programs. While it is good to have a realistic sense of one's quality, our voice alone is not adequate. We may need the affirmation of educational or government-level authorities. We definitely need the affirmation of the community we are trying to serve. But affirmation of quality from peer institutions leads to international credibility. And when an evangelical institution does well in preparing people for the ministries to which they have been called, the best affirmation is from God himself.

---

[16] From the ICETE website: https://icete.info/resources/sggete, section B1.4, p. 18.
[17] Ibid.
[18] From the ICETE website: https://icete.info/resources/sggete, section B4, p. 25.

About the Author

Steve Hardy has been a missionary educator since the mid-1970s in Ethiopia, Brazil, Mozambique, South Africa, the UK and the US. His love is teaching, and he has served as an educational consultant with SIM, Overseas Council, Langham, and ICETE. He did theological studies at Bethel in Minnesota and has a doctorate in missiology from Trinity in Chicago. He has written a number of articles and a textbook on educational administration, *Excellence in Theological Education* (Langham). He is married to LeAnne with two grown daughters and three grandchildren. Steve is sort-of retired and lives in the US.

Theological Education as Worship

Taras N. Dyatlik

1. My Personal Journey to Theological Education as Worshipping God

Questions concerning theological education began to trouble me seriously in 1993, when I started teaching Sunday school at the Church of the Good Shepherd in Rivne, Ukraine. It was then that I first realized the full responsibility of a teacher in the formation (or destruction) of the worldview of children and adolescents, especially in relation to worshiping God.

Feeling an urgent need, because of a lack of relevant knowledge and skills, I entered the one-year program at Donetsk Christian University in 1994. After completing the hermeneutics course, I transferred to the bachelor of theology program, so that I would have the opportunity to study New Testament Greek. During my studies, I led Bible study groups and preached in one of the local churches in Donetsk, where I tried to apply the knowledge and skills I had gained at the Christian university. At that time, I looked at theological education more from a student consumer perspective, wishing to grasp and master as much information as possible that I could pass along to other believers in sermons and in Bible study groups in the local church. I did not see any connection between theological education and worshiping God.

In 1997, after three years of study, I returned to Rivne, to my conservative Baptist church, and for a whole year I served as academic dean of Rivne Bible College, trying to make the most of everything I had learned in Donetsk. At the same time, I frequently visited other Baptist churches in the region for the purpose of student recruitment. Although worshiping God was, in my understanding, still limited to Sunday services and evangelistic activities, I started asking myself about the organic connection between the theological education I had received and the liturgical life of the local churches I was visiting.

In the summer of 1998, I returned to Donetsk, where I worked as the director of the library for four years and also taught courses in several subjects. In addition, I continued to lead a Bible study group in my church and preached. During this period, I asked myself, "What can students apply to the life and worship of their local churches from the subjects I was teaching—what information and what kinds of skills?" At this time, I was actively rethinking what I had learned during my studies, but from a different perspective: teaching. The question of the importance, role, and place of theological education in worship haunted me.

In 2002, I entered the master's program at the Faculty of Evangelical Theology in Leuven, Belgium, from which I graduated in 2004. During my master's studies, I tried to rethink my initial two years of experience in the theology program and my four years of teaching at a Christian university. I became even more concerned about the question: "How can theological education be made an organic part of the local church and worship?"

After completing my studies, I took a year off before applying for a teaching position. I needed to look for many answers about the connection between theological education and the liturgical life of the Church. During that period, I was engaged in youth work with teenagers in one of the small villages near our city. Every Wednesday, while leading a group, I asked myself whether this young man or that young woman needed theological education and how it might impact their worship of God and the life of their local church. Would their lives be changed (positively or negatively) if they graduated from a theological college? How might theological education be made an organic part of a local village church, where life issues and the practical application of the Gospel are in many ways different and more challenging than in churches located in an urban subculture?

In the summer of 2005, I returned to Donetsk to teach New Testament, and in June 2006, I became the academic dean of Donetsk Christian University. I then began attempting to comprehend theological education from a new perspective: "How can our theological programs be made more holistic, so that they will engraft students into the life and worship of the local church, rather than leading them away? And how can professors and students be brought together in such a way that their participation in theological education results in a theological seminary becoming an organic part of Church life and of worshiping God?"

From 2008 through 2011, I worked with the Euro-Asian Accrediting Association of Evangelical Theological Schools (EAAA) as the director of the EAAA Slavic Research and Resource Center (now registered as the Eastern European Institute of Theology in Lviv, Ukraine). From 2011 until now, I have served as the Regional Director for Eastern Europe and Central Asia of the Overseas Council–United World Mission, while continuing to help the EAAA with educational development and quality assurance. Having traveled through the region for ten years, visiting dozens of theological seminaries and local churches, I confess that I now have even more questions about the connection between theological education and the worship of

God in local churches in three geopolitical centers: pro-European, pro-Kremlin, and Central Asian. We, the evangelical church and the theological educators of Eastern Europe and Central Asia, have various socio-political views, making the life and ministry of local churches very complicated. But we remind ourselves daily of two things which do not change: our prophetic calling in the world and our spiritual gifts for building up the Church.

Thus, below I want to share two perspectives which have encouraged me during my twenty-five years of experience in theological education as a student, professor, manager, and developer. The first perspective is related to the practical prophetic ministry of theological education in the Christian community and secular society. The second one continually helps to keep my spiritual focus on the biblical foundations of theological education as the manifestation of spiritual gifts given by the Lord to the Church. The prophetic voice and spiritual gifts lead to the fulfillment of the mission of God, despite all the socio-political complexities, and they also continually serve as an invitation to the relationships of trust and love in the Kingdom of God in the world and in our local churches.

2. The Prophetic Role of Theological Education in Leading to the Worship of God

With regard to the worship of God, theological education has the prophetic task of being and doing *together with*, *in*, and *for* the Christian community. However, theological education cannot be considered mature if it does not also acquire a fourth prophetic ministry—*against* the Christian community—but, of course, not against the Church, since the Christian community and the Church, of which the community is a part, are two different phenomena, partially overlapping in their identity. Not everyone who belongs to the Christian community belongs at the same time to the Body of Christ, the Church, which is infallible. But the Christian community, consisting of people living in a secular society in the fallen world, is guilty of many sins, resulting from fallen human nature.

A prophet worships and serves the Lord:

- *Together with* the people of God,
- *In* the people of God,
- And also, for the *sake* of God's people.

But the fullness of the prophetic ministry also consists of proclaiming the mission of God against the sins of the human religious community, when the people of God begin worshiping other gods and idols. Therefore, to acknowledge and be against the sinful manifestations of the Christian community does not mean to be against God or the Church.

The prophetic role of theological education is not so much to protect the image of the Christian community vis-à-vis the government, society, other religions, and political ideologies as to proclaim the Kingdom of God, making it visible and evident, manifesting it in relationships of trust, love, and hope as the community of faith.

The community of faith is a community of practicing Christians who love, trust, and serve God and one another. They are followers of Christ who are not so much at war against the sins of secular society and other Christians as they are puzzled by questions about how, in worshiping the Lord, they can find their calling in the Body of Christ and manifest the Kingdom of God to the secular society in which we live.

Theological education should be directed not so much at intra-church or public dialogue as at *Church-public conversation* about how to worship God, and not so much in the form of dogmatics or systematics (which does not negate their significance), but in the form of narratives and parables about the Kingdom of God, understandable by the public, to fulfill the words of Jesus: "Worship the Lord your God, and serve him only" (Matt 4:10).

"The everlasting man" (humanity) is an integral part of the Kingdom of God, in which human beings worship God, because God created humanity not for humiliation and contempt, but for dignity and honor, which are restored through relationships of trust and love with the Lord and with the community of faith. Unfortunately, however, very often, in the pursuit of the divine and of being like God, we lose our humanity ("the everlasting man," according to G. K. Chesterton); we forget that a human is the one who was created by God, and the one in whose body God himself put on the Son, who was also resurrected in a new human body.

God does not expect us to humiliate ourselves and grovel before him. On the contrary, God, God himself, restores the dignity of humans, reviving the essence of their humanity, so that there is no groveling or humiliation in them. Humility before God has nothing to do with groveling and self-deprecation. To the contrary, humility before him is following his path, on which we acquire a natural human face, as intended by God, and acquire an "everlasting man." The humility of the Son before the Father is an integral part of his incarnation and his resurrection in a new body, the ascension of God the Son in a new body, his sitting at the right hand of the Father, and his abiding in eternity in a new body.

Thus, one of the most critical prophetic tasks of theological education with regard to the worship of God is glorifying the Lord and restoring human dignity in God. But this task is impossible to fulfill if we do not first recognize that the Christian community, as a "corporate unconscious" (not in the sense of the Body of Christ), sometimes humiliates and demeans people, no less than does secular society.

Theological education results in the worship of God only if it leads a person and the Christian community to the cross of Jesus Christ, where together we confess our sinful manifestations and recognize that being against the sins of the Christian community does not mean being against the Church. The cross is the starting point for restoring our dignity and honor in God, because the meeting of the Christian community with secular society should also take place only at the cross, where Christ does not kill humanity and humans, but restores them to the Father through his humility. It is at the cross that we accept the invitation to relationships of trust and love in the Kingdom of God.

The dehumanization of sinners in the era of digital information and social networks is one of the most challenging and ungodly sins of the Christian community (which differs from the Body of Christ, although it sometimes intersects with it in its identity). The dehumanization of sinners has nothing to do with worshiping God and is a form of rebellion against the Creator and "the everlasting man." One cannot worship the Lord and at the same time dehumanize a sinner who needs the restoration of the image of God through the invitation to relationships of trust and love in the Kingdom of God. If the Lord wants to resurrect sinners through the Holy Spirit, proclaiming to them through us the Good News and inviting people to worship him, why then do we want to humiliate and dehumanize people by adopting the attitude of the "Christian collective unconscious"?

The overwhelming majority of the prophets lived and worshiped God amidst the ongoing crisis of the people of God. Indeed, there has never been a single instance of a prophet and his ministry flourishing in a religious community. Even during the reign of the righteous Jewish kings such as Asa, Jehoshaphat, Josiah, and others, the prophets and their ministry were unprotected and challenged. Sooner or later, symbolically speaking, the prophet's head ends up on a tray for the institutions of religious and political powers, which worship their power, but not God.

Likewise, theological education today occupies the space between the Christian community and secular society. To be *between* and *against* means being always in crisis and unprotected, in situations where both the religious community and the secular society will try to get rid of it, putting its "head" on a tray. To be *between* and *against* means it is not so much looking for answers to the questions being asked by the Christian community and secular society, but rather looking for answers to the questions that God is asking.

Thus, an integral part of the path of theological education with regard to worshiping God and following Christ is the ability to admit and confess the sinfulness that exists within the Christian community, to refuse to defend an image of infallibility in the eyes of both secular and religious society; it is the ability to abandon an obsession with religious and political power in favor of unprotected prophetic faithfulness to Christ at his cross.

Following the path of Christ does not mean that we do not make mistakes and do not stumble or fall. No, following Christ implies that the righteous person is characterized not by the fact that he does not stumble but that he rises and that he also helps others who have stumbled to rise. Without vulnerability and openness to Jesus Christ at the cross, there is no resurrection of human dignity, the dignity of an "everlasting man" in Christ and with Christ for eternity with him. And theological education plays a crucial role in leading the Christian community to the cross of Christ, where humanity and humans are restored for the Kingdom of God through the invitation to relationships of trust and love with the Lord and with each other.

3. Theological Education as an Organic Part of Worship: Biblical Foundations

To fulfill the prophetic role of theological education in leading to the worship of God through the invitation to relationships of trust and love in the Kingdom of God, we need to realize that theological education is one of the gifts of the Holy Spirit. Theological education is the manifestation of such gifts as teaching, the word of wisdom, the word of knowledge, and others. Since spiritual gifts are given for the Church, the Body of Christ, to worship God and to serve both God and the people of God, theological education is an organic part of worship (in the broadest sense of the word), like all other spiritual gifts.

3.1. The local church as the Body of Christ: a living organism

In his epistles, the apostle Paul, under the guidance of God, formulated the teaching about the nature of the Church. Paul's hermeneutical key to understanding the nature (and, accordingly, the purpose) of the Church is to perceive it as the Body of Christ, consisting of people who are born again, of whom Christ is the Head, who live under the guidance of the Holy Spirit, and who participate in the fellowship of the three persons of the Holy Trinity. Summarizing the goals and objectives of the Church as a living organism of God in the context of human civilization, three main aspects of local church life become apparent:

- Glorifying God the Creator as the Holy Trinity (Father, Son, and Holy Spirit);
- Helping one other as believers to fulfill the purpose of mutual spiritual growth and transformation into the character of Jesus Christ (what we call "sanctification," "discipleship," and so on) for the building up of the Church, the Body of Christ;
- Participating in the mission of God through the fulfillment of one's calling, the realization of one's talents, and the discovery of one's spiritual gifts. Cooperation in the mission of God speaks of the missionary nature of the Body of Christ as a whole, even though each of us has different spiritual gifts.

Thus, the whole life of the Body of Christ in worshiping God, as a living organism through the application of spiritual gifts, is aimed at glorifying Christ, keeping oneself in a clean state as the Bride of Christ and as a testimony about Christ and his cross. "We preach Christ crucified: a stumbling block to Jews and foolishness to Gentiles, but to those whom God has called, both Jews and Greeks, Christ the power of God and the wisdom of God" (1 Cor 1:23–24).

3.2. The life of the Body of Christ: worship through calling

The Apostle Paul sets out the primary teaching about spiritual gifts in three epistles: Romans, 1 Corinthians, and Ephesians. In these three epistles, Paul speaks of the Church as the Body of Christ in the context of the spiritual gifts and calling that every believer receives after being born of the Holy Spirit.

Paul first openly expounds the doctrine of spiritual gifts in his first epistle to the Corinthians (c. AD 53–57), which he wrote from Ephesus during his third missionary journey (Acts 19). Most likely, it was because of a situation that arose in the Ephesian church that Paul began to formulate the doctrine of spiritual gifts. Next, arriving in Corinth, Paul wrote the epistle to the Romans (c. AD 58), in which he addresses the same issues as in Ephesus. Finally, from Rome (Acts 28), Paul wrote the epistle to the Ephesians (c. AD 60–62) from where he had written 1 Corinthians. In studying the issue of spiritual gifts, the sequence of the epistles is essential, since each subsequent passage on spiritual gifts complements what was written in the previous passage.

It is evident from the existing epistles of Paul that the issue of spiritual gifts had to be settled in at least three churches, and it is in the context of spiritual gifts that Paul speaks of the Church as the Body of Christ, a living organism. Each passage also mentions specific gifts that relate directly to theological education and its mission. These gifts include at least the word of wisdom, the word of knowledge, and teaching. The vocation of believers consists mainly of the living embodiment of their God-given and recognized talents and spiritual gifts for building up the Church, not only during its worship in a local church but also in its public activities, which are also missional—worshiping in a secular environment.

Our talents are the natural abilities with which God endows each person, and which we recognize and develop for our social and professional life. With particular skills and experience, a person becomes *a master of his craft*. The life of the priest Luka Voino-Yasenetsky (1877-1961) can serve as a notable example: he surprisingly combined the talents of drawing and surgery with the spiritual gifts of preaching and evangelism in the Gulag camps and during the Second World War.

Spiritual gifts are particular abilities with which God endows people during their spiritual birth. Then, with particular skills and experience, people become ministers in the Church. The purpose of spiritual gifts is to build up the Church as the Body of Christ. Unbelievers cannot fulfill their divine calling in the complete sense of the word because they lack spiritual gifts. However, at best, they try to use their talents "for the good of society," serving humanity with their skills and experience.

3.3. Theological education as an organic part of local church life and worship

Worshiping God cannot be limited to glorifying God during our Sunday meetings. We should not associate worshiping the Lord with directing the efforts of believers mainly to the inward life of a local church, because serving God implies the fulfillment of his mission by every member of the Body of Christ in the context of the missional vocation. Thus, theological education, as carried out through the gifts of teaching, the word of wisdom, and the word of knowledge, is also worshiping God and has the same importance and purpose as all other spiritual gifts, including the gifts of evangelism, counseling, pastoral ministry, and so on. (The New Testament lists at least nineteen spiritual gifts.)

Thus, just as the use of other spiritual gifts is an integral, organic part of the life of a local church in the Body of Christ, theological education is also an organic component of that life to fulfill its prophetic role in leading to the worship of God through the invitation to relationships of trust and love in the Kingdom of God. It is impossible to participate in the mission of God holistically if we do not realize that theological education is one of the gifts of the Holy Spirit and an organic part of the Church's worship.

4. Conclusion

Thinking about the practical application of the prophetic voice of theological education as worship, we need to remember that we are transformed into the image and likeness of who or what we worship.

Belief in the uniqueness of the origin of any nation, language, or race, or belief in the right of any nation to dominate other nations and races, controlling their natural and intellectual resources and defining for them what is good and evil, leads the Christian community to ruin the conciliatory nature of the Church.

The humbling of our racial and national pride before Christ leads the children of God to build up the Church by recognizing the diverse wealth of the Body of Christ, which consists of representatives of all races, nations, tribes, and languages, united by worshiping God together.

We do not deny our racial or national identities, but we overcome them, loving one other with the love of Christ, despite our differences. Racial, national, and linguistic distinctions in the Body of Christ bring varied blessings to all believers and glorify the Creator. These distinctions no longer dominate or divide the Body of Christ. Instead, all segments of Christ's Body worship the Lord together.

There is neither Jew nor Greek, Russian nor Ukrainian, male nor female, white nor black in Christ—not because we have renounced our nationality, language, or gender, but because our attitude toward one other is no longer based on our distinctions. It is rooted, rather, in the love of Christ, which he demonstrated on the cross. We worship God because we have accepted his love, and we express this love toward our neighbor, toward others, and toward those we consider to be our enemy or who consider us to be their enemy.

We are transformed into the image and likeness of who or what we worship. Theological education is a powerful tool for equipping Christian leaders and ministers, as well as laypeople, to be united in worshiping God, and for transforming our character into the character of Jesus. Theological education as a prophetic calling in the world and as the manifestation of the spiritual gifts for building up the Church leads us to the fulfillment of the mission of God, despite all the socio-political complexities, and is the invitation to relationships of trust and love in the Kingdom of God in the world and in our local churches.

About the Author

Taras was born into an Evangelical family with eleven children in the western Ukrainian city of Rivne. He graduated from Donetsk Christian University in 1997 with a Bachelor of Theology degree and earned his Master of Theology from the Evangelical Theological Faculty (Leuven, Belgium). Since 2011, he has served as the Regional Director of Overseas Council for Eastern Europe and Central Asia. His passion is to provide mission-minded theological education to fulfill the mission of God in the world. Taras also has more than 20 years of experience in teaching theology in Eastern Europe.

PART 3: THE WORD OF GOD, INTEGRITY AND HUMILITY

Itching Ears and Willing Learners: Balancing the Clarity and Complexity of Scripture

Bruce Barron

1. Introduction

The popularity of the "prosperity gospel," despite its tendencies toward simplistic and unbalanced theology, epitomizes one of the biggest problems in contemporary Christianity: how to provide adequately trained leaders for the global Christian movement, especially in the Majority World. This essay explores reasons why the problem exists, summarizes the contours of what all Christian leaders need to know, and identifies the Re-Forma organization cofounded by Manfred Kohl as a strategic solution.

2. How Deficient Theology Spreads

In 1987, I published *The Health and Wealth Gospel*, one of the first detailed studies of the strain of Christian teaching now widely referred to as the "prosperity gospel" or the "word-of-faith movement." At that time, the movement was largely a North American phenomenon, although a few disciples had taken the message overseas. In fact, Ray McCauley, a graduate of word-of-faith teacher Kenneth Hagin's Rhema Bible Training Center in Tulsa, Oklahoma, USA, was pastoring a large interracial congregation in South Africa and making positive contributions to racial reconciliation as that nation moved toward the close of its apartheid era.

Among the various criticisms of the prosperity gospel voiced during the 1980s, one common claim was that a message that couldn't go all over the world was not the true gospel. According to these detractors, the prosperity gospel was popular in rich, materialistic nations like the United States but could never survive in economically poorer areas.

By contrast, I thought the prosperity gospel could attract followers anywhere in the world, as long as prosperity was defined appropriately for the local context. For brash televangelists such as Kenneth Copeland or Jesse Duplantis, prosperity seems to mean a lavish lifestyle and multi-million-dollar jets; in rural Kenya, prosperity might mean a secure home, good health, two ample meals a day, and a few well-fed cows.

History has proved me right. During the last thirty years, the prosperity gospel has spread throughout the Global South and has overrun parts of Africa. After I began volunteering for the World Evangelical Alliance in 2015, two of its theological leaders asked me to consider updating *The Health and Wealth Gospel*; I said I could not do so properly without a global travel budget. I then asked a friend active in African relief work (ironically, a 1980s graduate of Rhema Bible Training Center whose theology had shifted over time) if he thought I needed to travel all over Africa to understand the impact of the prosperity gospel today. "No," he replied, "just go to Lagos or Nairobi and look at the billboards."

Of course, those aren't the only two cities impacted. For example, Yoseph Yisma, in his thesis at the Ethiopian Graduate School of Theology, has documented how the prosperity gospel migrated from Nigeria to Ethiopia and how it has affected the body of Christ there. In fact, it has spread so far and wide that one of the thirty-five outcomes identified by ReForma, the organization founded by Manfred Kohl and others to strengthen the quality of Christian instruction in parts of the world where church leaders receive little or no formal theological training, is that leaders should be able to "explain why the prosperity gospel is unbiblical and unethical." This is the only specific area of theological error identified in the thirty-five outcomes.

3. Teaching Good Theology Convincingly Can Be Hard

To a large extent, our problems with extreme versions of the prosperity gospel exist because of church leaders who are greedy for gain and followers with "itching ears" (2 Tim 4:3). But they also exist in part because of sincere Christians' desire to read the Bible and take it at face value. Therefore, we need to find a way to help these willing learners—especially those who aspire to become church leaders and teachers—to develop a sound theological foundation, even if they don't have the time or money to obtain formal seminary training.

Beliefs about divine healing provide a good illustration of the challenge. Christian believers read in Psalm 103:3 that God "heals all your diseases." They read Matthew's use of Isaiah 53:5, "With his stripes we are healed," in the context of Jesus' healings (Matt 8:17) and deduce that Jesus' atonement has guaranteed our physical as well as our spiritual health. They read of the many amazing miracles recorded in the book of Acts and see no reason why we should hope for less. They read of the broad New

Testament promises offered to believers (Mark 11:24; John 16:23; 1 John 3:22) and conclude that we too should receive whatever we ask if we exercise faith.

Direct efforts to convince such well-meaning believers that they may be misinterpreting the intent of Scripture often fail, because such explanations seem to deny the apparent meaning of the text. We might try to point out to them that God may heal all our diseases but not every time, or else we would never die. We might argue that Jesus' healings on earth demonstrated his messiahship but did not constitute a promise that all Christians henceforth would be healed. We might emphasize that the promises that we can move mountains (although I've never desired to relocate a mountain anyhow) or can have whatever we ask are all subject to our conformity to God's will. To such statements, our word-of-faith friend is likely to reply that we are making excuses rather than taking God at his word. Or, as Kenneth Hagin said more humbly when I pressed him to acknowledge that healings don't always occur even when we do everything right, "I'd rather aim high and get half of it than aim at nothing and get all of it."

4. "I Can Read the Bible for Myself" Has Its Limits

People who try to read the Bible for themselves, but without respect for the accumulated knowledge and experience of the Christian community, often go off the rails. The Jehovah's Witnesses, the "Jesus only" movement with Pentecostalism, and many others have departed from Christian truth in this way. To handle the word of God properly, we have to balance the Bible's clarity (the fancy theological word for this feature is *perspicuity*) and its complexity.

The perspicuity of Scripture was an important doctrine for the Protestant Reformation. Against the Catholic claim that laypeople could not be trusted to read the Bible for themselves and needed priests, bishops, and popes to explain it to them, Luther sought to make the Bible available to the people in their own language. He firmly defended the concept of "private judgment," or the right and duty of every believer to make their own informed decisions on matters of faith and doctrine.

The 1646 Westminster Confession of Faith expressed the principle of perspicuity in this way:

> All things in Scripture are not alike plain in themselves, nor alike clear unto all; yet those things which are necessary to be known, believed, and observed, for salvation, are so clearly propounded and opened in some place

of Scripture or other, that not only the learned, but the unlearned, in a due use of the ordinary means, may attain unto a sufficient understanding of them.

But even while stressing that the truths essential for salvation are clear, the Westminster divines also acknowledged that not everything in the Bible is clear. The condition of the contemporary Christian church makes this obvious. Today, dedicated Christians differ over the mode and appropriate age of baptism, church government, how to administer sacraments, speaking in tongues, and many other matters.

Even if these differences are not directly pertinent to salvation, error in non-essential matters can have enormous impact on individual lives and on the church's effectiveness. For example, those who anticipate Christ's return at a particular time or confidently anticipate a physical healing can be bitterly disappointed or publicly embarrassed when it doesn't happen. People who are not spiritually prepared for suffering may be tempted to abandon their faith when they face persecution. Some who trusted in a "modern-day prophet" have become trapped in authoritarian congregations or floundered spiritually when their leader went astray.

5. Keeping Zealous Believers on the Right Theological Track

To effectively deploy the next generation of Christian leaders, especially in areas where the church is growing but the number of trained pastors and teachers is insufficient, we must enable them to gain a firm grasp of foundational essentials, handle disputable matters with balance, and avoid fruitless rabbit holes.

Young Christians and new believers are the members of the body of Christ best positioned to communicate the gospel to outsiders. They have the greatest enthusiasm and the most personal contacts outside the Christian subculture. But they also usually have the least theological knowledge. In most places where Christianity is growing, scooping up such people and placing them in a seminary for three years—the prevailing approach to training in Western Christianity—is neither feasible nor culturally effective.

How can we best ensure that enthusiastic but still-learning Christians can guide others into spiritual maturity and holiness, not into serious error? The best answer seems to be to achieve a consensus on the essential biblical, theological, spiritual, interpersonal, and practical capacities needed for ministry leadership and to set up an efficient way to help people acquire those capacities, accompanied by ongoing discipleship.

One crucial ability often overlooked by those who claim they want to take the Bible at face value (and, in the process, often misinterpret it) is hermeneutics, or an understanding of proper interpretive principles. As a tongue-in-cheek way of demonstrating the need for good interpretive skills, I typically insist that the Bible does not let us eat at restaurants. When asked for proof, I turn to 1 Corinthians 11:34, where Paul tells his readers, "If anyone is hungry, let him eat *at home.*" I have yet to persuade anyone that Paul was warning believers to beware of the threat McDonald's posed to their spiritual lives. But the only way you can refute my goofy interpretation is by (1) showing that it is not consistent with the context of the verse and the cultural milieu of that time *and* (2) invoking the principle that interpretations that ignore the context, the surrounding culture, and the author's original intent are illegitimate. In the course of dispelling my silliness, you will realize that we must consistently watch out for creative, subjective interpretations that have no basis in the text—like some preachers' penchant for converting 3 John 2 from a friendly greeting into a guarantee of financial prosperity for all believers.

Where studying the Bible in its original languages is not possible, Christian leaders must be especially cautious about promoting new interpretive discoveries. Before I became a Christian, I was a nerdy, studious loner with poor social skills. When I began to read the Bible, I was excited to discover that Galatians 5:20 (in the Revised Standard Version) classified "party spirit" among the sins of the flesh. Only later, when I began to read the New Testament in other translations, did I discover that Paul was targeting people who sowed discord in the church, not people who enjoyed having fun in social settings. The correction of that error, which had resulted from reliance on a single English translation, had a dramatic impact. I actually began making a few friends and, eventually, even got married.

Theologically, Christian leaders must be able to explain to believers and inquirers alike why the church holds to complex convictions that can't be substantiated by a single proof text: why we affirm that God is a Trinity even though that word doesn't appear in the Bible; why we have overcome sin yet we still sin; why we still suffer and groan even though the kingdom of God has already come; and in what sense we are living in the "last days" when Jesus has tarried for two thousand years.

Spiritually, Christian leaders must sustain a daily, disciplined devotional life that keeps them humble, servant-like, and seeking the kingdom of God first. Interpersonally, they must express themselves with grace and sensitivity, articulating Christian truth unapologetically while never placing unnecessary obstacles in the way of belief or sending people on guilt trips (which the prosperity gospel has often done). Practically, they must apply the tools available to them, from liturgy to social media to cultural competence, so as to "by all means save some" (1 Cor 9:22).

That's a lot to learn. No wonder people go to seminary for three years—and even then they don't learn everything, especially in terms of practical ministry.

6. Conclusion: Thank You for This Solution, Manfred

There is a better way, and Manfred Kohl and Re-Forma have shown it to us. Without imposing any specific financial, travel, or course requirements, Re-Forma simply states, "This is what a collection of experienced Christians believe you need to know in order to function effectively today as a Christian leader. Show us that you know these things, or if you don't know them, we'll try to help you get there."

Re-Forma is an invaluable tool and a great legacy for which the church will be thanking Manfred for years to come. If widely embraced, it could empower willing learners for greater effectiveness, drown out the tempting siren songs that appeal to itching ears, and build greater unity in the global Christian movement.

About the Author

Bruce Barron (Ph.D., University of Pittsburgh) is senior editor for the World Evangelical Alliance and director of editorial services for the Society of Christian Scholars.

Confronting Lying Biblically in Honor- and Shame-Oriented Cultures

Ajith Fernando

1. Introduction

This essay seeks to find culturally sensitive and biblically driven ways to combat the epidemic of lying that is seen among Christians, especially in collectivist cultures, where shared community values are important and lying is often an acceptable value. A two-fold strategy is presented. First, make revulsion for lying a shared value. Then it would be considered a shame to lie, and shame is a powerful motivation for action in collectivist cultures. Second, let Christians know that the Bible teaches that God abhors lying and that lying will be judged.

It gives me great pleasure to write this in honor of my friend Dr. Manfred Kohl. He has sought to bring kingdom values to bear among Christians in the Majority World, especially through theological education. Among the values he paid attention to was integrity. So I thought I would make my contribution to this book by discussing ways to confront one of the commonest expressions of a lack of integrity in the church: lying.

2. An Acceptable Practice

Lying has become so acceptable in our nations that people do not hesitate before telling a lie. Every day many people in Sri Lanka recite, as part of their religious ritual, their resolve not to lie, but they break that resolution shortly after. It is a common practice to take sick leave when workers want to stay away from work for personal reasons or to agitate for their rights. Christians sometimes lie and add, "God is my witness," to buttress the lie.

A child cries when she sees her father leave home. Her Christian mother pacifies her by saying that he is going to a shop and will come back soon. Actually, he was leaving on a two-week trip. Some years later, when someone comes to the door and the daughter informs the mother about it, she tells her, "Tell him I'm not at home." This is the mother who introduced her daughter to Christianity. Over time, she comes to adopt the view that lying is acceptable for Christians.

The tendency to lie is part of our fallen nature and is adopted from the time a child learns to speak, even before he discovers that his parents lie. A two-year-old child who has just broken a glass is asked whether he is responsible for the accident. Without hesitation, he denies doing it.

There are also cultural motivations for lying in some societies. In most Asian cultures, honor and shame are major factors determining whether an action is right or wrong. This orientation that gives more prominence to honor and shame is growing in the West too. If an action brings shame on a person or a group, that action is considered wrong. According to this value system, if telling the truth brings shame, it is wrong to tell the truth.

The shame of telling the truth is especially seen when it comes to admitting that one has done something wrong. A friend of mine was falsely accused of being responsible for a costly mistake that happened in his office. His boss scolded him in obscene and insulting language in front of his colleagues when they were gathered for their tea break. Later a colleague told the boss that another member of the staff was responsible for the mistake. The next day, during the tea break, the boss praised my friend for the good work he is doing in the office. He did not accept his error. But he communicated my friend's innocence in a way that would make him not lose face.

3. Shared Values in Cultures with Strong Community Solidarity

How can we create a culture where lying is not tolerated? I will present two important biblical keys that are needed. The first key is related to the fact that because the Bible was written in a culture where honor and shame were important values, due attention was given to these values in the Bible.[1] Honor- and shame-oriented cultures are more community-oriented (or collectivist) than individualistic. Community solidarity is strong in these cultures. The community decides on what is honorable and what is shameful. Our challenge, then, would be to make truthfulness a shared honorable value in the community and lying a shameful value.

---

[1] This has been documented extensively by the writings of John J. Pilch and Bruce J. Malina. See especially Malina, *The New Testament World: Insights from Cultural Anthropology*, 3rd ed. (Louisville: Westminster John Knox, 2001); Pilch and Malina, eds., *Biblical Social Values and Their Meaning: A Handbook* (Peabody, MA: Hendrickson, 1993). See also David A. de Silva, *Honor, Patronage, Kinship, and Purity: Unlocking New Testament Culture* (Downers Grove, IL: InterVarsity Press, 2000).

The Bible is alert to the reality of the avoidance of shame being an important value. It uses this value to present sin as something shameful. The Bible often presents sin as shameful and righteousness as honorable. Matthew devotes a whole chapter to Jesus talking about the shamefulness of hypocrisy (Matt 23:1-39). Paul says, "But sexual immorality and all impurity or covetousness must not even be named among you, as is proper among saints. Let there be no filthiness nor foolish talk nor crude joking, which are out of place ... Take no part in the unfruitful works of darkness, but instead expose them. For it is shameful even to speak of the things that they do in secret" (Eph 5:3-4, 11-12).[2] In a section about family life, Paul presents neglect of elderly relatives as shameful. He says, "If anyone does not provide for his relatives, and especially for members of his household, he has denied the faith and is worse than an unbeliever" (1 Tim 5:8).

Applying the above to the problem that lying is not shameful in many societies, our task would be to help nurture attitudes within our Christian communities where lying is considered shameful and truth-telling honorable. We desire to see revulsion for lying becoming a shared value within our communities. That attitude would make its way into the behavior of Christians, who will find many disincentives to lying in the fellowship.

4. How the Bible Makes Revulsion for Lying a Shared Value

Though lying is not shameful in many communities, the Bible often presents it as a dishonorable act which is to be avoided.

4.1. Immediate confrontation

The first problem recorded in the Bible that the church faced related to the lie of Ananias and Sapphira. The response to that from the leader of the Church, Peter, was immediate confrontation: "Ananias, why has Satan filled your heart to lie to the Holy Spirit ...?" (Acts 5:3). A large gift had been given to the needy church. It was an act of generosity, as such gifts were voluntary (Acts 5:4). But Peter ignores the generosity and focuses on the lie they had told about having given all the proceeds from the sale of their land. Peter and God, through his harsh judgment, were sending a message to the church that lying was not tolerated.

---

[2] Unless otherwise indicated, Scripture quotations are from the ESV Bible (The Holy Bible, English Standard Version), Crossway 2001.

Usually when people, especially leaders, lie, others know that they have lied, but they overlook it. A leader comes late for a meeting one morning. The real reason for his coming late is that he got up late that morning. But it would be shameful to say that. So he says he was late because of the traffic he encountered. It is a religious holiday, and the people know that on such a holiday there is not much traffic on the road. They know their leader has lied. But no one confronts him, because they must protect the honor of the leader. They ignore the lie to keep up appearances. His earthly respect is preserved, but he has lost spiritual esteem which lies at the heart of biblical credibility. He will need to adopt earthly methods to maintain his honor in the church.

However, the Bible is sensitive to cultural issues when it comes to confronting sin and error in honor- and shame-oriented cultures. Confrontation must be done with sensitivity to the culture. In a passage on rebuking church members, the young pastor Timothy is told, "Do not rebuke an older man but encourage him as you would a father" (1 Tim 5:1). I have seen Westernized Christian leaders in Sri Lanka publicly rebuking older Christians in ways that humiliate them. I always felt that was an unnecessary violation of our cultural norms.

Significantly, Ananias and Sapphira lied about money. The Bible often warns about the dangers of loving riches (1 Tim 3:3; 6:9–10). Judas was dishonest about keeping accounts in Jesus' team (John 12:6). This is an area that has brought much scandal to the contemporary church. Christians distort the facts when applying for funding or when reporting about the use of funds. Some even doctor receipts to claim more than they spent. I have had salespeople, knowing that I will claim the funds from an organization, ask me how much they should write on the receipt. Inflating the price is considered almost a normal practice in society.

In an environment where lying is an acceptable practice, confronting it would be considered an example of disloyalty to people in the group. But Peter was willing to do this at a time when a member displayed great generosity.

4.2. God hates lying

Whatever culture Christians belong to, if they know God hates something, they would be careful to avoid it. God's hatred of lying is clear from the story of Ananias and Sapphira. Proverbs uses strong language when it says twice that "a lying tongue" and "lying lips" are an "abomination" to God (Prov 6:16–17; 12:22). Lying, then, is among those "abominations (*toʻebah*) that provoke loathing."³ This is shame language. It would be shameful for those committed to God to espouse something that God considers shameful. Preachers and teachers must be faithful in communicating to their people God's abhorrence of lying.

4.3. Lying violates our new identity

Our identity as Christians is very important to us. When we became Christians, there were some things we left behind because they violated our new identity. One of those things is lying. Paul said, "Do not lie to one another, seeing that you have put off the old self with its practices" (Col 3:9). Lying belongs to our old identity. Christians do not do that kind of thing anymore. It is contrary to our new identity as children of God. Like the previous point, this truth is something that must be communicated in preaching, teaching, discussions, and conversations. Because it may be distant from people's thinking when they become Christians, it needs to be communicated often. Sadly, many who pray to receive Christ do not realize that becoming a Christian includes a lifestyle of not lying. They received a message that was deficient in the area of repentance.

4.4. Lying violates Christian community

Corporate solidarity is a key value in community-oriented (collectivist) cultures. Members are expected to act as a unit in many situations. Corporate solidarity is an important aspect of Christian community too. But its essence is a spiritual unity coming out of union with Christ. We belong to his Body and our actions impact the Body. What is unique about spiritual unity is its emphasis on unity coming out of godly behavior. John said, "If we walk in the light, as he is in the light, we have fellowship with one another" (1 John 1:7). Walking in the light in the context of 1 John 1 included a sincere pursuit of God's ways and being honest about our failings.⁴ These two factors can be overlooked sometimes in collectivist cultures. One who fights on behalf of the community would be highly esteemed, even though everyone knows he is having an adulterous affair. In a biblical community, such a person would be disciplined and not permitted to represent the community. Christian solidarity includes spiritual accountability.

---

³ P. E. Koptak, *Proverbs,* The NIV Application Commentary (Grand Rapids: Zondervan, 2003), p. 190.
⁴ See John R. W. Stott, *The Letters of John: An Introduction and Commentary,* Tyndale New Testament Commentaries (Downers Grove, IL: InterVarsity Press, 1988), p. 79.

Included in walking in the light was truthfulness. Those who lie violate the Body and cannot have genuine "fellowship with one another." It is like a thumb sending a wrong message to the middle finger, thus making the hand dysfunctional. Paul says that being members of the Body of Christ is a reason for us to speak the truth: "Therefore, having put away falsehood, let each one of you speak the truth with his neighbor, for we are members one of another" (Eph 4:25). Conversely, when we lie to the body, we lie to God. Peter told Ananias that he lied to the Holy Spirit (Acts 5:3), not to man but to God (5:4).

Sadly, evangelical Christianity has been weak in its understanding of the doctrine of the Body of Christ. This has had many unhealthy effects on the life of the church. One of these is the loss of understanding that we violate the Body of Christ when we lie.

4.5. Lying is self-deception

John says, "If we say we have no sin, we deceive ourselves, and the truth is not in us" (1 John 1:8). In any culture it is shameful to deceive oneself. Only fools allow that to happen. Today many people lie to avoid shame. But in the new community we abstain from lying to avoid shame, because it is shameful to lie. It makes us into fools. Our cultures affirm that shame is an important factor in determining right and wrong. The Bible also affirms this, and it presents new criteria for shame. Lying was once honorable. But in the new community it is shameful.

4.6. Leaders set an example

At least six times Paul asked his readers to follow his example (1 Cor 4:16; 11:1; Phil 3:17; 4:9; 1 Thess 1:6; 2 Thess 3:9). He once told Timothy, "You, however, have followed my teaching, my conduct, my aim in life, my faith, my patience, my love, my steadfastness, my persecutions and sufferings that happened to me" (2 Tim 3:10-11). Donald Guthrie observes that the Greek word translated "have followed" (*parakoloutheō*) carries the meaning "to trace out as an example."[5] William Mounce explains that "almost every virtue ... [mentioned in 2 Tim 3:10-11] appears elsewhere in the [Pastoral Epistles] in an admonition to Timothy, either using the same word or the same concept."[6] Paul practiced what he preached and intended others to follow the example of his behavior.

---

[5] Donald Guthrie, *The Pastoral Epistles: An Introduction and Commentary*, Tyndale New Testament Commentaries (Downers Grove, IL: InterVarsity Press, 1990), p. 178.

[6] William D. Mounce, *Pastoral Epistles*, Word Biblical Commentary (Dallas: Word, 2000), p. 556.

The effect of the example of leaders is particularly powerful in collectivist cultures, where leaders are usually held in high esteem.[7] Their people trust them and are willing to follow them. When the people recognize that their leaders are holy people, there would be a major incentive to holiness in the community. It is matter of deep shame to me that many young Christians have told me that they cannot trust their leaders because they know they lie. Some have even told me that these leaders justify lying, using examples from the Old Testament. It would be dangerous to use narratives from exceptional situations and from an era lacking God's fuller revelation in Christ to disobey the explicit teaching in the Bible.

In a culture where lying is common, leaders who do not lie would stand out as a challenge to their people. The Bible talks of a person who is acceptable to God as one "who swears to his own hurt and does not change" (Ps 15:4). These are people who are known to be willing to suffer in order to keep their word and maintain their integrity. This is an attitude to the spoken word that stands in sharp contrast to the atmosphere of lying in the church.

I have a bad habit, when telling stories in a talk, of exaggerating to make the stories more striking. For example, I may describe a small meeting as a large gathering. I have learned to correct myself, then and there, when I do this. It is quite humiliating and usually the apology elicits a smile from the audience. But hopefully it gives people the message that lying is not tolerated in the church. For me, it also means that a hindrance to the free working of the Spirit through me is removed.

4.7. Habitual liars will change or leave

We said that community solidarity is an important factor in collectivist cultures. We said that we want this solidarity to extend to spiritual accountability. We also showed that for this extension of the idea of solidarity to spiritual accountability to take place, first, the community must teach the importance of truthfulness and the wrongness of lying. Second, it must require truthfulness from its members and confront lying when it appears. Third the leaders must demonstrate truthfulness by their exemplary lives.

In my forty-five years as a staff worker of Youth for Christ in Sri Lanka, I have tried to teach the importance of truthfulness often when I speak to volunteers and staff. I often say that in a youth movement we work

---

[7] For a fuller treatment of this theme see Ajith Fernando, *Discipling in a Multicultural World* (Wheaton, IL: Crossway, 2019), pp. 150–157.

through young volunteers who sometimes in their enthusiasm do unwise things and bring shame to the organization. I say that this is something that goes with youth work and that we are willing to bear that shame. But there is one thing we will not tolerate: lying. When a person lies, we cannot work with that person candidly. They cannot overcome their weaknesses as they do not admit to them, and we cannot trust them enough to have true Christian fellowship with them.

If a group pushes an abhorrence to lying in such an unmistakable way, people accustomed to lying will change or leave the group. We have seen both these scenarios in Youth for Christ. Some people have survived for a long period of time while lying. But it finally surfaces. And when confronted about it, they either change or leave.

A young man from a very dysfunctional background came to Christ in our ministry. He found great affirmation through the acceptance he received from his new Christian friends and through involvement in God's work. There was nothing he loved more than fellowship with our people and involvement in our work. But he continued to lie and use obscene language. He was often rebuked for this, but nothing seemed to help change him. Finally, he was disciplined and prohibited from getting involved in any of our programs. He felt like his world had come crashing down. He struggled for a time with deep anger and loneliness. But finally, God got through to him and he decided to follow Christ completely, renouncing the vestiges of his past life, including lying. Today, many years later, he is a leader who is having a wide and effective ministry.

Authentic biblical community life where truthfulness is a shared value, then, is a key to overcoming the cultural inclination to lying.

5. A Fuller Understanding of the Nature of God

The second key needed in creating a culture where lying is not tolerated in the church is a proper understanding of the nature of God.

5.1. The fear of judgment

Many people lie because they fear the consequences of telling the truth. Biblical Christians do not lie because they fear the consequences of lying. Paul said, "For we must all appear before the judgment seat of Christ, so that each one may receive what is due for what he has done in the body, whether good or evil" (2 Cor 5:10). This prospect elicits fear in the Christian, which motivates action. Paul continued, "Therefore, knowing the fear of the Lord, we persuade others" (5:11a). We are constantly aware of the fact that the "The Lord will judge his people" and that, "It is a fearful thing to fall into the hands of the living God" (Heb 10:30-31).

God has given us a glimpse of his attitude toward lying with the judgment on Ananias and Sapphira. That passage says twice that after their deaths "great fear came upon" the church (Acts 5:5, 11). Revelation 21:8 explicitly says, "But as for ... all liars, their portion will be in the lake that burns with fire and sulfur, which is the second death."

James explains how the prospect of judgment inspires us to be truthful. He urges his readers to be patient amid troubles and not to grumble (Jas 5:7-10). When things are getting tough, they may be tempted to escape from a dangerous situation. So he asks them to remain steadfast (5:11). Then he gives one aspect of being steadfast in tough times: "But above all, my brothers, do not swear, either by heaven or by earth or by any other oath, but let your 'yes' be yes and your 'no' be no" (5:12a). We must be truthful, however hard that is. And why? "So that you may not fall under condemnation" (5:12b). We live constantly with the reality that unrighteousness will be condemned. And that motivates us to be truthful even when the going gets tough.[8]

Of course, this fear of God's wrath is not a feeling that keeps us under bondage and destroys our freedom. It is a friend who alerts us to danger and directs us along the path to freedom.

5.2. The shame of judgment

Just as people lie because they fear the consequences of telling the truth, people also often lie to avoid the shame that comes from telling the truth. Yet the Bible teaches that the greatest shame is the shame that comes at the final judgment. I was able to find twenty-four passages in the New Testament which connect the judgment with shame. Those who were unprepared for the judgment are presented as fools (Luke 12:20; Matt 25:1-13), and there is going to be weeping and gnashing of teeth (Matt 8:12; 13:42, 50; 22:13; 24:51; 25:30).

While openness about confessing sin and telling the truth, regardless of the consequences, may be culturally distant to our people, shame is not! The prospect of extreme shame at the judgment would show them the folly of lying. So if the teachings about judgment in the Bible are true, we do people a favor by confronting them when they lie, because we help them to repent and avoid huge shame at the judgment.

---

[8] See Robert L. Plummer, *ESV Expository Commentary,* vol. 12, Hebrews–Revelation (Wheaton: Crossway Books, 2018), p. 279-280.

Today Christians do not die if they lie, as happened with Ananias and Sapphira. If that were to happen, many of our churches would be severely depleted! But during special revelatory periods God shows his will in unmistakable ways so that we know what he thinks. He has reserved his judgment to the end. There is a lot we do not know about judgment. But we know that Jesus clearly said, "Not everyone who says to me, 'Lord, Lord,' will enter the kingdom of heaven, but the one who does the will of my Father who is in heaven" (Matt 7:21). On the day of judgment, people will claim to have prophesied, cast out demons, and done many mighty works in Christ's name (7:22). But Christ will say to them "I never knew you; depart from me, you workers of lawlessness" (7:23). The prospect of shame at the coming judgment should encourage habitual liars to repent of their ways.

5.3. A culturally distant understanding of God

The above teachings about God are culturally very distant to people in both the West and the East. Many of the structures within Western culture were fashioned out of the belief that we are accountable to a supreme God who is morally pure and who will judge humanity. Humans are morally accountable to him. That enabled honesty and truthfulness to become part of the ethic of Western culture. Now, with the rejection of belief in a supreme God, we wonder how it will affect their understanding of morality. Already many revealed truths have been rejected and replaced by an ethic of inclusivity that regards some actions the Bible calls "sin" as human rights that must be affirmed. Already analysts are saying that the West is rejecting the idea of dependence on absolute truths to govern life. Shame is replacing ideas of sin and guilt.[9] One wonders how long the emphasis on truthfulness, which was generally considered a high value, will last.

In the East, often the gods are not viewed in terms of moral purity. In fact, certain behaviors of some gods could be characterized as grossly immoral. People follow the prescriptions dictated by the god or his representative to ensure that they receive a blessing from the god. They are not accountable to this god for all their actions. Often the gods are more like doctors to whom they go for help with specific needs, but who do not make moral demands of them. So you may find underworld figures who are

---

[9] Roland Muller, *Honor and Shame: Unlocking the Door* (n.p.: Xlibris Corporation, 2000), p. 52; Alan Mann, *Atonement in a "Sinless" Society: Engaging with an Emerging Culture* (Milton Keynes: Paternoster, 2005), pp. 31–59. Mann, however, says that shame in the post-industrialized West is different from that in shame- honor-oriented societies, being "an intensely private affair" (p. 37).

fervent devotees of a god and who contribute generously to this god's shrine. There is not much of the doctrine of a future judgment in Eastern religions. Many adherents believe in reincarnation or rebirth, but the karma that is carried on to the next birth is distant from the person born, who has no recollection of his previous life. So the prospect of judgment is often not a big motivating factor in behavior.

When people from such backgrounds become Christians, they often *transfer* their ideas of the gods to the Christian God. They also view him as a doctor to go to for needs, not as one to whom they are accountable for all their actions. Their understanding of God needs to be *transformed* to the biblical idea of a holy God to whom we are accountable regarding all we do. A lot of the preaching new believers hear is oriented toward promising God's blessings to them. And this can further buttress their idea of God being merely like a doctor who meets needs. Such "blessings preaching" must be augmented by preaching that incorporates the idea of accountability to a morally pure God.

The church must be proactive in helping to transform people's understandings of God to incorporate the idea of judgment and accountability. That must become part of their worldview, their approach to life.[10] An occasional sermon on judgment may not suffice to effect so major a change. Worldviews are imbibed through constant exposure more than incorporated through a stray sermon. The biblical approach to the issue is to include judgment as part of our approach to life and to mention it even while speaking about different topics. Sometimes it is given as an aside, a small part of a larger picture. We need to be talking about judgment in ordinary conversation. In this way it unconsciously becomes part of our approach to life.[11] Ideally Christians should be taking judgment into account in all the decisions they make. In the history of the church, judgment has been misused in Christian proclamation and presented in unbalanced ways. But misuse does not warrant disuse. If it is not part of the worldview of Christians, a major aid along the path to holiness has been overlooked.

6. Conclusion

We have presented a two-fold strategy to combat the epidemic of lying in the church. First, make revulsion for lying a shared value. Then it would

---

[10] See Martin E. Marty, "Hell Disappeared. No One Noticed. A Civic Argument," *Harvard Theological Review*, Vol. 78 (3–4) (1985), p. 386.
[11] See Ajith Fernando, *Crucial Questions about Hell* (Wheaton: Crossway Books, 1994), chapter 14, "Proclaiming the Message of Judgment."

be considered a shame to lie. And shame is a powerful motivation for action, especially in collectivist cultures. Second, let Christians know that the Bible teaches that God abhors lying and that it will be judged.

When a friend of mine heard that I was writing this article, he wrote to me to say that he regularly prays the prayer of Proverbs 30:8a: "Remove far from me falsehood and lying."[12] Jeremiah exclaimed, "The heart is deceitful above all things, and desperately sick; who can understand it?" (Jer 17:9). If that is so, it would be wise for all of us to pray that prayer regularly!

About the Author

Ajith Fernando holds a Th.M. in New Testament from Fuller Seminary. After leading Youth for Christ in Sri Lanka, for thirty-five years, Ajith now serves as its Teaching Director. His work includes teaching, mentoring, discipling, and counseling younger Christians and Christian leaders. His grassroots ministry is with the urban poor. He is the author of 20 books published in 24 languages and of numerous booklets. He serves as adjunct lecturer at Colombo Theological Seminary. Ajith and his wife Nelun live in Colombo, Sri Lanka and are active in the Nugegoda Methodist Church. They have two married children and four grandchildren.

---

[12] Personal correspondence with Dr Ebenezer Perinbaraj, 6th July 2021.

Faithful Ministry: An Exposition of 2 Timothy

Kevin G. Smith

1. Introduction

At the end of his life, Paul the apostle wrote a parting letter to his closest ministry partner, his true son and trusted apprentice, Timothy.[1] He found himself in a Roman prison, awaiting execution for the crime of preaching the gospel of Jesus Christ (Lea and Griffin 1992, 179). As the pressure mounted, he had seen trusted ministers turn aside to false teachings and witnessed faithful believers turning away from Christ. As he waited for the inevitable, his thoughts turned to his dearest ministry companion, his "true child in the faith" (1 Tim 1:2). As he remembered Timothy, two emotions dominated his frame of mind. First, he longed to see his son and apprentice one last time. He opens and closes with this human longing (2 Tim 1:3-5; 4:9-21). Second, he wanted to ensure that Timothy did not suffer the same fate as others who had drifted or deserted the gospel, to ensure that Timothy remained faithful to the Lord and the call of the gospel despite the pressures confronting him. This concern dominates the body of the letter as he charges and exhorts Timothy to remain faithful under fire (1:3-4:8).

What does it mean for a servant of Jesus Christ to remain faithful under fire? What should a departing apostle say to his true child before he dies? We do not need to guess because Paul left us his charge to Timothy in the letter we know as 2 Timothy. The body of the letter is an extended call to faithful ministry, designed to keep Timothy on track once his mentor was no longer present to guide him.

As we celebrate the twilight years of Dr. Manfred Kohl's life and ministry, there are similarities to Paul's context. Dr. Kohl has been a spiritual

---

[1] I take the truth claims of Scripture as innocent until proven guilty. The epistle purports to be a personal letter from Paul the apostle to Timothy his spiritual child and ministry partner, written while Paul was in prison anticipating his imminent death. Although the spirit of academia treats this implied situation with skepticism, the objections to Paul's authorship of the letter are too circumstantial to offer compelling grounds for believers to distrust the face-value claims of God's inspired Word.

father and mentor to many. What charge might he give them to help them remain faithful to the Lord and the gospel after he is gone? I humbly propose that Dr. Kohl's charge might run parallel to the apostle Paul's, casting a vision of what ministry faithfulness looks like, actively grounding it in a gospel-centered worldview.

Second Timothy is a personal letter from Paul to his protégé on the brink of the apostle's death. The majority of the letter consists of personal instruction as the master counsels and exhorts his student, painting a portrait of what faithful ministry ought to look like (Magnum 2014). The body of the letter divides quite naturally into six pericopes. The dominant tone of each is hortatory (Thompson 2016) because Paul is urging Timothy to live and minister in ways that are faithful to the nature of the gospel. The six exhortations offer a vision of faithful ministry that remains as relevant to contemporary pastors as they were to Timothy. They are as follows:

- Champion the gospel (2 Tim 1:3–18)
- Sacrifice for the gospel (2 Tim 2:1–13)
- Instruct false teachers (2 Tim 2:14–26)
- Avoid counterfeit ministries (2 Tim 3:1–9)
- Follow trustworthy sources (2 Tim 3:10–17)
- Preach the Word (2 Tim 4:1–8)

For the remainder of this chapter, I will expound 2 Timothy under these headings, showing how it paints a portrait of gospel-centered ministry and exhorts faithful ministers to live out that vision.

2. Champion the Gospel (2 Tim 1:3–18)

Do verses 3–18 cohere as a single section of the letter? Paul begins by giving thanks for Timothy's sincere faith (vv. 3–5). "For this reason" (δι' ἣν αἰτίαν, v. 6), he reminds Timothy to rekindle his gift without being afraid (vv. 6–7). "So" (οὖν, v. 8) he urges Timothy not to be ashamed of the gospel, but to join him in suffering for it (vv. 8–12), both following its sound guidance and protecting it as a sacred treasure (vv. 13–14). Paul concludes by reminding Timothy of two who abandoned him (v. 15) and one who was not ashamed of his chains (vv. 16–18). After a little reflection, the unity of Paul's thought in these verses becomes clear.

The unifying idea is "the gospel" (v. 8). The gospel lies at the center of all faithful Christian service. Paul briefly describes it in these words:

> He [God] has saved us and called us to a holy life—not because of anything we have done but because of his own purpose and grace. This grace was given us in Christ Jesus before the beginning of time, but it has now been revealed through the appearing of our Savior, Christ Jesus, who has destroyed death and has brought life and immortality to light through the gospel. (2 Tim 1:9-10)

This is the ideological bedrock of Christian ministry. God has saved us and called us to a holy life through Christ Jesus, who has destroyed death and brought life and immortality to light through the gospel. It calls forth zealous service (vv. 6-7), courageous suffering (vv. 8-12), and careful protection (vv. 13-14).

The message of what God has done in and through Christ remains the only firm foundation for Christian ministry. Like Paul, we believe that human beings are without holiness and without hope apart from grace. But God saves sinners and calls them to a holy life. This glorious grace is provided only through Jesus Christ, whose virgin birth, virtuous life, vicarious death, and victorious resurrection destroyed death and brought life and immortality. This message, the gospel, remains scandalous to the academic elite of our day. We may be tempted to soften it or syncretize it with more palatable modern philosophies to make our ministries more marketable to mainstream society, but we dare not (v. 15).

Paul's opening charge to Timothy has the gospel as its fulcrum. Because the gospel is the only message of life, he urges Timothy not to be afraid or ashamed of it. We can outline the big ideas in this way: The gospel is the only message of life (vv. 9-10). Therefore,

- believe it sincerely (vv. 3-5),
- proclaim it boldly (vv. 6-7, 11),
- suffer for it courageously (vv. 8, 12), and
- protect it diligently (vv. 13-14).

In short, be faithful and courageous like Onesiphorus (vv. 16-18), not unfaithful and cowardly like Phygelus and Hermogenes (v. 15).

Paul points out four implications of building our ministries on the gospel that are as relevant to contemporary believers as they were to Timothy. Let us unpack them.

We must believe the gospel sincerely (vv. 3-5). Their relationship left Paul with no doubt about Timothy's "sincere faith" (v. 5). Although it may seem surprising for Paul to mention this, the Pastoral Letters are sprinkled with previously trusted co-workers and leaders who turned from the truth of the gospel, raising doubts about the sincerity of their faith. Hymenaeus and Alexander (1 Tim 1:19–20), Phygelus and Hermogenes (2 Tim 1:15), Hymenaeus and Philetus (2 Tim 2:17), and Demas (2 Tim 4:10) are likely all men who seemed to have sincere faith but departed from it. The ministry institutions of our day are littered with men and women who have lost their sincere faith in the gospel, yet they remain as ministry "professionals." The problem is perhaps most acute in faculties of theology when professors have lost their faith and continue teaching so that they can help the students to lose theirs too. If you lose your sincere faith in the gospel as the only hope of the world, you should get out of ministry.

We must proclaim the gospel boldly (vv. 6–7, 11). God called Paul to proclaim the gospel as a preacher, apostle, and herald (v. 11). He had gifted and called Timothy to preach the gospel too, and Timothy needed to ensure that he never allowed his zeal for proclaiming the good news to diminish (v. 6). Love for Christ and the lost compel him to preach; fear of persecution must not silence him (v. 7). Every true minister needs to defend the primacy of the gospel in their ministry, not allowing anything to undermine its centrality—not the restless cult of novelty that plagues academia, not the quest for professional respectability that tempts pastors, and not the sophistication of political correctness that dominates the postmodern world.

We must suffer for the gospel courageously (vv. 8, 12). Paul was not ashamed to suffer for the gospel (v. 12). He urges Timothy not to be ashamed to suffer for the testimony of the Lord (v. 8). In Paul's case, the suffering was physical imprisonment that would soon culminate in martyrdom. In Timothy's context, it was cultural pressure to conform to the norms of a pagan society that found the gospel naïve and offensive. We face both threats and temptations in our twenty-first-century world. In some parts of the world, believers are violently persecuted and murdered for their faith in Jesus Christ. In the post-Christian Western world, we experience social and psychological pressure to compromise the gospel that our societies find abhorrent. Let us beware lest we confuse contextualization for compromise.

We must protect the gospel diligently (vv. 13–14). "By the Holy Spirit who dwells within us, guard the good deposit entrusted to you" (v. 14; cf. 1 Tim 6:20). The emphasis is to protect the gospel against false teachers and teachings that threaten to distort it (Knight 1992, 381).

In the light of Paul's suffering and imminent death as a minister of the gospel, Timothy must not be afraid to stand for it or ashamed to share it, but he should proclaim, persevere in, and protect the gospel with the help of the indwelling Spirit (Mounce 2000, 490). Paul's doctrine of election does not lead him to view the risks to Timothy as purely hypothetical. The contrasting examples of Phygelus and Hermogenes (v. 15) and Onesiphorus (vv. 16-18) show that faithfulness is possible but not guaranteed.

3. Sacrifice for the Gospel (2 Tim 2:1-13)

In the face of the related threats of desertion and persecution, Paul exhorts Timothy to stand strong, since the Christian minister is called to labor and to suffer for the gospel. The chapter opens with the words, "You then, my son" (Σὺ οὖν, τέκνον μου, v. 1). These words position it as a response to the situations described in chapter 1 (Wall and Steele 2012, 235). What situations? First, the threat of persecution is real. Paul is in prison awaiting execution for preaching the gospel. Persecution is in the air. Although he is in Rome and state persecution has not yet reached Ephesus, Jesus' disciples are in imminent danger. Secondly, the threat of desertion is real. Paul and Timothy know fellow workers who have turned from the truth, perhaps to avoid suffering and to make their message more politically correct in their context. To strengthen his resolve to remain true to the gospel, Paul offers his son four commands, three metaphors, and three examples.

The four commands (2:1-7).[2] This paragraph charges Timothy with four commands. They presuppose the twin threats of persecution and desertion. First, he must "be strong in the grace that is in Christ Jesus" (v. 1). I prefer to translate the passive imperative ἐνδυναμοῦ "be strengthened" to underline the fact that Timothy should allow God to strengthen his resolve through the grace that is in Christ. Faced with fear of suffering and temptation to compromise, Timothy must *be strong*; the resources to stand firm come from Christ and his grace. Secondly, Timothy must entrust Paul's message "to reliable people who will also be qualified to teach others" (v. 2). If only a few top leaders spread the gospel, the empire can easily cut off the head of the dragon, but if an underground network of trustworthy people disseminates it, organized persecution cannot scatter the sheep by striking their shepherds. Thirdly, Timothy must "join with me in suffering" (v. 3). The gospel calls for suffering and sacrifice. The faithful minister must be willing to endure suffering and embrace sacrifice. This is the central thought of the paragraph, so Paul unpacks it with the three metaphors (see below). Finally, Timothy must "reflect on what I am saying" (v. 7). The connection between faithfulness and suffering is counterintuitive. If you

---

[2] Although there are five imperatives—ἐνδυναμοῦ ("be strong," v. 1), παράθου ("entrust," v. 2), συγκακοπάθησον ("join in suffering," v. 3), νόει ("reflect," v. 7), and μνημόνευε ("remember," v. 8)—I am treating the last one as introducing three examples of people who embodied the response Paul was urging from Timothy.

faithfully serve your God, and he is the true God, you should prosper, right? Paul wants Timothy to think deeply about the biblical connection between gospel ministry and suffering because wrong expectations will derail his faith. If he reflects on Paul's teaching, the Lord will give him insight into it (v. 7).

The three metaphors (2:3–6). The willingness to suffer and sacrifice in service of the gospel lies at the heart of this passage. Paul drives it home with three metaphors—the *soldier* who disciplines himself and embraces hardship to please his commander (vv. 3–4), the *athlete* who must compete by the rules to win (v. 5), and the *farmer* who must work hard but then gets to enjoy the fruits of his labor (v. 6). The metaphors serve to galvanize the young pastor's resolve to please God, endure hardship, live by the gospel, work hard, and receive his reward at harvest time.

The three examples (2:8–13). After urging Timothy to be willing to suffer and sacrifice in service of the gospel, Paul encourages him to reflect on these things because the Lord will grant him insight (v. 7). In 2 Timothy 2:8–13, Paul drives these truths home by giving three examples to show that faithful disciples of Christ suffer. First, Jesus Christ suffered and died (v. 8). Secondly, Paul was suffering (vv. 9–10). He was in prison for the gospel. He was willing to "endure everything" so that the elect could "obtain the salvation that is in Christ Jesus." Thirdly, Paul quotes a trustworthy saying to show that it is normal for believers to face hardship and death with and for Jesus, needing to remain faithful so that they can live and reign with him (vv. 11–13). The flow is from the Head to the members—Jesus suffered faithfully for the gospel; Paul suffered faithfully for the gospel; believers must suffer faithfully for the gospel.

In our post-Christian world, all who lead God's people face temptations to desert or distort the gospel and pressures to make their message more politically correct than it is. Some endure full-blown persecution. The Lord calls all his disciples to be willing to sacrifice for the sake of the gospel. We find our strength in Christ's grace. We share our message with other faithful servants—not stars, just servants. We endure hardship like soldiers and work tirelessly like farmers. We think deeply about these things, realizing that the prosperity gospel holds out false hope—Jesus suffered, Paul suffered, all believers must be willing to die with Christ in order to live with him.

4. Instruct False Teachers (2 Tim 2:14–26)

The focus shifts from hardship to heresy as Paul instructs his protégé about how to deal with false teachers in the churches. He uses three metaphors to frame his vision of how to deal with false teachers—namely, the approved workman, the clean instrument, and the humble servant. Timothy should handle false teachers as an approved workman by rightly handling the Word (vv. 14-19), as a clean instrument by earnestly pursuing righteousness (vv. 20-22), and as a humble servant by gently instructing opponents (vv. 23-26).

The approved workman (2:14-19). The faithful minister must present himself to God as an approved workman who handles the Word of God correctly (v. 15). "Do your best" (σπούδασον, v. 15) refers to being "especially conscientious in discharging an obligation" (Danker et al. 2000, s.v. 3), having "keen interest" or "intense desire" (Thompson 2015, s.v. 1) to do something. The faithful minister has an intense desire to handle the Word of God correctly, and they work conscientiously to present themselves to God as worthy of approval in this duty. Sadly, many ministers evidence little conscientious effort or intense desire to present themselves as approved workmen who can handle the Scriptures well. We should be the ultimate lifelong learners.

Paul wants Timothy to prioritize the positive side of preaching and teaching the truth in the church over the negative temptation to become embroiled in fruitless debates with false teachers. He repeatedly cautions the young minister not to let discussions with them distract him from more fruitful uses of his time.

The clean instrument (2:20-22). To stand against the rising tide of error and temptation, the faithful minister needs to be a clean instrument, earnestly pursuing righteousness. Paul introduces this point by an analogy—a large house has vessels for noble use and vessels for common use (v. 20). Then he applies the idea to ministry usefulness—holy people are useful to the Master (v. 21). Last, he applies it to Timothy's ministry, especially his struggle against false teachers. Timothy must "flee the evil desires of youth and pursue righteousness, faith, love and peace, along with those who call on the Lord out of a pure heart" (v. 22). God works only through clean vessels. Purity and power go together.

The humble servant (2:23-26). When it comes to engaging with false teachers, the faithful minister should adopt the posture of a humble servant, gently instructing opponents. Paul again warns Timothy to steer clear of controversies and quarrels (v. 23). As "the Lord's servant" (δοῦλον κυρίου, v. 24), he must "correct his opponents with gentleness" (v. 25). Being kind and enduring evil makes it easier for them to repent if God convicts them (vv. 25-26). The entire approach is salted with humility. The gospel minister knows that it is not his powerful rhetoric that will bring a deceived person to their senses. Only the convicting power of God's Spirit can bring them to repentance and set them free from the devil's snare. Therefore, he avoids quarreling, endures insults, speaks kindly, and instructs gently, praying that God will break through the person's defenses.

Every Christian leader should make it their mission to represent Christ as an approved workman, a clean instrument, and a humble servant. To be approved workmen, our first duty is to "rightly handle the word of truth" (v. 15). This calls for a positive and a negative response. On the positive side, we must make every effort to acquire the knowledge and skills we need to rightly handle God's Word. On the negative side, we must guard against letting the good distract us from the best. While it may be good to engage the causes and philosophies of our day, they should not become our focus. Since only clean vessels are useful to the Master, we should prioritize holy living. When it comes to the work, he calls us to be humble servants. We should treat all people kindly, gently instructing opponents. If we realize that only God can grant repentance and open the eyes of the deceived, it frees us to be humble servants instead of egotistical saviors.

5. Avoid Counterfeit Ministries (2 Tim 3:1–9)

Despite the warning about "terrible times in the last days" (v. 1), Paul is not writing about the general deterioration of the world in the lead-up to Christ's return. "The last days" is the period between Christ's two comings (Van Neste 2008, 2341). The conjunction δέ, rendered "but," links this to the preceding discussion of how to handle false teachers. Δέ is a "development marker," signaling a distinct development in the argument about false teachers (Runge 2010, 31). Although Paul hopes the false teachers will come to repentance (old idea—2:23–26), he does not harbor unrealistic hopes (new development—3:1–9) (Fee 2011, 268).

This pericope is built around two imperatives, namely, "mark" (γίνωσκε, v. 1) and "avoid"[3] (ἀποτρέπου, v. 5b). They stand in a ground-inference relationship.

- Ground: Timothy should expect terrible times characterized by all kinds of sinfulness (3:1–5a).
- Inference: Therefore, Timothy should avoid such people (3:5b–9).

---

[3] The NIV renders it "have nothing to do with," which is accurate. I am using the shorter gloss "avoid" so that it is clear to the English reader that it is a single imperative in Greek.

Who are these people whom Timothy should avoid? Both Paul's theology and the context of the letter leave us in no doubt that he is not referring to outsiders (1 Cor 5:9-13). The crucial clue comes in verse 5a; Timothy must avoid people "having a form of godliness but denying its power." They have "a form of godliness" in the sense that they are religious and spiritual, presenting themselves as believers. They "deny its power" in that they do not believe or proclaim the true gospel, which is the only source of power that produces authentic godliness. Who are they? They are the false teachers, who present themselves as servants of God and ministers of the gospel, but whose lives and teachings do not follow the true gospel.

Paul's exhortation to Timothy is twofold. First, he should expect such counterfeit ministers and ministries. He should not be surprised or dismayed. He knows this is what will happen in the last days (Fee 2011, 268). Secondly, he should "have nothing to do with such people" (v. 5b), referring to fellowship or partnership. He should not legitimize their "ministries" by treating them as co-laborers or contaminate his ministry by partnering with "religious charlatans" (268).

What does this teach us about faithful ministry? First, we should not be surprised by anything the last days throw at us. We should not be shocked when sinners love and endorse sin or dismayed that fallen societies oppose God's ways. We should expect counterfeit ministries that have "a form of godliness but deny its power" (i.e., the gospel). Secondly, we should "have nothing to do with such people." We should gently instruct them (2 Tim 2:24-26), but we should not co-labor with them. This could take various forms. Bible-based ministries should not partner with liberal theological institutions that teach not from a gospel-centered worldview but from a set of presuppositions anchored in methodological naturalism (Carter 2018). We should be wary of words or actions that might legitimize ministries that we know to be doctrinally dubious. The immortal words of Ignatius to Polycarp echo Paul's caution to all pastors: "Those who appear to be trustworthy yet teach strange doctrines, do not let them amaze you. Stand firm, like an anvil being struck *with a hammer. It is the mark of a* great athlete to endure punishment and to achieve victory" (Ign. Pol. 3:1, trans. Brannan 2012).

6. Follow Trustworthy Sources (2 Tim 3:10-17)

How can Timothy avoid the traps that tripped up others? Under the social pressure to conform to Roman beliefs and values and the rising threat of persecution, other co-workers had yielded and compromised their message (1 Tim 1:19-20; 2 Tim 1:15; 2:17; 4:10). How can the departing apostle ensure that his best apprentice does not follow the same trajectory? Paul urges his protégé not to be like the false teachers, but to continue in the way he had learned because he knows that the two key sources, Paul and Scripture, are trustworthy.

This pericope is built around two occurrences of σὺ δέ, "but you," at the start of verses 10 and 14. They set Timothy in contrast to the deceivers mentioned in the preceding verses. The preceding verses warn about deceivers and deceptions, but Timothy has two firm bases for not following them—Paul's example (3:10-13) and the Holy Scriptures (3:14-17).

False Teachers	Contrast	Timothy's Experience
3:1-9	3:10	3:10-13
The last days will be characterized by false teachers with a form of godliness but without the gospel.	"but you"	Timothy's ministry is grounded on the example of Paul the apostle, who modeled godliness and sacrifice.
3:13	3:14	3:14-17
Evildoers and imposters will go from bad to worse, deceiving and being deceived.	"but you"	Timothy's ministry is grounded on the inspired Word of God, which has equipped him for every good work.

Timothy should not be like the false teachers because he has followed Paul's teaching and example (3:10-13). He knows what authentic gospel-centered ministry looks like because he has seen it firsthand. The NIV renders παρηκολούθησάς as "you know" (v. 10). Danker et al. (2000, s.v. 3) define it as "to conform to someone's belief or practice by paying special attention, *follow faithfully, follow as a rule*." Thompson (2015, s.v. 1) suggests "to attend or pay attention in minute and careful detail." Timothy knows everything about the master apostle's teaching, lifestyle, and suffering. He does not know it in a general sense; he knows it in meticulous detail. He does not know it intellectually; he has lived by the same values and experienced the same things. He has learned what to teach, how to live, and what to expect (persecution from men and protection by God). This firsthand knowledge of the real should help him not to fall for the counterfeit.

Timothy should not be like the false teachers because he has followed the teachings of Scripture (3:14-17). He not only knows Paul's example; he also knows the Holy Scriptures. He has known them since childhood (i.e., he knows them thoroughly). His wisdom and salvation are grounded upon his knowledge of the Scriptures (v. 15). Since the Word of God equips the man of God for faithful and fruitful works of service (vv. 16-17), Timothy's thorough knowledge of the Scriptures should inoculate him against deceivers and deception (v. 13).

What is the abiding challenge for ministers wanting to remain faithful? We should be careful about the people and books that we allow to influence us. We should not follow or imitate false teachers. They come in various shapes and forms, from the false prophets of hyper-charismatic groups to liberal theologians who have doctorates but no living faith.[4] Instead, we need two things. First, we need inspiring role models whose living faith we can follow in life and unto death. They may be present or past heroes of faith. Secondly, we need to know the Scriptures thoroughly and trust them completely. The Word of God makes us wise for salvation and equips us for service. When our go-to source for wisdom and guidance ceases to be the Bible and becomes other sources, whether books or people, we are on shaky ground.

7. Preach the Word (2 Tim 4:1-8)

Second Timothy 4 is the closing chapter of Paul's life and writings. A person's last words to their loved ones are extremely important, especially if they know they are speaking their last words. Although Paul hoped to see Timothy one last time, he knew these would likely be his final words to his beloved son. Therefore, he opens with the most solemn charge he can (Collins 2012, 265): "In the presence of God and of Christ Jesus, who will judge the living and the dead, and in view of his appearing and his kingdom, I give you this charge" (v. 1).

In discourse language, this is called a meta-comment—when authors interrupt their flow of thought to make a preparatory comment about what is to follow (Runge 2008; 2010, 101-24). Meta-comments signal that what is about to follow is especially important to the author. This is no ordinary meta-comment; it is an *uber* meta-comment conveying a solemn charge that is to be carried out in the full awareness that Christ, the Judge of the living and the dead, is watching. Paul is signaling that what he is

---

[4] I am not inherently opposed to doctorates or charismatics—I am charismatic and I have two doctorates.

about to say is *the most important thing* he wants to tell Timothy. If the apostle were forced to reduce his final letter to his protégé to a tweet, he would have tweeted 4:2a—Preach the Word!

This pericope has two paragraphs in an idea-ground relationship.

- Idea: Preach the Word (4:1-5)
- Ground: because the time for my departure is near (4:6-8)

In the light of his imminent death and the assured influence of false teachers in the last days, Paul charges Timothy to preach the Word. This is the foremost calling of a faithful minister.

Paul unpacks his exhortation for Timothy to preach the Word in verses 2-5. First, he must preach the Word at all times: "in season and out of season" (v. 2). Secondly, he must preach it in all ways: "correct, rebuke and encourage—with great patience and careful instruction" (v. 2). Thirdly, he must preach the Word because people need sound doctrine even if they don't want it (vv. 3-4). The loving parent gives children what they need without pandering to what they want. Finally, he must preach the Word as a crucial part of "discharg[ing] all the duties of your ministry" (v. 5).

There should be no higher priority for a faithful minister than to *preach the Word*. The apostles guarded it jealously (Acts 6:2). If only more pastors followed their example. The pastors I know seem to spend their time and energy managing the church or counseling its members. These are good things, but they often come at the expense of the best thing—learning and teaching God's inspired Word.

8. Conclusion

How amazing that the Holy Spirit saw fit to leave us the parting charge of a master apostle to his dearest protégé as part of our canon. How apt that it was written in the context of pressure, persecution, and desertion to paint a portrait of what it means to be faithful under fire as a servant of the gospel of Jesus Christ. Paul left us with an amazing portrait of what faithful ministry should look like. He opens with a challenge to put the gospel at the center of all ministry, being neither afraid nor ashamed, but determined to proclaim it, persevere in it, and protect it. He reminded us that the gospel calls forth sacrifice and suffering. Since false teachers will always be a threat during the last days, the faithful minister is to focus on rightly handling the truth of God's Word, cultivating righteousness, and gently instructing those who oppose the gospel. The final part of the letter emphasizes the central place the Scriptures ought to hold in the minister's life, climaxing with the challenge to "preach the Word" (2 Tim 4:2). According to tradition, Timothy served faithfully as bishop of Ephesus until AD 97. During a pagan festival, he was severely beaten for preaching against idolatry; he died two days later from his injuries (Foxe 1563, 10). If the tradition is true, Paul's charge bore fruit.

References

Brannan, Rick, trans. 2012. *The Apostolic Fathers in English*. Bellingham, WA: Lexham Press.
Carter, Craig A. 2018. *Interpreting Scripture with the Great Tradition: Recovering the Genius of Premodern Exegesis*. Grand Rapids, Michigan: Baker Academic. Scribd.
Collins, Raymond F. 2012. *1 & 2 Timothy and Titus*. Edited by C. Clifton Black, M. Eugene Boring, and John T. Carroll. The New Testament Library. Louisville, Kentucky: Westminster John Knox.
Danker, Frederick W., Walter Bauer, William F. Arndt, and F. W. Gingrich. 2000. *A Greek-English Lexicon of the New Testament and Other Early Christian Literature*. 4th edition. Chicago, Illinois: University of Chicago Press.
Fee, Gordon D. 2011. *1 and 2 Timothy, Titus*. Understanding the Bible Commentary Series. Grand Rapids, Michigan: Baker.
Foxe, John. 1563. *Actes and Monuments: [The Book of Martyrs]*. London: John Day. Kindle edition.
Knight, George W. 1992. *The Pastoral Epistles: A Commentary on the Greek Text*. NIGTC. Grand Rapids, Michigan: Eerdmans.
Lea, Thomas D., and Hayne P. Griffin. 1992. *1, 2 Timothy, Titus*. The New American Commentary 34. Nashville, Tennessee: Broadman & Holman.
Magnum, Douglas. 2014. *The Lexham Glossary of Literary Types*. Bellingham, WA: Lexham Press.
Mounce, William D. 2000. *Pastoral Epistles*. Word Biblical Commentary 46. Dallas, Texas: Word.
Runge, Steven E. 2008. *The Lexham Discourse Greek New Testament: Glossary*. Bellingham, WA: Lexham Press.
Runge, Steven E. 2010. *Discourse Grammar of the Greek New Testament: A Practical Introduction for Teaching and Exegesis*. Bellingham, WA: Lexham Press.
Thompson, Jeremy. 2015. *Bible Sense Lexicon*. Bellingham, WA: Logos Bible Software.

Thompson, Jeremy. 2016. *Longacre Genre Analysis of the Bible Dataset Documentation*. Bellingham, WA: Faithlife.

Van Neste, Ray. 2008. "1 and 2 Timothy." In *ESV Study Bible*, edited by Lane T. Dennis, Wayne Grudem, and J. I. Packer, 2231–2343. Wheaton, Illinois: Crossway.

Wall, Robert W., and Richard B. Steele. 2012. *1 and 2 Timothy and Titus*. Edited by Joel B. Green and Max Turner. The Two Horizons New Testament Commentary. Grand Rapids, Michigan: Eerdmans.

About the Author

Kevin Smith holds a Ph.D. in Theology from South African Theological Seminary (SATS) and a D.Litt. in Biblical Greek from the University of Stellenbosch. He served as a pastor before joining SATS as the Academic Dean in 2004. He is currently the Principal of SATS.

He is passionate about the Bible and theological education, having written and spoken widely on both topics. He is a lover of one God, a husband to one wife (Lyndi), a father to one son (Joshua), and a student for life.

God's Word for God's World: Toward a Gospel-Centered Faith

Samuel Richmond Saxena

1. Introduction

We live in unprecedented times, surrounded and pressed by life-related issues. It is difficult to predict what may happen next because of the prevailing circumstances. In the midst of all this, God's Word gives strength to overcome trials and temptations. The proper interpretation of God's Word helps people to walk in the will and purpose of God. In the Old Testament, believers have witnessed God's Word as an active agent during the creation of the universe, a commandment to live a righteous life, and a rebuke through the prophets that warned Israelites from time to time against their evil deeds. Since then, God's Word throughout the OT became the speech for the prophets, the standard for the faith, morals, and practical living.

Interestingly, God's saving grace allowed the Word to be incarnated in God's created world in the form of Jesus Christ, which shows that God has not forgotten his creation. By using the term *logos*, the apostle John conveys most expressively the mission of Jesus as the revealer of the Godhead (John 1:1, 14). According to St. Paul, God's Word is God-breathed and is useful for teaching, rebuking, correcting, and training in righteousness (2 Tim 3:16). Here Paul mentions the absolute authority of the Bible over our lives, and that the Bible does not merely contain the Word of God, but is the Word of God in its sum and in its parts.[1]

In his *Church Dogmatics*, Karl Barth, a renowned Protestant theologian, elaborates the Word of God in three forms—the preached, the written, and the revealed. Hence the "Word" implies action and communication which need to go together. Believers need to allow the incarnate Word to richly dwell and act accordingly. In the pluralistic New Age and immoral society, the proclamation of the Word of God should become the central theme of our mission, which requires boldness so that the world may identify the power of the revelation of the triune God.

---

[1] Jack Hayford, "The God-Breathed Word," https://www.jackhayford.org/teaching/devotional/the-god-breathed-word/.

This paper is divided into three sections: (a) exploring the authority of God's Word as a hope to the perishing world; (b) the supremacy of the Lord Jesus Christ in the pluralistic society; (c) power and communion of the Holy Spirit as an agent of transformation.

2. The New Age Spirituality

Since its inception, the Church as the body of the Lord Jesus Christ has faced challenges within (heresies) and outside (persecution). Still, the authority of the Word, the Lordship of Jesus Christ, and the transforming power of the Holy Spirit continue. The twenty-first century has witnessed several crises. Christian doctrines are under attack due to the rise of the New Age spirituality. In most of Western countries where Christianity is a dominant religion, there is an increase in nominalism and secularism, which has led many youngsters to drift away from their faith in God. According to the Pew Research Center's survey conducted in 2018 and 2019, the religious landscape of the United States continues to change. According to the report, 26% of American adults identify themselves as an atheist, agnostic, or "nothing in particular," a percentage which was only 17% in 2009. Many have started to believe in reincarnation, astrology, psychics, and spiritual energy in physical objects like mountains or trees.[2] The New Agers are trying to find god within the self rather than looking for him who is transcendent yet communicates through his Word and enters our lives through the incarnation.[3] Voddie Baucham Jr. identifies two competing worldviews in our culture: *Christian theism* and *secular humanism*. These worldviews raise "life's ultimate questions," which need to be addressed by the Church.[4]

---

[2] Claire Gecewicz, "New Age Beliefs Common among Both Religious and Nonreligious Americans," Pew Research Center, 2018, https://www.pewresearch.org/fact-tank/2018/10/01/new-age-beliefs-common-among-both-religious-and-non religious-americans/.

[3] David Wells, "The Supremacy of Christ in a Postmodern World," in John Piper and Justin Taylor (eds.), *The Supremacy of Christ in a Postmodern World* (Wheaton, Illinois: Crossway, 2007), 25.

[4] Piper and Taylor, *The Supremacy of Christ*, 52–55.

Questions	Christian Theism	Secular Humanism
God	God is the starting point; he is an intelligent, all-powerful being; Creator	Atheistic, man is the starting point. Man is supreme.
Human	Humans created in the Image and Likeness of God	Humans as a single-celled organism; a glorified ape; a cosmic accident with no real rhyme or reason
Truth	Truth as absolute	Rejects the absolute, objective truth of God's Word
Ethics	Moral rights and wrongs as absolute, since morality is rooted in the eternal and unchanging character of God.	Ethics as completely cultural and negotiable

The New Age spirituality finds its roots in secular humanism as well as religious pluralism, which promotes the idea that there are different ways to reach one God. The New Age spirituality tries to dilute the essence of Christian belief, and it has a new way of looking at the world. It involves a paradigm shift from theism to pantheism; from rationalism to mysticism; from separation to universalism; from patriarchism to feminism; from fragmentation to holism.[5] In the New Age spirituality, God is summed up in energy and force and permeates all of the natural world. They believe that as the human body and soul form one being, God and the universe form one (*Vasudhaiva Kutumbakam*), thus making everything divine. It is through consciousness that the New Agers can know themselves and experience God. For them, everything revolves around consciousness. Higher consciousness achieved through meditation and yoga leads them to transcendent reality where they feel that they have become gods. At this level, they realize that they have power to sense emotion and energy.[6]

For New Agers, the truth is relative and not absolute. Hence they reject the whole moral truth. Theologian John Drane observes, "The New Age has no place for sin."[7] Sadly, some New Agers have gone so far as to believe

---

[5] H. Christina Steyn, "An Example of a 'New Age' Interrelation of the Bible." *Religion & Theology* 4, no. 2 (1997), 111.
[6] Pat Collins, "New Age Spirituality," *The Furrow* 49, no. 2 (Feb. 1998), 93–94.
[7] Collins 1998, 95.

"that victims of any kind, e.g., of South African apartheid or the Nazi holocaust, suffer as a result of their own choices and spiritual karma."[8]

Often it has been noticed that the New Age movement people are inclusive. For them, there are many ways to attain ultimate reality and spiritual fulfillment. Even after having this belief, there is a general dissatisfaction underneath in the form of a vacuum that only God can fill. One of the crucial characteristics of New Age spirituality is that it "consists of a complex of spiritualities which are no longer embedded in any religion." For me, the New Age spirituality is an amalgamation of an individual's manipulation of different religions as well as their concept of self, which usually leads to illusion. The New Age spirituality generally concentrates on whatever is not associated with the traditional churches and their theologies, but is inclined towards Gnosticism, Western esotericism and monism. If New Age spirituality fades away, then to whom will the New Agers turn? Some feel that they will become atheists, while others predict that they will turn to the Ultimate Truth, which is rooted in Christianity.[9] We should be mindful that as Gnosticism was a threat to the early Church, similarly the New Age movement is a threat to Christians today. The present situation raises some very pertinent questions for the Church: How do we get the gospel across in a postmodern world? How to fulfill the Great Commission in the present context? How may we communicate God's Word to God's world? Do we need to rethink our ordinary way of sharing the gospel due to cultural changes?

3. The Authority of Scripture

For Pat Collins, when people get disillusioned with the traditional churches for one reason or the other, then they become attracted to New Age spirituality.[10] In the twenty-first century, "the rightful idea of authority has fallen on hard times."[11] Hence, to overcome the above challenges, it is required that we uphold and propagate the authority of Scripture. In the present scenario Christians are called to affirm the two claims that, (a) the Bible is authoritative and (b) God gave it through divine inspiration. According to Donald Hagner, "the Bible has evidently lost its authority in

---

[8] Collins 1998, 94.
[9] Wouter J. Hanegraaff, "New Age Religion and Secularization," *Numen* 47, no. 3 (2000), 303-6.
[10] Collins 1998, 96.
[11] Richard L. Mayhue, "The Authority of Scripture," *Master's Seminary Journal* 15, no. 2 (Fall 2004), 226.

our day. The beginnings of this loss go back to the period of the Enlightenment with the origin of the historical-critical method."[12] Ludwig Feuerbach (1804-72), in his work *Essence of Christianity* (1841), stated that God was an imagination of human beings to satisfy to themselves their deepest desires and cravings.[13] Unfortunately, with the rise of liberal theology, liberal theologians consider the Bible at par with other scriptures. Benjamin Jowett's 1860 essay "On the Interpretation of Scripture" argued that the Bible ought to be read "like any other book."[14] Henry Emerson Fosdick (1878-1969) preached a controversial sermon in May 1922 entitled "Shall the Fundamentalists Win?" Fosdick rejected core beliefs of fundamentalism, arguing that belief in the virgin birth was unnecessary, that belief in the inerrancy of Scripture was untenable, and that the doctrine of the Second Coming was absurd.[15] Later with the coming of Darwinism, followed by other scientific theories in the nineteenth century, science seemed to have triumphed over the authority of Scripture.

According to the Oxford Dictionary, authority is "the power or right to give orders, make decisions, and enforce obedience."[16] In the New Testament, the word "authority" is ἐξουσία (*exousia*), which means "the power exercised by rulers or others in high position by virtue of their office."[17] According to Richard, from the biblical worldview, "ultimate authority resides with God and God alone. God did not inherit His authority—there was no one to bequeath it to Him."[18] St Paul in 2 Tim 3:16-17 speaks of Scripture as "God-breathed" (*theopneustos*). In early Christian thought, such an idea was prevalent and even the Greek-speaking Jewish philosopher Philo of Alexandria regarded Scripture as fully inspired and upheld its authority.[19] The Greek word *theopneustos* occurs once in the Greek New Testament as mentioned in the above verse. It is composed of the noun *theos*, "God," and the verb *pneo*, "breathe into." Hence the etymology is "divinely inspired" or "breathed by God." Therefore it should be clearly understood by everyone

---

[12] Donald A. Hagner, "The State of the Bible in the Twenty-First Century," *Currents in Theology and Mission* (January 1, 2008), 18.
[13] Alister E. Mcgrath, *Christian History: An Introduction* (Oxford: Wiley-Blackwell, 2013), 240.
[14] Ibid, 246.
[15] Ibid, 294.
[16] Angus Stevenson, *Oxford Dictionary of English* (Oxford University Press, Kindle Edition).
[17] Mayhue, "The Authority of Scripture, 227.
[18] Ibid, 228.
[19] Marian Hillar, "Philo of Alexandria (c. 20 BCE.—40 CE)" *Internet Encyclopedia of Philosophy* (IEP) https://iep.utm.edu/philo/.

that Scripture originates from God and is filled with the breath of God.[20] The rabbinic tradition held that every part of Scripture is important, no matter how small. Whereas Paul writes that "every [or all] Scripture is God-inspired and is useful," there were some teachers who interpreted some parts of Scripture as myths (1 Tim 1:4); therefore, Paul emphasizes that Scripture is entirely inspired of God.[21] God's Word is helpful "for teaching, reproof, correction, and training in righteousness that the man of God may be completely equipped for every good work" (3:16–17). Since then, the Christian community has long held that the Old and the New Testaments are "inspired" by God and are the basis for faithful reflection in the Church.[22]

Although the Bible was read in the monasteries and cathedrals during the medieval period, ordinary people primarily did not have access to it personally.[23] During the Reformation period, William of Occam argued and promoted the idea that "the revelation of God in Scripture is the authoritative basis for Christian faith," and his argument influenced Martin Luther. Later, Luther made the famous claim, "Only the Holy Scripture possesses canonical authority." John Calvin agreed with this and said, "God bestows the actual knowledge of himself upon us only in the Scriptures."[24] Interestingly, during the Renaissance and sixteenth-century Protestant Reformation period, the invention of printing and translations of the Bible into vernacular languages led people to the Scriptures.[25] William Wilberforce (1759–1833), an English philanthropist who pressed for the abolition of slavery, in his *Appeal* (1823) for the slaves of the West Indies, appealed to "express authority of Scripture" to challenge the social basis of slavery. After Wilberforce died in 1833, Parliament finally abolished slavery throughout the British Empire.[26] Karl Barth sees that the Word of God has a threefold form: (1) the Word of God preached, (2) the written Word of God, (3) the revealed Word of God. The Word of God in all its three forms

---

[20] Bill Wenstrom, "Exegesis and Exposition of Second Timothy 3:16–17," Academia, https://www.academia.edu/34066370/Exegesis_and_Exposition_of_Second_Timothy_3_16_17.
[21] Paul M. Zehr, *Believers Church Bible Commentary: 1 & 2 Timothy and Titus* (Waterloo, Ontario: Herald Press, 1936), 210.
[22] Daniel L. Brunner, Jennifer L. Butler and A. J. Swoboda, *Introducing Evangelical Ecotheology: Foundations in Scripture, Theology, History and Praxis* (Grand Rapids: Michigan, Baker Academic, 2014), 23.
[23] Zehr 1936, 210.
[24] James C. Denison, 'Shaking the Foundations: The Shift in Scriptural Authority in the Postmodern World,' *Review and Expositor* 95 (1998), 547.
[25] Zehr 1936, 210.
[26] McGrath 2013, 234.

is God's speech to humans.[27] For Barth, the Word of God does not play a merely static role but a dynamic one. Barth says that in God's revelation God's Word is identical to God Himself.[28] According to Grenz, for Barth "the Word of God is not simply proclamation and scripture, but the dynamics of God's revelation in proclamation and scripture."[29]

The authority of God's Word helps us to live a righteous life and makes us perfect in our living. In the wilderness, Jesus emphasized the authority and power of God's Word from Deuteronomy 8:3: "It is written, 'Man shall not live by bread alone, but by every word that proceeds from the mouth of God'" (Matt 4:4). The Church's health depends upon the proper interpretation of Scripture. Scripture remains the principal authority by which Christians decide their beliefs, values, and practices. Contextual theology plays a vital role in addressing the ongoing issues, but the Scripture's authority helps the Church to be on the right track, because God's Word does not change with the times, the culture, the nation, or the ethnic. When "the authority of Scripture" is unpacked, N. T. Wright affirms that it expresses a picture of God's sovereignty and his saving act for the whole universe, which is dramatically inaugurated by Jesus himself and now implemented through the Spirit-led life of the Church.[30]

4. The Centrality of Jesus Christ

The centrality or the supremacy of Christ is one of the significant issues in the postmodern world. People belonging to New Age spirituality are not comfortable with the authority of God's Word and the centrality of Jesus Christ because it demands much more. One has to yield fully to God's will and also to the life of Christ instead of depending upon one's own will and intellect. It robs fleshly freedom and strives hard for a holy and righteous life. For the disciples of Christ, Jesus is "the Way, the Truth and the Life" (John 14:6); and "Salvation is found in no one else, for there is no other name under given to men by which we must be saved" (Acts 4:12). Our belief is firmly rooted in God's Word and well stated in the Nicene Creed of

---

[27] Karl Barth, *Church Dogmatics: Doctrine of the Word of God*, vol. I/1, ed. G. W. Bromiley & T. F. Torrance (eds.) (London: T&T Clarke, 2009), 125.

[28] Young Jun Kim. *A Reformed Assessment of the Revitalization of the Doctrine of Trinity by Four Leading Twentieth Century Protestant Theologian* (thesis, Department of Systematic Theology, Faculty of Theology–University of Pretoria, April 2008), 60.

[29] S. J. Grenz, *Rediscovering the Trinity in Contemporary Theology* (Minneapolis: Fortress, 2004), 37.

[30] N. T. Wright, *Scripture and Authority of God: How to Read the Bible Today* (Harper Collins e-book, 2011), 272.

AD 325, that the Lord Jesus Christ is "very God of very God ... of one substance with the Father ... who for us men, and for our salvation, came down from heaven ... and was made man." Such claims are accepted not only by many religious fundamentalists. Liberal theologians feel that believers cannot build their conviction on isolated verses to state the absoluteness of Christianity. One of them was an influential Indian theologian, Stanley Samartha, who objected to the use of biblical proof texts like these.[31]

Even amid the New Age spirituality, the Church has maintained the supremacy of Jesus Christ, because the Truth can be neither distorted nor destroyed. Since we claim that Jesus is the ultimate truth, there cannot be any other truth apart from this. Aristotle once said that the truth is one and not many.[32] Through incarnation and atonement, we recognize what God has done in Christ, and through this, we are looking for the new life and the new humanity called forth by faith. Incarnation reveals that God has not abandoned his creation but that through this act "God was reconciling the world to himself in Christ." In fact, through the coming of Christ, God becomes very personal to us (*ishta devata*).[33] Through Christ, we experience God in us, which is still a mystery for many people.[34] The centrality of Jesus Christ in the content, form, and method of Karl Barth's theology has long been identified as one of its most notable attributes.[35] For him, all theology finds its focal center in Christ and all knowledge of God is obtainable only through Christ.[36] According to Barth, Christology forms "the heart of the Church's dogmatics" and any deficiency or deviation here "would mean error or deficiency everywhere."[37] His emphasis on the centrality of Jesus Christ came as a breath of fresh air into a theological arena that had been dominated by liberalism.[38] In his commentary, F. F. Bruce makes a commendable assertion regarding Jesus' claim that "I am the way, the truth and the life, no one comes to the Father except through me." For him, "God has no avenue to communicate to the world apart from His Word and the same Word became flesh and dwelt

---

[31] Ajith Fernando, *The Supremacy of Christ* (Secunderabad: OM-Authentic Books, 2004), 20.
[32] Ken Gnanakan, *Proclaiming Christ in a Pluralistic Context* (Bangalore: Theological Book Trust, 2002), 23.
[33] Ken Gnanakan, "Creation, New Creation, and Ecological Relationships," in Timoteo D. Gener (eds.), *Asian Christian Theology: Evangelical Perspectives* (Manila, Philippines: Langham Global Library, 2019.
[34] Gnanakan 2019.
[35] T. F. Torrance, *Karl Barth, Biblical and Evangelical Theologian* (Edinburgh: T. & T. Clark, 1990), 138.
[36] Barth, *Church Dogmatics*, IV/1, 123.
[37] Barth, *Church Dogmatics*, IV/1, p. 3.
[38] Fernando 2004, 188.

among us in order to supply such an avenue (way) of approach."[39] According to Thomas à Kempis, "Without the way there is no going; without the truth there is no knowing; without the life there is no living."[40]

It is the task of the Church to propagate the centrality of Jesus Christ boldly and effectively without condemning any religion or movement. We are called to present the truth with love because the truth of Jesus Christ is the solution to every problem. A Hindu once asked Dr E. Stanley Jones, "What has Christianity to offer that our religion has not?" He replied, "Jesus Christ." Christians have confined Jesus Christ within the four walls of the Church. One of the biggest challenges the Indian Church faces is the crisis of "identity" where Christianity is considered a foreign religion and the Indian Christians are the product of this religion. Likewise, there are other countries with different contexts, and while propagating the gospel, we need to exercise extra precaution so that the gospel be communicated without any dilution. According to Mark Driscoll, "An incarnational Christology ... stresses the immanence of God at work here with us. It focuses on bringing about the new way of life offered to the citizens of the kingdom of God."[41]

5. New Life Through the Holy Spirit

Any spirituality that contradicts the Word of God and the centrality of Jesus Christ can be corrected through the doctrine of the Holy Spirit. The Holy Spirit helps people to believe in the Word of God and the supremacy of Christ. He is the Spirit of Truth, who reveals God's truth to those who are open to accepting the Truth. St. Thomas Aquinas once wisely observed that the truth, no matter by whom it is spoken, is from the Holy Spirit.[42] Jesus promised his disciples, "When the Spirit of truth comes, he will guide you into all the truth" (John 16:13). For F. F. Bruce, the truth the Spirit discloses is not any other truth than the truth as Jesus declares in John 14:6, but a further unfolding of the same truth.[43] The believers are called to be guided by the Holy Spirit so that they may speak truth in love, because God's mission on this earth is accomplished through the power of the Holy Spirit. We cannot ignore or sideline the work of the Holy Spirit from the day-to-day activities of Church. Where there is no Spirit, there is dryness, barrenness,

---

[39] F. F. Bruce. *The Gospel of John: A Verse-by-Verse Exposition* (1983; Kingsley Books, Kindle Edition), 402.
[40] Thomas à Kempis, *The Imitation of Christ*, 56.1, cited in Bruce 1983, 412.
[41] Piper and Taylor, *The Supremacy of Christ*, 128.
[42] Collins 1998, 96.
[43] Bruce 1983, 431.

hopelessness. For this reason many seminaries have become spiritual cemeteries, several church buildings have become shopping malls, and some prominent Christian organizations have become a center for social activities only. Pentecost brought a paradigm shift—the Spirit which was previously experienced as the Spirit of God was now also experienced as the Spirit of Christ. Only after Pentecost were the disciples able to witness to the gospel of Lord Jesus Christ boldly. The Holy Spirit helps present-day believers proclaim Jesus as Lord, live a Jesus-centered life, and uphold the authority of the Scripture amid New Age spirituality. It is the Holy Spirit that makes the resurrected Christ present to us in faith. He is the "Lord and the giver of Life" through whom we attain new life. The Spirit guides the Church to do mission in action in the contemporary world. According to the Lausanne Movement's 2010 Cape Town Commitment, the Holy Spirit is

> the missionary Spirit sent by the missionary Father and the missionary Son, breathing life and power into God's missionary Church. We love and pray for the presence of the Holy Spirit because without the witness of the Spirit to Christ, our own witness is futile. Without the convicting work of the Spirit, our preaching is in vain. Without the gifts, guidance and power of the Spirit, our mission is mere human effort. And without the fruit of the Spirit, our unattractive lives cannot reflect the beauty of the gospel.[44]

According to Karl Barth, the task of Christian theology is to proclaim the content of God's revelation through the Holy Spirit, without collapsing the essential distinctions within the triune God and between God and humanity.[45] Through the Holy Spirit, Barth shows God's redeeming work for humanity. Holy Spirit—the Redeemer—is he by whom we come to faith and in whom revelation is "being revealed." The Holy Spirit is God in life-giving presence. Although Scripture calls him the Spirit of Christ, he is not Christ. The Holy Spirit is a transforming agent which proceeds from the Father and the Son. He shapes our character so that we tend to become more like Jesus every day. The Spirit-led Church needs to be humble enough to address the present realities. The Spirit-led Church should be proactive in satisfying the inner spiritual needs of the people, which, unfortunately, the current technology, New Age spirituality, self-proclaimed gurus, and recent scientific

---

[44] Thomas K. Johnson, David Parker, and Thomas Schirrmacher (eds.), *In the Name of the Father, Son, and Holy Spirit: Teaching the Trinity from the Creeds to Modern Discussion.* World of Theology Series 17 (Bonn: Culture and Science Publishers, 2020), 90.

[45] Miyon Chung, "An Introduction to the Pneumatologies of Karl Barth and Eberhard Jungel (Part 1)," *Torch Trinity Journal* 7 (2004), 106, cited in http://www.ttgst.ac.kr/upload/ttgst_resources13/20124-197.pdf.

discoveries have failed to do. The primary mission of the Church is to proclaim sound spirituality centered on the gospel, through the Holy Spirit so that people's hunger be satisfied. The Spirit exactly knows when, where and how to meet the spiritual demands of the people. There are ways one may reduce stress and increase mindfulness by some physical activities, but the spiritual vacuum continues, unless it is filled by the presence of Christ that comes through the Holy Spirit. Mathematician Blaise Pascal said, "There is a God-shaped vacuum in the heart of each man which cannot be satisfied by any created thing but only by God the Creator made known through Jesus Christ."[46] Jesus said, "It is the spirit that gives life; the flesh is useless. The words that I have spoken to you are spirit and life" (John 6:63). Christian spirituality, however, focuses not only on seeking internal peace but also on the duty to reach out to others with the love of Christ. Thus, it is a holistic spirituality that is not self-centered, but Christ-centered, and the love of Jesus Christ impels Christians to love others.[47]

6. Conclusion

Human flesh and the human spirit are so well connected that people fail to distinguish between spiritual and physical needs. Seeking to satisfy themselves, ordinary people get easily deceived by those types of spiritualities that play with their emotions and ultimately affect their spiritual lives. In Colossians 2:4, Paul warns the Church, "I tell you this so that no one may deceive you by fine-sounding arguments." The New Age spirituality tends to bring together different schools of thought that ultimately contradict the authority of Scripture, the centrality of Jesus Christ, and the person and work of the Holy Spirit. Sadly, the New Age spirituality is secretly creeping into our churches. By deceptive and hollow arguments, the followers of this type of spirituality tend to influence those Church members who are not well rooted in the Scriptures. It is important for the believers to be well versed with God's Word. Jesus said in Matthew 24:35, "Heaven and earth will pass away, but my words will never pass away." God's Word is "alive and active" (Heb 4:12). Similarly, the incarnate Word of God in Jesus Christ reveals the will and purpose of God in the lives of believers. We are not gods as the followers of New Age spirituality think. We manifest God through the indwelling of Christ in us. We correct these false philosophies by recognizing that Jesus Christ is the

---

[46] Paul Asay, *God on the Streets of Gotham: What the Big Screen Batman Can Teach Us about God and Ourselves* (Colorado Springs: Tyndale House, 2012), 118.

[47] Reginald Alva, "The Spirit-led Church Mission in Action in the Contemporary World" *International Review of Mission* 108, no. 1: (June 2019), 172.

solution to the problems of the universe. The Holy Spirit is the spirit of discernment who helps believers not only to confront these false philosophies but also gives courage to profess the faith to the world, as Paul says in 2 Timothy 1:7: "For God did not give us a spirit of cowardice, but rather a spirit of power and of love and of self-discipline." We are commissioned to do three things simultaneously: "speak the truth in love" (Eph 4:15); proclaim the truth of Jesus Christ's uniqueness without any compromise, and witness to all people about his salvation with an attitude of sincere Christian love. Through love and care, which has always been an integral part of Christian missions, we may reach others along with proclamation.

About the Author

Samuel is presently an Academic Dean at Caleb Institute, Gurgaon, India. Prior to this he was University Chaplain and Head, Department for Advanced Theological Studies, Faculty of Theology at Sam Higginbottom University of Agriculture Technology and Sciences (SHUATS), Allahabad, India.

He holds a PhD in Theology from SHUATS, an MSc in Chemistry from Christ Church College, Kanpur, and an MA in Christianity from SAIACS, Bangalore.

Samuel is an Indian educator, environmentalist, musician and eco-theologian. He is a frequent speaker at workshops, seminars and conferences. He is an Honorary Secretary, Theological Commission of Evangelical Fellowship of India; Member, Theological Commission, World Evangelical Alliance; and Associate Member of International Society for Science and Religion. As an author he has written book on Contemporary Issues in Science and Theology published by ISPCK.

He is married to Delicia Howell and blessed with two children Jane Esther and Sam John.

Plumbing the Sacred: Narrative Approaches to Understanding Non-Western Christian Ethical, Political, and Theological Discourse

Thomas Alan Harvey

1. Introduction

Of every particular enquiry there is a narrative to be written, and being able to understand that enquiry is inseparable from being able to identify and follow that narrative.[1]

If MacIntyre is correct, it is only fitting that we begin with a story. This tale begins in Scott Atran's study of ISIS and Kurdish fighters in Iraq. An unorthodox Oxford evolutionary anthropologist, Atran and his team have entered into dialogue with Isis and Peshmerga fighters in Iraq to understand their inordinate willingness to kill, or be killed in combat, with a level of sacrifice that surpasses that of their rivals. Atran and his team interviewed captured ISIS fighters and their nemesis the Kurdish Peshmerga, using standard anthropological qualitative analysis.[2]

They began their interviews with the fighters by setting out laminated cards engraved with various images and phrases that the interviewee would then arrange. These would be worked through and ordered so as to plumb the identity, values, motivations, and assessments of the fighters. To the surprise of Atran and his team, the ISIS fighters "literally threw the cards down and ... refused to respond."[3] When the researchers pressed the fighters as to why they refused to put the cards in order, the combatants dismissed the cards as "incomprehensible" and thus useless to explain who they are, why they fight, kill, and die for ISIS.

---

[1] MacIntyre, Alasdair. *The Tasks of Philosophy: Selected Essays*, vol. 1 (Cambridge: Cambridge University Press, 2006), 168.

[2] Atran, Scott. "The Devoted Actor: Unconditional Commitment and Intractable Conflict across Cultures." *Current Anthropology* 57 – Supplement 13 (University of Chicago Press, 2016) 192–203.

[3] Howard, Jacqueline. *What Motivates ISIS Fighters—and Those Who Fight Against Them.* CNN, September 4, 2017, http://edition.cnn.com/2017/09/04/health/isis-fighters-human-behavior-study/index.html.

Thus, Atran and the team went back to the drawing board and, in further conversation with the combatants, redesigned the cards using the fighters' symbols, terminology, and sacred reference points. Gradually Atran and his researchers gradually gained insight into the combatants' thought world in a way that began to reveal the rationale behind their intense devotion to their cause. Where standard utilitarian cost/benefit analysis had failed, Atran's "devoted actor framework on infused identity" began to unearth why:

> People who are willing to sacrifice everything, including their lives—the totality of their self-interests—will not be lured away just by material incentives or disincentives. The science suggests that sacred values are best opposed with other sacred values that inspire devotion, or by sundering the fused social networks that embed those values.[4]

Given that utilitarian explanations were incomprehensible at best and at worst morally offensive to these combatants, Atran concludes that ISIS and Peshmerga fighters are "deontic agents" caught up in a violent struggle to establish a universal right and wrong. Atran sees this categorization as his only option given his assumption that "philosophers of moral virtue suggest that moral values may be either deontological (Kant) or utilitarian (Mill)."[5]

Describing "devoted actors" as "deontic agents" is ungainly at best, given that Kantian deontological liberal norms clash with Muslim and Christian pursuit of ends based on sacred values that reflect the norms, virtues, and excellences they embody.[6] Atran's epistemology confuses rather than clarifies, for it lacks lenses suited to plumbing the relationship between sacred value, human agency, and meaning. That being said, Atran is on the right track in his recognition that sacred value, devotion, and agency must be reconsidered epistemologically.

2. Devoted Actors and the Epistemological Turn

Atran is not the first scholar to note the uneasy relationship between modern secular scholarship and religious agency. Saba Mahmood shows how feminists' focus on agency as personal autonomy blinds them to the agen-

---

[4] Atran 2016.
[5] Ibid, 168.
[6] MacIntyre, Alisdair. *Three Rival Versions of Moral Enquiry* (Notre Dame, IN: University of Notre Dame, 1990), 164.

cy experienced and valued by women dedicated to the teaching of and submission to the *dawa*,[7] "the way of righteousness."[8]

Mahmood's research looks at the disciplines and discursive practices of women in the Cairo Mosque Movement. To better understand their experience of sacred agency, Mahmood followed three women teachers of the *dawa* and their pupils in Cairo. When the women gathered, the teachers and the pupils would first recite the Koran and then inquire as to how best to interpret the passages as sacred tools to gain the insight, agency, and power required to successfully navigate the shoals of modern Egyptian society faithfully. According to Mahmood:

> The participants of this movement often criticize what they consider to be an increasingly prevalent form of religiosity in Egypt that accords Islam the status of an abstract system of beliefs that has no direct bearing on the way one lives and structures one's daily life. This trend, usually referred to as secularization (*almana*) or Westernization (*taghrīb*) of Egyptian society, is understood to have reduced Islamic knowledge (both as a mode of conduct and as a set of principles) to the status of "custom and folklore" (*āda wa fūkloriyya*). The women's mosque movement, therefore, seeks to educate lay Muslims in those virtues, ethical capacities, and forms of reasoning that the participants perceive to have become either unavailable or irrelevant to the lives of ordinary Muslims.[9]

As Mahmood notes, in these sessions the teacher and pupil "exchange presents a situation far more complex than any simple model of 'religious indoctrination' would suggest, and requires an analysis of the micro-practices of persuasion through which people are made to incline toward one view versus another."[10] The embodiment of pious disciplines and teaching enables a "morphology of moral reflection and human agency."[11] As such, norms, virtues, excellences, and practical wisdom are embedded and embodied through teaching and informed devotional piety, so that the faithful might individually and communally reflect the *dawa* in Egyptian society. Herein, piety, reflection, and action are inextricably entwined to

---

[7] *Dawa* literally means "invitation" or missionally the "call to Islam." Some refer to *dawa* as "Islamic mission," though this is understood quite differently from standard Christian or secular understandings of mission.

[8] Mahmood, Saba. "Feminist Theory, Agency, and the Liberatory Subject: Some Reflections on the Islamic Revival in Egypt." *Temenos* 42, no. 1 (2006): 31–71.

[9] Mahmood 2006, 35.

[10] Mahmood, Saba. *Politics of Piety: The Islamic Revival and the Feminist Subject* (Princeton, NJ: Princeton University Press, 2005), 106.

[11] Ibid, 25.

afford sacred agency in an increasingly secular world. This form of agency contrasts sharply with feminist views that assume women's agency is gained by resistance to the patriarchal norms of religion that impede women's emancipation and by an autonomous self-realization. For women of the Mosque Movement, however, submission to Islamic norms and the disciplined embrace of Islamic piety are the linchpin of freedom and power, and thus a resistant political praxis to what they perceive as an incursive and defiling secularization of Egyptian society.

Mahmood's epistemological approach to understanding this agency required that she decouple the feminist link of agency to personal autonomy. Only in this way could she better understand an agency gained in discipline, teaching, and submission to the *dawa*.[12] Thus, like Atran, Mahmood set aside standard secular views of individual agency that "sharply limit our ability to understand and interrogate ... projects (that) have been shaped by nonliberal traditions." Nonetheless, unlike Atran, Mahmood takes a further step to identify the source of liberal epistemological blindness. At root, she argues, it is a modern subject/object orientation that catalyzes personal autonomy as a necessary stepping stone in progressive definitions of agency and self-realization. This liberating autonomy allows the agents to stand outside the *dawa* so they may question and abandon any restrictive norm, teaching, or form of piety that impinges upon their individual freedom. Naturally, such a view is directly at odds with an agency gained in habitual submission to the norms, teaching, and discernment gained in submission to the *dawa*. Mahmood concludes that these presuppositions that underpin feminist scholarship analysis blind it to the spiritual and disciplinary resources of Islamic identity, piety, and agency, which are then discounted by secular critics as absurd at best and at worst a regression into a servitude and subjugation. This secular aversion leaves standard feminist epistemologies unable to perceive the embodied emancipatory projects of women whose sense of self, desire, and lived lives are caught up in an agency enfolded within the *dawa* and the spiritual, familial, and societal agency it affords. As with Mahmood, only when researchers decouple notions of agency from liberal modern appeals to autonomy can they begin to fathom the nature and agency of devoted actors and pursue the "critical analytical questions crucial to understanding nonliberal projects, subjects, and desires whose logic exceeds the entelechy of liberatory politics."[13]

---

[12] Mahmood 2005, 14.
[13] Mahmood 2006, 33.

3. Epistemology: On Sense and Sensibility

This relationship between faith, self-realization, agency, and the pursuit of piety have been part and parcel of Christian monasticism from its origins. Talal Asad describes the agency of Cistercian monks gained through obedience and disciplines of "humiliation, instruction, and exercise" that train the monk to distinguish between truth and error.[14] Cistercian monks gain discernment and power through habits. These habits entail physical and spiritual exercises that nurture soul and body, taught, guided, and exemplified by the monastic superior. Only through following the master can the novice gain mastery over sense and soul. At first glance, these habits may appear as a form of "works-righteousness" or mere "dead ritual," yet in monastic orders they are seen as gracious gifts to be received in humility and refined by rigorous discipline wherein the true power of the agent is recovered. As such, their habitus reflects the original understanding of *religio* as rites performed that bring ontological blessing to the supplicant. In this way, discipline, virtue, and practice empower agency toward the order's shared ends as opposed to simply individual "choices ... *sui* generis and self-justifying."[15] Thus, according to Asad, within this habitus "agency emerges from within semantic and institutional networks that define and make possible particular ways of relating to people things and oneself."[16]

To understand agency within this social world, one must attend to the habits that form the embodied subject. Cultivation of the senses and sensibility lie at the heart of moral potentiality. Thus, the habitus is not simply a submission to an arbitrary order, but the necessary training of sense and sensibility essential to informed expertise, power, and wisdom.

In short, if one thinks of ritual not as an activity that denies choice by imposing formalities but as aiming at aptness of behavior, sensibility, and attitude, one may see the repetition of forms as something other than a blind submission to authority. For the aptness of formal performance (whether this be politeness or reverence) requires not only repeating past models but also originality in applying them in appropriate new circumstances. In other words, although at one level the cultivation of appropriate formality necessary to ethical virtues may not allow unlimited choice, it does require the exercise of judgment. Like the rules of

---

[14] Asad, Talal. *Genealogies of Religion: Disciplines and Reasons of Power in Christianity and Islam* (Baltimore and London: Johns Hopkins University Press, 1993), 157.
[15] Ibid, 126.
[16] Ibid, 34.

grammar, forms are at once potentialities and limits, necessary to original thought and conduct.[17]

Thus, to discern the agency of these devoted actors requires attention to the ways in which the order forms the individual and the community to achieve their end.

4. Epistemology, Agency, and Narrative

Mahmood and Asad's epistemological approaches require a narrative of agency nurtured by piety and the wisdom and power they afford. The narratives plot the disciplines, practices, reflection, and gradual perfection toward their shared end and their earthly and divine consequence that are at once practical and rational.

Naturally, narratives both in sacred texts and the lives they guide are more than mere collections of stories; they represent a form of religious and political embodiment whose performance within the public square is a "morphology of moral reflection and human agency."[18] They embody the norms, virtues, excellences, and practical wisdom of the body politic whatever its size or sacred/secular disposition. As Stanley Hauerwas and L. Gregory Jones note:

> The intentional nature of human action evokes a narrative account, that a narrative account is concerned with how those intentional actions are woven into the depiction of personal identity and character, and that because the language and moral notions of people use to describe their character and their behaviour are tied to the narratives of particular traditions, the notion of rationality itself is narrative-dependent.[19]

In this way, devoted actors embody rational claims to truth that combine word, deed, and identity of their habitus, which entail

> theological convictions [that] inextricably involve truth-claims that are in principle open to challenge. The claim that our existence has a teleological character that requires narrative display is a 'metaphysical' claim. ... I assume that Christian theology has a stake in a qualified epistemological realism. I certainly do not believe, nor did Wittgenstein that religious convic-

---

[17] Asad, Talal. "Thinking about Religion, Belief, and Politics," In *The Cambridge Companion to Religious Studies*, edited by R. A. Orsi (Cambridge: Cambridge University Press, 2013), 42.
[18] Mahmood 2005, 25.
[19] Hauerwas, Stanley, and L. Gregory Jones. *Why Narrative: Readings in Narrative Theology* (Grand Rapids, MI: Eerdmans, 1989), 12.

tions are or should be treated as an internally consistent language game that is self-validating.[20]

This relationship between narrative, moral agency, and rationality is set out by Alasdair MacIntyre in his "three-fold scheme" of narrative ethics.[21] Traditions of moral inquiry and agency lie between two poles: "human-nature as it happens to be" and "human-nature-as-it-could-be-if-it-realized-its-telos." What links "untutored human-nature" to "human-nature-as-it-could-be-if-it-realized-its-telos" are the precepts, excellences, practices, rituals, disciplines and virtues that both inform and serve as catalysts to the individual or community to transform individuals and communities toward their perfection.[22] This "three-fold scheme" forms an extended exemplum, i.e., a story that brings to light an agent's or community's character and, at least in matters of faith, brings out the individual, communal, and social lineaments of their devotion and agency. As such, they are both rational and political. They offer ethical, and rational alternatives in light of spiritual progress or regress toward or away from what they regard as the common good. Naturally, when tuned to a Jewish, Christian, or Muslim key, that relative advance or retreat proceeds along an ordained trajectory that situates their relative defeats and triumphs, trials and temptations along their tradition's path. Navigating this path that winds through the sacred and mundane dimensions of daily life requires an informed and discerning agency enabled by receiving the tradition through instruction and extended in reflection. This rational inquiry is then honed by discipline and embodied in humility, obedience, and applied practical wisdom. This way of life represents a tradition of rational inquiry embodied:

> A tradition of enquiry is more than a coherent movement of thought. It is such a movement in the course of which those engaging in that movement become aware of it and of its direction and in a self-aware fashion attempt to engage in its debates and to carry its inquiries forward. The relationships which can hold between individuals and a tradition are very various, ranging from unproblematic allegiance through attempts to amend or redirect the tradition to large opposition to what have hitherto been its central contentions.[23]

---

[20] Hauerwas, Stanley. *The Hauerwas Reader* (Durham, NC: Duke University Press, 2001), 99.
[21] MacIntyre, Alasdair. *After Virtue: A Study in Moral Theory* (Notre Dame, IN: University of Notre Dame Press, 1981).
[22] Ibid, 63.
[23] MacIntyre, Alasdair. *Whose Justice, Which Rationality.* (London: Duckworth, 1988), 326.

Thus, for devoted actors, traditions of inquiry are embodied narratives. They provide the means of informed interpretation, debate, and changes within that tradition of rationality. Furthermore, within these narratives and traditional matrices meaning, agency, and extension of movements by devoted actors are understood in light of how they inform their moral and political judgment. Attention to these provides thick accounts of the sacred scaffolding that defines and guides the agency and actions of devoted actors in the world. What the work of Atran, Mahmood, and Asad brings to the fore is epistemological approaches wherein these sensibilities and their distinctive attitudes, desires, and valorized senses that inform and enable the agency of devoted actors may be understood.

What should be apparent, however, is that the agency described by Asad, Mahmood, and even Atran rests uneasily with progressive liberal imaginaries of religion that view religious agency as distinctly private and their encroachment upon the public square a threat. As we shall note below, this is particularly problematic for Western Protestant evangelicalism given its tie to the English Reformation, the rise of European and North American imperial power, and the global Protestant missionary movement of the nineteenth and twentieth centuries.

5. The Political and Theological Roots of Secular Epistemology

The move to make religion a private domain of personal devotion was at once a theological and political campaign. John Milton's remonstrance against Charles I's imposition of "fixed prayers" viewed prayers recited from prayer books as

> tyranny that *depriv*[es] us the exercise of that Heav'nly gift, which God by special promise powers out daily upon his Church, that is to say, the spirit of Prayer ... is (to) imprison and confine by force, into a Pinfold of sett words, those two most unimprisonable things, our Prayers and that Divine Spirit that of utterance that moves them.[24]

The issue for Milton was not the words of the prayers themselves but the limit placed on free human spirits when required by king and clergy to surrender their conscience to the "outward dictates of men." For Milton, prayer was a private matter of the soul and thus a preserve of human

---

[24] Milton, John. "Eikonoklastes," 1649, in *Complete Prose Works*, 3:504 (New Haven: Yale University Press, 1962).

freedom. This emphasis upon the private nature of religious agency was taken up in John Locke's advocacy for strict boundaries between religious and political institutions so as to ensure that no confusion as to their distinct natures and roles would trouble society:

> I esteem it above all things necessary to distinguish exactly the business of civil government from that of religion and to settle the just bounds that lie between one and the other. If this be not done, there can be no end put to the controversies that will be always arising between those that have, or at least pretend to have, on the one side, a concernment for the interest of men's souls, and, on the other side, a care of the commonwealth.[25]

As William Arnal notes, this quarantine of belief and religious agency within the cloister of the individual soul apart from the public square came to define the cognitive character of religion and the secular nature of Western states,

> insofar as they assume a privatised and cognitive character behind religion (as in religious belief) simply reflect (and assume as normative) the West's distinctive historical feature of the secularized state. Religion, precisely, is not social, not coercive, is individual, is belief oriented and so on, because in our day and age there are certain apparently free-standing cultural institutions, such as the Church, which are excluded from the political state.[26]

In "modern society," at least in most Western European and North American societies, religion, religious knowledge and agency were reserved to "cultural institutions" distinct from secular government. Thus, allowing religion to intrude upon politics and intellectual inquiry was increasingly viewed as a political and epistemological categorical error. Thus, as Max Weber contends, secular inquiry makes the demand that

> principally there are no mysterious incalculable forces that come into play, but rather that one can in principle master all things by calculation. This means that the world is disenchanted. One must no longer have recourse to magical means to master or implore the spirits as did the savage for whom such mysterious powers existed. Technical means and calculations perform the service. This above all is what intellectualization means. This process of disenchantment, which has continued to exist in Occidental culture for

---

[25] Locke, John. "John Locke: A Letter Concerning Toleration," 1689, https://socialsciences.mcmaster.ca/~econ/ugcm/3ll3/locke/toleration.pdf.
[26] Arnal, William. "Definition." In *Guide to the Study of Religion*, edited by Willi Braun and Russell T. McCutcheon (London: T&T Clark. 2000), 21–34.

millennia, and, in general, this "progress," to which science belongs as a link and motive force.[27]

Religion's inability to provide the calculations and calibration that disenchanted reason, rationality, and agency afford meant that religious phenomena were increasingly housed within university departments of religious studies, social sciences, or psychology where rational inquiry was to elide any recourse to belief, theological opinion, or sacred value but was instead to be re-signified as matters of "belief" along secular methodological lines. As Stanley Fish notes, rationality and agency were the preserve of secular reason apart from religious opinion and superstition.

Let those who remain captives of ancient superstitions and fairy tales have their churches, chapels, synagogues, mosques, rituals and liturgical mumbo-jumbo; just don't confuse the (pseudo) knowledge they traffic in with the knowledge needed to solve the world's problem.[28]

6. Agency and Semiotic Ideology

According to the anthropologist Webb Keane, this modern distinction between secular reason and private religious opinion owes much to Western semiosis, i.e., a shared semiotic ideology of "underlying assumptions about what signs are, what functions signs serve, and what consequences they might produce." Given that all human communities operate under forms of semiotic ideology, Keane notes that they are not the possession of some to the exclusion of others, but refer to innate human reflexivity in its use of signs to communicate. Nonetheless, though general semiotic processes are universal, the particular social, cultural, and political frameworks of meaning vary and are often contentious within any given society and between societies given their religious, social, political and historical import. Thus, Keane notes:

> Clashes over the status of religious signs reveal the ontological and ethical entailments of semiotic ideologies, in which the very existence of a sign's object may be in dispute. Such ongoing semiotic processes help endow social existence with much of its constructive, uncertain, and conflictual character. ... Signs signify only on being interpreted and those interpretations will differ based on the relationship perceived between the sign and signified

---

[27] Weber, Max. "Science as a Vocation," in *From Max Weber: Essays in Sociology*, edited by H. H. Gerth and C. Wright Mills (Abingdon: Routledge, 1948), 129-158.
[28] Fish, Stanley. "Are There Secular Reasons?" *New York Times*, February 22, 2010, https://opinionator.blogs.nytimes.com/2010/02/22/are-there-secular-reasons/.

and thus set the understanding as to the content of the sign. Such interpretations and the perspective of the interpreters lead to different interpretations generated by those who present the sign.[29]

Thus, going back to early Protestant attempts to distance themselves from what they regarded as the dead Roman Catholic ritualism led them to employ, much like their later secular progeny, a semiotic ideology that separated religious ritual from true religion of the heart. As Keane notes, this semiotic ideology required a necessary subject-object distinction that would be adopted and adapted by Protestant mission movements of the nineteenth and twentieth centuries. Thus, in his study of the semiotic divide between missionaries and the Sumba people of Indonesia, Keane brings this point to light:

> Where the articulation of words and things plays a central role in non-Christian rituals, matter and materialism pose special difficulties for the more austere Protestants. Their efforts to regulate certain verbal and material practices, and the anxieties that attend them, center on the problem of identifying—and even becoming—a human subject that is at its core supposed to be independent of, and superordinate to, the world of mere dead matter. For them, getting their semiotic ideology right is no "academic question": it has eternal consequences for the immortal soul.[30]

For Protestant missionaries confronted with pagan fetishism where matter and spirit are inextricably fused, conversion to Christ requires a necessary spiritual and epistemological conversion that separates spirit and matter. For these missionaries, Christian mission requires a semiotic ideology that distinguishes between spiritual agency and material objects and that denies the agency of the latter. Thus, words communicate meaning via a distinction between sign and signified as well as subject and object so as to no longer be understood as ontological extensions in oaths, curses, or blessings by ritualist invocation. This epistemological gospel required a turning away from belief in the perceived power of blessings and curses and use of fetishes and an embrace of a Christian spiritual, intellectual, and epistemological view that true religion was a matter of heart and mind. Without this necessary epistemological conversion, there could be no liberation from the spiritual and intellectual bondage of pagan fetishism, ritualism, and ignorance of the "true" nature of the material world.

---

[29] Keane, Webb. "On Semiotic Ideology," 2018, https://www.journals.uchicago.edu/doi/pdfplus/10.1086/695387.
[30] Keane 2018.

Thus, as with their Reformed forebears, for these missionaries religion and religious agency are matters of the individual soul and separated from Catholic ritual and pagan fetish. Thus early Sumba understanding of religious agency that fused rite, physical object, oaths, curses, and blessings had to give way to religion, religious agency, and even knowledge as matters of the heart, and to give cognitive assent to sound doctrine about God, humans, and salvation. Nonetheless, as Keane carefully notes, the unintended consequence of this distinction between object and subject, substance and meaning, signifier and signified, form and essence soon informed secular ideologies and epistemologies untethered from their Protestant doctrinal and theological moorings, which led to secular resignification of the nature and agency of religion. It is important to note, however, that both austere Protestant missionaries and their secular antagonists share a common objective semiotic ideology that then gives way to contending moral and intellectual epistemological communities of inquiry. As Keane notes:

> For semiotic ideology implies that there is in principle no determinant ground of a sign. To say this is not to give up on the serious tasks of observation and analysis nor to cast doubt on the real knowledge to which they lead. Rather, it is to situate our knowledge within particular communities of inquiry and their asymptotic approach to something like conviction. ... But it does so while still accepting that signs in human worlds are inherently contestable and subject to historical transformation. For these processes are ineluctable features of semiotic mediation, as it functions within social projects and practices.[31]

Thus Protestant Calvinist missionaries and secular liberal modernists may share the view that religious faith is private and a matter of individual belief, yet they part company when it comes to their respective views of human salvation, intellectual inquiry, and their moral implications. For Protestant evangelicals, salvation is a matter of conversion to a religion of heart and mind that leads the convert out of the spiritual and intellectual darkness. For progressive secular liberals, emancipation leads the individual out of the intellectual and personal captivity of patriarchal religion that impedes autonomy, self-realization and progressive human discovery.[32]

---

[31] Keane 2018.
[32] Keane, Webb. *Christian Moderns: Freedom and Fetish in the Mission Encounter* (Berkeley: University of California Press, 2007).

7. The Recovery of Integral Mission

Certainly the global expansion of Protestant mission alongside the imperial expansion of the Western powers profoundly changed how individuals and societies beyond the European powers understand the world they live in and their lives within that world. Even if the expressed purpose of nineteenth—and twentieth—century Protestant missionaries was to save souls and plant churches in pagan lands now under Western imperial sway, they brought with them the epistemological secularizing disenchantment of Western semiotic ideology. Nonetheless, that encounter has proved dialectic. As Mahmood has noted, resistance to Western secularization is a motive force in non-liberal agency gained by submission to religious norms and practiced piety. I would argue that the same is true for many Asian, African, and Latin American Christians, whose non-Western perspectives on Christianity and mission have begun to redefine Christianity and mission along alternative semiotic trajectories. Note the Argentinian theologian Renee Padilla's definition of mission: its purpose is to incarnate the values of the Kingdom of God and bear witness to the love and the justice revealed in Jesus Christ, by the power of the Spirit, for the transformation of human life in all its dimensions, on a personal and community level.[33]

Padilla and other Latin American mission theologians have coined this understanding of mission as *Misión Integral*. It offers it as an alternative to what they regard as the inappropriate privatization of mission agency. Instead *Misión Integral* argues for "holistic transformation" and offers it as a gift from non-Western Evangelicals to recover what they regard as the richer biblical understanding of mission. They define mission as

> crossing the frontier between faith and no faith not only in geographical terms, but in cultural, ethnic, social, economic, and political terms for the purpose of transforming life in all its dimensions according to God's plan so that all people and human communities may experience the abundant life that Christ offers.[34]

Padilla's reorientation of mission directionally and missiologically does not dismiss conversion to Christ, but insists on its call to cultural, ethnic, social, economic, and political transformation—a way of being in the world that embodies and witnesses to "the abundant life that Christ offers." This

---

[33] Padilla, Rene. *What is Integral Mission?* (Oxford: Regnum, 2021), 8.
[34] Ibid.

is not mere pragmatic activism; it is an agency based on theological missiological reflection that evaluates what is being done and to be done to see if it "actually contributes to the goals of the Kingdom of God and its justice."[35]

The Great Commission, according to Matthew 28:16-20, is not an evangelistic commandment on which to base the idea that the church's main concern should be converting people and establishing churches; rather, it is a calling that the risen Lord gives to the church to concentrate on training men and women to recognize his universal lordship, to be part of God's people and to follow Jesus, which covers every aspect of human life. In other words, it is a call to integral mission, a summons to participate in training citizens of God's Kingdom who are willing to obey him in everything, for which the church can count on the Spirit (the other Jesus) "to the end of the age."[36]

Thus, rather than a semiotic ideology that would sever the tie between subject and object, faith and agency, piety and liberation, church and public square, it challenges these artificial distinctions. In contrast, they contend that the role of Christian witness and mission is to connect "word and deed." These mission emphases have faced headwinds from some North American evangelical mission institutions and spokespersons that seek to "reduce the church's mission to a form of evangelism equivalent to verbally communicating the Gospel."[37] Nonetheless, as Vinay Samuel argues,

> Mission is individuals coming to Christ, challenging corrupt and sinful systems, structures and cultures and enabling individuals and communities to experience God's Transforming Power. Transformation is to enable God's vision of society to be actualised in all relationships, social, economic and spiritual, so that God's will may be reflected in human society and his love be experienced by all communities, especially the poor.[38]

These concerns raised by non-Western evangelical theologians led to the founding of the International Fellowship of Evangelical Missionary Theologians (Infemit) and in 1983 of the Oxford Centre for Mission Studies. Together they sought to better understand and respond missionally to the challenges of social justice, global economic and political inequality, economic development and other critical challenges facing the churches

---

[35] Ibid, 12.
[36] Ibid, 18.
[37] Ibid, 29.
[38] Sugden, Chris. "Transformational Development: Current State of Understanding and Practice," *Transformation* 20, no. 2 (April 2003): 70-76.

around the world with students drawn largely from the Global South and East. Though unevenly, what has developed is a spectrum of research whose epistemological approach seeks to understand and empower holistic transformative mission. Like Mahmood and Asad, these scholars pursue epistemological perspectives that offer new lenses that might remove the missional and secular blinders that divide mission, epistemology and agency.

For example, Stephanie Goins's thesis on the "The Place of Forgiveness in the Reintegration of Former Child Soldiers in Sierra Leone" is a study on how "forgiveness functions in various dimensions of society, not merely as a spoken language but a language of action, an enacted process, which is significantly influenced by one's cultural orientation."[39] Herein, Word, agency, research, and epistemology inform each other. The epistemological approach offers thick descriptions of forgiveness as a transformative agency in Sierra Leone. One could turn as well to Kethoser Aniu Kevichusa's *Forgiveness and Politics: A Critical Appraisal,* which employs Scripture as it unpacks the relationship of forgiveness to politics in Nagaland, India.[40] Here, research into the biblical grounds of forgiveness informs the practice of politics, justice, and reconciliation in the work of peace-making in Nagaland. In this way, Kevichusa's research looks at the dynamics of missional agency fully engaged in the public square. Finally, Terence Garde's "Mining God's Way: Towards Mineral Resource Justice with Artisanal Gold Miners in East Africa" may be the first research project to consider the relevance of missional agency to ethical issues surrounding artisanal mining in the Global South.[41] Garde's final clause of his thesis title, "with Artisanal Gold Miners in East Africa," bears notice. Garde describes four stages of research framed by the names given to him by the Kenyan miners. First, he was referred to as "the stranger" who, even though present, could be safely ignored as neither a local nor an unobserved observer. Soon, however, he was called "the fool" "due to the 'stupid questions' asked by 'this idiot amongst us.'" In time, he was named the "student" as he came to understand their use of illegal explosives and their associated dangers. Finally, he became the "partner": a fellow miner with useful technical know-how on mining

---

[39] Goins, Stephanie. *Forgiveness and Reintegration: How the Tranformative Process of Forgiveness Impacts Child Soldier Reintegration* (Oxford: Regnum Studies in Mission, 2015).

[40] Kevichusa, Kethoser Aniu. *Forgiveness and Politics: A Critical Appraisal* (Oxford: Regnum, 2017).

[41] Garde, Terrence William. "Mining God's Way: Towards Mineral Resource Justice with Artisanal Gold Miners in East Africa" (dissertation thesis, Oxford Centre for Mission Studies, 2020).

and other matters of life and faith. As these names suggest, the research conversation changed. As "partner," these fellow miners were willing to share with Garde. They no longer told him what they thought he wanted to hear but began to confide in him, sharing their hopes and fears as artisanal miners. In this way, the gap between researcher and the researched was at least partially bridged in the fellowship formed through shared experience and faith. For the researcher, this inquiry led to a descent into the mine with miners that itself embodied an agency that afforded a thicker narrative of the relative agency of Christian miners in Kenya.

8. Conclusion: Plumbing the Sacred

From ISIS fighters to Christian artisanal miners in Kenya, we have considered the epistemological issues that haunt secular accounts of religious agency and considered alternative approaches to understand religious agency and devoted actors. Mahmood's attention to women's experience of agency and self-realization gained through submission to religious teaching, disciplined piety, and pursuit of the *dawa* showed that only through the decoupling of agency from personal autonomy can one begin to understand the nature of their agency and its moral and political import in Egypt. Talal Asad noted the relationship between habitus, sense, sensibility and agency. Asad approached agency not as a matter of liberal choice, but of disciplined discernment in the pursuit of a righteousness that is at once gift and practice. Finally, we looked at the alternative approaches to understanding mission and research of Global South scholars who have begun to probe new ways of research to understand and practice mission as holistic transformation.

As we have shown, the tensions that exist between rival epistemologies arise in part due to common denominators within these rival semiotic ideologies as well as the equivocal semiotic relationship of sign and signified. Keane argues that this makes ideological contention universal, ineluctable and irresolvable. Certainly, Keane's anthropological reflections do put austere Calvinist Protestantism and its missionary expansion in the dock. Nonetheless, recent missiological pushback with its growing emphasis upon integral mission offers alternative approaches to missiology that plumb sacred mission along epistemological lines that are neither a return to a semiotic innocence, nor a necessary epistemological privatization of religious agency, nor a capitulation to Western intellectualist appeals to mere "technical means and calculations," but instead offer incisive ways to understand the agency, ethics, and significance of religious agency and devoted actors in our world today.

About the Author

Thomas holds a Ph.D. from Duke University and serves as the Academic Dean of the Oxford Centre for Mission Studies. He has written extensively on Chinese Christianity as well on church, state and mission in Asia. As lecturer in systematic theology at Trinity Theological College in Singapore, he served on the National Council of Churches, Singapore.

He is passionate in working alongside Asian, African, and Latin American scholars in cutting-edge research, writing, and academic excellence that inform and empower global holistic mission and ministry. He is married to Judy, an ordained Anglican priest, and they have three grown children and three grandchildren.

Integrity and World Evangelization: What is the Connection?

David W. Bennett

1. Introduction

For nearly five decades the Lausanne Movement has been connecting influencers and ideas for global mission. Hundreds of networks and collaborative initiatives have sprung up, as evangelical leaders have linked arms and found ways to partner together to bear witness to Jesus Christ and all his teachings—in every nation, in every sphere of society, and in the realm of ideas.

In 2014, I was invited by Dr. Manfred Kohl and Bishop Efraim Tendero, leaders of a newly formed network, at that time called the Lausanne Integrity Network (before it became a collaborative effort with the World Evangelical Alliance, and named the Global Integrity Network), to participate in a workshop in Hong Kong. They asked me to address the connection between the focus of that network—on integrity and the struggle against corruption—and the historic emphasis of the Lausanne Movement on world evangelization. After all, there were other movements, networks and initiatives that had sprung up in recent years to stand for integrity, to call for higher standards of public morality, and to take aim at corruption. What, if anything, made the Lausanne Integrity Network (and now, the Global Integrity Network) distinct from the rest of them? And how was an integrity-focused network to be aligned with the Lausanne Movement as a whole? This chapter is based on the answers I provided in that workshop.

I would suggest three points of connection between integrity and world evangelization. The first is found in our fundamental *understanding of integrity*. The second point of connection is located in our *understanding of the gospel*, the good news of Jesus Christ. The third is based in our understanding of what may be the *single greatest hindrance to world evangelization*.

2. Our understanding of integrity

From its beginnings in 1974, the mission of the Lausanne Movement has been to call the *whole* church to take the *whole* gospel to the *whole* world.[1] Notice the repeated emphasis on "whole." Even though the Lausanne

Movement was launched by people like Billy Graham and John Stott, who represented wings of the church often described theologically as "evangelical," its intention has always been to be in conversation with, and to issue its calls to, the entire global church, including not only fellow evangelicals, but all Protestants, Catholics, Orthodox, independents—whatever groupings are marked by their common affirmation that Jesus Christ is Lord.

The Lausanne Movement has been calling the *whole church* to embrace the *whole gospel*—that is, the biblical message in all its fullness, with all its implications, for every dimension of life, and every sphere of society. In July of 1974, when the International Congress of World Evangelization was held in Lausanne, Switzerland, and I had just completed my first round of theological studies, I remember well that there were still many divisions between those who emphasized proclamation, evangelistic preaching, and personal witnessing, calling people to individual repentance and faith in Jesus Christ, over against those who emphasized the implications of the teaching and the example of Jesus for engagement in acts of compassionate service, involvement in social justice, and participation in public life. The Lausanne Movement attempted to bring these two streams together in the call to a "whole gospel" that combined word and deed. And that "wholeness" was expressed in the Lausanne Covenant, then fifteen years later in the Manila Manifesto,[2] and again in 2010 in the Cape Town Commitment.[3]

Furthermore, from the beginning, the Lausanne Movement had the *whole world* in view—all nations, all people groups, in all places, both men and women of all ages. The compendium of messages from the First Lausanne Congress was entitled *Let the Earth Hear His Voice*,[4] its title inspired by the phrase repeated by Billy Graham in his opening greeting: "We are gathered in Lausanne to let the earth hear his voice."

This word "whole" has been firmly embedded in the Lausanne Movement throughout the last five decades. And the concept of "whole" is fundamental to the understanding of "integrity."

The basic meaning of the English word "integrity" is "whole, not divided." It is related to the word "integer," which means a whole number,

---

[1] Section 6 ("The Church and Evangelism") of the Lausanne Covenant includes this statement: "World evangelization requires the whole Church to take the whole gospel to the whole world." https://lausanne.org/content/covenant/lausanne-covenant#cov.

[2] https://lausanne.org/content/covenant/lausanne-covenant#cov.

[3] https://lausanne.org/content/ctcommitment.

[4] J. D. Douglas, ed. *Let the Earth Hear His Voice: International Congress on World Evangelization, Lausanne, Switzerland* (Minneapolis: World Wide Publications, 1975).

not divided into fractions. Integrity is about wholeness, completeness, consistency.

The basic meaning of the Hebrew word *tōm*, translated "integrity" in the Old Testament, is completeness, fullness. Nothing is missing. Nothing is deficient. Nothing is out of alignment. The meaning of the Greek word *aphthoria*, translated "integrity" in the New Testament, is "morally sound, pure," literally, "without corruption." Integrity is in fact the opposite of corruption. To have integrity means to "have it all together" morally.

When asked to name the greatest commandment, Jesus quoted from Deuteronomy 6, saying in Mark 12:29-30, "The most important one is this: 'Hear, O Israel, the Lord our God, the Lord is one. Love the Lord your God with all your heart and with all your soul and with all your mind and with all your strength.'" All ... all ... all ... all ... the whole ... no admixture of other motives and agendas.

The Lausanne Movement has been calling the whole church to take the whole gospel to the whole world—a call to leave no one and nothing out. The call to personal integrity is about bringing the whole of life into alignment with the person, the teaching, and the example of Jesus Christ. Jesus is Lord of all. There is no corner of creation, no sphere of society, no sector of the workplace, no aspect of personal life that Christ does not claim as his. Not finances, not business, not sexuality, not motives. Integrity is about wholeness on the personal level.

So the first connection between the Global Integrity Network and the Lausanne Movement is in the core understanding of integrity as wholeness—the entirety of life brought into submission to Jesus Christ, who is Lord of all.

3. Our understanding of the gospel

The second point of connection comes in our understanding of the gospel, the good news of Jesus Christ. The Greek word *euangelizo*, which we have transliterated in English as "evangelize," means to announce good news. That good news includes the whole of the story of God and his interactions with the human race, from creation, to the fall, to redemption, to the final consummation—all centered in the person and work of the promised Messiah, Jesus, who lived a sinless life, died in voluntary sacrifice for our sins, was raised triumphantly from the dead, and has ascended to heaven, from where he will return to establish his eternal kingdom in a transformed heaven and earth. This story of global, cosmic and personal restoration, full of hope and purpose, is about the mission of God, into which we have been invited as participants.

This story is good news. It is not just words, but it is expressed in actions which are for the common public good, and for the individual's personal good—especially if people will embrace this message, personally surrender their lives to Jesus in trust and obedience, and become active participants in God's global mission.

Early in the history of the Lausanne Movement, a distinction was made between "evangelism" and "evangelization." Evangelism, as I have said, means the announcement of good news. It emphasizes the proclamation of the message about Jesus Christ. But the word "evangelization," which is not a biblical word, but one introduced into the Lausanne Movement early in its history, and endorsed at a meeting in Mexico City in 1975, is broader. It embraces all the active expressions of the life and teaching of Jesus, in compassion and justice and servanthood. Evangelization combines proclamation with demonstration, words with deeds.

Jesus was full of grace and truth (John 1:14). He was the embodiment of the fullness of God's character. All the fullness of deity dwelt in him (Col 1:19). As followers of Jesus, we are called to be full of grace and truth. Thus, everything we say and do is to be an expression of God's grace, his steadfast love. And everything we do and say is to be an expression of his truth. To have integrity is to be consistent, to be complete, to be free from corruption, in both grace and truth. And that kind of life is good news to those who encounter us.

At the beginning of his ministry, people spoke well of Jesus. The crowds flocked to hear his words. All who came to him for healing or deliverance were transformed. Children were embraced. Outcasts were welcomed. Jesus was able to challenge his adversaries without contradiction when he asked, "Can any of you prove me guilty of sin?" (John 8:46). During the trial of Jesus, Pilate had to concede, "I find no basis for a charge against this man" (Luke 23:4). The Roman centurion who saw Jesus tortured and executed concluded, "Surely this man was the Son of God" (Mark 15:39). The coming of Jesus was good news for those who would receive it. In him they encountered grace and truth.

The same was true with the early followers of Jesus. We read in Acts 2 that in Jerusalem the first believers enjoyed the favor of all the people (v. 47). When Philip the evangelist went to Samaria in Acts 8, there was great joy in the city (v. 8). In Acts 16, the jailer and his whole family were filled with joy because they encountered the living God through the witness and the example of Paul and Silas (v. 34). Through the followers of Jesus, people continued to see examples of integrity, full of grace and truth. When they were willing to receive the good news, both their personal lives and their communities were transformed and blessed.

Donald McGavran, the great missionary to India in the mid-twentieth century, documented the changes that happened when whole families and people groups began to turn to Jesus. He spoke of "redemption and lift."[5] That is, when people repented, believed and welcomed the good news of Jesus, and began to align their lives with Jesus' teaching, their whole community advanced. Their health improved, their educational level went up, public drunkenness and sexual debauchery went down, family life became more peaceful, they began to earn more and save more, and their treatment of the disabled and the weak became more compassionate.

In many parts of the world, we can see the contrasts between the Christian villages and the non-Christian villages, and between the Christian homes and the non-Christian homes. The gospel is good news, not just for individuals, but for entire communities. When people start to live lives of integrity, full of grace and truth, they serve the common good. They become good news to the contexts in which they function—their homes, their extended families, their neighborhoods, their businesses, their institutions, their civic lives.

There are many examples of this in Scripture. Joseph lived a life of integrity whatever the context. He did not give in to sexual temptation, despite insistent and repeated invitations to do so from his boss's wife. He handled Potiphar's affairs in ways that benefited his boss, such that his boss trusted him completely. Genesis 39:6 reports that Potiphar "left in Joseph's care everything he had; with Joseph in charge, he did not concern himself with anything except the food he ate." The same thing happened to Joseph in the jail. Genesis 39 records, "The warden put Joseph in charge of all those held in the prison, and he was made responsible for all that was done there. The warden paid no attention to anything under Joseph's care, because the Lord was with Joseph and gave him success in whatever he did" (Gen 39:22–23). Then later Pharaoh did the same thing with Joseph, putting him in charge of the palace, and of the whole land of Egypt (Gen 41:40–41).

When someone gives you the keys, when someone turns over full responsibility to you, it is because they believe that you will be acting in their best interests, you will not be trying to undermine them or usurp their leadership, you will be making decisions for the common good, and for their personal good.

Nehemiah is another example of a man of integrity whose public service brought good to those under his leadership.

---

[5] https://lausanne.org/about-the-lausanne-movement.

Daniel was a man of integrity, demonstrated in everything from the food he was willing to take into his body, to his refusal to worship or give ultimate allegiance to anyone except God alone. He was willing to speak the truth respectfully and graciously, without spinning it or shading it, even in the corridors of power, to intimidating leaders like Nebuchadnezzar and Belshazzar. His leadership was considered so beneficial that he continued to serve despite several changes of administration, and even changes of empire.

Psalm 78:72 says of David's public leadership, "David shepherded them with integrity of heart; with skillful hands he led them." Yet the pursuit of integrity does not imply the attainment of sinless perfection. Certainly not in David's case, where he lapsed into adultery with Bathsheba and premeditated murder of Uriah by proxy. Yet still David was described as a man after God's own heart (1 Sam 13:14; Acts 13:22). Why? Because the direction of his heart was toward God, and he returned again and again to loving the Lord with all his heart, soul, mind and strength—to integrity.

The living embodiment of the grace of God and the truth of God lifts a whole society. Consistent applications of grace and truth, expressed in straightforward business dealings, honest research, transparency in government leadership, fulfillment of contracts, concern for the last and least, and respect and kindness toward all the different segments of society (including race, ethnicity, national origin, age, gender, ability and disability, class and status), all contribute to *shalom*, that beautiful Hebrew word describing a state of peace, righteousness and wholeness toward which God's mission is aimed.

And this provides the common ground for the Global Integrity Network with other networks and movements in society as a whole working toward integrity and against corruption. In obeying and serving Jesus Christ as Lord in every dimension of life, in being embodiments of the grace and truth expressed fully only in Jesus Christ but awakened by his Holy Spirit's operation in us as well, we become agents for the common good. Many of the other Lausanne-related issue networks find this same common ground in working with others for the common good.[6] A few examples would be the issue networks for Children-at-Risk, for Cities, for Creation Care, for Disability Concerns, for Business as Mission, and for Freedom and Justice. Jeremiah called the Jewish exiles in Babylon to

---

[6] Donald McGavran devoted a chapter to the phrase "redemption and lift" in his definitive work on church growth philosophy, *Understanding Church Growth* (Grand Rapids: Eerdmans, 1970). This work was revised in 1980 and then revised again with C. Peter Wagner in 1990.

seek the peace, that is the *shalom*, and the prosperity of the city to which they had been taken (Jer 29:7).

Yes, people of integrity embody good news for the social sectors in which they live and work. And in so doing they make credible the more complete message of good news which they bring, about the redemptive work of God in Jesus Christ. Integrity means not only expressing grace and truth regarding issues and concerns of this present world, but also loving people enough to tell them about their eternal destinies, to let them know that they stand condemned as sinners before a perfect and holy judge, and that if they do not repent and turn to Jesus, they cannot be saved. Grace and truth mean loving people enough to tell them of the Savior's love for them, and of the possibility of life forever with God in the new heavens and earth. Complete integrity means living with heaven, eternity, and Christ's second coming in view. While Paul was imprisoned in Caesarea, he spoke frequently to Felix about righteousness, self-control and the judgment to come (Acts 24:25). That is, he spoke about integrity, not only in view of the common good in this life but considering the life to come. And Paul modeled integrity by refusing to pay the bribes that Felix kept hoping for.

It might be good to inject a reminder here that what sets the Global Integrity Network apart from many integrity and anti-corruption movements is its Christ-ward motivation, its awareness of eternal as well as temporal consequences flowing from integrity or its lack, and also its realism about how much human beings are likely to change, except as new creations, empowered by the Spirit of God. Simply calling people to "be good" and to "do the right thing" is necessary and helpful, but by itself it will not produce lasting results. The human heart is "deceitful above all things and desperately sick" (Jer 17:9). People cannot be changed permanently from the outside in. Change must come from the inside out. Only God can perform a spiritual heart transplant. Only he can replace the heart of stone with the heart of flesh.

Thus, a focus on integrity supplies us with common ground with those who seek the common good. It enables us to be good news to our societies, as agents of grace and truth, and it prepares the way for us to speak the more complete good news about God's revelation in Jesus Christ. Jesus called us to be salt and light. Integrity beams light into the darkness. Integrity preserves a society from decay.

What then is the connection between an emphasis on integrity, and the Lausanne Movement as a whole, with its focus on world evangelization? First, integrity speaks of the *whole*, so that in all of life, and every place, Jesus Christ is honored and obeyed as Lord of all. This corresponds to the Lausanne Movement's call for the whole church to take the whole gospel to the whole world. And second, a life of integrity both expresses and prepares the way for the gospel, the good news of grace and truth revealed in Jesus Christ.

4. Our understanding of what may be the greatest hindrance to world evangelization

In the third place, a focus on integrity addresses what may be the greatest hindrance to world evangelization—that is, the lack of integrity in the church. This was a major focus at Cape Town 2010, which led to the birthing of a new issue network around the theme of integrity and anti-corruption. Let me direct your attention to the Cape Town Commitment.

This document is arranged in two halves. The first part is a confession of faith, and the second part is a call to action. The first half of the Cape Town Commitment calls us to wholeness, to integrity, in our love for the triune God—Father, Son and Holy Spirit—based on his love for us. It affirms our love for God's Word, God's world, the gospel of God, the people of God and the mission of God.

The second half of the Cape Town Commitment shows the implications of this love—God's love and ours, as we participate in God's mission, bearing witness to Jesus Christ and all his teaching, in every nation, in every sphere of society, and in the realm of ideas—that is, living a life of consistent integrity, full of grace and truth. The more than thirty calls to action correspond to six areas that were highlighted at Cape Town 2010:

- Bearing witness to the truth of Christ in a pluralistic, globalized world,
- Building the peace of Christ in our divided and broken world,
- Living the love of Christ among people of other faiths,
- Discerning the will of Christ for world evangelization,
- Partnering in the Body of Christ for unity in mission, and
- Calling the Church of Christ back to humility, integrity and simplicity.

Let us examine the paragraphs from the Cape Town Commitment that introduce the call to integrity (Section IIE.1):[7]

> The Bible shows that God's greatest problem is not just with the nations of the world, but with the people he has created and called to be the means of

---

[7] https://lausanne.org/all-issue-networks.

blessing the nations. And the biggest obstacle to fulfilling that mission is idolatry among God's own people. For if we are called to bring the nations to worship the only true and living God, we fail miserably if we ourselves are running after the false gods of the people around us. ...

When there is no distinction in conduct between Christians and non-Christians—for example in the practice of corruption and greed, or sexual promiscuity, or rate of divorce, or relapse to pre-Christian religious practice, or attitudes towards people of other races, or consumerist lifestyles, or social prejudice—then the world is right to wonder if our Christianity makes any difference at all. Our authority carries no authenticity to a watching world.

This portion of the Cape Town Commitment then goes on to detail the call to

- Walk in love, rejecting the idolatry of disordered sexuality
- Walk in humility, rejecting the idolatry of power
- Walk in integrity, rejecting the idolatry of success
- Walk in simplicity, rejecting the idolatry of greed

In the paragraphs on integrity, it says, "We cannot build the kingdom of the God of truth on foundations of dishonesty. ... Let us strive for a culture of full integrity and transparency."

Hypocrisy is so destructive to the witness of the church. The Barna Group did a major research project on the increasingly negative reputation of evangelical Christians in the USA, especially among younger adults, resulting in a book entitled *unChristian*.[8] First on the list of six common points of skepticism and objection is the perception among people outside the church community that Christians are hypocritical, saying one thing and doing another, pretending to be something unreal, conveying a polished image that is not accurate—in other words, lacking integrity. I have heard similar statements numerous times in other countries as well, which substantiate the statement that the greatest threats to world evangelization do not come from the world but from the church itself.

Just as Jesus branded the religious leaders of his day as hypocrites, as play actors, so a similar prophetic voice is needed in many parts of the church today. In Romans 2:24, the apostle Paul warned the self-righteous Jewish leaders of his day by quoting from Isaiah 52: "God's name is blasphemed among the Gentiles because of you."

---

[8] https://lausanne.org/all-issue-networks.

In contrast, the apostle Peter instructed his readers, "Live such good lives among the pagans that, though they accuse you of doing wrong, they may see your good deeds and glorify God on the day he visits us. For it is God's will that by doing good you should silence the ignorant talk of foolish men" (1 Pet 2:12-13). In other words, live lives of integrity.

Similarly, Paul wrote to Titus, "In everything set them an example by doing what is good. In your teaching show integrity, seriousness and soundness of speech that cannot be condemned, so that those who oppose you may be ashamed because they have nothing bad to say about us" (Titus 2:7-8).

But if our lives do not express integrity, wholeness, and freedom from corruption, if there are inconsistencies and cracks, people will not believe or welcome our message. They will reject the good news as too good to be true, or as obviously not relevant. If people do not feel they can trust what we will do or say, if they are not assured that we are working for the common good, or for their personal good, they will not take seriously what we say about anything else—including the good news of Jesus Christ.

The stakes are immensely high. The Global Integrity Network has an opportunity not only to build common ground with those who do not yet believe, and to prepare the way for the proclamation and further demonstration of the gospel, but also to rally the global church and its leaders, so that the church does not, through its hypocrisy and its lack of integrity, undermine or undo all that is being done to bear witness to the good news of Jesus throughout the world.

What an opportunity! What a challenge! What an awesome responsibility! May God help us!

About the Author

As Global Associate Director for Collaboration and Content for the Lausanne Movement, David Bennett oversees the Lausanne Catalysts and leads the Content Team. He has served as Senior Pastor of globally involved churches in California, Oregon and Massachusetts. He holds a B.S. from MIT and M.Div., D.Min. and Ph.D. degrees from Fuller Theological Seminary. He has written three books on biblical principles of leadership, including *Metaphors of Ministry: Biblical Images for Leaders and Followers.*

His wife Phyllis serves as Director of the Women's Center for Ministry at Western Seminary in Portland, Oregon. They have two grown sons and eight grandchildren.

Living in Global Integrity:
Moral Wholeness for a More Whole World

Kelly O'Donnell and Michèle Lewis O'Donnell

In this chapter, we distill some of the lessons we have learned over the past twenty years in promoting integrity and confronting corruption. How can we better live up to our moral and ethical aspirations? As both Christians and psychologists, we reflect on the nature of integrity and corruption, highlighting the challenges and tactics of dysfunction, deviance, and self-deception (Part One). We then feature ten materials that have been developed within the Lausanne Movement (2010–2020), noting the importance of using and building upon these foundational resources (Part Two). We conclude with a summons to the international church-mission community (CMC) to resolutely and broadly collaborate toward a global integrity movement, marked by righteousness and relevance, We have also prepared an additional list of multi-sectoral resources that can be accessed via the Global Integrity section of the Member Care Associates website (www.membercare.org). We are the light—or the darkness—of the world.

> Do not fear. These are the things which you should do: speak the truth to one another; judge with truth and judge for peace in your courts. Also let none of you devise evil in your heart against another, and do not love perjury, for I hate all these things, declares YHWH. ... Therefore, love truth and peace. (Zech 8:14–19, excerpts)

The ubiquitous co-existence of good and evil. Escher, 1960[1]

---

[1] M. C. Escher, "Circle Limit IV" (1960), https://www.wikiart.org/en/m-c-escher/circle-limit-iv.

1. Part One—Exploring Integrity and Corruption

How much integrity do you have? If you are like most people, your response is a definite "lots!" Yet in spite of our character strengths such as courage, humility, and perseverance, our self-appraisals of integrity can be seriously influenced by our own self-serving distortions; namely rationalizing away inconsistencies between our purported values and our actual actions. "I am a moral person and a model person" can be one of the greatest self-evident truths of human history. At least to ourselves.

We define *integrity* as *moral wholeness*—living consistently in moral wholeness. Its opposite is *corruption*: the distortion, perversion, and deterioration of moral goodness, resulting in the exploitation of people and the planet. *Global integrity* is moral wholeness at all levels in our world—from the individual to the institutional to the international and everything in-between.

Living in *global* integrity is essential for sharing the good news and good works among all peoples and spheres of society. It is also requisite for fostering sustainable development-transformation, health-well-being, and peace-security in our world. Integrity is not easy, it is not always black and white, and it can be risky.[2]

1.1 Searching for Integrity

Fifteen years ago I (Kelly) was engrossed in a conversation with one of my closest friends. It was a cold winter's day as we walked along the icy gray water of Lake Geneva. I was lamenting, with candid fervor, why it can be so hard for good people to simply try to do good in an organizational context. "Why can organizational life, especially in *Christian* organizations, sometimes be as bleak as this winter day?" I mourned. Why can integrity be so elusive?

An hour into this somber discussion—dominated by concerns about leadership hubris, systemic dysfunction, selfish self-interests, and wrongful dismissals—my friend stopped and turned his gaze at me. He gently offered me two words of advice: "Read Machiavelli."

---

[2] See the twenty-five entries on "Global Integrity: Moral Wholeness for a Whole World" in CORE *Member Care: Reflections, Research, and Resources for Good Practice* (2016), http://coremembercare.blogspot.fr/search/label/global%20integrity.

1.2. Manipulating Vice and Virtue

My friend was referring to the sixteenth-century treatise on power by Niccolò Machiavelli, *The Prince*.[3] Machiavelli resolved to develop a reasoned argument for leadership that was practical and reality-based, and not simply idealistic or solely virtue-centered. Power could be "legitimately" unencumbered by ethical values.

So I read and reread Machiavelli, determined to upgrade my understanding of how the organizational world often works. Especially illuminating was a core principle from Chapter 15: "A man who wishes to act entirely up to his professions of virtue soon meets with what destroys him among so much that is evil. Hence it is necessary for a prince wishing to hold his own to know how to do wrong, and to make use of it or not according to necessity."[4]

Machiavelli's work was a major influence in the *realpolitik* thinking that has impacted leadership and governance practices for the last five centuries. It has also crept into the CMC and has undermined the global integrity so desperately needed in our world today.[5]

1.3 Exposing Dysfunction and Deviance

Unfortunately, we can all be seriously duped and disabled by Machiavellian-type people and processes (Luke 16:8). We call these *DD Realities*: personal and organizational *dysfunction* (distortion of reality for one's own ends) and *deviance* (exploitation of others for one's own ends).[6]

DD is often disguised as being "virtuous" or "necessary for the greater good." In organizations, managing DD is especially tricky when there is insufficient understanding, accountability, or political will to resolutely

---

[3] Niccolò Machiavelli, *The Prince* (1515), http://www.gutenberg.org/files/1232/1232-h/1232-h.htm.

[4] Ibid. Chapter 15 concisely summarizes, in about 500 words, much of Machiavelli's advice for maintaining positions of power: "Concerning Things for which Men, and Especially Princes, Are Praised or Blamed," http://www.gutenberg.org/files/1232/1232-h/1232-h.htm#link2HCH0015.

[5] Many of the references to "integrity" from the Cape Town Commitment (2010) are cited in "Global Integrity—21," *CORE Member Care: Reflections, Research, and Resources for Good Practice* (November 12, 2016), http://coremembercare.blogspot.fr/search/label/Cape%20Town%20Commitment.

[6] See the various terms used in the New Testament to describe evil people *within* the church and warnings to not be naïve. "Member Care: Tares, Tears, and Terrors," *CORE Member Care*, http://coremembercare.blogspot.fr/search/label/na%C3%AFve.

enforce good practice standards. Above all, DD is reinforced when people compromise their integrity by looking the other way, rationalizing their responsibility, and ultimately becoming polluted themselves (see Prov 16:2, 25:26).[7]

1.4. Tactics for Sustaining DD

The following grid of five more D's helps to identify the presence and progression of DD in organizational and other settings. These five tactics can overlap. The grid can also be used as a mirror into one's own integrity.[8]

Deny. Conceal DD. "Don't ask about problems (even obvious ones), don't talk about problems, and don't rock the boat" is a pervasive, core, unwritten rule.

Downplay. Minimize DD's negative impact. State that it is probably "normal." Relational unity and conformity trump truth and genuine relationships.

Distract. Distract from the real DD issues. "Feign pain" and get sympathy, or admit that something is "not exactly right" and refer to problems as being largely a matter of having different perspectives/preferences—a need to agree to disagree.

Discredit. Belittle those who point out or inquire about DD. Silence them. Blacklist them. Instill an atmosphere of fear of reprisals and intimidation to prevent people from speaking up or calling for good practice.

Destroy. Demolish people's reputations, contributions, relationships, and well-being. Use half-truths, spin, lies, rumors, threats, false accusations, and dismissals. Reap the benefits of control, position, respect, status quo, and revenue streams.

---

[7] The lesson from Machiavelli was a prelude to the learning we were to undergo in dealing with corruption. In 2007 we joined with colleagues to publicly expose a long-term, international fraud. Together we contacted and consulted with four governments and called upon the assistance of several organizations and people primarily in the CMC to disclose how they had been affected. See PETRA People for updates: http://petranetwork.blogspot.com/.

[8] Adapted from Kelly O'Donnell, "Wise as Doves and Innocent as Serpents? Doing Conflict Management Better," *Evangelical Missions Quarterly* 43.1 (2007), pp. 40–49. This article is available in 12 languages on the Reality DOSE web page (https://sites.google.com/site/mcaresources/) and is expanded in Part Two of *Global Member Care* (vol. 1): *The Perils and Perils of Good Practice* (Pasadena, CA: William Carey Library, 2011), pp. 83–99, https://www.amazon.in/Global-Member-Care-Pearls-Practice-ebook/dp/B00IK71QM6,and *Member Care in India: From Ministry Call to Home Call* (Vellore, TN: Missionary Upholders Trust, 2012), pp. 111–126.

1.5. Practicing Self-Deception[9]

Cognitive dissonance is a powerful concept from social psychology that can help us understand our propensity to deceive ourselves while still believing we are living in integrity (Jer 17:9). It refers to the self-serving rationales that we use to calm our disturbing, internal incongruence and harmonize discrepant thoughts about ourselves—who we want to be versus who we actually are.

Illustration courtesy of Marc Rosenthal (www.marc-rosenthal.com)

Tavris and Aronson (2007) shed light on how our inner moral maneuvers help us feel good about ourselves:

> Most people, when directly confronted by evidence that they are wrong, do not change their point of view or course of action but justify it even more tenaciously. Even irrefutable evidence is rarely enough to pierce the mental armor of self-justification. ... Yet mindless self-justification, like quicksand, can draw us deeper into disaster. It blocks our ability to even see our errors, let alone correct them. It distorts reality, keeping us from getting all the information we need and assessing issues clearly. It prolongs and widens rifts between lovers, friends, and nations. It keeps us from letting go of unhealthy habits. It permits the guilty to avoid taking responsibility for their deeds.[10]

---

[9] Adapted from: Kelly O'Donnell, "Integrity and Accountability for United Nations Staff: Navigating the Terrain," *UN Special*, Issue 767 (March 2017), pp. 40–41, https://membercareassociates.org/wp-content/uploads/2017/04/Integrity-and-Accountability-parts-1-and-2-UN-Special-March-and-April-2017-ODonnell.pdf.

[10] Carol Tavris and Eliot Aronson, *Mistakes Were Made (but Not by Me): Why We Justify Foolish Beliefs, Bad Decisions, and Hurtful Acts*, (Orlando, FL: Harcourt, 2007), pp. 2, 9–10. This book is now in its third edition (2020).

1.6. Bad Leaders Are Bad News

Self-justification to minimize cognitive dissonance is a big reason why any leader can become a "bad" leader—Machiavellian. One international survey assessing the experiences and views of Christian leaders identified three main categories of negative characteristics of fellow leaders: "Prideful, always right, and always the big boss; Lack of integrity, untrustworthy; Harsh, uncaring, refused to listen, critical."[11]

Robert Sternberg's extensive research consistently finds that bad leaders see themselves as being above accountability—"ethics are for other people." They do not avail themselves of needed input from others to complement, balance, and correct themselves. They lapse into an unrealistic and often disguised sense of omnipotence, inerrancy, unrealistic optimism, and invulnerability. They become entrenched in their ways, even when it is obvious to others that these leaders are digging a bigger pit of mistakes into which they and others will fall.[12]

1.7. Tactics for Feigning Integrity

The four tactics discussed below illustrate what *not* to do when we are asked to give an account for a possible mistake or misconduct. Use this as a mirror into your own life and integrity. We encourage you to describe a few more tactics based on your experience and self-reflection.

- Distance yourself from the issue. Dodge, reword, or repackage it. Obfuscate the facts, talking tentatively or vaguely about concerns or "mistakes in the past." Disguise any culpability. Agree to some type of "review" but either never do one at all or do it with biased reviewers.
- Appeal to your "integrity" and your practice of acting with the "highest standards." Point out your past track record, your current contributions, and that you are doing your best. Punctuate it all

---

[11] Lausanne Movement. "We Have a Problem!—But There is Hope" (2010), https://www.lausanne.org/content/we-have-a-problem-but-there-is-hope-results-of-a-survey-of-1000-christian-leaders-from-across-the-globe.

[12] This summary of bad leader qualities is based on a presentation by Robert Sternberg given at Tufts University in 2009. A longer summary is in Kelly O'Donnell, "Resources for Good Practice" (chapter 8, p. 144), *Global Member Care* (vol. 2): *The Pearls and Perils of Good Practice* (Pasadena, CA: William Carey Library, 2011), https://www.amazon.in/Global-Member-Care-Pearls-Practice-ebook/dp/B00IK71QM6.

with the language of transparency and accountability without demonstrating either.
- State that you are being attacked and being treated unfairly, and that people don't understand. Be sure to remind folks that leadership is hard and full of ambiguities and tough choices. Mention other peoples' problems; question their motives and credibility.
- Hold out until the uncomfortable stuff goes away. Sack staff but don't change the system or the culture of complicity. Maintain your self-interests, lifestyle, affiliations, and allusions of moral congruity. Remember, you are special. Cognitive dissonance applies to others but not to you.

1.8. Multi-Sectoral Resources for Confronting Corruption

Corruption is commonly defined as the abuse of entrusted power for private gain.[13] It especially preys on the poor, with estimates of over one trillion dollars being siphoned off each year from countries in development.[14] Within the CMC, Zurlo, Johnson, and Crossing (2021) estimate that $55 billion each year is stolen through "ecclesiastical crime," defined as the "amounts embezzled by top custodians of Christian monies." This figure is more than the estimated $49 billion of income generated for "global foreign missions"![15]

Corruption is not just about financial fraud.[16] It also manifests as "bribery, law-breaking without dealing with the consequences in a fair manner, unfairly amending election processes and results, and covering mistakes or silencing whistleblowers (those who expose corruption in hope that justice would be served)."[17]

---

[13] This is Transparency International's succinct definition of corruption. See https://www.transparency.org/what-is-corruption.

[14] ONE, "Trillion Dollar Scandal Report" (2014), https://www.one.org/international/policy/trillion-dollar-scandal/.

[15] Gina Zurlo, Todd Johnson, and Peter Crossing, "World Christianity and Mission 2021: Questions about the Future," *International Bulletin of Mission Research* 45.1 (2021), pp. 15–25, https://journals.sagepub.com/doi/pdf/10.1177/2396939320966220. See also Todd Johnson, Gina Zurlo, and Albert Hickman, "Embezzlement in the Global Christian Community," *The Review of Faith and International Affairs* 13.2 (2015), pp. 74–94, https://www.researchgate.net/publication/277977397_EMBEZZLEMENT_IN_THE_GLOBAL_CHRISTIAN_COMMUNITY.

[16] See the list of sixty categories in Transparency International's Anti-Corruption Glossary.

[17] Time and Date, "International Anti-Corruption Day," https://www.timeanddate.com/holidays/un/international-anti-corruption-day.

The Zero Rupees banknote, part of a major anti-corruption campaign in India.[18]

In the humanitarian sector, corruption extends into "nepotism/cronyism, sexual exploitation and abuse, coercion and intimidation of humanitarian staff or aid recipients for personal, social or political gain, manipulation of assessments, targeting and registration to favor particular groups, and diversion of assistance to non-target groups."[19]

Fortunately, many publicized scandals and campaigns have sensitized us to the grim realities of corruption.[20] To combat corruption, we urge colleagues to: (a) cultivate a life of integrity: "Your task is to be true, not popular" (Luke 6:26, *The Message*);[21] (b) appreciate your own vulnerability to

---

[18] For more information on the Zero Rupees banknote campaign against corruption, see https://www.weforum.org/agenda/2015/12/the-power-of-a-zero-rupee-note/.

[19] Feinstein International Center, Humanitarian Policy Group, and Transparency International, *Preventing Corruption in Humanitarian Assistance: Final Research Report* (2008), http://www.odi.org.uk/sites/odi.org.uk/files/odi-assets/publications-opinion-files/1836.pdf.

[20] For a composite case study on corruption, including biblical and psychological perspectives, see Kelly O'Donnell and Michèle Lewis O'Donnell, "Loving Truth and Peace: A Case Study of Family Resilience in Mission/Aid Corruption," in *Family Accountability in Missions: Korean and Western Case Studies* (New Haven, CT: OMSC Publications, 2013), pp. 175–186, http://membercareassociates.org/wp-content/uploads/2017/11/Loving-Truth-and-Peace-Mission-Aid-Corruption-ODonnells.pdf. See also the anti-corruption efforts and materials by Transparency International (https://www.transparency.org/), ONE (https://www.one.org/international/), Faith and Public Integrity Network (https://fpinetwork.org/), Into Integrity (https://intointegrity.blogspot.com/), and the EXPOSED Campaign (https://www.eauk.org/current-affairs/news/exposing-corruption.cfm).

[21] See the resources for developing integrity in Kelly O'Donnell, "Integrity and Accountability for United Nations Staff: Staying the Course," *UN Special Issue 768* (April 2017), pp. 40–41 https://membercareassociates.org/wp-content/uploads/2017/04/Integrity-and-Accountability-parts-1-and-2-UN-Special-March-and-April-2017-ODonnell.pdf.

temptation, including propensities to distort and justify mistakes and misdeeds (Prov 20:6); (c) connect and contribute across sectors as people of integrity, keeping current with multi-sectoral resources on integrity and corruption such as the more than 75 multi-sectoral resources available. Many are provided in this chapter; contact us for more information.[22]

2. Part Two—10 Resources from the Lausanne Movement (2010–2020)

> Let us strive for a culture of full integrity and transparency. We will choose to walk in the light and truth of God, for the Lord tests the heart and is pleased with integrity. —Cape Town Commitment, 2010, Part 2, IIE. 4

We now share ten examples of integrity and anti-corruption resources that have been developed within the Lausanne Movement for or since its third Congress in 2010.[23] These practical resources are part of the collective roadmap--foundational building blocks—to help preserve the Lausanne institutional memory about integrity advocacy and commitments and to inform collaborative efforts to promote moral resilience and relevance within the international CMC. We encourage you to review the various references related to "integrity" in the Cape Town Commitment[24] and to connect with the Integrity and Anti-Corruption Network, coordinated by the Lausanne Movement and the World Evangelical Association.

---

[22] For suggestions about connecting and contributing across sectors, see these two resources: Kelly O'Donnell, "Charting Your Course through the Sectors," chapter 2 in Kelly O'Donnell and Michèle Lewis O'Donnell (eds.), *Global Member Care* (vol. 2): *Crossing Sectors for Serving Humanity* (Pasadena, CA: William Carey Library, 2013), https://www.amazon.com/Global-Member-Care-Crossing-Humanity-ebook/dp/B00HX6WZLQ/); Kelly O'Donnell and Michèle Lewis O'Donnell, "Global Grids: New Strategies for Staying Informed," *Global Integration Updates* (October 2016, Issue 11), https://us10.campaign-archive.com/?u=e83a5528fb81b78be71f78079&id=417e55ffc6.

[23] "Ten years ago in Cape Town, South Africa [October 2010], over 4,000 Christian leaders from 198 countries gathered as one body to call the global church to action, shaping world missions as we know it today. ... The Cape Town Commitment [CTC, the main resulting document] is the conviction and voice of a multitude hailing from nearly every nation on earth. As our roadmap for the past ten years, the CTC has been the touchstone for countless global gatherings, publications, and collaborative initiatives." "Our Roadmap and Touchstone," Lausanne Movement, https://lausanne.org/best-of-lausanne/our-roadmap-and-touchstone.

[24] The references to integrity are featured in "Christian Integrity: Moral Wholeness for a Whole World," *CORE Member Care* (November 12, 2016).

Global Integrity and Anti-Corruption Network, website homepage[25]

2.1 Resources from the Lausanne Congress (2010)

1. "We have a Problem!—But There Is Hope!"[26] by Jane Overstreet, an Advance Paper for the Lausanne Congress in Cape Town based on a survey about Christians in leadership (2010). "Too often evangelism is done successfully, a church is planted and begins to flourish, but then a leader is appointed who sadly destroys everything that was built, and the fruit is lost. While there are many variations on the story, its theme is much too familiar." See also the summary and perspectives about this study in *CORE Member Care* (February 14, 2016). For example: "When asked to describe their worst experiences working under [Christian] leaders, and what characteristics those poor leaders had, 1,000 leaders answering the survey gave these three main comments: "Prideful, always right, and always the big boss; Lack of integrity, untrustworthy; Harsh, uncaring, refused to listen, critical."

2. "Salt and Light: Christians' Role in Combating Corruption,"[27] Paul Batchelor and Steve Osei-Mensah, *Lausanne Global Conversations* (2010).

---

[25] Home page, Integrity and Anti-Corruption Network, Lausanne Movement and World Evangelical Alliance, https://www.globalintegritynetwork.org/. Header image courtesy of and ©2019 Erin Noelle O'Donnell.

[26] "We have a Problem!—But There Is Hope!" https://lausanne.org/content/we-have-a-problem-but-there-is-hope-results-of-a-survey-of-1000-christian-leaders-from-across-the-globe.

[27] "Salt and Light: Christians' Role in Combating Corruption," https://documentcloud.adobe.com/link/track?uri=urn%3Aaaid%3Ascds%3AUS%3Af6314f13-2b59-4de4-a433-e1a5e33c7a28.

"What part does corruption play in *your* life? That may seem a strange question to ask an audience such as this. Many may answer that, of course, as Christians, we would have nothing whatsoever to do with it. But others among us live with the dire consequences of corruption every day. Our assertion in this paper is that, whether we recognize it or not, we are all caught up in one form or another of corruption or its consequences and, as Evangelical Christians, we need to do more to prepare and engage in the fight against it."

3. "'Good News' in the Fight Against Corruption,"[28] Roberto Laver, *Review of Faith and International Affairs* (November 2010, volume 8, issue 4). Dr. Laver shared this article in a blog (*Lausanne Global Conversations*) for the Lausanne Congress 2010. "The World Bank, along with other international development institutions, is giving growing attention to good governance and anti-corruption. These efforts provide a unique opportunity for evangelical faith leaders and institutions to play a stronger advocacy role. Corruption is receiving far more attention from secular organizations than religious ones. The evangelical church can engage through advocacy and by building character within its own members. It needs to work locally on relevant and appropriate ways to engage the people it serves with the truth of scripture; to teach ethics and encourage public integrity; and to help reduce the gap between law and practice."

4. "Blogs Promoting Integrity and Health,"[29] Kelly O'Donnell, *Lausanne Global Conversations*, Lausanne Congress (2010).

"Mixed Blessings: Healthy and Unhealthy Organizations in Global Mission": "Virtue does not have to be so painful, if it is sensibly organized" (Charles Handy, *Understanding Voluntary Organizations*). "How healthy is your church, mission, NGO, and so on? Here are five brief quotes [not reproduced in this chapter] about organizational life to help explore this question. Remember: in mission as in life, we reproduce who we are."

"Confronting Corruption in the Church-Mission Community": "Yesterday they prayed for us. Today they preyed on us. Major fraud and other forms of corruption are a fact of life. Just think of the bogus solicitations that you get regularly in your email inbox, sincerely asking for your sympathy, help, personal financial information, and ultimately your money. People get duped all the time. And even the financially savvy can become the prey of experienced fraudsters. No one is immune to being exposed to

---

[28] "'Good News' in the Fight Against Corruption," https://drive.google.com/file/d/1tVZHc6786sFAvEAO1IsDDwqHYkP5t8LN/view.

[29] "Blogs Promoting Integrity and Health," http://coremembercare.blogspot.com/p/member-care-at-lausane-3-seven-mca.html.

fraud's far-reaching toxins, including people/organizations in the faith-based community."

"Porn as Mission and Porn in Mission: We are as Healthy as our Secrets": *"Porn as Mission? You bet.* In fact, there is a major multi-billion dollar industry whose mission is to convert you into a regular, paying, porn-using consumer. And Porn in Mission? You bet too. Its insidious, ensnaring tentacles pop up almost everywhere it seems—in our daily lives, media, our thoughts—and even if we do not seek it."

5. Video: "Confronting Our Idols,"[30] Chris Wright, Lausanne Congress, October 23, 2010. "This 22-minute plenary challenges the people of God to confront the idols of power and pride, popularity and success, and wealth and greed. He calls the Church to repentance and simplicity" (video description from Lausanne website).

Defending the exploited. Exposing the darkness.[31]

2.2. Resources from the Lausanne Movement (2010–2020)

6. "Choosing to be Salt and Light: Can the Church in India Become a Model in the Fight for Anti-Corruption?"[32] Arpit Waghmare, *Lausanne Global Analysis* (November 2012, volume 1, issue 1). This article explores one form of

---

[30] "Confronting Our Idols," https://lausanne.org/content/confronting-idols?_sft_post_format=post-format-video&_sft_post_tag=integrity-anti-corruption&_sfm_wpcf-groupings=Session+Videos&_sfm_wpcf-select-gathering=2010+Cape+Town.

[31] Image courtesy of and ©2006 Kelly O'Donnell. Statues are from the International Red Cross and Red Crescent Museum in Geneva, Switzerland.

[32] "'Choosing to be Salt and Light: Can the Church in India Become a Model in the Fight for Anti-Corruption?" https://lausanne.org/content/lga/2012-11/choosing-to-be-salt-light-can-the-church-in-india-become-a-model-in-the-fight-for-anti-corruption.

corruption—financial corruption—with reference to Indian churches and auxiliary Christian organizations. It also explores attempts being made to address the issue with particular reference to the Operation Nehemiah Movement facilitated by Transition Network in collaboration with the Lausanne Movement.

7. "Integrity, the Lausanne Movement, and a Malaysian Daniel,"[33] David Bennett, *Lausanne Global Analysis* (January 2015, volume 4, issue 1). "Integrity prepares the way for us to speak the more complete good news about God's revelation in Jesus Christ. A focus on integrity addresses what may be the greatest hindrance to world evangelization—that is, the lack of integrity in the church. Hypocrisy is so destructive to the witness of the church. If our lives do not express integrity, people will not believe or welcome our message. If people do not feel they can trust what we will do or say, if they are not assured that we are working for the common good, or for their personal good, they will not take seriously what we say about anything else—including the good news of Jesus Christ."

8. "A Summons to a Global Integrity Movement: Fighting Self-Deception and Corruption,"[34] Kelly O'Donnell and Michèle Lewis O'Donnell, *Lausanne Global Analysis* (March 2018, volume 7, issue 2). "In this article we distill some of the lessons we have learned over the past 15 years in promoting integrity and confronting corruption. Why is it hard to live up to our moral and ethical aspirations? We reflect on the reality of dysfunction and deviance, highlight the challenge of self-deception, describe anti-corruption resources, and summon the church-mission community (CMC) to a global integrity movement marked by righteousness and relevance."

9. "Do We Care about Corruption? How Integrity Can Tame the Beast of Bribes and Extortion,"[35] Manfred Kohl, *Lausanne Global Analysis* (May 2019, volume 8, issue 3). "In recent days I have asked more than a dozen individuals for their definition of the term 'corruption.' ... I received a great variety of answers. The term is defined by the Webster dictionary as: 'to bribe,' 'to spoil,' 'morally unsound,' 'perverted,' 'wicked,' 'evil.' These are disturbing terms. Yet we have become immune to them because we hear almost

---

[33] "Integrity, the Lausanne Movement, and a Malaysian Daniel," https://lausanne.org/content/lga/2015-01/integrity-the-lausanne-movement-and-a-malaysian-daniel.

[34] "A Summons to a Global Integrity Movement: Fighting Self-Deception and Corruption," https://www.lausanne.org/content/lga/2018-03/summons-global-integrity-movement.

[35] "Do We Care about Corruption? How Integrity Can Tame the Beast of Bribes and Extortion," https://lausanne.org/content/lga/2019-05/do-we-care-about-corruption.

daily in the media of scandals and financial scams involving government officials, businesses, and individuals. Our tendency is to say, 'So what?' When we hear about corruption and scandals within Christian denominations, para-church organizations, or even local churches, we quickly look beyond the headlines for names we might recognize. Even then the effect on us tends to be minimal."

10. Video: "The Greatest Threat to Your Ministry Is You: Calling the Church Back to Humility, Integrity, and Simplicity,"[36] Michael Oh, Lausanne Global Consultation on Prosperity Theology, Poverty, and the Gospel (Atibaia, Brazil, 30 March—2 April 2014). "In our sharp attention to the culture wars around us, have we lost our ability to see the wars that rage in our own churches and in our own hearts? Michael Oh, Global Executive Director/CEO of the Lausanne Movement, calls believers to lives of radical distinctiveness grounded in humility, integrity, and simplicity." Note: This video message was sent out again in 2020 by the Lausanne Movement.

3. Conclusion—A Summons to a Global Integrity Movement

Our globalized world is marked by extraordinary progress alongside unacceptable—and unsustainable—levels of want, fear, discrimination, exploitation, injustice and environmental folly at all levels. ... We have the know-how and the means to address these challenges, but we need urgent leadership and joint action now .... I urge Governments and people everywhere to fulfill their political and moral responsibilities. This is my call to dignity, and we must respond with all our vision and strength. —UN Secretary-General Ban Ki-moon (2014)[37]

---

[36] "The Greatest Threat to Your Ministry Is You: Calling the Church Back to Humility, Integrity, and Simplicity," https://lausanne.org/best-of-lausanne/the-greatest-threat-to-your-ministry-is-you.

[37] Ban Ki-moon, *The Road to Dignity by 2030: Ending Poverty, Transforming All Lives, and Protecting the Planet*, Synthesis Report of the Secretary-General on the Post-2015 Sustainable Development Agenda, December 2014, paragraphs 11, 13, 25, https://sustainabledevelopment.un.org/majorgroups/post2015/synthesisreport. For additional quotations from international organizations regarding the urgent need and responsibility to address the issues facing our world, see Kelly O'Donnell and Michèle Lewis O'Donnell, "Doomsday: Next Stop, Global Dis-Integration?" *Global Integration Update*, June 2017, http://mailchi.mp/24d24e690a01/doomsday-global-integration-update-special-issue-1013925.

Global Integrity Day, June 9, 2021[38]

We believe our common identity and shared responsibility as Christians who are global citizens can be leveraged to integrate integrity into the individual-institutional-international levels, and everything in between.[39] We believe it is a propitious season to invest in global integrity, wisely, resolutely, courageously.

We envision a growing, sustainable *Global Integrity Movement*, with the potential to be catalyzed by the Lausanne Movement, World Evangelical Alliance, and other international organizations[40] in collaboration with other major groups. It would be a platform for "connecting influencers, *integrity*, and ideas for global mission."[41]

Such a movement would also align with broader global efforts to confront corruption. Three examples are: (a) International Anti-Corruption Day (9 December); (b) the United Nations' Sustainable Development Goals (in particular SDG 16 on peace, justice and strong and inclusive institutions along with anti-corruption/crime); and (c) the recently launched Global Integrity Day (June 9), endorsed by the Lausanne Movement and World Evangelical Alliance's Integrity and Anti-Corruption Network (the 2020

---

[38] Global Integrity Day, June 9, 2021. Header image from website. Courtesy of Nancy Ford Duncan. https://sites.google.com/view/global-integrity-day/.

[39] Over the past seven years we have been developing and widely sharing about Global Integration (GI). Integrity is a core component. GI is a framework to help us connect relationally and contribute relevantly on behalf of human well-being and the major issues facing humanity, in light of our integrity and core values (e.g., ethical, humanitarian, faith-based) for God's glory. For more information and examples, see http://membercareassociates.org/?page_id=373.

[40] The Global Integrity Network, for example, was set up by the Lausanne Movement in response to the Cape Town Declaration and Congress in 2010. See https://www.lausanne.org/networks/issues/integrity-and-anti-corruption.

[41] This is the Lausanne Movement's strap line. We added the word "integrity" as it is also a central part of the Lausanne Movement's values as well as a moral safeguard and missional strategy.

theme was Corruption and Racism and the 2021 theme was Corruption and Poverty). Global Integrity Day's strategic potential is seen in its fourfold purpose, as described on the official website's home page:

> [Global Integrity Day] is ... a *positive day* to reflect, teach, and collaborate on ways to integrate integrity in all we do *throughout the entire year.*
>
> ... a *strategic day* to promote (a) cultivating lifestyles, cultures, and systems of integrity from the individual through the international levels; (b) joining together to understand and address the causes and consequences of corruption in its many forms; and (c) working towards just and equitable societies marked with wellbeing for all people and for the planet.
>
> ... a *solemn day* to consider our ways: if we are lying and/or stealing in any way big or small, then we need to stop it. If we need to right a wrong we have done, then do so. If we need to prudently confront wrongdoing, preferably in solidarity with colleagues for mutual support and greater impact, then do so.
>
> ... a *companion day* to complement UN International Anti-Corruption Day, December 9 (and vice versa). Both days are rallying points, six months apart, for fostering common ground, organizing events, sharing initiatives, and involving the public.
>
> We call upon righteous and relevant people, committed to Jesus Christ and the good news, to resolutely work together and across sectors on behalf of the well-being of all persons, peoples, and the planet. As people of truth and peace, seek common ground for the common good, *ad majorem Dei gloriam*.
>
> Global integrity requires ongoing, honest reflection at all levels—gazing regularly into the global mirror. Like the character and virtue in which it is embedded, it is refined in the caldron of life's tough challenges and choices.
>
> We are the light—or the darkness—of the world. We can be roadmaps or roadblocks for influencing moral wholeness for a more whole world.[42]
>
> We commit to integrate the inseparable areas of our character (resilient virtue) and competency (relevant skills) with compassion (resonant love) ... The world will not be a sustainably better, transformed place unless better, transformed people of integrity make it so.[43]

---

[42] For more ideas on a Global Integrity Movement, see "Global Integrity—25: Moral Wholeness for a Whole World," *CORE Member Care: Reflections, Research, and Resources for Good Practice* (2016), http://coremembercare.blogspot.fr/search/label/global%20integrity.

[43] Kelly O'Donnell and Michèle Lewis O'Donnell, "Following Jesus Globally," *Lausanne Global Analysis* (January 2020), https://lausanne.org/content/lga/2020-01/following-jesus-globally.

Living in Global Integrity: Moral Wholeness for a More Whole World 351

Gazing into the global mirror, contemplating our global integrity ...[44]

Readers can access additional multi-sectoral resources related to this article in the Global Integrity section of the Member Care Associates website (www.member care.org).

This chapter is based on updated versions of two articles published in the Lausanne Movement: K. O'Donnell and M. Lewis O'Donnell, 'A Summons to a Global Integrity Movement: Fighting Self-Deception and Corruption' [https://www.lausanne.org/content/lga/2018-03/summons-global-integrity-movement], Lausanne Global Analysis (March 2018), used by permission; and K. O'Donnell, 'Ten Resources for Integrity and Anti-Corruption: Moral Resilience and Relevance for the Church Mission Community' [https://www.globalintegritynetwork.org/post/ten-resources-for-integrity-and-anti-corruption-1], Lausanne-WEA Integrity and Anti-Corruption Network (GIN) (November 2020). To receive the bimonthly Lausanne Global Analysis, you can subscribe for free at https://lausanne.org/lga. Our emphasis on these two Lausanne articles reflects Dr. Kohl's ongoing connections and contributions to the Lausanne Movement since the 1970s, including as Co-Catalyst of GIN.

---

[44] Image source: https://images1.novica.net/pictures/15/p249899_2a_400.jpg. We encourage colleagues to reflect on the Scriptures referenced in this article as well as the two sets of "tactics" described for sustaining dysfunction-deviance and for feigning integrity. Confessing our sins to one another and praying for one another should be a normal, ongoing process for Christians.

About the Authors

Kelly and Michèle O'Donnell are consulting psychologists based in Geneva with Member Care Associates, Inc. (MCA). They studied psychology and theology at Rosemead School of Psychology, Biola University, where they received their doctorates in psychology. Kelly and Michèle focus their international, multi-sectoral work on staff well-being and effectiveness, global mental health, integrity/anti-corruption, and sustainable development. For the past five years they have been representatives at the United Nations for the World Federation for Mental Health. Their resources, including publications, presentations, and monthly *Member Care Updates* and *Global Integration Updates* are listed and linked on the MCA website (https://membercareassociates.org/). Email: MCAreseources@gmail.com.

The Book of Romans as a Charter for World Missions—Why Mission and Theology Have to Go Together: Thoughts on the Relationship of Theology, Missiology and Mission

Thomas Schirrmacher

1. Foreword

I live in a country in which the theology of evangelization has been harmed more than anywhere else. Constantly, new liberal blueprints are arising which have so weakened the proclamation of the gospel that many Christians and churches lack the power of conviction necessary for any type of missions effort. Moreover, the disputes caused by both liberals as well as devout Christians are leading to paralysis. Might it not be appropriate to simply make theologizing the main culprit?

And yet, even though emotionally and instinctively, more teaching and doctrine and theology have led to less evangelization for many Evangelicals in Germany—because even among us Evangelicals, contention has hindered us from moving ahead and tackling issues—teaching which is directly antagonistic to evangelization cannot be answered by an absence of theology. Rather, it can be answered only by true, healthy, and well-thought-out biblical teaching and through more biblical and Reformational theology. I would like to illustrate this claim by reference to the letter to the Romans.

2. Paul: Theologian and missionary

"What is at issue in the letter to the Romans? It all has to do with God's plan for the world and how Paul's mission to the Gentiles belongs in this plan."[1] This close relationship between the letter to the Romans and the practice of missions has been too seldom considered by commentators.

---

[1] Krister Stendahl. *Der Jude Paulus und wir Heiden: Anfragen an das abendländische Christentum.* Chr. Kaiser: München, 1978. p. 42; Stendahl, ibid. pp. 43-49, for this reason holds Romans 9-11 to be the center of the letter.

Emil Weber, in his important contribution entitled "The Relationship between Romans 1–3 and Paul's Missionary Practice,"[2] did not get beyond Romans 3, and other authors have only sketched out the topic.[3] Nils Alstrup writes in this connection, "Paul is identified as the first Christian theologian and the greatest Christian missionary of all time. However, researchers have not often appreciated how closely these two aspects are related to each other."[4]

Similarly, Robert L. Reymond calls Paul the "missionary theologian."[5]

At the same time, however, texts from the letter to the Romans played a major role in the history of missions.[6] Thus, for several hundred years Romans 10:14 ff. was one of the favorite texts for missionary sermons.[7] Among Calvinist Puritans in Great Britain and the USA from the sixteenth to the eighteenth centuries, back to which the great majority of modern,

---

[2] Emil Weber. "Die Beziehungen von Röm. 1–3 zur Missionspraxis des Paulus." *Beiträge zur Förderung christlicher Theologie* 9 (1905) Issue 4, Gütersloh: C. Bertelsmann, 1905.

[3] Z. B. Walter B. Russell III. "An Alternative Suggestion for the Purpose of Romans." *Bibliotheca Sacra* 145 (1988): 174–184; Paul S. Minear. "The Obedience of Faith: The Purpose of Paul in the Epistle to the Romans." *Studies in Biblical Theology* 2/19. SCM Press: London, 1971, especially both appendices on missions, pp. 91–110; Nils Alstrup. "The Missionary Theology in the Epistle to the Romans." pp. 70–94 in: Nils Alstrup. *Studies in Paul: Theology for the Early Christian Mission*. Augsburg Publ.: Minneapolis 1977; Krister Stendahl. *Der Jude Paulus und wir Heiden*. op. cit.; L. Grant McClung. "An Urban Cross-cultural Role Model: Paul's Self-image in Romans." *Global Church Growth* (Corunna) 26 (1989) 1: 5–8; Gottlob Schrenk. "Der Römerbrief als Missionsdokument." pp. 81–106 in: Gottlob Schrenk. *Studien zu Paulus. Abhandlungen zur Theologie des Alten und Neuen Testaments* 26. Zwingli-Verlag: Zürich, 1954; Charles Van Engen. "The Effect of Universalism on Mission Effort." pp. 183–194 in: William V. Crockett, James G. Sigountos. *Through No Fault of Their Own?* Baker Book House: Grand Rapids, 1993 (1991 reprint). pp. 191–193 (very good); Karl Müller. "Das universale Heilsdenken des Völkerapostels nach dem Galater- und Römerbrief." *Studia Missionalia* 9 (1955/56): 5–33 (rather general but good); Chris Schlect. "Romans as a Missionary Support Letter." *Credenda Agenda* 6 (1994) 3:9; Robert L. Reymond. *Paul: Missionary Theologian*. Geanies House (GB): Christian Focus Publ., 2000. pp. 208–213.

[4] Nils Alstrup. "The Missionary Theology in the Epistle to the Romans", op. cit. p. 70.

[5] Robert L. Reymond. *Paul: Missionary Theologian*, op. cit.

[6] Documented in A. F. Walls. "The First Chapter of the Epistle to the Romans and the Modern Missionary Movement." pp. 346–357 in: W. Ward Gasque, Ralph P. Martin (eds.). *Apostolic History and the Gospel: Biblical and Historical Essays Presented to F. F. Bruce on his 60th Birthday*. Eerdmans: Grand Rapids, 1970.

[7] Ibid. pp. 346–347.

Protestant global missions efforts trace themselves,[8] the concern of missions sermons found a point of entry in the exegesis of the letter to the Romans. Otherwise, the exegesis of Romans remained untouched by the intense promotion of world missions.

Paul presumably wrote Romans in AD 57, at some point in the three months mentioned in Acts 20:2-3 prior to his trip to Jerusalem. His letter was thus composed after he had collected funds from all his congregations in order to help the congregation in Jerusalem. From Jerusalem, he wanted to travel to Rome to use the church there as his starting point for his additional missions plans, particularly an outreach to Spain (Rom 15:27-31).

3. Romans 1:1-15

Paul does not waste much time before mentioning his missionary plans (Rom 1:8-15). Paul wants to proclaim the gospel to all people without exception, regardless of language, culture, or ethnicity ("Greeks and non-Greeks," Rom 1:14) as well as regardless of education or social class ("the wise and the foolish," Rom 1:14). Furthermore, it is for that reason that he comes to Rome (Rom 1:15). Paul moves from these practical missions concerns directly to the "real" topic. In the famous verses of Romans 1:16-17, Paul begins his teaching with "for ..." (NASB). He thus doctrinally justifies what he wants to practically do in Romans 1:8-15. There is no indication that Paul changes the topic at hand between verses 15 and 16.

The first fifteen verses of Romans relate to Paul's concerns. The letter does not begin with Romans 1:16: "I am not ashamed of the gospel." As early as the greeting in Romans 1:1, Paul describes his mandate to preach God's gospel. His mandate is stated more precisely in Romans 1:5: "to call people from among all the Gentiles to the obedience that comes from faith." He wants to visit the church so that he can also preach in Rome, since "I am obligated both to Greeks and non-Greeks" (Rom 1:14). He explains why he wants to proclaim the gospel to everyone beginning in Romans 1:16, as well as in the following chapters.

Romans 1:15 is not a superfluous introduction. Rather, it gives us the actual reason for composing the book of Romans, namely to demon-

---

[8] Comp. Iain Murray. *The Puritan Hope: Revival and the Interpretation of Prophecy*. Banner of Truth Trust: Edinburgh, 1971 and Thomas Schirrmacher (ed.). "Die Zeit für die Bekehrung der Welt ist reif: Rufus Anderson und die Selbständigkeit der Kirche als Ziel der Mission." Verlag für Kultur und Wissenschaft: Bonn, 1993. pp. 31, 35 and often.

strate that the expansion of world missions is God's very own plan. Anders Nygren writes in this regard, "While in declaring this Paul is holding firmly to the thought of the introduction and rebuffs suppositions about the cause of the long delay of his trip to Rome, he has already gotten around to his major theme of the gospel as God's saving power. 'It is almost inaudible how he glides from making a personal address to a lecture.'"[9]

4. Romans 5:7–16:27

We find the same thing at the end of the actual teaching portion of his letter. In Romans 15:14, Paul seamlessly segues from Old Testament quotations about the peoples of the world directly to his practical mission plans, and he repeats a lot of what he has already said in the introduction.

In chapters 15 and 16, the reason for the composition of the letter becomes even clearer. Beginning in Romans 15:7, Paul demonstrates that Christ has come as much for the Jews as for the Gentiles. After the general verses about the calling of the Gentiles, his own personal plans begin in Romans 15:14. He reports why he can think about nothing other than the mission among the Gentiles. And even here (Rom 15:18), he mentions that his central task is to bring obedience to faith to the Gentiles in word and deed.

This becomes clearer when one contrasts the introduction of Romans 1:1–15 with the complete final section of Romans 15:14–16:27. This framing of Romans actually identifies the reason for and the topic of the letter in the beginning and ending verses (Romans 1:1–6; 16:25–27): the "obedience that comes from faith" has to be proclaimed among all peoples and planted, just as the Old Testament foretold (for example, compare Romans 15:21 to Isaiah 52:15 and the broader context of Isaiah 52:5–15, from which Paul frequently quotes in Romans). The parallels between Romans 1:1–15 and 15:14–16:27 show that Paul does not lose sight of the practical missionary considerations of his letter during the entire epistle.

---

[9] Anders Nygren. *Der Römerbrief*. Vandenhoeck & Ruprecht: Göttingen, 1965. pp. 53–54, at the end with the use of a quote from "Jülicher."

On the framework of the letter to the Romans: Parallels between Romans 1:1–15 and 15:14–16:27		
1:1–6	The gospel was foretold in the Old Testament.	16:25–27
1:5	The obedience that comes from faith has to be proclaimed to all nations.	16:26; 15:18
1:7	Grace and peace to you …	16:20
1:8	The faith of the Roman Christians is known throughout the whole world.	16:19
1:8–13	Travel plans to Rome via Jerusalem.	15:22–29
1:11–12	Paul seeks to be spiritually encouraged by the Christians in Rome.	15:14, 24
1:13	In spite of his wishes, Paul was prevented from traveling to Rome up to this time.	15:22
1:13–15	The gospel has to be proclaimed to all peoples.	15:14–29; cf. 16:26

The letter to the Romans has too often been interpreted as a theological treatise without observing these points that frame the letter. "Most authors actually ignore the introductory and concluding declarations of his intention and concentrate on the theological interpretation of the core of the letter."[10]

5. The misuse of the letter to the Romans as pure doctrine

Like no other New Testament book, Romans has played a central role at the crossroads of Western church history. For centuries the letter to the Romans stood in the center of dogmatic battles, and we have become accustomed to reading it completely against this background. It has become Christians' first "doctrinal theology."

In the process, Romans was often seen *only* from this vantage point, as the first significant doctrinal theology. In addition, complete parts of Romans were concealed or overlooked without further ado. People acted as if Paul were above all an important theology professor who had a teaching

---

[10] Walter B. Russell III. "An Alternative Suggestion for the Purpose of Romans," op. cit. 175.

chair in Jerusalem or Antioch and had composed a textbook. We know, however, that Paul had a completely different calling, as a church planter and missionary with body and soul, very much an apostle. "The missionary of the New Testament is the Apostle Paul."[11] He traveled throughout the world and started as many churches and missionary centers as possible. If a church anywhere had become halfway independent, Paul moved on to the next city.

We could ask what relationship the fascinating doctrinal developments in Romans had to Paul's calling and sending. Why did Paul write such a labor-intensive letter in light of the situation in his churches, the stress of traveling, and his responsibility for a large number of fellow workers within the entire Roman Empire? The answer to this question is found, as we have seen, in the letter to the Romans itself, above all in the first and last two chapters.

Gottlob Schrenk has aptly emphasized, "The letter to the Romans is the most important declaration of the leading missionary of the Christian church."[12] "To what extent is Romans a missions document? If we now attempt to test this key concept as a methodological norm of interpretation, then it is necessary to more precisely define the exercise. As is the case with every utterance by Paul, this has also grown out of unmitigated missionary activity. However, this letter much more than all others contains the summary of the foundational missionary convictions the apostle has. That is the matter before us now."[13]

6. Doctrine and world missions

This is why I, as a missiologist and systematic theologian, have written a book about Romans, a book that is normally left to exegetes.[14] This most systematic and "most theological" of Paul's letters was written out of the context of concrete missions work and substantiates, in comprehensive fashion, the justification and necessity of missions in unreached areas through the use of systematic theology and a study of the Old Testament. As a result, we can reach the following conclusion:

---

[11] Einar Molland. "Besaß die Alte Kirche ein Missionsprogramm und bewußte Missionsmethoden?" pp. 51–67 in: Heinzgünther Frohnes, Uwe W. Knorr (eds.). *Die Alte Kirche. Kirchengeschichte als Missionsgeschichte* 1. München: Chr. Kaiser, 1974. p. 59.
[12] Gottlob Schrenk. "Der Römerbrief als Missionsdokument," op. cit. p. 81.
[13] Ibid. p. 83.
[14] Thomas Schirrmacher. *Der Römerbrief*. 2 vols. Hänssler: Neuhausen, 1994¹; RVB: Hamburg & VTR: Nürnberg, 2001².

Whoever only pragmatically conducts "missions" and for that reason dispenses with "doctrine" in the end conducts missions in their own name and does not look after *what God* has said and written about missions.

Whoever teaches a "set of doctrines" which does not have missions at the center and does not lead to practical missions work presents a teaching in their own name and disregards *why God* said and wrote particular things.

Practical missions work always begins with healthy, foundational doctrine and Bible study, and healthy, foundational teaching will always lead to practical missions work!

Gottlob Schrenk has formulated this best with respect to the letter to the Romans: "And furthermore: How will the missionary church be equipped? Out there the big wide world is surging ahead. Should we not be rushing about in some hasty fashion? To what end, then, is our immersion in the self? No, missionary centers only develop by the fact that in them the message we have is taken very seriously. In addition to that, there also have to be sharp, deeper efforts at achieving knowledge."[15]

World missions: the fulfillment of the Old Testament[16]

Two special messages that more precisely explain what is at stake in world missions should now be underscored with the help of Romans 15-16. The first message is the meaning of the Old Testament, to demonstrate that world mission is desired by God. The second message is that world mission seeks above all to reach the unreached—the major message of the letter to the Romans.

Let us first turn to the meaning of the Old Testament. Paul reminds the "strong" Gentile Christians "that Christ has become a servant of the Jews" (Rom 15:8), which is to say that he submitted himself to the law and in particular to Jewish ceremonial law. With that said, "the promises made to the patriarchs ... [were] confirmed" (Rom 8:15). Astonishingly, Paul directly changes from the "promises made to the patriarchs" with reference to the Jewishness of the Messiah to the fact that "the Gentiles might glorify God for his mercy," which relates to non-Jews: "As it is written: 'Therefore I will praise you among the Gentiles; I will sing the praises of your name'" (Rom 15:9). He thus reminds Gentile Christians of Romans 9-11, where he has already made it clear that Gentiles have Christ's work and the history of Israel to thank for their salvation.

---

[15] Gottlob Schrenk. "Der Römerbrief als Missionsdokument." op. cit. p. 83.
[16] See Robert L. Reymond. *Paul: Missionary Theologian*, op. cit. pp. 373-384, "The Old Testament Roots of the Pauline Gospel."

In Romans 15:9–12, Paul quotes five texts from the Old Testament that demonstrate that the nations will one day glorify God: 2 Samuel 22:50; Psalm 18:50; Deuteronomy 32:43; Psalm 117:1; and Isaiah 11:10. After Paul has repeatedly made it clear in the entire letter that the proclamation of the gospel and world missions do not contradict the Old Testament, there is a last bit of machine-gun fire in the form of Old Testament quotations. This is because the Old Testament actually underpins and calls for proclamation of the gospel and world missions. Adolf Schlatter wrote the following about these five quotations:

> The joint prize of God, in which all people participate, is the goal of God which the Scriptures proclaimed. In 2 Samuel 22:50, Paul presumably heard Christ, who wants to profess God among the peoples and sing to the praise of his name. It is the work of Christ that the church does this. Deuteronomy 32:43 is quoted because this dictum calls peoples to jointly praise God with Israel. Psalm 117:1 proclaims that indiscriminately and without exception all peoples are invited to praise God. Isaiah 11:1 justifies the worship which people will bring with the fact that they are under the lordship of Christ. ... Paul underpins his intercession with the promises of Scripture.[17]

The many Old Testament quotations should have not only convinced (and should still convince)[18] the Jews; they were and are of significance for Gentile Christians who not only rejoice about their personal salvation but who are to bring the gospel to all peoples of the earth in salvific continuity. C. E. B. Cranfield writes in this connection, "Neither the continual use of the Old Testament, which is found throughout the entire letter, nor the use of the words 'I am speaking to men who know the law' in Romans 7:1 demonstrates that Paul wrote to a predominantly Jewish Christian church. This is due to the fact that the Old Testament was the Bible of the Gentile Christians just as it was for the Jewish Christians, and it is important that Paul presuppose a familiarity and reverence for the Old Testament in his letters to the Galatians and the Corinthians."[19]

---

[17] Adolf Schlatter. *Gottes Gerechtigkeit: Ein Kommentar zum Römerbrief*. Calwer Verlag: Stuttgart, 1975⁵. p. 383.

[18] Comp. "Die Dreieinigkeit im Alten Testament und der Dialog mit Juden und Muslimen." *Bibel und Gemeinde* 94 (1994) 1: 19–27; "Trinity in the Old Testament and Dialogue with the Jews and Muslims." *Calvinism Today* 1 (1991) 1 (Jan): 24–25, 21, 27 = *Field Update: GR International* (Apr/May 1991): 6–8 + (Jun/Jul 1991): 5–8; "Der trinitarische Gottesglaube und die monotheistischen Religionen." pp. 113–151 in Rolf Hille, E. Troeger (eds.). *Die Einzigartigkeit Jesu Christi*. Brockhaus: Wuppertal, 1993.

[19] C. E. B. Cranfield. *A Critical and Exegetical Commentary on the Epistle to the Romans*. 2 vols. *The International Critical Commentary* 11. T & T Clark: Edinburgh, 1989 (1979 revised

The question is often asked why Jesus' Great Commission (Matt 28:18-20; Mark 16:15-16) is not quoted by the apostles after Pentecost, even if reference is made to the Great Commission a few times by speaking of Jesus' "command" (e.g., Acts 1:2; 10:42). Was the mission among all peoples never a disputed issue within the New Testament church, such that pointing to Jesus' command was superfluous? On the contrary, the mission among the Gentiles was something that only slowly got into gear and was for a long time very controversial (as shown by the Jerusalem council and the letter to the Galatians). If, however, we look at the New Testament discussions about the justification of missions, we are astounded to realize that at that point where we would have quoted Jesus' Great Commission, the Old Testament is almost always cited.

In other words, global mission is not primarily justified by Jesus' Great Commission but rather by the Old Testament.

Jesus' Great Commission was in a certain sense the initial declaration of that which had long been announced and prepared for, and which now was to be finally put into gear. The letter to the Romans and in particular Romans 15 are an obvious example of this, since Paul incessantly quotes Old Testament passages.

The election of the Old Testament covenant people happened with a view to all peoples, such that global mission is already a topic in the Old Testament.

The promise to the patriarchs that through them all the peoples of the earth should be blessed (Gen 12:3; 18:18; 22:17; 26:4; 28:14) is repeatedly drawn upon as a justification for mission work among non-Jews (Luke 1:54-55, 72; Acts 3:25-26; Rom 4:13-25; Eph 3:3-4; Gal 3:7-9, 14; Heb 6:13-20; 11:12). In Acts 13:46-49, it is reported that Paul and Barnabas were rejected by the Jews and, for that reason, were orienting themselves toward the Gentiles in Antioch. In this connection they quote Isaiah 49:6 (equivalent to Acts 13:47): "For this is what the Lord has commanded us: 'I have made you a light for the Gentiles, that you may bring salvation to the ends of the earth.'" The context in Isaiah makes it clear that the apostles are taking up an Old Testament command for missions: "It is too small a thing for you to be my servant to restore the tribes of Jacob and bring back those of Israel I have kept. I will also make you a light for the Gentiles, that you may bring my salvation to the ends of the earth" (Isa 49:6).

---

reprint). vol. 1. pp. 18-19; similarly Otto Michel. *Der Brief an die Römer. Kritisch-Exegetischer Kommentar über das Neue Testament* 4 (14th edition). Vandenhoeck & Ruprecht: Göttingen, 1978[5]. p. 36; John Murray. *The Epistle to the Romans.* 2 vols. *The New International Commentary on the New Testament.* Grand Rapids: Eerdmans, 1984. B. 1.

In his concluding address at the Council at Jerusalem in Acts 15:13–21, James justifies Paul's right to tell the Gentiles about the gospel by referencing Amos 9:11–12 (similarly expressed in Isa 61:4; Ps 22:27–28; Zech 8:22). This is where David's "fallen tent" will be restored—which for James is the church—and it brings together the remnant of Jews and the Gentiles who were also coming in ("and all the Gentiles who bear my name"). As a justification for preaching the gospel to the Gentiles, especially Cornelius, Peter connects the Great Commission from Jesus by pointing to the Old Testament: "He commanded us to preach to the people and to testify that he is the one whom God appointed as judge of the living and the dead. All the prophets testify about him that everyone who believes in him receives forgiveness of sins through his name" (Acts 10:42–43).

There are many places in the Old Testament where Gentiles heard the message of God via Jews and found faith in the one true God. At the same time, many texts, particularly in the Old Testament prophets, are directed at Gentile peoples.

The book of Ruth reports on the conversion of a Gentile, the book of Jonah tells of a successful missionary journey to Nineveh, and almost all Old Testament prophets call upon Gentile peoples to convert. Naaman the Syrian, Jethro the father-in-law of Moses, and the prostitute Rahab are just three examples among many people born as Gentiles who converted to belief in the living God. Circular letters from world rulers to all peoples, in which they praise the God of Israel, are frequently found in the Old Testament (above all in Daniel, Esther, Ezra, and Nehemiah).

Accordingly, world mission cannot be presented and practiced independently of the Old Testament, nor can it be presented and practiced independently of Old Testament salvation history and the destiny of the Jewish people.

Paul documents this primarily in Romans 9–11. In the process, two factors must be considered concerning the relationship of Christian missions to the Jewish people: the election of the Jews, on one hand, and endemic disobedience on the other hand. "As far as the gospel is concerned, they are enemies on your account; but as far as election is concerned, they are loved on account of the patriarchs" (Rom 11:28). Paul also makes it clear that the future turning of the people of Israel to their Messiah Jesus Christ will have unimagined positive repercussions on missionary work relating to all peoples (Rom 11:15, 24–26).

	Direct quotations from the Old Testament in the letter to the Romans (not in italics)
	Allusions and phrases from the Old Testament found in the letter to the Romans (in italics)
1:17	Habakkuk 2:4
1:23, 25	Deuteronomy 4:15–18; Jeremiah 2:11; Psalm 106:20
1:25	Genesis 9:26; 1 Samuel 25:32
2:5	Zephaniah 1:18; 2:3; Psalm 110:5
2:6	Proverbs 24:12; Psalm 62:13; Jeremiah 50:29
2:15	Jeremiah 31:33; Proverbs 7:3
2:21–22	Exodus 20:12–17; Deuteronomy 5:16-18
2:24	Isaiah 52:5
3:4	Psalm 116:11
3:4	Psalm 51:6
3:10	Ecclesiastes 7:20; Psalm 4:3; Psalm 53:2–4
3:11–12	Psalm 14:2-3
3:13	Psalm 5:10
3:13	Psalm 140:4
3:14	Psalm 10:7
3:15–17	Isaiah 59:7–8; *Proverbs 1:16*
3:18	Psalm 36:2
3:20	Psalm 143:2
3:29–30	Deuteronomy 6:4; Isaiah 37:16, 20
4:3	Genesis 15:6; *Psalm 106:31*
4:5	Exodus 23:7
4:7–8	Psalm 32:1–2
4:9	Genesis 15:6
4:11	Genesis 17:5, 10–11
4:13+16	Genesis 12:7; 13:15, 17; 24:7; 26:4 and often
4:17	Genesis 17:5

4:18	Genesis 15:5
4:19	Genesis 17:17; 18:11–12
4:22	Genesis 15:6
4:25	Isaiah 53:4, 11, 12; 1 Samuel 15:25; 25:28
5:1	Isaiah 53:5; 57:19; Micah 5:4; Numbers 6:26
5:19	Isaiah 53:4, 11, 12; 1 Samuel 15:25; 25:28
6:12, 14	Psalm 119:133; Genesis 4:7
6:21	Ezekiel 16:61+63
7:1	Genesis 2:16–17; 3:1; Proverbs 9:17
7:2–3	Deuteronomy 24:1-4
7:7	Exodus 20:12-17; Deuteronomy 5:16–21
7:10	Leviticus 18:5; Ezekiel 20:11, 13, 21
7:11	Genesis 3:1-7, 13
8:20	Ecclesiastes 1:2, 14; all of chapter 2
8:27	Jeremiah 11:20; 17:10; 20:12; Psalm 7:10; 26:2
8:33	Isaiah 50:8–9
8:34	Psalm 110:1, 5
8:36	Psalm 44:23
9:5	Genesis 9:26; 1 Samuel 25:32
9:7	Genesis 21:12
9:9	Genesis 18:10; 18:14
9:11	Genesis 25:21-22
9:12	Genesis 25:23
9:13	Malachi 1:2-3
9:15	Exodus 33:19
9:17	Exodus 9:16
9:18	Exodus 33:19
9:20–22	Jeremiah 18:3–6; Isaiah 45:9; 29:16; 64:7
9:22	Jeremiah 50:24; Isaiah 13:5; 54:16

The Book of Romans as a Charter for World Missions

9:25	Hosea 2:25; *1:6-9; 2:3*
9:26–27	Hosea 2:1
9:27–28	Isaiah 10:22–23
9:29	Isaiah 1:9
9:30–31	Isaiah 51:1
9:32–33	Isaiah 28:16; Isaiah 8:14; 10:5; Leviticus 18:5
10:6–8	Deuteronomy 30:12–14
10:11	Isaiah 28:16; Isaiah 8:14
10:13	Joel 3:5
10:15	Isaiah 52:7
10:16	Isaiah 53:1
10:18	Psalm 19:5
10:19	Deuteronomy 32:21
10:20	Isaiah 65:1
10:21	Isaiah 65:2
11:2	Psalm 94:14
11:3	1 Kings 19:14, *10*
11:4	1 Kings 19:18
11:8	Isaiah 29:10; Deuteronomy 29:3
11:9–10	Psalm 69:23–24
11:11, 14	Deuteronomy 32:21
11:16	Numbers 15:20; Ezekiel 44:30; Leviticus 23:10 and often
11:16-17	Jeremiah 11:16; Psalm 52:10; Zechariah 4:3, 11, 12, 14
11:25	Proverbs 3:7; Isaiah 5:21
11:26–27	Isaiah 59:20–21; Isaiah 27:9
11:34	Isaiah 40:13
11:35	Job 41:3
12:9	Amos 5:15; Psalm 97:10
12:14	Psalm 109:28

12:16	Proverbs 12:15; 24:12
12:16	Proverbs 3:7; Isaiah 5:21
12:17	Proverbs 3:4
12:19	Deuteronomy 32:35
12:20	Proverbs 25:21–22
13:9	Exodus 20:13 = Deuteronomy 5:17
13:9	Exodus 20:14 = Deuteronomy 5:18
13:9	Exodus 20:17 = Deuteronomy 5:21
13:9	Leviticus 19:18
14:11	Isaiah 45:23
14:13	Isaiah 8:14
14:20–21	Isaiah 8:14
15:3	Psalm 69:10
15:9	Psalm 18:50; 2 Samuel 22:50
15:10	Deuteronomy 32:43
15:11	Psalm 117:1
15:12	Isaiah 11:10
15:21	Isaiah 52:15
16:26	Genesis 21:33

The Old Testament justification of New Testament missions shows that global missions is a direct continuation of salvation history, animated by God's action since the fall of mankind into sin and the election of Abraham.

According to the Great Commission as related in the gospel of Luke, Jesus expressly confirmed the Old Testament justification of New Testament mission work. As he said to them, "This is what I told you while I was still with you: Everything must be fulfilled that is written about me in the Law of Moses, the Prophets and the Psalms." Then he opened their minds so they could understand the Scriptures. He told them, "This is what is written: The Christ will suffer and rise from the dead on the third day, and repentance and forgiveness of sins will be preached in his name to all nations, beginning at Jerusalem. You are witnesses of these things" (Luke 24:43–48). According to these words of Jesus, there is not only talk of his coming and the cross in all parts of the Old Testament. Rather, there is also mention of world missions: forgiveness must be proclaimed to all the nations.

7. Systematic theology and "the Scriptures"

What is the significance of the fact that Romans bases so much of its message on the Old Testament? The answer is simple. Systematic theology seeks nothing other than to be a complete view of things—that is to say, not to invent new theology but rather to see God's entire historical revelation and apply it to the current situation and the world.

Paul does not want to bring about anything new, although as an apostle he was charged by God to reveal what up to that time had been a "mystery" (Rom 11:25; 16:25; 1 Cor 15:51; Eph 1:9; 3:3, 4; Col 1:26, 27; 2:2).[20] Rather, he was to convey only what God had always revealed and proclaimed. At the beginning and at the end of Romans, Paul emphasizes that his gospel is in accordance with what God had revealed through the prophets and in the "Scriptures" (Rom 1:2; 16:26). In the entire letter he repeatedly introduces evidence for this, often with express reference to "the Scripture" (Rom 1:2; 4:3; 9:17; 10:11; 11:2; 15:4; cf. "prophets in the Holy Scriptures" in Rom 1:2; "the prophetic writings" in Rom 16:26, and "the law and the prophets" in Rom 3:21). If Paul had, for instance, been of the opinion that he could simply place something new on top of something old and faded, he would not have had to delve into the future of Israel so comprehensively. As it was, he had to show that the gospel for the Gentiles was compatible with everything that the Old Testament says about the Jews. This is because it is unthinkable that "God's word had failed" (Rom 9:6), for "the one who trusts in him will never be put to shame" (Rom 9:29). To such belong "the adoption as sons; theirs the divine glory, the covenants, the receiving of the law, the temple worship and the promises ... [and] the patriarchs and from them is traced the human ancestry of Christ" (Rom 9:4–5).

In this respect, *Hebrews 11 is an outstanding example of systematic theology*. The writer sees the thread of "faith" in the history of innumerable men and women of God found in Old Testament salvation history, regardless of whether the Hebrew equivalent for faith is found in the respective historical account or not. In some of the prominent examples,

---

[20] With the word "mystery" Paul can also mean truths that have already been revealed but which are intellectually difficult to understand. See 1 Corinthians 2:1, 7; 4:1; Ephesians 5:32; 1 Timothy 3:9; cf. Ephesians 6:19; Colossians 4:3; Revelation 3:16.

faith is expressly mentioned (e.g., Abraham, Moses), though in others it is not (e.g., Abel, Rahab).

8. The diversity of styles in the Bible

The letter to the Hebrews begins with these famous words: "In the past God spoke to our forefathers through the prophets at many times and in various ways" (Heb 1:1). Whereas the Koran[21] was written in one style in a short time and revealed to a single person, the Bible has texts alongside each other that demonstrate literary, historical, geographic, and ethnological diversity. Even within individual books, such as Psalms and Proverbs, there are texts from the most diverse group of authors, collected from the entire surrounding environment of the time. Since all Scripture has been inspired by God's Spirit (2 Tim 3:16), God can use many very different ways and styles to reveal himself, his being, and his will: proverbs, love songs, songs of lament, records of endless discussions (Job), archived documents, descriptions of visions, historical accounts, biographies, personal and official private letters, circular letters, and comments on current situations and questions.[22]

The pathway from this literary diversity to an ordered summary of biblical teaching, not to mention a "scientifically" thought out "theology," appears to be somewhat obscure. And as a matter of fact, Western theology has to allow itself to be "enlightened." It has to recognize that God does not speak only through systematic treatises and that to address actual problems a systematic presentation is often not the most useful approach. For example, we must not reduce Job or the Lamentations of Jeremiah to just a collection of proof texts for our doctrine, as much as these topics are taught there. Rather, first of all they have to fulfill their actual character. Thus, we for instance see the lamentations of an individual who lived completely for God, take them seriously as such, and draw upon them with respect to our own failures in the present day.

Most of Paul's epistles are occasional letters in which he does not set out to present systematically and summarily what he wants to say. Rather, he is guided by prevailing problems and questions in situ. Thus we have

---

[21] Comp. Thomas Schirrmacher. "Bibel und Koran als 'Wort Gottes': Das Offenbarungs- und Inspirationsverständnis im Christentum und Islam." *Islam und christlicher Glaube—Islam and Christianity* 5 (2005) 1: 5–10 (there also the English edition).

[22] Comp. Thomas Schirrmacher. *Die Vielfalt biblischer Sprache: Über 100 alt- und neutestamentliche Stilarten, Ausdrucksweisen, Redeweisen und Gliederungsformen*. Bonn: VKW, 1997¹; 2001².

Pauline teaching on the Lord's Supper in 1 Corinthians 11 only because there were practical problems with the Lord's Supper. Therefore, the path from historical problems in Corinth to doctrinal formulations on the Lord's Supper must be repeatedly trod and discussed. This method applies equally to us today: we do not have to say everything about what is important in the Christian faith in every sermon, in every evangelization, in every counseling conversation. Rather, we are permitted to address concrete issues relating to a particular situation. Whoever compares the common criticism after a sermon—"You didn't mention the love of God at all"—with the New Testament will be astonished at what the apostles do not mention in individual New Testament letters and would be forced to designate Paul's address in Athens (Acts 17:1–16) as error.

So-called "narrative theology," to mention just one theological model that has grown out of a literary style found in the Bible, is correct insofar as large parts of biblical revelation are revealed in a narrative fashion. Life histories, folk histories, and indeed world history have the important task of illustrating God's actions. Narrative theology is incorrect only insofar as other forms of God's oral revelation are eliminated.

Different cultures have a preference for certain types of biblical literature. African Christians love the book of Proverbs, the Old Testament narratives and all the reports of wonders, but they do not love the more systematic letters; the situation is the other way around for Christians from the West. Both sides have their justification, if they do not deny the complete breadth of biblical revelation or hold up their own preference as the more spiritual orientation in a one-sided manner.

Fortunately—for Western theology—we have the letters to the Romans and the Ephesians, the two systematic doctrinal letters of the New Testament. They are clearly broken down into a dogmatic portion and, beginning with "therefore, I urge you, brothers" (Rom 12:1; Eph 4:1), an ethical and practical portion. It is no wonder that Western theology has raised Romans to the level of a norm and turned other letters, such as Galatians, into a similarly pure doctrinal letter, stripping it of its original practical context.[23]

When we start out from the breakdown of styles in the Holy Scriptures, even if it can surely not be a normative process, we reach this conclusion: *Systematic theology is a justifiable and apparently necessary way of bringing God's revelation to humanity and into the heart of the individual. This must be declared to everybody who would rather get along without doctrine, dogma, and theology.*

---

[23] Comp. Thomas Schirrmacher. *Gesetz und Geist: Eine alternative Sicht des Galaterbriefes*. Hamburg: RVB, 1999; *Law or Spirit? An Alternative View of Galatians*. Hamburg: RVB, 2001.

However, systematic theology is only one of the available ways of revealing God to humanity and not even always the most important one, let alone the most frequent.

A good example of how a biblical writer who was rather unsystematic in his thinking and writing refers to the doctrinal letters of Paul, which often call for much intellectual effort, appears at the end of 2 Peter. There Peter writes, "Bear in mind that our Lord's patience means salvation, just as our dear brother Paul also wrote you with the wisdom that God gave him. He writes the same way in all his letters, speaking in them of these matters. His letters contain some things that are hard to understand, which ignorant and unstable people distort, as they do the other Scriptures, to their own destruction" (2 Pet 3:15–16). The human side of the Bible—in this instance, the distinctiveness of the Petrine and Pauline styles—does not detract from the divine side whatsoever. Even Peter has difficulty understanding Paul's letters. And yet there is no question for Peter that Paul is writing in the name of God and that a person who distorts Paul's letters does so to his own doom.

Peter's opinion is thus an important text for understanding the inspiration of the Bible. The Bible thoroughly mirrors the differences in character among its authors. Peter writes in short, concise sentences and gives warnings that can easily be remembered, changing the topic frequently and appearing to follow no overarching outline in his letters. Paul, in contrast, writes within the framework of protracted outlines, often using long, nested sentences that occasionally were left unfinished because they became too long. He justifies one thing from the previous thing. Peter is easy reading, and Paul is not. Even Peter can see this with respect to Paul, since Peter himself has difficulty understanding Paul.

9. Excursus: The example of the "Summit" project of New Tribes Mission[24]

Among tribes with whom they worked, missionaries of the New Tribes Mission simply began by building upon topics found within salvation history. They thus did not begin at the end, with the resurrection, Pentecost, or with the churches started by the apostles. Rather, they started at the beginning, with the creation, the building of the Tower of Babel, the flood, and the Patriarchs. The entire history of Israel and finally the time which Jesus spent living with his disciples came later. Only then did they get to

---

[24] The following text is essentially my "foreword" on p. 9 in: Trevor McIlwain, Nancy Everson. *Auf festen Grund gebaut: Von der Schöpfung bis Christus*. Hänssler Verlag: Neuhausen, 1998.

"the real objective." Additionally, they did not only recount God's history to the newly converted, but rather also to non-Christians. Thus they told about the Christian faith to everyone who wanted to know.

Is that not demanding too much? Should it not be the case that one comes to speak of the cross and resurrection as quickly as possible? Is the presentation of salvation history not rather a problem of "post-treatment" than of evangelization?

It would surely be seen as progress if every new convert received a good overview of salvation history as part of discipleship (or as "post-treatment"), and the material[25] available from New Tribes Mission is ideally suited for this purpose. However, even given the necessity of "post-treatment," the need for "preparatory work" prior to conversion is not refuted. The cross and resurrection, Pentecost, and the New Testament church can be rightly understood only by someone who already has understood God's history with humanity. For example, how does one expect to explain Jesus' sacrifice on the cross if one does not talk about the sacrifices of Cain and Abel, the patriarchs, and the Israelites? How does a person explain what sin is if one neither talks about the fall from grace nor the law of Sinai in which God defines what is and is not sin?

One reason, among others, why I am so glad to be a missiologist is that there is an enormous amount to learn for church work and theology from the experiences of missionaries. From early church history onwards, theology has been substantially shaped by the actual situation of evangelizing and conducting apologetics vis-à-vis the non-Christian world. Missionaries from New Tribes Mission have made their experience in teaching tribal peoples accessible, not by writing long treatises about it, but rather by making their program and teaching materials available for Western churches and audiences. Whoever studies the materials establishes very quickly that what they have in their hands comes from practical experience and is written for practical use.

Systematic theology is important and permissible and finds its paradigm in the carefully thought-out and systematically constructed letter to the Romans—although this, too, begins with creation and leads to the fall from grace, the law, and Israel and then all the way to redemption through grace. However, it is not by chance that only a small portion of the Bible is systematically written. The larger part of the Bible recounts the events of salvation history and the life histories of men and women with whom God has written his history.

---

[25] Trevor McIlwain, Nancy Everson. *Auf festen Grund gebaut: Von der Schöpfung bis Christus*. Hänssler Verlag: Neuhausen, 1998.

10. Excursus on fragmented fields of study[26]

The strict separation of fields of study has greatly contributed to "overtheorizing" and overspecialization within theological education and theology itself.[27] On one hand, systematic theology often completely breaks away from exegesis, while on the other hand it breaks away from a practical orientation towards missions and the church. It is all too easy for each area of theology to view its own subject as the hub of the Kingdom of God. As a result, it is too easy to judge students exclusively by what they achieve in one "discipline" and not according to their overall development in life and doctrine.

In theology, what is at stake is the overall picture that arises from comprehensive religious service, which is repeatedly tested against the spirit of the age, or the *Zeitgeist* (Rom 12:1-2). This comprises everything from personal heart piety all the way to a large-scale worldview, from the invisible peace an individual has with God to the future of the earthly creation, from an individual's everyday existence to the meaning of the state.

Paul A. Beals rightly calls the fragmentation of disciplines within theology "educational provincialism."[28] From the obligation to pursue an orientation toward the church and missions, he correctly does not even make an exception for exegesis.[29] In many an evangelical educational institution, the sacred cow of exegesis does not have to account for itself, what end it serves, and how it fits into a comprehensive Christian worldview. But exegesis should not be sacrificed to "biblical criticism." Rather, it should defer to the biblical claim that all Scripture is "useful for teaching" (2 Tim 3:16). In other words, exegesis, though it is certainly important, should always have the function of service to an overall objective.

In 1787, Johann Philipp Gabler claimed that "biblical theology" had to be separated from "dogmatic theology."[30] Since then, the exegesis of bibli-

---

[26] See also Thomas Schirrmacher. "Plädoyer für eine alternative Ausbildung von Missionaren und Pastoren." pp. 145–163 in: Thomas Mayer, Thomas Schirrmacher (eds.) *Europa Hoffnung geben: Dokumentation*. VTR: Nürnberg, 2004.

[27] Especially also John M. Frame. *The Doctrine of the Knowledge of God*, op. cit., pp. 206–214.

[28] Paul A. Beals. "Educational Provincialism," *A People for His Name: A Church-Based Missions Strategy*. Pasadena: William Carey Library: 1995,² p. 200.

[29] Ibid. 201–202.

[30] Johann Philipp Gabler. "De iusto discrimine theologiae biblicae et dogmaticae regundisque recte utriusque finibus." Inauguralrede an der Universität Altdorf. Altdorf, 1787; comp. to Gabler: Otto Merk. "Anfänge neutestamentlicher Wissenschaft im 18. Jahrhundert." pp. 37–59 in: Georg Schwaiger (ed.). *Historische Kritik in*

cal texts and the presentation of the contents of the Christian faith have increasingly grown apart. Modern, critical theology would be unthinkable without this separation.

Evangelical educational facilities were often started in conscious opposition to historical-critical educational institutions; this was certainly the case in my home country of Germany. Evangelical educational establishments have, however, left the canon of disciplines and the subjects' independent existence untouched. Hence, they have adopted one of the significant consequences of historical-critical theology instead of introducing a revolution that delineates and makes clear the path from interpretation of the Word of God, via systematic theology and dogmatics, ethics, and apologetics, all the way to practical theology, counseling, and missions.

John M. Frame has rightly reacted against the view emanating from philosophy that the division of knowledge and scientific disciplines stands at the beginning of science or at least is of central importance.[31] For him, the division is a question of pure utility. In the process, he also speaks out against otherwise very revered Reformed thinkers from the Netherlands, Abraham Kuyper and Hermann Dooyeweerd, for whom the division of sciences and the correct classification of theology were preconditions for the correct understanding of this world.

Missions should be an important part of basic courses on the faith as well as in theological curriculums, and an orientation toward building a church and world missions should pervade every institution of Christian and theological education.[32]

---

der Theologie. Studien zur Theologie- und Geistesgeschichte des Neunzehnten Jahrhunderts 32. Vandenhoeck & Ruprecht, 1980, here p. 57. However, this separation was primed in the Lutheran realm. From Robert Scharlemann. "Theology in Church and University: The Post-Reformation Development." Church History 33 (1964) 23ff. Melanchthon already differentiated between academic theology, which works historically, and kerygmatic theology, which is preached by the present-day church and which Lutheran orthodoxy built upon, e.g., B. Johann Gerhard (1582-1637), (comp. ibid.). In contrast, Reformed theology, based on the model of John Calvin, kept academic exegesis and preaching more strictly together and more significantly united for a longer period of time (so also in E. K. Karl Müller. Symbolik. A. Deichert: Erlangen, 1896. pp. 340-343, 389, 454-463).

[31] John M. Frame. The Doctrine of the Knowledge of God. op. cit., pp. 91-92.
[32] See Lois McKinney. "Why Renewal Is Needed in Theological Education." Evangelical Missions Quarterly 18 (April 1982) 93-94; also the collective volume of Harvie M. Conn, Samuel F. Rowen (eds.). Missions and Theological Education. op. cit., part. therein David Bosch. "Missions in Theological Education." pp. xiv-xlii; Horst Engelmann. Mobilmachung für die Mission: Wie können Mitarbeiter für den Missionsdienst

Every subject should contribute to strengthening the church and missions and should convey to learners the fascination of being allowed to participate in the building of God's great work domestically and internationally. "Independent of his special academic discipline, every faculty member of a theological school should give class instruction with a view to the mission of the church."[33] The late, esteemed South African missiologist David Bosch saw the role of the missiologist primarily in a critical function relative to all other subjects, and in a way that should penetrate all other subjects like leaven.[34] However, he also critically observed, "It is a significant problem that the present division of theological subjects was canonized at a time when the church in Europe was completely introverted."[35]

The following illustration[36] should make it clear that missions should actually provide orientation and motivation to all other disciplines.

Illustration 1: Thinking about missions should motivate and determine theological work in other areas of studies

---

gewonnen werden? Missionshaus Bibelschule Wiedenest: Wiedenest, n.d. (approx. 1983).
[33] Paul A. Beals. *A People for His Name*. op. cit., p. 199.
[34] David Bosch. "Missions in Theological Education." op. cit., pp. xxxi–xxxii.
[35] Ibid. xxx–xxxi.
[36] Following Paul A. Beals. *A People for His Name*, op. cit., p. 201.

11. Reaching the unreached

Having looked at the significance of the Old Testament in the letter to the Romans, I will turn to my second point enumerated above, which remains to be addressed: the purpose of world missions is to reach the unreached—which is the major objective of the letter.

It was not just any type of mission work that prompted Paul to write Romans. For Paul, "mission" meant his pioneering efforts aimed at unreached territories and peoples. Naturally, there were full-time workers on Paul's team who looked after new churches, such as Apollos and Timothy, while others, such as Timothy and Titus, themselves had to move from place to place in due course (2 Tim 4:21; cf. Titus 1:5; 3:13). Needless to say, there were also local evangelists. However, missionaries and apostles[37] did not limit themselves to local evangelization in their own area. Rather, they moved on and continued to plant, as long as there were still areas without their own Christian churches where work was to be done.

When Paul writes in Romans 15:19 that "from Jerusalem all the way around to Illyricum, I have fully proclaimed the gospel of Christ," he does not mean that he proclaimed the gospel to every single individual. Rather, he means that he has founded churches in all the strategically important locations. The same applies to the statement that "there is no more place for me to work in these regions" (Rom 15:23). For that reason, Paul does not seek to go to areas where Christ is known and where preaching is occurring (Rom 15:20). Rather, he wishes to go where no one has yet proclaimed the gospel and no indigenous church exists.[38]

Paul does not have people in existing churches in mind when it comes to his area of interest. Rather, he thinks about people who can be reached only if a missionary goes there: "It has always been my ambition to preach the gospel where Christ was not known" (Rom 15:20). Paul likewise confirms the primacy of missions to unreached areas by reference to the Old Testament: "Rather, as it is written: 'Those who were not told about him will see, and those who have not heard will understand'" (Rom 15:21, from Isa 52:15).

Paul calls upon the church in Rome "to join me in my struggle" (Rom 15:30) and reach the inhabitants of the world who are outside the range of existing churches.

---

[37] The word "Missionar" (English: "missionary") is known to be the Germanization of the Latin; "Apostel" (English: "apostle") is the Germanization of the Greek word for "Gesandter" (English: "envoy").

[38] Comp. L. Grant McClung. "An Urban Cross-cultural Role Model: Paul's Self-image in Romans." *Global Church Growth* (Corunna/USA) 26 (1989) 1:5-8.

Apparently, the best way of calling upon churches to collaborate is to thoroughly demonstrate from the Old and New Testaments that the expansion of the gospel to the far reaches of the earth belongs to the essence of Jesus Christ's church.

If mission work had more closely considered Paul as a role model, the spiritual map would doubtless look different nowadays. Fortunately, since the International Congress on World Evangelization (Lausanne 1974) and the World Consultation on Frontier Missions (Edinburgh 1980), mission work has more strongly moved into the central focus of Evangelicals.[39]

In evangelical missiology, a people group is understood to be an ethnic or sociological unit of individuals that is comprehensive enough to view itself as a group and that possesses a sense of belonging on the basis of linguistic, religious, economic, geographic, or other factors. From an evangelical point of view, it is the largest respective group within which the gospel can expand as a movement of church planting without running up against a wall of misunderstanding or lack of acceptance.[40]

I do not mean to imply that Paul had modern missiological or cultural-anthropological definitions in the back of his mind. However, I am convinced that today Pauline principles have well been cast into what are nowadays manageable forms through these definitions.

The enormously rapid expansion of Jesus' church at the time of the apostles can only be explained if one takes the Pauline guidelines noted above into consideration. After all, by AD 65, what was then the known world had been reached by the apostles and other Christians. Had the apostles remained in the churches they planted or if they had blanketed their own provinces with evangelization, they would never have made it "to the ends of the earth" (Acts 1:8). The churches were rather called on to send workers as mission teams ("representatives of the churches," 2 Cor 8:23) and to complete the work of the apostles in their surroundings. Paul communicated the same message to the Thessalonians. It was Paul's

---

[39] Comp. Thomas Schirrmacher. "Mission unter unerreichten Volksgruppen." pp. 23–26 and "Vorwort." pp. 11–12 in: Patrick Johnstone. *Gebet für die Welt*. Hänssler: Holzgerlingen, 2003⁵ (also in all earlier editions beginning with the 2nd edition). This handbook also contains detailed information about unreached people groups in all the countries of the world. See Thomas Schirrmacher (ed.). *Gospel Recordings Language List: Liste der Sprachaufnahmen in 4273 Sprachen. Missiologica Evangelica* 4. Verlag für Kultur und Wissenschaft: Bonn, 1992 and later online editions "GRID."

[40] This paragraph corresponds to a definition that leading Evangelical mission leaders and missiologists produced at a conference of the Lausanne Committee for World Evangelization in March 1982.

primary mission strategy to start churches in centrally located cities, to install elders trained by him at an early stage, and then to travel on. The more complete penetration of a region with the gospel was something that he left to a metropolitan church. As he told the church in Thessalonica, "And so you became a model to all the believers in Macedonia and Achaia. The Lord's message rang out from you not only in Macedonia and Achaia—your faith in God has become known everywhere. Therefore we do not need to say anything about it" (1 Thess 1:7-8).

12. The relationship between the church and missions in Romans: Paul seeks the church's support for world mission by appealing to teachings and doctrine[41]

What does the letter to the Romans have to do with the topic of the local church and world missions? Whoever consults a concordance or conventional commentaries will surely not find anything immediately. At first glance, Romans, as an instructional letter, has a lot to do with what the church believes and what missions should proclaim—i.e., the gospel—but ostensibly little to do with the practical relationship between the church and missions. But in actuality, this apparent absence is related to the one-sided interpretation of Romans that has already been mentioned as an aspect of church history.

Whoever knows Paul's missions strategy knows what we have already seen above with respect to Romans 15-16: Paul wanted to plant churches in strategic locations, and they in turn were to attend to the further tasks of evangelization and planting churches in their regions. Years after he had moved on, Paul wrote the following to the Thessalonians, who lived on the border between two Roman provinces: "The Lord's message rang out from you not only in Macedonia and Achaia—your faith in God has become known everywhere" (1 Thess 1:8).

After the churches were already in existence, Paul said, "But now that there is no more place for me to work in these regions" (Rom 15:23). On his way to Spain, he wanted to be strengthened by the church in Rome. Paul and his team had made mission plans, but he sought support from the churches, beginning with evangelization in Rome and extending to the

---

[41] The following text is a reworking of my "Gemeinde und Mission im Römerbrief." *Transparent* (SMD) 2/1999: 6 = *Evangelikale Missiologie* 16 (2000) 3: 109-110 = *Sounds* (ISM) Oct 2002: 1-2.

additional missions in new regions. He knows that as a missionary he has something to offer the church.

Paul was thus apparently of the opinion that he could gain broad support from the church in Rome for his mission work in Spain, just as he had received support from the church in Antioch for his earlier mission activity. In seeking this support, he broadly and systematically presents the gospel and demonstrates that it was in line with scriptural revelation up to that point.

Even nowadays, it has never harmed a church to allow missionaries to bring a "spiritual gift" (see Rom 1:11). Missionaries have knowledge and experience to contribute that we do not have—how they have experienced God where new churches emerge, where impossible situations are forced open, but also the challenges, the uncomfortable situations, and the reminders of persecution.

Paul does not, however, only want to bring the church something spiritual (Rom 1:11), and he does not only want to receive spiritual care or encouragement from the church (Rom 1:12). As a missionary, he expects not just logistical but also financial backing from the church. His goal is that the church may become an ingredient in missions, in that it makes the work of missions its personal issue. Even if it is unable to be geographically or culturally present where a missionary is active, the church can place itself spiritually in the center of mission efforts. It is for this purpose that Paul wrote his letter to the Romans, explaining in great detail that the proclamation of the gospel among all Gentiles is not to be a peripheral matter of faith and theology. Rather, mission work is to be at the church's center and indeed its legitimization.

13. Summary

What was the objective of the letter to the Romans and its detailed and systematic theology? Paul calls on the church in Rome "to join me in my struggle" (Rom 15:30) and reach the inhabitants of the world who are outside the range of existing churches.

Romans demonstrates that the best way to call churches to collaboration is to thoroughly demonstrate from the Old and New Testaments that world missions and the expansion of the gospel to the far corners of the earth belong to the essence of Jesus' church.

(For a biography of Thomas Schirrmacher, see the end of his earlier article in this volume.)

Part 4:
Biblical Ministry and Servant Leadership

Dissent: Global Transformation on Shaky Ground

Janet Wootton

1. Introduction

Congregational or Independent churches have their roots in the radical Reformation of England and Wales in the sixteenth and seventeenth centuries. The movement led to regicide and civil war and to an attempt to establish a commonwealth, which ultimately failed. Nonconformists were subsequently excluded from participation in ecclesiastical, academic or civic society. Their subsequent energetic involvement in new academies, travel/exploration and trade contributed to British expansionism and colonization, intertwined with global mission, in the context of the development of science, education, human rights and industry. This nexus of ideas served to spread dissenting or nonconformist Christianity, as a political as well as a religious system, throughout much of the world. This article explores the heritage of this form of dissent and its impact on the world of today, bringing it up to date in the author's experience as President of the Congregational Federation and in a number of international settings.

It is an honor to be invited to contribute to this volume. I have known and admired Reverend Dr. Manfred Kohl since I first heard him address a conference of the International Congregational Fellowship (ICF), thirty or more years ago, and have co-chaired the ICF Theological Commission with him since the turn of the last millennium!

The Congregational Way is rooted in a more than 400-year tradition of dissent. Of course, dissent itself is probably as old as the human race. Wherever people have held power or authority over each other, those who are in the position of subjects have claimed the freedom to express opposition. It is a complex matter, as we shall see. An individual or group will be powerful in some settings while being, and feeling, powerless in others, or may move between dissent and power over time. Dissenters take issue not only with the actions of the powerful, but also with the social structures that put them in the position of power. It is systematic as well as specific and can give rise to seismic shifts in what seemed like solid ground.

This article pinpoints a period in history when it seemed hard to find any solid ground at all, and when a relatively small group of people took up their freedom to dissent. Because of the specific time and place when this happened, the actions of these Dissenters and their heirs helped to shake and shape the world.

2. A Radical Reformation

There has been dissent in the Church pretty well from its birth. Even the New Testament epistles and accounts of the earliest Christian communities carry undercurrents of disagreement (for example, Acts 15, Gal 2), and indications of wrestling with notions of authority and power. Indeed, its DNA can be traced back far into the Hebrew Scriptures, where the institution of monarchy is stoutly resisted (1 Sam 8; Deut 17:14-20), and where the return from exile is described not only in terms of the solid, traditional structures of temple and priesthood, but also in a radical vision of an open, inclusive community, with no need for either institution (compare Ezek 40-47 with Isa 56-66 and Jer 31:31-34).

Throughout Christian history, attempts to institutionalize uniformity have given rise to dissent, from those whose views were eventually condemned as heretical as well as from new movements seeking further freedoms or reforms.

Through the centuries, reforming movements were variously tolerated or suppressed, but the pressure for radical change eventually became unstoppable. The point from which the start of the Reformation in Europe is traditionally marked is the moment when Martin Luther (1483-1546) nailed his Ninety-Five Theses to the door of the Wittenberg Castle Church in 1517, as celebrated on its 500th anniversary in 2017. Though the actual nailing of the Theses may be in doubt, their publication was real enough, and explosive, as they encapsulated the growing discontent with the Church's practices of the time.

England, under the turbulent reign of Henry VIII (1509-1547) and his successors, culminating in the long Elizabethan Era (1558-1603), reflected the complexities and uncertainties of European Reforming movements. The Elizabethan Settlement of 1559 was designed to tread a middle way between Catholics and Protestants. In the end, it left unsatisfied a group of Protestants who desired a far more radical Reformation.

Radical reformers formed small, illegal congregations, worshipping and meeting under threat of arrest and imprisonment or execution. They looked for support to others outside the restrictive laws of England, in places like the more liberal Protestant Netherlands. It was in Middelburg, in Holland, where he and others had fled persecution, that Robert Browne

(c. 1550–1633) printed his treatise: *Reformation without tarying for anie.*[1] The treatise was then distributed in England at great risk to its supporters, two of its distributors, Elias Thacker and John Copping, being hanged at Bury St Edmunds.

Browne had graduated from Corpus Christi, Cambridge in 1572. The two ancient universities of Oxford and Cambridge were places of lively scholarly debate, and he would have come under the influence of Puritan scholars such as Thomas Cartwright (1535–1603), whose lectures on the book of Acts had drawn unfavorable comparisons between the dynamic organization of the first churches recorded in Scripture and the formalities of the Church of his time. Though deprived of his living, Cartwright continued to support radical reform. Some years later, in 1627, the Dutch Calvinist Isaac Dorislaus, the first holder of a very short-lived chair of history at Cambridge, gave a series of lectures in which he drew on the Roman Republic as an example of a non-monarchic form of government. There was even talk of regicide and civil war.

Among the students at Cambridge at this time was Huntingdon landowner's son Oliver Cromwell (1599–1658). He attended Sidney Sussex College, Cambridge, which "offered a sound Protestant upbringing, the Master and Fellows being required by the Statutes to abhor 'Popery and all heresies, superstitions and errors.'"[2] His fellow students included "a number of early pioneering colonists in America such as the poetical George Moxon, ... John Wheelwright, and Sir John Reynolds, one of Cromwell's finest soldiers."[3]

It was not only the intellectual elite who had access to new ideas. In the background of religious and political change were huge technological advances in communication that increased the range and speed of change dramatically. Primary among these was the printing press, which enabled books and pamphlets to be reproduced in large numbers and made available for mass readership. In particular, the Bible, translated into modern European languages, was made available to ordinary people.

> What is less well known is that one of the most common forms of printed matter in European Protestant Churches consisted of hymns and hymn books. These provided access to popular theology in a form that congre-

---

[1] Robert Browne, *Reformation without tarying for anie, Etc.* (Middelburg, Holland: Richard Painter, 1582).
[2] Nicholas Rogers and Christopher Parish, *Cromwell and Sidney Sussex* (Cambridge: Sidney Sussex College, 1999), p. 1.
[3] "College History," Sidney Sussex College, University of Cambridge, https://www.sid.cam.ac.uk/about-sidney/college-history.

gations could sing together, and become familiar with. It took longer for hymns to become accepted in Calvinist England and Wales, but in continental Europe, Luther encouraged the congregational hymn-singing, writing to Georg Spatulin: "Following the example of the prophets and fathers of the church, I intend to make vernacular psalms for the people, that is, spiritual songs so that the Word of God even by means of song may live among the people."[4]

Small printed collections of hymns that people could carry with them spread the influence of this form of popular religious expression and put a vernacular theology in the hands of ordinary people.[5]

Printing not only made it possible to produce and distribute material. It also created an informed readership, opening a route for the widespread dissemination of ideas and knowledge that had remained safely in the hands of the rich and powerful up to that point. Now, with the ready availability of printed material, literacy was spreading, and with it the democratization of knowledge.

An untutored tinker's son, growing up in Bedfordshire, England, in the seventeenth century with no interest in religion, came to represent the influence of the new radical ideas through preaching and the printed word, and he reached out through the same means to touch the world.

John Bunyan (1628-1688), according to his own admission, "the very ringleader of all the Youth that kept me company, in all manner of vice and ungodliness,"[6] was swept up in the civil war, and joined the army under Oliver Cromwell on the side of Parliament. He was most likely a conscript as the tide of war swept through Bedford, and he ended up serving in the nearby garrison town of Newport Pagnell from 1644 to 1646.

Historian Anne Laurence reminds us that the civil war was political as well as religious. "The fight against [King] Charles was also a fight against a system of laws imposed by the Normans which had held the English in subjection."[7] Bunyan, a young man, skilled but without education or

---

[4] Martin Luther, *Works*, vol. 53, *Liturgy and Hymns*, Ulrich S. Leopold (ed.) (Philadelphia: Fortress Press, 1965), p. 512, cited in Robin Leaver, *Elisabeth Creutsiger: The Magdeburg Enchiridion 1536 and Reformation Theology*, the Kessler Reformation Lecture, October 18, 1994, Occasional Papers of the Pitts Theological Library, p. 4.

[5] See Janet Wootton, *This is Our Song: Women's Hymn-Writing* (London: Epworth Press, 2010), pp. 29-53.

[6] John Bunyan, *Grace Abounding to the Chief of Sinners* (London: 1666), p. 5.

[7] Anne Laurence, "Bunyan and the Parliamentary Army," in Anne Laurence, W.R. Owens and Stuart Sim (eds.), *John Bunyan and His England, 1628-1688* (London: Hambledon Press, 1990), p. 27.

direction, seems to have responded warmly to the discipline of the army and fervor of Cromwell's cause.[8]

While in the army, he would have heard talk about the redistribution of authority, wealth and power, as well as the purification of the Church. Although conditions in Cromwell's service at that time were dreadful and most of Bunyan's fellow conscripts deserted, it appears that the young tinker thrived. He would have had access to a *Soldier's Bible*,[9] and quite possibly he learned to read it. And he would have experienced "prophesyings" (radical preaching based on the exposition of Bible passages), prayer, and the singing of psalms, particularly the more warlike verses—all rousing stuff!

3. Exclusion and Beyond

Bunyan's story serves well to illustrate the period that followed. He returned, demobilized from the Army despite his willingness to continue to serve, and joined a radical congregation, under the ministry of John Gifford (1547–1620). Following Cromwell's death in 1658, the Monarchy was restored in 1660, and everything changed. Gifford's congregation found itself homeless and persecuted. Bunyan was himself imprisoned in Bedford in 1661 for twelve years, during which time he wrote his most famous work, *The Pilgrim's Progress,* published after his release in 1678 and 1684, in which Gifford appears in the character of "Evangelist."

The new king, Charles II, re-enforced the requirement of conformity to the established Church. Nonconforming clergy were ejected from their churches in 1662. The Great Ejectment, as it was known, was an extremely painful time, as well-loved ministers were removed from congregations, and all hope of an accommodation over contentious points of church discipline and practice seemed to vanish. Historian Geoffrey Nuttall describes the effect on what had grown up as an honorable tradition of Dissent, whose ministers "represented a type of Christian piety of long standing which at these points was different and recognizably different. In the 1650s, during the Commonwealth and Protectorate, they had enjoyed freedom under Cromwell to put into practice the principles of worship and church order which they cherished. This freedom the Restoration abruptly halted."[10]

---

[8] John Mullett "Bunyan's Life, Bunyan's Lives," in Michael Davies and W. R. Owens (eds.), *The Oxford Handbook of John Bunyan* (Oxford: OUP, 2018), pp. 21–35.

[9] *The Souldier's Pocket Bible* (London: 1643). This is a pamphlet containing verses selected for the spiritual life of the soldier.

[10] Geoffrey Nuttall, *The Beginnings of Nonconformity 1660-1665* (London: SPCK, 1962), p. 10.

Many expressed terrible grief at their parting, as, for example, in this sermon preached at the termination of fifteen years of ministry by Richard Fairclough: "*Farewel* this house; and *farewel* this Seat forever: and (within a little while) *farewel* your discourse, and your faces; *farewel* my pleasant habitation and this sweet air of Mels."[11] The Puritan theologian Richard Baxter (1615-1691) wrote a poignant poem, dated December 3, 1663, part of which is still in use, most commonly as a funeral hymn. It is headed, "Psal. 119:96. *Written when I was Silenced and cast out &c.*" and begins, "Lord, I have cast up the Account / What it will cost to come to thee," and it goes on to lament the loss of his books and livelihood, but most of all the company of his friends.[12]

Ejected clergy, along with nonconformist laypeople, were shut out of public life. They were prohibited from entering Parliament, or most forms of public office, or teaching or studying in the ancient universities, through the Corporation and Test Acts of the 1660s and 1670s, which required attendance at worship that conformed to the Church of England (hence the designation "nonconformist").

Despite legislation gradually loosening the restrictions placed on them, it was to be another two centuries before the Dissenters gained full access to the powers from which they had been excluded. Their exclusion and its impact, not only national but global, is one of the world's untold stories, as unable to engage in public life, nonconformists vigorously embarked on other routes to education and employment.

Daniel Defoe (c. 1660-1731), born Daniel Foe (he added the "De" to give an aristocratic veneer to his name) was born to a Dissenting family, and attended the Dissenting Academy (see below) at Newington Green, at that time a village on the northern outskirts of London. He made his living as a general merchant but was also involved in espionage. Outside the Establishment in every sense, he lived an exciting and precarious life.

His writings were prolific and brilliant. His novel *Robinson Crusoe*, published in 1719, was immediately popular and is still a classic. A lively commentator on the political and religious issues of his age, particularly the position of Dissenters in English law, he entered the debate on the

---

[11] David J. Appleby *Black Bartholomew's Day: Preaching, Polemic and Restoration Nonconformity*, (Manchester, Manchester University Press, 2007), p. 38, citing Richard Fairclough, *A pastor's legacy to his beloved people: being the substance of fourteen farewel sermons* (1663), p. 140, author's italics.

[12] *Mr Richard Baxter's Paraphrase on the Psalms of David in Metre with Other Hymns* (London: 1692). The hymn is "He wants not [that is, lacks not] friends that hath thy love."

"Occasional Conformity" Act[13] in a number of pamphlets, including an *Enquiry into Occasional Conformity: Shewing that Dissenters are no way concern'd in it*. Here, he describes the people he represents, making it clear that they are not monsters or outcasts, but fellow citizens: "People Born in the same Climate, submitting to the same Government ... link'd together in the same Common Interest, by Intermarriage continually mixt in Relation, concern'd with the same Trade, making War with the same Enemies."[14]

Indeed, he goes on to argue, they make a valuable contribution to national life and, in particular, to the growing economy of Britain at the beginning of the age of global trade, industry and discovery:

> Get a Law made we shall Buy no Lands, that we may not be Freeholders and see if you could find Money to Buy us out. Transplant us into Towns and Bodies and let us trade by ourselves; let us Card, Spin, Knit and Work and see how you will maintain your own poor without us. Let us Fraight our Ships apart; keep our money out of your Bank; accept none of our Bills ... and see how you can go on without us.[15]

The Dissenters were not, as sometimes depicted, a ragbag of ill-educated bigots, but skilled and literate traders, merchants, educators, and eventually, explorers, adventurers, and campaigners for the transformation of society. In Erik Routley's assessment, even though "Dissenters were still very much in the minority," yet, "being the kind of people they were—not often nobly born, but uncannily successful and not infrequently wealthy—they had plenty of influence."[16] It is as if the energy released through their exclusion from the traditional means of education and advancement became a driving force for new ideas.

The Dissenting Academies, founded to offer education to nonconformists, pioneered new forms of education through debate and experimentation, rather than the transmission of ancient traditions. The Newington Green Academy was run by Charles Morton (1627–1698), one of the ejected ministers, and offered access to scientific instruments, and Dr. Aikin's

---

[13] Debated in 1702 and 1704, and enacted into law in 1711, designed to prevent the practice of Dissenters' occasional attendance at mass to fulfill the requirements of office while also frequenting nonconformist meetings for worship.

[14] Daniel Defoe, *Enquiry into Occasional Conformity: Shewing that Dissenters are no way concern'd in it* (London: 1701), p. 9.

[15] Ibid, p. 18.

[16] Erik Routley, *English Religious Dissent* (Cambridge: Cambridge University Press, 1960), p. 128.

Warrington Academy in the north of England included lectures on chemistry and anatomy.[17]

The famous prison reformer John Howard (1726–1790) attended another London Dissenting Academy, and its influence can be seen in his life and work. A member of Bunyan Meeting Church in Bedford, he was appointed to the role of High Sheriff of Bedfordshire, despite being technically disbarred by his uncompromising Dissenting position.

Howard devoted his life to the cause of prison reform, pioneering a new scientific method of sociological research, based on measurement and statistics and hundreds of firsthand visits and interviews throughout Britain and Europe, all carefully recorded in tables and written evidence. Using these data, he campaigned to end the worst abuses of the prison system, while all the time under threat of denunciation for his own religious Dissent.

This combination of scientific method and a burning desire to root out the injustices at the heart of society was typical of the great nonconformist social reformers of Howard's time and beyond. Without their groundbreaking work, the world we live in now would be very different.

4. A Transatlantic Trade, a Shared Shame

One of the greatest campaigns of the age sought to end the shocking and brutal trade in enslaved people across the Atlantic. Here, the best known British names are Anglican Evangelicals, John Newton, William Wilberforce, William Cowper, Hannah More. But there was an equally active and effective network of Dissenting campaigners, whose emphasis and theology were notably different.

Anna Laetitia Barbauld (1743–1825, née Aikin) was the daughter of Dr. John Aikin, of the Dissenting Academy at Warrington. She married a Huguenot, Rochemont Barbauld, and they moved to Palgrave in Suffolk, where she as well as her husband taught. When his health broke down, they relocated to Newington Green, where they joined the Unitarian Congregation, and there is a plaque to her inside the church.

Mrs. Barbauld was an incisive political writer, closely involved in the campaign to end the slave trade. She wrote anonymously, often under the pseudonym "A Dissenter." Like many Dissenters, she supported both the French and American Revolutions and applauded their attempt to replace the old European hereditary monarchies and aristocracies with more egalitarian and democratic societies.

---

[17] See J. W. Ashley Smith, *The Birth of Modern Education: The Contribution of the Dissenting Academies, 1660-1800* (London: Independent Press, 1954).

For her, the trade in enslaved people was inextricably bound up with the injustice of an unequal society, a symptom of the "hard, impenetrable avarice" that ran through the old European societies, with their "Prejudice, Superstition and Servility," which must give way, when "Man *as* man [sic] becomes an object of respect."[18]

Barbauld's works were widely read in America, a fact that William McCarthy attributes to "her being, at home in England, a Dissenter."

As the president of Harvard College, Joseph Willard, wrote to Richard Price in 1788, British Dissenters "are the strenuous assertors of religious liberty; and I look upon them to be very great supporters of the civil liberties of your nation." Leading British Dissenters deplored the war to keep America. They saw it as an attempt to subject their fellow Britons there to tyranny.[19]

But in fact the battle between Establishment and Dissent, institutionalism and freedom was complex on both sides of the Atlantic. Chris Beneke warns against "the mistake of assuming that Britain's North American colonies began as cradles of religious freedom," when "it would be more accurate to say that many of the early colonies began as sanctuaries for religious *dissenters*." He goes on, "Some of these dissenters proved perfectly capable of systematic intolerance themselves."[20]

The descendants of the Dissenters in congregational Massachusetts acted like an established church:

> [They] enjoyed the tax support of their own towns and a monopoly on the main sources of institutional power in the colony. To many of those at the time and for most of us today, this arrangement had all the trappings of an establishment ... the conventional grammar of establishment and dissent still shaped public rhetoric well into the eighteenth century.[21]

And, to the astonishment of English Dissenters like Barbauld and the chagrin of American intellectuals, the exploitation of enslaved people survived in America long after the British abolition of the Atlantic trade. You can read the frustration at this dissonance in John Greenleaf Whittier's poem:

---

[18] *Address to the Opposers of the Repeal of the Corporation and Test Acts* (London: March 3, 1790), by A Dissenter, pp. 32–33, italics in original.

[19] William McCarthy, "How Dissent Made Anna Letitia Barbauld, and What She Made of Dissent," in Felicity James and Ian Inkster, *Religious Dissent and the Aikin-Barbauld Circle, 1740-1860* (Cambridge: Cambridge University Press, 2012), p. 53.

[20] Chris Beneke, *Beyond Toleration: The Religious Origins of American Pluralism* (Oxford: Oxford University Press, 2006, 2009), p. 17.

[21] Beneke, *Beyond Toleration,* p. 138.

> Shall every flap of England's flag
> Proclaim that all around are free,
> From 'farthest Ind' to each blue crag
> That beetles o'er the Western sea?
> And shall we scoff at Europe's kings,
> When Freedom's fire is dim with us,
> And round our country's altar clings
> The damning shade of Slavery's curse.[22]

But Britain was working hard to change its own narrative of the abolition of the slave trade, with consequences on a global scale. During the commemoration in 2007 of the ending of the Atlantic slave trade in 1807, a book and TV documentary by Adam Hochschild reminded audiences of the untold story of the vigorous campaign by the Dissenters, which had been all but expunged from the history, and the difference it might have made if their voices had continued to be heard in shaping the future. He argues that, as the more radical campaigners have been written out of the narrative, so the ideology of paternalism and grateful servitude prevails over that of equality and justice:

> For many Britons, the idea that emancipation had sprung from the benevolence of a wise elite was deeply comforting. Such confidence in British good intentions was gradually transformed into justification for more than a century of conquests and colonialism in Africa and a dramatic and often bloody expansion of British imperial holdings in India and the Far East.[23]

5. Mission and Empire

This was the era of global colonialism and the expansion of empires. Britain and America were growing immensely wealthy through industrialization, scientific development, and the exploitation of local and global populations, including the brutal trade in enslaved people, at least partially driven by the newfound confidence of those very people who had been excluded from traditional access to power and wealth in Britain.

Now, Dissenters themselves often became cruel exploiters of people and wealth in other parts of the world. Even where Christian mission

---

[22] Vicki L. Eaklor, *American Antislavery Songs: A Collection and Analysis* (New York: Greenwood, 1988), no. 190, cited in Janet Wootton, "Redemption Song: Hymns and Slavery" *Hymn Society Bulletin* 254, vol. 18, no. 9, January 2008, pp. 306–318; 255, vol. 18, no. 10, pp. 305–315.

[23] Adam Hochschild, *Bury the Chains: The British Struggle to Abolish Slavery* (London: Pan Books, 2006), p. 351.

followed in the footsteps of colonization, the cultural riches, ideas, wisdom and experience of the nations were routinely ignored, or discounted as ignorant barbarism. The gospel call to "go ... and make disciples of all nations" (Matt 28:19) did not seem to include listening, learning or mutual respect.

It is not enough simply to lionize or villainize the missionary endeavors of the eighteenth and nineteenth centuries. If we listen hard enough, there are yet more hidden stories to emerge from the narrative, more voices to be heard.

> Both the missionaries-as-Saints and missionaries-as-imperialists approaches to protestant missions leave little room for indigenous Christians. In the first interpretation, Anglo-American missionary activity was emphasized to glorify and memorialize the philanthropic efforts of a more "civilized" people. On the other hand, the newer scholarship emphasizes resistance, often violent, to Christian missions. In both accounts native Christians and indigenous Christianities they create are rarely taken seriously.[24]

These accounts of complex interaction show how the idea of dissent and nonconformity can permeate across cultures in surprising ways.

In Korea, as described by Korean historian Lee Mahnyol, Western missionaries trained local Christians as "Bible men" or "Bible women." These were alumni of the schools and training institutions founded by missions, who were taught to carry the gospel message into rural areas or to communities that were hard for foreign missionaries to reach. Lee tells how the *kwonseo* (Bible men/women, colporteurs) would smuggle portions of the Bible, translated into Korean, into remote areas. This meant that European and American missionaries would often find churches already established when they arrived.[25]

What is less well known is that the missionary endeavors of Korean Christians helped to foster active engagement in the movement for

---

[24] Edward Andrews, *Christian Missions And Colonial Empires Reconsidered: A Black Evangelist in West Africa, 1766-1816* (History Department faculty publications, Paper 3, 2009), p. 2, cited in Jonathan Kangwa, "The Contribution of Indigenous African Women to the Growth of Christianity in North Eastern Zambia: The Case of Helen Nyirenda Kaunda," *Feminist Theology* 26, no. 1 (September 2017), p. 41.

[25] Lee Mahnyol, "A study on *Kwonseo*, Korean Colporteurs," trans. Lee Lily and Lee Ha Yeon, *Dongbanghakji*, no. 65 (March 1990), (Institute of Korean Studies, Yeonse University), pp. 77-173, reprinted in *The International Congregational Journal*, Part I, 7, no. 1 (Winter 2007), pp. 17-36 and Part II, 7, no. 2 (Fall 2008), pp. 13-23. The quotation is from Part I, p. 18.

independence from Japan, which led to the March 1st Declaration of 1919. Bible men and women faced imprisonment as dissidents, and Christian churches and schools were attacked.[26] Recent articles by Min Heui Cheon and Seon-yi Lee highlight the impact of this work particularly among Korean women, and its legacy for the Church in Korea today.[27]

Lee Mahnyol argues for a shift of perspective. Rather than seeing the nineteenth century through the narrative of European and American expansion, he suggests being alert to the many other viewpoints, from which a far more richly textured narrative can be woven:

> In contrast to [the] missionary-centric view, an understanding of the Christian history that focused on national and mass-oriented positions has arisen. There have been some brilliant scholarly achievements related to the nationalistic standpoint. Yet, there is virtually no historical research related to mass oriented point of view and specification of it.[28]

Those words were written in 1990. Other similar narratives are now emerging. Jonathan Kangwa of the United Church of Zambia University has written a number of articles retelling the story of missionary work in Zambia from the perspective of the indigenous people.[29] Here too, missionaries were sometimes surprised to reach "new" territories only to find that mission stations were already running, founded and staffed by local leaders. One of these, the Mwenzo station, had been established by African teacher-evangelists in 1879, but was attributed to the Scottish missionary Alexander Dewar, who arrived some fifteen years later![30]

Kangwa highlights the complex relationship between colonializing mission and religious and political Dissent. He tells the story of Helen

---

[26] Lee, "A Study on *Kwonseo*," Part II, pp. 19–22.
[27] Min Heui Cheon, "The Life of Jo Ahra, 'Mother of Gwangju', 'The Godmother of Democratisation' and the implication of her life-giving to the Korean Church," translated and summarized by So Young Jung, in Janet H. Wootton (ed.), *Constance: Pioneer, Pastor, Preacher* (London: United Reformed Church, 2021), pp. 44–47; Seon Yi Lee, "Korean Women under the Impact of Imperialism," in Janet Wootton, *Cultural History of Women in Christianity: The Age of Empire (1800-1920)* (London: Routledge, 2022).
[28] Lee, "A Study on *Kwonseo*," Part I, p. 18.
[29] Kangwa, "The Contribution of Indigenous African Women"; see also "Christianisation of Female Initiation Rites by the London Missionary Society: The Case of Northern Rhodesia, 1883-1920," in Wootton, *Cultural History of Women in Christianity*.
[30] Peter Snelson, *Educational Development in Northern Rhodesia 1883-1945*, 2nd. edn. (Lusaka: Kenneth Kaunda Foundation, 1990), p. 59, cited in Kangwa, "The Contribution of Indigenous African Women," p. 35.

Nyirenda, a student at the Overtoun Institution (which had been opened under the aegis of the Livingstonia Mission), who came from a family already engaged in campaigns against British imperialism. She and her husband, David Kaunda, were active in establishing schools and increasing learning and literacy among local people. Kangwa notes:

> Indigenous Africans who were able to read started a search for positive values from African culture which were not found in mission churches. The Bible became a source of positive criticism levelled against the missionaries and the colonial masters. Values countering injustice and discrimination were found within the complex diversity of the Bible.[31]

Helen and David's son, Kenneth Kaunda, was born on the mission station and went on to lead the struggle against British rule and to serve as the first president of independent Zambia, from 1964 to 1991.

6. Shaky Ground

We are still living with the legacy of radical Dissent, rooted in sixteenth- and seventeenth-century England and Wales. This relatively small group of reformers shook the world more profoundly than we generally recognize. The English Civil War gave rise to one of the first regicides and earliest revolutions at the dawn of the modern world. They began life on shaky ground and then produced a set of seismic shifts, which reverberated through later revolutions and upheavals.

Their failure to establish a successful, lasting government led to the exclusion of Dissenters from public life for two centuries, during which time they turned their energies to trade, industry, science, and transformations in education and society, shaking the foundations of the world that had repudiated them.

They were as capable as anyone of exploitation, brutality, greed and injustice. And yet they carried with them an enquiring mind, and a thirst for freedom, as well as a fierce desire to see justice prevail. It is worth uncovering their story, where it is hidden, and it is worth listening for the echoes of Dissent where it emerges as new voices are heard.

---

[31] Kangwa, "The Contribution of Indigenous African Women," p. 45 referring to Hastings, *A History of African Christianity 1950-1975*, p. 19.

7. Conclusion

I will end with two contemporary references, which, like seismographs on opposite sides of the world, track the vibrations of Dissent in the present day.

Annelien de Dijn's *Freedom: An Unruly History* explores "the prolonged political struggle triggered by the Atlantic Revolutions of the late eighteenth century," which, she argues, "played a crucial role in establishing our modern, democratic political systems. But ... also inspired a formidable reaction against democracy."[32] She charts a profound change: "For centuries Western thinkers and political actors identified freedom ... with exercising control over the way one is governed. Theirs was a *democratic* conception of freedom: a free state was one in which the people ruled itself."[33]

But as democratic principles began to threaten cherished freedoms, an argument arose that

> [t]he best way to preserve freedom was not ... to expand popular control over government but to create roadblocks against government interference in people's lives. In a democratic context, then, individual liberty could best be protected by institutions and norms that curtailed popular power. This idea, it is safe to say, would have stunned earlier freedom fighters.[34]

Both interpretations of freedom can be traced back to the principles forged in the persecutions of sixteenth- and seventeenth-century England and Wales, in the debates in Cambridge colleges, the pamphlets and prophesyings that informed illegal congregations, and the heat of the civil war, capturing the allegiance of people like John Bunyan. They fought and died, lost their friends, and emigrated over unimaginable distances, to ensure that people had the democratic right to participate in their own government, and also that the state should not have undue control.

These are live issues that are shaking our certainties at the present time. Understanding their deep roots in this much-shaken ground may help to see where the language of dissent brings clarity or simply acts as an ideological mascot. Are the true heirs of the radical Dissenters those who campaign for racial justice and greater inclusion, or those who uphold the right to liberty from the interference of the state?

---

[32] Annelien de Dijn, *Freedom: An Unruly History* (Cambridge, MA: Harvard University Press, 2020), p. 3.
[33] Ibid, pp. 1–2, italics original.
[34] De Dijn 2020, p. 4.

On the other side of the Atlantic, a young South African congregational minister and Ph.D. student gave an interview as part of the 2021 online conference of the International Congregational Fellowship. Euodia Volanie described her work with African Independent or African Initiated Churches. These are churches that are not descendants of missionary movements but have their origins in indigenous African communities. She describes an ideological resonance, in which the new churches reflect the experience of independency back to organizations that had their roots in European nonconformity but have become institutionalized. Interviewed about her work, she says:

> Most of the pastors have started their own church in their homes or in schools, or in temporary structures in their areas. And what is fascinating is that the Congregational Way started out like this, congregating in open fields and under trees ... if we change the lens through which we view these churches then we actually discover our own roots.[35]

This chimes with my own experience as a congregational minister for many years and biblical tutor in ministerial training. We try hard not to let the ground solidify under our feet. We recognize the echoes of Dissent each time a new church springs up, or an existing church calls someone into a new form of leadership. Our task is not to teach them to conform to set patterns but to follow where the Spirit leads, with the openness and enquiring mind that we learn from our heritage.

In our international work, we look for the new and hidden voices, disturbing the foundations of history, questioning our own traditions and seeing God break open new ground, new understanding and new hope. We are still on shaky ground, for which we praise God!

---

[35] Euodia Volanie, "African Initiated Churches," *International Congregational Journal*, 19, no. 1 (2022).

About the Author

Rev. Dr. Janet Wootton (M.A., Oxon; Ph.D., London) has ministered in Congregational churches in rural and inner-city settings, and as Director of Studies for ministerial training. She has served as Moderator of the Churches Commission on Mission (UK), Moderator of the International Congregational Fellowship, and Founder Co-chair (with Dr Manfred Kohl) of the ICF Theological Commission.

She is a hymnwriter, broadcaster, author, and speaker at national and international conferences on worship and mission. She supports the Congregational Way as a powerful expression of church, enabling God's Spirit to speak to and through all God's people.

Jesus Inaugurates the Kingdom: Proclaim the Gospel in Word and Deed

Richard Howell

1. Introduction

The vision for the universal dimension of the Christian ministry for the flourishing of life for every person and the entire world finds its basis in the foundational text of Jesus' inauguration of the kingdom of God: "The time has come," he said. "The kingdom of God has come near. Repent and believe the good news!" (Mark 1:15). The kingdom is both a future event (Matt 13:36–43; 47–50) and present reality (Luke 11:20; 12:32). Miroslav Volf comments, "Jesus' healing miracles are a sign of the in-breaking kingdom. As deeds are done in the power of the Spirit, healings are not merely symbols of God's future rule but are anticipatory realizations of God's present rule. They provide tangible testimony to the materiality of salvation."[1]

God dwelling with his creation became a historical reality when God became man. Indeed "the Word became flesh and made his dwelling among us ... full of grace and truth" (John 1:14). And the permanent dwelling of God with his people awaits future fulfillment. As John wrote, "Look! God's dwelling place is now among the people, and he will dwell with them. They will be his people, and God himself will be with them and be their God ... He who was seated on the throne said, "I am making everything new!" (Rev 21:3, 5). The Christian life must be lived in a way that the world becomes God's dwelling place. Considering the foundational text, the *praxis* of ministry must affect everything in the light of God's self-revelation in Jesus Christ.

John also emphatically states, "God is love" (1 John 4:8), as the origin and source of all love God creates a good creation, and when humanity separated from the life of God (Eph 4:18; 1 John 4:10), God in his holy love redeems the world through his Son, who from the cross prayed, "Father forgive them" (Luke 23:34), and died for our sins (1 Cor 15:3), and "through him, we have both have access to the Father by one Spirit" (Eph 2:18). Jesus died even when we were enemies of God (Rom 5:10); this is why the love of

---

[1] Miroslav Volf, *Work in the Spirit* (Eugene, OR: Wipf & Stock, 2001), 104.

the enemy, not just love for the neighbor, is essential for the Christian life. And so, Christian ministry is not exclusively oriented towards God but is also oriented towards the world. As Barth wrote, "The aim of creation is history ... God wills and creates the creature for the sake of his Son or Word. And creation is not only the expression of divine love and grace, but the precondition of the outworking of God's purposes of grace, but the precondition of the outworking of God's purposes of grace through Christ in history."[2] Christian ministry participates in God's redemptive purposes for all creation and seeks to saturate the world with God's love and make it God's dwelling place.

The gospel of the kingdom of God must be faithfully proclaimed and lived with cultural sensitivity, and as it addresses contextual needs, holding together the twin themes of transcendence and immanence. The disciples did not go searching for the text in the context or consider context as text. Whereas the study of sociology and anthropology helps contextualize the gospel, it needs to be stated that theology is not anthropology, as Feuerbach suggested.[3] The kingdom is utterly transcendent and supernatural; it comes from above, from God alone, and it is God's gift, even as repentance is God's gift.

2. Call to Repentance

Sincere repentance may be one of the most demanding acts for a person, let alone a community, to achieve; repentance is a gift of God. There can be only one clarion call to repent and turn to God in anticipation of God's activity, which involves redemption and judgment. Repentance is closely linked with the expectation of divine judgment and the need for forgiveness of sins. The Lord taught that failure to repent would result in judgment and death (Matt 3:10, 11:20–24; Luke 13:3, 5). Repenting is changing one's mind and direction. Jesus gave an object lesson on repentance when he placed a child among his disciples and said, "Unless you change and become like little children, you will never enter the kingdom of heaven" (Matt 18:3). He contrasted the trust and humility of a child with

---

[2] Karl Barth, *Church Dogmatics,* edited by G.W. Bromiley and T.F. Torrance, 14 vols (Edinburgh: T&T Clark, 1957-75), III:1, 41, 59, sec. 40, 26–27.

[3] Ludwig Feuerbach says unambiguously, "Consciousness of God is self-consciousness, knowledge of God is self-knowledge. By his God thou knowest man, and by the man his God; the two are identical." *The Essence of Christianity,* translated by George Eliot, based on the second German version of 1843 (New York: Harper & Row, 1957), 12.

pride and self-seeking. Jesus said, "You cannot serve God and Money" and "Love your enemies and pray for those who persecute you" (Matt 6:24; 5:44). Jesus' teaching on money and violence shows us that repenting has social relevance.

Believers can break from the trap of sinful values and practice and live the new values of God's kingdom with repentance; this enables them to participate in authentic social transformation. That is why Jesus said the first action a person experiences on the coming kingdom of God is to have their heart made pure and receive the promise that they will see God (Matt 5:8). Forgiveness can happen only through the mediation of Christ, the Son of Man to whom God has given the authority to declare forgiveness (Mark 2:10).

Jesus illumined hope in the hearts of the oppressed when he proclaimed that God's unconditional love was available to those who repent; for example, the Samaritan woman (John 4) suffered from double oppression, first by gender, for she was a woman, and also racial, for she was a Samaritan, the outcast of her times. Although she was much sinned against, she also needed to repent, for she too had committed sin. All need to repent, forgive and reconcile. The oppressed tend to inherit the values of the oppressors. For an oppressor to repent requires a desire to change and make restitution to those wronged, and to remove the injustice that triggered the original violation. There is an irrefutable connection between the hope Jesus provides to the oppressed and the complete change of life he demands of them. Miroslav Volf writes:

> For a victim to repent means not to allow the oppressors to determine the terms under which social conflict is carried out, the values around which the conflict is raging, and the means by which it is fought. Repentance thus empowers victims and disempowers the oppressors. Repentance creates a haven of God's new world in the midst of the old, and so makes the transformation of the old possible.[4]

Repentance ushers in a reconciled community serving and reconciling in society.

3. Jesus Confers Identity

Jesus' proclamation of the blessedness of the kingdom of God is an affirmation of the unique identity of the disciples, which depends on the

---

[4] Miroslav Volf, *Exclusion and Embrace* (Nashville, TN: Abingdon, 1996), 116.

gracious activity of their heavenly Father. Jesus told his disciples, "You are the salt of the earth" (Matt 5:13) and "You are the light of the world." (v. 14). Identity answers the question "Who am I?" while dignity answers "What am I worth?" The Bible makes the subject of identity the prior question. It emphasizes that both the creation of humanity and redemption are acts of God's grace. There are no human elements, however meritorious or sinful, involved in our creation or redemption. Grace confers identity. The seventy-two messengers sent by Jesus returned excited by their experience of the reality of supernatural and spiritual power. Jesus admonished them that the ultimate issues of the kingdom of God are not power issues but the sheer privilege of entry into the kingdom of God.

Identity-related issues are major concerns that Christian ministry has to address, for it causes injury to people created in the image and likeness of God. Charles Taylor comments:

> Our identity is partly shaped by recognition or its absence, often by the misrecognition of others, and so a person or group of people can suffer real damage, real distortion if the people or society around them mirror back to them a confining or demeaning or contemptible picture of themselves. Non-recognition or misrecognition can inflict harm, can be a form of oppression, imprisoning someone in a false, distorted, and reduced mode of being.[5]

Jesus deliberately invited people to table fellowship as he transgressed social boundaries that excluded those considered social outcasts, people who practiced despised trades, Gentiles and Samaritans, calling these boundaries part of systemic evil, sinful, and outside God's will.

Human dignity cannot be given to a person by the kindness of others. It involves freedom of conscience, equality dignity of every human being, freedom and economic empowerment and relations of mutual respect among people and conscious participation in the life of the society. Such a universal theological vision of the Christian is important in addressing politically colored, identity-driven struggles among groups.

Identity is not, first of all, an individual identity. Christian identity is affirmed through relationships in the new household of Christ. Believing women and men in the household of Christ are all priests enjoying equal access to God. The Church engages in ministry to live the new values of God's kingdom; this enables them to participate in authentic social transformation.

---

[5] Charles Taylor, "The Politics of Recognition" in *Multiculturalism: Examining the Politics of Recognition,* edited and introduced by Amy Gutmann (Princeton: Princeton University Press: 1994), 1.

4. Messianic Compassion and Market Values

The messianic compassion of Jesus was manifested when, as the good shepherd, he taught the harassed and helpless crowds (Matthew 9:36) to keep them from straying from God. Jesus positively assured them, "You will know the truth, and the truth will set you free" (John 8:32). The truth of God's Word, when obeyed, empowers communities and transforms lives.

Jesus was concerned about human bodies, just as he was about souls. He fed four thousand, besides women and children (Matt 15:32ff.). He raised to life the dead son of the widow at Nain (Luke 7:12-15), demonstrating his concern for the world's sorrow. God's compassion is rooted in his free love and grace. The content of this compassion is not just an attitude but a bestowal of benefit. It has a concrete expression with real results: deliverance from sin, disease and death, abundant life, justice for the oppressed. God's compassion was indeed made humanly visible in the incarnation of Jesus Christ.

So how does compassion then exist in the marketplace? According to Robert Heilbroner, the nature of our society is the accumulation of wealth as power, and the logic of our society is the exchange of commodities.[6] The market is an arena where cutthroat competition guided by self-interest and individualism is the norm, where weakness is despised, and success is defined by the power one possesses and exercises. To survive in a free market economy, one must have capital or skills; people at the bottom of society have neither capital nor skills and are thus beyond the scope of survival in a market economy. In such a context, Christians are called upon to question the priorities of the market society and challenge the mammon that takes the place of God in human lives and reduces humankind to slavery, lust and greed. Jesus focused on the little ones and took special care of the losers. The Church should be at the forefront of empowering the cause and aspirations of the poor and the marginalized, for this is true neighborliness (Luke 10:25-37). The transformational ministry of compassion compels Christians to confront hopelessness and despair with word and deed. Until we learn that in seeking reconciliation with God, we must walk side-by-side in horizontal reconciliation, we shall not participate in the New Creation.

---

[6] Robert Heilbroner, *The Nature and Logic of Capitalism* (New York: W. W. Norton, 1985), 31-32, 141-48.

5. New Creation in Christ

Christ Jesus brought a radically new thing in the world: God's "new creation." At the heart of the biblical teaching of the human person stands the belief that God's creative power imparts new birth (John 3:3–8), a new creation (2 Cor 5:17), and creates a new heaven and new earth (Isa 65:17; Rev 21:1–5). The newness can be brought about by God's grace and holy love working in human life and material creation. The argument of the apostle Paul in 1 Corinthians 15:34, "Some people have no knowledge of God," rings in hope. The ground of belief in the possibility and conceivability of a resurrection mode of existence is "the infinite resourcefulness of God as already demonstrated in his sovereign power and wisdom as Creator ... A dead person cannot contribute to his or her 'being brought to life.'"[7] The emphasis on the "newness" of divine creativity speaks relevantly to human experience in situations where individual persons or humankind seems to have lost control of human well-being and destiny; arguably, the Covid-19 pandemic, global warming and other ideological forces invite a creative change of kind greater than mere correction or self-regulation.

The members in the body of Christ are "members of God's household" (Eph 2:19), and the church is indeed a family of families. The church members are united in Christ-like vines, rooted in him and gathered in one eternal and spiritual life. The unity of the church overcomes all barriers, including racial, linguistic, and social differences. We need to regain the horizon for approaching the nature of the church that is the corporate vision of the biblical writers rather than the individualism characterized by the Enlightenment of the West. And so, Geoffrey Wainwright rightly grounds the corporate dimension in God's mission, to the world through his people.[8] The church is the materiality described as being-in-Christ as one. *Koinonia* (Acts 2:42; 1 Cor 1:9; 10:16; 2 Cor 6:14; 8:4; 9:13; 13:13, 1 John 1:3–4) denotes not simply "companionship," but, writes Thorton, "common and material and participation in a common object."[9] Moltmann stresses both the theological dimension of Koinonia because it denotes "the messianic way of life" lived "in the power of the Spirit," the practical aspects of "fellowship among the congregations' rank and file," and

---

[7] Anthony C. Thiselton, *The First Epistle to the Corinthians: A Commentary on the Greek Text*, NIGTC series (Grand Rapids: Eerdmans; Carlisle, UK: Paternoster, 2000), 1264–65.

[8] Geoffrey Wainwright, *Doxology: A Systematic Theology-The Praise of God in Worship, Doctrine, and Life* (London: Epworth, 1980), 122–46.

[9] L. S. Thorton, *The Common Life in the Body of Christ*, 3rd edn. (London: Dacre, 1959), 31.

"friendship ... from the grassroots."[10] Moltmann described the fellowship of the church as in principle "a fellowship of friends," in aim and task. He writes, "The church will not overcome its present crisis through reform of the administration of the sacraments, or from reform of its ministries. It will overcome the crisis through the rebirth of practical fellowship ... and friendship."[11] The message of salvation is to be proclaimed to all nations to bring them into one fold, to unite them by the power of faith and the grace of the Holy Spirit (Matt 28:19-20; Mark 16:15; Acts 1:8).

6. Integrity of Creation

As people created in the image and likeness of God, we have the desire and the capacity to investigate God's world and live human life within the created order, with all its joys and sufferings, and to participate in the groaning of the creation, for "We know that the whole creation has been groaning as in the pains of childbirth right up to the present time" (Rom 8:22). The suffering of the creation is like birth pangs culminating in a glorious new creation rather than a dying creation. The redemption that Christ brings has cosmic scope. It is not limited to individuals, but rather to the whole cosmos (cf. Rev 21:1-5). "It is the will of God that gives meaning to our life, and God's will is precisely that a person should fully live his or her life as a free, creative, passionate participant in the cosmic dance."[12] As the community of Christ, situated in the nexus of science and faith, engages in ministry, the thirst for understanding and wisdom of the natural order equips them to work for the integrity of creation.

With contextual awareness, Christian ministry must engage with the natural sciences. Douglas John Hall states, "The natural sciences learned from this same Judeo-Christian ontology that human spirituality is cheapened when it fastens on the divine in such a way as to exclude nature and even history from the realm of transcendent wonder."[13] The present world is valued for what it is as God's good creation.[14] Interconnectedness and particularity are distinctive features *within* the life of the triune God—the

---

[10] Jurgen Moltmann, *The Church in the Power of the Spirit: A Contribution to Messianic Ecclesiology*, trans. Margret Kohl (London: SCM., 1977), 317; cf. 114-32, 272-75; 314-17.
[11] Moltmann 1977, 317.
[12] Guiseppe Del Re, *The Cosmic Dance: Science Discovers the Mysterious Harmony of the Universe* (Radnor, PA: Templeton Press, 2000), 391.
[13] Douglas John Hall, *Imaging God: Dominion as Stewardship* (Grand Rapids: Eerdmans, 1986), 138.
[14] See Jurgen Moltmann, *The Coming of God: Christian Eschatology* (Minneapolis: Fortress Press, 1996), 270-275.

Father, the Son and the Holy Spirit—who brought creation into existence in the freedom of his love. And as Graham Buxton posits, "The scientific discoveries of quantum physics, evolutionary emergence, chaos and complexity, posit a natural world that mirrors the life of God in all its perichoretic richness, wonder and mystery."[15] Buxton further states, "Perhaps human beings might concede that nature is more constant in its response to the Spirit than they are and to that extent a more faithful witness of *imago Dei*."[16]

The integrity of creation is also undermined when duality between the empirical and spiritual is promoted. Within the West, the sacred and the secular are often clearly demarcated. However, this is not the case worldwide: some countries continue to acknowledge rightly that all aspects of our lives are sacred. For example, travelling through Ghana, in Africa, one can observe many shops and advertisements that stand out, such as "Jesus is Lord Business Centre and Internet Cafe," "Give Thanks to God Tailoring Shop," "Riches of Glory Guest House" and the "Jesus Is Lord Fabric Shop." It is the same throughout much of sub-Saharan Africa, which is now 70% Christian. The secular, sacred, and material and spiritual lines are drawn very differently in Asia and Africa than in Western culture, influenced by enlightenment philosophy and theology, which divide the empirical and the spiritual worlds.

The biblical concept of *shalom* presents a harmonious integration of all things while maintaining the distinction. Shalom implies peace for all while focusing on the notion of individual-in-community, and the idea of "completeness" suggests wholeness brought about by the coming together of different parts. Shalom also presents two further goals for life: liberation for creation and justice for humanity.[17] Robert McAfee Brown expounds on Micah 6:8, arguing that the verse is not about "three different assertions being made, but one assertion being made in three different ways." He expresses the logic of his argument in the form of three equations: to act justly means to love tenderly and walk humbly with God; to love tenderly means to walk humbly with God and to act justly; to walk humbly with God means to act justly and love tenderly.[18] While proclaiming the gospel of the kingdom of God in word and deed, Christian ministry addresses the issues of caring for planet earth and social justice.

---

[15] Graham Buxton, *The Trinity, Creation and Pastoral Ministry* (Milton Keynes, UK: Paternoster, 2005), 282.

[16] Buxton, 282.

[17] Ulrich Duchrow and Gerhard Liedke, *Shalom: Biblical Perspectives on Creation, Justice and Peace* (WCC Publications, 1989) gives a complete explanation of these themes.

[18] Robert McAfee Brown, *Spirituality and Liberation: Overcoming the Great Fallacy*, (London: Hodder & Stoughton Ltd., 1988), 70.

People who are beaten down, stuck in deprivation, and on the margins on account of age, gender, race, caste, or class often have internalized a false, negative sense of self, including powerlessness. Sin in this world owes much to powerlessness, pride and the lust for power, especially since inequalities are institutionalized and imposed. The other side of pride, explains Moltmann, is hopelessness, resignation, weariness, and timidity, all of which result in falling away from the living hope that God promises. The sin that most profoundly threatens us is not the evil we perpetrate with power but rather the good that we do not do with the power we have.[19]

Shaull found Christianity in the Pentecostal movement in Latin America, which engaged the primal struggles between order and chaos. He described such Christianity as flourishing at "ground zero" of this struggle. This new paradigm of Christianity he described as

> [a] reconstruction of life in the power of the Spirit. This power to reconstruct life is profoundly manifest in those places where the most basic forms of life in the community—the family, local neighbourhood, social, economic and political structures are becoming unglued, leaving masses of poor people in both rural and peripheral urban areas without stable work, medical care, or education opportunities.[20]

The Holy Spirit renews our mind and imparts the capacity to discern the dominant culture's destructive powers and claim the freedom to act apart from or against those unjust structures. All our ministry initiatives for transformation have intrinsic value and significance as they relate to the eschatological new creation. The kingdom of God addresses the issues of power.

7. Power to Serve

The cross of Jesus reflects God's power at work. According to Barth, "Power in itself is not merely neutral. Power itself is evil."[21] Therefore, as we study the biblical narrative, we see God's unlimited power is in the incarnation and the self-giving nature of God. We hear Jesus in the Scripture, asking us to denounce self-referential, repressive, imposing, and one-sided power.

---

[19] Moltmann, Jurgen. *Theology of Hope*, trans. James W. Leitch (New York: Harper and Row, 1967), 22–23.

[20] Richard Shaull and Waldo Ceaser, *Pentecostalism and the Future of the Christian Churches* (Grand Rapids, MI: Eerdmans, 2000), 116.

[21] Karl Barth, *Church Dogmatics*, trans. and ed. G.W. Bromiley and T. F. Torrance (Edinburgh: T&T Clark, 1957-1975), II/1, 524.

He asks us to exercise power in collaborative, creative, relational and constructive ways. Jesus also offers a set of warnings (seven woes!) for people who enjoy systemic advantages at the expense of the disadvantaged (Matt 23:13-39).

Considering the self-sacrificial nature of God's love, the community of Christ in its intended form is marked by equality that has implications for church leadership. When we think of leadership, we often think of power, and when power is conceptualized as "power *over*," we imply that relationships characterized by domination and subjugation are desirable. Hierarchy as a system of power is rooted in such thought. In contrast, the church should shape its understanding of power guided by the Trinitarian language of interdependence and not domination. Churches should be a place where differences and similarities are celebrated instead of a place where power is solely vested.

Creating space for children, youth, and women in the church's ministry demands the leadership's generosity and a demand for justice. Jesus' understanding of power in the kingdom of God is in stark contrast with popular culture and popular practice.

8. Experiencing the Kingdom as a Little Child

In the Gospel of Mark (9:33-37), we witness Jesus placing a little child in the disciples' midst, saying, "Whoever welcomes one such child in my name welcomes me, and whoever welcomes me does [not only] welcome me but the one who sent me." The child noticeably trusted Jesus and was completely dependent upon Jesus. By doing as Jesus asked, the child was modeling the behavior Jesus expected from his disciples (Mark 9:37).

Traditionally, the accent fell on "the receptiveness of a child" as the key for understanding the analogy between the phrases "as a little child" and "receiving the kingdom of God." However, according to James Bailey, the current scholarly consensus is that Mark 9:33-37 and Mark 10:13-16 must be read with reference to each other and understood in light of their historical frame of reference.[22] In this setting, Jesus was introducing the child as among "the least ones" in the society, who needed to be sought, received, and embraced actively.[23] When we respect the excluded, we respect God, for welcoming a child is akin to welcoming God (Mark 9:37).

---

[22] James Bailey, "Experiencing the Kingdom as a Little Child: A Rereading of Mark 10: 13-16," *Word and World*, vol. 15, No. 1 (1995), 58-67.

[23] Chad Myers, "The Ideology and Social Strategy of Mark's Community," in *Binding the Strong Man* (New York, Orbis: 1988), 413-448.

Pleased by the child's behavior, Jesus was telling his disciples that "You need to change! You need to become like this child!"

Luke 22:24-27 introduces us to Jesus' conversations about greatness during his last Passover meal. The meal is an anticipation of the eschatological banquet of the kingdom of God, which gives Jesus' comments an eschatological perspective. Jesus insists that—in contrast to Gentile leaders who use power and authority to abuse or exclude—among his followers, the greatest become like the youngest and the leader like the one who serves. Jesus identified himself with the excluded groups when He said that "I am among you as one who serves" (v. 27). In this context, Jesus called attention to two of the most excluded people on the margins in that social context; the child (the youngest) and the slaves. During the conversation, Jesus said, "I confer on you, just as my Father has conferred on me, a kingdom, so that you may eat and drink at my table" (Luke 22:29-30).

In contrast to the dominant status quo, where authority is located among those already at the table, he conferred on the excluded groups a kingdom, with dignity and respect: now they "may eat and drink at my table" (v. 30). The triune God, who created all humanity with dignity and respect, redeems his creation in the person of Jesus Christ, the One who ushers in the reign of God and invites all to the table without discriminating. On the day of Pentecost, these excluded groups of children and slaves—and women—were equal partakers of the power of the Holy Spirit. Our refusal to see children, youth and women as co-equal in the body of Christ and as co-equal ministry partners is negated and reconstituted by the Holy Spirit; our ego defenses are transformed when the self is centered in Christ. The community of Christ is to call out one another in love, including children, youth and women, to be what God intends.

The traditional understanding of ministry as a vocation is changing, and emphasis is on the concept of charisma, giftedness as the cornerstone of the praxis of ministry. Instead of emphasizing that a person has been "called" to do certain work irrespective of their inclinations, prominence is given to engaging in work for which the Holy Spirit has gifted us.

9. God and the Diversity of Cultures

At Pentecost, we discern that the Holy Spirit empowers language to be what it is created to be: a tool to facilitate communion between man and God, for interpersonal communication and fellowship, and communication of truth. However, "This is not done by reverting to the unity of cultural uniformity but by advancing toward the harmony of cultural diversity. The miracle of overcoming broken communication is the fulfilment of a prophecy by Joel."[24] On the day of Pentecost, God revealed that all languages are worthy of divine communication (vv. 6–7). Andrew Walls underlines the importance of translatability of the gospel: "When God in Christ became man, Divinity was translated into humanity, as though humanity were a receptor language."[25] The engagement of Christian faith with languages and cultures of the world has the transcendent God at the centre of the universe of cultures, "implying equality among cultures and the necessarily relative status of cultures vis-à-vis the truth of God. No culture is so advanced and so superior that it can claim exclusive access or advantage to the truth of God, and none so marginal and remote that it can be excluded. All have merit; none is indispensable."[26]

10. Conclusion

In our understanding of ministry, we have considered God as the source of all ministry. Therefore, outdated concepts (old wineskins) of ministry, which ascribe responsibility for various dimensions of church life to only a few, must be replaced by an understanding of ministry based on the enabling of the Holy Spirit, irrespective of age, gender or class (new wineskins). When Christian ministry is understood from the perspective of its instrumentality, God's ministry is cast in terms of its usefulness. This understanding privileges purpose over existence and instrumentality over ontology. Thus people are often sent to the margins due to their perceived performance value. In reality, our performance must issue from our worship. Due to the church's participation in the divine life, the church is first an ontological reality (what church is) before an instrumental reality (what the church does).

We are also called to see our identity "in Christ," where we can participate in the life of God. The Spirit restores their identity as co-equal in the body of Christ, co-workers with God and locates them at the center of God's ministry in the world.

The Holy Spirit brings revival and renewal, transforming lives always within the particularity of social, cultural, racial, caste and religious, economic, political contexts of the world, and also affects those contexts. The lives made new are scattered like seeds born by the wind of the Holy Spirit to witness what they have heard, seen and experienced in word and deed.

---

[24] Miroslav Volf, *Exclusion and Embrace* (Nashville, TN: Abingdon, 1996), 114.
[25] Andrew F. Walls, *The Missionary Movement in Christian History: Studies in the Transmission of Faith* (Maryknoll, NY: Orbis, 1996), 27.
[26] Lamin Sanneh, *Disciples of All Nations* (Oxford: Oxford University Press, 2008), 25.

About the Author

Richard Howell holds a Ph.D. from Sam Higginbottom University of Agriculture, Technology and Science (SHUATS) in Paryagraj, India. He is the Principal of Caleb Institute at Farrukh Nagar, Gurugram, and a visiting Professor of Christian Studies at SHUATS. Earlier, he served as the Principal of Allahabad Bible Seminary (1990–1996), as General Secretary of Evangelical Fellowship of India (1997–2016) and as the General Secretary of Asia Evangelical Alliance for ten years and Vice President of the World Evangelical Alliance for four years. He is a founding member of the Global Christian Forum, and he writes a weekly column on Christianity in the *Sunday Guardian*.

Lifelong Learners in the School of Grace: The Pedagogy of Grace

Paul Sanders

1. Introduction

The word "grace" is commonly employed in religious terminology and in daily parlance in a wide variety of languages, including English. Expressions such as "to be in someone's good graces," "to fall from grace," "to be granted a grace period," and many others have found their way into everyday conversation.

For historical and theological reasons, evangelical Protestantism's emphasis on the doctrine of grace (*sola gratia*) has often accentuated God's grace in justification to the detriment of its role in the ongoing sanctification of the believer. The revivalist roots of evangelicalism have favored an emphasis on the "crisis" nature of conversion and focused the doctrine of grace on the initial conversion experience.

Popular evangelical piety echoes this tendency. A cursory examination of evangelical hymnology, for example, shows that most of our evangelical hymns highlight the justifying dimension of God's grace as revealed in Christian conversion. However, a concordance search of the 150 occurrences of "grace" (*charis*) and its cognates (two-thirds of them are found in the epistles of Paul) reveals that the majority of these passages focus on the role of grace *after* conversion. A key example of this usage is found in Titus 2:11-14:

> For the grace of God has appeared that offers salvation to all people. It {grace} teaches us to say "No" to ungodliness and worldly passions, and to live self-controlled, upright and godly lives in this present age, while we wait for the blessed hope—the appearing of the glory of our great God and Savior, Jesus Christ, who gave himself for us to redeem us from all wickedness and to purify for himself a people that are his very own, eager to do what is good. (NIV)

I propose in this contribution devotional and personal reflections on the Titus 2 passage as applied to theological education. Two main themes unfold in this text and are consistent with the emphasis of the New Testament as a whole:

1. Grace is the foundation for the *conversion* of the Christian believer.
2. Grace is the basis for the *education* of the Christian believer.

At the outset, rather than an exhaustive theological description, let us retain the following simple definition of grace: "an undeserved blessing freely bestowed on man by God."[1]

2. Two Facets of Grace

2.1. God's grace justifies

As a citizen of both France and the United States, I know that the heads of state of these two countries have the authority to grant a "presidential pardon" or, as we say in French, *"une grâce présidentielle."* Thus, in exceptional instances, a person who has been found guilty of a crime may be liberated from incarceration or receive a reduced sentence—or even, such as in the United States, be freed from the death penalty (now abolished in the European Union).[2] Such clemency is granted rarely and in very specific circumstances. A pardon does not expunge the offense committed or erase the guilt of the transgressor but rather revokes the punishment that he or she should have suffered for their crime.[3]

Paul first emphasizes the justifying dimension of grace, the *sola gratia*, in the first phrase of this text: "For the grace of God has appeared that offers salvation to all people" (2:11). Indeed, God's grace that "appeared" (*epephanē*) is here personified in Christ who is "full of grace."[4] The Greek aorist tense refers to a precise event or group of occurrences taking place in the past. Christ's "appearing" here encapsulates a series of events related to the first advent of Christ (incarnation, life, teaching, suffering, death, resurrection, ascension and glorification). The totality of God's New Covenant work of grace takes place between Christ's first coming (*epephanē*—"has appeared") and his second advent (*epiphaneian*—"the appearing"; 2:13).

Unlike the rare pardons granted by human heads of state in exceptional circumstances, the New Testament tells us that God's pardon is

---

[1] P.E. Hughes, "Grace," in Walter A. Elwell (ed.), *Evangelical Dictionary of Theology* (Grand Rapids: Baker, 1984), 479.
[2] https://www.eu-logos.org/2020/10/21/death-penalty-in-neighbouring-countries-what-is-the-eu-doing/.
[3] https://www.service-public.fr/particuliers/vosdroits/F780.
[4] John 1:14, 16–17.

offered to all mankind (*pasin anthrōpois*). God's grace in Christ is universal in scope and is available to all those who place their trust in him, regardless of their sex, race, culture and language, and irrespective of the number and gravity of past offenses committed. Yet, like a human presidential pardon, God's offer of grace is conditioned upon the guilty party's acceptance; it is never forced upon the offender. Here is dual freedom: God is never obligated to grant his grace, always freely given, and human beings are not constrained to accept it. Both divine and human freedom are fully respected, yet God remains sovereign.[5]

After Paul's reminder on justifying grace, a closer look at the following verses (12–14) reveals a second key emphasis relative to God's grace. This second theme shall be our focus in the remainder of this contribution.

2.2. God's grace educates

After reminding his readers of God's grace in offering salvation, Paul clearly points to its ongoing nature, that is, the "sanctifying" dimension of grace in operation during the entirety of our Christian lives.[6] Because God's grace continues after conversion, it is thankfully available to meet believers' daily needs. Indeed, all of God's educational processes are based upon his grace. As Bridges has expressed it:

> This means that all our responses to God's dealings with us and all our practices of the spiritual disciplines must be based on the knowledge that God is dealing with us in grace. And it means that all our efforts to teach godly living and spiritual maturity to others must be grounded in grace.[7]

Paul's letters are replete with texts that describe grace in its "post-conversion" benefits to the believer. Here is a brief sampling:

- Grace provides strength amid our weakness as well as consolation and hope in times of need (2 Cor).
- God's grace is the source of the gifts of the Spirit for the edification of the Body (1 Cor; Rom).
- This same grace makes deep joy possible despite unfavorable circumstances (Phil).

---

[5] J. I. Packer, *Evangelism and the Sovereignty of God* (Inter-Varsity Press, 2010).
[6] Wayne Grudem, *Théologie systématique. Introduction à la doctrine biblique* (Charols: Éditions Excelsis, 2010), 200–202.
[7] Jerry Bridges, *The Discipline of Grace* (Colorado Springs: NavPress, 2006, Kindle edn.), 72–73.

We could continue this enumeration for pages on end! Overall, God's grace gives believers a life worth living and makes available to us a continual growth process throughout our lives.[8]

To apply this understanding of the pedagogy of grace to theological education, we propose to employ illustrations from the world of education, comparing the work of grace in the Christian life to enrollment and learning in the "School of Grace."[9]

3. Lifelong Learning in the School of Grace

3.1. The nature of education in the School of Grace

At conversion, when we believed in Christ, we were duly and definitively "enrolled" in the School of Grace. We might even say that we have "dual registration" in this school: in the School of Grace for the duration of our earthly journey, and in eternity, in the Book of Life.

Enrollment is only the beginning of our educational sojourn, for after invoking Christ's appearing in 2:11, Paul adds in the same breath that grace teaches (or "educates") us (*paideuousa*). Christ the Savior is also Christ the Educator. But what is meant here by the term "educates"?

In many contexts, the translation of *paideuousa* by "educates" may connote the mere acquisition of information. Liefeld prefers to translate *paideuousa* by "trains" to better reflect the scope of this comprehensive Greek term for education.[10] However, the English word "train" often refers principally to the development of practical competencies, whereas the Pastoral Epistles, indeed the New Testament in general, make it clear that God's desired educational outcomes also refer to the quality of Christian living and virtues.

---

[8] "Au vu de ces enseignements, nous ne pouvons guère conclure que le Royaume de Dieu ... est une récompense accordée en reconnaissance d'une obéissance aux enseignements de Jésus. C'est le don de la grâce de Dieu. Mais le Royaume n'est pas seulement un don futur ; il est aussi un don actuel à ceux qui veulent renoncer à toutes autres choses et se livrer sans réserve à la grâce de Dieu." George E. Ladd, *Théologie du Nouveau Testament* (Charols: Éditions Excelsis, 2010), 130–131.

[9] Canon Hay Aitken in *The School of Grace: Expository Thoughts on Titus 2.11-14*, 1880. See John R. W. Stott, *The Message of 1 Timothy & Titus* (Nottingham: Inter-Varsity Press, 1996), 193.

[10] W.L. Liefeld, *1 & 2 Timothy/Titus*, NIV Application Commentary (Grand Rapids: Zondervan, 1999), 337, 339.

In French, a rich word, *formation*,[11] connotes both process and content and covers the acquisition of knowledge, capacities and attitudes. This *formation* takes place continuously and is intended to last one's entire life.[12]

The more holistic notion of "transformative education" as used by Perry Shaw seems to be more accurate here, as incorporating the learning of attitudes, behavior, knowledge and competencies.[13] In keeping with the Lord's own example as Master Teacher, we conclude that this "pedagogy of grace" relates to formational and transformational education.[14] The apostle uses the same word *paideuousa* in Ephesians 6:4 in his exhortation to fathers to devote themselves to the training and instruction of their children:[15] "Fathers, do not exasperate your children; instead, bring them up in the training and instruction of the Lord (*en paideia kai nouthesia kyriou*)." The use of the present participle "educating"[16] in Titus 2 implies an ongoing process of transformation, which, as we have indicated, is lifelong in duration. This progressive inner renovation corresponds to the "metamorphosis" described by Paul in Romans 12:2 and 2 Corinthians 3:18.

3.2. The curriculum of the School of Grace

As we reflect upon the educational nature of God's grace, a second question comes to mind: *What* specifically does God's grace teach us? What is the content of God's curriculum? The answer is found in verses 11 and 12: "For the grace of God ... teaches us to say 'No' to ungodliness and worldly passions, and to live self-controlled, upright and godly lives in this present age."

In other words, God's curriculum on our behalf is both corrective and affirmative in intention, learning how to say "No!" and "Yes!" On one hand, God's grace provides the strength to renounce choices, behaviors and desires that are contrary to God's heart and will. On the other hand, while we say "No," we must also say "Yes!" to developing virtue, to choosing right

---

[11] This French word has different connotations from "formation" in English. See https://www.larousse.fr/dictionnaires/francais/formation/34643.
[12] Paul Sanders, "Formation," *Dictionnaire de théologie pratique* (Charols: Excelsis, 2021), 475.
[13] Perry W. H. Shaw, *Transforming Theological Education: A Practical Handbook for Integrative Learning* (ICETE Series) (Carlisle: Langham Global Library, 2014).
[14] Shaw, Transforming *Theological Education*.
[15] Bridges, 71.
[16] Liefeld, *1 & 2 Timothy/Titus*, 337.

and healthy life habits. Marvin Oxenham's excellent contribution on character and virtue in theological education develops this theme.[17]

The School of Grace is governed and managed by the Trinity. To express this in institutional imagery, we could assert God the Father is the "Founder and Owner"; Jesus Christ is the "Principal" (for his death and resurrection made our admission possible). The Holy Spirit, the Paraclete, is the "Director of Studies" who monitors progress and provides needed educational resources. Note that this is only a metaphor, not an attempt to present a modalistic or subordinatist view of the Trinity!

According to Titus 2, the core curriculum of the School of Grace includes two major modules: (1) how to reject destructive life choices, and (2) how to live in light of the life to come.

4. Yes and No

4.1. Learning to say "no!"

Paul's first learning outcome is corrective: "It [grace] teaches us to say 'No' to ungodliness and worldly passions." In the School of Grace, believers learn to renounce or deny[18] "ungodliness" (*asebeian*). This latter term basically refers to "disregarding God, ignoring him, or not taking him into account in one's life."[19] Such attitudes may result in detestable behavior fed by ignorance, forgetfulness and passions that the world system incites or encourages (*kosmikas epithymias*). The play on words is significant: *asebeian* is contrasted in the following verse with *eusebeia*, that is, life choices pleasing to God. The worldly passions referred to involve "the inordinate desire for and preoccupation with the things of this life, such as possessions, prestige, pleasure, or power."[20] In every age, the Christian life is lived in a morally dangerous context—this includes theological teachers and students, who also must live in the sphere of grace—that is, God's resources for human needs. The stakes of this learning are immense, for how can future pastors and church/ministry leaders truly lead if they themselves have not learned to say "no" to ungodly behavior and the thinking that underpins it?

---

[17] Marvin Oxenham, *Character and Virtue in Theological Education. An Academic Epistolary Novel* (Carlisle: Langham Global Library, 2019).
[18] Liefeld, *1 & 2 Timothy/Titus*, p. 339, points out that this denial or renunciation is the same word used in Peter's denials of Christ.
[19] Bridges, 77.
[20] Bridges, 77.

Renouncing *worldly desires* (*kosmikas epithymias*) constitutes a second "corrective" learning outcome. Present and future Christian leaders need to resist these desires that lie so close to our doorways. They appear to have an element of attraction but are in reality part and parcel of a "human society that ignores or despises God."[21]

An important curricular question we might ask of our schools is the following: Where in our study programs do we deal with the twin temptations of ungodly and worldly behavior?

4.2. Learning to say "yes!"

The second learning outcome presented by Paul is "positive" in nature. The Christian life cannot simply say "No!" for such renunciation should be the result of positive Christian character. The pedagogy of grace is progressive, just as good learning in its essence must be gradual. Specifically, grace teaches three virtues: "to live self-controlled (*sōphronos*), upright (*dikaios*) and godly (*eusēbōs*) lives in this present age."

George W. Knight has suggested that the first virtue refers to one's personal growth, that is, the ability to focus on the positive and worthy things of life. The second virtue focuses on growing in relationship with others, making choices that reflect both God's justice and his righteousness. The third virtue emphasizes our "vertical" relationship to God, implementing the integrative principle of God's glory.[22] Here indeed are three key "units" in the "course" on saying "Yes." These three areas' "growth itineraries" are lofty outcomes statements that are certainly worthy of the spiritual formation program of any theological school.[23]

In short, the foundation of the curriculum of the School of Grace involves learning how to *live*: "For the grace of God ... teaches us ... to live" (2:11–12).[24] God's pedagogy of grace aims to promote life.[25] This is a clear outcome statement. The Scriptures as a whole (and in the Pastoral Epistles in particular) develop the specific content of God's curriculum of grace which educates and corrects and, in doing so, teaches believers to live differently.

---

[21] Liefeld, *1 & 2 Timothy/Titus*, 339.
[22] Cf. George W. Knight, *The Pastoral Epistles* (Grand Rapids: Eerdmans, 2013), 320.
[23] Bénétreau, *Les Epîtres pastorales*, 321.
[24] *Hē charis tou theou sotērios ... paideuousa hēmas ... zēsomen.*
[25] *Hina ... zēsomen en to nyn aioni.*

4.3. The methodology of the School of Grace

After emphasizing the nature of "education" and the "curriculum" in the School of Grace, Paul's next words answer a third question: *How* does grace educate us? The passage identifies or implies three ways by which we are educated or trained concerning God's grace.

4.3.1. By reminding us of the cost of grace

Paul reminds Titus and all Christian believers that Jesus paid an infinite price to free us from sin and death. The implication is clear: it is unthinkable that we should fall back into a life of sin in light of the cost of Jesus' sacrifice: "Our great God and Savior, Jesus Christ … gave himself for us to redeem us from all wickedness" (2:13–14a).[26]

Theological teachers and students are not immune to the tendency to forgetfulness which may breed ingratitude. Being immersed in the study of the sacred texts and of theological reflection may even contribute to a spirit of familiarity. This danger reinforces the need in our theological institutions for board, faculty, staff and students to maintain a strong emphasis on gospel witness as well as personal and corporate piety.

This retrospective look at Christ's first coming and work should arouse in believers a sense of immense gratitude (note the linguistic link in English and many other languages between "grace" and "gratitude").

4.3.2. By informing us of God's overall intention in giving grace

God's grace also educates as we become aware that his grace is God's means for transforming the Church as a whole into a new humanity: " and to purify for himself a people that are his very own, eager to do what is good" (2:14b).

These verses place before us a double challenge regarding the consistency and the quality of church leadership, as well as the impact of our theological training on the society around us. In his concise book *Connecting Curriculum with Context*,[27] Rupen Das has distinguished between "output," "outcome," and "impact" in the evaluation of curricular effectiveness. Whereas output refers to the quantitative results of our training

---

[26] Tou megalou theou kai sōtēros hēmōn Iēsou Christou, hos edōken heauton hyper hēmōn hina lytrōsētai hēmas apo pasēs anomias.
[27] Rupen Das, *Connecting Curriculum with Context* (Carlisle, Langham Global Library, 2015).

(number of students, professors, graduates, books in the library, buildings, and so on), outcome indicates the transformation taking place in the lives of the graduates, who in turn influence the churches and ministries they lead. And finally, impact denotes the influence exercised by the churches and ministries led by our graduates on their surrounding societal contexts. In the School of Grace, God's primary concern is the transformational training of leaders in their ministries whose ministries lead in turn to the transformation of their environments. The forging of a "people" implies influence and impact that is collective in nature. As N. T. Wright has so aptly put it:

> Now that we have glimpsed in Jesus the way things are actually going to be, we can see how we should live in the present. The Christian who understands what God's grace is all about—the powerful love which will turn the world the right way up, and has begun to do so in Jesus—will not be able to stand idly by and watch injustice at work.[28]

Beyond the personal piety of the individual believer, there is a clear social, collective dimension in the transformational learning program of the School of Grace.

4.3.3. By setting God's grace within its eschatological context

The third means by which God's grace educates his people relates to the eschatological dimension of this enterprise. Grace teaches us to live between the already and the not yet: "while we wait for the blessed hope—the appearing of the glory of our great God and Savior, Jesus Christ" (2:14). The hope of the second advent of Christ mentioned in this text is qualified as *makarion elpida* (happy, blessed hope) and a second term, the glory (*tēs doxēs*) of Christ, described both as "great God and our Savior" (*tēs megalou theou kai sotēros hēmōn*). Paul here emphasizes the exultation of believers contemplating the second coming of Christ in infinite splendor. After being reminded of the "already" of Christ's finished work, we are invited to reflect on the "not yet" of his return. It is the contemplation of both the "already" and the "not yet" which should impact the moral choices of believers.

The notion of awaiting Christ's Second Coming also involves a sense of "blessed incompleteness" or "holy dissatisfaction" that should move us to

---

[28] Quoted in https://setsnservice.files.wordpress.com/2017/04/grace-its-complicated.pdf.

progress[29] in the integration of the virtues of self-control, uprightness and godliness. Christ's return is a "happy hope" (*tēn makarian elpida*) and a "glorious appearing" (*epiphaneian tēs doxēs*). This beatitude of hope is not focused on our desires, even the most legitimate ones, but on the consummation of all things initiated by the *parousia*.

In the School of Grace, we are transformed[30] as we learn contentment while awaiting Christ's return. Learning to wait, to renounce destructive choices in light of the blessed hope, is a key outcome of God's curriculum.

The "glorious appearing" of Christ will be the gateway to eternal life in all its fulness. God's grace has "appeared" in Jesus' first coming and we await its full realization upon his return. The two epiphanies (vv. 11, 13—*epiphanein, epiphaneian*) form a coherent whole, including the incarnation, Jesus' earthly life and ministry, his glorification and triumphal return.[31]

The development of Christian virtue and character is thus set in the context of our future hope. Some, in the Thessalonian church for example, neglected both responsibility and morality under the pretext that Christ's return was imminent. Paul is setting forth the opposite implication here: because we have this blessed hope, we learn to live lives that are worthy of it. As Liefeld puts it, "All of this—manner of life and expectation of heart—is the content of the training that grace gives us."[32]

In summary, God's transformational curriculum possesses cosmic dimensions. Much more than this present life is at stake!

5. The Intended Overall Outcome of God's Educating Grace

A fourth important question from our passage relates to the "why" of the School of Grace curriculum. Modern education is focused on "learning

---

[29] Phil. 3:12-14: "Not that I have already obtained all this, or have already arrived at my goal, but I press on to take hold of that for which Christ Jesus took hold of me. Brothers and sisters, I do not consider myself yet to have taken hold of it. But one thing I do: forgetting what is behind and straining towards what is ahead, I press on towards the goal to win the prize for which God has called me heavenwards in Christ Jesus."

[30] 2 Cor 3:18; 4:16: "And we all, who with unveiled faces contemplate the Lord's glory, are being transformed into his image with ever-increasing glory, which comes from the Lord, who is the Spirit. ... Therefore we do not lose heart. Though outwardly we are wasting away, yet inwardly we are being renewed day by day."

[31] Cf. Bénétreau, *Les Epîtres pastorales*, 321.

[32] Liefeld, *1 & 2 Timothy/Titus*, 339.

Lifelong Learners in the School of Grace: The Pedagogy of Grace

outcomes"—predefined results in our educational programs for which we mobilize our energies and our resources. Titus 2:14 stipulates an overall learning outcome in the School of Grace: to free, to purify and to qualify a people.[33] This redemptive purpose is akin to that of Israel's exodus. The Older Covenant people were to conquer and inhabit a land in which they would be free to worship and serve Yahweh and to bear witness to Yahweh to the surrounding nations. The New Covenant people are to fulfill God's desire for a "holy nation" under the lordship of Christ (1 Pet 2:9), a people characterized by freedom from every form of lawlessness (*anomia*). This is made possible by the liberating (*hina lytrosetai hēmas*) and purifying work of Christ (*katharisē heautō*), resulting in a people that are exclusively his (*laon periousion*).[34] The adjective *periousios* highlights God's sovereign choice and his desire to have a people who are especially dear to him, who are family. God's people, conscious of the grace given to them, thus desire to accomplish good works (*kalōn ergōn*) on Christ's behalf and thus be motivated to grow in grace throughout their life.[35]

It is noteworthy that the formation of a people is central, taking us beyond an individualistic understanding of this passage. This collective dimension of the pedagogy of grace is both multi-individual and greater than the sum of its individual parts. Fostering a "collective perspective" is indispensable as we train students for ministry. Indeed, we are all enrolled together!

Grace educates us during a lifelong program in the School of Grace. This curriculum is continuing education at its utmost.[36]

All educators know that education involves not only teaching, but also learning, testing and evaluation. During our study programs, we may resist God's grace (Heb 12:15)[37] and repeat certain courses until we can accomplish the Spirit's intended learning outcomes. These "tests" are God's means for measuring our progress, as well as for deepening and enriching our lives, developing Christian virtues and giving us greater meaning and purpose. These assessments stimulate us to move beyond the status quo to

---

[33] Liefeld, *1 & 2 Timothy/Titus*, 324.
[34] Titus 2:14: "who gave himself for us to redeem us from all wickedness and to purify for himself a people that are his very own, eager to do what is good."
[35] 2 Pet 3:18: "But grow in the grace and knowledge of our Lord and Savior Jesus Christ. To him be glory both now and for ever! Amen."
[36] Compare the current understanding of lifelong learning in the European Higher Education Area: http://www.ehea.info/pid34427/lifelong-learning.html#:~:text=The%20Leuven%2FLouvain%2DLa%2D,as%20work%2Dbased%20routes%E2%80%9D.
[37] Heb 12:15: "See to it that no one falls short of the grace of God and that no bitter root grows up to cause trouble and defile many."

greater dimensions of Christian living and witness. They prepare us for "graduation," which will take place in the life to come.

6. Conclusion

We have attempted to demonstrate from Titus 2:11–14 that the biblical doctrine of grace extends to the totality of the Christian life, individual and corporate. The use of the image of the "School of Grace" frames the passage in educational terms including the nature of education in the School of Grace, its divine curriculum, its methodology and overall outcome. Other pedagogical concepts such as testing, evaluation and lifelong learning may enrich our understanding of God's program of individual and corporate grace.

The School of Grace is an image of the process of sanctification whose aim is to teach believers to live while awaiting their departure from the earth or Christ's return, whichever should come first. Education in the School of Grace is holistic, involving the (trans)formation of attitudes, virtues, behavior, knowledge and skills. It focuses on our relationship to God, to others and on worthy choices.

Let us help one another to remember the cost of grace. Let us balance any individualistic outlook on grace with its role in the formation of God's people. Let us frame God's entire educational program in the light of our blessed hope.

May our Lord encourage you in your life and ministry as you continue your education in the School of Grace and participate in God's curriculum on behalf of others!

About the Author

Paul holds the *Doctorat* from the Université Paris—Sorbonne. He has also led the Institut Biblique de Nogent, the Arab Baptist Theological Seminary in Beirut, the European Council for Theological Education, the Middle East North Africa Association for Theological Education and the International Council for Theological Education.

Since his retirement in 2013, he continues to serve as instructor, consultant, translator, and course writer. He is passionate about the empowerment of younger national leaders in the Francophone and Arab worlds. Married to Agnès, a French physician and author, Paul has three grown children and 7 grandchildren.

Re-Forma: Solving a Desperate Need

Reuben van Rensburg

1. Introduction

During the Third Lausanne Congress on World Evangelization in Cape Town in 2010, Dr. Ramesh Richard called an informal, lunchtime meeting of those in pastoral training, whether through formal programs or non-formal methodologies. So many came that the doors were eventually closed, and a second meeting was held for those who could not fit into the first. As a result of these meetings, a document entitled Pastoral Trainers Declaration was released, the concluding paragraph of which says:

> Since the formal and non-formal sectors of pastoral training have knowingly and unknowingly allowed ourselves to be divided in heart and efforts, we declare together that we shall endeavor to build trust, involve each other, and leverage the strengths of each sector to prepare maturing shepherds for the proclamation of God's Word and the building up of Christ's Church in all the nations of the world.[1]

During this meeting, Richard proposed a global conference, which eventually took place on June 15-22 2016 in Bangkok, Thailand, and was called the Global Proclamation Congress (GProCongress). In his opening address, Richard shared the results of research conducted by the Center for the Study of Global Christianity, which revealed that there are "5 million pastors/priests in all Christian traditions worldwide (Catholics, Orthodox, Protestants, and Independents, including bi-vocational)." They further estimate that "5% (250,000) are likely to have had formal theological training (undergraduate Bible degrees or master's degrees)."[2] Of the 5 million, the research estimated that about 2.2 million were evangelical pastors (some put that number as high as 3.4 million).

The problem is exacerbated when one considers that the Global Alliance for Church Multiplication (GACX) has as its goal "to help start at least

---

[1] https://rreach.org/wp-content/uploads/2017/05/Pastoral-Trainers-Declaration-Cape-Town-2010.pdf.
[2] Based on incomplete responses in survey results from colleges and seminaries in their Global Survey on Theological Education, available at https://www.globethics.net/web/gtl/research/global-survey.

five million multiplying biblical churches and faith communities,"[3] each of which will need a pastor. In addition, Richard points out that Dr Thomas Schirrmacher of the World Evangelical Alliance Theological Commission estimates that worldwide there are 50,000 new baptized believers daily.[4] That equates to between 500 and 1000 new churches every day, each of which needs a pastor!

When taken together, these factors spell out a massive crisis in the global church. How will it supply enough trained pastors to keep up with the demand? What is being taught from the pulpit of churches with untrained or inadequately trained pastors? It is a matter of urgency that something significant needs to be done!

Furthermore, it has always been a troubling thought that every other discipline requires its practitioners to have some form of training which is recognized; think of the medical field, engineering, plumbing, and so on. One simply cannot practice in these fields unless one is registered with the appropriate professional body. But when it comes to the pastorate, in many countries anyone can rent a small building somewhere and start a church! There are simply no standards. Now, not all those who are pastors and who do not have a formal qualification are not trained—many are well trained in non-formal settings, but sadly some are very poorly trained, and some are not trained at all. Again, no standards.

2. Re-Forma: A Solution

Toward the end of 2016, Dr. Manfred Kohl, burdened by the realities of the research highlighted at the GProCongress, called a meeting of like-minded leaders from various countries in Halifax, Nova Scotia, which gave birth to an organization tasked with making a significant contribution towards solving the above issues—Re-Forma. Several meetings followed, which led to the formulation of the Re-Forma Statement, which sets out several key principles to guide the thinking and praxis of the organization. Among them are the following:

> Re-Forma does not tell ministry organizations what to do or how to do it, but rather provides resources to assist them in achieving the goals they have formulated. It does not focus its work on traditional, formal theological education, but rather on non-formal/informal leadership for-

---

[3] https://gacx.io/about/framework.
[4] Ramesh Richard, "Training of Pastors: A High Priority for Global Ministry Strategy," https://www.lausanne.org/content/lga/2015-09/training-of-pastors#_edn2.

mation needs which exist at all levels, from grassroots upwards. The outcomes we prescribe are extremely simple and can be demonstrated by students at any level, including those who only have a primary school education.[5]

With respect to governance, the Statement says that Re-Forma

- is constituted as an independent entity (a self-governing organization). It is not subject to any other organization but is affiliated with the WEA.
- has an Advisory Council with representatives from different continents.
- has a legally constituted international Board with representatives from various continents, organizations, and church groups. The Board is solely responsible for the governance of Re-Forma.[6]

As far as delivery of the program is concerned, Re-Forma provides training of trainers, and its website enables partner educational organizations to connect and to facilitate delivery. It includes:

- Extremely simple, creative and innovative outcomes
- Standards
- Links to providers
- A network of program providers and teachers
- Resources

Providers can use various delivery methodologies, e.g.,

- Multi-format (written, digital, visual, audio)
- Online, multi-platform
- Hybrid[7]

2.1. Statement of faith

Re-Forma subscribes to the Lausanne Covenant and the Statement of Faith of the World Evangelical Alliance (WEA).

---

[5] Re-Forma Statement, formulated in Frankfurt, Germany, March 2019.
[6] Ibid, pp. 1–2.
[7] Ibid, p. 4.

2.2. Outcomes

After several meetings, thirty-five key competences for effective pastoral ministry were identified and a learning outcome was attached to each, as follows.

Knowing the Scriptures, usually called Biblical Theology, Old Testament and New Testament Surveys

- Recount ten of the main events in the Old Testament and share the stories of at least ten of the main characters in the Old Testament
- Explain by using five examples how Jesus fulfils Old Testament prophecy
- Summarize at least five major teachings of Jesus
- Explain why the death and resurrection of Jesus is so important
- Explain the significance of Jesus' relationship with his disciples for discipling others today
- Describe ten main events in the book of Acts
- Explain at least three of Paul's key teachings

Living by Faith, usually called Practical Theology, Hermeneutics, Children's Ministry, Church Management, Relationships

- Preach or teach effectively
- Successfully explain a Bible passage to a group of people
- Bear the fruit of the Spirit in all areas of life and practice humility, integrity and simplicity
- List, explain and exercise the spiritual disciplines
- Apply biblically ethical principles to relationships with the congregation
- Demonstrate compassion, welcome and forgiveness in all relationships, including with people who have special needs
- Practice kindness and hospitality

Outreach, usually called Evangelism, Missions, Discipling

- Motivate others for mission
- Effectively share the gospel with family, friends and strangers
- Mentor at least one person in a specific form of evangelism or mission
- Explain why the Bible is more important than culture
- Use technology and social media for ministry
- Demonstrate servant leadership

- Identify and train at least three others to serve in some form of church leadership

Listening and Encouraging, usually called Counseling, Family

- Comfort and assist others in times of crisis, namely death, marital problems, illness, and so on
- Help a couple prepare for their marriage
- Recount at least seven stories in the Bible where God used children
- Explain how Jesus' attitude towards children should change the church
- Involve themselves in ministry to, with and by children
- Nurture faithfulness and love in marriage and family
- Describe the impact of absentee fathers

Trustworthy Faith, usually called Systematic Theology, Ethics, Church History, Stewardship

- Believe and practice sound doctrine
- Summarize and explain the key doctrines of the New Testament
- Explain three of the most important events in the history of the Church
- Describe how their denomination (or church movement) came into being
- Explain the biblical basis for stewardship, giving and offerings
- Explain why the prosperity gospel is unbiblical and unethical. (Note: If the prosperity gospel is not a problem in your region, then select the most important issue that is.)
- Describe the importance of the church

2.3. Leadership

An internationally representative Board and Advisory Council were appointed, with Dr. Kohl serving as the first President. When I retired as President of the South African Theological Seminary (SATS) in 2018, I was asked to direct the project. Non-profit companies were registered in Germany and South Africa, and the plan is to do the same in the US, Asia and South America so that the organization is truly global.

2.4. Advocacy

The next task was to make the program known across the globe. The following methods were deployed:

- A comprehensive website was developed, where potential groups can enroll, download materials, and so on.
- Thousands of pastors, leaders, denominations, missions agencies, church planters, among others, were contacted via email and a range of social media platforms.
- Presentations were made about the program at international conferences, both in person and via Zoom.
- Several articles have been written and published.
- An explanatory video was uploaded to YouTube and the Re-Forma website.

2.5. Enrollment

The first group enrolled in September 2019, and since then there has been an ever-increasing stream of applications. By early November 2020 the number of enrolled groups already stood at 500 and in early February 2022, at more than 1100. It is envisaged that eventually thousands of similar groups will enroll.

3. Resources for Facilitators

In the early stages of development, new facilitators were sent the outcomes, suggested questions, and assessment sheets, and they were able to find helpful resources on the Re-Forma website, www.re-forma.global. If they were already teaching a different curriculum, they were asked to compare its content with the Re-Forma outcomes and then simply teach the balance. In this regard, Tim Keep, the President of Shepherds Global Classroom,[8] kindly made his curriculum of eighteen courses available, free of charge, to Re-Forma facilitators.

Re-Forma also provided a set of optional suggested questions which facilitators can use to help them teach the outcomes.

However, it soon became clear that many facilitators still struggled to find suitable materials to help them teach, and so I decided to write comprehensive notes for each of the outcomes, which are sent to each facilitator when the group enrolls. These notes have been well-received and are being widely used.

It should be stressed that although these notes are supplied by Re-Forma, because this is an outcomes-based program, they are not compulsory. In explaining the situation to facilitators, we use the example of a

---

[8] https://www.shepherdsglobal.org.

driver's license test; when one goes for the test, the examiner does not ask whether one learned how to drive from one's father, or uncle or even a driving school—all he or she is interested in is whether one meets the standards set for the test. With the Re-Forma program, the same principle applies—if one can demonstrate the outcome successfully, it does not matter how one gets there.

To further assist the facilitators, we produced a PowerPoint explaining, with sound bites for each slide, exactly what the role of a facilitator is, and this is distributed to facilitators on enrollment. It explains in detail how to teach the outcomes and how to do the assessment.

4. Quality Assurance Institutes

Re-Forma conducts regular Quality Assurance Institutes in various places around the world. At these events, those who teach the outcomes, whether they be pastors, teachers, or other qualified facilitators, are given specific training in various aspects of group facilitation and assessment. With respect to the latter, because Re-Forma offers a global standard for biblical, ministry training, it is imperative that a common approach is adopted and maintained by all the groups.

At the time of writing, two such Institutes have been held, one in Cape Town in March 2020 for facilitators from Southern African countries, and one, because of COVID restrictions, in Johannesburg in November 2020 for facilitators from South Africa. During 2021, institutes are planned for Nairobi, Kenya for East African facilitators, Accra, Ghana for West African facilitators and two in Asia. Re-Forma pays for each delegate's accommodation, conference fees and materials, but delegates have to find their own way to the venue.

5. The Certificate of Biblical Training for Ministry

It was important to ensure that the program becomes the global standard for non-formal ministry training, and after seeing the content, the World Evangelical Alliance underwrote the Certificate of Biblical Training for Ministry, which is awarded to those students who can successfully demonstrate all thirty-five outcomes—thus making it the first-ever global standard. However, students are urged to place much greater value on the training and what it achieves than on the Certificate.

The Certificate has the Re-Forma logo as well as that of the Theological Commission of the World Evangelical Alliance and is signed by the leaders of both organizations. There is also a place for the facilitator to sign. For security reasons, the Certificate is embossed with the Re-Forma logo and a unique security number is printed on each one.

Although the program is free, for the Certificate to be issued students are required to pay a nominal fee of $5 plus postage in developing countries and $10 plus postage in first-world countries.

6. Funding

As a non-profit organization, Re-Forma is obviously dependent on donor funding, but God has used donors to generously supply all its needs. This has enabled the organization to fund the Quality Assurance Institutes, translations into multiple languages, office expenditures and the salaries of the project director and his assistant. It is clear that the donors involved are of the opinion that God is doing something significant and are keen to get behind it.

7. Conclusion: The Way Ahead

As we have spoken to thousands of Christian leaders and organizations around the world, and as we contemplated what God would do through Re-Forma, our early thoughts have been confirmed: there is a desperate need for a global standard in non-formal ministry training, and when leaders see the Re-Forma program, they agree that it meets a critical need and are eager to enroll their groups. We project that in the future thousands of these groups will enroll and tens of thousands of pastors will go through the program. Naturally this will require careful planning, an increase in staff and the need for greater resource provision, but because this initiative is under God's direction and clearly has his blessing, we know that he will provide all that is needed.

About the Author

Reuben holds a D.Th. from UNIZUL. Before serving as the President of South African Theological Seminary, he was responsible for the policy development of religious education at a national level. After he retired in 2018, he was appointed as Project Director of Re-Forma.

He has spoken at several national and international conferences. He is passionately concerned about the lack of a biblical worldview among Christians and about ministry to, with and by children. He is married to Bev, who still teaches at the seminary, and has three grown children and four grandchildren.

Transregional Mission from Bad Liebenzell: Piety, Pioneering and Priority of Maria Von Rausch in Hong Kong Mission

Wai-Yip Ho

1. Transregional Mission: From Bad Liebenzell to the World

In the formative period of his spiritual formation, Manfred Kohl studied and was personally influenced by Pietism, as reflected in his 1969 Harvard University dissertation, *Studies in Pietism: A Bibliographical Survey of Research since 1958/1959*. This chapter acknowledges the importance of his early spiritual home and heritage of South German Pietism at Bad Liebenzell, but also celebrates his pioneering spirit of inaugurating multifaceted, innovative ministries, as well as appreciating his strategic insights in prioritizing key topics in his transregional mission (e.g., child advocacy, Re-Forma, and Lausanne Catalyst for Integrity and Anti-Corruption). The chapter explores the long-neglected importance of Maria von Rausch, who was born and raised in Bad Liebenzell, in the same region of South Germany as Manfred. Her life and mission reflect godly piety, pioneering spirit and strategic priority.

2. Introduction: Significance of Hong Kong

In the early nineteenth century, Hong Kong consisted of several foreign non-Chinese-speaking communities. Among them, the British were the largest community, the Macau-based Portuguese were the second largest, and Germans were third, followed by the Americans.[1] In the late Qing Dynasty, after the Chinese defeat in the Opium War, Hong Kong was ceded by Qing China to Britain in 1842, becoming a Crown colony of the British government in the Far East until 1997. It has been serving as the meeting point of East and West, in particular as China's window to the world. In the eyes of the missionaries, Hong Kong was different from but closely connected

---

[1] Smith, Carl T. 1994. "The German Speaking Community in Hong Kong 1846-1918." *Journal of the Royal Asiatic Society Hong Kong Branch*, 34:1–55.

to China. Because of the geographical proximity of Hong Kong to China, and being ruled by Britain since 1842, Hong Kong has been considered by missionary societies as the first springboard, or the steppingstone to the "interior" mainland China. In the eyes of Western missionary enterprise, there were reasons to choose Hong Kong as an entry point for the West entering China, which was best illustrated by Jee Gam, the first Chinese ordained as a Congregational pastor in the United States. He wrote to the American Board of Foreign Missions, conveying the wish of California Chinese Christians, to send a missionary to Hong Kong:

> On the evening of the 4th of Aug., 1882 (the same day the Chinese Restriction bill went into effect), the good news came through our superintendent that the American Board had consented to establish the Hong Kong Mission. ... And now, why we so earnestly desired this mission, and why Hong Kong is chosen rather than any other city? ... Having Hong Kong for headquarters, missionaries and teachers can be sent from there to preach and teach in the villages from which our young men come. Besides this, the English language is used more in Hong Kong than in any other part of China, and the Chinese living there, or those visiting that place, could not be reached in a more effective manner by opening the same kind of free schools for them that you have opened for us here. They feel that they need to know the English language. Of course, there are public schools, where both the English and Chinese languages are taught by the British Government, but all have their sessions in the daytime; consequently, the children are the only ones benefitted by these schools. There remains the laboring class unreached. If a free evening school is opened, I have no doubt that much good could be done among them. Moreover, Hong Kong is a great highway to all foreign ports, especially San Francisco. Through Hong Kong nearly all the Chinese in the United States have come and will return. If a general mission could be established at this port, much co-operating work could be accomplished between our missions here and that at Hong Kong. Christian Chinese retuning home, would receive letters of introduction to the superintendent of the Hong Kong mission. This superintendent would have pastoral care over them, and be a very great help in time of persecution. Converts would be made firmer in faith, and more earnest in leading others to Christ.[2]

Hong Kong was chosen due to the strategic importance of Hong Kong's location. Though small, Hong Kong has been considered a strategic site for several reasons. It is a point from where missionaries can be sent to mainland China, it also shelters missionaries from the interior when they are persecuted, and they can come back to Hong Kong for protection. In Hong

---

[2] *The Pacific*, vol. 32, no. 8, February 21, 1883.

Kong, English is one of the official languages and it was taught in the school curriculum under British rule. It was also the free port enabling labor mobility between China and the rest of the world. All that explains why various missionary societies operating evangelistic activities in colonial Hong Kong, including Catholic and Protestant missionary societies, deployed stations in Hong Kong. Jee Gam's appeal was accepted by the American Board of Council for Foreign Missions (ABCFM) and it resulted in sending Charles Robert Hager, Maria von Rausch's husband, to establish the Hong Kong mission on March 31, 1883. Perhaps more than the anticipated strategic considerations of Jee Gam and ABCFM, after one year of Charles Robert Hager's arrival in Hong Kong, he reported to ABCFM about having baptized a young Chinese student, Sun Yat Sen, who became the second member of the mission church:

> At present there are some seven members in the interior belonging to our mission, and two here. One I baptized last Sabbath, a young man who is at attending the Government Central School. He held a very pleasant communion service yesterday.[3]

Most importantly, the lasting impact of baptizing the young Sun Yat Sen is that he became a Christian revolutionary, mobilized like-minded Christians and reformers from Hong Kong and South China leading several uprisings against the Qing Dynasty, and finally established the Republic of China in 1911. Dr. Sun Yat Sen is well-known as the father and the first President of modern China. Among the Protestant missionary societies, Anglo-Saxon Christian missionaries predominate including the London Missionary Society, Baptist Missionary Society, Methodist Society, and ABCFM. But there are other missionary societies from three German-Swiss societies including the Berlin Missionary Association, Basel Missionary Society, as well as Barman Missionary Society which were also in Hong Kong.

The Basel Missionary Society (Basel Mission) was founded in Basel, Switzerland in 1815, and missionaries were sent to do outreach and preach the gospel to the Chinese in 1847, serving mainly the Hakka people in Hong Kong and South China's Guangdong area. To trace the legacy of the work of Basel Mission in Hong Kong, two male Basel missionaries, Rudolf Lechler and Theodore Hamberg, were responsible for taking care and resettling many refugees fleeing after the Taiping Rebellion and its defeat (1850–1864) by the Qing Dynasty. Through their pioneering efforts, the gospel

---

[3] Letter of Rev. Charles Robert Hager from Hong Kong to Rev. Dr. Nathan George Clark at Boston, May 5, 1884, Reel 260, Letter no. 17, American Board of Council for Foreign Mission Papers (ABCFM Papers), p. 3.

was preached, churches established, hospitals and schools built. After a good foundation was laid by the missionaries, an indigenized Chinese Christian church, Tsung Tsin Mission, was established in Hong Kong. By opening Basel Mission archives (BM Archives) and the microfilm of ABCFM plus other sources for transregional analysis,[4] this chapter attempts to explore the untold legacy of Maria von Rausch, a missionary of Bad Liebenzell origin as well as the first female Basel missionary sent to Hong Kong, South China.

3. Möttlingen at Württemberg: Piety as Spiritual Drive of Transregional Mission

Maria von Rausch (1863–1918) was born on March 6, 1863 and raised at Möttlingen, in the district of the town Bad Liebenzell in the Calw district in Württemberg, now Baden-Württemberg. She spent much of her childhood and adolescence in the parsonage in Möttlingen and the Daughters' Institute in Korntal, where the pastors in the boarding school and the hometown pastors played a central role in her spiritual development and orientation toward overseas mission. Besides the direct pastoral care of Maria von Rausch, Möttlingen has been the cradle of spiritual revival and the root of German pietism. One cannot ignore the lasting influence of the spiritual revival of the region, even before Maria von Rausch was born. Möttlingen, within the Bad Liebenzell district, is a place that has gained a reputation in Christian circles beyond the borders of Germany. In understanding Maria von Rausch's life and work, her biography and life mission must firstly be put in the context of nineteenth-century Möttlingen in Bad Liebenzell, where several renowned pastors in that region consecutively impacted the spiritual life and transregional mission-orientation of Möttlingen within Bad Liebenzell, and they marked Maria von Rausch's life and mission.

First, Christian Gottlob Barth (1799–1862) was widely regarded as a representative of Pietism in South Germany. He served as a pastor of Möttlingen from 1824 to 1838. He is famous for promoting evangelical youth literature, especially a children's Bible, believing that children should be taught and led to the Bible. In addition, Barth was deeply committed to promoting world mission.[5] Under this general aura of pietism, Maria von

---

[4] Jenkins, Paul. 2018. "Opening up Transregional Analysis in the Basel Mission Archive" in *The Routledge Handbook of Transregional Studies*, edited by Matthias Middell. Abingdon: Routledge, pp. 555–565.

[5] Blumhardt, Christian Gottlieb and Barth, Christian Gottlob, 1845. *Christian Missions, or, A Manual of Missionary Geography and History: African, Mohammedan Countries,*

Rausch was brought up to focus on early childhood education. As she presented in her curriculum vitae to the Basel Mission:

> From my earliest youth I was urged to fear God and to pray and learned to love the Savior. It was especially the confirmation class, which was taught by our dear Pastor Benz, and especially the confirmation day itself, which became a lasting blessing for me. After the confirmation, the private lessons, which I had already received from the local teacher, were continued until my transfer to Korntal; the rest of the time I dedicated to the children at the parsonage. Here I learned to understand children, to love them and to interact with them.[6]

Second, it is perhaps not by accident that Maria von Rausch applied to the Basel Mission, largely because former pastors were in the ministry of Basel Mission. Christian Gottlieb Blumhardt was the co-founder and inspector of the Basel Mission, which was founded in 1815–1816, and he was the cousin of the father of Johann Christoph Blumhardt (1805–1880). Before serving as a pastor of Möttlingen and Bad Boll, young Johann Christoph Blumhardt became a missionary teacher in Basel Mission from 1830 to 1837. Succeeding to the position of Christian Gottlob Barth in 1838, he started serving as the pastor in Möttlingen. After being in office for three years, Pastor Blumhardt, after many visits, interpreted the illness of a sick woman, Gottliebin Dittus, as not being a physical symptom which could be healed by taking medicine. His famous motto "Jesus ist Sieger" (Jesus is Victor) originated from the exorcism of this lady in 1842 at Möttlingen. He recalled in his writing on Gottliebin Dittus, a widow, who was demon-possessed for two years, killed two children and buried them in a field. She was ill until the night when the demon exclaimed "Jesus is the Victor," and Gottliebin Dittus regained her consciousness. This incident of faith healing led the whole region and beyond to a spiritual revival, where it attracted many from all parts of Germany to seek healing, conversion and repentance,[7] which prompted believers in deep devotion to Lord's mission. One of the lasting impacts of Blumhardt was his delivery of addresses at the yearly Korntal festival, where Maria von Rausch was spiritually influenced by the festival when she

---

Australia and Polynesia. London: Religious Tract Society. For a brief biography of Christian Gottlob Barth, see https://www.kirche-moettlingen.de/unsere-kirchengemeinde/barth-christian-gottlob-1799-1862/.

[6] BMA (Basel Mission Archives), PF (Personenfaszikel) Maria von Rausch (Curriculum Vitae of Maria von Rausch sent to Basel Mission), March 14, 1892.

[7] Zündel, Friedrich. 2010. *Pastor Johann Christoph Blumhardt: An Account of His Life*. Eugene, OR: Cascade Books. For a brief biography of Johann Christoph Blumhardt, see https://www.kirche-moettlingen.de/unsere-kirchengemeinde/blumhardt-johann-christoph-1805-1880/.

studied at the Daughters' Institute in Korntal after the early death of her father. Later the Daughters' Institute was named Blumhardt-Haus, after Blumhardt.[8] Maria later stated:

> The first thought that I wanted to serve the Lord in mission awakened in me through the mission lessons and festivals in Korntal, which I always attended with the greatest interest. Especially the blessing of a mission daughter made a deep impression on me and from then on, I included this wish, the Lord may also make me useful to his ministry, in my daily prayer.[9]

Third, the church minister who wrote and recommended Maria von Rausch was Pastor Theodor Schauffler (1835-1897), who succeeded Pastor Barth and Pastor Blumhardt. According to the Basel Mission archive, Pastor Theodor Schauffler, before coming to Möttlingen, served as a Basel missionary at Calicut (now Kozhikode in the state of Kerala) in southwestern India with faithfulness from 1860 to 1879. After theological training (1879-1881), he ministered to that congregation at Möttlingen for fourteen years from 1882 to 1896,[10] during which Maria von Rausch was under his pastoral care. With the zeal of overseas mission, he at first recommended her to take part in the Zenana Mission in India,[11] eventually when he learned there was a suitable position in Hong Kong:

> In addition to her inner development, which was a completely normal one, she expresses herself in the enclosed curriculum vitae, which she handed over to me for forwarding. She writes about her experiences and about how she feels in her heart. In case the esteemed committee reaches the joyful conclusion of sending Miss von Rausch to Hong Kong, it would still be appropriate for her to attend an institution for the training of children's teachers for a short time, and to take part in a course in nursing.[12]

It is believed that Maria von Rausch grew up under this social aura of pietism, child-caring and overseas-mission oriented worldview, cultivated in

---

[8] Ising, Dieter. 2009. *Johann Christoph Blumhardt, Life and Work: A New Biography.* Eugene, OR: Cascade Books, p. 30.
[9] BMA, PF Maria von Rausch, Curriculum Vitae of Maria von Rausch to Basel Mission, March 14, 1892.
[10] *Evangelische Missionsgesellschaft in Basel.* Indische Mission (1898) *The Fifty-Eighth Report of the Basel German Evangelical Mission in South-Western India For the Year 1897.* Mangalore: Basel Mission Press, pp. 22-24.
[11] BMA, PF Maria von Rausch, Brief von Pfarrer Schauffler (Letter of Pastor Schauffler to Basel Mission), February 15, 1892.
[12] BMA, PF Maria von Rausch, Brief von Pfarrer Schauffler (Letter of Pastor Schauffler to Basel Mission), March 14, 1892.

Möttlingen, in the region of Bad Liebenzell. For Maria von Rausch, the pastors in the Daughters' Institute and the pastors in her hometown played a central role in shaping her spiritual development and orientation toward overseas mission. As a young woman in her twenties, she was already working as a governess for a family, and she cared for her niece after the death of her sister. In 1892, Maria von Rausch applied to the Basel Mission.

4. Women in Mission: Pioneer as the First Single Female Basel Missionary to China

There were discussions of the Basel Mission Home Board on the idea of "Women's Mission" (*Frauenmission*), an overseas missionary enterprise by and for women, and the objective was to propagate overseas a model of Christian femininity.[13] According to the Basel Mission Record, Maria von Rausch was the first single unmarried missionary lady sent to China,[14] and pictures of three other pioneering single unmarried ladies sent to different continents are displayed in the Basel Mission Archive, entitled "Women in the Mission" (*Frauen in der Mission*).

Figure 1: Maria von Rausch (second from left) honored as one of the pioneers of "Women in Mission."[15]

---

[13] Sill, Ulrike, 2010. "The Basel Women's Mission in the European and the Basel Context" *Encounters in Quest of Christian Womanhood: The Basel Mission in Pre- and Early Colonial Ghana*. Brill: Leiden, p. 35.

[14] Mission 21. 2015. "Chronologie 1815–2105: 200 Jahre Basler Mission" in *Pioniere, Weltenbummler, Brückenbauer: Geschichten zum Jubiläum der Basler Mission; Jubiläumsmagazin 200 Jahre Basler Mission*. Basel: Evang. Missionswerk, p. 110.

[15] Photo taken by author at Basel Mission Archives on August 9, 2018.

Maria von Rausch was admitted to the Basel Mission in 1892, departed in September and arrived in Hong Kong on 28 October 1892,[16] to be the first single, unmarried female missionary teacher sent to China. It was a trail-breaking move for Basel Mission to send an unmarried mission teacher to China. To understand the significance and the breakthrough of sending a single female to overseas mission, one has to understand some tragic and painful precedents; some Basel missionaries became ill and died very soon after arriving at their destination[17] and Basel Mission was then more cautious and careful in selecting the single female unmarried missionary, making sure she was spiritually and physically strong to undergo the challenges of overseas mission. Eventually, Maria von Rausch passed rigorous examination as affirmed by the Headmaster of the Daughters' Institute of Korntal[18] and a medical examination before embarking on the journey to Hong Kong.[19] In the first letter sent after her arrival, she immediately prepared herself to go local by learning the Chinese language:

> It is with great joy and profound thanks to God that I can inform you that yesterday we arrived safely in our new homeland. Despite the fact that the weather was good during our whole trip and despite us only getting to know seasickness during the last few days, the journey felt very long and we are very happy to have reached our destination. We were most warmly welcomed by our dear brothers and sisters. Mrs. Bender, Mr. and Mrs. Gussmann and Mr. Kircher picked us up at the Sachsen. The Reusch family and Mrs. Kircher welcomed us into the beautifully decorated mission house, which will certainly become a dear home to me. Of course, we think Hong Kong is beautiful, by which I mean the location, because we haven't seen anything of the city yet. We were already accustomed to the Chinese on the Sachsen and got an idea of their life and activities, because from Singapore on we had over a hundred deck passengers. I will probably start learning the Chinese language next week.[20]

---

[16] BMA, Schwesternverzeichnis, SV 30 (Directory Entry of Basel Mission Sisters), Maria von Rausch.
[17] I am thankful for the kind remarks and wonderful assistance of Basel Mission Archivist Andrea Rhyn.
[18] BMA, PF Maria von Rausch, *Zeugnis des Mädchen-Instituts Korntal* (School Report Card of the Daughters' Institute in Korntal to Basel Mission), July 29, 1883.
[19] BMA, PF Maria von Rausch, *Ärztliches Zeugnis* (Medical report endorsed by Doctor Jahn at Calw to Basel Mission), February 13, 1892.
[20] BMA, PF Maria von Rausch, Brief von Maria von Rausch (Letter of Maria von Rausch to Basel Mission), October 29, 1892.

Figure 2: Maria von Rausch (right) with a Chinese language teacher (left)[21]

5. Children Come First: Priority of Initiating the First Kindergarten in Hong Kong

Maria von Rausch applied to Basel Mission in 1892, and Basel Mission intended to open nursery schools in Hong Kong and needed nursery school teachers to do so. In the same year, Maria left for Hong Kong in September and was responsible for teaching infants. Her character and spiritual quality of caring and teaching children were praised by a kindergarten teacher at Basel:

> Will now catch up in any case and tell you how pleased I am that Miss von Rausch is currently being sent out for this post. I have the impression that she is specially equipped for this by the Lord. She has shown a great deal of love and compassion for the weakest among the little ones, has worked daily with new, untiring, cheerful devotion in school, and has done the lowest services of her own accord. ... Her Christianity seems to be of deep devotion, selfless humility and love and of a very special, rare sincerity. This conviction will make it easy for her to guide adults to the same service and to supervise them later. The Lord will bless her.[22]

---

[21] "Schwester Maria v. Rausch mit Sprachlehrein," BM Archives, http://www.bmarchives.org/items/show/63886.

[22] BMA, PF Maria von Rausch, Brief von Marie Müller (letter of Marie Müller to Basel Mission), September 23, 1892.

She was the first single female staff member sent to China by the Basel Mission. In her letter sent to the Inspector of Basel Mission Board in summer 1893, she reported a kindergarten was getting ready to start in the Chinese New Year (1894) and she called for the donation of books, charts and toys for the teaching children in Hong Kong:

> Mr. Reusch thinks that the kindergarten can be started in the Chinese New Year, and for this purpose he has already envisaged premises near the Mission House. However, since one needs so many things for the establishment of a kindergarten, which are not on the list of allowances, I take the liberty of addressing you, dear inspector, with the request for picture books or charts. The most suitable would perhaps be the biblical pictures from Esslingen, as well as pictures for visual instruction. Furthermore, I would like to ask for all kinds of toys for boys and girls, for example dolls, which we could dress ourselves here, building sets, bowling games, animals, cottages etc. Since one could use all kinds of toys, just like the ones the children have back home, many a child, if the matter were known, would perhaps like to give up some of their superfluous toys. It would be very welcome if we could have the things here by our New Year so that everything could be put in order. May God bless this new work.[23]

Figure 3: Maria von Rausch (middle, last row) with children of the kindergarten in Hong Kong[24]

---

[23] BMA, PF Maria von Rausch, Brief von Maria von Rausch (letter of Maria von Rausch to Inspector Oehler in Basel), August 14, 1893.

[24] "*Kinderschule* in Hong Kong," BM Archives, https://www.bmarchives.org/items/show/63887.

According to the report of Dr. Ernst Johann Eitel, the Inspector of Schools of Hong Kong Government (Dr. Eitel himself was also a Basel Missionary [1862-1865] and Sinologist), a first kindergarten was founded in 1894 to offer teaching to young Chinese children at Sai Ying Pun, "not only combining play with work but giving useful instruction in the rudiments of industry by systematic training of hand and eye."[25] Maria von Rausch was sent to take up the position of director of the kindergarten (Figure 3) and served at Sai Ying Pun kindergarten from 1892 to 1896. One has to appreciate Maria von Rausch's contribution in the Chinese context in the nineteenth century. The significance of Maria von Rausch's work is two-fold. First, this was the first kindergarten to appear in Hong Kong and South China, and Maria von Rausch was indeed the pioneer of introducing early childhood education to Chinese people. Second, the period of her initiation in the kindergarten coincided with the outbreak of bubonic plague that started in 1894, one of the most disastrous calamities that affected Hong Kong for three decades. During the period, she single-handedly struggled to overcome adversities so that the mission of operating the kindergarten education could continue when there was a recurrence of the plague in 1896:

> This summer, my school readiness was strengthened again by the plague which unfortunately occurred again in Hong Kong. As soon as we were up and running in the new school year, many families left Hong Kong for an indefinite period, so that the number of my students decreased from 40 to 24. Under such circumstances one lacks the joy for work and the courage and enthusiasm for the school decreases rather than increases. Looking to the future I am often anxious, because I had hoped to be able to start a second school soon and now this one can hardly be continued. But the Lord will make it happen, and will find ways and means, that the little work we started must not perish.[26]

6. Conclusion: Pietism, Pioneering and Priority in Future Christian Mission

In 1896, Maria was engaged to Dr. Charles Robert Hager, the missionary physician of the ABCFM. At her request, she was released from her commitment to the Basel Mission until the end of 1896. According to the

---

[25] Sweeting, Anthony, 1990. *Education in Hong Kong, Pre-1841 to 1941: Fact & Opinion: Materials for a History of Education in Hong Kong.* Hong Kong: Hong King University press, p. 215.

[26] BMA, A-01.30 (1896), Hongkong, 2. Bericht vom Maria von Rausch (Report from Maria von Rausch to Basel Mission), August 4, 1896.

Committee Minutes of Basel Mission, she was then allowed to marry Dr. Hager on 31 December 1896.[27] He offered on behalf of his society to reimburse the costs of sending her out, and several members were in favor of accepting the offer, as the Basel Mission Board expected that Maria would work significantly longer than four years (1892–1896). However, it was decided not to claim any compensation, partly in view of the faithful services of Maria and the valuable services her fiancé had recently provided as physician to Mrs. Kircher, the wife of Pastor Kircher, the Basel Missionary in Hong Kong.

Figure 4: Rev. Charles Robert Hager and his wife Mrs. Maria von Rausch Hager[28]

After her marriage, Maria joined her husband's mission in ABCFM and pledged to share Dr. Hager's heavy mission workload in the Hong Kong and South China mission of ABCFM. In her letter written to ABCFM on February 15, 1899, she focused on working among women and prepared herself to share in the burden of work:

> The work among the women in the country I regarded as my own work, but the Lord has for the present given me other duties to perform. It is possible that I shall hereafter be able to undertake this work, when new strength and new opportunities are given me to labor for Christ I should be devoutly

---

[27] BMA, Komiteeprotokoll 1896, § 780 (Committee Minutes No. 780, 1896).
[28] "Herr und Frau Dr. Hager," BM Archives, https://www.bmarchives.org/items/show/63872.

thankful. If anyone in the South China Mission needs help it is Dr. Hager with his increasing growing work.[29]

After the death of her husband in 1917, Mrs. Maria von Rausch Hager lived with her children, two sons and a daughter in their home at Claremont, California, but she died shortly afterwards on November 22, 1918 in the United States. Her missionary devotion to Hong Kong and South China was highly appreciated and respected in the words of Rev. Charles A. Nelson, the senior member of ABCFM South China Mission:

> She was active in kindergarten work for Chinese children; also in Sunday school and church work. Her regret was deep when in 1910, because of Dr. Hager's failing health that had led him to seek the advantage of a change of climate, she was compelled to leave the mission in order to join him in California. Though never physically strong, she was ever ready to spend and be spent for the Kingdom of God. "She hath done what she could.[30]

It is widely known that the idea and institutional heritage of kindergarten traced its roots in Germany back to 1840 with Friedrich Froebel, and nowadays most Hong Kong children are nurtured by more than a thousand kindergartens and nursery schools registered at the Education Bureau (EDB) in Hong Kong. Despite this, the origin of and who initiated the kindergarten in Hong Kong and China largely remain unknown and forgotten by most of the Hong Kong people.

The chapter highlights the pietist background in South Germany that prompted Maria von Rausch to make history by courageously becoming the first unmarried female Basel missionary to China, and by faith creatively inaugurating the first kindergarten in Hong Kong and China. Through the unsung legacy of Maria von Rausch being rediscovered, her life still speaks today about how religious pietism and a pioneering spirit as well as strategic prioritization quietly but decisively impacted the success of the future Christian mission. Yet it also reflects the life and mission of God's chosen servants in every generation:

> He will not quarrel or cry out; No one will hear his voice in the streets.
> A bruised reed he will not break, and a smoldering wick he will not snuff out,
> Till he has brought justice through to victory.
> (Matt 12:19–20)

---

[29] Letter of Mrs. Maria von Rausch Hager from Hong Kong to Dr. Judson Smith at Boston, February 15, 1889, Reel 260, Letter no. 321, ABCFM Papers, pp. 3-4.
[30] "Death of Mrs. C. R. Hager," *The Missionary Herald*, vol. 115, no. 1 (1919): 6.

About the Author

Wai-Yip Ho is currently the François Chevalier Fellow, Madrid Institute for Advanced Study; Correspondent Member, Nantes Institute for Advanced Studies; Honorary Research Fellow, Institute of Arab & Islamic Studies, University of Exeter. His works include *Islam and China's Hong Kong: Ethnic Identity, Muslim Networks and the new Silk Road* (Routledge: London, 2015, paperback) and *Islam* (Religious Studies in Contemporary China Collection; Leiden: Brill, 2017). His research interests include Islamic studies, China's Christian-Muslim relations, new media and China's Islam, Gulf-China relations, the Middle East in China and contemporary Muslim youths in Chinese context.

The Bible as the Foundation of Life: Sacramental Realism

Sergii Sannikov

1. Introduction

I would like to start my paper with personal notes.

There are people I feel I have always known. It's hard to say when I first met such a person. Of course, it's possible to recall the time that person came into my life, but in fact, at the very first encounter with him I feel as if we had known each other for a very long time, maybe, even, forever. Manfred Kohl is one of these people.

I think that we first met in Odessa in 1989 or 1990 in a small room in the Serov St., 34, in the courtyard of an ordinary residential building in which the entire academic department of Odessa Bible School was located. Our school still functioned half-legally, and Manfred was one of the first foreigners who had somehow learned about it and was brave enough to come to the Soviet Union and find us.

We have known each other for over thirty years, but it seems that I have known him all my life. This does not mean that we have worked side by side in the same office all this time. We have been seeing each other once in a while, but on a regular basis. In general, it is difficult to imagine Manfred sitting in the office, despite his strict punctuality, scrupulousness, and unbending purposefulness. We have met in very unexpected parts of the world, in different countries, and probably on all the continents: in my native Odessa (Ukraine), in his native Germany, in America, Africa, Russia, Croatia, Great Britain, Chiang-Mai, and even Australia. Everywhere Manfred has been the same—strict, collected, but approachable like a father. He knows how to combine his incredible industry with attention to the family of each of his colleagues. He is interested not only in the outcomes of the work, but also in the personal life and spiritual growth of all his friends. His dedication to the Kingdom of God has always amazed and inspired me.

Many times I met him at the airport after a twelve or fourteen-hour flight and he was ready to go to the conference or lecture right away. I asked him how it was possible. How do you overcome jet lag? He would smile and say, "Don't pay attention to the time. Pay attention to Christ and

His Kingdom." One of Manfred's secrets is the reading of the Bible here and now, and not there and then, and that way of thinking has worked miracles in his life and in the lives of those whom he has served around the globe.

He has often said that most theologians express themselves in all the moods and tenses except the present indicative. They tell us of the things that were done in ancient times. They tell us of the things which are yet to come, or which might or would have happened under certain circumstances. But of the actual reality in which we live at present, we hear very little. The facts of experience do not fit in well with theological theories.

Such theologians know how biblical heroes behaved in difficult situations, but do not know what to say to a mother of five children who turns to them for advice. Manfred emphasizes the importance of living according to the Bible here and now, and not only studying the biblical text in the context of the first recipients. It is no longer enough for theology to encourage a Christian to live according to the rule enunciated by the White Queen to Alice, "Jam tomorrow and jam yesterday—but never jam today."[1] The stress on the immanence of God in each experience allows Manfred to implement biblical sacramental realism in his life.

2. Sacramentality in Evangelical Discourse

Sacramentality is an unpopular concept in Evangelical theology because of the fear of sliding into Catholic or Orthodox terminology. However, the connotation of this phenomenon has always been present among Evangelicals.

The very word "sacrament" implies a mysterious presence of the spiritual in the material, incomprehensible to the human mind. A sacrament indicates the integrality and indivisibility of the spiritual and material world, the presence of the sacred in the profane through some objects which play a mediating part in this mysterious presence. Christ himself, who has revealed the mystery of the Incarnation, is a sacrament ("God appeared in a body," 1 Tim 3:16). The Church, as a mystery hidden for ages and generations, is a sacrament (Col 1:26), and, of course, the Bible is undoubtedly a sacrament, being a result of the act of both God and humans, and such synergism is always unexplainable and unfathomable (2 Pet 1:21).

If we deny the mysterious, sacramental nature of the Bible, the latter becomes a mere book of wisdom and collective spiritual experience of mankind. In this case, one can draw lessons and instructions from it, but

---

[1] Lewis Carroll, *Alice in Wonderland and Other Favorites* (New York: Pocket Books, 1951), 175.

this approach "forgets" that God really works through the Bible. According to John Colwell, if people refute the sacramentality of the Bible, they expect to be informed, but not transformed; they expect understanding, but not action (something to happen to a reader)."[2] Anti-sacramental strategy in regard to the Bible makes it a mere object of an academic analysis.

On the other hand, if the Bible is perceived as a sacred word dictated by God from the first to the last letter, and, therefore absolutely unavailable for any hermeneutical and historical-critical analysis, it becomes not a sacrament but an idol. One can either worship such a Bible or fight with it, but one cannot have fellowship or a dialogue with it. The soundest course is to perceive the Bible as a sacrament, i.e., as the mediating presence of the Holy Spirit in the biblical text in three modes—in the processes of writing, determining which books should be included in the biblical canon, and of reading the canonical text. This approach helps avoid two extremes—the idea of the direct dictation and the idea of the discrepancy between the Bible of faith and the bible of academia—while encouraging to understand the Inspiration as a synergic cooperation of God and humans.

Manfred Kohl is capable of keeping a sound balance between all the aspects of inspiration in everyday life in various denominational contexts. He communicates with all the mainstream Christian denominations, while preserving his Evangelical identity.

3. The Bible as a Sacrament

The sacramental nature of Scripture is rarely articulated in Evangelical Christianity, although the latter constantly points to the meaning and the divine power working through the biblical text. At practically every Eastern European Evangelical worship service, regeneration through the Word alone is proclaimed. The regenerating significance of the Word of God is emphasized not only by Evangelicals, but by modern Catholics as well, especially after Vatican II. If previously Catholicism used to emphasize that the Bible is the holy book in itself, now it underscores the impact Scripture makes on the reader. In his Post-synodal Apostolic Exhortation *Verbum Domini* (*The Word of God*), Benedict XVI (Joseph Ratzinger) dedicates an entire section to the Bible as a sacrament:

> We come to see that at the heart of the sacramentality of the word of God is the mystery of the Incarnation itself: "the Word became flesh" (John 1:14),

---

[2] John Colwell, *Promise and Presence: An Exploration in Sacramental Theology* (Eugene, OR: Wipf and Stock, 2011), 88.

the reality of the revealed mystery is offered to us in the "flesh" of the Son. The Word of God can be perceived by faith through the "sign" of human words and actions. Faith acknowledges God's Word by accepting the words and actions by which he makes himself known to us. The sacramental character of revelation points in turn to the history of salvation, to the way that word of God enters time and space, and speaks to men and women, who are called to accept his gift in faith.[3]

Thus, the Bible is regarded as an interlocutor, by talking to whom humans find God. It leads them to believe, if they respond to the action of God. It is an instrument by which God's grace works. Therefore, *Verbum Domini* notes, "Here it might be helpful to recall the analogy drawn by the Fathers of the Church between the word of God which became 'flesh' and the word which became a 'book.'"[4]

The sacramental presentation of the Bible was seriously criticized after the structuralism of Ferdinand de Saussure and post-structuralism of Jacques Derrida. They showed that when a modern reader begins to peruse a text—especially an ancient one written in a completely different cultural context in a different, already dead language, with other paradigms of thinking—it is impossible to guarantee the right understanding of the meaning and significance of what is written. Regarding the same text as a physical object with unchanging letters, printed identically, each reader finds a different meaning. In his brilliant novel *Small World: An Academic Romance*, David Lodge shows in a subtle and clever way the futility of the quest for the true and only exact meaning of any fixed text:

> To understand a message is to decode it. Language is a code. But every decoding is another encoding ... and even if I were, deviantly, to indicate my comprehension by repeating back to you your own unaltered words, that is no guarantee that I have duplicated your meaning in my head, because I bring a different experience of language, literature, and non-verbal reality to those words, therefore they mean something different to me from what they mean to you.[5]

In other words, the gap between an utterance and understanding is real and often rather significant.

In regard to the written text, the gap between the author and the reader is even deeper than in oral speech; therefore, it is not surprising

---

[3] Benedict XVI, *Verbum Domini* (2010), 56.
[4] Ibid, 18.
[5] David Lodge, "Small World: An Academic Romance," 2021, *BooksVooks*, https://booksvooks.com/nonscrolablepdf/small-world-pdf-david-lodge.html?, p. 34.

that structuralism loudly proclaimed "the death of the author." It is true that a written text loses its "parent,"[6] who would have been able to explain and defend it, and, thus, the reader is left alone with the text. Hence, the plurality of connotations and the absence of an objective criterion of the exact meaning. This relates to ordinary, secular texts. But the situation changes significantly when the biblical text is perceived as a sacrament, i.e., if we acknowledge the dual nature of the authorship of the text. In this case, the text loses its parent, the author who has materialized (fixed physically) it, while remaining under the protection and guardianship of the divine father who has breathed its meaning into it. This father is really present during the reading, and he is never "dead." He explains the text and helps the reader understand the message that he has meant to communicate to a concrete recipient. To put it in biblical terms, the Spirit opens the eyes of the reader (Ps 119:18) and speaks to him through the text, revealing to him the meaning, significance, and essence of what is written. Therefore, the reading of Scripture is fundamentally different from the reading of any other texts, because of the omnipresence of the divine Author.

The interpreting action of the Spirit provides that understanding of the biblical text which God desires in all times and in all cultures, because it presents the divine ideas of the text in the form of the semantic concepts which are the most comprehensible to a particular reader as they are in accordance with his level of knowledge. Such an understanding allowed Vanhoozer to state:

> I reject any plurality that assumes the meaning of a text changes at the behest of the reader, at the influence of an interpretive community, or as a result of the Spirit's leading. On the other hand, I affirm a "Pentecostal plurality," which maintains that the one true interpretation is best approximated by a diversity of particular methods and contexts of reading. The Word remains the interpretive norm, but no one culture or interpretive scheme is sufficient to exhaust its meaning, much less its significance.[7]

---

[6] In the dialogues of Plato, Socrates showed this really well, as he said that when written works "are maltreated or abused, they have no parent to protect them; and they cannot protect or defend themselves." Plato, *Phaedrus, The Internet Classics Archive*, http://classics.mit.edu/Plato/phaedrus.html.

[7] K. J. Vanhoozer, *Is There a Meaning in This Text? The Bible, the Reader, and the Morality of Literary Knowledge* (Grand Rapids: Zondervan Academic, 2009), 419.

4. The Performative Role of Scripture

Thus, the perception of Scripture as a mediator allows one to obtain a hermeneutical key to the quest for the particular meaning and significance of the text which the divine Author wishes to reveal "here and now." This leads to another important aspect of the understanding of the Bible as a sacrament: *the Bible is performative* without being the speech in the literal sense of the word. This is what Manfred Kohl often emphasizes when he says that oral speech can be not only informative but also performative, i.e., it may include words and phrases that produce actions. But a written text does not have performative properties, although it may contain performative utterances.[8] When a reader utters any text, he performs a standard locutionary, and not performative act. At the moment of speaking, which takes place as a locutionary act, any text inevitably produces an illocutionary effect, i.e., it achieves certain communicative goals (it accuses, proposes, demands), but the listeners or readers of the text may still remain unchanged. They may participate in the process of communication without being transformed. In other words, the perception of the text may fail to become an action. But sometimes a text, as a locutionary act, produces a *perlocutionary* effect, i.e., it affects the listeners so as to perform certain actions in or through them.

As John Colwell has shown, since Scripture is a mediator of the action of the Holy Spirit, it becomes a "speaking" text, "And in this expectation of the Spirit's active speaking lies the true basis for the Church's anticipation of the reading and hearing of Scripture as a performative and transformative event: that which is anticipated is the Spirit's speaking and acting."[9] The transformative action of God performed through Scripture is effective not only in the context of the Church, where, according to the Bible, it is "mixed with faith in them that heard it" in contrast with the unbelieving Israelites coming out of Egypt (Heb 4:2), but also outside the church walls as it encounters those unacquainted with the Church. The word of Scripture heard with the heart forms faith. As the apostle Paul says, "So then faith cometh by hearing, and hearing by the word of God"

---

[8] As is known, Derrida was not able to express the final opinion on the performativity of the Declaration of Independence of the USA and he believed that this undecidability (dark spot) should be preserved. In other words, it is still unclear whether the text of the Declaration establishes independence or simply announces it. Therefore, the possible performativity of the written text remains uncertain. See Jacques Derrida, "Otobiographies. I. Declarations of Independence," *Ad Marginem* 93 (1994), 174–85.

[9] Colwell, *Promise and Presence*, 96–97.

(Rom 10:17). It produces an effect, although not always comprehensible to people, and "it shall prosper in the thing whereto I sent it," says Yahweh to his people (Isa 55:11). In other words, Scripture transforms and, thus, produces a sacramental effect. As Francis Watson put it, "The scriptural texts converge on this divine speaking because they mediate this divine speaking."[10]

Speaking of the sacramental nature of the Word, one should understand that to limit it exclusively to the materialized biblical text means not only to impoverish it, but also to create a favorable environment for numerous distortions and erroneous interpretations. As has already been noted, a naïve idea that one can read and understand the meaning and significance of any written text, especially the one separated from the reader by many millennia, is clearly wrong. The sacramental nature of the Word presupposes the unity of the written biblical text and its interpretation. This interpretation can be explicit, i.e., in the form of a denominational tradition, or implicit, i.e., in the form of a personal or group hermeneutical key.

5. Criteria of Interpretation

It is well known that each Christian denomination, including Evangelical Christianity, has its own interpretive tradition or traditions, which mostly concur with each other but still have significant differences. Long before Scripture became a text, it had been the oral sacramental word that affected sinners through the preaching of the first Christians, freeing from sin and forming local congregations of the saints. The oral word of the apostles was passed on to the disciples and constituted the nucleus of the common Christian tradition. With time, the tradition preserved a part that arose from the teaching of Christ and the apostles and made the essence of Christianity, but there also appeared some additional narratives, foreign principles, and pagan rules adopted in the course of history.

This natural historical process of the formation of the "living tradition" reminds one of the growth of a vine, the branches of which spread far and wide, but not all of them bear fruit for the owner of the vineyard. This is why Christ calls God the husbandman: "Every branch in me that beareth not fruit he taketh away: and every branch that beareth fruit, he purgeth it, that it may bring forth more fruit" (John 15:2). In other words, if we liken the life of the Church to the pruning of the vine, then, according to the words of Christ, it needs correction. This is why during the time of the significant spread of Christianity in the fourth and fifth centuries, there

---

[10] Ibid, 98.

arose a need to determine a certain fixed standard to be used as the most authoritative criterion of truth in different cultural environments and in different historical periods. Thus, from the mainstream of traditions the inspired part was singled out which was written down and called Scripture. The rest of the tradition was to remain flexible and open to changes, depending on time and culture.

The question that remains the most controversial in Christianity is the one regarding the epistemological criterion that allows us to distinguish the inspired part of traditions from purely human ones and, thus, to confirm the sacramental impact from above made through this instrument. Most Christian theologians choose antiquity, unchangeableness, and apostolicity for that. In other words, all try to show that the doctrines of their denominations are based on the true and unchangeable teaching of Christ and the apostles. This is done by Roman Catholics who refer to the authority of Peter entrusted with the keys of the Kingdom, by Eastern Orthodox who point to the absence of any alterations in the teaching of Church Fathers, and by Baptists who are sure that they have been able to purify Christianity from historical deposits and make it the way it was during the time of the apostles. These indications of truth are undoubtedly right in themselves, but the problem arises when they are being interpreted and applied.

It is known that antiquity in itself cannot guarantee the veracity of the apostolic teaching. There is a statement attributed to Cyprian of Carthage, "For antiquity without truth is the age-old error." Antiquity should be universally and unanimously accepted. This is the formula indicating the catholicity (*sobornost* in the East) that Christianity came to in the fourth century. It is expressed by Vincent of Lerins (d. before 450), an obscure monk and theologian, who lived in the time of heated theological debates. In his apparently only work, called *Commonitorium* (*Commonitory*, i.e., *Remembrancer*), he sums up the criteria that help to distinguish right teaching from wrong teaching:

> I have often then inquired earnestly and attentively of very many men eminent for sanctity and learning, how and by what sure and so to speak universal rule I may be able to distinguish the truth of Catholic faith from the falsehood of heretical pravity; and I have always, and in almost every instance, received an answer to this effect: That whether I or any one else should wish to detect the frauds and avoid the snares of heretics as they rise, and to continue sound and complete in the Catholic faith we must, the Lord helping, fortify our own belief in two ways; first, by the authority of the Divine Law, and then, by the Tradition of the Catholic Church.[11]

---

[11] Vincent of Lerins, *Commonitorium*, https://www.newadvent.org/fathers/3506.html.

In other words, the criterion to be used to test true and false teachings is, first of all, the canon of the Holy Scriptures, and also the Tradition, which facilitates the right understanding of Scripture, because all the heretics, as he says, refer to the Bible as well. But, at the same time, Vincent takes a sensible view of the Tradition, pointing out that it needs to be used selectively. He says:

> Moreover, in the Catholic Church itself, all possible care must be taken, that we hold that faith which has been believed everywhere, always, by all (*quod ubique, quod semper, quod ab omnibus creditum est*). For that is truly and in the strictest sense Catholic, which, as the name itself and the reason of the thing declare, comprehends all universally. This rule we shall observe if we follow universality, antiquity, consent.[12]

In other words, Vincent believes that the main epistemological criterion is catholicity, which he describes with the help of such terms as universality, antiquity, and consent.

The article about Vincent of Lerins in the Orthodox Encyclopedia explains, "Universality (*universitas*) means to accept as true only the faith that the universal Church (*universalis Ecclesia*) professes. Antiquity (*antiquitas, vetustas*) implies the faithfulness to the teaching approved by the holy fathers. Consent (*consensio*) means to follow—in the antiquity itself—the definitions and judgments of all or almost all of those who are entrusted with priesthood and teaching."[13] Rostislav Tkachenko sums up the criteria of Vincent of Lerins by paraphrasing the main theses of the latter: "A Christian who wishes to remain faithful to the truth should be loyal and persistent in keeping to the principles related in the Holy Scriptures, further explained and confirmed by the Holy Tradition, and accurately professed by the Christian Church everywhere and by all her members."[14]

---

[12] Ibid.

[13] А. Р. Фокин, «Викентий Леринский», *Православная энциклопедия под редакцией Патриарха Московского и всея Руси Кирилла*, просмотрено 15 апреля 2021 г., http://www.pravenc.ru/text/158480.html.

[14] Ростислав Ткаченко, «Писание, Предание и богословие: Определения и принципы взаимодействия согласно учению одного отца церкви. Анализ произведения Викентия Лиринского "Commonitorium"», *Esxatos* (blog), просмотрено 15 апреля 2021 г., http://esxatos.com/articles/pisanie-predanie-i-bogoslovie.

6. Interpretation in Radical and Magisterial Reformation

The use of the maxim of Vincent of Lerins—"faith which has been believed everywhere, always, by all" (sometimes called "the Vincentian canon")—helps create a field inside which the Word is certain to become an acting sacrament, while taken out of it, it remains a denominational doctrine and its own tradition. Still, the interpretation of Scripture in the Radical Reformation tradition is based on principles different from the ones of the Magisterial Reformation tradition.

One of the most prominent researchers of Anabaptist hermeneutics, Dr. Stuart Murray, lists the most important principles of the interpretation of the Bible for this group:

- The Bible as self-interpreting (the Bible explains itself)
- Congregational hermeneutics (the right extrication of meaning is possible only when there is a correcting interaction of the congregation)
- Hermeneutics of obedience (true meaning of Scripture can be discerned only when Scripture is obeyed)[15]

In other words, God reveals the right understanding of the biblical text only in the community of the saints, and not in the solitude of the university, as long as there is holistic (canonical) reading of the Bible as it is and complete obedience to its demands. Only in this case, Christ is present with his disciples personally, in the sacral way, in the Spirit (Matt 18:20), revealing the meaning of the written evidence about him.

The hermeneutical system of Luther and the supporters of the Reformed theology was built in a different way, and it started with the historical-grammatical analysis and historical background. It also avoided allegorizing and any "spiritual" interpretation whenever possible. In his dissertation on this topic, Larry Shelton says that in his hermeneutics Luther

> attempts to determine what the writer generally wishes to communicate. In this process he deals with history and geography as they relate to and

---

[15] Stuart Murray, "Biblical Interpretation among the Anabaptist Reformers," in *A History of Biblical Interpretation*, vol. 2: *The Medieval Through the Reformation Periods*, edited by Alan J. Hauser and Duane F. Watson (Grand Rapids: Eerdmans, 2009), 403–23.

illuminate the text and the relationship of God to man. Secondly, he attempts to elucidate the grammatico-philological meaning of a particular passage. In doing so, he conscientiously seeks the exact meaning of the words and warns against construing meanings to fit one's own theological presuppositions. Thirdly, he searches for the primary thought contained in the text, and attempts to reproduce in his own soul the religious atmosphere and experience of the writer.[16]

That was a completely different approach to the understanding of the biblical text which kept its sacramental nature in the shadows. Manfred Kohl often criticized that approach, pointing out its limitations, although the Reformation hermeneutics is actively forcing out the Anabaptist and Pietistic ones in the theological educational institutions of Eastern Europe.

7. Conclusion

Considering the suspicious and skeptical attitude of modern people toward the intelligible discourses and scientific approaches that originate from the Enlightenment and Modernism, we should admit that the sacramental attitude toward the biblical text is the best response to the needs of the epoch of post-truth. This is why Manfred Kohl's focus on the real impact of the biblical text as well as the demand to understand and apply the text "here and now" is a productive and blessed way to strengthen the Kingdom of God and glorify Christ.

---

[16] R. Larry Shelton, *Martin Luther's Concept of Biblical Interpretation in Historical Perspective* (Pasadena, CA: Fuller Theological Seminary, 1974), 218.

About the Author

Rev. Sergii Sannikov, Ph.D. in Philosophy; Dr. habil. in Theology (Doctor of Science in Theology); Baptist theologian, pastor, chaplain.

Senior Research Fellow at the Center for the Study of Religions, National Pedagogical Dragomanov University (Kyiv, Ukraine); Professor at Odessa Theological Seminary (Odessa, Ukraine); Visiting Professor at different theological institutions in the former Soviet Union. Dr. Sannikov was a Fulbright Scholar-in-Residence (2005) and was a founder and, from 1989 to 1997, the first President of Odessa Theological Seminary; from 1997 to 2011, he was Executive Director of the Euro-Asian Accrediting Association (EAAA), and after 2011 he was EAAA President for six years.

Married, with two adult children and three grandchildren.

Humble Integrity:
The Work of God in the Life of Job

Brad Smith

1. Introduction

God desires to build whole-life integrity within us. The journey He takes us on is custom-made for exactly what we need. The path God took Job on was certainly confusing to Job and his friends. It has also been confusing to many readers of the book of Job for thousands of years. The key that unlocks understanding the journey God prepared for Job is understanding God desires integrity of our actions, emotions and motives.

2. Integrity in a World of Lies

As a college student, I worked one summer for the CEO of a large oil company. After observing this oilman meeting with one of his staff, we got back into his Cadillac car to drive back to the office. I said, "Mr. B., it appeared to me that perhaps you did not trust that person. Why?"

The Texas oilman replied, "Well, Brad, you need to know that there are two types of liars in this world. The first kind is an 'honest liar.' When they are lying, *they* know they are lying, and *you* know they are lying. I can trust an honest liar. But then there are 'dishonest liars.' They've lied to themselves long before they lie to you. They scare me. I cannot trust a dishonest liar. That is why I don't trust that man."

A friend of mine who lives in Ukraine shared an apocryphal quote from Russian President Vladimir Putin. Supposedly speaking to Russian citizens, he said, "We all know that American politicians lie. We all know that Ukrainian politicians lie. And of course, as your leader, I lie too. But it is better for you to believe Russian lies than American or Ukrainian lies."

"Honest lying" is a way of life in our world. It is part of political corruption, media economics, legal courts, and business deals. This should not surprise us. In John 8:44, Jesus says, "You are of your father the devil, and your will is to do your father's desires. He was a murderer from the beginning, and does not stand in the truth, because there is no truth in him. When he lies, he speaks out of his own character, for he is a liar and the father of lies."[1]

In John 12:31, Jesus refers to Satan as the "ruler of this world." Second Corinthians 4:4 reads, "In their case the god of this world has blinded the minds of the unbelievers, to keep them from seeing the light of the gospel of the glory of Christ, who is the image of God."

Various English translations of 1 Peter 2:11 label Christians as aliens, strangers, foreigners, sojourners, temporary residents, exiles, pilgrims, immigrants, visitors, and refugees in this world. We live in a world of lies. As Jesus followers, we are alien people in this world.

In the same chapter where Satan is identified as the father of lies, Jesus says, "If you abide in my word, you are truly my disciples, and you will know the truth, and the truth will set you free" (John 8:31b-32). Later in John 14:6, Jesus says, "I am the way, and the truth, and the life. No one comes to the Father except through me." Satan personifies lies. Jesus personifies truth.

3. The Impossible Road of Self-integrity

As followers of Jesus desiring to live with integrity, we must first recognize that we are surrounded by lies in every aspect of our world. We seek integrity by recognizing lies, not getting caught up in lies, and by speaking out against lies. It is our role to call that out and advocate for justice and integrity. But integrity is not just about pointing out the lies of others. It also seeks to find the lies within ourselves. Too often we become prophetic against "honest liars" while we ourselves are rampant "dishonest liars."

If we underestimate the power and prevalence of lies in our world, we are tempted to think *our* self-discipline and commitment to integrity will prevail. That way of thinking is a lie. If our goal is to white knuckle ourselves to a life of integrity, we have lost before we even begin. If our hope is in our own integrity, then we've already bought a lie about where our hope should be. By focusing on *our* integrity, we have become "dishonest liars" ... the most fearsome kind of liar. Self-integrity is neither the ultimate goal, nor the primary means of a life of integrity.

As a result of so many lies in our world, any discussion about integrity must recognize that none of us rise above the lies that saturate our world. It is the polluted sea in which we swim, and it is difficult to recognize what truth actually looks like, smells like, and tastes like. That alone would cause

---

[1] All biblical quotes in this article are from the English Standard Version Bible (2001).

all of us to be "dishonest liars" to some degree. Yet as much as we have threats to integrity outside of us, we have even greater threats within. No one rises above self-deceit. Recognizing our propensity to lie to ourselves changes how we approach our pursuit of integrity.

Mark 2:16-17 reads, "And the scribes of the Pharisees, when they saw that he was eating with sinners and tax collectors, said to his disciples, "Why does he eat with tax collectors and sinners?" And when Jesus heard it, he said to them, "Those who are well have no need of a physician, but those who are sick. I came not to call the righteous, but sinners." In this case the scribes were "dishonest liars" about their health. In truth, they desperately needed Jesus as their physician, but they lied to themselves that they had no need.

In Luke 7, Jesus' feet are anointed by a prostitute, and he forgives her as the Pharisees judge his lack of integrity for allowing her to do that. In truth, they needed forgiveness as much as she did, but they were "dishonest liars" about their need.

In Luke 16, Jesus tells a parable of a rich man living in luxury who goes to hell after death, and a poor beggar, hungry and full of sores named Lazarus who goes to heaven after death. The rich man had no earthly need, which made him a "dishonest liar" about his true spiritual needs. The beggar had every earthly need which allowed him to be honest about his spiritual needs.

Jeremiah 17:9 reads, "The heart is deceitful above all things, and desperately sick; who can understand it?" That verse doesn't just apply to the politician, or the drunkard, or the prostitute or the Pharisee. It even applies to the person most committed to integrity. The person most committed to being honest will not be totally honest with themselves. The person most committed to being whole, acting in private in the same way as in public, will have shortcomings, even if they are unaware of those shortcomings.

4. Human Integrity Is Humble, Imperfect and Relational

As a result of so many lies in our world and in our own hearts, any discussion about integrity must understand that true integrity must be *humble*, *imperfect* and *relational*.

Humility is not seeing ourselves with less worth or thinking less of ourselves. Humility doesn't come from adjusting our self-image or increasing our self-awareness. Humility comes from seeing God more and more for who He is—good, just, powerful, holy, and loving. We are so impressed with God that it doesn't make sense to think a lot about ourselves. When we do think about ourselves, we see ourselves through the lens of God. We are created, loved and fully adopted by God as his sons and daughters. How could any human accomplishment compare with being adopted into God's family? We don't take our titles or accomplishments very seriously, but we are very serious about obeying and being dependent upon God.

Integrity for anyone who is not God is *imperfect*. The *Merriam-Webster Dictionary*'s definition of integrity includes "the state of being complete or whole"; "firm adherence to a code of especially moral or artistic values"; "an unimpaired condition"; "the quality or state of being complete or undivided." Only God can fully fit the definition of integrity. We rarely use the word *holy* to describe a person since only God is holy. In the same way, any time we describe a person as having integrity, it will never be perfect.

Integrity can only be experienced in an ongoing, growing *relationship* with God. Only Jesus is the truth. Only by abiding in the vine do we produce fruit of integrity. A branch of a vine trying to make it on its own is withered and burned (John 15). Real integrity doesn't celebrate my integrity, but points to the truth of God's character. Real integrity is so focused on who God is that our own shortcomings are easily seen. But we don't lose hope in our shortcomings because they are not the point of integrity. Our relationship and our focus on God are the point. The result is that we will grow in integrity as we grow in receiving the love of God.

5. The Story of the Book of Job

In the book of Job, we learn of a man who very much wanted to obey God with integrity. The rest of this article will explore a way to understand the book beginning with Job as self-deceived. In the narrative of the story, God takes Job on a journey that opens up a new level of integrity for him that is humble, aware of its imperfections, and relational.

The book of Job has many mysteries. Some say it is the oldest book in the Bible due to its archaic Hebrew styling. The date of the story has been often identified as the time of Abraham. The book is narrative. That doesn't mean it didn't actually happen historically. Instead, it means that the events are told in the style of a story. From the ancient epic of the *Iliad* to modern movies, the formula of story almost always has a protagonist on a heroic journey that entertains us as we live vicariously through their struggles and eventual success. The formula also includes an antagonist who opposes the protagonist. There are supporting players and sidekicks. And often there is a guide who helps the protagonist reach their goal. The

Humble Integrity: The Work of God in the Life of Job

protagonist is often the hero. But in some stories, they are not the true hero of the story. Often the *guide* is the hero as they provide direction, arrange circumstances, or even define the goal the protagonist needs to reach to be successful. If we mislabel the true hero in a story, we will lose much of its meaning.

One of the most confusing aspects about the book of Job is that many commentary writers and teachers make Job the hero of the book. They lift up Job as the quintessential example of a man of integrity. The first verse of the book states, "There was a man in the land of Uz whose name was Job, and that man was blameless and upright, one who feared God and turned away from evil."

At first glance, it appears as if even God identifies Job as the quintessential man of integrity. Job 1:8 reads, "And the Lord said to Satan, "Have you considered my servant Job, that there is none like him on the earth, a blameless and upright man, who fears God and turns away from evil?"

What follows is one horrendous disaster after another as Job's children are killed, his riches are destroyed, and he loses everything. Yet, even after all this, verse 20 reads, "Then Job arose and tore his robe and shaved his head and fell on the ground and worshiped. And he said, 'Naked I came from my mother's womb, and naked shall I return. The Lord gave, and the Lord has taken away; blessed be the name of the Lord.' In all this Job did not sin or charge God with wrong."

God again praises Job for keeping his integrity. Job 2:3 reads:

> And the Lord said to Satan, "Have you considered my servant Job, that there is none like him on the earth, a blameless and upright man, who fears God and turns away from evil? He still holds fast his integrity, although you incited me against him to destroy him without reason."

It looks as if Job is the hero of integrity. But Satan pushes the trial to another level. Verse 7 and 8 read, "So Satan went out from the presence of the Lord and struck Job with loathsome sores from the sole of his foot to the crown of his head. And he took a piece of broken pottery with which to scrape himself while he sat in the ashes."

Even with this, Job demonstrates he is the man of industrial strength integrity. Verse 9-10 state: "Then his wife said to him, 'Do you still hold fast your integrity? Curse God and die.' But he said to her, 'You speak as one of the foolish women would speak. Shall we receive good from God, and shall we not receive evil?' In all this Job did not sin with his lips."

People reading Job often draw a straight line between this statement that "Job did not sin" and God's words much later in the book in Job 42:7-8:

> The Lord said to Eliphaz ... : "My anger burns against you and against your two friends, for you have not spoken of me what is right, as my servant Job has. Now therefore take seven bulls and seven rams and go to my servant Job and offer up a burnt offering for yourselves. And my servant Job shall pray for you, for I will accept his prayer not to deal with you according to your folly. For you have not spoken of me what is right, as my servant Job has."

As a cherry on top of the notion that Job is the quintessential man of integrity, James 5:11 is often quoted: "You have heard of the steadfastness of Job, and you have seen the purpose of the Lord, how the Lord is compassionate and merciful."

Reading Job 3, skipping over 39 chapters to land on Job 42 and then reading James 5, it appears as if Job is a hero of integrity to God and James, the brother of Jesus. But are we missing something about the story of Job?

6. The Plot Thickens as We Change Our Focus from Job to God

In Genesis 3, Satan says that if Eve eats the fruit she will be like God. After that fateful fruit salad, every human is born with the desire to be god in their own lives and in the lives of others. We spend so much of our lives trying to arrange circumstances, so we are god and we are the hero. We lie constantly to ourselves that we and our side, our tribe, our way of thinking, our political party, our theology is the way of the hero and superior to our "enemies" who don't think or act like us. No wonder that we attempt to make characters in the Bible heroes as well, even if there are clues screaming at us in the narrative of the Bible that God is the only Hero. Always. No exceptions.

The Bible reveals the dark sides and sins of Abraham, Moses, David, Peter and Paul on purpose. It is amazing that these flawed people are put in places to be bit players and sidekicks to the real Hero in the biblical narratives. It is humbling that God has chosen that role for us as well in His work on earth. Yet we still want to be the hero. We are always usurping God even if we are "dishonest liars" about doing so. It is not surprising that we would attempt to make Job the hero of the book named after him.

There is no doubt that Job is a remarkable example of obedience. He recognizes God as his Creator who has the full rights as Creator to give him bad circumstances as well as good. Losing his family and his health does not shake his faith in God. Job is an example of integrity at a level that most people will never reach. However, there was something missing in his full trust in God. God knew what was missing in Job's heart and exactly what was needed to bring Job into full integrity. God used Job's friends to reveal Job's primary hidden fault. If we don't recognize Job's shortcomings, we miss the amazing work of God in Job's life. When we make Job the hero of the book, we miss God's definition of integrity.

In the narrative of Job, the crack in Job's integrity is surprisingly revealed by Satan saying something truthful in the midst of his many lies. In Job 4, one of Job's friends, Eliphaz says, "Now a word was brought to me stealthily; my ear received the whisper of it. Amid thoughts from visions of the night, when deep sleep falls on men, dread came upon me, and trembling, which made all my bones shake. A spirit glided past my face; the hair of my flesh stood up. It stood still, but I could not discern its appearance. A form was before my eyes; there was silence, then I heard a voice."

When an angel of God shows up, it is all about light, brightness, and commanding presence without any hiding. The first thing angels always say is "Do not be afraid." This creature in the dark of the night is sneaky and sly and causes the hair on the back of Eliphaz's neck to raise up. It is the manner of Satan.

In Job 4:17-21, Satan says (through Eliphaz):

> Can mortal man be in the right before God? Can a man be pure before his Maker? Even in his servants he puts no trust, and his angels he charges with error; how much more those who dwell in houses of clay, whose foundation is in the dust, who are crushed like the moth. Between morning and evening they are beaten to pieces; they perish forever without anyone regarding it. Is not their tent-cord plucked up within them, do they not die, and that without wisdom?

Satan is saying, "Who does Job think he is in his delusional pride that he is blameless? How can any puny human be righteous compared to God?"

Actually, Satan has a point. It is very interesting that the antagonist in the story reveals the core plot of the story. Satan is jealous of God, but he is livid that some mere, mortal, stupid human thinks he is above everyone, including Satan himself. Satan is furious that Job is being lifted up by God as a model of integrity while God blames Satan for wrongdoing.

It gets even more personal for Satan. God has charged the most beautiful and powerful angel on earth with the sin of pride. Isaiah 14:12-16 provides the back story of Satan's fall:

> How you are fallen from heaven, O Day Star, son of Dawn! How you are cut down to the ground, you who laid the nations low! You said in your heart, "I will ascend to heaven; above the stars of God. I will set my throne on high; I will sit on the mount of assembly, in the far reaches of the north; I will

ascend above the heights of the clouds; I will make myself like the Most High." But you are brought down to *sheol*, to the far reaches of the pit. Those who see you will stare at you and ponder over you: "Is this the man who made the earth tremble, who shook kingdoms?"

It takes a prideful person to fully recognize another prideful person. Satan reveals that perhaps the hope of Job is Job's integrity, not God's integrity through Job. Perhaps Job's steadfastness in the midst of suffering was fueled by his self-pride, not a desperate dependence upon God and a deep trust of God's goodness. Over the next 38 chapters, Job's motives will be revealed, and it is not a pretty sight inside his heart. Job is not humble. Job is not relationally in desperately dependence upon his God. He doesn't fully trust God's character. The story is about to go into 35 chapters of his friends goading him, and his veneer of impeccability starts unraveling.

As a side note, it is interesting to see Satan saying, "Even in his servants he puts no trust, and his angels he charges with error." Satan said to Eve in Genesis 3:4-5, "But the serpent said to the woman, 'You will not surely die. 5 For God knows that when you eat of it your eyes will be opened, and you will be like God, knowing good and evil.'" I always thought that Satan was an "honest liar" in that moment. I assumed Satan knew that God really was good and had the best interests of Adam and Eve in mind. I thought Satan lied directly hoping to disrupt God's plan. Yet this passage in Job 4 reveals that Satan is a "dishonest liar." He believes that God is NOT good. He actually believes that God does NOT have the best interest of his created angels nor his created humans in mind.

Satan is captured by his own lie. He lied to himself about God's goodness long before he lied to Eve. This is perhaps why in Matthew 4 Satan made the audacious move to tempt Jesus as if somehow, he could drive a wedge between God the Son and God the Father. The acts of dishonest liars are delusional. But those who believe their own lies are often the most convinced, and the most convincing, liars.

7. The Recurring Dialogue Between Job and His Friends Reveals Deeper Motives

Starting in Job 4 and extending for the next 28, chapters there is a reoccurring dialogue like an endless carousel going around and around. Job's three friends say God is good and just, so there is no way these bad circumstances could have happened to Job unless Job had a hidden sin. Job vehemently defends himself as not having a hidden sin with detail after detail about his good works and integrity.

Job had unparalleled discipline, strong will power, and a deep desire to obey God. He probably did not have a hidden sin that he was aware of. However, Job could have said to his friends, "Only God is perfect, so I am the first to acknowledge I have an unknown shortcoming. All human integrity is imperfect and so am I. I don't think your sanctimonious judgments will help me find my faults. Instead, give me space to be angry, confused and imperfect and receive God's grace." However, Job did not go in that direction. Instead, Job insisted more vehemently in the midst of the accusations that he was faultless.

Job's three friends were not guiltless either. They were caught up in a lie that God is two-dimensional. If you do right, they insisted, God is obligated to bless you. As such, God is controlled like a genie in a bottle to do only what is determined by human actions. The more Job denied their accusation, the more they dug into the proof of their argument that God was bound by man's actions. The lie about God becomes more intense as the chapters progress.

God uses these friends and their lie as unwitting instruments of his grace toward Job to show Job his sin of pride. Job is obedient to God and has many reasons to be proud of his outstanding character and life choices. But this pride is the Achilles' heel of Job's integrity. Job is convinced he is righteous, making him self-righteous, which is one of the most difficult sins to see. He has a veneer of impeccability and knows exactly the right things to say. Yet his friends relentlessly keep poking at this weak spot until something in Job snaps. Job begins to accuse God of wrongdoing. Job's deeply hidden root of arrogance and distrust of God is revealed.

In Job 9:22-24, Job states his cynicism about God's character, fairness and justice, accusing God of being non-caring and mean spirited: "Therefore I say, [God] destroys both the blameless and the wicked. When disaster brings sudden death, he mocks at the calamity of the innocent. The earth is given into the hand of the wicked; he covers the eyes of its judges—if it is not he, who then is it?"

In Job 29, Job lists his impressive accomplishments. The focus is on himself, not God. Even in suffering, Job remains impressed with his own righteousness.

Job 31 details Job's argument against God. In verse 6 Job states, "Let me be weighed in a just balance, and let God know my integrity!" The implication is that God is wrong about Job's integrity, but that if there was a third-party balance more just than God, then God would be corrected.

In Job 31:13-14, Job states, "If I have rejected the cause of my manservant or my maidservant, when they brought a complaint against me, what then shall I do when God rises up? When he makes inquiry, what shall I answer him?" Job is saying, "My track record of integrity is so good, it can stand up to even God's cross-examination."

In Job 31:35, Job arrogantly demands that God answer him. "Oh, that I had one to hear me! (Here is my signature! Let the Almighty answer me!)

In Job 33:12, Elihu who has been a quiet listener for most of the argument points out the real problem with Job. Elihu doesn't accuse Job of a hidden sin but instead challenges Job's lack of trust in God: "Behold, in this you are not right. I will answer you, for God is greater than man. Why do you contend against him, saying, 'He will answer none of man's words'?"

In chapters 34-37, Elihu changes the focus of the narrative away from Job's refusal to confess a hidden sin to God's righteousness, foreshadowing God's rebuttal of Job starting in Job 38.

Job believes in *his* integrity and that somehow God has made a mistake. If only God would show up in a courtroom scene, then Job could convince God of his mistake. Job trusts God in so many ways, but he trusts his own integrity even more. For Job to have full integrity, that trust must be shifted. God does exactly that.

8. God Shows Up and Everything Changes

God interrupts the debate between Job and his friends in chapter 38:

> Then the Lord answered Job out of the whirlwind and said: "Who is this that darkens counsel by words without knowledge? Dress for action like a man; I will question you, and you make it known to me. "Where were you when I laid the foundation of the earth?

After two chapters of questions, God pauses in chapter 40: "And the Lord said to Job: "Shall a faultfinder contend with the Almighty? He who argues with God, let him answer it."

Job had envisioned that this courtroom scene with God would have gone much differently. Job imagined that his integrity would allow him to convince God that he had wrongfully punished Job for sins he did not commit. Job pictured himself making wise and convincing counterarguments, resulting in God saying, "Thank you. Your wisdom has convinced me of my wrong and vindicated yourself before me and your friends."

But after seeing God in the storm, Job's only response in verse 3 is "Behold, I am of small account; what shall I answer you? I lay my hand on my mouth. I have spoken once, and I will not answer; twice, but I will proceed no further."

Humble Integrity: The Work of God in the Life of Job

After two more chapters of God revealing his goodness, justice and strength, Job responds in 42:1-6:

> I know that you can do all things, and that no purpose of yours can be thwarted. "Who is this that hides counsel without knowledge?" Therefore I have uttered what I did not understand, things too wonderful for me, which I did not know. "Hear, and I will speak; I will question you, and you make it known to me." I had heard of you by the hearing of the ear, but now my eye sees you; therefore I despise myself, and repent in dust and ashes.

At this moment, Job is now a man of full integrity. He is no longer a "dishonest liar" placing too much trust in his own integrity fueled by his own self-discipline. His worldview has shifted. He now knows that God's integrity is his hope. He is *humble*. He knows that only God has *perfect* integrity. He understands integrity comes in a *relationship* of desperate dependence upon God. That makes him a man with whole integrity like never before.

From this position of complete and utter repentance, he can now oversee his friend's sacrifice to God for their lies about God.

The book of Job ends with the account of God restoring Job's fortunes to even greater than before. Yet let us imagine Job at age 140 being asked, "Isn't it wonderful that God restored your fortunes to even greater than before?" Job's response might have been, "God did that out of His limitless love and goodness. I deserve none of this. All those disasters were used by God to clean up my heart in ways that I so badly wanted, but I didn't see how self-deceived I was. God's greatest grace to me was to destroy me so I could trust him more fully. I am grateful God gave me blessings since that time. But in a way, these blessings are a distraction. My greatest moment of joy in my whole life was when I was destroyed, covered with boils, and God was in front of me chastising me. At that moment I felt the full joy of knowing my true place of desperate dependence before God. It is all about God, not me. That is the highlight of my life. Everything since then is downhill from that moment."

Integrity is *humble* because it recognizes that the hero of integrity is always God, the only true Person of Integrity. Integrity is *imperfect* because we are redeemed humans, re-created and growing toward Christlikeness but caught up in old habits, living in a slurry of lies all around us. Integrity is *relational* because it is only true when abiding in Jesus.

About the Author

Brad holds a D.Min. from Bakke Graduate University (BGU) and a Th.M. from Dallas Theological Seminary. He currently serves as BGU's President and directs the World Evangelical Alliance Global Institute of Leadership. In previous roles, Brad has served on the staff of two U.S. Senators and a U.S. Congressman; planted an urban church; and served as the President of Leadership Network, which facilitated peer learning for U.S. and global church leaders.

Brad is married to Debby and has three grown children.

The Power of Servant Leadership

Dan Aleshire

1. Introduction

Servant leadership is a way of understanding leadership that, contrary to what some Christians have come to believe, does not have its origins in the Bible or Christian antiquity. In the United States the term was introduced by Robert Greenleaf, an engineer and mathematician who spent much of his career as an executive with a large American corporation. Over several decades, as he observed leaders and consulted with corporations, foundations, and higher education institutions, he came to believe that what was needed in the leadership of these institutions was servants who were leaders. Greenleaf was not an academic, and he wrote only one book—*Servant Leadership: A Journey into the Nature of Legitimate Power and Leadership* (1977)—that was a collection of essays and speeches he had written over many years.

Though Greenleaf became a Quaker in middle adulthood, and though his Quaker values are evident in his work and perceptions, the deepest resource for his thinking appears to be his observations of American business and institutions at a time of social crisis—in the 1960s and 1970s. Out of those observations, he advocates for a kind of leadership that can address social problems and contribute to a common good. Since Greenleaf was the first to use the term, I think it appropriate to begin with his definition. He writes about the servant who is a leader, more than he does about servant leadership, because for him "servant" defines a kind of leader rather than leadership defining a kind of servant. "*A great leader is seen as a servant first*, and that simple fact is the key to his greatness" (italics in original).[1] He expands: "The servant leader is servant first. ... It begins with the natural feeling that one wants to serve. ... That person is sharply different from the one who is leader first" (p. 13).

The opening essay in his book summarizes qualities that characterize the leader who is a servant: "Servant leaders ... hear things (they are good listeners), see things (they are perceptive in ways that others are not),

---

[1] Robert Greenleaf, *Servant Leadership: A Journey into Legitimate Power and Greatness*. New York: Paulist Press, 1977), p. 3. This book is referenced many times in the essay, and in succeeding uses I have simply noted the page numbers in parentheses following the quotations rather than footnote the same text repeatedly.

know things (especially about what it means to be in community and contribute to a common good), and their intuitive insight is exceptional (a leader who has a sense of the unknowable and able to foresee the unforeseeable)" (p. 43; parentheses are mine, based on statements elsewhere in the essay).

The topic of servant leadership was suggested to me for this contribution to a volume in honor of Manfred Kohl, who in a long and incredibly productive career as advocate for and leader of theological education throughout the world personified the qualities of the servant leader. The idea of servant leadership has been an interest of mine for several decades, particularly as I observed leaders of theological schools in North America. The assignment, in addition to giving me the opportunity to honor Manfred Kohl, allows me to explore how servant leadership might be understood biblically, especially in the ministry of Jesus, who taught his disciples: "Whoever wants to be first must be last of all and servant of all" (Mark 9:35).[2]

Leadership, whether in the form of a servant or autocrat, is about getting communities or organizations from one place to another. If no movement is needed, stewardship is appropriate, but leadership is unnecessary. Because no institution or organization can be moved without the exertion of some form of power, power is a central part of leadership. Greenleaf writes that the kind of power most associated with servants who are leaders is the power of "persuasion and example," a power that is used "to create opportunity and alternatives." The key to understanding leadership is how the leader uses power, and the servant who is a leader uses power in a particular way.

2. Leadership, Power, and the Bible

The Old Testament does not have much to say about leadership other than in the stories of leaders, and the New Testament gives limited direct attention to it other than noting the qualifications for leaders in the first-century church. The Bible, however, has a lot to say about power. It is a characteristic of the one true God; it is a means by which God engages the world; and people of faith implement God's mission by the power that has been shared with them. While the Bible recognizes the presence of malevolent power, it gives most of its attention to the power of God and the good to which that power is marshaled.

---

[2] All biblical references are taken from the New Revised Standard Version of the English Bible.

2.1. Power for good and for evil

Power is a characteristic of God according both to the Hebrew Scriptures/Old Testament and the New Testament. The Psalmist declares, "Great is our Lord, and abundant in power" (Ps 147:5). Paul understands the power of God to be a witness to those who have not known the law of Moses: "Ever since the creation of the world his eternal power and divine nature, invisible though they are, have been understood and seen through the things he has made" (Rom 1:20). Power is an integral part of the God of the Bible.

The life of the individual Christian begins with power: "But to all who received him, who believed in his name, he gave power to become children of God," (John 1:12). Power provides the resources necessary for living the Christian life once it begins: "His divine power has given us everything needed for life and godliness, through the knowledge of him who called us by his own glory and goodness" (2 Pet 1:3).

The Christian witness to the world began with power: "But you will receive power when the Holy Spirit has come upon you; and you will be my witnesses in Jerusalem, in all Judea and Samaria, and to the ends of the earth" (Acts 1:8). The continuing witness to this gospel first proclaimed at Pentecost has power: "For I am not ashamed of the gospel; it is the power of God for salvation to everyone who has faith, to the Jew first and also to the Greek" (Rom 1:16). And in the end, the consummation of the Christian story will be seen in power: "Then the sign of the Son of Man will appear in heaven, and then all the tribes of the earth will mourn, and they will see 'the Son of Man coming on the clouds of heaven' with power and great glory" (Matt 24:30).

Power is a central characteristic of God; it is the reason anyone is able to become a Christian and lead a Christian life; and it is the resource that has brought the gospel into being, giving it the capacity to shape human lives for good, and unmistakably attends to the consummation of the Christian story. Power, by every measure in these passages, *is* good and *does* good for the human family. In fact, no good thing can be done without power.

Power, however, also exists outside of the nature of God and apart from those upon whom God bestows power. A more malevolent version of power opposes the purposes of God. This more sinister power is mentioned infrequently in the Bible, but when it is, it is typically in the form of a warning, such as this text in Ephesians: "For our struggle is not against enemies of blood and flesh, but against the rulers, against the authorities, against the cosmic powers of this present darkness, against the spiritual forces of evil in the heavenly places" (Eph 6:12).

Citing individual passages, as I have, can fail to reflect or even distort the biblical themes of which the passages are part. In this case, however, I think the passages are faithful to broad biblical themes. The dominant perception in the Bible affirms the fundamental goodness of power as part of God's identity and a necessary resource for doing any good, and a subordinate theme that construes power as gone bad and doing evil.

2.2. Contemporary perceptions of power

While the Bible gives greater emphasis to the goodness of power, contemporary Christian perceptions seem to be preoccupied with its potential for evil. For example, Richard Foster wrote from a more conservative Christian perspective about three things that lead Christians astray: sex, money, and power—a catalog that has been noted time and again in Christian history. He concludes his discussion on power with the affirmation of its contributions to creativity and ministry, but he begins the discussion with the capacity of power to do evil, particularly in religious communities. Christian feminists, writing from a more liberal Christian perspective, have critiqued power. Their criticisms are about the unjust distribution of power on the basis of gender or the use of power that unfairly advantages men and disadvantages women. Christianity in the United States—from Roman Catholics to Southern Baptists—has experienced the trauma of sexual misconduct by priests and ministers. Once considered primarily a form of sexual immorality, sexual misconduct has increasingly become seen not only as sexual sin but also as abuse of power, and for some, the abuse of power becomes a greater evil than the sexual immorality, although comparative patterns of sinful acts are always dubious.

While evil in the three perspectives above is the abuse of power, there is a modern tendency to think of power itself as normatively destructive if not intrinsically evil. The concern about the destructive, evil quality of power can be so great that religious institutions have sometimes organized themselves such that power is so widely distributed that it is difficult for the institution to accomplish its mission—as if the cure for misused power is no power. Understanding power as primarily evil truncates any understanding of servant leadership because servant leadership requires power.

3. Power and Servant Leadership

What does servant leadership mean in a power-drenched faith? Its value emerges from two sources. The first lies in how power is used, and servant leadership exercises power in several ways. One way is the disciplined *non-*

use of power, even though it is available and could be used to the advantage of the person with the power. Another is using power to do good for others and contribute to human flourishing or giving it to others to use in generative and creative ways. The second source of value is the effect of using power in these ways: it cultivates certain virtues that make the work of the leader more authentically human and faithfully Christian.

I have not been enamored of efforts to explicate the work of Jesus in order to discern a model for leadership of twenty-first-century religious institutions or communities of faith. The work and words of Jesus, however, elegantly illustrate the way in which servants who are leaders exercise power.

3.1. The discipline not to use available power

According to Matthew's gospel, Jesus was led into the wilderness after he was baptized and there was tempted. Much has been written about this event—its connections to similar events in Scripture, like the forty days and nights that Moses and Elijah spent in the wilderness, the forty years the children of Israel wandered in the wilderness, the manna that was provided during their decades of wandering, and Jesus' use of passages from Deuteronomy in response to each of the temptations. Of the many ways this wilderness experience has been interpreted, the most instructive from the perspective of servant leadership is that Jesus began his ministry removed from the intensity of the work that will follow and dealt with power that is a central feature of two of the temptations.

Robert Greenleaf discusses the value of such withdrawal for servants who want to be leaders. "The ability to withdraw and reorient oneself," he writes, "presumes that one has learned the art of systematic neglect, to sort out the more important from the less important" (p. 19). Jesus began his ministry by withdrawing for a prolonged period of time. It is a pattern to which Jesus returned from time to time. Maybe he took these moments away to avoid the press of crowds or because he was tired and needed respite, or perhaps, as Greenleaf suggests, these were times when a sensitive and observant leader needed to sort out what was more important from what was less important, to reflect on what needed to be done or said. Some people think of the servant pastor as someone who is always with people or engaged in tasks, relentlessly present and busy. That often may be the case, but the true servant is also the pastor in a study thinking about the needs of individuals, the congregation, and the community.

The first two of the three temptations focus on power. In the first, Jesus is tempted to make stones into bread. No doubt Jesus had the power to do this. Bread is nourishment for all humans, and Jesus must have needed food after weeks of fasting. Who would have faulted Jesus had he used his power to make something so necessary for life as bread? Jesus would. He had the personal need and the power, and the temptation was whether or not he had the discipline not to use his power for his own comfort. While Jesus used his power to feed the multitudes, he resisted the temptation to use it for his own need. Resistance to this first temptation, and others like it, involved the disciplined non-use of his power.

The second temptation is for Jesus to use his power to demonstrate that he is the Son of God by jumping from the highest point of the temple and allowing the angels to bear him up. Who would have faulted Jesus for using his power to show who he in fact was? Jesus would. After all, he wanted people to decide for themselves who he was, and once again, he did not want to use his power for his own purposes. He reprimanded the tempter by quoting Scripture that the "Lord God should not be put to the test," which was a way of affirming Jesus' identity without using power to display it.

What was true of Jesus at the beginning of his ministry was even more true of him at its conclusion. When Jesus was on the cross, religious leaders taunted him: "Let him come down from the cross now, and we will believe in him. He trusts God, let God deliver him now, if he wants to" (Matt 27:42b-43). Jesus had the power to do what they were taunting him to do, and had he used that power, it would have proved his identity. A part of Jesus' passion was the discipline not to use his power to rescue himself. It would have proved a point at the expense of failing to accomplish the mission for which he had come.

Note from these examples that servant leadership is not powerless leadership. It is leadership that uses power in particular ways, and in the case of these three passages, the particular way is the disciplined *non-use* of available power. How does this affect the leader over time? Aristotle argued that virtues of character develop by habituation. Learning to do justly, for example, requires doing justice. The more one acts justly, the more just one becomes in one's dealings with others. What virtue might accrue to the disciplined non-use of the power? It seems to me that humility is one, and humility is an important virtue in handling power. It entails honesty about what the leader can or cannot do and respect for the power of power. Humility reminds individuals that there is something more important than one's own needs, wants, and desires.

3.2. Sharing power and using power for good

I had a friend and colleague, now of blessed memory, whose youngest son lived with the consequences of the rubella his mother suffered with during pregnancy. The son was partially sighted and had coordination limitations. We were members of the same church, which had a horseshoe balcony, and during Advent, banner bearers led the processional hymn and then placed the banners in cleats on the balcony rail. One year, Christmas fell on Sunday, and someone had forgotten to identify persons to carry the banners. My colleague's son, then a teenager, was standing nearby and volunteered. I watched as the son carried the banner down the sanctuary aisle, sometimes swinging it precariously. He made it to the chancel and up the stairs to the balcony where his father met to help him. The son struggled to get the banner pole into the cleat and his father stood behind him with outstretched arms, ready to intervene. Finally, the son anchored the pole in the cleat. It took a great deal of discipline on my friend's part not to take hold of the pole as the banner swayed above the people seated below. By disciplining his own power, he gave his son power to do something he had very much wanted to do. One of the outcomes of a leader's disciplining his or her use of power is that their restraint often allows others to use their power or come into power.

Words and deeds that both conveyed his power and empowered others characterized the ministry of Jesus. Some Bible readers prefer the words and find themselves troubled by some of the deeds. Thomas Jefferson, the author of the Declaration of Independence and the Bill of Rights in the U.S. Constitution, famously devised a New Testament that included only the teachings of Jesus. He was impressed with Jesus as the teacher of morals but offended by miracles that contradicted reason. The Gospels, however, unite the words and deeds and Jesus' power is best understood by both of them together.

Words are instruments of knowledge and wisdom. As a boy, Jesus' parents took him to the temple, and there he became engrossed with the teachers, with the result that "all who heard him were amazed at his understanding and his answers" (Luke 2:47). The Sermon on the Mount is a prolonged account of Jesus' knowledge and wisdom. He is the teacher who knows the law and whose teaching rescues the law from shallowness that makes it easier to obey and takes it to the deep level that God intended for it. There was a law about murder, for example, but Jesus went to the root cause of murder, and that is anger and poisoned relationships. Later in his ministry, the Sadducees confronted Jesus with a trick question about marriage in heaven, and Jesus responded with knowledge of the tradition and an answer that turned the trick question into a teaching moment (Matt 22:23-33). The examples go on and on through the Gospel accounts.

Jesus used words, and words are conduits of power. Words can be the vehicle of malevolent power and can be used to cut down the hearer or to demonstrate how much the speaker knows. The words that Jesus uttered, however, never did that, not even his most stern words. He used words to instruct, to build up, to set straight, but never to advance himself or belittle others. Jesus' words were expressions of power that benefited others—at times in instruction, at times in comfort, and at times in rebuke. With wisdom and love, his words became the foundation for a faith and guidance for individuals' daily lives. He used words to point to truth as great as the goodness of God and to give that truth away. In this century, words are protected for the economic benefit of the author or speaker. Not so with the words of Jesus. He gave them away for anyone to use, and in using them, others could discover the power that they convey.

The Gospels are full of mighty deeds—most often incidents of physical and emotional healing. Sometimes, Jesus initiated the healing, but much of the time, it was in response to a desire either by the person in need of healing or a relative or friend of that person. Sometimes Jesus was physically present and at other times he was at a different location from the person receiving the healing. Sometimes the faith of someone reached out to Jesus for healing. At other times, it was the faith of others. Healing, like words, embodied and conveyed power, so much so that Jesus could even feel the power pass from him when a healing had occurred, as was the case with the woman ill with a chronic hemorrhage: "For she said, 'If I but touch his clothes, I will be made well.' ... Immediately aware that power had gone forth from him, Jesus turned about in the crowd and said, 'Who touched my clothes?'" (Mark 5:28, 30). The incidents of healing taught people about the power to which Jesus had access, but more importantly, they were gifts. Jesus used the power to heal to do good, not create spectacles. Lame persons walked, deaf persons heard, blind persons saw, lepers had lesions removed and social contact restored. Jesus did not limit this do-gooding to the people near him. In commissioning the disciples to their mission, he gave these gifts of power to them, instructing them, "As you go, proclaim the good news, 'The kingdom of heaven has come near.' Cure the sick, raise the dead, cleanse the lepers, cast out demons" (Matt 10:7-8a). A stunning characteristic of servants who lead is that they exercise power to the benefit of others and to give it away. Many (if not most) people with power keep it to themselves for their own financial or reputational benefit. Servants who lead, however, give their power away. And in giving it away, they multiply its impact. Power that is given away expands to others but does not diminish the power of the one who gives it away. Power given away to do good breeds more power to do good.

If the discipline not to use the power that one possesses for personal gain contributes to humility, then what is the effect of using power to do good or of giving it away to others? The practice of using power for good, among other things, cultivates the virtue of compassion. The Gospel accounts often note that Jesus was moved to compassion. It does not seem that compassion is so much the prior condition of his mighty deeds as it is a corollary. It goes along with the healing or the feeding of the multitudes. Doing mighty deeds grows Jesus' already generous compassion. Doing good for others makes persons sensitive both to the presence of others and to the good that they may need done for them. When youth return from a mission trip in which they have used their ability (power) to help others in need, for example, they often report to their church how the experience changed them, how they now see people differently, how they see themselves differently in light of what they did: they developed compassion. And what virtue accrues from the practice of giving away the power we have? I think that it cultivates a sense of generosity in the giver. Like compassion, generosity is not so much the reason we first give something away as it is a consequence of the repeated act (the habituation, as Aristotle would put it) of giving something of value away. In my career in theological education, I have had the opportunity to observe people with considerable financial resources give gifts to theological schools. They may have given their first gift to honor someone or because a special need arose, but over time, as they experienced the gladness that comes with giving and saw the good that their gifts did, they became truly generous.

4. Conclusion

A meeting at a seminary many years ago included an appreciative discussion about servant leadership. The Christian community of this school had limited roles of ministry that women could fill and gave virtually no authority to women to exercise leadership. Some women approached me after the session to ask how they could be servant leaders in this context. These women could be servants—a role to which they had been relegated—but they could not serve as authorized leaders. It was the first time that I realized that servant leadership, like all forms of leadership, assumes either the possession of or access to power and authority. Servant leadership is not possible without power.

The servant who has power to lead knows when not to use that power, how to use it to do good for others, and how to give it away. Servant leaders use power so differently than other kinds of leaders that they are sometimes perceived as weak. The apostle Paul seems to have anticipated this perception and wrote that the Lord said to him, "My grace is sufficient for you, for power is made perfect in weakness" (2 Cor 12:9). Servants who lead have power, and how they use it generates a whole new kind of power: one that persuades more than commands; one that keeps attention on the mission more than the leader; and one that stays with the task until it is accomplished.

Servant leadership is not a "get-things-done-quickly" kind of leadership. Greenleaf tells the story about eighteenth-century John Woolman. In the early 1700s, many Quakers in the American colonies owned slaves, and Woolman spent thirty years of his life trying to change that. By the time Woolman concluded his efforts, no Quakers in the American colonies held slaves and the Society of Friends formally condemned slave-holding. Greenleaf was interested in the leadership that Woolman engaged:

> He didn't raise a big storm about it or start a protest movement. His method was one of gentle but clear and persistent persuasion. The burden of his approach was to ask questions: What does the owning of slaves do to you as a moral person? What kind of an institution are you binding over to your children? Man by man, each by each, by persistently returning and revisiting and pressing his gentle arguments. (pp. 29–30)

Woolman was a servant who was a leader, and the same can be said for Manfred Kohl. He has traveled extensively, written thoughtfully, and worked tirelessly on behalf of global theological education. By example and persuasion, he has enhanced its quality, increased its capacity, and informed its vision.

About the Author

Daniel Aleshire served on the staff of the Association of Theological Schools in the United States and Canada (ATS) from 1990 until 2017, first as associate director for accreditation, then associate executive director, and became executive director in 1998. Prior to joining the ATS staff, Aleshire was a seminary professor for twelve years and, before that, a research scientist for three years. Among his publications are *Being There: Culture and Formation in Two Theological Schools* (Oxford University Press, 1997) with Jackson Carroll, Barbara Wheeler, and Penny Long Marler; *Earthen Vessels: Hopeful Reflections on the Work and Future of Theological Schools* (Eerdmans, 2008); and *Beyond Profession: The Next Future of Theological Education* (Eerdmans, 2021).

The Churches Need Healthy, Well-Formed Leaders—How Shall We Now Train?[1]

Paul Allan Clark

1. Introduction

From this vantage point, 2,000 years into the history of the Church, and at the junction of world-shaking incidents surrounding the COVID-19 pandemic, we see churches being planted in areas of the globe which were once out of reach of the message of the Gospel of Jesus Christ. We are seeing missionaries being sent from many nations that a few decades ago were termed mission fields. We are seeing the people of God mobilized to evangelize in Jerusalem, Judea, Samaria and to the ends of the earth (Acts 1:8). And we see God's people suffering under persecution, under poverty, and under the power-wielding hands of unhealthy leaders. We also see the effects of self-proclaimed leaders, of self-promoting pastors, and of self-serving teachings. We also see the weakness of churches because of a lack of healthy, well-formed leaders and pastors. We are at another crossroads in the history of the Church.

People are following Christ and forming churches in Africa at such a rate that by 2050 approximately half of the world's believers will reside on the African continent (Zurlo 2020). Latin America and Asia show signs of sustained church growth over the last decades, leading to countries like Brazil and South Korea sending missionaries to the rest of the world, and the movement of missions from everywhere to everywhere is growing (Yeh 2016, 2018). We can rejoice in this effect of the gospel, and in the growth of the churches as a result. This is truly a sign of God at work.

To sustain the missional impact of the churches being planted, they need to be led by men and women who are healthy on the inside, and well-formed as leaders, thinkers, and servants of Jesus Christ and his people. This is not only a historical challenge, but it is a missiological challenge. The Cape Town Commitment recognized the reality that "rapid growth of the Church in so many places remains shallow and vulnerable, partly because of the lack of discipled leaders, and partly because so many use their

---

[1] Based on the "Diversity of Theological Education Programs in Majority World Seminaries" Survey—Overseas Council, 2019.

positions for worldly power, arrogant status or personal enrichment" (Lausanne 2010, II.D.3). This recognition was matched with a call to "whole-person training" and to a movement of discipling in churches, in order to provide the training that the church leaders need.

The training and forming of Christian leaders in, with and for the churches has long been a focus of missionary work. In the days of the renewal of the modern missionary movement, the formation of Bible institutes was a key strategy, knowing that the churches would only flourish with healthy, well-formed pastors and leaders. In the days of the original missionary movement, the apostle Paul encouraged the formation of local leaders to care for the flock (Acts 20; 1 Tim 3; Titus 1). His instructions to Timothy connect the health of the church to the life of the leaders.

Even with this emphasis, the explosive growth of churches has created a tremendous problem—there are not enough healthy, well-formed leaders to pastor these churches, and the churches are at risk of losing their missional effectiveness in their communities and beyond. It is estimated that there are 5 million pastors around the world, and that 90% or more have little or no formal theological training for their pastoral role (Johnson 2017). This would indicate that those churches in areas in which the greatest growth is occurring may be pastored by men and women without sufficient theological training for their ministry work. In recent years, there have been efforts to increase the nonformal training of pastors, which may lower that percentage a bit.[2] However, there is still a need to bring training to a vast majority of men and women who are pastoring churches around the globe. This vantage point in history gives us perspective—God is at work, the churches are growing, the effect of the Gospel is spreading, and the need for more healthy, well-formed leaders is increasing. Though the work of the churches is advancing, along with the training of leaders in, with and for the churches, the leader training gap looms large. So, how shall we now train?

---

[2] ReForma (https://www.re-forma.global/) and GProCommission (Global Report 2021—https://gprocommission.org/) are two of the organizations promoting the use of nonformal training to assist in the formation of pastors and Christian leaders who do not have access to formal, degree-granting theological education programs. One type of nonformal training is "Theological Education by Extension"; Increase Association (https://www.increaseassociation.org/) and SEAN International (https://www.seaninternational.org/) are examples of providers of theological education by extension. Other organizations will contribute to the discussion in this volume, providing great insight into the need and diversity of theological training in the Majority World.

Responding to the "how" question requires a substantive discussion. This chapter will draw on the findings of a survey of over 100 theological schools in the Majority World to provide material for this broader discussion. While pointing to the diversity of forms of theological and ministry training, this survey also highlighted the tremendous need for forming Christian leaders in, with and for the churches and their ministries. Our hope is that the insights you gain in your reading here will spur on your thinking and working to address this leader training challenge.

2. Developing Theological Education

Overseas Council (OC) has been partnering with theological seminaries since 1974, to promote excellence in theological training for Christian leaders who will lead churches and ministries for the Gospel transformation of lives, families, communities, and societies.

Growing from the variety of approaches to train leaders that the missionaries took with them, the "theological seminary" became a standard for higher theological education. As testimony to the importance of this institution, today we find seminaries in all corners of the globe. Their presence also carries a certain stereotype with it. Seminaries are often seen as the primary force for equipping Christian leaders for the churches and ministries. As a result, the term "theological education" is often synonymous with the activity of theological seminaries. The model that comes to mind is "four years and four walls" in a residential campus, distant from the local church setting and local cultural context. Negatively, it is viewed as an "ivory tower" of academic excellence though with little connection to the local church ministry or the life of the congregant. While based on a model of Western education transplanted by missionaries and foreign-trained nationals, this model has become foundational for theological training for many decades.

The OC ministry to support and promote excellence in theological education in the Majority World parallels a movement to renew theological education (Ferris 1990), to transform it (Shaw 2014), and to give it missional orientation (Ott 2001, 2016; Banks 1999). Among evangelicals, this movement has roots in the "ICETE Manifesto" (ICETE 1984). There have been other movements to shape alternatives to the institutional theological education, by way of Theological Education by Extension (TEE) and other forms of nonformal and nontraditional training modes. These responses to the *status quo* have had at their core a desire to effectively train Christian leaders so that the churches will be strengthened, to have an impact in their communities, in the society and around the world.

Alongside the formal training model, alternative models of forming and equipping Christian leaders developed. Through the application of trends in professional education and vocational training, a divergent and often dichotomizing language developed, such as "formal versus nonformal" or "traditional versus nontraditional" or "academic versus grassroots." These spectrums of models expressed their roots in education and mission activity. The classification of "formal," "nonformal" and "informal" education developed in the twentieth century and was applied to theological education by Ted Ward (1972, 1982) and Lois McKinney (1975, 1982), and later revisited by others (Ferris 1987; Kinsler 2008; Shaw 2014). Another way of depicting the needs for theological training among leaders of the churches and their ministries originated with Donald McGavran (1974), was reinforced and revised by McKinney (1975) and Elliston (1989, 1996), and formed a foundation for the India Leadership Study (David 2002) and the Africa Leadership Study (Priest and Barine 2017). The image of a pyramid of leader groupings emerged that describes both the sphere of influence of different types of leaders and the probable training needs of each level of leaders. We are now in an opportune time to evaluate our development to this point, so that we can discover cooperative and collaborative pathways to equip, train, and form the coming generations of leaders of the churches around the world.

Through decades of experience with theological seminaries in the Majority World, we perceived a changing reality. OC field staff worked with seminaries and their formal programs but hypothesized that these seminaries have increasingly offered or supported nonformal programs bringing an extension of their equipping ministry to those without access to traditional modes. To check this hypothesis, the OC team conducted a survey of the state of theological training programs among OC-related schools.

3. Theological Training by Seminaries in the Majority World

The 2019 Survey of Diversity of Theological Training Programs in the Majority World[3] was developed to ascertain the numbers of students and graduates in OC-related programs, to perceive the shape and variety of these programs (both formal and nonformal), and to seek to understand

---

[3] This survey was reported in *InSights Journal for Global Theological Education*, vol. 6, no. 6 (June 2021) and is foundational for this chapter. The article may be accessed at: https://insightsjournal.org/the-churchs-leader-training-challenge-more-than-one-way-to-address-the-need/.

the perception of the leader training gap in the context of these programs. One hundred and thirty-five OC-related theological training programs received an invitation to respond to the survey, conducted online. Ninety-six completed responses were compiled for analysis, a response rate of 73%. It should be noted that 11 additional schools provided only student and graduate statistics, for a response rate of 82% on the enrollment and graduation data. Four snapshots describe the scope and diversity of the theological training occurring in the Majority World—pointing to the "how" of theological education at this time.

Snapshot 1: Seminaries are training tens of thousands of Christian leaders in the Majority World.

The first picture that appeared was of a mighty throng of Christian leaders in training and formation in the Majority World. The survey asked for data on the number of students and graduates from the formal theological education programs in these schools. For this survey, we defined "formal theological education programs" as "programs in your seminary that lead to a certificate or degree that is recognized (or could potentially be recognized) by an accrediting agency or government ministry of education" (Survey, p. 2). Several examples were given to help clarify this definition, including Bachelor of Theology and Master of Divinity. Using this definition, programs could be offered through non-residential modes (such as through intensive modules or through online courses) and still be described as "formal," if the courses lead to recognized credentials.

The 107 schools that provided student body data had enrolled in their formal programs during the most recent school year a total of 49,035 students and graduated 13,265 in their most recent graduation from all their formal programs. While these numbers point to a significant contribution of these schools, we recognize that this is only part of the total picture of leader training throughout the world.

The survey also requested data on the programs and participants in "nonformal theological training programs" that may be affiliated with and/or supported by these schools. For this survey, "nonformal theological training programs" were defined as those "programs of instruction offered by your institution that aim to provide practical training, rather than qualification for an accredited degree" (Survey, p. 5). Again, several examples were given to clarify this definition.[4]

---

[4] Great care was taken to provide simple definitions for the terms "formal theological education programs" and "nonformal theological training programs."

From the 96 schools that completed the survey, 76% identified that they also had "nonformal theological training programs" (73 schools). During the most recent year, these nonformal theological training programs (NFTPs) accounted for an additional 33,221 participants, receiving specific and practical training, outside of the formal degree programs (Fig. 1). This table indicates an interest in developing alternative modes and programs to equip Christian leaders—through skill training programs, training for women leaders in local church ministries, local church-based and extension programs, along with a variety of arrangements to train leaders in, with and for the churches and their ministries. While some of these programs are part of degree programs, a significant number of them are not, and thus are categorized as nonformal training programs. This is significant as an indication of the variety of means and modes that theological schools are utilizing to fulfill their mission in support of the churches in their context. The chapter will delve deeper into this question of diversity of theological programs as we progress with the analysis.

Region	Full Time Students (Survey)	Part Time Students (Survey)	Total Students (Survey)	Total Students (Partial Report)	TOTAL STUDENTS (Reported)	Total NFTP Participants (Survey)	TOTAL LEADERS TRAINED
Anglo. Africa	7085	6154	13239	4230	17469	3137	20606
Franc. Africa	1125	413	1538	309	1847	639	2486
E. Eur & C. Asia	462	3714	4176	1741	5917	728	6645
W. Europe	163	304	467	0	467	4065	4532
Latin America	6111	4988	11099	1161	12260	19791	32051
M. East, N. Africa	168	951	1119	129	1248	2009	3257
South Asia	2415	2771	5186	215	5401	1793	7194
SE & E Asia	2528	847	3375	1051	4426	1059	5485
TOTAL	**20057**	**20142**	**40199**	**8836**	**49035**	**33221**	**82256**

Figure 1: Table of Statistics of Students and Participants in Formal and Nonformal Theological Training Programs[5]

During Cape Town 2010, one of the motivations for a renewed emphasis on the role of theological education was that over 100,000 churches are

---

Although it is possible to use many details to make the distinction, we believed that the key dividing line was the question of accreditation of some sort. For reviews of the multiple layers of definition of these two categories, consult Smith (2002), Spear (1982), Ward (1982), and McKinney (1982).

[5] In Figure 1, the first five columns indicate the different classifications of students in the survey and email responses. "Total NFTP Participants" is the number reported for participants in the nonformal theological training programs.

starting each year around the world. While this number of students in the process of formation is significant, it is not nearly enough to supply the need of the growing churches around the world, especially in the regions of greatest growth. Nor can we diminish the 90% of pastors without training. We can praise the Lord for this first snapshot, but we must see the need for more healthy, well-equipped leaders for the churches.

Snapshot 2: Seminary leaders perceive the training need for leaders in churches in their context.

While the survey sought to gather data on the schools, another purpose was to gain insight into the perception of these schools and their leaders concerning the training of Christian and church leaders in their specific context. The survey asked the respondents to describe the gap in the training of leaders for the church by comparison to "the number of churches with the number of adequately trained pastors." This wording was used to ascertain the perception by the school leaders of the need of current pastors and church leaders for training, and to avoid the many distinctions of the necessary training for pastoral positions and/or ordination. The definition for "adequate training" is an important one for further investigation, as a follow-up study.

Each one rated their own perception of the leader training gap in their context using a range of terms: no perceived training gap; small gap; moderate gap; significant gap; and very serious gap. Seventy percent of the respondents indicated that they perceived this training gap to be either "very serious" or "significant" in their context. When adding the responses of a "moderate" training gap, 90% observe the existence of a training gap in their context. The purpose of asking this question was to measure the perception of a gap, not the percentage of leaders who lacked adequate training. It was believed that the perception stated by the school leaders would be an indication of the severity of this situation. This is significant in pointing out that these school leaders have a clear perception of a leader training gap in the Majority World among Christian churches.

Snapshot 3: School leaders responded to the training gap for leaders in churches in their context.

In a follow-up question to all who indicated a perceived training gap, the survey asked if their leadership team and/or governance body had considered a response to this gap during the last three years. Ninety-five percent of them responded positively—this matter had been considered at the highest levels of leadership. This indicates that the school leaders not only perceive church leaders' need for training but also considered how to respond to it.

Figure 2: Word-cloud Representation of Responses to the Perceived Training Gap

Those who responded "Yes" were then asked to describe their responses. These open-ended responses were analyzed qualitatively, yielding a good picture of the kinds of actions considered and/or taken. The word-cloud graphic (Fig. 2) portrays by the words the type of actions, and the size of the font indicates the relative quantity of each type of response.

While these responses indicated the kinds of actions taken in response to the perceived training gap, the motivation of these leaders in responding was not measured. Their motivation may have come from the perception of the need, from institutional factors of sustainability, from conversations with churches and pastors, or from other contextual pressures.

4. Desire to Serve the Churches in Partnership

The responses of the school leaders and church leaders indicate the pathways of their actions—both formal and nonformal programs, both extension and church-based training options, as well as adding mentoring, women's training, and specializations. The responses evidence an impulse to stretch the mold of traditional educational models because of the local churches. Seminaries in Croatia (Evangelical Theological Seminary), the Middle East (Nazareth Evangelical College), Nigeria (West Africa Theological Seminary), the Philippines (Asian Theological Seminary), and Togo (West Africa Baptist Advanced School of Theology) reported that their responses grew out of discussions with churches in their countries. The qualitative research study, entitled "Unconventional Models in Theological Education" (Macleod 2013),[6] indicated the motivation for innovation in "serving the church by providing accessible theological education for the working adult student" (p. 10). This motivation to serve the churches opened these leaders up to respond to their perception of the training needs of those churches. The models of partnership that have surfaced in the current survey will need further study in the localities to describe their development, extract principles, and promote further partnership development for the sake of equipping Christian leaders—and make a positive contribution to reducing the leader training gap.

5. Perception of Training Needs

One motivation evidenced in this survey is the school leaders' perception of the need for training for Christian leaders in different areas of ministry. Their response was to follow the normal pattern of higher education to develop an area of specialization to meet that need. However, as the perception of a leader training need continues, these leaders in contact with the churches adopt some nonformal programs to assist the churches in training leaders in the local setting. While the perception of a leader training need is a good sign, the present reality begs us to look deeper into the problem. In responding to this need, the school leaders and church leaders in the Majority World may need to address other areas of training, education, learning and development as they focus on equipping leaders in the Body of Christ—both locally and globally.

Bringing the Church of Jesus Christ into focus in theological training is a motivation behind this survey. The findings point to a perception of the leader training need in the global church and in the local context, and they indicate that a diversity of means and modes are being used to address that

---

[6] The research behind this report was commissioned by Overseas Council with the aim of learning about nontraditional models of theological education. Using an appreciative inquiry model of qualitative research, it focused on ten OC-related seminaries around the world.

need. It would be valuable to investigate this question of motivation in a qualitative study through interviews with these leaders. We have hopeful signs from these findings, along with challenging lessons.

Snapshot 4: Evidence of the diversity of theological education programs in the Majority World

The fourth snapshot reveals a wide-ranging diversity of theological education and training expressions through these formal theological education schools. This diversity surfaced in ways that should challenge us to think and work differently as we equip Christian leaders for the Church around the world. In this section, we will explore the diversity of formal theological education programs, the diversity of modalities of theological training, and some of the possible reasons for this evident diversity in the theological training programs in the Majority World. Consider, now, the evidence of this diversity of mode and program for equipping Christian leaders in the Majority World.

Diversity of Formal Theological Education Programs

The survey used the definition of "formal theological education programs" as "programs in your seminary that lead to a certificate or degree that is recognized (or could potentially be recognized) by an accrediting agency or government ministry of education" (Survey, p. 2). The programs reported were identified in five academic levels—Certificate, Diploma, Bachelor's, Master's, and Doctorate. Schools reported using the names of the programs with both academic level and area of study.

In the list of formal theological education programs that the schools offered, the diversity was remarkable. At the Certificate level, there were 24 areas of study; at the Diploma level, 25 areas; at the Bachelor program level, 33 areas; at the Master's degree level, 44 areas; and at the Doctoral level, 11 areas. These 137 areas were categorized into 25 broad areas of study. These categories include some of the traditional areas of theology and biblical studies, as well as specific ministry skill areas, and areas that intersect with ministry in the marketplace, as seen in the following list:

- Theology / Theological Studies
- Christian Ministry / Pastoral / Practical Theology
- Bible / Biblical Studies / OT and NT

- Biblical Theology
- Counseling / Psychology
- Leadership / Organizational Leadership
- Youth Ministry / Youth Counseling
- Christian Education / Religious Education / Discipleship
- Women in Ministry
- Holistic Child Development / Community Development
- Preaching / Exegesis / Expository Preaching
- Missions / Evangelism / Church-Planting / Apologetics
- Islamic Studies / Religions / Messianic Theology
- Translation / Linguistics
- Theological Education
- Historical Theology / Church History
- Systematic Theology
- Ethics / Governance / Public Policy
- Apologetics
- Education and Teaching
- Social Ministry / Urban Ministry
- Media Leadership
- Christian Studies / Basic Studies
- Sign Language
- Church Library
- Basic English

When considering this diversity of areas of study alongside the other findings, it is possible to affirm that in part this diversity of programs is a result of the responsiveness to the contextual need for equipping Christian leaders for the churches and their ministries. Ukraine Evangelical Theological Seminary (UETS) in partnership with other seminaries developed a short program for training military chaplains in response to the conflict in Ukraine. This has now expanded into a peace-building initiative involving seminaries, chaplains, churches and other ministry organizations. In areas where bivocational pastors are common, seminaries like Institut Biblique du Benin (IBB) have developed professional skills courses alongside their pastoral training programs. This responsiveness has enabled these institutions to stretch their practice beyond the traditional categories and areas of study of theological education in its formal programs.

Diversity of Theological Training Program Types (or Educational Modes)

The survey also sought to understand the involvement of these schools with "nonformal" theological training. In this survey, "nonformal theological training programs" (NFTP) were defined as those "programs of instruction offered by your institution that aim to provide practical training, rather than qualification for an accredited degree" (Survey, p. 5). Since these programs are not oriented to the normal categories of academic and accredited degrees, the categorization of these programs is more difficult.

The surprising finding is that 76% of schools characterized by formal theological education programs also support, affiliate with and/or partner with nonformal training programs. This points beyond a diversity of formal program study areas, to a diversity of modes of teaching and learning. This finding offers a new perspective on theological education institutions, which shows the effects of years of investing in renewal and innovation on the part of the theological education community. Influences in the development of this diversity of modalities can be attributed to the practice of many nonformal trainers around the globe. The processes for this development need further study to ascertain models of partnership and collaboration that may be helpful in expanding this development. Alongside this investigation, further conversations that include leaders representing different modalities could help to bridge the divide that has widened over the years (Richard 2015; Ortiz 2021).

The table in Figure 3 provides some of the data on the nonformal programs and participants in the seminaries that reported in the survey. This shows the presence of a diversity of modality of theological training in 76% of the schools, with an average of 455 participants in nonformal programs in addition to their formal programs.

Region	Schools Reporting	# Schools with NFTP Program	NFTP Participants	% Schools with NFTP Program	Average # NFTP Participants per School
Anglo. Africa	23	16	3137	70%	196
Franc. Africa	10	9	639	90%	71
E. Eur & C. Asia	11	9	728	82%	80
W. Europe	4	2	4065	50%	2032
Latin America	18	15	19791	83%	1319
M. East, N. Africa	8	5	2009	63%	401
South Asia	11	9	1793	82%	199
SE & E Asia	11	8	1059	73%	132
TOTAL	96	73	33221	76%	455

Figure 3: Table of Nonformal Theological Education Data by Region

The qualitative analysis of the nonformal programs yielded an array of types and areas that further demonstrates the diversity of theological training programs in the Majority World. The table in Figure 4 shows the diversity of types of nonformal training programs with the number of different programs reported in those analytical categories. A map of the different areas of study across these types of nonformal program does not easily fit here.

CERTIFICATES	32
Pastoral Ministry	9
Specific Ministries (Other)	7
Bible/Biblical Studies	5
TEE	3
Theology	3
General Certificates	3
Missions	1
Apologetics	1

Figure 4: Types of Nonformal Training Programs

A sampling of this diversity of areas of study can be seen in the analysis of the 32 "certificates" that are offered, when depicted as a word-cloud (Fig. 5).

NonFormal Theological Training Program	
SKILL TRAINING PROGRAMS	71
CERTIFICATES	32
NON-RECOGNIZED DEGREE PROGRAMS	25
WOMEN'S TRAINING PROGRAMS	24
CONFERENCES	10
ORG./MIN. PARTNERSHIPS	9
PASTORS' MEETINGS	4
OTHER TRAINING PROGRAMS	7

Figure 5: Word-Cloud of Nonformal Programs of "Certificate" Type and Data Table

This diversity goes beyond areas of study within a modality. The evidence indicates the diversity of modalities along with the diversity of areas of study. It also may point to the potential within theological schools to innovate toward those perceived contextual needs. Often, there are other factors that turn the potential to innovate into real action. OC's "Unconventional Models" research revealed factors of leaders who were willing to take a risk, of a proactive approach to local churches and their ministries, and of an openness to new ideas (Macleod 2013, 10–12). The survey results indicate an evident diversity of formal theological education programs, compounded by the development of a diversity of modalities that these schools are using to equip Christian leaders in their context.

The presence of this multilayered diversity of programs means that we must adjust our perspectives on theological education and seminaries in the Majority World. In this reality, many questions are arising and we must investigate more deeply to understand the dynamics of these changes. One of these questions concerns the role of partnerships in this development of diversity. What was the role of outside organizations in this development? Were there formalized partnerships or informal ones that played a role in this process? How did organizations more involved with nonformal theological training play a role or become involved in partnership with the seminary? While this development speaks of an internal process of response to the contextual need through external and nonformal programs, it may be possible to explore further the partnerships involving formal institutions and nonformal training organizations that have accelerated or enhanced nonformal training on the part of seminaries.

6. A Developing Problem: Tendency to Formalize Theological Training

Analysis of the survey data revealed a possible correlation between the academic levels of formal programs and the degree of involvement with nonformal programs. A pattern of involvement with nonformal theological training programs surfaced, which correlates directly with the level of formal theological education that the school provides. Generally, we discovered that schools which offer formal programs with lower academic level (Certificates—Secondary School equivalence) appear more likely to also offer nonformal theological training programs. The inverse is also demonstrated—the more focused a school becomes in upper-level academic programs, the less likely it is to be involved with nonformal training programs.

The data (Fig. 6) form a pattern based on the academic level of the formal programs offered. We can see that 100% of the schools that offer only a formal Certificate-level program also offer nonformal training programs. When we consider all the schools together that offer Certificate-level programs, 82% also offer nonformal training programs. When we consider all the schools that offer Bachelor's-level programs, 75% of them also offer nonformal training programs. For the postgraduate programs (Master's and Doctoral levels), 62% of those schools offer nonformal training. However, when considering the programs that are exclusively at the highest academic levels, only 50% of those offer nonformal theological training. While this finding may be understood as a critique of postgraduate theological education (i.e., Master's and Doctorate), more that needs to be studied about this pattern.

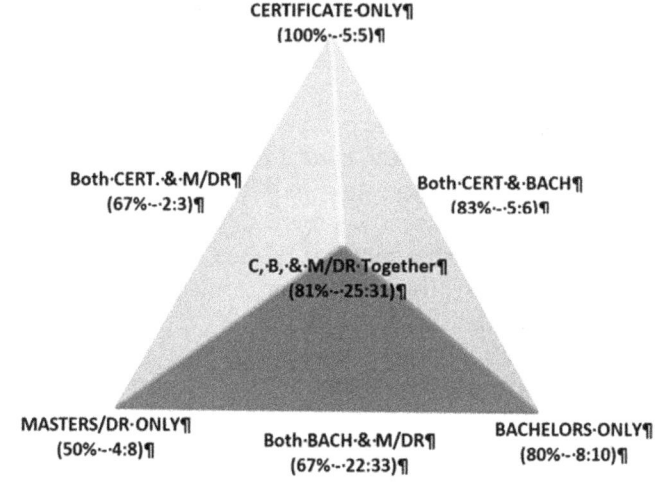

Figure 6: Correlation of Academic Level of Formal Programs with Nonformal Program Offerings

On one side, our intuitive sense affirms that there is a normal tendency to think in the direction of higher levels of academic endeavors. This human tendency to improve and advance spreads to our human institutions. However, as an expression of the people of God imbued with the Spirit of God expressing love and unity, it could be hoped that the value of equipping the less prepared would also be a part of our higher-level theological programs. Indeed, the survey shows that there are some clear examples that would demonstrate a strong connection of schools which offer postgraduate programs along with their involvement with nonformal programs. In Latin America, FIET (Instituto Teológico FIET, Argentina) and SETECA (Central American Theological Seminary, Guatemala) provide theological training at the Master's and Doctoral levels, while most of their students are involved in church-based or prison-based nonformal training. In the South Pacific, at CLTC (Christian Leaders Training College, Papua New Guinea), over half of the students are part of TEE courses in the local setting. This opportunity is part of an integrated learning pathway that may lead to continued studies in a formal program. These and other examples merit further investigation to discover the practices and motivations that would counter this general pattern. It might be possible to see developments soon that will change this finding through intentional partnerships to expand the diversity of training programs and modalities.

7. Implications of the Diversity of Theological Education Programs

I would like to suggest four holistic perspectives that we can gain from this study of diversity of theological education programs in the Majority World. These perspectives relate to mindsets, which set our practice in motion. Consider these perspectives for your own situation and for the sake of God's global work that requires trained leaders to move forward and be effective in bringing the gospel transformation into our communities, societies, and world.

7.1. Whole-life transformation

In considering this growing diversity of theological education programs in the Majority World, each one needs to draw on trends in higher education that point to the rise of the "lifelong learner." Leslie Scanlon (2019, 16) points to lifelong learning in which "the focus increasingly comes from listening to congregational leaders and the community about their current needs." One aspect of lifelong learning is that students may take shorter bursts of training but, over a lifetime, piece together the training they need at the time they need it. This adds intrinsic motivation to the studies and often gives opportunity for a problem-based learning approach. But whole-life transformation will only be available through the increasing diversity of theological education offerings in terms of courses, programs, and modalities. Through online courses, intensive modules, extension centers, pastors' conferences and church-based training, Christian leaders can continue their theological formation for life and ministry transformation over their whole lives. This movement toward greater diversity of options for theological training will require this lifelong learning perspective, by looking beyond the "four years" of higher education. This will require the continuing adjustments of theological school models—both curricular and business—to provide an integrated learning pathway for whole-life transformation (Green et al. 2018, 249–253).

7.2. Whole-being formation

In surveying the reality of theological training programs in the Majority World, we discovered a sensitivity to the need for whole-person formation. The program offerings in different settings provide the opportunity to take advantage of the benefits of the local church for spiritual formation, the local community for social outreach, and the academic community for the rigors of academic studies in areas of theology and biblical studies. This blending of learning contexts capitalizes on the dimensions of formal, nonformal and informal learning settings to bring together the forces for shaping the whole being of Christian leaders in formation. The creation of opportunities to address competencies in the affective, behavioral, and cognitive areas of development shapes students, faculty, and other leaders in competencies in their whole person (Shaw 2014), understanding the dimension of "character and virtue education" as vital to this whole person development (Oxenham 2019). This diversity brings us to the implication of looking beyond the four walls to embrace these other environs as part of the formational model of our theological institutions. To stretch beyond those physical barriers for the sake of holistic learning, theological training programs will need not only more diversity but more partnerships to sustain the kind of whole-being formation that is needed in Christian leader development.

7.3. Whole people of God in training

In digging into the realities of the theological schools in this survey, you will find a recognition that theological training is needed by the whole people of God, not just the leaders. Yes, we have a leader training gap that is perceived by 90% of the leaders in this survey, but that gap involves the rest of the congregations and assemblies of God's people around the world. One implication of this need is to include a focus on "training trainers" in the seminaries, so that the ministry graduates will be able to mobilize a trained people of God for ministry in the local congregations and ministries. This may require more involvement in nonformal kinds of training to prepare them to multiply the training opportunities in the local areas. As we observe some of the rapidly growing movements of Christianity, we discover that there is an ethos of training and releasing people for ministry without formal training. The formal training can be added later to augment their competence and capacity as they develop in ministry leadership. The seminaries in partnership with churches and training programs in churches can work toward developing Christian leaders who will train the body of Christ, so that the people will be able to influence the world around them toward God's ways. It will take more than the seminaries, and it will take more than the existing programs—but it will demand a working together toward the goal of a people of God trained to influence their communities, their nations and the world.

7.4. Whole-church responsibility for leader training

The responsibility for leader training is on the whole church. For too long there has been a separation between the theological education programs and the churches. This survey points to some good news in the formation of partnerships with local churches for the sake of training leaders. But it is time to get theological training closer to the churches, and the churches closer to the theological training. One of the responses to this divide has been that churches have sought to form their own Bible schools or have invested in importing "content dump" programs. This may threaten the theological seminary leaders, or, on the other hand, it may open the door to conversation about how we can work together to sustain the training of God's people in ways that fit the context. The seminary exists to serve the Church, as it serves the mission of God. Therefore, we should not permit this divide to exist any longer. It is time for the churches and the seminaries to look on each other as members of one body, with mutual respect and mutual responsibility. For solid partnerships to sustain the needed training of leaders for Christ's churches, partnerships must become more a reality in the world of theological education. This opportunity for partnerships must include other modalities of training programs, from church-based training to nonformal and mentoring models of training.

There is evidence of diversity; now we need to develop the foundation of unity in that diversity for the sake of transforming theological education. This will provide opportunity among the diversity of training programs for the practice of whole-life transformation, through whole-person formation, for the whole people of God, guided by partnership of whole-church responsibility. The stereotype of four walls and four years for theological education is yielding to this reality and must increasingly do so. So how shall we now equip leaders for Christ's churches?

8. Conclusion

As these holistic perspectives guide us, four imperatives can be identified which challenge each of us to consider what we must do, now that our awareness has been raised about both the current need and the developing diversity.

8.1. We must build bridges to connect schools, churches, and programs

Through investigation of some of the good models, partnerships may surface that will help to shape future connections for training. In the investigations, we can learn from their stories of building bridges. But the bridges must extend outward to include other schools, other churches, and other types of training programs. These bridges will begin with conversations that lead to a developing trust. From the trust, it may be possible to test some new ways of working together for training leaders (pilot partnerships or pilot projects). As we gain experience in these pilots, it will be possible to learn how to share resources and support each other; testing and learning together, so that existing equipping ministries can be more effective. Building bridges is an investment that will require cooperation, built on mutual respect and dialogue.

The results of this bridge-building will bring challenges—adaptability and flexibility on one side, and assessment and standards on the other side. But the bridges will also bring the opportunity to develop leaders who can be effective trainers of trainers and bring a multiplication effect to the theological training ministry of the church. The bridges may create an environment in which nonformal training ministries can identify leaders and needed competencies that may be developed through their joint effort. And the competence gained may not have a title or degree but may bring the leader into a fuller ministry through the practice of lifelong learning.

8.2. We must support a diversity of training programs

Support speaks of the necessary resourcing and scaffolding for development to occur. In supporting a diversity of training programs, theological educators who are accustomed to the classroom will need to adapt to other learning environments. That kind of personal adaptation will require support within the current programs for their faculty to apply new models of teaching and learning. Developing this diversity of modalities of theological training will no doubt take us out of our comfort zones and require of us the virtues of humility and cooperation.

Taking advantage of the diversity of theological programs to equip the current and future leaders of the churches may require support structures (scaffolding) to sustain the scaling up of these training efforts. Not only will it require materials and finances, along with personal investment, but it will also require developing new forms of sustainability to support the diversity of programs. These new forms of sustainability might include collaboration among institutions and coordination between the diverse modalities of theological training. While partnerships are a probable part of these forms of sustainability, there may be other ways to sustain this diversity and assist in the reaching of fruitful outcomes in favor of the mission of God through the Church, for this and the next generation of Christ-followers.

8.3. We must drop our false dichotomy of modes of theological training

In 2010, a group of pastoral trainers released a declaration as part of the Lausanne Cape Town Congress, which called on all educators and trainers to "endeavor to build trust, involve each other, and leverage strengths of each sector to prepare maturing shepherds for the proclamation of God's Word and the building up of Christ's Church in all the nations of the world" (Pastoral Trainers Declaration 2010). To accomplish the first three imperatives, we must adopt a change of mind as it relates to the modes of education that we use in theological training—the "how" of theological education and ministry training. For too long, a false dichotomy has divided our training efforts. It will hinder the building of bridges, the sustainability of the diversity, and even the investigation of the current models of diversity.

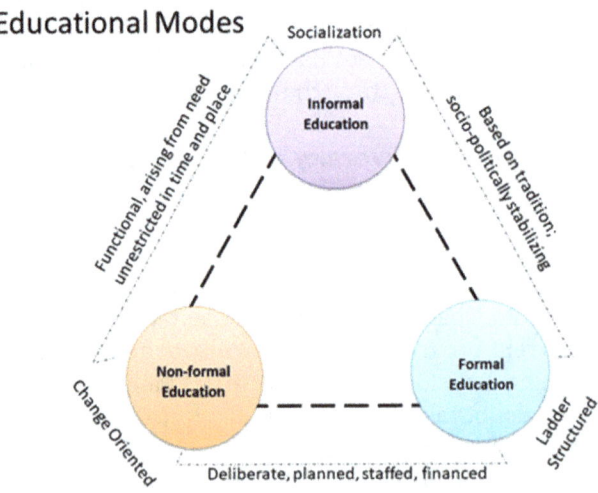

Figure 7: The Modes of Education—Formal, Nonformal and Informal (adapted from Elliston, 1989, p. 243)

Let us look toward a starting point at which we can gain a mutual respect for other modes of education. This respect will only develop as we honestly look at our own practices and models, to evaluate them frankly. From a place of humility and the posture of a learner, we can then enter into dialogue across the modalities, so that we can learn from each other. This willingness to learn must necessarily grow from a humble heart that has recognized its own responsibility for the divide. The goal of dialogue will not be a homogenized model of theological education and ministry training, but a development of mixtures of modalities to meet leader training needs based on the context and the needs of the leader. We may even learn together to apply the variety of modalities of education and learning within our current practices of training trainers and leaders.

8.4. We must continue to investigate this diversity in theological education

Further studies with some of the key schools that are practicing both formal and nonformal education models may give us insights into the motivations, methodologies, mindsets and models. From their practice of integration of learning, paths may be discovered toward overcoming some of the false dichotomies prevalent today. Motivations that build resilience so that the schools can adapt their programs and processes may open doors to motivate others to develop their own pathways to more effective leader training. A way of thinking may be uncovered that helps us to hold differences in tension, supported by relationships in brotherly love. The pathway to responsiveness to the context may be marked out, to aid in other places in the world. Along with these potential fruits of investigation, we will learn to listen to and learn from each other.

Through the process of investigation—listening and learning together—we may discover how to apply multiplication principles through training trainers of leaders (in both formal and nonformal modalities). This multiplication of trainers of trainers may be a new key to address the large gap in leader training around the world, in the churches.

In this world of diverse models of theological education and training, I return to the question, "How can we work together in equipping leaders with the Church of Jesus Christ?" This need for trained leaders is too important to go alone! While some people are interested in a quick solution, the African proverb may be good to keep in mind: "If you want to go fast, go alone; if you want to go far, go together. I believe the evidence shows us that we have a lot going for us, to go together." I believe the situation we face demands that we find ways to go together. The mission of Jesus Christ through his Church in the world is too important—and his Church needs adequately trained leaders to flourish in that mission. It is all too important—the mission of God, the Church of Jesus Christ, the working of the Spirit, and our part in equipping leaders—to go alone. So let's work together, amid this diversity, for the sake of God's work in this world.

References

Banks, Robert. *Reenvisioning Theological Education: Exploring a Missional Alternative to Current Models.* Grand Rapids, MI: Eerdmans, 1999.

Clark, Paul Allan. "The Church's Leader Training Challenge: More than One Way to Address the Need." *InSights Journal for Global Theological Education* 6, no. 2 (June 2021): 72-89. https://insightsjournal.org/the-churchs-leader-training-challenge-more-than-one-way-to-address-the-need/.

David, D. R. "India Leadership Study: A Summary for Indian Christian Leaders." https://firstfruit.org/india-leadership-study/.

Elliston, Edgar. "Moving Forward from Where We Are in Missiological Education." In Woodberry, J. Dudley et al. (eds.). *Missiological Education for the Twenty-First Century.* Maryknoll, NY : Orbis, 1996. Pp. 232-256.

Elliston, Edgar (ed.). *Christian Relief and Development: Developing Worker for Effective Ministry.* Dallas: Word Publishing, 1989.

Ferris, Robert W. "Linking Formal and Nonformal Education." Address delivered at 1983 PAFTEE Annual Meeting; later published in *Theological Education Today* (July-Sept, 1987, pp. 1-9).

Ferris, Robert W. *Renewal in Theological Education: Strategies for Change.* Wheaton, IL: Billy Graham Center, 1990.

Green, Tim, Hanna-Ruth van Wingerden, and Graham Aylett (EDS). *TEE in Asia.* Kuala Lumpur, Malaysia: INCREASE Association, 2018.

ICETE Manifesto for Renewal of Evangelical Theological Education, 1983. https://icete.info/resources/manifesto/. Published in *Theological Education Today* 16, no. 2 (1984): 1-6.

Johnson, Todd. *Quick Facts about Global Christianity 2017.* Center for the Study of Global Christianity. https://archive.gordonconwell.edu/ockenga/research/Quick-Facts-about-Global-Christianity.cfm.html#pastors.

Kinsler, Ross (ed.). *Diversified Theological Education: Equipping All God's People.* Pasadena, CA: William Carey Library, 2008.

Lausanne Committee. *The Cape Town Commitment* (2010). https://www.lausanne.org/content/ctc/ctcommitment.

Macleod, Meri. "Unconventional Educational Practices in Majority World Theological Education." Indianapolis, IN: Overseas Council, 2013.

Unpublished research study, used in the Institutes for Excellence; available by request to pclark@overseas.org.
McGavran, Donald. "Five Types of Leaders." Lecture presented at Columbia Bible College, 1969.
McGavran, Donald. *Understanding Church Growth.* Grand Rapids: Eerdmans, 1970.
McKinney, Lois J. "Plan for the Church's Leadership Needs." *Evangelical Missions Quarterly* 11, no. 3 (July 1975). https://missionexus.org/plan-for-the-churchs-leadership-needs/.
McKinney, Lois J. "Leadership: Key to the Growth of the Church." In Vergil Gerber (ed.), *Discipling through Theological Education by Extension.* Chicago: Moody Press, 1982. Pp. 179-191.
Ortiz, Michael A. "The Global Call to Untrained Pastors." Video presentation at Dallas Theological Seminary, June 8, 2021. https://www.youtube.com/watch?v=ipBX0GWTTgk.
Ott, Bernhard. *Beyond Fragmentation: Integrating Mission and Theological Education.* Eugene, OR: Wipf & Stock, 2017.
Ott, Bernhard. *Understanding and Developing Theological Education.* ICETE Series. Carlisle, UK: Langham Global Library, 2016.
Oxenham. Marvin O. *Character and Virtue in Theological Education.* ICETE Series. Carlisle, UK: Langham, 2019)
"Pastoral Trainers Declaration." Cape Town, 2010. https://rreach.org/wp-content/uploads/2017/05/Pastoral-Trainers-Declaration-Cape-Town-2010.pdf.
Priest, Robert J., and Kirime Barine (ed.). *African Christian Leadership: Realities, Opportunities, and Impact.* Carlisle: Langham, 2019.
Richard, Ramesh. "Training of Pastors: A High Priority for Global Ministry Strategy." *Lausanne Global Analysis* 4, no. 5 (September 2015). https://www.lausanne.org/content/lga/2015-09/training-of-pastors.
Scanlon, Leslie. "Continuing Education is Central to the Mission." *In Trust,* Spring 2019, pp. 14-16.
Shaw, Perry. *Transforming Theological Education: A Practical Handbook for Integrative Learning.* Carlisle, UK: Langham Global Library, 2014.
Smith, M. K. Informal, Non-formal and Formal Education: A Brief Overview of Different Approaches. *Encyclopedia of Informal Education,* 2002. http://infed.org/mobi/informal-non-formal-and-formal-education-a-brief-overview-of-some-different-approaches/.
Spear, George. Lifelong Learning: Formal, Nonformal, Informal and Self-Directed. Columbus: ERIC/ACVE and NCRVE, 1982. http://files.eric.ed.gov/fulltext/ED220723.pdf.

Ward, Ted. "Nonformal Education—What Is It?" In Ward, T., Joesting, L., and Horton, L.D., *Handbook for Nonformal Education*. East Lansing, MI: Institute for Studies in Nonformal Education, College of Education, Michigan State University, 1982. Pp. 8-12.

Ward, Ted, and Samuel F. Rowan. "The Significance of the Extension Seminary." *Evangelical Missions Quarterly* 9, no. 1 (1972): 17-27.

Yeh, Allen. *Polycentric Missiology: 21st-Century Mission from Everyone to Everywhere*. Downers Grove, IL: IVP Academic, 2016.

Yeh, Allen. "The Future of Mission Is from Everyone to Everywhere." *Lausanne Global Analysis* 7, no. 1 (January 2018). https://lausanne.org/content/lga/2018-01/future-mission-everyone-everywhere.

Zurlo, Gina A. (2020). "African Christianity." Blog post on the World Christian Encyclopedia, 3rd ed. https://www.gordonconwell.edu/blog/african-christianity-101/

About the Author

Paul holds a Ph.D. from South African Theological Seminary. Before joining Overseas Council as an education consultant in 2014, Paul served as a missionary in Brazil, leading the Alliance Biblical Seminary and mentoring emerging pastors in São Paulo.

He has coordinated workshops for theological educators in the Majority World. He desires to see holistic Christian leader development, so that their churches and ministries bring grace-filled transformation to their communities and the world. He is married to Karen, who works in Levine Children's Hospital, and they have five grown children and 11 grandchildren.

Servant-Leadership of Ezra and Nehemiah

Joseph Shao

1. Introduction

Ezra and Nehemiah lived in a challenging era. They illustrated their servant-leadership as they led the returnees to Jerusalem. Both of them had different roles in the post-exilic community and could easily assert their leadership, demanding that the people respect them. Nevertheless, each showed their servant attitude. Both of them had honorable character and missional duties. Their personalities differed, but both of them exercised team building, engaging in collaborative leadership and encouraging weak team members to join them in fulfilling the tasks ahead of them. In today's global church, we need both Ezra (vocational fulltime pastor) and Nehemiah (bi-vocational leader) to build up God's church.

There are many leaders in the Old Testament who illustrated servant-leadership in their divine tasks from the Lord. They were leaders and also servants of God. They led the people with their spiritual gifts and with the spirit of servanthood. Their purpose in life was to serve the people they lead, instead for having the people serve them. All the Old Testament leaders had their own role to point the people to the Lord God. Many were described as God's servants.[1]

I would like to focus on Ezra and Nehemiah who lived in the post-exilic era.[2] It was a difficult and challenging time for them. With so many uncertainties, both of them led the people to a life of hope and love. They exercised their gift of leadership in leading the remnant back to Jerusalem. Ezra led the second group of returnees to Jerusalem in 458 BC, whereas Nehemiah directed the third group of returnees in 445 BC. They both had their special role to play in the community. It was not easy for the people to be

---

[1] Out of God's servants, the nomenclature of "The Lord's servant" (*ebed yhwh*) is given only to Moses (Deut. 34:5; Josh.1:13; 8:31, 33), Joshua (Josh. 24:29; Judg. 2:8) and David (Ps/ 18:1 [MT]; 36:1 {MT}). See HALOT 2:775.

[2] I am so glad to dedicate this article to Dr. Manfred Kohl, who has been both my mentor and friend for more than thirty years of my theological ministry in Asia and beyond Asia. His exemplary servant-leadership is a great model for many leaders and budding leaders to follow. I especially appreciate his straightforward counsel that is often balanced with his unique sense of wisdom and wit. He is a friend who dares to speak the truth because he cares.

convinced to come back home, since they had followed the suggestion of Jeremiah to live in their sojourn place (Jer. 29:4-9). But with a servant heart, both Ezra and Nehemiah were able to convince a group of people to work closely with them and rally the people back to Jerusalem. In this article, we shall focus on a few topics illustrating their servant-leadership, such as their honorable character, missional duties, and their personalities and roles, and their modus operandi for team ministry.

2. Honorable Character

In Old Testament character studies, most spiritual giants start with an inner distinctive character that yields outer spiritual behavior. The introduction to the servant-leadership of Ezra and Nehemiah starts with their honorable character.[3] In Asia and the global village, honorable leaders gain respect that begins with their internal character.

In Eastern society, the background and character of a potential leader are carefully scrutinized before any leadership tasks are assigned. The simple reason is that the one leading should be a respectable leader for others to follow him. Ezra is introduced by his priestly genealogy and then identified as the priest (Ezra 7:11-12, 21; 10:10, 16). His ancestral roots can be traced back to Zadok, Phinehas, Eleazar, and Aaron (Ezra 7:1-5). Zadok is the priestly line that remained faithful during the time of David while the line of Eli went astray (1 Kgs. 2:27, 35; Ezek. 44:15-16). Phinehas is the decisive priest who asserted his zealous devotion to the Lord's honor at a crucial stage in the wilderness to avert a plague (Num. 25:6-18; Ps. 106:30-31). Eleazar is the faithful priest who supported Joshua (Josh. 24:33). Aaron, of course, was the chief priest during the time of Moses. This impressive priestly line certifies that Ezra is qualified to serve as the priest. The genealogical record ensures that Ezra is a legitimate servant-leader who can lead the returnees back to Jerusalem.

Ezra was a scribe ("teacher," niv) who was well-versed in the law of Moses (Ezra 7:6). He is introduced as a model learner who teaches by his exemplary character (Ezra 7:10). Ezra internalizes God's instruction and teaching by devoting himself to careful study, probing and seeking for the truth, and then living out the truth himself before teaching the law to others. Moreover, Ezra is known to King Artaxerxes as "the priest, a teacher of the law of the God of heaven" (Ezra 7:11-12, 21), and so he is

---

[3] See Joseph Too Shao and Rosa Ching Shao, *Ezra and Nehemiah: A Pastoral and Contextual Commentary*, Asia Bible Commentary Series (Carlisle, Cumbria, UK: Langham Global Library, 2019), pp. 5-6.

entrusted to teach the law and to bring back the articles of worship to God's house. At the square before the Water Gate, all the people of God invite Ezra to read God's law (Neh 8:1, 4). Ezra's integrity is widely known, and he is accepted as trustworthy, both to the king and to ordinary people. Hence Ezra's inner quality makes him a leader in the community. Having earned respect and honor because of his exemplar character, we later learn that the reputable titles of "priest" and "scribe" are given to him (Neh. 10:1; 12:36).

Likewise, Nehemiah is introduced as a man of prayer with honorable character (Neh 1:4-11; 2:5). His service for God starts with his written prayer that conveys his trust in God for the task in which he desires to participate (Neh 1:8-9). His inner preparation over four months confirms his upright character (Neh 1:1, 2:1). As a trusted cupbearer, he can speak freely to the King Artaxerxes even while his queen is present (Neh 2:6). In the ancient Near East, it is not common. As a man of prudence, he carefully examines the broken wall before he persuades the crowd to join the cause of rebuilding the wall of Jerusalem (Neh 2:12-15).[4] This really elucidates his inner character. He displays a discipline of silence before acting outwardly (Neh 2:12, 16). Having established Nehemiah's character, he is later identified as the governor and the leader of the third returnees (Neh 8:2, 9, 13).

3. Missional Duties

During the seventh year of King Artaxerxes (458 BC), the king commissions Ezra to return to Jerusalem. This royal edict from a non-Jewish ruler gives Ezra both extensive authority as well as comprehensive support for his mission. The king's letter of authorization assigns Ezra four specific missional duties in Jerusalem. First, Ezra's *administrative mission* is to lead the Israelites who want to return to Jerusalem (Ezra 7:12-13). Second, Ezra's *didactic mission* is to conduct an inquiry into Judah and Jerusalem regarding obedience toward the law (Ezra 7:14). Third, Ezra's *cultic mission* is to bring back gifts and sacrifices for the temple of the God of heaven (Ezra 7:15-24). Fourth, Ezra's *social mission* is to appoint magistrates and judges to administer justice and to teach God's laws (Ezra 7:25-26).

In the book of Ezra, we can observe that Ezra fulfills all four missional duties. In his memoirs, Ezra records the family heads and the number of

---

[4] See Joseph Shao, "An Asian Reading of the Theological Themes of Nehemiah," in *Light to Our Path: The Authority, Inspiration, Meaning and Mission of Scripture*, ed. Bruce Nicholls, Julie Belding, and Joseph Shao (Manila: Asia Theological Association, 2013), pp. 119-129.

descendants who return with them (Ezra 8:1-14). His didactic mission can be seen clearly during his direct reading of the law of the Lord at the Water Gate (Neh 8:1-8). He also has an intensive biblical study with the heads of the families, along with the priests and the Levites during the feast of Tabernacle (Neh 8:18). His cultic mission is carefully implemented as he leads the group back to Jerusalem. He gives clear guidance on how to transport the articles for the temple with twelve of the leading priests and twelve Levites (Ezra 8:24). He also gives them direct and clear instructions about what is expected of them (Ezra 8:28-29). As such, worship can be conducted with the vessels and gifts that are brought back from the exile to the temple. Although we cannot know exactly how Ezra assigned magistrates and judges during his time in Jerusalem, we can assume that he did since he knew the teaching of the Torah (cf. Deut. 17:8-13).

With royal blessings and four missional duties, Ezra could easily lord it over the community and implement the changes in the community. Yet upon hearing the intermarriage issue, Ezra humbles himself and pours out his confession to the righteous God of Israel (Ezra 9:6-15). Instead of making his own decision in dealing with intermarriage, he listens and accepts the suggestion of Shecaniah, another leader, to make a covenant before the Lord, in accordance with the counsel of those who fear God and commands of God (Ezra 10:2-4). His humility demonstrates his servant heart!

On the other hand, Nehemiah's first missional duty is to build the wall (Neh 1:1-6:19). As Nehemiah's brothers inform him about the plight of Jerusalem with its broken city wall and burned gates, Nehemiah begins his personal account within the secured walls of the Persian palace. His memoirs, which are our most valuable and authentic source on the history of the post-exilic age, record his journey from Susa to Jerusalem and describe how he restored the city walls and gates of his ruined hometown in the land of Canaan. Nehemiah's missional duty is to return to Jerusalem and Judah to commence the rebuilding of the city wall and gates. Nehemiah knows his role as God's servant as he waits upon the Lord to grant him the opportunity to serve (Neh 1:6. 11). He could have easily used other means such as monetary contributions to support God's work as the cupbearer of King Artaxerxes. But he knows that God's missional work starts with a dedicated servant of God who is willing to give his time and effort to do his work. As God's servant, Nehemiah waits upon his Lord for his time and clearance, since King Artaxerxes is the person who makes edicts (Neh 1:11; cf. Ezra 4:21). Nehemiah only not only faces external oppositions from his enemies but also deals with internal issues with the rebuilding project. Despite personal threats to his life, he rallies the people to finish the project in fifty-two days.

The second missional duty of Nehemiah is to rebuild the faith of the people (Neh 7:1-13:31). With the wall project finished after such a short period of time, Nehemiah could have immediately initiated a dedication ceremony. His first task, however, is to ensure the welfare and prosperity of Jerusalem by appointing responsible and leaders of integrity (Neh 7:1-3). By recording the first returnees, Nehemiah shows his respect for the previous generation who are the first returnees. The difference between the lists in Ezra 2 and Nehemiah 7:4-73 is quite significant as Nehemiah uses the list for the repopulation of the city of Jerusalem (Neh 11:1-36).

Nehemiah works closely with Ezra on rebuilding the people through the law of Moses so that they can live faithfully as the people of God. The community renewal project begins when the community gathers to listen to the law of Moses so that they can understand God's teaching (Neh 8:1-12). The next day, the family heads, priests, and Levites gather to gain deeper insight into the words of the law (Neh 8:13-18). After this time of learning, the community gathers to confess their sinfulness before God (Neh 9:1-37). Then they renew their commitment to the Lord by making a pledge to observe the commandments, ordinances, and statutes of God and to support the work of the priests, Levites, and temple servants and the house of God (Neh 9:38-10:39).

The community goes through a threefold stage of separation (Neh 8:1-12), transition (Neh 8:12-9:37), and reincorporation (Neh 9:38-10:39). They are reconciled with God and in solidarity with one another. As a renewed people wanting to live according to the covenant, the community is now ready to live in the city, and so Nehemiah sets about the work of repopulating Jerusalem and appointing provincial leaders (Neh 11:1-36). Once the people are established in Jerusalem, they are ready to dedicate the wall (Neh 12:27-30). Though the story could end here, Nehemiah continues to challenge the people and instruct them about the law of God (Neh 12:31-44, 13:1-30).

4. Personalities and Roles

Ezra and Nehemiah were great leaders, but they had different personalities. The Lord used both of them to accomplish the tasks assigned to them. With the experience that the gracious hand of God was upon them, both of them were very serious in following the guidance of the Lord (Ezra 7:9; 8:18, 22; Neh 2:8, 18). This really shows their attitude, walking closely under the leading of the Lord.

As Ezra starts the journey to Jerusalem, even with the edict of Artaxerxes, he hesitates to ask the king for soldiers and horsemen to protect him. To illustrate his full trust in the Lord as he testifies about God's gracious hand, Ezra leads the people to fast and petition the Lord for protection; and the Lord answers their prayer (Ezra 8:22-23)! On the other hand, Nehemiah interprets what the king did for him including sending escorts and calvary, as God's generous provision of his gracious hand (Neh 2:8). Nehemiah even uses this experience to rally the people to rebuild the wall with him (Neh 2:18). Their personalities dictate their way of life and decision making. God's gracious hand is interpreted differently. But still we can see how both of them are dependent on God and appreciated his provision.

Their servant-leadership differences can be seen too in how they handle the intermarriage issue. Ezra responds to the intermarriage problem with compassion, whereas Nehemiah is more assertive. Ezra tears his own tunic and cloak and pulls his own hair and beard (Ezra 9:3), whereas Nehemiah rebukes the people, hits them and pulls their hair (Neh 13:25). Moreover, Ezra responds to the problem of intermarriage by fasting and making a private confession before the Lord (Ezra 9:3, 5-15), whereas Nehemiah deals with the matter in the public square (Neh 13:25). Their different roles in the community shape their approach in responding to the situation. As the priest in the community, Ezra prays to the Lord and expresses his emotional sorrow. As the teacher of the Torah, Ezra knows that the words of the Lord are the proper guidance of the people. The people should obey them. Ezra's sorrowful quietness and his self-abasing sincerity in praying before the Lord show his spiritual maturity in handling the case. Nehemiah, on the other hand, is the governor. He has to show his decisive action in the community and teaches them through uncompromising actions. Obedience and understanding of God's words need to translate into daily lives. To ensure that such an intermarriage issue will not happen again, he makes the people take an oath (Neh 13:25). Nehemiah also gives a historical lesson about Solomon's sinful interracial marriages and their ongoing unfaithfulness to God (Neh 13:26-27). Though their distinctive personalities and roles lead them to respond differently, God uses their leadership skills in the community.

5. Servant-Leadership in Action

Both Ezra and Nehemiah were gifted in their leadership skills. The spirit of their servanthood can be seen in how they built up a team, collaborated with people in leadership ministry, and encouraged marginalized team members to fulfill God-given task. Through team building, their work could be sustained. Collaborating with people in leadership ministry ensures that other people in the leadership position are partners and not

5.1. Exercising team building

With authority from King Artaxerxes, Ezra could easily implement the tasks himself and command subordinates to listen to his instruction. Nevertheless, he leads a second group of returnees to Jerusalem with earnestness (Ezra 8:1-14). In the list of second returnees, Phinehas (Ezra 8:2a) defends the true worship of the Lord and thereby becomes a model of godly leadership for subsequent generations (Num 25:7; 31:6; Josh 22:13; Judg 20:28). The Lord bestows priesthood on Phinehas and his descendants and all the priestly factions (Aaronites, Levites and Zadokites). Ithamar (Ezra 8:2b), on the other hand, is in charge of the Levites, the lesser clans of Gershon and Merari in particular (Exod 38:21; Num 4:28, 33; 7:8). Thus, Phinehas and Ithamar represent two branches of priests who are descendants of Aaron (1 Chron 24:1-3). Aside from priestly descendants, the royal descendants are part of the caravan (Ezra 8:2c).

As Ezra assembles the people at the Ahava Canal, he notices the complete absence of Levites. To ensure that the Levites can join the caravan, he takes pains to search for them (Ezra 8:15-20). The whole team should include priests, Levites and the people. The Levites have special responsibilities on the march to Jerusalem, for without their service, worship in the post-exilic period cannot be carried out in accordance with the Mosaic Law. The people are the basic unit of the covenanted family; the priests lead them in worship; the Levites assist the priests in the worship service. His servant-leadership skills enable him to build a team to carry out the reformation.

Likewise, Nehemiah as a cupbearer of Artaxerxes could easily do the rebuilding of the wall with the authority and blessing from the King. He, however, builds up a team to support him. His team-building strategy includes three important features. First, Nehemiah *chooses a team* of trustworthy persons whom he can count on to face strenuous challenges and to labor closely with him. This team is composed of his brothers (Neh 1:2), his men (Neh 2:12), and his guards (Neh 2:9). His brothers give him clear information about the condition in Jerusalem (Neh 1:3). The guards escort him to return to Jerusalem without any trouble (Neh 2:9-10). His men help him to survey the site in the middle of the night in order to observe what

---

[5] Shao and Shao, *Ezra and Nehemiah*, pp. 17-20.

he needs to do with the wall (Neh 2:11-16). His men are a trusted group of confidants who work together to look at the damaged portion of the wall. The group he gathers is loyal, reliable, and dependable. His team stands behind him to support him and to help implement the rebuilding efforts.

Second, Nehemiah *commands his team*, giving them clear instructions and earning their respect. When he faces opposition at the wall, his men work and equip themselves with weapons to defend (Neh 4:16). As he commands the people to work longer in order to repair the wall quickly (Neh 4:21) and to stay in Jerusalem to avoid propaganda schemes (Neh 4:22), he orders his team members to watch diligently and to act responsibly by preparing for a possible attack by their enemies (Neh 4:23). By staying close, each with a weapon, they are not only protecting the wall, but are also prepared to fight a possible skirmish. Hananiah, Nehemiah's brother, is a trustworthy person whom he puts in charge of Jerusalem (Neh 7:2). When Nehemiah wants to implement Sabbath keeping among the people, he orders his men to stand at the gate at sundown to make sure that it remains shut until after the Sabbath so that no one can work or conduct business (Neh 13:19).

Third, Nehemiah *compliments his team*. In his memoirs, which summarized his accomplishments, he includes his brothers as part of his faithful team. Unlike previous governors, who put heavy tax burdens upon the growing community by demanding food, wine and silver from them, no one on his team demanded the governor's food allowance (Neh 5:14); rather, they forfeited that right without complaint. With their privileged position close to him as the governor, they could have used their power to acquire land and appoint more landlords, leaving more landless people in the community (Neh 5:16). Their faithful, diligent, and focused service amplifies Nehemiah's leadership. Nehemiah's team clearly follow his servant-leadership.

5.2. Engaging in collaborative leadership

Ezra sets apart twelve leading priests and twelve Levites to deal with the offerings that he is bringing to Jerusalem (Ezra 8:24-27). They help Ezra in handling the articles to two priests and two Levites at the temple (Ezra 8:33). This is collaborative leadership as Ezra confidently lets them share the responsibility. He delegates the responsibility to both priests and Levites, for their roles in the worship are very different. Both groups ensure that the vessels they bring with them would be put to good use in the worship service. The using of plurality of leaders is to ensure the transparency of transaction.

Before Nehemiah arrives on the scene as governor, there are already key political leaders in the community (Neh 2:10, 19). Although Nehemiah has a team consisting of his brothers, men, and guards who may be able to assist him in the rebuilding of the wall (Neh 4:23), he also recruits new leaders from their Jewish community such as the priests, nobles, and officials to join him in the rebuilding project. Servant-leadership skill can be seen here. Through his recruiting of the existing leaders in the community, they become partners in the ministry.

With a passion to rebuild the work after his night visit to the wall, Nehemiah *challenges the leaders* to support his work (Neh 2:16-17). Nehemiah shares his own experience of how the Lord's gracious hand blesses him. The testimony becomes a rally point for the community leaders to join in. Secondly, as the people start rebuilding the wall, Nehemiah *calls the leaders* to make strategic plans in facing difficulties (Neh 4:14, 19). He clearly informs the nobles and the officials of the strategy. Thirdly, Nehemiah *commits the key leaders* to push for positive changes (Neh 5:7, 12). Nehemiah is a great leader who understands the dynamics of the post-exilic community.

Moreover, as a political leader and building manager, Nehemiah works closely with Ezra, the priest, teacher, and scribe. After Nehemiah and his leadership team complete the wall, Ezra can fulfill his duty as the teacher of the law. Nehemiah and Ezra serve together at the Water Gate as Ezra reads the law of Moses to the people. Then both Nehemiah and Ezra call the people to a celebratory feast (Neh 8:9). The spiritual gifts of Nehemiah are different than those of Ezra. The Lord uses both leaders' gifts. With the rebuilding of the wall of Nehemiah, the people can have a peaceful place such as the Water Gate to listen to God's word. With the proper teaching of the Word of God through Ezra, the faith of the people surely is strengthened. Though they have different viewpoints (Ezra 8:22; Neh 2:8-9) and different ways of handling their anger regarding intermarriages (Ezra 9:3; Neh 13:25), they collaborate with one another, and both take part in the festive group as they dedicate the wall to the Lord (Neh 12:33).

5.3. Encouraging weaker team members

In the post-exilic community, there are more priests than Levites. In fact, during the second return with Ezra, there are initially no Levites in the caravan (Ezra 8:15). The Levites have lower status in the temple service and perform the more menial tasks, but without them, the worship of the post-exilic community cannot be handled properly. Ezra recruits some Levites to join him (Ezra 8:16-18).

Some of the returning Levites settle in Jerusalem, while others settle in their ancestral properties outside Jerusalem. But for the dedication of the wall, the decision is made to seek out all the Levites from their scattered dwellings to come to Jerusalem for the celebration (Neh 12:27–30). Inviting the "weaker" Levites to participate restores their role as part of the team. Instead of shaming the Levites, the invitation allows the Levites who have left their ministry to come back and participate honorably in the celebration.

After the wall dedication, another decision is made to provide them with respectable provisions (Neh 12:44–47; 13:13). The provisions ensure the livelihood of the Levites. When Nehemiah returns to Jerusalem after a short period of absence, he again restores the Levites to serving the Lord (Neh 13:10-11). Together, Ezra and Nehemiah make sure that all the Levites, musicians, and gatekeepers join together to serve God and the people. The healthy financial system of tithes and offerings strengthens the longevity and service of the entire community.

6. Conclusion

In today's global church, the servant-leadership of Ezra and Nehemiah is our model. We need both Ezra, who may represent the vocational, full-time pastor and missionary, and Nehemiah, who may represent the bi-vocational leader, to build up God's church. Such servant-leadership in action is the key not only to church growth, but also to exhibiting Jesus' model of unity and humility in God's kingdom ministry. May the Lord raise up more Ezras and Nehemiahs today, all for his honor and glory!

About the Author

Dr. Joseph Shao is the President Emeritus of the Biblical Seminary of the Philippines, where he served for 30 years. He holds a Ph.D. from Hebrew Union College, Ohio. He is the fourth General Secretary of the Asia Theological Association. He has served as a visiting professor in Asia, Spain, Australia, and North America. He was one of the ten recipients of the *"Qianbei"* (Senior Scholar) award at the International Congress of Ethnic Chinese Biblical Scholars.

Together with his wife Rosa, they now serve with the Global Mission Seminary in California. They have three grown children and four grandchildren.

Part 5:
The Church

The Covid-19 Pandemic as a Test Case for the Unity of the Worldwide Church and for Solidarity in Ecumenical Diakonia of All Christian Churches—15 Theses

Dietrich Werner

1. Introduction

The global Coronavirus pandemic—which is far from over—is more than a stress test for all national health, economic, financial and social systems; it is a fundamental challenge to reconsider the ethical foundations of our global model for development, our goals for education, and it is a test case for the unity of the one worldwide fellowship of churches. It is not making churches irrelevant or the great losers of the pandemic today (as some have argued), but on the contrary, like almost never before, the truth of the Gospel and its integral and holistic approach for reconciliation, justice and peace in all its relational dimensions of God, humankind, nature and our earth is required and extremely relevant for the key issues the whole of humankind is dealing with in terms of reflecting on the conditions for its survival on this threatened earth. Spelling out some fifteen theses on the relation between the challenges of the pandemic and the essence of the Gospel should start a broader reflection process by churches, mission networks and theological education circles on their contribution to public theology and ethical orientation in the current period of transition and crisis.

2. We Can Only Cope with the Pandemic Together as One Body of Christ (1 Cor 12:12)

When on March 11, 2020, the World Health Organization (WHO) declared Coronavirus Covid-19 to be a pandemic, nobody could have anticipated the graveness of the consequences to be faced by so many countries in the world. The unfolding of the pandemic has shown the fragility of our world as well as the vulnerability of the human species to an unprecedented extent. It has also drawn attention to some grave risks ignored for decades, including inadequate health systems, gaps in social protection, gaps between rich and poor, structural inequalities, and environmental degradation. Efforts in several regions which had led to significant developmental gains and progress towards eradicating poverty have been set back years, in a matter of months. Poverty, even outright hunger, has been on the increase in recent months in an unexpected manner. Although humanity has faced grave pandemics in earlier centuries, and memories of what this has meant are gradually revived and brought back again, the speed and exponential growth of the impacts of the pandemic on almost all areas of life have taken many by surprise. Thus, the pandemic in its global spread, grave impact and rapid circulation is an unprecedented event in the contemporary era, emphasizing the fragility and vulnerability of human existence.

Churches, since their earliest beginnings, were confronted with the fragility and vulnerability of human existence. Churches have as built-in assets what societies are eagerly waiting and looking for in this pandemic: they bring with them a gospel of hope, which encompasses even experiences of suffering and death, and centuries of experiences with diaconal care and counseling to those who experience sickness, trauma and even death. The diaconal services of churches and church-related organizations have contributed immensely to responding to this unprecedented crisis—from attempts to provide medical and protective equipment, to visits to lonely people, to elderly care in homes, or old age homes. While the need for assistance has increased globally, the ability of churches and communities has often also been hampered, because of restrictions on gathering, working, and responding. Nevertheless, this crisis has also offered inspiring responses from faith communities to chart the way forward, to bring healing and transformation, with love, faith, hope, courage, and persistence.

The virus does not make a distinction between a Chinese, an American, a Russian, a Rwandan or a Pacific Islander; it does not know borders nor denominational dividing lines, but transcends social, cultural, confessional and ideological borders. Once again we are reminded that humanity has to stand together, and there is no blessing for approaches that focus on "my nation first" or "my nation only" slogans. Again, Christian churches are uniquely positioned to reinforce this message of a common responsibility and of multilateralism to be enforced in terms of how to answer to the global crisis. Christian churches from their earliest beginnings share the conviction that we all belong to the one Body of Christ as the apostle Paul stated in his first letter to the Corinthians. We can only cope with the pandemic if we stand together in solidarity and remember the message of St, Paul that we are one body (1 Cor 12:12). We cannot overcome the crisis in isolation. Solidarity in ecumenical diaconia therefore has to go beyond just the local context, as the pandemic is having a dramatic impact on vulnerable populations in every society and is crippling lives and livelihoods of societies and countries that are already disadvantaged socioeconomically. Therefore, assistance, sharing in solidarity, and advocacy and accompaniment have to be broadened and put into an ecumenical context, a context in which churches collaborate in all regions of the inhabited world and enrich each other though coming from different denominational backgrounds. The apostle Paul in 1 Corinthians 12:26-27 stated, "If one part suffers, every part suffers with it; if one part is honored, every part rejoices with it. Now you are the body of Christ, and each one of you is a part of it." These words take on strong meaning and resonance in the context of the global pandemic, and they have a strong resonance in the life and work of Manfred Kohl.

He always felt touched (or moved by the Spirit) if he received signals of need from churches in other parts of the world. He has a passion for the wider horizon in which churches are giving witness, struggling for authentic service and mission and the need to strengthen their learning and competences by theological education. Being attentive to the suffering of different parts of the body of Christ on the global scale makes one humble, service-oriented, and strongly determined—all of these are attitudes which I found shining through the work of Manfred Kohl. And there is a kind of basic lesson to be learned on what empowers us for greater service in Christ's mission which we might have in common and on what also brought us together: "Once you can pray together, you can also act together!" Once, visiting me in the years after 2007 in the office of the World Council of Churches with a group of colleagues from Evangelical backgrounds, some of the benefactors of which might have criticized a visit to the WCC in those years, we soon realized that we could share many passions and visions together, particularly that we could sit and simply open our hearts to God and allow him to use us and transform us for his purposes. Praying like this together laid the foundation to become open to being used in God's mission, though we would to some extent also come from different worlds. The sincerity and honesty of common prayer and subsequent personal sharing on how God has been working in our lives probably provides the most essential basis for wider solidarity in diaconal action and international solidarity.

What applies for the area of theological education—and we have both attended several international meetings and joint ventures to bring circles together on theological education from the various church families in World Christianity, particularly the Global Forum of Theological Educators

(GFTE) conferences[1]—applies even more to the area of joint diaconal action and common reflection on the answers to the Covid-19 pandemic. The subsequent reflections are an attempt to highlight some crucial areas in which collaboration and specific joint action are needed for churches to stand together, to provide ethical leadership in their societies, and to act together in ecumenical diakonia in the context of the pandemic in the way the apostle Paul has suggested to Christianity in his letter to the Corinthians.

3. The Coronavirus Crisis Is Aggravating, Not Solving the Effects of the Climate Crisis

In a highly provocative article in *The Guardian*, the UN Chief of Environment, Mrs. Inger Andersen, in March 2020 warned the community of nations, "Nature is sending us a message with the coronavirus pandemic and the ongoing climate crisis."[2] Humanity is placing too many pressures on the natural world with damaging consequences. Failure to take care of the planet means not sufficiently taking care of ourselves. Seventy-five percent of all emerging infectious diseases come from wildlife. In many cases in former centuries, the spread of diseases was hindered by mountains, rivers, and natural boundaries between different species. In this new pandemic, the virus has infected the most cosmopolitan, extremely individualized and highly interconnected species that has ever emerged on earth, the human species—exposing its vulnerability in an unprecedented manner. It is quite likely that the Coronavirus crisis is not just a single, one-time event, but that similar zoonosis-based diseases have not only occurred before (e.g., Ebola, Nile Virus), and they might occur much more often in the future, as they exploit the consequences of a globalized and highly intrusive, industrialized human culture, which is fundamentally disturbing sensitive balances between the realm of humanity and the realm of animal life. It was not just tragic coincidence or fate or even God's intentional punishment that brought this catastrophe on humanity. The Coronavirus pandemic is the expression and a result of a type of human behavior which is based on fundamental imbalances between humanity and nature. The intrusive style of human industrialized agriculture and animal breeding in combination with a heavily meat-oriented culture of nutrition has multiplied the opportunities which exist for pathogens to

---

[1] http://gfte.org/wp-content/uploads/2018/04/GFTE-FINAL-REPORT-Merged-Oct 2016.pdf.

[2] https://www.theguardian.com/world/2020/mar/25/coronavirus-nature-is-sending-us-a-message-says-un-environment-chief.

pass from wild and domestic animals to people. Humans are at war with nature. Unless humanity ends this war-like relationship toward nature and particularly animals, the dangers will continue to threaten the future of global society. Ethical leadership of churches on the global scale is therefore demanded to guide and provide orientation for the transition from a narrow anthropocentric notion of development which negates the ongoing dependency of humanity on the integral whole of the biosphere, to an ecological civilization which recognizes humanity as being an integral part of organic life on earth. Churches of all denominational backgrounds which follow the direction of St. Paul's dictum in 1 Corinthians 12:26–27, "If one part suffers, every part suffers with it," are called to speak up together to become advocates for suffering wildlife, suffering rainforests, and suffering animals in industrialized agriculture.[3]

4. Coronavirus Is No Relief for Nature Yet—Rethinking Priorities in Terms of the Protection of Biodiversity

There are those who rejoiced at the news that in the canals of Venice one could observe dolphins and felt excited about the lessening of ecological pressures on the water channels of the city,[4] as well as those who have praised the Coronavirus crisis for reducing Greenhouse Gas Emissions (GHG) due to a major reduction of international air traffic. Unfortunately, the story from Venice about the dolphins was deliberate fake news, and applauding the Coronavirus crisis with simplified slogans like "nature has hit the reset button," "animals are taking over" and "wildlife making its comeback where humanity is withdrawing" while pointing to some singular regional phenomena might be a romantic projection, but is far from describing the true and complex picture, which altogether is not at all rosy for nature. Both the direct and the indirect impacts of the Covid-19 pandemic might not be at all positive for nature and the biosphere, and the wildlife might be under even greater threat than before.[5] The Coronavirus

---

[3] See on this last issue the recent new publication of EKD churches from 2020 which was co-authored by the author: Livestock and Fellow Creatures. Animal Welfare, Sustainability and the Ethics of Nutrition from a Protestant Perspective, EKD-Texte 133, 2020, in: https://www.ekd.de/ekd_en/ds_doc/ekd_texte_133_en_2020.pdf.
[4] https://ilglobo.com/news/mother-nature-hits-reset-button-venice-canals-run-clear-as-italys-quarantine-measures-lead-to-less-pollution-47540/.
[5] https://www.aljazeera.com/indepth/opinion/coronavirus-good-nature-200508120555480.html.

might affect different species of apes in disastrous ways nobody can clearly predict or assess yet. It has for instance already started to infect populations of minks in northern Denmark, which led to a further mutation of the Coronavirus and transmission of this new type of a Coronavirus to human beings with yet unknown consequences.[6] With drastically reduced tourism, investments for wildlife conservation are being drastically reduced in several regions. The economic downturn because of lockdown is leading to a boost for the criminal poaching of wildlife species in many tropical areas. The breaking up of regional food supply chains is increasing pressures on regional populations to go out hunting and kill whatever promises to assuage increasing hunger. The removal of key surveillance measures on rainforest destruction due to the shifted focus of security forces to Coronavirus lockdown measures has led to a dramatic increase in illegal logging, as enforcement agencies are unable to conduct raids due to restrictions on movement. (Government data suggest that deforestation in the Brazilian Amazon rose 30 percent in March 2020.)[7] A heavy focus of certain governments on getting their economy restarted quickly and getting "back to normal" raises serious concerns that the kairos will be missed to reformulate policies for economic recovery in a way that reflects the need for social ecological transformation. Instead, old patterns of destructive, extractionist, and expansionist, industrialized patterns of agriculture and society will be continued. Again, ethical leadership and common efforts in lobbying and advocacy are needed by churches from all backgrounds to promote a comprehensive rethinking of priorities of social and political development in terms of the protection of biodiversity, which has becomes a "must" in our current situation, not just an optional extra.

5. Covid-19 Is No Relief for the Poor Either, But Is Like a Burning Glass Exposing Global Economic Inequalities and a Looming Hunger Catastrophe and Food Crisis

The Coronavirus crisis has led to an exponential growth of the contradictions and tensions between rich and poor in the world. Millions of migrant workers have been laid off, struggling to find transport to return home.

---

[6] https://www.who.int/csr/don/06-november-2020-mink-associated-sars-cov2-denmark/en/.
[7] https://news.cgtn.com/news/2020-04-12/Deforestation-rises-in-Brazil-despite-coronavirus-PCFrJITHgc/index.html.

Foreign remittances of migrants to their families in Asian or African countries have stopped, thereby leaving millions on the brink of starvation. Lockdown scenarios which have been applied in the majority of Western countries do not work in settings in which up to 40% or 50% of the populations work at a daily subsistence level. The lockdowns prevent people from looking for daily small-scale jobs in the informal economy; this literally puts them in a situation without any livelihood. The Coronavirus pandemic has brought hunger to millions of people around the world.[8] National lockdowns and social distancing measures are drying up work and incomes and are likely to disrupt agricultural production and supply routes—leaving millions to worry about how they will get enough to eat. Having to stay at home, often in appalling conditions of overcrowding or loneliness, and threatened by fear of violence, hunger and deprivation, leaves thousands in a situation of great uncertainty, with worries and even sometimes aggressions caused by too-confined living conditions. While richer countries can mobilize billions of Euros or dollars for economic stabilization and recovery measures, poorer countries are left behind. (The German government has mobilized 156 billion Euros as a rescue package for the economy, but still the Federal Ministry for Economic Cooperation and Development is struggling to get permission for the small amount of 3 billion to be made available as a special fund for Coronavirus support mechanisms for poorer countries.) Countries like Malawi have one intensive care (ICU) bed for every one million people, Sierra Leone has no ICU beds at all, and South Sudan has two ventilators for 12 million people, whereas richer countries have thousands. While there are some signs that the G20 governments want to reduce the debt burdens for poorer countries, the agreed debt relief of $125 million USD for poorer countries is offset against official development assistance (ODA), i.e., what these countries gain in terms of more debt relief they are losing at the same time in terms of support by ODA means. Thus the emerging global economic recession will be eating up many of the successes of past development decades, and the gulf between rich and poor countries most likely might be widened in the decades to come, although it is clear to everybody that the threat of the Coronavirus can be overcome only by fighting it together and in each and every country in the world with the same intensity. Ethical leadership by Christian churches, visionary thinking by civil society actors and political determination by political authorities and institutions are needed to chart a way toward real global solidarity and ecumenical sharing.

---

[8] See: https://www.wfp.org/publications/2020-global-report-food-crises.

6. Covid-19 Is Exposing Misleading Myths of Industrialized Neo-liberal Modernity

The Coronavirus pandemic also provides a fundamental challenge to rethink traditional narratives that have informed the exuberance of high-tech lifestyles in late modernity. The myth that God chose human beings to be the center of all creation, the myth that the future of humanity is intrinsically independent, separate from nature and always in our own hands, the myth that the growth of our affluence knows no limits, the myth that the market alone will be able to provide regulations to solve all tensions and inequalities, the myth that technology alone will provide all the necessary solutions to the problems of global human survival and justice for all, the myth that globalization essentially is good and serves the benefit and wellbeing of all—all these myths have lost credibility to an enormous degree. We are humbled and disillusioned; the optimistic belief that everything in our future can be determined by us and is firmly in our hands has crumbled. The optimistic future security and self-confidence of modernity, assuming that everything is in our control, seems to be broken. The feasibility of solving all things through science and technology is fundamentally questioned. There was a time BC (before Coronavirus) when people thought that progress was infinite and human technological advance would soon solve all the problems of humanity. There also was a time BC when people thought that humanity could leave behind all dependence on our biosphere simply by having the technological means to become emancipated from being tied up with biological strings and conditions, but in the new era AC (after Coronavirus) no sober mind would deny that our self-optimistic technological worldview is thoroughly challenged again. The pandemic is teaching us not to superficially trust and lean on modern technologies as the sole provider of solutions, but to seriously look at the root causes of the current dilemmas. The "new normal" everybody seems to be pressing for cannot be a return just to the "old normal," but ethical leadership by Christian churches is needed to underline the interrelatedness of the well-being of humanity, creation and animals to form an equally important component in a new approach to holistic concepts of development and a "one health approach" as outlined by the World Health Organization.[9] We are challenged to move toward a conceptual mindset which integrates much more honestly the fragility of the human species into our political and

---

[9] https://www.who.int/news-room/q-a-detail/one-health; https://www.cdc.gov/onehealth/index.html.

ethical concepts, and the Christian churches are key providers of ancient insights which humanity desperately needs for its survival.

7. Strengthening Multilateralism and Global Governance Over Against Narrow-minded Protectionist Nationalism and Populist Ideologies

It is irritating to realize that despite early warning signals (the German government had a major study on the likelihood of a pandemic already in 2012; the WHO had studies available on earlier pandemics; there were early warnings sent to certain governments already by the end of 2019), there was almost a complete failure at global governance levels to read carefully early warning signals of previous pandemics and to prevent the grave lack of precautionary measures and disaster preparedness. This is despite long debates having taken place in the international discourse on humanitarian assistance, and about the need to strengthen early preparedness and resilience in local communities. The pandemic can be fought only by multilateral approaches and combined and tuned efforts and measures of national governments. The discussion about who gets access to medical means first and who can buy up the first series of vaccinations is an embarrassing sign of captivity in outdated ideologies of "my country first" mentalities and nationalistic strategies which are completely outdated and unethical at a time of global threats. The lack of strengthening and support for national public health systems, along with the vast discrepancies in available access to sufficient medical care systems and social security in many countries which are less privileged, presents a scandal which needs to be addressed urgently for the sake of the protection of the whole of humanity. Playing dirty party politics with multilateral agreements on common health care and leaving the WHO in a period when it is needed most is unethical and disgusting, while open and critical discourses are needed on how to strengthen and improve this precious instrument of the UN. Ethical and moral leadership is demanded of all faith leaders from the religious traditions of this world to remind governments that there is no alternative to an inclusive approach toward global health which follows the key intention of the Sustainable Development Goals (SDG) agenda to leave no one behind.

8. Discerning Professions Which Are "System-relevant": Re-evaluating the Fundamental Value of

an Economy of Social Care Over Against an Economy of Individualized Possessiveness and Materialist Consumerism

There has been a discourse about key professions which are to be regarded as "system-relevant" in times of a national or global crisis during the lockdown period. This provides a healthy lesson for many as the "masters of the universe" are not any more just the big VIPs of international finance, trade and military power. What counts in the end are people—often referred to as "heroes of everyday life" and "heroes of solidarity"—who are ready to stay in frontline ministries to provide emergency assistance and social or medical care. Never have people all over the world been reminded so strongly that in periods of severe health crisis it is human care which supports us. During the first month of our lives, and during the last and final weeks of our life, during severe and unexpected periods of crisis in our lives, what counts to strengthen us and help us to survive are the manifold dimensions of social, medical and psycho-social care—often, but not exclusively provided by women, often hugely underpaid and unrecognized in terms of their societal value. The Christian churches have been knowledge bearers and providers of human care for centuries; they bring an indispensable competence in this field. National Christian Health Associations and networks of Christian hospitals in several countries of the Global South form the majority of health providers in society. Thus, we need ethical and moral orientation from churches to reassess the key values and priorities in our ranking of professional fields and also the priorities we give to realms of professional life related to the sector of health, medical and psychological support of people.

9. The Global Health Inequality and the Vulnerability of Migrants, Refugees and Marginal Groups Are a Call to Strengthen the Reform of the Global Health System

Widespread reports of the disproportionate impact of the Covid-19 pandemic among already vulnerable communities worldwide underscore the ethical and political dilemmas which are being exposed even more by the still-unfolding crisis. Low-income and middle-income countries, which are home to more than 80% of the world's population, will face a high likelihood of famine and under-nourishment. Disadvantaged people are at higher risk of infection and death from Covid-19, while having less access to care due to systems that treat health as a commodity and not a human right. This is in addition to the fact that most health-care systems are not prepared to handle a pandemic of this magnitude. Despite widespread acts of solidarity, we are witnessing unconscionable stockpiling of vaccines and materials by wealthy countries and attempts by many to extract profits from the crisis. Hoarding and speculation should be condemned in the strongest terms and measures taken globally to ensure equitable access for countries with fewer resources. Ethical and political leadership is urgently needed to provide equal access to quality generic diagnostics, medicines, vaccines, supplies, and protective equipment, and the abolishing of any pandemic-related patents. Steps to strengthen universal health-care systems globally and to address the economic disparities that have led to this appalling inequity are needed more than urgently. The unequal impacts of the pandemic could well lead to an intensification of regional as well as global conflicts, an increased spread of feelings of anger, desperation and hatred or even outright violence. Church leaders and the leaders of different faiths have to stand up together to demand basic rights to medical care as well as the social security of marginalized groups, and to pave a way toward models of genuine sharing and inclusivity in sharing the burdens of this disease.

10. Broadening and Deepening a New Culture of Thoughtfulness—Balancing One's Own Freedom with the Well-being of Others

As people in all societies are experiencing this pandemic as an intense learning process about new forms of social behavior, of social distancing and new forms of greetings, this also provides a new chance for spelling out new attitudes of self-restriction and consideration. There is a movement toward a new culture of thoughtfulness. Individuals are considering the limits of one's freedom and adopting new forms of social behavior which are marked by thoughtfulness and consideration in order not to risk harming others. At the same time, there are also incidents of a new attitude of ruthlessness where people immediately see attitudes of thoughtfulness as an illegitimate imposition of state authorities, and would protest the limitation of personal freedom, or would even deliberately risk becoming infected, as the limitation of personal freedom is seen as illegitimate from the very start. Broadening an emerging new sense of thoughtfulness and self-restriction out of an attitude of respect and the "do-not-harm" principle from individual social behavior to collective aspects of general environmental stewardship would strengthen the commitment to sustainability for our future and that of our children and grandchildren. Highly differentiated ethical and political leadership is needed to spell out the narrow middle line between the necessary protection of essential values of individual human rights and the equally important collective rights of public health and security. Rarely has a major emergency led to so many new and unparalleled situations of ethical dilemmas and the need for careful balancing of different rights as we are experiencing in this period. Highly focused attention needs to be given to any false attempt to legitimize the restriction of individual personal freedoms by sinister interests of autocratic governments to suppress civil-society rights on the one hand, while on the other hand warning against an absolutization of individual rights of freedom over against the rights of vulnerable parts of the population to remain protected. There is also the need to weigh and balance the rights and interests of the older generations over against the rights of young families and children, the rights and interests of schools over against the rights and interests of industrial enterprises, and so on. We are forced to spell out again in more detail what the basic social contract demands and entails for our societies both in legal as well as in political and ethical terms. This is a huge task which can be answered by churches together with all people of God's will, as churches have the attitude of serving others and of nurturing a culture of thoughtfulness in their DNA.

11. Slowing Down Capitalism and Rethinking Globalization—Inventing New and Smart Forms of Globalization?

Nobody could have imagined some months ago in the BC era that global air traffic would be reduced by 80% or more in some regions. De-escalating the speed of global mobility and traffic is an unwanted and unplanned global experiment with ambivalent and complex outcomes, which need to be accompanied by ethical and political reflection and careful monitoring to a large extent. On one hand, we learn by this dramatic slowing down of global capitalism that the free global circulation of money and goods in itself does not automatically create a more just and equitable world. On the other hand, we are realizing that an enforced and ill-prepared slowing-down of huge areas of modern industries occurs at a huge social price, with millions of people forced into unemployment and facing huge social insecurity. The upswing of teleconferencing and communication technologies which are now predominantly used to convene international as well as national conferences, workshops and webinars is at the same time posing the question as to what amount of international and national travel is actually really needed to maintain a similar quality level of international work and communication exchange. While not idealizing the limited conditions of working from an office at home, and also being aware of the huge negative effects of narrowing down human communication to audiovisual digital technologies started from tiny individualized home office cells, the future needs intensive ethical considerations, guidance and leadership in terms of combined sets of criteria for the sustainability, the integral human dimensions and the effectiveness of modern methods of collaborating and work ethics for the AC era which we have entered. What is decent work? This question needs to be spelled out in relation to the complementary ethical dimension. What are decent and responsible forms of mobility and interconnectivity? What kinds of goods really need to be transported around the whole globe to be marketed on other continents instead of being sold in regional markets, where there can be a move toward more glocalized forms of consumption and production? The voice of churches and Christian development actors is urgently needed in this regard to provide critical stimulation of new thinking and a kind of a new consensus on changed models of globalization.

12. Dethroning the Masters of the Universe: How to Provide Hedge Fund Owners and Global Capital Managers with Sufficient Guidance and Regulation to Serve the Common Good

Every global crisis also has its hidden or overt actors who benefit from the crisis. Without playing the game of searching for easy scapegoats, or pinpointing only one group, one is tempted to read with interest news which has described how in the first weeks of the Coronavirus crisis global investors withdrew hundreds of billions of USD from countries in the Global South and safeguarded their funds from being located in high-risk areas which soon might be affected by drastic consequences of the crisis. Others have speculated on falling prices of bonds and assets, assuming that an economic recession and collapsing bigger companies might provide a useful chance to get rid of or swallow an economic competitor in the market. The question which needs to be asked here is, who is going to cover and participate in the costs of developing emergency answers to the main victims of the Coronaviruis crisis? Are those who have proved to be major benefiters from the crisis, as it boosted the digital means of communication, also participating in a meaningful manner in the social burdens and the costs of answering the global crisis? How do we carry on with the huge amounts of debts now to be covered by national governments? Who is to share in the increased burdens that will undoubtedly fall on the shoulders of future generations? The question of who is going to bear the long-term costs, and whether equal and balanced sharing is going to envisaged, is an immensely difficult ethical question. We are waiting for more deliberate voices of churches, ecumenical bodies and church leaders about how the international financial system and its players need to be called to reform so as to make the financial system into a vital and reliable partner in solving the crisis, and not simply beneficiaries of the dilemmas created.

13. From Neoliberal Deregulation and Individualism to a New Appreciation of the Role of the State as Provider of Social Security and Emergency Preparedness

There was a time BC when people thought that neo-liberal deregulation was the key to more economic progress and vitality. There also was a time BC when people thought that individual stakeholders in the global markets would seek out the best solutions to issues of inequality and providing for essential human needs. But in the new AC era, no sober mind would deny that the ideology of neoliberal deregulation has led us astray. States that follow this line are usually those where infection rates are much higher and the responses to the pandemic are chaotic, and no clear strategy is recognizable and effective. The Coronavirus pandemic has also given many people a more skeptical view of excessive individualism and of beliefs about leaving the economy unregulated, and more open and positive reflection on the essential role of state authorities in securing social security and emergency preparedness in collaboration with civil society organizations (CSOs). Good governance of national authorities is essential—CSOs cannot do the whole job. While the state needs to encourage civil society organizations and their role in an open and democratic society, the form of responses needed in a very short and dramatically tight time span can come only from a functioning national state or regional associations of states which have a good mechanism for agreeing on terms of rapid response policies (such as the EU). New ethical leadership and reflection are needed on the balance between reappreciating the need for a clear role for national state authorities, principles of good governance, democratic rights and the strengthening of freedom of religion and civil space of CSOs, which have their unique role in all this.

14. The Spread of Conspiracy Theories, Fake News Attacks on Public Truth and the Need for a New Ethic of Honest and Reliable Communication

As has happened in other periods of global threats and pandemics in earlier centuries, encountering the global pandemic now has incited thousands of private propagandists to spread fake news, sell the most weird versions of conspiracy theories, and offer explanations of the crisis which add to feelings of fear and disorientation—all this being an expression of the widespread insecurity and disorientation spreading within and between societies. Apart from the drastic economic impacts of the pandemic, this is probably one of the most serious dangers and consequences the pandemic has already created, as it leads to a weakening of trust in the reliability of public communication and a widespread sense of obscurantist ideologies. The infodemic has ramifications and disorientating implications which might even surpass the negative economic as well as the health-related impacts as it leads to a general inner erosion of social cohesion and dialogical approaches to negotiating the future course of our societies. This is an area which needs determined ethical leadership, expertise and trust-building and public apologetic work by faith leaders, which cannot be overestimated in its relevance, as faith leaders in many contexts are trusted more than political leaders. To counter distorted pictures, and to correct any misinformation and scapegoating as well as discriminating pictures of people suffering from Covid-19 as well as targeting those who allegedly are responsible for carrying the virus into certain regions or ethnic communities (many instances of very dangerous and even deadly assaults on innocent people who have been accused of carrying the virus have been reported already), is one of the main ethical and moral tasks of religious leaders as well as faith-based organization representatives. Think tanks such as Globethics.net or WCC as well as major ecumenical international organizations such as world confessional families, global evangelical networks related to WEA, and regional ecumenical organizations have a crucial task in this area of providing an ethics and honest practices of appropriate information and enlightenment in the best sense of the word and have come up already with strong and prophetic common statements in this regard.

15. Covid-19 as Deepening the Global and Social Digital Divide—Moving Toward a Lost Generation for Education?

With the Covid-19 pandemic, an unprecedented run to digital methods of communication and education has emerged. People look to information and communications technologies (ICTs) to adapt to the evolving uncertainty and operate with minimal disruption. Suddenly, companies are being forced to embrace remote working arrangements facilitated by various productivity and videoconferencing tools. School closures have led to moving classes online. Quarantine restrictions have intensified the use of digital technology to mediate effective communication among family members and friends. But who is able to profit from these technologies? Who is excluded? Who is late to jump on the fast train of digital communication and to be linked to virtual networks? Experience both from cities in the West and countries in the Global South shows that many people are still without access to any ICTs and are now even more disadvantaged than before. The lifeline provided by technologies is only available to those who can access them. The digital divide unfolds itself into a major social barrier and an educational divide. Home schooling is not accessible and possible for those either illiterate in computer technologies or simply not in a position to have several technological devices at home, as they are unaffordable. It was estimated at the end of 2019 that around 3.6 billion people remain offline. The situation is much worse in the Least Developed Countries, where only an average of two out of every ten people are online.[10] Although progress has been made in bridging the digital divide, Covid-19 has brought to the fore how precarious access to ICTs is in many parts of the world, and that access to unfettered and empowering ICTs remains a challenge to many people. The old problem of the global digital divide therefore is exponentially aggravated and worsened by the Coronavirus crisis to express itself as a major educational and social divide in terms of access to any human communication in lockdown situations and particularly access to educational programs.[11] There is a high risk that educational inequalities will widen with less than half of the refugee children worldwide having the chance to still attend school programs during school closure periods.[12] We need commit-

---

[10] https://cs.unu.edu/news/news/digital-divide-covid-19.html.
[11] https://www.nytimes.com/2020/03/17/technology/china-schools-coronavirus.html.
[12] https://www.unhcr.org/news/stories/2020/5/5eb94dd14/refugee-children-hard-hit-coronavirus-school-closures.html.

ted ethical, religious and political leadership to prevent a further widening both of the global and educational divide and to avoid a "lost generation" in Covid-19 times![13]

16. Imagineering a World Beyond Coronavirus Converted to New Standards of Ecological Sustainability—Flattening the Bigger Curve

"What about the long-term implications of Covid-19? Life as we've known it is unravelling and becoming frighteningly unpredictable and precarious. What happens once we have flattened the curve and our health-care workers have gone home for an uninterrupted night's sleep? The long-term prospects are still terrifying: unemployment, hunger, poverty, financial collapse, debt, depression and anxiety, a depleted health care system and dysfunctional schools with unequal and lost learning opportunities. How do we rebuild our lives and our communities out of these ashes? Will our children ever know a time without crisis when the world we bequeath to them is one of continual and worsening environmental and social dislocation? Will we ever find the hope and courage to dream of a future?"[14] While the world might become different with the Coronavirus, many religious representatives base their hope on the vision that it will not end with Coronavirus. There is a sentiment of hope based on core religious convictions of the enduring love of God for his creatures that there will be a future—it might be with Coronavirus staying for ever to a certain extent (as it will not disappear totally from the scene even with a vaccine)—but there could be a future without the imminent life threats of Coronavirus. There could be a future to rebuild our planetary home with new, more solid foundations. "When we are through with Covid-19, there is going to be an even bigger curve to flatten. Climate change will require the greatest sacrifice and adaptive response that the human family has ever mustered."[15] The bigger curve to be flattened is the sustainability curve indicating excessive use and exploitation of our natural resources and the depletion of ecolo-

---

[13] https://www.nytimes.com/2020/04/16/opinion/coronavirus-schools-closed.html; https://www.washingtonpost.com/education/2020/04/21/do-we-really-have-covid-19-lost-generation-one-educators-message-stop-panicking-get-grip/.

[14] Kate Davies from SAFCEI, South Africa in her meaningful blog on Covid-19 and sustainability: https://www.facebook.com/notes/safcei/faith-hope-and-love-in-a-time-of-covid-19/3105341986172245/.

[15] https://www.facebook.com/notes/safcei/faith-hope-and-love-in-a-time-of-covid-19/3105341986172245/.

gical resources given to us in the realm of plants, trees, mineral resources and animals. We need visionary political leadership and proper ethical leadership of churches as well as scientists to prepare visions of how to reorganize our life in order to strengthen the ability of humanity to act together, to overcome narrow-minded nationalism as well as ethnocentrism, and to face together the huge tasks which we have in front of us to curb the destruction of our planetary systems, as otherwise humanity cannot survive. Christians and churches around the globe as well as interfaith ethical think tanks are encouraged and should proclaim that this new common ethical thinking and envisioning of an alternative model of globalization and strengthening of an ecological and responsible civilization in living within the given planetary boundaries are inspired by biblical faith. This tells us that God wants us not to sink in fatalism and fear, but to be inspired by his love for the whole of his beautiful earth.

17. Conclusion

It has become clear that the pandemic is challenging us to address core issues and ethical orientation questions, which have to do with the core of our Christian faith. Christian networks, churches and associations for theological schools should be courageous not to avoid the public discourse, but to raise their voice loudly so as to address the key issues at stake which humanity has to face in the current global crisis, including an interconnected health crisis, social crisis, economic crisis and ecological crisis. We are reminded of the words of the apostolic admonition and encouragement: "But in your hearts honor Christ the Lord as holy, always being prepared to make a defense to anyone who asks you for a reason for the hope that is in you" (1 Pet 3:15).

About the Author

Rev. Prof. Dr. Dr. Dietrich Werner, Senior Theological Advisor, Bread for the World, Berlin; Ordained Pastor of a Lutheran Church in northern Germany; former Director of Ecumenical Theological Education Program of the World Council of Churches, Geneva; primary thematic fields: ecumenism, ethics, missiology, theological education, World Christianity studies.

Lessons Drawn from the Precarious Existence of the Church under Pressure

Peter Kuzmič

In June 2007, Evangelical Theological Seminary in Osijek, Croatia bestowed a special award upon the deserving recipient of this *Festschrift*. The two-paragraph text published on the celebratory diploma follows immediately below, without any commentary. (A more detailed commentary was read at the ceremony.)

Dr. Manfred Kohl has distinguished himself as a transformative evangelical leader and a key strategist in the areas of world evangelization, humanitarian (World Vision) and Educational (Overseas Council International) executive ministries. His commitment to the global extent of the call of God and to the normativity of biblical revelation was matched by a rare grasp of history and a first-rate mind, sharp to perceive and quick to discern the issues of the day, "anchored to the rock, but geared to the times."

We also gratefully recognize his unique vision and strategic contribution to the growth of our Seminary and advancement of theological education in post-Communist Eastern Europe.

Dogmatic Marxism and historic Christianity have by and large consistently viewed each other as irreconcilable enemies because of fundamental differences in their worldviews, though one could also argue that they are actually relatives—relatives historically and philosophically at odds with each other. Oswald Spengler, for example, claimed that "Christianity is the grandmother of Bolshevism," while Nicolas Berdyaev argued that communism and Christianity were rival religions, and William Temple explained the similarity of Christian and Marxist social ideas by pronouncing the latter a Christian heresy.[1] One thing is sure: "Generally speaking, Marxists hate all gods, including the Christian God-man Jesus Christ."[2]

---

[1] See David Lyon, *Karl Marx: A Christian Appreciation of His Life and Thought* (Tring: Lion Publishing, 1979), 11–12.

It is a well-known fact that wherever Marxist communists came to power, their long-term goal was not only a classless but also a non-religious society. Consistent with their politics, derived from the philosophy of dialectical materialism and joined with revolutionary practice, they viewed the Christian faith as superstitious, obscurantist, obsolete, pre-scientific, and thus a totally irrelevant way of thinking and living. Christian institutions were treated as reactionary remnants of the old social order and a hindrance to the progress of the new society and full human liberation of their citizens. Since the Communist Party and its members had a monopoly on both power (which they abused) and truth (which they distorted), they developed comprehensive strategies and powerful instruments for the gradual elimination of all religion. This included restrictive legislation, comprehensive programs of systemic atheization of younger generations through educational institutions and fully controlled media, manipulation of selection of Church leadership, and effective monitoring of their activities. In contrast, for example, to the government-sponsored educational agencies and youth organizations pursuing a comprehensive campaign of indoctrination of children and youth in "scientific atheism," Christian organizations for youth and children were forbidden, Sunday schools outlawed, and youth under the age of eighteen years old forbidden to attend church services. As late as the 1980s, the Soviet government proudly claimed that one of the successes of its educational system was evident in the fact that around 90 percent of young people aged sixteen to nineteen adhered to atheism as their worldview.

Within communist-dominated nations, specialized legislation regulated and restricted the status and practice of religious communities. The USSR first introduced a "Law on Religious Associations" in 1929, after Stalin consolidated power. The law contained some sixty articles that stated what religious organizations could or could not do and what the rights and duties of believers were. During the Stalinist period of intense persecution, especially up to World War II, limiting articles were vigorously applied and almost regularly over-enforced through common abuse of political power by ambitious regional and local administrators and police. The Law on Religious Associations became a model for similar legislation that was introduced in the late 1940s in other Eastern bloc and socialist countries. More instruments for the control and oppression of Christian communities were introduced, such as central government offices, administrative apparatuses at all levels of governance, and specialized police and judicial depart-

---

[2] Peter Kuzmic, "How Marxists See Jesus," in Robin Keeley (ed.), *Handbook of Christian Belief* (Tring: Lion Publishing, 1982), 108.

ments. Cooperative leaders of registered Christian bodies were given some incentives and government-controlled unions were imposed on smaller Christian denominations. The best known among these was the All-Union Council of Evangelical Christians and Baptists (AUCECB) in the former Soviet Union, composed of Evangelicals, Baptists, Pentecostals, and Mennonites. Their unregistered counterparts were treated as enemies of the state, exposed to harsh treatment and periodic physical persecution. Waves of comprehensive and vigorous national anti-religious campaigns, such as during the Khrushchev era in the early 1960s, did not succeed in eliminating religious life but contributed rather paradoxically to a resurgence of spirituality and the growth of all religious communities.

It must be pointed out, however, that practical policies differed from country to country and, in different periods of time, even within the same nation, depending on what was considered to be politically expedient during various historical periods and in diverse regions. Generalizations are problematic, for Eastern Europe has never been totally monolithic regarding the treatment of religion, due to the complexity of the national, cultural, and religious history of different nations, and at times depending on international relationships and considerations.[3] It is legitimate, however, to conclude that, at best, Christian faith was reluctantly tolerated, with its adherents socially marginalized and discriminated against as "second-class citizens," while, at worst, practicing believers were brutally persecuted, church buildings closed or destroyed, and their institutionalized religion outlawed. In Albania, for example, all visible expressions of religion were, by force of law, totally eradicated, with that small neo-Stalinist country at that time (following 1967) priding itself as being the "first atheistic state in the world."

What lessons can be drawn from the precarious existence of the Church under pressure? Christians who live under repressive political (or religious, as in case of countries with Islamic governments) systems that are antagonistic to their faith face serious trials and severe temptations. Valuable lessons have been learned in observing and comparing how Christians in their vulnerable existence responded to the challenges of a totalitarian society. I shall briefly outline the experience of the churches under communism through three different kinds of responses, fully aware that there were occasional overlaps and circumstantial inconsistencies in all of them. These observations are partially based on my first-hand experience and study of the social behavior of minority Protestant communities, their

---

[3] One of the most reliably balanced studies of the topic is presented by Trevor Beeson, *Discretion and Valour* (London: Collins, 1974).

encounter with the challenges of the Marxist rule in general, and communist treatment of Christian churches and believers in particular.[4]

The first impulse of many Christian communities who suddenly found themselves surrounded by an aggressive enemy and ruled over by an atheistic system was to react by fighting back, taking a posture of active opposition to the government and its policies. The simple reasoning was that the new system was ungodly and evil, inspired by the devil, and so should neither be obeyed nor tolerated, but rather actively opposed in the name of Christ. At times it was simply the fight for Church property and resistance to revolutionary overthrow of the established order. There are obvious dangers in this posture of unrelieved hostility in any context of social change. In Eastern Europe, such opposition was recurrently based on an oversimplified political and correspondingly spiritual division of the world, with the accompanying character of an eschatological struggle between the children of light and the children of darkness. "During the times of the 'Cold War' when the political antagonism between the Western and Eastern bloc countries came to a very critical and dangerous climax, there was in fashion much over-generalized and simplistic speaking of the 'Christian West' and 'atheistic East' and mutual denunciation in almost mythological terms."[5] History records that in most countries the first years of the communist takeover were marked by bitter and at times violent confrontations. In some cases the state resorted to the most brutal repressive measures, producing countless Christian martyrs, and causing enormous devastation of Church property and institutions. Christians who were trapped into the assumption that their major task was to fight communism (modern-day Crusader mentality) handicapped themselves by becoming incapable of practicing forgiveness and being a living witness to the communists.

The second, materially and physically less costly, reaction was to withdraw from the social scene, literally to "flee the world." This posture of resignation in order to avoid confrontation and compromise took place by either internal or external emigration. Both are caused by fear of engaging with the new system that was conceived as evil, powerful, and bent on the

---

[4] See Peter Kuzmic, "Evangelical Witness in Eastern Europe," in Waldron Scott (ed.), *Serving Our Generation: Evangelical Strategies for the Eighties* (Colorado Springs, CO: WEF, 1980), 77-86; and "Pentecostals Respond to Marxism," in Murray A. Dempster, Byron D. Klaus and Douglas Petersen (ed.), *Called and Empowered: Global Mission in Pentecostal Perspective* (Peabody, MA: Hendrickson, 1991), 143-64.

[5] Peter Kuzmic, "Christian-Marxist Dialogue: An Evangelical Perspective," in Vinay Samuel and Albrecht Hauser (ed.), *Proclaiming Christ in Christ's Way: Studies in Integral Evangelism* (Oxford: Regnum, 1989), 161.

total destruction of those who dared to oppose it. Most of the communist countries practiced a "closed borders" foreign policy and thereby refused to allow their citizens to emigrate to other lands. Yet history records periods in which the governments granted passports and encouraged "undesirable elements" to leave their homelands on the grounds of ethnic or religious differences. The best-known cases were the Jews and, among Christians, large numbers of Pentecostal emigrants from the Soviet Union in the late 1980s.[6] Those who opted for the easier internal withdrawal by isolating themselves from the surrounding secular society, though spiritually motivated like the monastic communities, were by and large lost for any effective social impact. They very often developed a ghetto mentality, with a passive if not reactionary lifestyle, and were conspicuous by a high degree of legalism and insulation that made them incapable of a positive "salt and light" influence on their society. They often developed their own pietistic subculture with its own pattern of behavior, language, dress code, and even hymnology. Among the neo-Protestant groups (Baptists, Pentecostals, Adventists, and Mennonites), such internal withdrawal was very often doctrinally under-girded by apocalyptic, escapist eschatologies that, in their general outlook on life, seemed to validate certain aspects of Marxist criticism of religion as offering only a "pie in the sky." Extreme examples of such isolated groups of conservative Christians, both Orthodox and Protestant, have at times been highlighted in Soviet and allied anti-Christian propaganda to prove the socially and mentally harmful effects of Christian faith. This internal withdrawal universally tends to lead to a loss of relevance, denies the mission of the Church, and undermines the Christian impact on culture, for it deals with outdated issues, answers questions that are no longer asked, and has very little to say to its contemporaries and their society.

The third model of responding to the new ideological environment was to conform or compromise, to tailor the message and the method to the new situation, thereby accommodating to the prevailing ideology. Some Christian leaders were denigrated by others for yielding ground theologically and otherwise establishing rapport with the new rulers and gaining some concessions, if not privileges, in the areas of limited religious freedom, social status, international travel, and so on. Charges of opportunism and selfish careerism by the suffering believers and religious dissidents were not uncommon. In all Christian churches, but especially within the neo-Protestant camp, different degrees of accommodation and resistance

---

[6] Kent R. Hill, *The Puzzle of the Soviet Church: An Inside Look at Christianity and Glasnost* (Portland, OR: Multnomah, 1989), 292-93.

often led to splits between those denominations that registered with the government and agreed to observe the restrictions of the letter of the law and those that rejected the legal regulations and operated in a (semi-)clandestine way and thereby became known as "underground churches."

The compromising approach may appear to have been naïve at times and motives questionable, though in many cases it also provided evidence of the diplomatic skills of Church leaders who were able to negotiate settlements that led to a temporarily beneficial (to critics: morally and theologically dubious) modus vivendi between Church and state. The obedient attitude to the government by some apparently sincere leaders was additionally justified by their patriotism (as is frequently done today in China) and by appeals to the apostolic admonition to "submit to the governing authorities, for there is no authority except that which God has established" (Rom 13:1).

A brief concluding theological observation about the most important lesson from and for the Christians under pressure: the Church of Jesus Christ is a pilgrim community—*communio viatorum*—"in the world" but not "of the world," still on the journey to the eternal city and, therefore, never comfortably at home in any society. As Jan Milic Lochman, a Czech theologian, reminded us at that time, "Any attempt to relate the gospel too closely to an ideology is dangerous for its integrity and its identity."[7] An uncritical identification with the world inevitably leads to critical loss of both identity and spiritual authority and thereby discredits the preserving and transformative mission of the Church in the world.

Challenges for the post-communist-era Christians and their churches in Eastern Europe are many. With the rather sudden collapse of totalitarian regimes, as dramatically illustrated in November 1989 by the tearing down of the most powerful symbol and physical expression of a divided Europe—the Berlin Wall—a new spirit of hope filled the widened horizons of unexpected freedom. Many Christians all across Eastern Europe interpreted those events as *The Gospel's Triumph over Communism*, to borrow the title of Michael Bourdeaux's book,[8] describing them as the providential work of the Lord of history who has seen their suffering and longing for freedom, answered their prayers, and provided them with a special kairos period to call their nations back to God and to the spiritual foundations for a free and truly "new society."

---

[7] Jan Milic Lochman, Encountering *Marx: Bonds and Barriers Between Christians and Marxists* (Philadelphia: Fortress Press, 1977).

[8] Michael Bourdeaux, *The Gospel's Triumph over Communism* (Minneapolis, MN: Bethany House Publishers, 1991).

The general euphoria of East Europeans with a newfound freedom in the early 1990s, however, has been quickly replaced by the sober encounter with many grim realities that appeared to threaten the prospects of free, peaceful, and prosperous societies. Lack of developed political culture and other obstacles to the consolidation of democratic institutions are key reasons why some nations of Eastern Europe are still going through the very difficult political transitions away from one-party totalitarian regimes toward stable multi-party parliamentary democracies. Transition continues to be equally painful economically as several nations have moved too rapidly and in ethically dubious ways away from the centrally planned "command" economies toward desired viable free-market economies. Large-scale corruption in the process of privatization of formerly state-owned factories and land has created new injustices, causing massive unemployment and social disparities as a result of chaotic "wild capitalism." Social unrest, disillusionment of the impoverished masses, and the general mentality of dependence has created environments conducive to new authoritarian rulers, as well as to manipulations by populist politicians hungry for power and personal enrichment. Unfortunately, by and large, East European churches failed to provide effective and credible ethical correctives to these dubious processes. Developing a spirituality for transformative social engagement remains one of the priority tasks of the churches if they are to be credible and effective instruments of the Kingdom of God among the broken kingdoms of the post-communist world.

One of the major problems for the national churches is the temptation to return to a quasi-Constantinian model of Church–state relationship. After prolonged periods of external persecution, societal marginalization, and internal weaknesses, the Church is again favored by (frequently former communist!) rulers and receives privileges of public treatment incompatible with modern democratic societies. For example, in 2007, the government of Serbia passed a law that does not recognize Baptist, Pentecostal, and Adventist religious communities as churches and refuses to give them legal status. Russia, Belarus, and several other countries have in recent years adopted similar restrictive legislation. Although the intensive process of replacement of a singular communist ideology by nationalistic ideologies did lead to partially valid rediscoveries of ethno-religious identities, the discernible shifts "from totalitarianism to tribalism" (issuing in inter-ethnic conflicts and wars) and "from rights to roots" threatened democratic processes and diminished the liberties and human rights of vulnerable minorities. In such contexts, some national Orthodox churches seemed to still operate with the outdated view of canonical authority over a territory, which caused many tensions, such as in Russia where both Catholics and Protestants were accused of proselytism and illegitimate encroachment on areas supposedly under their control. A competent scholar of religion in Eastern Europe has identified and described this phenomenon as follows:

> Ecclesiastical nationalism consists in several distinct aspects of church activity: in the church's preservation and development of the cultural heritage, in the church's use of a special language for liturgy and instruction, in the advancement of specific territorial claims on putative ethnic grounds, and in the cultivation of the social idea itself, that is, the idea that a given people, united by faith and culture, constitutes a nation.[9]

Since the fall of communism, both Orthodox churches (in the republics of former Soviet Union and Yugoslavia) and Catholic churches (in Poland, Hungary, Slovakia, and Croatia) have in varying degrees reasserted their claims to a monopoly over the religious life of their nations. In these countries, belonging to the national Church has become less a question of doctrinal persuasion or moral conviction, and more an issue of national identity, patriotism, and ethno-religious folklore.

Protestant churches are small minorities in most of these nations and are in general looked upon with suspicion as adherents of that radical movement that in the past has divided Christendom, and as a modernized, Western faith, and thus a foreign intrusion that in the present, in its various fragmented forms, threatens the national and religious identity and unity of the people.[10] Democratically and ecumenically illiterate clergy, with intolerant militant fanatics among them and in their flocks, are fiercely opposed to evangelizing evangelicals and their Western partners, for they view them as disruptive sectarians involved in dangerous proselytizing and unpatriotic activities. Most traditional Protestant churches are in decline, while Baptist, Pentecostal, and charismatic churches are attracting young people and flourishing in countries like the Ukraine and Romania.

Since the Iron Curtain came down, most East European nations, for reasons of security and economic prosperity, aspire to membership in NATO and the European Union (EU). Although the enlargement of these transnational entities and Europe's integrating processes cause tensions with Russia and its neighbors, further unification of the continent is inevitable. In

---

[9] Pedro Ramet, "Autocephaly and National Identity in Church–State Relations in Eastern Christianity: An Introduction," in Pedro Ramet (ed.), *Eastern Christianity and Politics in the Twentieth Century* (Durham, NC: Duke University Press, 1988), 10.

[10] See the excellent symposium of John Witte, Jr. and Paul Mojzes (eds.), "Pluralism, Proselytism, and Nationalism in Eastern Europe," *Journal of Ecumenical Studies* 36/1-2, special issue (Winter–Spring 1999).

addition to political and economic reasons, it is obvious that the common Christian history and culture make it unacceptable for the continent to be divided permanently between the more advanced Western part, marked by democracy, economic prosperity, and general vitality, and the Eastern part, as less democratic, prosperous, and stable. Such a division is unsustainable and would do damage to both. The new and united Europe and its churches need each other to rediscover the full meaning and respect for life and personhood, provide for protection of human rights of minorities, work for social justice, practice solidarity, and bear witness to a future that transcends the vision of a common economic and political space. Europe also needs, as frequently reminded by the late Pope John Paul II, an intensive re-evangelization and rediscovery of the gospel.

About the Author

A native of Slovenia and a citizen of Croatia, Dr. Kuzmič is the foremost evangelical scholar in Eastern Europe and an internationally recognized authority on Christian ministry in post-Communist contexts. He has ministered in more than 80 nations on every continent and has authored several award-winning books and articles. His global platform has included plenary addresses at Lausanne II in Manila (1989), Urbana (1990), and the European Leadership Consultation (1992). He has spent past two decades working for reconciliation among the people of the war-torn former Yugoslavia, including founding the humanitarian organization Agape. His work in peacemaking has earned him several national and international awards.

A Tribute to Manfred Kohl: A Developer of Leaders

Theresa R. Lua

> Leadership is all about growing other people, developing people, and lifting and raising people. Leadership means developing other people to their potential. —Brandon A. Cox[1]

Manfred Kohl has made a lasting difference in the realm of international theological education because he inspires others by example, by gracious personal encouragement, and by friendly intimidation. He has been an integral player in my development for 20 years.

I first met Manfred in 2001, when I attended the Overseas Council's (OC) Institute for Excellence for the first time. The OC is dedicated to enhancing the quality of theological education, especially in developing countries. Manfred was the OC's vice president and director of the Institute, which brings leaders of OC partner schools together on a regional basis to strengthen their leadership skills and organizational expertise. I was the newly installed academic dean at the Alliance Biblical Seminary (now Alliance Graduate School) in the Philippines.

Before the opening session, a colleague introduced me to Manfred, and I quickly discovered his passion for awakening theological school leaders to what they don't know. "How did you become academic dean?" he asked me, followed by "How did you prepare for the role?" and "What books did you read?"

So the first thing I learned about Manfred was to be scared of this rather gruff German man's tough questions. I would soon learn that this was typical behavior on his part. Manfred understood painfully well that many leaders in theological education are well trained and highly competent in their academic discipline, but inadequately equipped for such leadership responsibilities as curriculum development, financial management, or governance.

---

[1] Brandon A. Cox, "How to Expand Your Capacity as a Leader," *Outreach*, June 4, 2019, https://outreachmagazine.com/features/leadership/43352-how-to-expand-your-capacity-as-a-leader.html?utm_source=omag-om-daily-nl&utm_medium=email&utm_campaign=omag-om-daily-nl-20190605&utm_content=button.

As the Institute began, I found that Manfred was equally candid and constructively confrontational in his public messages. He expressed his dissatisfaction with the quality of training in theological schools, illustrating his complaints with numerous examples. He strongly urged us to make theological education relevant by ensuring that our curriculum addresses issues that the church is facing and effectively equips leaders for practical ministry. Repeatedly he emphasized that seminaries must serve the church and that if we're not producing people who can lead churches, we are failing.

I emerged from that first Institute experience feeling both challenged and inspired. I would come back for many more OC events. They played an indispensable role in my professional development.

Over time, I came to discover that this tough and serious-looking German guy actually has a soft heart, which was reflected in Institute programs. The schedule always included a group tour, shopping in the host city, and other opportunities for informal fellowship and building friendships with seminary leaders from various countries.

Manfred and my leadership at AGST Philippines

In 2006, I became dean of the Asia Graduate School of Theology (AGST)-Philippines, a consortium of eight seminaries in the Philippines that offer collaborative postgraduate training programs. I learned that Manfred was scheduled to be in Manila around the same time as my installation, so I invited him to participate. It was a privilege to have him as the guest speaker at the event.

Manfred was an invaluable supporter and encourager during my time at AGST. He paved the way for us to become an OC partner school for the first time—something the school had long wanted to do but for which it could not qualify while under interim leadership—several months after my installation. As a result, OC provided scholarship assistance that enabled leaders from various Asian countries to pursue postgraduate study at AGST.

Manfred enjoyed having AGST as a partner because of his heavy emphasis on partnership and collaboration. He has frequently criticized duplication of programs, believing that having nearby seminaries competing with each other is not an effective use of Kingdom resources. Our consortium was, for him, a good example of what he wanted to see.

As a result, he blessed us with an extra challenge. While at AGST for my installation service, he told me, "I have a gift for you. I have been envisioning a Doctor of Ministry program in peacemaking, and I would like AGST to offer it." Manfred was on the board of Peacemaker Ministries at the time and wanted to see peacemaking become a more prominent part of seminary curricula.

We enjoyed observing another of Manfred's classic traits along the way: his impatience. He hoped we could launch the program within a year, but because of its novelty, locating qualified faculty, developing library resources, and recruiting students all took longer. During one of his visits to Manila, he met with me and our program director for an update. After listening to our status report, he responded (in jest, but with his typically serious voice), "I could bring along some dynamite to help things move faster!"

Manfred skillfully goaded us forward. By nature, he looks at opportunities, not hindrances. Where we were somewhat cautious about our approach to launching a new program, feeling that we didn't know exactly what we were doing, he encouraged us to commit to offering the program and continue refining things as we initiated operations. After all, if we waited until everything was in place, we would never get started.

In September 2007, we launched the D.Min. program, now called Peace Studies, with design and curriculum assistance from Peacemaker Ministries. The International Graduate School of Leadership is hosting this program. After the first cycle, we added a Ph.D. track. Manfred significantly promoted the program internationally. We have graduated students from Asia, Africa, and North America who have become experts in building a biblically based, Christ-centered culture of peace all over the world.

One of our graduates, Chrisso Handy, is now General Superintendent and Chairman of the Assemblies of God in Sri Lanka. He developed a model of reconciliation based on Hosea 1-3 that he has already shared effectively with fellow leaders and is planning a broader rollout in his home country. Chrisso explained how the program affected him: "I learned about the Peace Studies program when I was feeling sad about the violence in Sri Lanka. On my first day attending class in Manila, I felt I had made some mistake. I was looking for insight on how I could bring communal harmony to Sri Lanka, and they were focusing on my inner life instead. But as it turned out, that was exactly the best beginning point as I realized the many cords of disharmony that were prevalent within me. As the classes progressed through organizational peace to mediation and community peace, the program enriched my life, outlook and maturity beyond measure. When I enrolled, I had no plans for denominational leadership, but that's where I am today. The peace studies curriculum and course content are such a wonderful resource for leadership development."

Villo Naleo, another graduate, now teaches theology and ethics at the Shalom Bible Seminary in Kohima, Nagaland (northeast India). But when he talks about the Peace Studies program's impact, he starts with how it transformed his personal life.

"My marriage was not a coming together of two families; it was a separation of two families," he explained. "After I joined the Peace Studies program, I took the initiative to make peace with my wife's family members who were estranged from us because of our marriage.

"What I learned in the program also helped me bridge the relationship between my mother and her father, who abandoned her when she was a little girl. I took my mother to meet him, and we had precious moments of forgiveness and reconciliation.

"The practicum and exercises were very intentional in addressing the relational problems people are facing. The program has changed my attitude toward my children, my wife, and others."

All this started with Manfred's challenge to us at AGST.

Manfred's ongoing encouragement

Despite his considerable global obligations, Manfred has still found time to be a personal inspiration. For example, when I was appointed as General Secretary of the Asia Theological Association in July 2016, he wrote to me:

> I am very sorry that I cannot be with you in person, but I will be with you in thoughts and prayers. I still remember very vividly when you were installed into the leadership of the Theological Consortium and from everything, I have heard over the years you did an outstanding job. ... I wish you God's richest blessing for your new assignment. May the Lord guide and direct you. I pray that you will be successful, but also humble so that you depend on the Lord daily.

I received a similar personal note from Manfred when I became director of the World Evangelical Alliance's Department of Global Theology in 2021.

Manfred can be tough. Just looking at his intense, determined face can be scary at times. But I value the extra effort he made to support me, and I know he has done the same for countless others. He is never too busy to offer personal exhortation and encouragement to his brothers and sisters in Christ.

The vision of Re-Forma

In 2020, I returned the favor by becoming a board member of Re-Forma, perhaps the capstone of Manfred's lifetime of service to the church globally. I was somewhat surprised when he invited me to join the board, as I am not an expert in non-formal theological education. But I certainly appreciated the need. Seminaries are meeting only a small fraction of the need for trained Christian leaders in Asia. Our theological schools often have to respond to requests for accreditation or recognition from church-based training programs. Moreover, many candidates apply to enroll in our seminaries without the standard formal educational qualifications. The Re-Forma certificate process is helping to provide assurance that such candidates have completed credible non-formal training.

Re-Forma is pioneering ways to produce trained leaders to keep up with church growth in areas of the world where the Christian faith is flourishing. In its focus on essential competencies, it amplifies Manfred's vision for theological education that helps the church fulfill its mission. Re-Forma has introduced practical, relevant ways to assess individual competencies and is also helping church-based programs evaluate the suitability of their own training activities. I know no better way to respond to what both Re-Forma and I consider the greatest crisis facing the evangelical church globally—the inadequate supply of trained pastors and church leaders.

Willing to be tough for the Lord

One more unpopular topic from which Manfred has never shied away is fundraising. He knows this is an uncomfortable topic, but he has also seen seminaries all over the world struggle financially. He has tirelessly stressed that knowing how to approach donors and articulate a vision that will inspire them to give is an indispensable part of school administration. Where people were not skilled in that area, he told them to create a development department—an idea that wasn't always well received since hiring a director of development feels like an additional financial burden. But Manfred never holds back when he encounters theological leaders who, though they may care deeply about teaching and learning, are overlooking the administrative aspects of running a school. He knows that a school that operates in that way probably won't survive for long.

Manfred may have offended a few people along the way, but in my observation, they were hurt because he spoke painful truths with authority, based on his vast knowledge and experience. Manfred can be blunt and hard-hitting, but he is not insensitive. He knows how to connect with people individually, showing clearly that he cares about individuals, not just projects. I am very grateful that I sensed the compassion, along with the exemplary commitment to excellence, that lay behind those first tough questions he asked me 20 years ago.

About the Author

Theresa holds an Ed.D. from the Asia Graduate School of Theology (AGST), Philippines. She is serving as the General Secretary of the Asia Theological Association (ATA) and as the Director of the Global Theology Department of the World Evangelical Alliance. Prior to these roles, she served as the ATA Secretary of Accreditation and Educational Development and as AGST Dean for many years.

She is married to Dr. Fernando Lua, Vice President for Administration and Finance and professor of pastoral studies at the Asian Theological Seminary. They have two adult sons, Timothy and Joshua.

A Prayer for Manfred Kohl

Bill Houston[1]

We pray for Manfred, a husband, a father, a brother in Christ, a boss, and a friend.

O Lord, our God and father, we give thanks to you for the evidence of your grace in Manfred's long life. From the ravages of the destructive Second World War on Germany which plunged the Kohl family into hardship and hunger, you produced an iron will in the young Manfred and moulded it to achieve much for your Kingdom. From his apprenticeship as a master cabinet maker you produced the drive for excellence and an aversion of sloppy work. You gave Manfred the unusual ability to see the big picture and to welcome new possibilities while other languished in yesterday's solutions. You gave him the ability to bubble over with 101 ideas.

Thank you that Manfred has lived for a purpose greater than himself in terms of aligning his life to your mission and purposes for the world.

It has been a long journey made possible through the incredible support of Barbara who kept the home fires burning while Manfred was away from home on his extensive travels. We thank you for her steadfast life and gracious witness.

And now, Lord, we pray for your continuing grace in these last years going forward, when aches and pains catch up with us, when the stimulation of meaningful work comes to an end and the sense of being worthless niggles away at one's self-worth. When the hectic round of doing gives way to just being, may Manfred know that he is loved by You. In these circumstances, Lord, we pray for your abundant grace and your never-failing presence. We pray that Manfred may live "to the praise of your glory" to the end of his days.

We ask this knowing that in Christ you are our Father, our brother, our Lord and Saviour, and our friend.

---

[1] Bill Houston holds a D.Min. and has been in theological education for decades, having lectured in the UK, in South Africa and as a visiting lecturer in Nairobi. He was recruited by Dr. Kohl into the Overseas Council International in 2005 as their first Regional Director for Africa. After retirement, he now helps Langham Scholars (a division of John Stott Ministries) as a scholar caregiver. He has been married to Joan for 50 years and has three adult children—a pastor, a doctor and a teacher.

APPENDIX: BIOGRAPHY AND BIBLIOGRAPHY

Manfred Waldemar Kohl

Personal Data:

Born: March 24, 1942, in Arnsberg, Germany.

Parents: Telephone Engineer Waldemar Kohl (from Nordhausen/Harz). Deceased.
Housewife Maria Kohl, née Dietz (from Arnbach/Baden). Deceased.

Siblings: Older brother, Hans-Dieter Kohl (born in Berlin). Deceased. Younger sister, Rosemarie Methner, née Kohl (born in Arnsberg), now living in the Black Forest, Germany.

Married: 1969 to Barbara Marie Kohl, née Meisner (from Nova Scotia, Canada). Teacher, Guidance Counselor. B. A., M. Div., D. Min.

Children: Waldemar Roy (1972); Jonathan Manfred (1975); and six grandchildren.

Address: 5022 Hwy 329 Blandford
RR 1, Hubbards
Nova Scotia B0J 1T0, Canada

Office / Home tel: 902-228-2288
E-mail: Manfred@overseas.com
Skype address: mwkohl

Education:

Vocational/business school and later adult educational courses, Pforzheim, Germany (1956-59), certificate.

Mission seminary, Bad Liebenzell, Germany (1963-65), certificate.

Gordon Divinity School, Hamilton, Mass., U.S.A. (1966-68), M. Div.

Ordination as Congregational pastor, Peabody, Mass., U.S.A. (1968).

Harvard University, Cambridge, Mass., U.S.A. (1968-73), Th. M.
Thesis: *Studies in Pietism: A Bibliographical Survey of Research Since 1958-69.*

American Center for Congregational Studies, Los Angeles, Calif. (1978-92), Th. D.
Thesis: *Congregationalism: History and Outreach.* The required coursework was completed at Harvard Divinity School.

Management courses and seminars (1975-94), including: Lewis Allen School of Management, U.S.A. (1980), certificate; Management course for Presidents – The European Management Association, Italy (1984), certificate.

Gordon-Conwell Theological Seminary, Hamilton, Mass., U.S.A., D. (1994), D. Min.
Thesis: *Fund-Raising Principles for Maintaining Continuous Giving to Christian Humanitarian Ministries.*

Various courses, seminars, and self-study programs (1995-2020) in the areas of Institutional Development, Fundraising/Generosity, Leadership Development and Practical Theology with numerous papers published in professional journals and books.

Experience Highlights:

Apprenticeship and examination in cabinet making, Handelskammer Karlsruhe, Germany (1956-59).

Various positions in the trade in Germany and overseas (1960-65).

Director of the Youth Ministry of the City Mission, Pforzheim, Germany (1962-65).

Teacher of languages at Gordon College, Wenham, Mass. (1966-68).
Teaching and lectures as Director of the German Language Division: courses in language, literature, theological German, etc.

Teaching Fellow at Harvard University, Cambridge, Mass. (1969-70).
Staff Member and Assistant of the Theology and History Division under supervision of the Hollis Chair Professor, Dr. George Hunston Williams.

Pastor of the First Congregational Church in Middleboro, Mass. (1970-77).
Building the congregation. 25 active members and their families increased to more than 200 active members.

Field Director of World Vision in West Africa for Development Work (1976-79).
Building and managing more than 100 development projects in 10 countries of West Africa. Annual budget: US $ 2 million. Project staff: 80. Training of local personnel.

Executive Director of the aid agency World Vision Germany (1979-1993).

Vice President of World Vision worldwide ministry (1986-1993).
Founding of the German aid agency World Vision, also founded WV Austria, 1981; WV Switzerland, 1983; and WV Netherlands, 1986. At end of service in 1993 Germany alone had 25,000 sponsors supporting the work in the Third World by monthly contributions, and 150,000 additional friends and donors contributing to relief and development aid. Managing six offices with a total of 100 full-time employees and an annual donation income of US $ 20 million.

Vice President of International Development, Overseas Council International for Theological Education and Mission (1994-2008).

Co-director Institute of Excellence, Overseas Council International for the leadership of theological institutions for the majority world (2000-2008).

Ambassador, Overseas Council International (2008-present).

Founder and President, ReForma (2016-present).

Additional Activities and Special Awards:

Recipient of the Handwerkskammer Preis (an award for the best youth carpenter in the state), Karlsruhe, Germany (1959-60).

Member, Board of Trustees of the Liebenzell Mission, U.S.A. (1968-78).

Chairman, Middleboro Area Clergy Association (1973-74).

Recipient of the Holzner Fellowship Award, Harvard University (1973-74).

Moderator, Mayflower Ministerial Association (1975).

Chairman, National Association of Congregational Christian Churches – World Christian Relations Commission (1975).

Executive Secretary, International Congregational Fellowship (1975-80).

Member, Pietism Group – American Academy of Religion (1975).

Chairman, American Commission for Pietism Studies (1975).

Member, Academy of Religion (Guest Lecturer, Chicago, 1975).

Member, International Conference on Church and State (Guest Lecturer, New York, 1974/75).

Member, International Conference on Revivalism (Guest Lecturer, Oxford 1974/75).

Participant, International Congress on World Evangelization (Lausanne 1974/Amsterdam 1982/Manila 1989).

Chairman, Frankfurt Christian Leadership Group (1980-83).

President, International Congregational Fellowship (1984-88).

Member, Society of Church History, Society of Biblical Literature, Evangelical Theological Society, American Academy of Religion, Winthrop Club, Phi Alpha Chi.

Director/moderator of the Fourth International Congregational Conference (Leiden, 1989).

Founding member of the German Society of "Wirtschaftsethik" (ethics in business) in connection with the University of Mainz. Speaker at their conferences (1990/91).

Founding member of, teacher at, and Chairman of the Board of Grace College of Christian Ministry, Halifax, Canada (1995-2005).

Founding member of Overseas Council Europe, Frankfurt, Germany (1998) and Chairman of the Board, Heidenheim, Germany (2012-2020).

Founding member of the Theological Commission of the International Congregational Fellowship (1999).

Member of the Board of Directors, Peacemaker Ministries, Billings, MT (2000-2015), Vice-chair (2009- 2015).

Co-editor of the *International Congregational Journal* (2001-present).

Co-founder of the MBA program in Biblical Stewardship and Christian Management – Manila, Philippines and Londrina, Brazil (2005).

Recipient of honorary doctor degree from Seminario Sudamericano (Seminary of South America) and the University of Ecuador, Quito, Ecuador (2006).

Member of Overseas Ministry Study Center – Research for Mission Leaders, New Haven, CT (2005-present).

Recipient of the "African Theology Award," NEGST, Nairobi, Kenya (2006). First non-African to receive this award.

Recipient of honorary doctor degree from the Evangelical Theological Seminary, Osijek, Croatia (2008).

Honorary naming of an academic building and an academic chair at Evangelical Theological Seminary, Allahabad, India (2008).

Vice-chair of GlobaLink program of the Lausanne Movement (2008-2010).

Chairman of the Planning Committee of and speaker at the *Christ at the Checkpoint* conferences, Bethlehem, Palestine (2010). Member of the planning committee (2016-present).

Participant and workshop speaker at the Lausanne Congress of World Evangelization, Cape Town, South Africa (2010).

Participant and plenary speaker at the Vision Africa conferences, Ouagadougou, Burkina Faso (2011) and Brussels, Belgium (2015).

Co-Founder and member of Project Nehemiah – Integrity in India, Bangalore, India (2012).

Co-Catalyst (with Bishop Efraim Tendero) of the Integrity and Anti-Corruption Lausanne Network (2014-present).

Advisor to Bishop Efraim Tendero, Executive Secretary and CEO of the World Evangelical Alliance, New York, NY (2014-2017).

Co-Founder, member of, and speaker at the Global Forum of Theological Educators, Dorfweil, Germany (2016-present).

Member of Peacemaker Mediators – a global peacemaker initiative, London, England (2016-present).

Selected to two congresses to celebrate the 500th anniversary of the beginning of the Reformation, Wittenberg, Germany (2017).

Recipient of Presidential medal from the President of the Central African Republic, Bangui, CAR (2017).

Participant and workshop leader at the Lausanne Conference on Nominalism, Rome, Italy (2018).

Founder and President of Re-Forma. Registered in Germany (2019), South Africa (2020) and North America (2021).

Co-founder of the Galilean Movement/Mandate (2021).

Co-chair of the workshop on "Future of Theological Education" at the Lausanne Europe Conference, Wisla, Poland (2021).

Co-chair of Muliplex on "Integrity – A Personal Issue" at the Lausanne Europe Conference, Wisla, Poland (2021).

Participant and speaker at the ICETE Conference 2021 on the topic "How to deal with the GAP/BRIDGE between the Formal and Informal Theological World"

Lectures, Presentations, Keynote Addresses (universities, colleges, theological institutions)

on the topic of institutional development, theological education, biblical stewardship, Christian management, biblical leadership, etc. in the following countries:

Africa: Burkina Faso, Central African Republic, Chad, Ethiopia, Ghana, Ivory Coast, Kenya, Malawi, Mozambique, Namibia, Nigeria, Sierra Leone, South Africa, Sudan South, Togo, Uganda, Zambia, Zimbabwe

Latin America: Argentina, Brazil, Ecuador, Bolivia, Chile, Colombia, Costa Rica, Guatemala, Haiti, Jamaica, Mexico, Peru, Venezuela

Asia: Bangladesh, Cambodia, China, Guam, Hong Kong, India, Indonesia, Japan, Korea, Malaysia, Micronesia, Sri Lanka, Philippines, Singapore, Taiwan, Thailand, Viet Nam

Middle East: Armenia, Cyprus, Dubai, Egypt, Iran, Israel/Palestine, Jordan, Lebanon, Sudan North, Tunisia, Turkey

Europe & Eurasia: Austria, Bulgaria, Croatia, Czech Republic, England, France, Germany, Holland, Lithuania, Moldova, Poland, Portugal, Romania, Russia, Ukraine

North America: Canada, United States

Preaching, Devotional Addresses, Pastors Conferences:

Preached in more than 100 countries, churches of multiple denominations, from small fellowship groups and open air services in Africa to congregations of more than 5,000 in China.

Served on the pastors' conference team with World Vision and with Overseas Council International in many countries.

Publications:

1. "Imago Dei," The Speculum: A Student Journal of Gordon Divinity School 1:3 (Fall 1967), pp. 18-23.

2. "Spare the Criticism" (Liebenzell: Liebenzeller Mission, 1968).

3. "Studies in Pietism: A Bibliographical Survey of Research since 1958-59" (Masters Thesis Harvard University, 1969).

4. Lagoon in the Pacific: The Story of Truk (Schönach, Germany: Liebenzell Mission, 1971).

5. "Newsletter of the Church History Department of Harvard Doctoral Alumni in Church History and Related Fields" (1971).

6. "In the Shadow of Promise" (Middleboro, MA: First Congregational Church, 1971).

7. "Ecclesia in Middleboro: The Doctrine of the Church and Its Implication for the Local Parish" (September 1971).

8. "The Road from Scrooby to Plymouth" (Yarmouth Port, MA: The Massachusetts Congregational Christian Fellowship, 1972).

9. "I am Because I Am: Bacalaureate Address Middleborough High School, Class of 1972" (Middleborough, MA: First Congregational Church, 1972).

10. "Wiedergeburt as the Central Theme in Pietism," The Covenant Quarterly (November 1974).

11. "Who and What Am I? I Am Because I Am - A Baccalaureate Sermon," The Congregationalist (June 1975).

12. "Pietism as a Movement of Revival," The Covenant Quarterly (August 1975).

13. "Spener's Pia Desideria – The Programmschrift of Pietism," The Covenant Quarterly (February/May 1976).

14. "Charismata – Unity in Variety," Currents 35:3 (May 1976)

15. "Long-Term Preparation-Practicing the Presence of God," Mayflower Devotions for Lent (Oak Creek, WI: NACCC, 1976), p. 15. Based on Luke 2:52.

16. In the Shadow of God's Promise (Oak Creek, WI: NACCC, 1976), p. 31-37.

17. "Welcome to New England, the land of the Pilgrims, Puritans and Patriots. Congregationalists return to the Bay State, their birthplace, "The Congregationalist 136:5 (1976), pp. 14ff.

18. "To See Beyond," Mayflower Devotions for Advent (Oak Creek, WI: NACCC, 1976), p. 28.

19. Many articles and interviews on development work in newspapers and magazines.

20. Congregationalism in America (Oak Creek, WI: The Congregational Press, 1977).

21. "Westminster Abbey – A Miracle," The Congregationalist (January 1977), p. 12.

22. "Take Up Your Cross," So Great Salvation. Mayflower Devotions for Lent (Oak Creek, WI: NACCC, 1979), p. 44.

23. HILFE DIREKT – quarterly magazine since 1983 on sponsorships and development work.

24. The First Six Years of World Vision – A Marketing Study (Frankfurt: GGK, 1985).

25. Menschenskinder HILFE DIREKT. (Stuttgart: Hänssler, 1986).

26. Kinder der Welt sagen danke (Stuttgart: Hänssler, 1990).

27. „Mehr als ein Nachwort," Heidelberger Dritte Welt Studien 29: Soziale Arbeit und Entwicklungsrelevanz (Heidelberg: Heidelberger Verlagsanstalt, 1990), pp. 300-310.

28. „Das Gemeindeentwicklungsprojekt in Nyikavanhu, Simbabwe," Pädagogisches Forum (4/1991).

29. "Congregationalism: History and Outreach" (Doctoral Thesis Center for Congregational Studies, 1992).

30. „Grundlagen erfolgreicher Hilfe" in Lachmann, Werner and Reinhard Haupt (eds.), Entwicklungsförderung: Ost-West-Anpassung und Nord-Süd-Ausgleich (Moers: Brendow Verlag, 1992), pp. 13-29.

31. Como Melhorar seu Estilo de Lideranca. Trans. Heloisa Helena Goncalves Dusilik from Towards a Better Understanding of Christian Leadership (Belo Horizonte: Missao Editora, 1993).

32. "Filling the Leadership Void in the Post-Communist Church," Contact (Spring 1994), pp 3-5.

33. "Fund-Raising Principles for Maintaining Continuous Giving to Christian Humanitarian Ministries" (Doctoral Thesis Gordon-Conwell Theological Seminary 1994).

34. „Dreißig Dörfer und kein Pastor," Entscheidung (German version of Billy Graham's Decision magazine) 2:194 (1996), pp. 20-23.

Appendix: Biography and Bibliography 573

35. "Sensation: Luther's Testament," Entscheidung (German version of Billy Graham's Decision magazine) 2:194 (1996), pp. 26-29.

36. Several articles on development ministry and leadership training in German journals and newspapers.

37. "Responsible Stewardship in Theological Education: Guidelines for Resource Development in Post-Communist Countries," Christian Education Journal (Spring 1998), pp 57-74

38. "Motivation – Designation. Historic Glimpses into Donations and Fund-Raising for Christian Ministry" in Rodney L. Petersen & Calvin Augustine Pater (eds.), The Contentious Triangle. Church, State and University. A Festschrift in Honor of Professor George Huntston Williams (Kirksville, Missouri, USA: Thomas Jefferson University Press: Truman State University, 1999), pp 319-337

39. "Renewing Congregationalists" in Are We Who We Say We Are? Toward a definition of the mission of the Congregational Church in the New Millennium: A Collection of Papers Given for the Second Congregational Symposium (Derry, N.H., 2000).

40. "Trends in Theological Education" (translation), published in Russian (Odessa, Ukraine: Odessa University and Odessa Theological Seminary, 2000).

41. "Current Trends in Theological Education," International Congregational Journal 1:1 (February 2001), pp. 26-40.

42. "Mission – The Heart of the Church for the New Millennium," International Congregational Journal 1:2 (August 2001), pp. 87-107.

43. "Towards a Theology of Land: A Christian Answer to the Hebrew-Arab Conflict," Phronêsis ATS (Philippines) 9:2 (2002), pp. 7-26.

44. "Towards a Theology of Land: A Christian Answer to the Hebrew-Arab Conflict," International Congregational Journal 2:2 (August 2002), pp. 165-178.

45. "Theological Education: What Needs to be Changed," in Kohl, Manfred Waldemar, and N. Lal Senanayake (eds.), Educating for Tomorrow: Theological Leadership for the Asian Context (Bangalore,

India: SAIACS Press and Overseas Council International, 2002), pp. 29-48.

46. "Liderança criativa: Modelos no Novo Testamento," in Kohl, Manfred Waldemar, and Antonio Carlos Barro (eds.), Liderança para um novo século (Londrina, Brazil: Descoberta Editora, 2003), pp. 87-114.

47. "An Encounter with the Theologian of Hope" and "Reflections on Hope: A Mosaic," International Congregational Journal 3:2 (August 2003), pp. 139-141 and 185-202.

48. "Current Trends in Theological Education," UBS Journal (India) 3:1 (March 2005), pp. 37-49.

49. "Reflections on Hope: A Worldwide Mosaic," The South African Journal of Theology, Vol. 14 (2005), pp. 206-212.

50. The Church in the Philippines: A Research Project with Special Emphasis on Theological Education (Manila: OMF, 2005).

51. "Towards a Theology of the Land," Meate Journal (Jordan), 1 (2005), pp. 17-29. Edited with Antonio Carlos Barro the 5 volume series on transformation in Portuguese, Ações Transformadoras (Londrina, Brazil: Descoberta, 2006). I had one article in each volume:

52. "Missão: o Coração da Igreja para o novo Milênio" in Vol. 1, Missão Integral Transformadora, pp. 45-68.

53. "Transformação Radical na Formação do líder Cristão" in Vol. 2, Liderança Cristã Transformador, pp. 41-64.

54. "Educação Teológica: o que necessita ser Mudado" in Vol. 3, Educação Teológica Transformadora, pp. 87-108.

55. "O Papel do Pastor na Transformação da Sociedade" in Vol. 4, Ministério Pastoral Transformador, pp. 103-122.

56. "Introdução" in Vol. 5, Aconselhamento Christão Transformador, pp. 7-14.

57. "Educating Leaders to Minister in Asia's Multi-Faith, Multi-Denominational Context," Naming the Unknown God (Manila: OMF and Asian Theological Seminary, 2006), pp. 26-43.

58. "Mission: The Heart of the Church for the New Millennium," Journal of Asian Mission 8:1-2 (March-September 2006), pp. 3-21.

59. "Radical Transformation in Preparation for the Ministry," International Congregational Journal 6:1 (Fall 2006), pp. 42-50.

60. "Worship for the Church," an article in a book published in Russian, 2006.

61. "Various concepts in Theological Education," an article published in Russian, 2007.

62. "Biblical Stewardship and Its Various Historical Interpretations," The South African Baptist Journal of Theology, Vol. 16 (2007), pp. 73-88.

63. The Effectiveness of Theological Education in Ukraine: Research Project. I was part of the research team producing this volume, edited by S. V. Sannikov (Odessa: EAAA, 2007). Published in English and Russian.

64. "Radical Transformation in Preparation for the Ministry," Haddington House Journal, Vol. 9 (2007), pp. 155-178 (The Lausanne Covenant is included as an appendix.)

65. "Theological Education: What Needs to be Changed," in Kohl, Manfred Waldemar, and N. Lal Senanayake (eds.), Educating for Tomorrow: Theological Leadership for the Asian Context (Bangalore, India: SAIACS Press and Overseas Council International, 2007, New Expanded Edition), pp. 29-55.

66. "Radical Change is Required for the Leadership of the Church Today: 'Let's Get Back to Basics'," The Church: Born for a Time Like This. The Fifth Congregational Symposium, ed. Rev. Steven A. Peay (Oak Creek, WI: NACCC, 2007), pp. 113-118.

67. "Mission – The Heart of the Church for the New Millennium," Mission Mandate II, ed. Bishop Dr. Ezra Sargunam (Ayanavaram, Chennai, India: Mission Educational Books, 2008), pp. 95-114.

68. "Mission to Small Islands: Congregationalism comes to the South Pacific: A Different Introduction," International Congregational Journal 8:1 (Spring 2009), pp. 9-11.

69. "Regaining a Prophetic Voice for the Church Today: Training Leaders to Impact PostModern Culture," International Congregational Journal 8:2 (Fall 2009), pp. 73-78.

70. "Theological Education: What Needs to Be Changed," Torch Trinity Journal 12:1 (November 2009) pp. 149-162.

71. "International Partnership and Funding Principles in Theological Education in Evangelical Perspective," Handbook of Theological Education in World Christianity: Theological Perspectives, Ecumenical Trends, Regional Surveys, ed. Dietrich Werner, David Esterline, Namsoon Kang, and Joshva Raja (Oxford: Regnum, 2010), pp. 325-328.

72. "Theological Developments: Examples from Around the World," International Congregational Journal 9:1 (Spring 2010), pp. 37-42.

73. "Theological and Philosophical Understanding of Church Liturgy/Worship," International Congregational Journal 9:2 (Winter 2010), pp. 69-77.

74. "Biblical Stewardship: Fund-Raising for Christian Ministry," in The Earth is the Lord's: Reflections on Stewardship in the Asian Context, ed. Timoteo Gener and Adonis Abelard Gorospe (Manila: OMF, 2011), pp. 131-144.

76. "Towards a Better Understanding of Church Liturgy/Worship Today," in Haddington House Journal 13 (2011), pp. 105-114.

77. "A Vos Profética da Igreja do Futuro," in A Igreja do Futuro, ed. Manfred W. Kohl and Antonio Carlos Barro (Londrina, Brazil: Descoberta, 2011), pp. 259-270.

78. "The Holocaust and the Evangelical Movement: from German Pietism to Palestinian Christians," International Congregational Journal: Looking Backward and Looking Forward 10:2 (Fall 2011), pp. 51-60.

79. "Towards a Better Understanding of Church Liturgy/Worship Today," Zhejiang Theological Review 5 (Hangzhou, China, 2011), pp. 73-80.

80. "Excellence in Theological Education in Bible Schools and Seminaries," in Moise Napon (ed.), Vision Africa Conference: The Church Commits Herself to the Integral Development of Africa (Ougadougou, Burkina Faso: Visionafrica, 2011), pp. 124-127.

81. "Biblical Stewardship: Fund-raising for Christian Ministry," in Timoteo Gener and Adonis Abelard Gorospe (eds.), The Earth is the Lord's. Reflections on Stewardship in the Asian Context (Manila: OMF and ATS, 2011), pp. 131-144.

82. "Towards a Theology of the Land: A Christian Answer to the Israeli-Arab Conflict," in The Land Cries Out: Theology of the Land in the Israeli-Palestinian Context, ed. Salim J. Munayer and Lisa Loden (Eugene, OR: Cascade, 2012), pp. 265-281.

83. "Every Christian Institution Needs a Strategic Plan," in International Congregational Journal: Deed and Word 11:2 (Winter 2012), pp. 19-40.

84. "The Holocaust and the Evangelical Movement: from German Pietism to Palestinian Christians," in Paul Alexander (ed.), Christ at the Checkpoint: Theology in the Service of Justice and Peace (Eugene, OR: Pickwick, 2012), pp. 12-22.

85. "Gathering and Using Finances Responsibly: A Biblical Approach," in International Congregational Journal: A Pilgrim People – We Are on the Way 12:2 (Winter 2013), pp. 107-110.

86. "Children and Ministry – an Integral Part of Theological Education," in Dan Brewster and John Baxter-Brown (eds.), Children & Youth as Partners in Mission (Penang, Malaysia: Compassion International, 2013), pp. 245-248.

87. "Biblical Stewardship: Biblische Haushalterschaft," in Robert Badenberg and Friedemann Knödler (eds.) Evangelisation und Transformation: Zwei Münzen oder eine Münze mit zwei Seiten? (Bonn: VTR, 2013), pp. 135-140.

88. "Strategic Planning in Theological Education," in Fritz Deininger and Orbelina Eguizabal (eds.), Foundations for Academic Leadership

(Hamburg: VTR, 2013), pp. 151-180. Republished in Fritz Deininger and Orbelina Eguizabal (eds.), Foundations for Academic Leadership, in Riad Kassis (series ed.), Leadership in Theological Education (Carlisle: Langham, 2017), Vol 1, pp. 151-181.

89. "Theological Education in Africa Needs Money," in Isabel Apawo Phiri and Dietrich Werner (eds.), Handbook of Theological Education in Africa (Oxford: Regnum, 2013), pp. 1106-1110.

90. "Bibliographical Resources for Action in the Public Arenas," in Darrell Bock (ed.), The Cape Town Commitment: A Confession of Faith, a Call to Action: Bibliographical Resources (Eugene, OR: Wipf & Stock, 2013), p. 49.

91. "A Boy Called Jesus," in Jesudason Baskar Jeyaraj, Rosalind Tan, Shiferaw Michael, and Enrique Pinedo (eds.), Repairer of Broken Walls: Essays on Holistic Child Development in honour of Dr. Dan Brewster (Delhi: Allianz Enterprises, 2014), pp. 15-29.

92. "Strategic Planning in Theological Education," in Zhejiang Theological Review 7 (Hangzhou, China: 2013), pp. 76-88.

93. "Strategies in Theological Education" (in Chinese), in Jason Lim (ed.), Theological Education and Theological Issues in the 21st Century Chinese Churches (Kuang, Malaysia: MBS, 2014), pp. 24-49.

94. "Biblical Stewardship: Fund-raising for Christian Ministry," in Zhejiang Theological Review 8 (Hangzhou, China: 2014), pp. 68-74.

95. "Congregationalism and Evangelism/Mission.Outreach," in International Congregational Journal: Congregationalism in Spirit and Practice 13:2 (Winter 2014), pp. 53-64.

96. "A Boy Called Jesus," in Zhejiang Theological Review 9 (Hangzhou, China: 2015), pp. 66-72.

97. "From a Lagoon in the Pacific to the Pulpit in Westminster Abbey: An After Dinner Talk at the John Bunyan Church in Bedford, England," in International Congregational Journal 14:1 (Summer 2015), pp. 40-42.

98. "From a Lagoon in the Pacific to the Pulpit in Westminster Abbey: An After Dinner Talk at the John Bunyan Church in Bedford, England," in The Congregationalist 167:3 (September 2015), pp. 27-29.

99. "A Boy Called Jesus," in Haddington House Journal: An International Theological Journal 18 (2016), pp. 77-78.

100. "A Tribute to Revd Dr William (Bill) P. Fillebrown: I have lost a special friend," in International Congregational Journal: Liberating Learning 14:2 (Winter 2015), pp. 7-10.

101. "A Boy Called Jesus," in International Congregational Journal: 14:2 (Winter 2015), pp. 115-124.

102. "The Inception of EGST: Preliminary Preparations. One Graduate School for All Ethiopia," in EGST Succession Chronicles: Institutional Memories (Addis Ababa: EGST, 2015), pp. 6-8.

103. „Was hilft es, wenn ich alles über Luther weiß," in idea Spectrum: Nachrichten und Meinungen aus der evangelischen Welt 21 (25 May 2016), p. 13.

104. "An Encounter with the Risen Lord," in Speak to Us: Messages from the Torch Trinity Chapel (Seoul: Torch Trinity Graduate University Press, 2016), pp. 268-284.

105. "Sensational Discoveries: A Contribution to the 500th Anniversary Celebration of the Reformation," in International Congregational Journal: Always Reform 15:2 (Winter 2016), pp. 29-35.

106. "A Unique Encounter – Meeting the Moltmanns," in International Congregational Journal: God's Healing Love 15:1 (Summer 2016), pp. 53-54.

107. With Antonio Carlos Barro, "A Educação Teológica e os Recursos Financeiros," in Práxis Evangelica 27 (2016), pp. 135-146.

108. "A Unique Encounter – Meeting the Moltmanns," in Zhejiang Theological Review 11 (Hangzhou, China: 2017), pp. 69-70.

109. "Sensational Discoveries: A Contribution to the 500th Celebration of the Reformation," in Zhejiang Theological Review 11 (Hangzhou, China: 2017), pp. 88-90.

110. "As Goes the Seminary So Goes the Church," in Priorities for Evangelical Theological Education, Essays in Honor of Reuben van Rensburg. Festschrift. (Johannesburg, South African Theological Seminary Press: 2018), pp. 65-96.

111. "The Significance of a Theological Commission," in International Congregational Journal: Called to Freedom 16:1 (Winter 2017), pp. 126-129.

112. Edited with Munther Isaac, Christ at the Checkpoint. Blessed are the Peacemakers (Bethlehem, Palestine, Diyar Publisher: 2018)

113. "What Can We Tell When We Return Home,?" in Christ at the Checkpoint. Blessed are the Peacemakers (Bethlehem, Palestine, Diyar Publisher: 2018), pp. 65-74.

114. "Sensational Discoveries. A Contribution to the 500th Celebration of the Reformation," in Haddington House Journal: An International Theological Journal 20 (2018), pp. 91-102.

115. "Do We Care About Corruption," in Lausanne Global Analysis 8:3 (May 2019), pp. 1-10.

116. With Michael Biehl and Dietrich Werner, "Christianity in Germany" in World Christian Encyclopedia, 3rd Edition (Edinburgh: University Press, 2019), pp. 141-147.

117. "The Lord is Risen ... The Lord is Risen Indeed!," in Haddington House Journal 21&22 (2019/2020), pp. 163-175.

118. "China: A Brief Introduction to the History and Current Status of Christianity and the Congregational Church," in International Congregational Journal 17.2 (2019), pp. 93-97.

119. "Integrity Begins With Us," in Visa Journal (Radcliffe College, 2020), pp. 105-114.

120. "Re-Forma: Solving a Key Issue in Global Training of Pastors and Church Leaders," in Evangelical Review of Theology 45:2 (2021), pp. 103-112.

121. "The Beginning of the Lausanne Movement," in Haddington House Journal 23 (2021), pp. 11-18.

122. "Dau Gyfyng-gyngor Christnogol (Two of Christianity's Dilemmas)" (in Welsh), in the newspaper Y Tyst (The Witness), (2021), pp. 1-2.

123. "Foreward," in David W.T. Brattston, The Rise of Bishops. From Parish Leaders to Regional Governors (Eugene, Oregon, WIPF & STOCK: 2021), pp. xi - xiv.

124. "A Global Standard for Ministry Training. Re-Forma's response to the crisis of poorly-equipped church leadership," in Lausanne Global Analysis 10:6 (November 2021), pp. 1-9.

www.ingramcontent.com/pod-product-compliance
Lightning Source LLC
Chambersburg PA
CBHW052043290426
44111CB00011B/1597